MW00441998

Voices from Four Directions

Voices from Four Directions

Contemporary Translations of the Native Literatures of North America

Edited by Brian Swann

UNIVERSITY OF NEBRASKA PRESS | LINCOLN AND LONDON

An earlier version of "The Oekuu Shadeh of Ohkay Owingeh" was published in the *American Indian Culture and Research Journal*, volume 24, number 4, and is used by permission of the American Indian Studies Center, UCLA © Regents of the University of California.

Excerpts from *The Power of Kiowa Song: A Collaborative Ethnography*, by Luke E. Lassiter © 1998 The Arizona Board of Regents. Reprinted by permission of the University of Arizona Press.

"Prophecy at Lytton" originally appeared in *Write It on Your Heart: The Epic World of an Okanagan Storyteller*, edited by Wendy Wickwire (Vancouver: Talonbooks, 1989).

"The Sealion Hunter" is reprinted from *Nine Visits to the Mythworld: Ghandl and the Qaayahl Llaanas*, translated from Haida by Robert Bringhurst, by permission of the University of Nebraska Press. © 2000 Robert Bringhurst. Published in Canada by Douglas & McIntyre Ltd. Reprinted by permission of the publisher.

© 2004 by the Board of Regents of the University of Nebraska

"The Sealion Hunter" © 2004 by Robert Bringhurst

"Two Children Adrift" © 2004 by Edna Ahgeak MacLean

"Coyote Stories" © 2004 by Rex Lee Jim

"Umâyichîs" © 2004 by Julie Brittain and Marguerite MacKenzie

"Rabbit Frees the People from Muskrat" © 2004 by Jimm G. GoodTracks

All rights reserved
Manufactured in the United States of America

Library of Congress Cataloging-in-Publication Data
Voices from four directions : contemporary translations of the Native literatures of North America / edited by Brian Swann.
p. cm.
Includes bibliographical references and index.
ISBN 0-8032-4300-6 (cloth : alk. paper) —
ISBN 0-8032-9310-0 (pbk. : alk. paper)
1. Indians of North America — Folklore.
2. Folk literature, Indian — North America.
3. Indian mythology — North America.
4. Tales — North America.   5. Legends — North America.   I. Swann, Brian.
E98.F6V665   2004
398.2′089′97 — dc22
2003019698

There are four voices coming
from four directions
        the center is harmony
        the center is beginning.

Peter Blue Cloud, from "Wolf"

Contents

Introduction

This volume is a follow-up and extension of *Coming to Light: Contemporary Translations of the Native Literatures of North America.*[1] The present collection continues both the format and the method of *Coming to Light.* The introductions that preface each translation give readers as much information as possible so that they can contextualize and understand the work that follows. Although much of the material may be familiar or comprehensible without special knowledge, much is also compellingly different. Also familiarity can sometimes be misleading: what we take for granted will often need interpretation since meanings change across cultures.

The present collection includes retranslations of "classical" literature as well as translations of recent material. It is made up of new work both by contributors represented in *Coming to Light,* and by those, the majority, who are not. Of the former, Paul Zolbrod contributes more Navajo work and Herb Luthin more Yana. Robert Leavitt, whose Passamaquoddy work appeared in the earlier volume, presents Mìgmaq (Micmac) stories, this time with E. Nàgùgwes Metallic and Jennifer Andrews, while Richard and Nora Dauenhauer add to their Tlingit work and Judith Berman gives us more Kwakwaka'wakw (Kwakiutl)literature. Julian Rice provides a Lakota story, while Robert Bringhurst is present again with Haida work. This time Blair Rudes contributes, not Tuscarora, but Catawba material.

The contributors new to the venture include John Enrico (Haida), David Kozak and David Lopez (O'odham), Monica Macaulay and Marianne Milligan (Menominee), Lawrence Kaplan, Tadataka Nagai, and Minnie Gray (Iñupiaq), Edna MacLean (Iñupiaq), and Rex Lee Jim, a Navajo poet who reminds us that a number of contemporary Native writers are also working with traditional materials in original ways. "It may not be what you expected," he wrote, "but it is the Coyote way." Then there are Philip LeSourd (Maliseet), Rand Valentine (Ojibwe), Wendy Wickwire (Okanagan), Virginia Hymes (Sahaptin), Katherine Turner (Miguelino Salinan), Eleanor and Tom Nevins and Paul and Genevieve Ethelbah (Western Apache), Catherine Callaghan (Lake Miwok), Amy Miller and Millie Romero (Quechan), Ives Goddard (Meskwaki), Crisca Bierwert (Lushootseed), Jimm

GoodTracks (Iowa-Otoe-Missouria), Willard Walker and Wesley Proctor (Cherokee), Mary Linn, Jason Baird Jackson, Josephine Barnett Keith, and Josephine Wildcat Bigler (Yuchi), Eric Lassiter (Kiowa), Hao Huang (San Juan Pueblo–Tewa), Wallace Chafe (Seneca), Herbert Lewis (Oneida), William Seaburg (Upper Coquille Athabaskan), and Julie Brittain, Alma Chemaganish, Margaret MacKenzie, and Silas Nabinicaboo (Naskapi). By including Alexander King's contribution (Koryak), I have taken it upon myself to extend our northern boundaries into Siberia, where cultural contacts with Alaska are being renewed. I have, however, illogically left our southern borders in place.

As with all such collections, much is present, but much is also absent. For example, although I tried hard to recruit translators of Southeast materials for *Coming to Light,* only one is represented in that volume. I made extra efforts to obtain Southeast translations for the present volume, but again with only limited success. For the most part, Native communities seem to be directing more effort toward preservation and renewal than to translation. For instance, the Choctaw Nation of Oklahoma informed me that their language program was involved in so many projects that it would be a hardship to start anything else, and the Kiwat Hisinay Foundation, Preserving Caddo Culture, told me that they could not participate because they were "madly" trying to get down "all we can, knowing that careful editing of our CDs, DVDs, and other formats to come can be done for decades and centuries to come." Such responses were typical, not just specific to the Southeast.

In gathering material for this book I was dependent on the vagaries of who was working on what and who was interested in sharing the fruits of his or her labors. From the responses to my hundreds of letters, e-mails, faxes, notices in journals, and phone calls, I learned just how busy everybody is in an understaffed field, one in which a vast amount of work remains to be done. Apart from fieldwork there are archives full of materials that need attention, and fragile audiotapes and wax cylinders that need re-recording in new formats. In addition, language experts are frequently called on in law cases involving land rights and claims.

Adding to the difficulty of recruitment, some experts, particularly linguists, are simply not interested in literature or translation. One prominent Algonquinist wrote me: "I am only interested in the original texts themselves, and see translations only as keys into the original." He preferred "the stuff in the raw."[2] One or two translators even said they didn't want their translations to be accessible or fully understood, in an effort to resist assimilation. Some linguists refused to participate in a project that does not use a bilingual format: "What does it say to the Native communities when we tell them 'Your literature is only valuable when it is in English'?"

Finally, not everyone can translate well. "In this translation I am attempting to suggest the syllable-counting metrics of the original . . . and reveal the over-all pattern," one song translator wrote me. In the hands of a skilled practitioner, this approach could work. But the result in this case was not successful. For this translator, style was simply pattern. For his purposes, as for many other linguists, any "text" was as good as any other. "Plain translation," a latter-day Boasian approach, sufficed for more than one. Franz Boas, the grand figure of American anthropology and anthropological linguistics, saw texts as primarily for linguists and ethnographers. Translation was something of a necessary evil. Literary merit counted for little, and Boas thought style was difficult to translate, being bound up with peculiarities of language and culture, a position he shared with his famous student Edward Sapir.[3] At a time when languages were disappearing and expert collectors in the field were few, when many previous translations were loose and inaccurate, "direct," "close," "literal" texts were the aim. But today, after a few decades of ethnopoetics, plain, close, literal translations surely miss a number of important points. "There are pitfalls to this romance of plainness," as Willis Barnstone notes.[4] For one, if an original is regarded as "beautiful," however the term is defined, the translation is no translation at all if it is not also "beautiful." So, when another linguist wrote of the work he sent in: "I am afraid the poetry may be left out in the process of trying to be faithful to the original," he had not been faithful at all. How can the translation of something acknowledged to be "poetic" omit the poetry?

The history of Native American translation has been written about extensively in recent years. For convenient and accessible accounts I refer the reader to essays in the Smithsonian's *Handbook of the American Indian,* volume 17, *Languages.*[5] At this point it might suffice to note that the visibility of Native cultures and languages is quite a new phenomenon.

According to some estimates, at the time of contact the American continent contained as many as one-third of the world's languages, but from the conquest until the early nineteenth century, these languages were not regarded as worthy of much attention. For practical purposes word lists and vocabularies had been recorded from the earliest period of contact, but it took some time for many people to acknowledge that the languages they heard were not Hebrew or Phoenician, Irish or Welsh, or even that the Natives had any language at all. From the first, Europeans looked at the indigenes and saw projections of themselves, outlines of their wishes and desires, wisps of assumptions. Despite our modern tendency to see a new world, these Europeans were largely indifferent to the new and unique. So in a certain sense Indians were invisible and inaudible. Indians had to be fitted in because Europeans were not capable of conceiving of the "other." As Anthony Pagden has noted, sixteenth- and seventeenth-century observers believed in social unity among the various races.[6] They were not looking for "otherness" but for a way of eliminating it, and thereby bringing the disturbingly new within an anthropology made authoritative by its origin in Greek thought. Indians were placed in the familiar category of "barbarian," implying inferiority, someone distinguished by a lack of ability to speak, someone who can only make animal-like noises (well into the twentieth century Indian languages were often dubbed "barbarous dialects"). Since the Greeks made the close connection between intelligible speech and reason, barbarians were de facto devoid of logos, or reason. Columbus said the natives had no religion and no language. Thus in 1492 he planned to carry off to Spain six of them "that they may learn to speak."[7]

Comparative linguistics started in Europe in the eighteenth century, about the same time in America interest in indigenous languages developed, as in the case of Franklin and Jefferson and other Enlightenment intellectuals. But it was not until the nineteenth century that a blooming of interest in the languages occurred, as well as attempts at translating them, mostly within the intellectual structure of evolutionary thought and the idea of the "dying race." The Smithsonian Institution was founded in 1846 to house Native American materials and linguistic artifacts, while the Bureau of American Ethnology, established in 1879, stressed linguistic research. "Salvage anthropology" attempted to preserve what could be preserved as fast as possible before the Indian passed from the stage in a process of natural selection. Many collections were made in this way, before Franz Boas arrived at Columbia University in 1899 and began the scientific training that was to produce many of the most prominent names in American anthropology.

Today it is fair to say that Indian literatures are being treated more seriously than ever before. As far as translation is concerned, two figures stand out as seminal: Dell Hymes and Dennis Tedlock. Most translators today have been influenced in some way by these two men. In essence, Hymes, who elevates translation to a primary aim, works primarily with Native-language texts, whereas Tedlock uses recent tape recordings and performed narrations. Hymes looks for organization by recurrent patterning, from structural particles to, more importantly, clusters of number patterns, mostly three, four, and five, depending on the culture, and treats them as markers signifying distinct segments of the narration, or song, which he then sets up in lines and stanzas, frequently dramatic and poetic.[8] On the other hand, Tedlock, using a tape recorder, tries to recover the voices and patterns of the original performance, and for him the length of the pause indicates line and stanza.[9] When he transfers the material to print, he vivifies the page, making it gestural with typographic devices. Tape recording can help overcome certain difficulties encountered in the field. Even Boas, despite his phonetic skills, was sometimes frustrated. Writing down a phrase, checking with the teller or singer, sometimes drove Boas to distraction, and he lamented what he called the unnatural simplicity of diction resulting in something that even he, who wasn't concerned with the literary quality of translation, found inadequate.[10]

The whole question of translation is problematic. It has always had a political and social dimension.[11] Apart from difficulties in rendering oral language on the page—the "shadow survivance"—and apart from English's inability to translate adequately language such as the Navajo Yellowman's "pretty languages" or beautiful archaic therapeutic vocabulary, much cultural baggage and many encumbrances exist, ranging from what might be considered the mundane (property rights, who owns what) to the larger context of a history of suppression and exploitation.[12] And there is sometimes opposition to translation from within the Native community itself. Access is frequently not "open." More than one translator has voiced to me the necessity of checking to see if the stories he or she wished to work on were in fact available for translation. One said that since the stories he was considering were part of a cosmological cycle, he wanted to make sure they were not part of a ceremony for initiates only. The general feeling among the people he was working with, he noted, was that the stories should not be publicized at this time, even though they had been published previously in several anthropological treatments. An older, well-respected scholar had to withdraw from this project because of changing attitudes among the people she had long worked with. Copyright questions had arisen, she wrote, and a litigious attitude had developed, especially among people who did not live on the reservation.[13]

A related dimension to the problem of translation is the way many of the early texts were obtained, the "hidden colonialism."[14] Fraud, threats, and deceit were sometimes involved. The great collector John Peabody Harrington, for instance, often manipulated his consultants or "informants."[15] But the story is seldom simple. Recently the indigenous community of San Juan Capistrano expressed its gratitude for materials that resulted from Harrington's field procedures by hosting a conference of linguists and anthropologists devoted to his work.[16] Tribes and individuals have also used materials gathered under suspicious circumstances for language revitalization and development.

There are other questions such as payment and the right of even well known informants to recount materials that were not theirs by genealogical inheritance. Judith Berman has analyzed the situation of Boas's collector George Hunt in this regard.[17] In addition, anthropologists and Native informants are often at cultural cross-purposes. Many speakers of Tohono O'odham, for instance, believe that Juan Gregorio died not of old age but because of what he told Donald Bahr about the way animal spirits can be offended, thus attracting evil forces.[18] In the case of Barre Toelken's work on Navajo Coyote stories with the Yellowman family, his Native fieldwork partners believed his investigations were responsible for certain repercussions: accidents, injuries, even death.[19]

While Native languages are under continual pressure, a number are in pretty good shape. Navajo, for instance, has over one hundred thousand speakers, and Cree is spoken by some eighty thousand people in Canada. Approximately the same number speak Iñupiaq in Canada and Greenland, while in the United States Choctaw-Chickasaw has about twelve thousand speakers, as does Creek.[20] Many efforts are under way to strengthen and revitalize languages on a number of fronts, from colleges and universities, to Native communities and tribal colleges.[21] On the academic front the exemplary Society for the Study of the Indigenous Languages of the Americas (SSILA) publishes a newsletter as well as a bulletin (http://www.ssila.org) and acts as a clearinghouse and notice board. It is also a resource center, producing learning aids, dictionaries, grammars and tapes, bilingual narratives, and so on. Groups of specialists meet regularly at conferences, including the Algonquian Conference, (whose thirty-third annual meeting was held in 2001), the Athabaskan Conference, the Hokan-Penutian Conference, the Siouian and Caddoan Conference, and many others. In addition, a number of Native-based production companies and broadcast channels, such as the Canadian APTN (Aboriginal People's Television Network), are devoted to using Native languages. The Internet provides valuable resources, and there are many language-related Web sites. *Nativeculture.com* is a comprehensive portal site, a good place to start. There are also CD-ROMs, videos, a whole variety of educational means whose purpose for Native peoples is, in the words of the Blackfoot educator Duane Mistaken Chief, "to rediscover who we are."[22]

Despite these efforts, the danger of linguistic mass extinction is very real. As the opening statement of the Endangered Languages Fund noted in 1995: "Never have we faced the mass extinction that is threatening the world right now. . . . We are faced with a stark reality: Much of what we study will not be available to future generations. The cultural heritage of many people is crumbling while we look on."[23] Half the world's languages are moribund, that is, not being passed on. Such attrition is sobering if we consider that language is at the core of what it means to be human since cultures are largely passed on through language. As the policy statement by the Linguistic Society of America noted in 1994: "The loss to humanity of generic diversity in the linguistic world is . . . arguably greater than even the loss of genetic diversity in the biological world, given that the structure of human language represents a considerable testimony to human intellectual achievement."[24]

Those of us studying Native American cultures, who hold them to be precious, need access to the original languages, so we have to be involved with their preservation and strengthening. Everyone pays homage to "the oral tradition," but unless it is grounded in native languages, it could well become, as more than one critic has pointed out, a catchall phrase whose main function would be to name the source of the difference between Native writers and Euro-American writers. The final step would be when the oral tradition (which, it should be noted, is still alive and flourishing) becomes synonymous with anything that is *told,* mostly in English. The great tradition that defined a culture to itself in its own language will disappear into the thin outlines of itself. As the Anishinabe writer Gerald Vizenor has pointed out, "the tribes were born in language." [25] Words are worlds and vice versa.

But, as with most Native American issues, things are not that simple. What about those Native storytellers, who may or may not know their own language, who choose to tell their stories in English? Or what about those like E. Nàgùgwes Metallic who write their stories in English, or others, such as Harry Robinson, who translate their own stories? This volume, while devoted to the art of translation, also includes such stories; it should be noted that English in the United States and largely in Canada has become the lingua franca of Native peoples, and varieties of Indian English have arisen that are of value in their own right.[26] Moreover, even precontact monolingualism was probably a rarity among many Indian peoples on the continent because of trade, travel, and overlap among many languages. One sixteenth-century observer in Latin America remarked that in a single village two or three different languages were spoken. It should be noted that in certain North American groups who have lost their languages, Native culture continues largely in English. However, as Dell Hymes has pointed out in correspondence, the stories told in those cultures are not just English-language stories. Many are shaped by cultural habits and structures. Hymes perceives aboriginal organization and patterning in English-language narration, particularly the use of the numbers three and five in Northwest stories, and surmises that the same is true among other western cultures. "In many cases," he wrote me, "English is the envelope, as it were, not the shape of the message."

In accordance with this book's title, I have ordered the voices by the cardinals, north, south, east, west, but rearranged in a large circle, north, west, south, east. This is not entirely logical nor satisfactory if one goes by culture areas. Southeast cultures are distinct from Southwest and Californian from North Pacific Coast, for instance. But the question of language and cultural affinities is, for the most part, taken care of in the individual introductions, and the fourfold division, if it is understood as pure convenience, works to balance the contents and give the reader a rough orientation among materials from so many different cultures.

Finally, in this collection I have attempted to create something of a dialogue, an interplay of voices as diverse as the cultures they come from. I hope the "totality of intentions," in the translated words of Walter Benjamin, "supplement each other," and that the necessarily monolingual format doesn't flatten the diversity or reduce the distinctions too much.[27] The richness and inventiveness of the languages and cultures represented here is only a small, a tiny part, not only of what has been lost, but of what remains.

I am immensely grateful to all contributors for their skills and generosity and not least for their equanimity and good humor in the face of not infrequent editorial badgering.

NOTES

1. *Coming to Light: Contemporary Translations of the Native Literatures of North America,* ed. Brian Swann (New York: Random House, 1994). It is also the result of the cancellation of my Smithsonian Institution Press series The Smithsonian Series of Studies in Native American Literatures, which I had hoped would focus on individual volumes devoted to specific languages, thus obviating the need for another general anthology. So far, however, only three of the orphaned volumes have made an appearance: *Translating Native Latin American Verbal Art: Ethnopoetics and Ethnography of Speaking,* ed. Kay Sammons and Joel Sherzer (Washington DC: Smithsonian Institution Press, 2000); *Our Voices: Native Stories of Alaska and the Yukon,* ed. James Ruppert and John W. Bernet (Lincoln: University of Nebraska Press, 2001); and *Surviving through the Days: Translations of Native California Stories and Songs: A California Indian Reader,* ed. Herbert W. Luthin (Berkeley: University of California Press, 2002).

2. The phrase is Edward Sapir's, quoted in Regna Darnell, "The Boasian Text and the History of Anthropology," *Culture* 12, no. 1 (1992): 42. He wrote: "I am not particularly interested in 'smoothed-over' versions of native culture. I like the stuff in the raw, as felt and dictated by the natives. The genuine, difficult, confusing primary sources, these must be presented, whatever else is done." Sapir was not arguing against translation but against the kind of translations that preceded him and Boas. He stressed knowledge of and immersion in sources.

3. While Boas was not primarily concerned with aesthetics, Dell Hymes credits him with being a pioneer "in discovering recurrent relations among grammatical elements and the patterns of words constituted by them," in his essay "Boas on the Threshold of Ethnopoetics," in *Theorizing the Americanist Tradition,* ed. Lisa Phillips Valentine and Regna Darnell (Toronto: University of Toronto Press, 1999), 91. For Sapir on style, see the chapter "Language and Literature" in his 1921 volume *Language: An Introduction to the Study of Speech* (New York: Harcourt, Brace & Co.).

4. Willis Barnstone, *The Poetics of Translation: History, Theory, Practice* (New Haven: Yale University Press, 1993), 37. Barnstone's excellent study is typical of all the books I have read on translation and translation theory. It omits any mention or discussion of Native American literatures or oral literatures, being mostly concerned with written literary texts in the "Western" tradition. Concomitantly, most scholars of Native American literatures, especially linguists and anthropologists, rarely show any interest in translation theory and seldom evince any familiarity with its texts, demonstrating a refusal to integrate disciplines, something essential in Native American studies.

5. *Handbook of North American Indians,* ed. William C. Sturtevant, vol. 17, *Languages,* ed. Ives Goddard (Washington DC: Smithsonian Institution, 1966). See in particular Ives Goddard, "The Description of the Native Languages of North America before Boas," 17–

42; and Marianne Methun, "The Description of the Native Languages of North America: Boas and After," 43–63. Also useful is M. Dale Kinkade and Anthony Mattina, "Discourse," 244–74, especially the pages on translation and presentational format. For a brief overview I refer the reader to my introduction to *Coming to Light,* xxi–xxix; and to Arnold Krupat's essay "On the Translation of Native American Songs and Stories: A Theorized History," in *On the Translation of Native American Literatures,* ed. Brian Swann (Washington DC: Smithsonian Institution Press, 1992), 3–32. Finally, I recommend William M. Clements's *Native American Verbal Art: Texts and Interpretations* (Tucson: University of Arizona Press, 1966).

6. Anthony Pagden, *The Fall of Natural Man: The American Indian and the Origins of Comparative Ethnology* (Cambridge: Cambridge University Press, 1982), 5 and passim.

7. An equally strange notion, to us, was expressed by the Rev. Richard Eburne in 1624 in a tract advocating the establishing of plantations in Virginia, which was, he says, a tabula rasa, a no-place, until the English arrived: "So you may find England where now is, as I may say, no place" (*A Plain Pathway to Plantations,* ed. Louis B. Wright [Ithaca NY: Cornell University Press], 125). For more on this and related subjects, see David Murray, *Forked Tongues: Speech, Writing and Representation in North American Indian Texts* (Bloomington: Indiana University Press, 1991), as well as Eric Cheyfitz, *The Poetics of Imperialism: Translation and Colonization from 'The Tempest' to 'Tarzan'* (New York: Oxford University Press, 1991).

8. Dell Hymes, *"In Vain I Tried to Tell You": Essays on Native American Ethnopoetics* (Philadelphia: University of Pennsylvania Press, 1981).

9. Dennis Tedlock, *The Spoken Word and the Work of Interpretation* (Philadelphia: University of Pennsylvania Press, 1983).

10. See Boas's essay "Stylistic Aspects of Primitive Literature," *Journal of American Folklore* 38 (1925): 329–39.

11. In the words of André Lefevere, "translation is never innocent" (*Translation, History and Culture,* ed. Susan Bassnett and André Lefevere [London: Pinter Publications, 1990], 11). "Translation," he notes later, "is one of the most obvious forms of image making, or manipulation, that we have" (27).

12. The phrase "shadow survivance" is Gerald Vizenor's, from his essay titled "The Ruins of Representation: Shadow Survivance and the Literature of Dominance," *American Indian Quarterly* 17, no. 1 (winter 1993): 7–30. He notes that "[t]he wild unities of heard stories and the pleasures of performance are unbodied in translations. The shadows and tribal experiences that are *heard* in stories, and variations on natural reason, are transformed in publications that are *seen* as cultural representations" (9). Regarding the limitation of English translations of Native material, see Barre Toelken and Tacheeni Scott, "Poetic Retranslation and the 'Pretty Languages' of Yellowman," in *Traditional American Indian Literatures: Texts and Interpretations,* ed. Karl Kroeber (Lincoln: University of Nebraska Press, 1981), 65–116.

13. Recently some tribes have attempted to copyright their languages. See "The Linguist List: Archives of Siouan" (http://listserv.linguistlist.org/archives/siouan.html), a mirror of the Siouan list at Siouan@Lists.colorado.edu, especially the archives for June 2001, "Language as Property."

14. Roger Sanjek has studied this issue in "Anthropology's Hidden Colonialism: Assistants and Their Ethnographers," *Anthropology Today* 9 (1993): 13–18.

15. For two opposing viewpoints on Indian-anthropologist relations, see David Brumble

and Karl Kroeber, "Reasoning Together," in *Smoothing the Ground: Essays on Native American Oral Literature,* ed. Brian Swann (Berkeley: University of California Press, 1983), 347–64. Recently the question of collaboration between Native and non-Native has resulted in the first collection of essays on the subject: *Native American Oral Traditions: Collaboration and Interpretation,* ed. Larry Evers and Barre Toelken (Logan: Utah State University Press, 2001).

16. See Jane H. Hill, "The Meaning of Writing and Text in a Changing Americanist Tradition," in *Theorizing the Americanist Tradition,* 182.

17. Judith Berman, "George Hunt and the Kwak'wala Texts," *Anthropological Linguistics* 36 (1994): 483–514.

18. Donald Bahr, *Piman Shamanism and Staying Sickness* (Tucson: University of Arizona Press, 1974).

19. See Swann, introduction to *Coming to Light,* xxx.

20. For this and other language topics, see *American Indian Languages: Cultural and Social Contexts,* ed. Shirley Silver and Wick R. Miller (Tucson: University of Arizona Press, 1997).

21. *Tribal College* 11, no. 3 (spring 2000) is devoted to "native languages" and contains a very useful summary of the situation in tribal colleges. See also Rand Valentine on "some exemplary programs" in his essay "Linguistics and Languages in Native American Studies," in *Studying Native America: Problems and Prospects,* ed. Russell Thornton (Madison: University of Wisconsin Press, 1998), 171–74. It should be noted that there are some imaginative approaches to teaching children in Native communities. For instance, Fort Peck Community College in Montana has two very successful Montessori Native Language Immersion Schools, which combine Montessori methods with ancient indigenous methods. The languages taught are Nakota, the language of the Assiniboines, and Dakota, a Sioux language.

22. *Tribal College,* 2. While language loss is real, a new collection of essays shows ways to mitigate the crisis and avert the direst predictions: *The Green Book of Language Revitalization in Practice,* ed. Leanne Hinton and Ken Hale (New York: Academic Press, 2001).

23. Quoted in David Crystal, *Language Death* (Cambridge: Cambridge University Press, 2000), vii.

24. Quoted in Crystal, *Language Death,* 10. An interesting recent development in an integrative conservation approach is the establishment of the organization Terralingua: Partnerships for Linguistic and Biological Diversity. See Luisa Maffi, ed., *On Biocultural Diversity: Linking Language and the Environment* (Washington DC: Smithsonian Institution Press, 2001).

25. Gerald Vizenor, "Dead Voices," *World Literature Today* 66, no. 2 (spring 1992): 241.

26. William Leap has suggested that distinct forms of English exist for each of the tribal languages in "American Indian English and Its Implications for Bilingual Education," *Georgetown Round Table on Language and Linguistics, 1978: International Dimensions of Bilingual Education,* ed. James E. Alatis (Washington DC: Georgetown University Press, 1978), 657–69.

27. Walter Benjamin, "The Task of the Translator," in *Illuminations,* ed. Hannah Arendt, trans. Harry Zohn (New York: Schocken Books, 1973), 135.

Voices from Four Directions

1. North

Koryak

Raven Tales from Kamchatka

Introduction by Alexander D. King

Raven is the main mythological cultural hero of the Koryaks and their Chukchi neighbors to the north and their Itelmen neighbors to the south. Although these people are indigenous to Kamchatka and Chukotka, in Russian northeast Asia, their mythology has remarkable continuities with mythologies of Native American peoples across the Bering Strait, especially on the North Pacific coast. Some may find it odd to see narratives from Asia among a collection of stories from Native America, but the cultural similarities among peoples of northeast Asia and northwest America are so strong, especially in terms of oral literature, they led Waldemar Bogoras to state a century ago, "from an ethnographical point of view, the line dividing Asia and America lies far southwestward of Bering strait."[1] Sometimes translated as "Big-Raven," the trickster-hero's name in Koryak is Quyqinyaqu. In many stories he exhibits the same characteristics as Raven, Coyote, and other trickster-transformers in North America — an unwavering desire to search for food, sex, and mischief, but also special wisdom and power. Quyqinyaqu differs in key respects from his Native American counterparts, however, for he is not a lone adventurer. He is a father and head of a household. His wife, Miti, son Amamqut, daughter Yiniangawgut, and other children and their spouses and children are featured in many of the stories collected at the turn of the twentieth century and still being told today.

In the two stories presented here, Quyqinyaqu represents the center of the social world. His daughters and sons are the most desirable spouses, and outsiders like Little-Bird-Man, Raven-Man, and the Ermine-People wish to join his household. In other stories Quyqinyaqu can also be a scoundrel as is Raven-Man or the fool as played by Ermine-Man. I have selected these two stories by Paqa for retranslation for two reasons. First, we have the original Koryak versions, published as part of a collection of linguistic texts in 1917.[2] An ethnopoetic analysis based on the original language can transform what at first appears to be just a cute story in prose translation into a powerful work of art. Attention to the form of the original Koryak elucidates deeper subtleties of formal patterning and symbolic organization — a glimpse into the way Koryak people organized the universe and their aesthetics of language. By working back and forth between the small details of linguistic structure of the Koryak language and the larger patterning of relations within the narrative, one can see how all the parts fit together, parts that seem disconnected in a prose translation. The second reason is that Paqa seems to have been an exemplary storyteller. She is one of the few people to have her stories published by both Bogoras and Waldemar Jochelson. Paqa's stories are well crafted on several levels, from grammatical subtleties to cosmic symbolism.

Bogoras and Jochelson were two of the leading ethnographers working on the Siberian side of the famous Jesup North Pacific Expedition, sponsored by the American Museum of Natural History in New York. The two men had been living in northeast Asia for several years as political exiles, and Bogoras had already developed a high level of proficiency in Chukchi, which is closely related to the variant of Koryak represented by these texts.[3] Thus, I believe that the transcriptions he produced are as reliable as any of the best transcriptions by Americanists from that era. Bogoras was working on describing the grammar of the language, and he elicited stories in typical Boasian fashion, publishing them as interlinear texts for linguistic data. Jochelson was documenting Koryak culture, and he was interested in the stories as evidence of Koryak cosmology, religion, and folklore.[4] He published over two hundred stories in English, but because his notes have been lost, we have no record of the original Koryak versions told to him. Thus, we cannot be sure that the version of "Bird-Men" published by Jochelson, with the order of the second and third acts transposed and other minor changes from the version published in Koryak by Bogoras, reflects Paqa's creative improvisation or Jochelson's editing; most likely both were at work.[5]

Paqa was a young or middle-aged woman living in the village of Waikenan (called Kamenskoe or Kamenki by Russians) on the north shore of Penzhina Bay, which is the northernmost part of the Sea of Okhotsk. With a population of about 160 people, Waikenan was the largest native village for several hundred miles and the largest concentration of Koryak speakers anywhere. People spent winters in semisubterranean, octagonal houses in the village and summers along the banks of the many rivers or the seacoast, harvesting salmon and various sea mammals. Village-dwelling Koryaks (or Nymylans, after the Koryak word for 'settlement') frequently traded with reindeer-herding friends and relatives, who migrated across the interior tundra, exchanging seal skins and other trade goods for reindeer hides and meat. In this area those herders who personally owned many hundreds of deer were considered the richest individuals; a few of these herders owned up to two or three thousand reindeer. Herders lived in dome-shaped, reindeer-skin tents. The Koryak word *yayanga* was (and is) used for all domiciles (and now any building), and I have translated it as 'house' or 'home', although Paqa may have had a skin tent in mind when she used the word in the final part of "Bird-Men" (line 245).

Following Dell Hymes and Dennis Tedlock, I believe that oral narratives are best represented on the page as verse. As Hymes has recognized for Native American narratives, I have found that lines are combined into larger units following consistent patterns. I mark verses by successive indentations when several lines constitute a single verse. Verses are grouped into stanzas, marked by a capital letter in parentheses. Scenes are marked by a small Roman numeral and acts by capital Roman numerals. Scenes, acts, and the narratives themselves are defined by the onset of a problem and its eventual resolution. These openings and closings operate at many levels, producing patterns of bracketing and symmetry. The opening and closing brackets are almost always constructed of pairs—two lines or two verses, and patterns of two are found throughout Paqa's narratives.

Paqa artfully drew on a variety of linguistic resources at her disposal in her construction of this narrative. Most of these devices are lost in the prose, and my translation recovers these patterns. I have tried to translate Koryak words consistently with the same English word or phrase in order to give the reader a sense of the pattern created by Paqa's use of *vayuk* 'so then', *qonpa* 'all the time', for example. Words in square brackets are not in the original Koryak but are added for the benefit of the English reader. Paqa often uses the Koryak word *vayuk* 'so then' to mark the beginning of a stanza or other major unit. Scenes often begin with this word, particularly in the second story, "Ermine-People." Various interjections (*toq, go, to,* etc.) also mark the beginnings of major units. I have chosen to leave interjections untranslated because they provide some flavor of the original.[6] *Toq,* for instance, is often used before the speaker starts doing something and may be translated as 'well', 'okay then', 'heads up', or 'cheers'. I use boldface type to render words that are emphasized by a shift of stress to the final syllable. These words may be louder or more drawn out as part of the emphasis, but not always.

One of Paqa's more subtle uses of language includes her choice of verb tense. Scenes ii and iii of act I of "Bird-Men" provide us with a particularly apt example. Looking at lines 28–36, Raven-Man's attempt is in a verb tense analogous to the English present continuous, as I have translated it here, and this produces a sense of Raven-Man running around and doing a lot but accomplishing nothing. In Koryak the verbs are at the ends of the lines and thus rhyme with one another (word order is not as strict in Koryak as it is in English). In contrast, Little-Bird-Man's action is expressed in a narrative past tense and connotes that the activities are "finished."[7] Thus in lines 55–65 and again in lines 74–80, Little-Bird-Man got things done. He finished one thing after another while Raven-Man was just doing nothing useful.

Paqa's story of Raven-Man and Little-Bird-Man is a narrative of social and cosmic order; the universe must be kept in balance, a balance of conjugal pairs. Koryak society does not have clans or lineages, and marriage was (and continues to be) primarily an issue of personal or household choice based on the qualities of the individuals concerned. Bringing a stranger into the household was fraught with physical and spiritual danger, and the snowstorm is a metaphor for this. When a young man was interested in marrying a woman, he would go to her father or the head of the household and "serve" for a period of time that typically lasted one year. This labor was not payment for a bride but a test of the prospective son-in-law's character. He was made to work hard and perform unpleasant tasks, not so much for the benefit of the household, but in order to test his strength, endurance, and intelligence. Fixing the hole in the sky is exactly this kind of test. With two suitors, the son-in-law service becomes a competition between the two bachelors. Changing the weather is a typical shamanic competition to establish who is more powerful. Judging from Raven-Man's ineffectiveness and his sneaking off to eat alone in the first scene (a selfish and immoral act all across the North), we should surmise that his claim to hunting the furs is a lie, but Little-Bird-Man just keeps silent (as he does again after witnessing Raven-Man's duplicity) and lets his actions speak for him. However, Little-Bird-Man succeeds not alone but in co-operation with Quyqinyaqu; even heroes aren't prima donnas. I can't say whether Raven-Man's peeing in his boots is an index of his cowardice or just his general grossness. While ravens are sacred, they are also disgusting—eating shit and decayed animals isn't pretty. Contemporary Koryaks and Nymylans to whom I have shown these stories find Raven-Man pretty funny.

The women in this story (and in Koryak culture in general) are not helpless damsels. Yiniangawgut's sister Chanyai is powerful enough to conjure water out of a dry riverbed and thus attract River-Man's help and wed him. While River-Man can only bring forth a little light, Yiniangawgut restores the daylight completely. Raven-Woman appears as the most pitiful creature in the story, wailing her brother's death yet forced to accept it and rationalize it. In Koryak narratives most people in her situation avenge the murder of a relative, revive him through shamanistic power, or both. The fact that Raven-Woman simply "left" makes her pitiful, but she is not weak because she is a woman. Indeed, women (like Yiniangawgut here or her mother, Miti, in other stories) are usually the most powerful agents in a story. Raven-Woman is weak and pitiful because she is alone.

Anyone familiar with narratives of the Northwest Coast of America will recognize the motif of Raven carrying the sun in his mouth and releasing it, although here Raven-Man carries the sun to hide it, not release it. On the other hand, the sun's liberator, Yiniangawgut, is also a raven, as are all of Quyqinyaqu's family. In other stories Quyqinyaqu parallels the American trickster in many raunchy respects. Even though Quyqinyaqu is always an important household head, he is not above the crude acts concerning food, sex, and general mischief common to tricksters in America. In this story the trickster is separate from the culture hero.

Raven-Man (the fool) is a fool through his orality. He eats shit, talks a lot, and is generally concerned with food above all else. He puts the sun in his mouth, and when Yiniangawgut puts his head on a house post, she refers to the inside of his mouth ("spotted palate") as a metaphor for the sky, which it was while the sun was there. Thus, Raven-Man and his bad mouth are a symbol of bad weather, as Bogoras notes in his transcription.[8]

Raven-Man orders several pairs of boots for his journey to the sky. This reminds one of the Chinook "Sun's Myth" translated by Dell Hymes in the volume *Coming to Light,* where the protagonist orders ten pairs of moccasins and leggings for a long hike to the sun. Jochelson points out that this motif is also found on the southern British Columbian coast and in Greenland.[9] The motif of Raven-Man and Little-Bird-Man's competition for a wife is also found up and down the coast of British Columbia.[10] This narrative differs from most Koryak stories with its "happily ever after" statements in the final verse (lines 262–65), providing a closure (epilogue) to a long narrative not found in the other, shorter stories. Notice the repetition of the verb in present tense through every line of this verse. We also see this kind of repetition in the rhyming stanzas of act I. Here it gives the listener a definitively happy ending, which is only partially successful in translation. Also, the penultimate line is the formula "they were living," which is often used as an opening to narratives. No other Koryak narrative in Bogoras's collection of texts uses this device.

The second narrative, titled "Ermine-People," opens with the formula "X were living" and closes like the first narrative with the Koryak word *achoch,* which Bogoras translates as 'that is all'. I have found this word to occur only as a closing to narratives, and thus I believe it is best translated as 'The End', which is an equivalent English formula. "Ermine-People" is divided into five scenes according to the same principle of problem introduction and resolution used with "Bird-Men." Scene i is defined by the problem of cutting the new child's umbilical cord. This scene seems to show that these Ermine-People are fools or worse. Aside from everyone having names meaning 'stinky', they use an ordinary axe to cut the umbilical cord instead of the sacred knife kept for that purpose in every household's collection of sacred objects. However, Koryak traditions concerning childbirth and other close interactions with spirits makes this scene ambiguous. During births, funerals, and while traversing spiritually powerful landmarks, people say and do things in an opposite manner from the intended meaning. Thus, in a wax-cylinder recording of a narrative of a birth (made by Jochelson), women tease an expectant mother as being dirty and a stranger. However, this other narrative does use the Koryak word for the sacred umbilical cord-cutting knife (*kiləčvineŋ*), whereas the Ermines in the narrative presented here use an ordinary ax (*a-al*). The rest of this narrative is not as clear-cut in terms of problem onset and resolution as the Bird-Men narrative because there are no resolutions to the problems. Scene ii begins with the start of the birth feast and relates the misadventures of an Ermine-Girl trying to carry some food to Quyqinyaqu, which she ultimately fails to accomplish. Thus, the rest of the narrative is organized by successive failures to resolve problems.

On the surface this story strikes me as a sort of Koryak version of the Three Stooges. The Ermine-People are stupid, disgusting, and all-round fools. At a more cosmic level the narrative opens with a birth and closes with a death. Ermine-Man's death is connected to someone eating inappropriate food. This is symbolically reminiscent of the demise of Raven-Man in the first story by Paqa. Food is also connected to the birth through the birth feast. Making the expected connection between sharing food and sharing social relationships, the Ermine-People try to establish sociality with Quyqinyaqu's household by sharing their food. Quyqinyaqu finds their food unfit, and they are consistently rebuked as disgusting. They smell like shit, and their food is fit only for dogs. The Ermine-People are buffoons, and since they can't act like people, they turn into real animals forever. This is a theme common to much of North America, where the mythic age is populated with a variety of beings who crisscross the boundaries between human and animal. Some beings ultimately become people with some sort of spiritual connection with the animal whose form they had periodically assumed. Others end up permanently animals that reflect one or more inherent traits of the beings. Thus, we see that Raven-Man and Little-Bird-Man change shapes but are ultimately ancestors of contemporary Koryak people, while the Ermine-People end up as ermine because they are inherently more erminelike.

Unlike many of the contributions by elders and senior scholars to this collection and the *Coming to Light* volume, my translation and editing of these two stories are just the beginning of my work with oral narratives. I have recorded several contemporary narratives in Kamchatka, and publication of those stories is planned. Presently I am transcribing and translating several narratives recorded by Jochelson on wax cylinders in 1901 (including the one mentioned earlier) with the help of the last few elders who understand well the dialects of Koryak on those recordings. Evidence of direct connections between northeast Asian languages and those of the Americas is still lacking, and definitive relationships may never be demonstrated.[11] However, this does not invalidate the cultural connections that seem obvious. As Franz Boas and his students demonstrated nearly a century ago, people can be unrelated physically or linguistically but still participate in a common general culture. Although anthropologists have abandoned the concept of culture area as not being useful, many native people in Kamchatka think of themselves as part of a culture area that includes Alaska and other parts of northwestern America as they compare their rituals of the first salmon, funerary practices, mythologies, and other practices and beliefs with those of American Indians. Native Kamchatkans and Siberians are communicating with and visiting Native Americans in Canada and the United States. The present generation of elders, activists, and indigenous scholars are sharing stories, material goods, and political strategies back and forth. The Pacific is not a barrier; it's a highway.

A NOTE ON ORTHOGRAPHY AND PRONUNCIATION

The letters *ng* represent a single sound similar to the final sound in the English word *sing,* as opposed to the two sounds in *finger.* Koryak and Chukchi do not have voiced stops. The letter *g* alone represents a voiced fricative, articulated in the back of the throat and sounding similar to a French *r. Q* represents a back velar, which sounds like a *k* to English speakers, but is made farther back and contrasts phonemically with *k* in Koryak. *V* is made with just the lips and is softer and sounds more like *w* than in English. The letters *ny* represent a single sound (palatalized *n*) similar to the sound in the word *canyon.*

NOTES

The translations and this introduction have benefited from discussions with Dell Hymes, Virginia Hymes, Brian Swann, Christina Kincaid, Valentina Dedyk, and Nina Milgichil. My work on Koryak narratives has been partially funded by grants from the National Endowment for the Humanities and California State University, Chico, Office of Sponsored Programs.

1. Bogoras, "Folklore of Northeastern Asia, as Compared with That of Northwestern America," 579.

2. Bogoras, *Koryak Texts.*

3. For a general introduction to the cultures and the anthropology of the North Pacific, see relevant chapters in Fitzhugh and Crowell, *Crossroads of Continents.* Rethmann's *Tundra Passages* is an interesting ethnography of Alutor Koryaks focusing on women's lives. A description of Koryak language and culture, as well as a full bibliography, pictures, an index of scholars working in the area, and links to other resources can be found at *http://www.koryaks.net.*

4. Jochelson, *Koryak.*

5. Jochelson, *Koryak,* 250–53.

6. Tedlock, "On the Translation of Style in Oral Narrative," 43–46.

7. These statements are based on both studying publications by Bogoras and Zhukova on Koryak grammar and talking to Koryaks themselves on why they chose one tense instead of another. Note also that since these stories occurred in a mythic era, this distant past tense (or Past II) functions as a narrative past tense.

8. Bogoras, *Koryak Texts,* 20.

9. Jochelson, *Koryak,* 369.

10. Franz Boas, *Indianische Sagen,* cited in Jochelson, *Koryak,* 372–82.

11. The most comprehensive investigation to date is Fortescue, *Linguistic Relations across the Bering Strait.*

SUGGESTED READING AND REFERENCES

Bogoras, Waldemar [Bogoraz, Vladimir G.]. "The Folklore of Northeastern Asia, as Com-
    pared with That of Northwestern America." *American Anthropologist* 4 (1902): 577–683.
———. *The Chukchee.* Parts 1, 2, 3. 1904–9. Reprint, New York: AMS, 1975.
———. *Koryak Texts.* 1917. Reprint, New York: AMS, 1974.
Fitzhugh, William, and Aron Crowell, eds. *Crossroads of Continents: Cultures of Siberia and
    Alaska.* Washington DC: Smithsonian, 1988.
Fortescue, Michael. *Linguistic Relations across the Bering Strait: Reappraising the Archaeo-
    logical and Linguistic Evidence.* London: Cassell, 1998.
Jochelson, Waldemar [Iokhel'son, Vladimir I.]. *The Koryak.* 1908. Reprint, New York: AMS,
    1975.
King, Alexander D. "Reindeer Herders' Culturescapes in the Koryak Autonomous Okrug."
    In *People and the Land: Pathways to Reform in Post-Soviet Russia,* edited by Erich Kasten.
    Seattle: University of Washington Press, 2002.
———. *Koryak Net.* http://www.koryaks.net.
Rethmann, Petra. *Tundra Passages: History and Gender in the Russian Far East.* University
    Park: Pennsylvania State University Press, 2001.
Tedlock, Dennis. "On the Translation of Style in Oral Narrative." In *The Spoken Word and
    the Work of Interpretation.* Philadelphia: University of Pennsylvania, 1983.
Worth, Dean S. *Kamchadal Texts.* The Hague: Mouton, 1961.

Raven-Man and Little-Bird-Man Compete for Yiniangawgut's Hand

Told by Paqa
Translated by Alexander D. King

ACT I

Raven-Man and Little-Bird-Man both want a wife from Quyqinyaqu.   (A)
Quyqinyaqu wants Little-Bird-Man,
   he says,
    "I will give my daughter to Little-Bird-Man."
Miti says,   5
   "I will give my daughter to Raven-Man."

So then Raven-Man is going out secretly,   (B)
He's eating shit,
   he's eating dog carrion.
They wake up,   10
Lying about are wolverine skins and a pair of wolf skins.
They are asking both,
   "Who killed them?"
Raven-Man,
   "I did it."   15

So then came a snowstorm.   ii (A)
All the time it's not getting better.

Quyqinyaqu was saying to both,   (B)
  "*Toq*, make it better!
  Whoever will make it better,   20
    to that one I'll give the wife."
Raven-Man,
  "I'll make it better."
He says,
  "Prepare provisions for me."   25
They prepared a number of boots.

He left.   (C)
There he is staying under a cliff,
  eating.
Little-Bird-Man is going out,   30
There he is staying,
  eating.[1]

Of course, Raven-Man is scowling at Little-Bird-Man.   (D)
Little-Bird-Man comes back in.
  Inside he's not talking.   35
Raven-Man stays there.
All the time it's storming,
  not getting better.

Go, so then he entered.   (E)
All his boots were frozen,   40
  because he had been peeing into his boots.
Thus his boots were frozen.
"Impossible,
  heaven is broken."

So then he said to Little-Bird-Man,   iii (A)   45
  "*Toq*, you now, **make it better**."
"Impossible,
  shall I go out like you?
  Shall I pee in my boots?"
Quyqinyaqu said to them,   50
  "Go away,
    stay there unmarried."

1. Little-Bird-Man observes Raven-Man eating his traveling provisions.

So then [Little-Bird-Man] said,   (B)
  "Well now."
He took a small bit of fat,   55
  a stopper,
    a small shovel,
He left for the sky,
  he flew up,
    he arrived,   60
He stopped up the cleft in heaven with a stopper,
  he threw the bit of fat at the sky,
For a while it was fine.

Again he came home,   (C)
  again it stormed.   65
That stopper was thrust out into the house.
  The small one, that is to say.
He says,
  "Impossible.
  Heaven is broken."   70

Quyqinyaqu made another, a big stopper,   iv (A)
  gave it [to him],
    gave him also a big piece of fat.
He went again;
  he flew up to the same place.   75
    He arrived.
Another time he stuffed in that stopper really well;
  he struck it with the mallet;
    he threw that fat at the sky.
Again he shoveled up snow,   80
  [over] the hole.
All the time [the weather] was fine.

[Raven-Man] arrived;   v (A)
  that Raven-Man hated [them].
He is sitting close to Miti.   85
She is saying to Raven-Man,
  "Why are you here?
    You **really** smell like shit!"
"Why, I have been without any bread for a long time."
She said,   90
  "Enough, go away!
  You didn't even make it better!"

He left.   (B)
Little-Bird-Man married Yiniangawgut.

                                      ACT II

Toq, summer arrived,   i (A)   95
Then it rained.

Raven-Man used the sun as a chaw [of tobacco].[2]
So it became dark all the time.

So then they said to her,   (B)
  "Chanyai, fetch water!"   100
"How, namely, shall I fetch water?"

So then they said to her,   (C)
  "Why we are very thirsty.
So then we will die."

She left groping.   105
Thus in the dark.

So then she stopped;   (D)
  she began to sing.
She says,
  "All small rivers are stingy."   110

2. Koryaks traditionally preferred to chew tobacco.

So then a small river was made in that place;   (E)
   it began to bubble.
She filled the Russian pail;
   she went to the house.
She carried the Russian pail on her back.   115
A man arrived.

She could not do it,   (F)
He says,
   "**I, I** will carry it."

She went home in the dark.   120
That one followed,
   River.

They asked her,   (G)
   "Who is this?"
He says,   125
   "I am River-Man.
   I had compassion for that singer."

They began to scold their daughter.
That one, River-Man married her.

To, so then they were living in total darkness.   ii (A)   130
They said to River,
   "Why are we living in darkness?"
He says,
   "Why indeed?"
He put on a ringed-seal headband,   135
   went out,
At least a little light began to come out—
   dawn was created.

So then they were saying,   iii (A)
   "How shall we do it?"   140
Yiniangawgut began to prepare.

She arrived at Raven-Man's,
   "Hello, is Raven-Man here?"
Raven-Woman says,
   "He is."   145

She said to Raven-Man,   (B)
   "Since you left,
   I am sad all the time."
She found Raven-Man,
   said to him,   150
     "You're not so sad?
     Will you stay that way?"

He turned his back,
   she turns him to the front.
Again he turns his back.   155

So then she began to tickle him in the armpits,   (C)
   she put her hands under his armpits.
His sister told him,
   "What is the matter with you?
   Enough.   160
   This one is a good woman."

So then he began in that direction,   (D)
   "*Gm, gm, gm.*"
She turns him to this side.

So then he laughed loudly,   (E)   165
   "*Ga, ga, ga!*"
The sun peeped out,
   it fastened itself to the sky,
     it grew light all the time.

So then those two slept together, Yiniangawgut [and he],   iv (A)   170
   she asked,
     "Now what is here,
     is there a tent here?"
"No."

"Now is a fork here?"   175
He says,
   "No."

"Is a plate here?"
Again he says,
   "No."   180

She says,
   "Let's go home.
   My home has these things."
There those two moved on toward Quyqinyaqu's.

She began to say to Raven-Man,   (B)   185
   "*Ay-en,* [you're] a good man."
He was feeling flattered.

So then she killed him there.   (C)
Yiniangawgut stuck Raven-Man's head on the roof.
She says,   190
   "Let your spotted palate grow to be a fine sky,
   let it grow into a fine sky."[3]

She came home.   (D)
They asked her,
   "How were you?"   195
She says,
   "I killed Raven-Man.
   He used the sun for a chaw."
From then on [the weather] was fine all the time.

Raven-Woman says,   v (A)   200
   "**Ingay!** Does brother think of me?
   He is eating well."
She says,
   "Let me visit him!"

She visited him.   205
Ay-en, he was dead.

3. Used as an incantation against bad weather.

She began to cry,
  "He annoyed other people first."
She left him.

How was she to act?   (B)   210

Those people were saying to Little-Bird-Man,   i (A)
  "You two go home."
They said to the couple,
  "Have a caravan of sledges (you two)."
He said thus,   215
  "Better on foot."
The couple left on foot.

So then they came upon a big river.   (B)
Little-Bird-Man says to the woman,
  "I will carry you!"   220
The woman told him,
  "No need."
He says,
  "It's all right."
He carried her.   225

So then Little-Bird-Man died.   (C)
Yiniangawgut arrived at [some] pine bushes to spend the night,
  [she was] **almost** frozen.

The next day it dawned;   ii (A)
  at that place a herd was walking around,   230
    with iron antlers.
A man is also walking at that place.

He said to her,   (B)
  "*Toq*, come!"
She told him,   235
  "**I won't come!**
  My real husband died."

He said to her,   (C)
  "This I am,
    I am your husband."   240
He took out gloves.
  "You made these.
  This I am,
    I am Little-Bird-Man."

At that place, there's a home,   iii (A) 245
  again reindeer.
He told her,
  "Let's go to Quyqinyaqu's.
  Openly they might say,
    'She has a bad man.'"   250

Those two went by [deer sledge] caravan,   (B)
  those two arrived.
They all began to talk,
  "**Daughter**!
    She came   255
      with a caravan!"

They said,   (C)
  "Our daughter went away on foot with him."
She said,
  "Here I have all this.   260
  Little-Bird-Man brought me."

EPILOGUE

Little-Bird-Man created many driving-sledges all of silver.
There together they lived,
  in all directions they traveled around with a caravan.
They were living in joy,   265
  they were living.
Achoch (**The End**).

Ermine-People

Told by Paqa
Translated by Alexander D. King

Ermine-People were living.

So then a woman of the Ermine-People gave birth.   i (A)
Ermine-Man says,
  "Ermine-Woman gave birth."

He says,   (B) 5
  "With what shall we cut the navel string?"
"Smell-Pusher-Away has an axe."

"Smell-Pusher!   (C)
  Do you have an axe?"
"No."   10

He arrived at Odor-Pusher-Away.   (D)
  "Hello!
    Is there an axe here?"
"No.
  Odor-Averter has one."   15

He arrived at Odor-Averter.   (E)
"O Odor-Averter!
  Is there an axe here?"
"Here it is!"

He took the axe;   (F) 20
  he came home.
Only then was the umbilical cord severed.

They began to arrange the birth feast.   ii (A)
They cooked for Ermine-Man.
They said,   25
   "Take some meat to Quyqinyaqu's people!"
They carried some meat.

[Ermine-Girl] went,   (B)
  she arrived.
He [Quyqinyaqu] said,   30
   "Why did you come here?"
"[Our] mother gave birth."
He said,
   "Why did you come?
   You smell like shit!"   35
He threw the meat to the dogs.
He gave her back the empty dish.

Again she went home.   (C)
She said,
   "**Hello!**   40
    Miti ate it all herself,
    gave nothing to the old one."
"Poor thing, that old man!
   Again, a second time, take meat over there."
She took the meat.   45

He said to her,   (D)
   "Why did you come?"
Again Quyqinyaqu threw her outside together with her dish.
She remained there unconscious all day.

So then afterward she came home.   (E) 50
"Why did you stay there so long?"
"Amamqut held me back all the time,
   [saying], 'a very good girl.'
  Moreover Amamqut says,
   'Go there, live together!'"   55

"**Ingay!** I have just now given birth to a child!"   (F)
"Don't worry, I will carry it warmly wrapped."

They set off,   iii (A)
   they all arrived.
"Why have those Ermine-People come here?   60
   They smell like shit."

They came [in],   (B)
   they began to enter the house.
They began to strike them.

"They refuse us!"   (C) 65
"They welcome you!
   Let Mamma enter first!"

Again Quyqinyaqu began to strike them with a stick.   (D)
The daughter says,
   "I will go first."   70
   "**Oh**! old man,
     Why are you welcoming me so?
     I can shake [my parka] myself."

They were rejected.   (E)
They went away.   75

So then,   iv (A)
   "Where will we go?
     We'll go to a cave."
They went to a place rich in edible seaweed.

[Ermine-Man] fell off a cliff,   (B) 80
   he fell unconscious.
"Hello, it's good,
   it's stunning,
    it's good!"
They descended into a cave;   85
   they slept there.

He went out during the night to pee.   (C)
There ice blocks were submerged in water.
"Hello, Stone-Face!
   What success have you had [fishing]?"   90

He went back into the house,   (D)
"With whom have you been talking?"
He says,
   "[I asked,] "Stone-Face,
    how is it fishing with a net?'"   95
  He says,
   'All right!'"
She says,
   "Now we'll eat some cooked fish."
They went to sleep.   100

So then the seawater was coming to them.   v (A)
"You peed."
He says,
   "It is you who peed."
They looked around.   105
They said,
   "We are caught by water."

They began to climb up the cliff;   (B)
   all the children's straps broke.
They climbed up.   110
  He climbed first.
His flank fell off,
  [as if] chopped off.
They climbed up.

"Cook this meat!"   (C)   115
She asked,
   "Where does this come from?"
He says,
   "The Chukchi passed by,
   here they left a flank."   120
They began to cook the meat.

As soon as the kettle began to boil,   (D)
   he began to feel unwell.
The woman asked,
   "What is the matter with you?"   125
He says,
   "I feel unwell."
They ate the meat.
He died.

The woman saw it,   (E) 130
   his flank, that one is missing.
"[We ate] that whole flank without knowing it!
   To where will we go?"
"To every cache,
   to other people's caches."   135
They turned into real ermine forever.
Achoch (**The End**).

Tlingit

Raven Stories

Introduction by Nora Marks Dauenhauer and Richard Dauenhauer

Raven stories comprise the comic genre in Tlingit oral literature, in contrast to the clan histories and legends, which might be compared to tragedy. Raven is a trickster figure, and in Tlingit tradition the trickster role merges with that of culture hero or demiurge. As the accompanying stories demonstrate, the Tlingit Raven cycle contains both elements, and this combination has frustrated two centuries of scholars. The Boasians, Jungians, Freudians, structuralists, and "other-ologists" have all had a shot at capturing Raven in English, German, Russian, and French, but Raven eludes them all in his liminal romp at the boundaries of everything imaginable. The most significant feature of Tlingit Raven is his dual, if not multiple, personality.

In our opinion, Raven is not a god or a divinity, or even a creator, although he is sometimes described as such. Rather, he is a great rearranger of things. Lévi-Strauss calls him a "bricoleur," a mythic handyman who fixes things up out of cosmic leftovers, and who in so doing makes the world more user-friendly for humans. Thus, the stories happen in myth time, and there is usually some etiological component explaining how something came to be the way it is. But as a moral or ethical model, Raven is ultimately a negative example, a good example of how not to behave. He is ambivalent at best in his attitude toward humans and others. Raven is driven primarily by hunger, greed, and lust. He is manipulative and incapable of any honest, significant, or enduring relationship. In Tlingit the stem for *Raven* and *liar* are the same. Any benefits to humans and fellow creatures are secondary and accidental rather than altruistic. The stories included here are examples of this.

Raven's personal thirst drives him to steal water, although he also benefits humans and all life on earth by creating streams, rivers, and the hydrogen cycle. Ganook suffers mainly a blow to his ego and self-esteem, along with the loss of exclusive rights to water. He now has to share water with all of creation, but he still comes out of his encounter with Raven alive. In contrast, Mr. and Mrs. Brown Bear die gruesome deaths with no benefit to anything but Raven's gluttony and greed. Such episodes are grim and sobering examples of the darker humor in the

Raven cycle. Other episodes are pure buffoonery, as when Raven loses his beak or nose to gluttony and has to invent an elaborate deception to get it back. Even though he suffers a major setback, he lands on his feet and flies away to further adventures.

The themes in the samples here are found in other stories. Raven benefits the people by bringing fire, salmon migration up the streams, tide change, sun, moon, stars, and daylight; but beware the fellow creature who stands in the way of his gluttony and greed. Deer is lured into a deathtrap so raven can eat him. Raven flies into the blowhole of a whale to eat all the fish the whale is swallowing, and when the fish are all gone, he lives off the whale's internal organs until the whale dies and floats ashore, where Raven tricks the villagers into abandoning the carcass so he can eat that too.

Raven stories were and are traditionally told to people of all ages. They can be didactic and entertaining for children, but as with all great literature, adults can grow with the stories and learn to be on guard against elements of Raven lurking in others and especially in themselves. Even those stories that are told so often as to become hackneyed (such as "Raven and the Box of Daylight," not included here) can remain enduring and powerful examples of human behavior and relationships. For more about Raven and tricksters, please see the suggested readings.

The stories presented here were tape-recorded in small group performances, transcribed in Tlingit, and translated into English (except for the story that was told in English). They will be included in our volume of Tlingit Raven stories, forthcoming from University of Washington Press and Sealaska Heritage Institute. Willie Marks told his story at home at the request of his daughter, Nora Marks Dauenhauer, with his wife, Emma, present. Katherine Mills was recorded at the request of her niece, Edna Lamebull, director of the Anchorage School District Indian Education program. She told six stories in Tlingit and one in English to an audience of four people. Austin Hammond told his story in the context of a museum conference on Northwest Coast art.

The line turnings reflect pauses in delivery. Shorter lines reflect a slower pace, with more pauses. A longer line reflects faster delivery. Katherine Mills's lines 50 and 112 show run-on grammar, with two sentences in the same breath unit, emphasizing Bear's gullible eagerness in line 50 and Raven's fast-talking sales pitch to Mrs. Bear in line 112. Indented lines indicate a continuation of the nonstop breath unit of the preceding line.

The physical and cultural setting of the stories is important. The Tlingit people live in southeast Alaska, in the middle of the largest temperate rain forest in the world. This is a land of rocky ocean shoreline, and Raven stories often open with Raven walking along the beach in search of food. Many episodes take place in the wood-plank clan houses, with a smoke hole in the roof. Many episodes involve fishing and ocean-going canoes.

Kinship is a very important part of the cultural context and is used by the storytellers and Raven. The storytellers use kinship for humor, following joking relationships in the culture and establishing a three-way interaction of themselves, the story, and the audience. Tlingit social structure is divided into two halves, called moieties, and traditionally people married into the opposite moiety. Following his mother's line, Willie Marks is Chookaneidí, of the Eagle moiety. In line 114 he humorously refers to Raven as his paternal uncle, his father's brother, of the opposite moiety. In line 97 he teases his daughter about transcribing stories. At the end of his story, Austin Hammond, a leader of one of the Raven moiety clans, jokingly apologizes to the women of the opposite moiety, whom he calls his paternal aunts. Raven stories are the comic genre of Tlingit oral literature and can be told by persons of either the Raven or the Eagle moiety, whereas the clan legends are owned by the clans and performance is restricted. All three of these performances are characterized by audience chuckles and laughter throughout.

Raven manipulates the kinship system to establish comembership with his target and secure a position of trust from which he can deceive his victim. In line 26 of "Raven and the Brown Bears," Raven explains that "Your wife is my aunt through my father" (i.e., his paternal aunt), and in line 29 he calls his fishing partner "My aunt's husband."

These stories also include stylistic features common to oral literature in general and worth commenting on here. These features are repetition, variation, and understatement. Repetition seems to be a universal feature of oral composition, and all three stories contain many examples. Variation means that versions of the story may differ from telling to telling. For example, *kéel*, the Tlingit word used by Willie Marks, means either 'auklet' or 'murrelet'. There is also a tradition of G̲anook being a petrel. All of these birds nest on remote rocky islands. Some versions have Bear using other parts of his genitalia for bait. Understatement is also universal in oral literature. Storytellers may omit explicit details they know their audience understands. In line 32 Willie Marks, knowing that his audience knows what he's talking about, is evasive or indirect. Raven brings in dog excrement and smears it on the sleeping G̲anook. We have supplied this information in the text. But in contrast to his own understatement as storyteller, Marks has his character doing quite the opposite: in line 53, G̲anook uses verbal abuse to match Raven's literal abuse of G̲anook. On a botanical note, we don't know the English name of the plant mentioned by Willie Marks in line 107. It grows on the top of cliffs and similar high points. One possible contender is parsley fern, also called mountain parsley (*Cryptogramma crispa*), but the most likely is mountain fern (*Thelypteris limbosperma*).

SUGGESTED READING

Babcock-Abrahams, Barbara. 1975. "A Tolerated Margin of Mess: The Trickster and His Tales Reconsidered." *Journal of the Folklore Institute* 9: 147–86. (Good survey of critical theory and very important suggestion of trickster as a liminal figure.)

Boas, Franz. [1916] 1970. *Tsimshian Mythology.* New York: Johnson Reprint. (The classic Northwest Coast comparative study.)

Dauenhauer, Nora Marks, and Richard Dauenhauer. 1998. "Tlingit Origin Stories." In *Stars Above, the Earth Below: American Indians and Nature,* edited by Marsha C. Bol, 29–46. Published for the Carnegie Museum of Natural History. Niwot CO: Roberts Rinehart. (Our most recent published work on Raven.)

Goodchild, Peter. 1991. *Raven Tales: Traditional Stories of Native Peoples.* Chicago: Chicago Review Press. (The most recent collection; uses the Tlingit Raven cycle as a departure point for comparative study.)

Pelton, Robert D. 1989. *The Trickster in West Africa: A Study of Mythic Irony and Sacred Delight.* Berkeley: University of California Press. (Good survey of critical theory; suggests that tricksters help humans become aware of their own potential for divinity.)

Radin, Paul. [1956] 1972. *The Trickster: A Study in American Indian Mythology.* With commentaries by Karl Kerényi and C. G. Jung. New York: Schocken Books. (This is a classic study; the 1972 reprint has an introduction by Stanley Diamond.)

Swanton, John. [1909] 1970. *Tlingit Myths and Texts.* New York: Johnson Reprint. (This is the classic collection for Tlingit.)

Raven and Water

Told by Willie Marks
Translated by Nora Marks Dauenhauer

There didn't used to be water
long ago.
Maybe after it rained
then there was water
for people to drink.   5
I don't know exactly where.
Now, G̲anook used to live
around Deikee Noow.
He's the only one who has water.
G̲anook   10
is what they call an auklet.
That's what he is.
An auklet.
He's the one Raven happened across
way out there.   15
Deikee Noow, you see,
is far from shore.
That's where Raven's visiting.
He went out there on vacation.
That man owns the water.   20
He's always sitting by it.
He sits by the lid
of the spring.
I saw that island.
It's not long.   25
Was it eventually
Raven began to study the situation?
He wants G̲anook to get up from there.
But meanwhile G̲anook

fell asleep. 30
While he was sleeping
Raven brought in by him something no good [dog mess].
After Raven messed him up
he said to Ganook,
"What did you do? 35
You did something!
Yuck! Go outside!"
That's why he went outside like Raven told him.
While he was outside, Raven ran
to the water. 40
But the cover
of the water
is on it.
He pushes it aside.
He drinks 45
with all his strength.
You all know how skinny Raven is.
Just the same, he drank how many gallons?
While he's still drinking
Ganook opens the door of the house 50
on him.
"Are you at it again?
Are you, you shit-assed Raven?
You'll pay for this!"
There used to be a smoke hole, you see. 55
The smoke rises through it.
That's what's called *gaan* — the smoke hole.
That's where he flew.
Caw!
Caw! 60
"My Smoke-hole Spirit, grab him!"
Ganook said.
He was flapping his wings in one place.
He just stayed there.
But that Raven 65
was white then.
He was still flapping his wings.
The water is still inside him.
Finally, Ganook makes a fire under him.

With sapwood, the sapwood people used to have, see,   70
he makes a fire there.
Raven was still flying in it.
It's tough for him.
It was he, it was he,
who did godlike things then.   75
Tough.
It was for the sake of the people.
It was for the sake of the people of this whole world,
so they could drink the water.
That's why Raven   80
suffered for it.
Only when he had turned as black as coal
then he let him go.
"Let him go now, Smoke-hole Spirit," he said.
He was like a little hunk of coal.   85
He's flying away from there.
These—these dribbles from around his mouth—
these are the rivers here.
That's what a river is.
Maybe the first one   90
was the Copper River, maybe.
He spit it down.
But maybe to the North, maybe
it was the big rivers he spurted out.
Then he named them,   95
"This is such and such a river."
But who was there to transcribe it?
Then he named them.
This is how fresh water came to be.
Raven spit it out throughout the world.   100
But those that fall off the mountain peaks
don't have any lakes at the head.
Even so, you can see they never run dry.
Where does it flow from,
this mountain grass?   105
Perhaps it's called *shaa lukalít'gi.*
But I don't know what this *lít'k* is called in English.
That's what he spun into a wheel.
He squirted some water on it.

That's when he rolled it down.

That's why water flowing from a mountain peak flows in a circle.

He was the one who made it that way.

That's why it never runs dry.

Pretty smart guy, huh, my paternal uncle?

Raven and Brown Bears

Told by Katherine Mills

The Raven with the fish tail:
he was
carrying it around,
walking
on the beaches.   5
And all of a sudden he saw Mr. and Mrs. Bear.
This is
Mr. and Mrs. Bear,
I'm telling it in English.
And   10
he came to the place.
Both of the bears
were growling at him.
They didn't want him around.
And then the Raven kept on trying to be friendly.   15
So,
Mr. Bear had
some halibut hanging
in his smokehouse.
And   20
the Raven says to this Bear,
"If you want to get more halibut,
I have just the right bait for it."
But he didn't tell them that it was a fish tail.
"I have just the right kind of bait for it.   25
Your wife is my aunt through my father.
We can go,
we can go out.
My aunt's husband,
you can go out with me,   30

and
I'll fill up your boat in no time.
Then you'll bring it ashore.
We'll help your wife hang them up,
clean them up and everything."   35
And so he finally convinced the Bear. They went out.
The Raven has another sidekick, it was the
Cormorant bird.
He was sitting behind him [Raven], or
up in front,   40
up in front, behind
Mr. Bear.
And then
he didn't let the Bear see what he was baiting his hook with.
He [Raven] let it go down.   45
He was using this fish tail.
And then he kept on getting fish after fish until that boat was loaded.
Finally the Bear asked him,
"What do you have
for a bait, anyway? I want to try your style of baiting."   50
"You wouldn't do that,
you wouldn't do that,"
the Raven said.
"It's very—
it's a very crucial thing."   55
And so, [Bear said]
"Even if it's that crucial, let me try it.
Just tell me what to do."
[Raven:] "You won't like it a bit. It hurts, [audience laughter]
it hurts."   60
So the Bear kept on begging the Raven
to show what kind of bait he was using.
And finally
the Raven said,
"Allllllll right!   65
You have to
cut part of your penis out,
and put it on your bait.
It will hurt you,
but it's just for a little while.   70

It will hurt you."
And so—
and so the Bear did that.
He was screaming and hollering.
[Raven:] "It won't hurt any more.   75
So put it on your hook and
let it go down into the water."
And so he did.
But the Bear died before he caught a fish.
That was the purpose.   80
And so
he towed the Bear ashore
on the other side of the point.
And then
the Cormorant   85
was saying, "You did something wrong!
His wife's gonna find out about [it]
from who I am, I'm going to tell on you!"
And so the Raven said,
"You better not!"   90
[Cormorant:] "No, I will.
I will!"
And then
the Raven told the Cormorant,
"Stick your tongue way out!"   95
And then, the Cormorant did that.
He stuck his tongue way out,
and the Raven pinched it off
as far back as he can reach.
And then [Raven:] "Now, talk!"   100
[Cormorant:] "Errrrrrrr!"
Nobody would understand him.
So he took the Cormorant
and the load of fish
back to the lady.   105
And she was so happy
that they got a boatload first time.
And the Raven said,
"I'm gonna cook the stomachs of this fish,
this halibut   110

stomachs.[1]

So just throw the bigger ones to me. I'm going to do the cooking while you're
    cleaning the fish."

[Mrs. Bear:] "Where is my husband?"

[Raven:] "Oh, he's on the other side of the point.

He's making new   115

halibut hooks

because we broke all of ours.

He's going to come around pretty soon, maybe by dinnertime or after dinner."

And so

she went to work on the fish.   120

And

the Raven,

he cut all the halibut stomachs.

He put little rocks in them.

He heated them.   125

He put the halibut stomach

around the

little rocks.

And then

he put it in that boiling water,   130

around the rocks.

The halibut stomach was already cooked.

And so he called the lady, "It's time to eat now.

People don't chew my food,

they just swallow it.   135

They just swallow it

whole.

It's no good to chew

my cooking.

So you have to swallow it hard   140

just the whole thing."

And so

those hot rocks:

she was swallowing them

right after another.   145

And then

he gave her some cold water to drink.

1. The storyteller uses the English singular "this," implying a "batch of stomachs." Such usage is common among Tlingit speakers of her generation when speaking English.

And then
it started to steam in her stomach.
And she stood up and   150
running around
her stomach was real
warm.
[Raven:] "Cold water. Some more cold water. It will go away now.
Some more cold water."   155
And
she died too.
And so Raven brought the other,
Mr. Brown Bear.
He skinned it and cleaned it.   160
The lady too.
And
he lived there for a while
until he finished aaalllll the halibut
and the two bears.   165
That's the way the story ended.

Raven and His Nose

Told by Austin Hammond
Translated by Nora Marks Dauenhauer

Raven
didn't do any deep-sea diving.
Even so, this story
about it exists.
They say he heard about   5
this fat,
where people are using it for bait, for jigging halibut.
Raven really loved to eat only fat.
But even with this he was still thin.
He saw   10
where people were baiting their hooks for halibut.
This was when,
he went there.
The sea,
for example, he lifted like a cloth.   15
He went under it.
After this
he would untie them
where they had tied on the bait.
Long ago, they only tied   20
the bait
on the hooks.
Well,
people couldn't feel it
when he untied them.   25
When the hooks were pulled up,
there was nothing on them.
Then as soon as they were baited—into the sea again.
Well,

after a while,   30
the same thing again.
He's untying them again.
How many times was he doing this?
Yes, they don't feel
this Raven there.   35
This is when that fisherman
is thinking about it.
That's why
this
bite expert   40
was just the man.
They rowed ashore for him, so they say.
So once again,
when they went to get the bite expert,
Raven went down again.   45
Here he was just
trying to work on them lightly.
But he overdid it. He put his mouth to it as he was removing the bait.
That man, the bite expert,
felt it.   50
As he felt it
suddenly
he told his hook to get it.
This was when that hook
caught Raven through the nose, they say.   55
They're pulling him up.
He's watching the bottom of the boat, just like it's this ceiling,
like here.
As he was getting closer to it, he kicked the bottom of the boat.
They pulled the line.   60
(Whoever is Raven's paternal uncle,
please forgive me.)
He kicked the bottom of it.
They pulled the line.
All of a sudden   65
it fell into their hands.
This nose of his
was stuck to it.
They didn't know what it was.

When they went ashore   70
all the people looked it over.
But that Raven, poor thing, swam ashore without his nose.
He carved
a piece of bark.
He stuck his nose in it.   75
Could anyone guess how it came into his hands?
"Visor hat" is what it's called.
He started walking again.
He started from the house at the end of town,
asking,   80
"Where did they jig
the Alien Nose?"
So he goes from door to door.
"It was caught next door," they say, giving him the brush off.
That's why he'd start out again. He'd come to another one.   85
"Was it here that someone brought up
an Alien Nose?"
"No. That was next door."
He goes to all the houses.
Finally he gets here   90
right to the place where it's sitting.
He asks,
"Was it here that someone brought up an Alien Nose?"
"Yes. It's right here,
over there."   95
This
down was put all around it.
That was when he looked it over.
"My!
Oh!"   100
It was amazing to him, too. "My!
This is great!
Not too shabby,
the way it is."
Just as he was looking it over   105
he pulled out
the bark.
He stuck his nose back on in place of it.
This was when he ran outside.

That's why Raven's nose— 110
you can see the way it is—
doesn't fit too well there.
Well, this is how it was told to me.
Please excuse me,
my paternal aunts. 115

Iñupiaq

The Young Woman Who Disappeared

Introduction by Lawrence Kaplan and Tadataka Nagai

This story was told by Minnie Gray (Aliitchak) to her sister, Clara Lee (Paaniikaa-luk), in Ambler, Alaska, on August 28, 1999. It was transcribed in Iñupiaq (the language of the Northern Alaskan Iñupiat) and translated by Minnie Gray and Tadataka Nagai. The village of Ambler is located at the confluence of the Kobuk and Ambler Rivers in northwest Alaska and is called Ivisaappaat in Iñupiaq, mean-ing 'redstone river mouth', since *ivisaaq* is a type of red stone used for its color. The population of Ambler is about three hundred, and there are two other villages nearby, Shungnak and Kobuk. Ambler was established in 1958 by people from Shungnak, located not far up the Kobuk River, in the search for a better hunting place. Shungnak, in turn, had been established by people from Kobuk, a village upriver from Shungnak. The Kobuk River people are called Kuuvaŋmiut, mean-ing 'people of the Kobuk'. The inland Iñupiat do not hunt sea mammals such as seals, whales, and walrus like most other Alaskan Iñupiat. They mostly subsist on game animals, such as caribou, moose, and bear, as well as fish, such as salmon, trout, and pike, and berries and edible plants. They trade with the coastal people for seal oil, skins, and other supplies. Subsistence activities follow the seasons. In summer the Kobuk people set up camps away from the village to hunt game ani-mals, to seine for fish, and to pick berries. In this season they acquire most of the food they need for an entire year and prepare it for storage, cutting and drying the meat and fish. Summer is a very busy time. In winter people eat what they have gotten in summer for the most part, although there is some hunting and ice fishing. The traditional subsistence lifestyle retains its time-honored importance in this region.

The Kobuk dialect of the Iñupiaq language has been traditionally spoken in this region and is now spoken primarily by older people. Iñupiaq literally means 'real person' from the noun stem *iñuk* 'person' and the suffix *piaq* 'real'. Minnie Gray and Clara Lee are sisters and fluent speakers of Iñupiaq. Originally from nearby Shungnak, they moved to Ambler in 1958. This story was told to Minnie as a child by her mother and was originally a very long story that took several nights to fin-ish. It was a favorite story of Minnie's, and this version is also rather long, taking about twenty minutes to tell. The story tells of a young woman, Kigvalu'uutchik, who is taken by geese, becomes a goose herself, is told by an old man how she can go home again, is later turned back into a person, and travels all the way back to her parents. She floats home on the river in a hollow log that serves as a dugout canoe. When she passes a village and a person approaches, she twice gives away pairs of gloves as she was instructed to do, in order to be allowed to pass. At last she reaches her parents, who know of her arrival in advance because a bird has called her name. She must stay in the log canoe for four days without letting her parents touch her, or she will be unable to remain with her parents. They wait the required four days, and then she can finally return to her parents.

In the story animals and humans change form with relative ease. Geese become humans and humans, geese. Humans can fly after they are transformed, and geese can talk. Even the language sometimes expresses the ambiguity of the human and bird forms of characters in the story; one particular linguistic coincidence stands out. When Kigvalu'uutchik is approached and kidnapped by two young males, are they geese or men? The word *nukatpiaq* is used and can mean either a young man or a male goose. They are perhaps geese in the form of young men. The "old man" who advises Kigvalu'uutchik on how she can return to her parents is also a goose, and we sometimes refer to him as "the old one," acknowledging the ambiguity of form. Although the name Kigvalu'uutchik has no meaning per se, the first part is reminiscent of *kigvaluk* meaning 'muskrat'.

Iñupiaq stories may serve multiple purposes, with entertainment being an important aspect of storytelling. Storytellers often explain how much they themselves enjoyed hearing and learning stories when their parents or elders told them, and Minnie Gray has told of her pleasure in listening to this story. Many stories also provide instruction on how to live and cope with the world. This story is an *unipkaaq* (or *unipchaaq* in the Kobuk dialect), meaning an ancient legend involving people and events not directly connected to today's world. In this story Kigvalu'uutchik must negotiate her way through a complicated series of events that threaten to remove her from her family forever. She enters a magical world of geese who carry her off, and her only hope comes from an old goose who explains to her what she must do in order to leave the geese and return home, overcoming obstacles along the way. The wise old goose teaches self-sufficiency, helping her find a dugout among the driftwood and caulk it. He also tells her how to cope with the magic forces that have taken her away, so that she can overcome them by following strict instructions, such as the requirement that she remain in the hollow log for four days. Living in the ancient world of the Iñupiat required subsistence skills (here, berry picking), inventiveness (finding a log to use for a canoe), and consideration of the rules of the nonempirical universe (not allowing herself to be touched for four days). This story, like many other Iñupiaq legends, incorporates all these aspects.

A NOTE ON ORTHOGRAPHY AND PRONUNCIATION

In the Iñupiaq orthography used in this story, $ġ$ is like a back g, and q is like a back k, both pronounced in the uvular area at the back of the mouth. $ŋ$ is the *ng* sound. Double letters, like the *aa* in *unipchaaq*, are pronounced long. An apostrophe (') indicates a glottal stop.

SUGGESTED READING

Asatchaq, Tukummiq, and Tom Lowenstein. *The Things That Were Said of Them: Shaman Stories and Oral Histories of the Tikiġaq People.* Berkeley: University of California Press, 1992.

Burch, Ernest S., Jr. *The Iñupiaq Eskimo Nations of Northwest Alaska.* Fairbanks: University of Alaska Press, 1998.

Cleveland, Robert. *Unipchaaŋich Imaġluktuġmiut.* Anchorage: National Bilingual Materials Development Center, 1981.

Fitzhugh, William, and Susan Kaplan. *Inua: Spirit World of the Bering Sea Eskimo.* Washington DC: Smithsonian Institution Press, 1988.

Gray, Minnie et al. *Unipchaallu Uqaaqtuallu: Legends and Stories.* Anchorage AK: National Bilingual Materials Development Center, 1979.

Lee, Linda, Ruthie Sampson, and Edward Tennant, eds. *Qayaq, The Magical Traveler.* Kotzebue AK: Northwest Arctic Borough School District, 1991.

Lee, Linda, et al, eds. *Lore of the Inupiat: The Elders Speak.* Vols. 2–3. Kotzebue AK: Northwest Arctic Borough School District, 1990–92.

Mendenhall, Hannah, et al., eds. *Lore of the Inupiat: The Elders Speak.* Vol. 1. Kotzebue AK: Northwest Arctic Borough School District, 1989.

The Young Woman Who Disappeared

Told by Minnie Gray
Translated by Minnie Gray, Tadataka Nagai, and Lawrence Kaplan

I will tell a long story about a young woman who disappeared.
While she was gone, her parents became quite old and sorely missed their
daughter.

I will tell a long story about this.
According to the story, Kigvalu'uutchik was the young woman's name.

It is said that once a man and his wife lived on the banks of a river.
Their daughter used to go berry picking out on the tundra when early fall
finally came.
When early fall came and the geese began to take flight, she would say to them,
"How I wish I could fly for such a long time as you do!"
for she was all by herself and felt very lonesome.

And then one time in fall, when the geese were finally starting to fly away,
she went back out on the tundra to pick berries again.
She picked berries until her little basket was full.
After she had filled it, some geese suddenly landed below her.
Quite a number of geese came down on the tundra,
as she was trying to pick berries.

And then two young male geese suddenly came to where she was.
They began to take her by the hand.
The two of them quickly grabbed onto her,
and taking her by the hand, they began to lead her away with them.
It is said that she didn't want to go and tried in vain to hold herself back.
She had to leave behind the basket she had filled.

And when she reached the place where they were going, the geese took her
along with them.

She did not know how to travel like them,
but they all traveled together in their way.
When it would be time to quit traveling for the day, they would just camp
overnight.
It is said that they always had lots to eat,
and that the geese had very good food.

And that's the way they all traveled.
I don't know how long they spent traveling.

One time when they had made camp for another night, an old male started
slowly telling her,
"Don't go beyond the place that we have arrived at.
That place is like a glacier, a long, steep, icy hill that never melts.
You will not be able to go any farther,
for then it will be time for you to return.
You will go back to your own place.

You must go eastward toward the place where the sun rises
and travel a long time.
And you will reach a river, a river that has no more ice in it.
When you get to the river's edge, you must check the driftwood there.

There among the driftwood you will find something you can use for a boat,
a tree that has been hollowed out.
There is earth there that you can use to plug any holes.
You should plug any leaks in the boat and get in.

There will be two pairs of new gloves there.
After you float downriver a long time, you will come upon people.
When you reach these people and they approach you,
give those gloves to the person who reaches you,
and say to him, 'It is not good wood.'"
This is what the old one told her.

"Then you will travel further,
and you will pass by places where other people live,
and you will travel again for a long time.
When you stop, check around that place.
Finally, you will stop at your parents' place.

When you arrive and they find out you are there, don't let them touch you for
four days.
You will still be in that hollow log.
Do not leave it without letting four days pass."
This is the advice the old one gave her.
"Don't let your parents touch you," he said.

The geese stayed overnight and had slept all night long when they awoke.
When daylight came, she could see the place she was told not to pass through.
There was a tall piece of ice up above, and she wouldn't pass by there.

Then she began to watch the geese.
They went to where the ice was and started slowly going up.
That goose from before, the old one, turned into a person.
When they stopped making any noise and she could no longer see them, she
started to leave that place.

She went toward the sunrise
and began traveling steadily.
The snow was melting, and the tundra had bare spots.
When she reached the bare spots where the snow had melted, she found berries
and would eat these thawed berries.

That is how she traveled.
When she got sleepy, she would lie down and go to sleep on bare ground where
there was no more snow.
She would sleep a long time.

I don't know how long it was, but she must have traveled for a very long time,
since there were no longer individual bare spots on the tundra.
Now everything was thawing.

She traveled that way for a long time,
and at last she got tired from traveling too much.
Then one time as she was continuing to travel, she reached the bank of a river.
When she reached the river's edge,
she spent a long time looking among the driftwood there.
She inspected the pieces of driftwood for quite a while, walking among them
for a long time.

In that way she came across a tree that was the right size for a person.

When she looked inside it,
what she found was a big, hollow tree into which a person could fit.
There was nothing else she could possibly do,
so she had to try and get into the log.

She pushed it down to the shore and got in.
There was something with which she could plug its holes.
There must have been something that would prevent leaks so she used it to seal the boat.
And right there were those two pairs of new gloves!

Then she fell asleep.
She started floating downriver like that.
She went around with the current, wherever it took her.
One time, as she was traveling,
she began to hear people talking.
"Oh, there is good wood down by the shore,
because there is no ice there," they said.
She had started out on her journey in fall.

Somewhere upriver could be heard a splashing sound.
The person whose paddling sound could be heard reached where she was.
She showed him the new gloves.
"'It is not good wood,' tell them. These gloves are for you," she said to the man in the boat.
He went back the way he had come.

Then she finally began traveling again.
The current was said to be slow.

She traveled for quite a long time again that way,
when she gradually became aware of a person talking.
"This is good wood," they said, somewhere upriver,
and another person must have pushed his boat off.

He could be heard paddling and then reached her.
"'It is not good wood,' tell them. These gloves are for you," she said once again and gave him the gloves.

She traveled again for a long time.

When she went to sleep, I don't know how long she slept.
A person would really get tired of lying down.
How many days did she travel?

She must have slept many times, since she was traveling a long while.
Then, she realized that she was no longer moving.
When it seemed that she had come to a stop, she started to get out of her
dugout.
She started to get out and when she got out, she began looking at something.
There were her parents!
She had drifted to that place.
She didn't make herself known but stayed there for a long time.

As for the parents,
their daughter had been missing since the previous fall.
They had found her berry basket all right, up on the tundra,
but they didn't know what had happened to their daughter.
The two of them wept for their daughter a long time, and they had gotten very
old as well.
Their only daughter was now a young woman.

She stayed standing where she was.
As for her parents,
they became aware that a bird was calling their daughter's name.
"Kigvalu'uutchik, Kigvalu'uutchik," the bird was saying.
Then the parents began to suspect that their daughter was nearby.
The bird took them along when it flew away.
They went along with the little bird and continued following it.
And what a surprise! There was their daughter, sitting on that log.

Then her parents wanted to grab her.
But she told them not to take hold of her.

"Don't! Don't grab me!" she told them.
"I will come back.
For four days I must remain here.
Stay still, just like that!" she pleaded with them,
because she couldn't come back.
She would be unable to come back, if they ever touched her.
Then her parents began to cry.

They remained still.
She had told them to do that and said nothing more to them.
She didn't allow herself to be touched.
Her parents began staying with her.
She slept there four times, four days.
After that she came back to her parents.

The story tells that she had gone with the geese for quite some time.
She had flown with the geese, turning into a goose herself.
That is the end of the story.

Two Children Adrift

Introduction by Edna Ahgeak MacLean

Iñupiaq is part of the Inuit language, a continuum of dialects that extend all the way across the American Arctic from Unalakleet to Nome to Kotzebue to Barrow to Barter Island in Alaska; from Aklavik, Northwest Territories, to Rigolet, Labrador, in Canada, and into all of Greenland.[1] The Inuit language is called Kalaallisut in Greenland, Inuktitut in Canada, and Iñupiaq in Alaska.

Iñupiaq narrative texts are called *unipkaat* (plural form), stories that have been told and performed for Iñupiaq audiences from generation to generation. This story was narrated by Ericklook and Suvlu of Barrow, Alaska, in the early sixties. Ericklook is the primary storyteller, and Suvlu makes comments and additions as Ericklook tells the story. Ericklook learned this story from his father.

When Ericklook moved to Barrow, Alaska, from the Colville River area (located toward Canada) with his extended family in the late 1950s, he found that the Native store managed by Lee Suvlu was the place where Iñupiaq legends were told. Suvlu and his wife, Mary, were enthusiastic recorders/collectors of *unipkaat* 'legends' and *quliaqtuat* 'life experience stories' from older Iñupiaq residents of Barrow, Alaska. *Quliaqtuat* become *unipkaat* with the passage of time.

Before the arrival of Christian missionaries, *unipkaat* were told in the *qargi* (singular form, pronounced "kargi"), the traditional social and educational institution organized by and for whaling captains and their crews and families. Each community had two or more *qargit* (plural form). Membership in a *qargi* provided a sense of belonging and identity to an Iñupiaq, especially for men. When schools replaced the qargit and Western teachers replaced the participation of family and community members as the primary educational providers of the Iñupiat, the Native store took over as one of the places to tell *unipkaat*. Ceremonial rituals that sometimes involved shamanism were held in the *qargit*, so they were targeted by missionaries for destruction. Thus, in the 1960s Ericklook found himself in a Native store telling *unipkaat*.[2] Ericklook's audience is Iñupiaq, and they share the cultural and linguistic knowledge necessary to appreciate the *unipkaaq* that Ericklook tells, creating images of scenes that the audience observes.

I transcribed and translated this *unipkaaq* from a tape recording done by Ericklook. Before I made the final translation from Iñupiaq to English, I performed a morpheme-by-morpheme analysis to facilitate more correct and uniform translations of Iñupiaq morphemes and concepts into English. Interlinear translations showed the linguistic basis of the translations and interpretation of Iñupiaq into English.[3] Discovering the narrative structure of this *unipkaaq* was facilitated by the identification and classification of each linguistic element according to its form, meaning, and function.[4] During this process I paid close attention to the syntactic structure, especially the role of demonstratives as verbs and markers of discourse; to syntactic and semantic parallelism; and to repetition of sentences and phrases. In the final translation presented here, I accorded a line to sentential structures, to syntactic and semantic parallelisms, and to repetitions.

I adapted the scene/act/part format from Hymes for the overall text organization.[5] The line-by-line translations were analyzed for grouping of lines into verses, sets of verses into larger groupings forming scenes, scenes into acts, and acts into parts. To achieve the narrative structure I relied on the principle that "narratives, as linguistic representations of past experiences . . . contain stories with chronologically related events experienced by the characters in the story."[6] In this endeavor I was guided by the work that Labov and Fleischman have done on identifying elements of narrative structure.[7]

Suvlu, as the coperformer, had the liberty to insert comments as Ericklook told the story. Suvlu's comments are accorded lines and are followed by an asterisk (*). Ericklook made many of the repetitions as he worked to incorporate and accept Suvlu's comments into the story. Sometimes Ericklook merely acknowledged Suvlu's comments with an affirmative response *ii* 'yes'. I have chosen not to include the affirmative *ii* acknowledgments in this translation. Ericklook agreed with Suvlu's comments most of the time, but in line 358 he contradicts Suvlu because his comment would have made the return journey impossible. Right after Ericklook states that the *aŋatkuq* is planning to take care of the children, Suvlu makes the comment that the *aŋatkuq* decides to nurture the children into adulthood.

Ericklook, as the performer of this *unipkaaq,* had two tasks. First, he had to tell the story as accurately as he had learned it from his father. Second, he had to keep his audience engaged in the story not just as listeners but as observers of the events unfolding in his telling. He accomplished these two tasks through the creative use of Iñupiaq demonstratives, which can function as discourse markers as well as devices to help the audience focus on events in the *unipkaaq.*

North Slope Iñupiaq *unipkaat* are replete with demonstratives. Iñupiaq demonstratives are used to express "distinctions of reference, particularly with respect to location" spatially and temporally.[8] Demonstratives form an elaborate system of reference in the Iñupiaq language. They indicate a person, an animal, an object, or an area by reference to its position with respect to the speaker and the addressee, and the position of the speaker and addressee in reference to the concept of "downness" represented by a body of water, a river or a downslope in the outside environs, or the door inside a dwelling.[9] Iñupiaq demonstratives are also used as markers of linguistic units in *unipkaat*.

Several demonstratives and one evidential feature prominently in "Two Children Adrift." An evidential is used to assert that the information one is giving has been observed and reported by someone else. For the Iñupiaq listener the use of the evidential *gguuq* 'it is told' indicates that Ericklook heard and learned the story from another storyteller. The utterance of *gguuq* establishes the authenticity of the story. The evidential *gguuq* begins the *unipkaaq* and appears frequently throughout the telling as Ericklook brings the events that happened in the past to the present through the narrative. Another function of the evidential *gguuq* is found in lines 35 and 373, where Ericklook uses it to indicate indirect speech. Instead of creating or quoting the speech of a story character, he chooses to frame the speech act with *gguuq* 'it is told she/he said'. This function occurs several times in the story.

Major developments in the story are marked by demonstratives in combination with the evidential *gguuq*. The demonstrative *tavra* 'then' in combination with the evidential *gguuq* is used nine times to signal major developments in the story once the children are adrift. In line 121 it indicates a change of activity from only crying to crying and sleeping; in line 157 it marks the end of drifting for the children and marks the beginning of their adventures on land; and in line 250 it marks the change of the girl from a victim to a protagonist. Up to now she and her brother have been adrift at sea, have been in hiding once on land, and have been forced to venture out only at night. In this section the girl reaches the village where the *aŋatkuq* lives, enters a passageway and ventures into the main part of a house, and begins stealing food.

The climax of these major developments is signaled by another marker *kiisaimmaa* 'finally' in combination with *gguuq* in line 287. *Kiisaimmaagguuq* 'finally then, it is told' indicates the action now taken by the girl is the result of a succession of prior actions and marks the outcome—the beginning of the interaction of the *aŋatkuq* with the children.

In part 2, the combination *tavragguuq* 'then, it is told' (line 396) marks the beginning of the series of encounters that the *aŋatkuq* and the children have on their journey returning to the children's home. It marks where the *aŋatkuq* awakens and instructs the girl to cover her young brother's face with his hood as they encounter the first set of hostiles.

Throughout the *unipkaaq* the audience is made to observe the events of the story from afar or in close proximity. Ericklook deftly incorporates adverbial demonstratives such as *uvva* 'right here' (e.g., line 1) and *tamarra* 'there all around' (e.g., lines 11 and 177) and the demonstrative pronouns *una* and *uuma* 'this one here' (e.g., lines 280, 316, and 320) to accomplish this effect. The abundant use of demonstratives creates the sensation that has prompted numerous Iñupiat to say that listening to an *unipkaaq* is like watching a movie. Much of this effect is lost in translation, but I have incorporated many of the demonstratives, although doing so made the translation a bit choppy.

In addition to the use of demonstratives to create a sensation of being near or far from a scene in the *unipkaaq*, Ericklook also uses tense to create this effect. The use of the present tense at the beginning of the *unipkaaq* and throughout the story makes the audience "feel as if they were present at the time of the experience, witnessing events as they occurred."[10] The past tense is used to describe established states of being, or attributes. This technique is best exemplified in lines 51 to 54. Lines 52 and 53 describe the items the man frantically runs after in line 54.

Line 572 is italicized since Suvlu is comparing the clothes that the woman is sewing for the *aŋatkuq* to the clothes that modern Iñupiaq people on the north slope of Alaska wear. Line 424 is also set in italics because it describes the action of a member of the audience in response to events in the *unipkaaq*.

Iñupiaq people transmitted generations of knowledge to their children through the telling of *unipkaat* such as the one that Ericklook tells here. Ancient societal and cultural values as well as beliefs about the relationships of the natural and the supernatural in a universe that encompassed both were learned from the *unipkaat*. In this *unipkaaq* the arrival of the wind initiates the transition process from the natural to the supernatural realms and vice versa. The wind stays with the travelers until they reach their destinations. During both journeys the children sleep a lot. It is as though the state of sleep facilitates the transition process. Sleep or semiconsciousness or even death plays a part in the *unipkaaq* as the parents are rendered immobile in the *iglu* 'sod house'.

In Iñupiaq society children are given freedom to explore the environment, and parents usually do not interfere unless the children place themselves in danger. In this *unipkaaq* we are told right away that the father is carefully watching the children as they play in the boat on the beach but is distracted by the activity of emptying the cache of its contents. During this brief period of distraction, the children are whisked away by the wind. At the loss of their children, the parents are rendered immobile by grief. They crawl into the warmth of the house and lay in fetal positions facing each other. It is as if they have crawled back into the *iglu*, forsaking life at the loss of their children.

One of the cultural traits of the Iñupiat that is disappearing fast is the reluctance to state explicitly what one means especially in terms of affecting human behavior. Traditionally, a mother never gave direct commands to a child but instead made hints. For example, if a mother was butchering a seal and her *ulu* (pronounced "olo") 'crescent-shaped knife' became dull and she needed another *ulu* from the house, she would hint for it. She might say, "I sure could use that sharp *ulu* that is on the table next to the stove right now." Likewise in the telling of this *unipkaaq*, Ericklook never explicitly states the main theme of the *unipkaaq*. Each listener is free to make an interpretation of the *unipkaaq* in his or her context. If I were to extrapolate a meaning or theme from this *unipkaaq*, I would say that it is a lesson in life informing us that hardship (see line 12) is part of life. Another interpretation could be that no matter how careful one is in structuring and controlling one's environment, there are forces that one has no control over, such as the supernatural.

In an Iñupiaq universe *aŋatkut* could fly out of their bodies to travel to the *tatqiq* (pronounced "tatkik") 'moon' and back; manipulate the elements of the natural world such as the wind and the activities of animals and humans; and heal the sick. The Iñupiaq drum, the *qilaun* (pronounced "kilaun"), was used by *aŋatkut* in the ceremonial rituals where acts of shamanism occurred. In this *unipkaaq* the *aŋatkuq* uses the drum to manipulate the wind to bring the children to her from their home and then to take them back to their parents. She also uses the drum to lull the occupants of the house who are always conversing into silence as she leaves to take the children back to their parents. In another story titled *Ataatalugiik* (Grandchild and grandfather) told not by Ericklook, but by another Iñupiaq named Nageak, the *aŋatkuq* is able to make a *qilaun* no larger than his hand grow larger as he wets it with his saliva.[11] Through song and drumming he creates a crack in the ocean ice through which two sets of huge jaws come tearing. The Iñupiaq drum when possessed by an *aŋatkuq* is a powerful tool.

The traditional North Slope Alaska Iñupiaq *iglu* (pronounced "igloo") 'house' was constructed primarily of sod, supported by whalebone and wooden planks made of driftwood found along the beach. The *iglu* had a long semisubterranean entrance passageway dug several feet into the permanently frozen ice to create cold storage for food and furs. Smaller ribs of the *aġviq* 'bowhead whale' were used to create an archway over the passageway, which was long enough to accommodate several storage alcoves and a cooking area. The entry into the *iglu* from the passageway was through a hole in the floor called the *katak* 'the drop'. Ventilation for the airtight sod house was accomplished by the manipulation of the cold air in the entrance passageway and the hot air of the main house by opening both the *igalaaq* 'skylight' of the main house and the entry into the passageway from the outside.

In the *unipkaaq*, in line 250, the "little mother-sister" comes upon an *iglu* that has two passageways. One is an entrance passageway, and the other is an escape passageway. The escape passageway was used primarily in times of combat between different villages and whenever anyone had to make a quick getaway from the *iglu*. The "little mother-sister" secures a hiding place for herself and her little brother in the escape passageway and is able to observe the comings and goings of those using the entrance passageway. She is able to remain in hiding with her brother and steal food from the house since the escape passageway does not get much traffic.

In line 504 the *aŋatkuq* climbs up the *iglu* to the skylight instead of going through the entrance passageway to check whether there is anyone in the *iglu*. She is able to lift the corner of the skylight cover, which is made of dried intestines sewn together and stretched over a wooden square frame laid into a square hole in the sod. Looking in, she sees the couple lying in fetal positions facing each other. Through the power of her voice and the triple reference to the children she revives the parents. Some of the more powerful *aŋatkut* were able to bring those who had died back to life. Ericklook does not specifically say that this is what the *aŋatkuq* does, but one may infer that this is the case. The fact that the *aŋatkuq* is female in this *unipkaaq* is significant because she is the caregiver of the children while they are away from home and because she is the one to give the "breath of life" to the couple lying in fetal positions in the *iglu*.

In Iñupiaq culture children are said to *qauri* (pronounced "kauri") 'come into consciousness' after they reach a certain age, usually around two or three years old. During the time before the onset of *qauri*, it is believed that the life force of the namesake, the *atiq*, that the child has been given is dominant. The child is not strong enough spiritually or mentally to resist the presence of the spirit or the life force of the person he or she is named after. In the *unipkaaq* the *aŋatkuq* transmits her power through the young brother and "little mother-sister" over the hostiles they encounter on their journey home. In line 407 the *aŋatkuq* tells the "little mother-sister" to make her little brother cover his face as well as her own face. The hostiles they encounter also cover their faces and are rendered harmless, unable to attack. The *aŋatkuq* transmits her power over the hostiles twice through the young brother. Just as she is able to transmit her power over the children, the *aŋatkuq* is also able to manipulate a stick to do her hunting for her. In line 373 the *aŋatkuq* allows the girl to observe the stick, her hunter, bring home a seal. There is no further reference to the stick in the *unipkaaq*. The *aŋatkuq* may have just been showing the girl that she, the *aŋatkuq*, had magical powers.

Ericklook does not indicate which direction the children drifted in the ocean, but it can be inferred from the description of the *aŋatkuq*'s all sealskin clothing that they drifted into the land where there were a lot of seals, where the inhabitants used beads as trading goods, and where cottonwood trees drifted ashore with their roots still attached (line 194). The *aŋatkuq* accepts the new clothing that the couple offer her but refuses to throw away her old clothes, which seems to signify her identity as an *aŋatkuq* and as a person from another place. This interpretation is suggested by another, more recent story of an *aŋatkuq* who became a Christian but continued to perform his role as an *aŋatkuq*. For Christian-related events he wore one set of clothing and for his role as *aŋatkuq* he wore another set. The *aŋatkuq* in the *unipkaaq* finds the new clothes uncomfortable, is not willing to throw away her old clothes, and insists on saving them. She leaves the young family and goes home but returns again the following year. This time the woman makes the new clothes for the *aŋatkuq* more beautiful than the first set. She lives with the young family for a while again but eventually forsakes the new home that she has created with the couple and their children and returns to her own land to stay. This particular theme of the *unipkaaq* is especially meaningful to many contemporary Iñupiat as we struggle to maintain our identities as rural village people but with a dependence on urban Alaska. The glamour of the city is there, but the pull of the familiar and family is stronger.

The Iñupiat have a rich tradition of performing *unipkaat* that needs to be nurtured. The pleasure that one experiences as one listens to a masterful performance such as the one by Ericklook and Suvlu should be enjoyed by all young Iñupiat. Studies and analyses of *unipkaat* do not detract from their beauty and enjoyment but instead enhance the understanding between the storyteller and the audience. As one learns more about the linguistic devices that Iñupiaq storytellers use to exert their "magical" influence over the mind of their audiences, one begins to grasp the magnitude of the investment of the Iñupiat in their oral traditions. Only through detailed study and analyses can the structure and content of narratives begin to reveal the richness of the language and themes used to engage the audience in the performance of each story.

NOTES

1. Krauss, Alaska Native Languages, 49.
2. MacLean, Revitalization of the QARGI, 1–2.
3. MacLean, *Inupiaq Narratives*, 301–88.
4. Hymes, "Breakthrough into Performance," 11–74.
5. Hymes "In Vain I Tried to Tell You," 149–52.
6. Traugott and Pratt, Linguistics for Students of Literature, 248.
7. Labov, "Transformation of Experience in Narrative Syntax", 363; Fleischman, *Tense and Narrativity*, 135.
8. Trask, Dictionary of Grammatical Terms in Linguistics, 75.
9. MacLean, *Inupiaq Narratives*, 98–99.
10. Fleischman, *Tense and Narrativity*, 75.
11. Nageak, *Ataatalugiik*, 85–86.

SUGGESTED READING AND REFERENCES

Fitzhugh, William W., and Susan A. Kaplan. *Inua, Spirit World of the Bering Sea Eskimo.* Washington DC: Smithsonian Institution Press, 1982.

Fleischman, Suzanne. Tense and Narrativity: From Medieval Performance to Modern Fiction. Austin: University of Texas Press, 1990.

Hymes, Dell H. "Breakthrough into Performance." In *Folklore: Performance and Communication,* edited by Dan Ben-Amos and Kenneth Goldstein, 11–74. The Hague: Mouton, 1975.

————. "In Vain I Tried to Tell You": Essays in Native American Ethnopoetics. Philadelphia: University of Pennsylvania Press, 1981.

Kaplan, Lawrence. *Ugiuvangmiut Quliapyuit, King Island Tales, Eskimo History and Legends from Bering Strait.* Fairbanks: King Island Native Community and Alaska Native Language Center, College of Liberal Arts, University of Alaska, 1988.

Krauss, Michael. *Alaska Native Languages: Past, Present, and Future.* Fairbanks: Alaska Native Language Center, University of Alaska, 1980.

Labov, William. "The Transformation of Experience in Narrative Syntax." In *Language in the Inner City.* Philadelphia: University of Pennsylvania Press, 1972.

Lowenstein, Tom. *Ancient Land: Sacred Whale.* London: Bloomsbury, 1993.

MacLean, Edna Ahgeak. "Inupiaq Narratives: Interaction of Demonstratives, Aspect, and Tense." Ph.D. diss., Stanford University, 1995.

————. "The Revitalization of the QARGI, the Traditional Community House, as an Educational Unit of the Inupiat Community." Paper presented at the Alaska Anthropological Association Symposium on Policy and Planning for Alaskan Languages, Fairbanks, Alaska, March 8, 1986.

Nageak, Vincent. *Ataatalugiik.* Fairbanks: Alaska Native Language Center, University of Alaska in Fairbanks, 1975.

Nelson, Richard K. *Shadow of the Hunter.* Chicago: University of Chicago Press, 1980.

Ramoth-Sampson, Ruth, and Angeline Newlin. *Unipchaaŋich Imaġluktuġmiut Stories of the Black River People.* Anchorage: National Bilingual Materials Development Center, University of Alaska, 1980.

Trask, R. L. A Dictionary of Grammatical Terms in Linguistics. London: Routledge, 1993.

Traugott, Elizabeth Closs, and Louise Pratt. *Linguistics for Students of Literature.* New York: Harcourt Brace Jovanovich, 1980.

Two Children Adrift

Told by Ericklook with Lee Suvlu
Translated by Edna Ahgeak MacLean

Two persons, it is told, these two are here,   1
by the edge of the ocean,
close to the mountains.
One wonders where.
Probably in the east somewhere.*
They are probably in the east.

The area around there, it is told, their place is a long, gentle slope.   7
The bottom of the slope has sand, very fine sand.
The area by the ocean, the low area of the bluff,
has very fine sand, very fine indeed.
There it is all around.

They did not have hardships, these two.   12
They are alone.
Alone by themselves.*
Alone by themselves.

They did have children, a boy and a girl.   16
They had children, it is told.
The little girl was his "little mother-sister,"
she being the eldest.

COMPLICATING ACTION
PART 1: JOURNEY OUT ORIENTATION

Now then,   20

after some time,

when they have grown a bit,
when they learn to entertain themselves regularly down there,
when it becomes warm,
when it begins to warm up considerably one morning;
they, in fact, have a house at the top of the hill;
her husband begins to think of taking things down from the meat cache.

Things, items here and there, including fox skins—
he begins to set them about for the heat to cleanse.
All around down there.*
All around here and there,
he takes them all down from the meat cache.

Down around there, the two are playing.   32
She climbed up quickly, it is told, after some time,
that little mother-sister of his
and tells her father that they two would really like to go boating, it is told she
said.

Then, because he loves his daughter very much, it is told,   36
turning their boat right side up,
placing the bow of the boat out of the water,
he lets them use the boat.

They cleverly use the boat.   40
Sometimes they row.

He watches them.   42
Since they are amusing themselves rowing down there in the boat,
he relaxes all day long.
In the heat, he leisurely cleans the contents of the large meat cache.
The other contents, it is said, are clothing
made by the woman in the course of their livelihood.

ACT I: SUDDEN WIND COMES

Then without warning, a very gusty one,   48
while they are not paying attention,
comes upon them, a wind.

Those laying here and there,   51

the items it sent flying about,
the items they had set about to be cleansed,
he begins to run frantically after them; her father does.
Her father begins to run frantically after them, thus it is.

Here and there,   56
into crevices,
and small depressions,
he quickly stuffs them in;
he quickly begins to secure the items that it sent flying about.

Suddenly, his wife scolds him, it is told: 70
"Alas! Our children!
Look!
They are way out there!"

It had already taken them far out to sea.   74
Breaking into a fast run, he proceeds out to them.

Still very close to the shore, it is told,   76
when he begins to encounter waters up to here;
and they are so far down there,
his wife scolds him.
She calls to him:
"Let them be, those two down there!
You are about to leave me alone, thus it is."

What to do . . .   83
after being indecisive about what to do,
he slowly begins to head back to shore.

Then,   86
coming to shore . . .
after coming on shore,
after methodically changing his clothes,
he begins to watch them from the top of that bluff.
SO TINY DOWN THERE!!!!
They become smaller and smaller.
It is blowing them out to sea.*
It blows them out to sea;

there they are way down there.

Finally then,   96
after being visible for a while,
they can no longer be seen.

Then after sitting motionless continuously like that,   99
after some time, they begin to go inside,
since his wife said to him:
"We will not stay outside.
Go inside . . . let us go inside,
let's do so.
We cannot do anything for them."

Then after they enter,   106
facing the rear of the house they lie down.
They lie down facing the rear of the house,
letting their knees touch.
They begin to watch each other.

Then like that,   111
watching each other they remain lying down,
with their knees touching, facing each other.

CHILDREN ADRIFT

Then those two there.   114
Crying continuously, but to no avail.
They cannot do anything.
Crying, but to no avail.
While [she was] trying to comfort her young brother;
as before, both of them would begin hard again.
While [she was] trying to comfort her young brother, it would be as before.

Then, it is told,   121
when becoming sleepy . . .
when they become sleepy eventually,
when they have no other recourse,
she begins to place her young brother into the skirt of her parka, his head.
And after some time they eventually fall asleep
[she] tucking his head inside like that,

placing it into the skirt of her parka.

Then waking . . .   129
they both once again become quite awake
after sleeping for some time, but . . .
Then like before there is crying.
Trying to console her younger brother . . .
like before, [she] trying to comfort him,
it would be like before.

Because of him, it is impossible for both.   136
Following . . . following his lead,
both of them would cry hard and loud like before.
[She] Trying to comfort her young brother, it would be like before:
both of them would cry hard again.
Then having no other recourse,
after trying to place her young brother into the skirt of her parka,
after she places his head inside,
they would eventually fall asleep, after some time,
when they are weary from crying,
when they have no other recourse.

Then . . .   147
they are also hungry, probably;
it is hunger that is the cause of their crying,
her younger brother crying hard, like that.
But he probably did not cry for a long time initially, her younger brother . . .
like that crying . . . ;
that one cried easily, the youngest one did . . . ;
both of them would cry hard.

Those two were like that for several days, thus it was;
while their boat is drifting sideways, because of the waves.

ACT II: CHILDREN LAND

Then, it is told,   157
like before she had fallen asleep with her young brother,
she begins to wake up, his little mother-sister.
[TAT]
Then she realizes that their boat is being made

to hit land rhythmically.
[TAT]
[TAT]
It had become lodged in shallow water.*
[TAT]
[TAT]

It begins to awaken her, the movement like that.
She realizes they are rocking to and fro.

So then,   169
quickly waking her young brother up —
look! they are on land!
She realizes it had brought them to land, to very fine sand.

Then,   173
upon taking her young brother out of the boat
she looks both ways, but . . .
there is nothing for her to see.

There they are,   177
following the shoreline they begin to proceed.
Look! They begin to eat worms.
Then like that, they continue to eat until they are full.
Those that have been washed ashore.*
Those that have been washed ashore.

Suddenly, she begins to see a person over there in motion.   183
Over there in motion in the area ahead of them.
Their boat is here, close by.
Not knowing what to do, it is told thus, [she] with her young brother,
since someone is coming along the shore over there,
realizing that it is coming toward their area,
toward them,*
yes, toward them,
she proceeds to take him toward the grass, it is told,
to that area up there,
to the grassy area of the fine sand,
when suddenly she discovers this cottonwood with its roots still attached,
positioned landward, like that,

washed ashore by waves.

And so,   197
to that extended area,
to its elevated portion,
she hides with her young brother.

Passing by . . . the person proceeds to pass by.   201

There the person goes;   202
the girl watches it surreptitiously.
She tells him not to cry, her young brother, that one.
She tells him not to begin crying.
After she hides with him.*
They remain hiding like that.
The person does not look toward here.

There it goes,   209
the person keeps going toward their boat.
When it reaches their boat, it is told,
the person pulls it up landward.
And begins to return home;
there it goes.
The person is probably going to go home.
Because it is returning.

Then when the person disappears,   217
over there she sees many things, right over there, in view at the land point;
she had been looking at them previously,
very close to the edge of the ocean in what looks like a land point,
in a dark area,
in something dark.

And so thus it is,   223
to that area over there,
to those over there,
when any sign of human activity ceases,
when it begins to get dark,
she proceeds to take her young brother to that area there,
following its path.

Look!   230
She suddenly realizes the meat caches . . . like her parents' . . .
that the meat caches around here are like the ones her parents had!
And what looks like a house is there by their ocean side,
very close to the ocean.

CHILDREN IN HIDING

Then,   235
not wanting to take her young brother, this one, all the way,
among the old objects washed ashore,
among those things around there.
In the area that is piled the highest,
she proceeds to dig a place for him.

And after they both can get in by digging out the fine sand,   241
she says:
"Stay right there for a while.
I will go and observe them.
Don't you move.
Don't you dare move."

After admonishing her young brother,   247
she proceeds to go to observe them
when they cease any signs of activity.

Then, it is told,   250
Without reaching that one, the house,
the one she saw along the shore,
it had an escape passageway, this one,
she proceeds to enter slowly climbing down.
Climbing down . . . climbing down . . .
she slowly begins to enter after climbing down.
Proceeding along the entranceway . . .
then at the trapdoor she proceeds to look in up from below.
These are sleeping ones, she realizes, on the sleeping platform!
People.*
People.

Then as she quietly turns to look . . .   262
as she turns to look . . .

as she turns to look exposing herself this much,
here on this side, she realizes, is boiled meat on a platter.
Quickly taking some, it is told, as she climbs up,
she quickly climbs down with some.

And so then they begin to eat eagerly.

Then, it is told,   269
she does this again and again
whenever night comes.

Whenever night came, it is told,   272
she would go to get food.
When they all fall asleep.*
When they all fall asleep.
They sleep a lot, it is told,
because it is so peaceful.

Wonderfully, like that, they no longer experience hunger.

Then, like that,   279
her younger brother, this one, is not permitted to move, thus it is.
She brings him food.*
She brings him food.

During the nights, it is told, she would take him outdoors though.   283
She would do that for him.
Around here in this immediate area, she took walks with him though.
When time for them to wake up drew near, they would return to their little
place.

Finally then, it is told, when it became night again,   287
she said to her young brother:
"Don't you dare move from there.
Here is the situation,
I will go and prepare a place for us in the entrance-passageway."

Then when any sign of activity ceases,   292
through the elevated back area of and between these two support beams,
she begins to dig;

making sure there is just enough space,
she prepares a place for themselves.

She brings her young brother to that place there. 297
To their entrance passageway.*
She made sure that she was able to observe through that area.
Because it is dark, it is told.
The entrance passageways are dark.

CHILDREN DISCOVERED

It was then, it is told, that . . . 301
conversing . . . the conversing ones inside, however, could be heard.
She would listen to them.
They would converse at length inside there, for some time.

They had been conversing for quite some time,
it is told, when day came, 305
suddenly, carrying a large crescent-shaped knife, a woman comes out;
as the woman goes by, she carefully looks at her.
She becomes afraid.
One with a large crescent-shaped knife for a weapon!*

Then, taking it outside with her, the woman goes past them; 310
after being gone for some time, she arrives home.
Thus it was, she was not carrying her large ulu.

Then later on when it begins to darken, 313
drumming . . . , striking the drum,
a person begins to come down into the escape passageway.
Unexpectedly, it is one with clothing that is all sealskin, it is told, this one is;
when she peeks at the woman, it is like that;
the woman proceeds to enter, as soon as she hits the floor.

While she is full of fear, 319
suddenly, the woman casually looks in on them, it is told, this one does.
"Don't you two move.
I will take you two home when I leave,"
she tells them whispering softly.
She knew them.*
She knew them, thus it was.

And then,   326
inside there the woman drums for a while;
when she stops,
she comes out.

The girl realizes that any sign of activity had ceased, thus it was.   330
Then when the woman wants to take them outside,
she quickly takes her young brother outside.

Then, it is told, the woman told the people not
to come out that evening,   333
that one there with the drum did, the big woman.

And so then,   335
she takes them home to that house by the shore.
"There, you will stay there.
You will not go outside, though."

When she no longer got any meat, it is told, is the reason
she acknowledged them;*
she was being paid, that one;
when the platter no longer had any meat
she acknowledged them.*
When the expected meat began disappearing.*

Here, it is now clear;   345
She had come to pull their boat up because she knew of them.

It is without doubt that it was she who caused
them to become adrift; that one did.   347
"Here is what happened; it is I who caused you to come here."
She begins to tell them.*
"I caused you to come here;
it is I who caused you to come here by causing you to become adrift."
And there you will stay, thus it is.
There you will stay quietly,
without going in and out, though."

Then right there, she begins to take care of them.
She decides to nurture them to adulthood.*

Nurture . . . she decides not to nurture them to adulthood, thus it was.

Then before much time had passed,   359
she tells the people not to go out for the day when day came once again.

"I will take you home, thus it is."   361

Then she proceeds to take them to their boat   362
after telling the people not to go out.
Her clothes are all sealskins, it is told, it is thus.

The woman, this one, had a hunter, it is told, a stick.   365
When the girl was asked to look outside once,
by lifting the cover,
through right here,
the woman had a peephole toward the ocean,
the girl observed,
when the woman allowed her to look,
there, in motion, was a stick coming ashore with a bearded seal!

"There in motion is my hunter," it is told she said.

PART 2: JOURNEY BACK

ACT I: ENCOUNTERING HOSTILES

And so then,   374
the woman begins to take them home.

When the woman reaches their boat,
launching it
she tells them to get onboard.
"Get onboard."

She has her drum with her, this one.   380
She has her drum with her, thus it was.

Then after they get onboard, in the boat . . .   382
shoving the boat . . . their boat,
she gets onboard.

While it is gliding,   385 she slowly raises her arms, holding the drum.

It begins to get windy for them, thus it was.   387
They begin to sail swiftly, thus it was.
It becomes very windy for them.

So then they would sleep.   390
After sleeping for a while
they would eat
when they woke up.
Meanwhile their parents.*
Meanwhile their parents.

Then, it is told, while they are sleeping again, she told that one,   396
his little mother-sister:
"Do wake up with your young brother,
over there are people."

Along the ocean shore are many people, houses.   400
Seeing . . . seeing . . . all of a sudden she sees them crowd together, thus it was.
Yes! With bows and arrows!
They are going swiftly,
but still the people quickly get their bows ready.
The people reach the shore quickly all together.
They begin to wait for them crowded together.

Then, it is told, she calmly tells his little mother-sister, that one: 407
"Make your young brother cover his face
and cover your face too."

So she quickly does this and that to her young brother, it is told,   410
causing him to cover his face quickly
by causing him to bite his hood.
And she also quickly covers her face,
arriving . . . just as they begin to arrive.

Then, like that, while they have their faces covered   415
she tells that one, his little mother-sister:
"It is time for you two to open your eyes."

When his little mother-sister frees herself,   418

she realizes that they had left them far behind!
Suddenly, she realizes those over there had their faces covered!
They had left them far behind over there scattered,
with their faces covered like that, she realized.
Over there in that place, it is told, no one knows how they are doing.*
—*woman in audience laughs*—
They probably still have their faces covered.

Yes! They then sailed for a very long time.   426

Then while they are sleeping,   427
they were sleeping again undoubtedly
because they had been awake for some time;
they are not anxious, at least;
they are not experiencing hunger;
they are not experiencing hunger.*
She once again wakes that one up.
She once again awakens her, his little mother-sister.

"Over there," it is told she said, "are many people   435
and we are about to arrive again."

When she looked quickly,   437
sure enough there they are, like before!
She realizes that they had already reached the shore all together.
There they are with large weapons, harpoons!

Then, it is told, she once again quickly says to her: 441
"Your young brother.
Your dear young brother,
make him put his arms inside.
Both of you put your arms inside."

She makes him put his arms inside, thus it was,   446
as quickly as she can,
then she quickly puts her arms inside.

These, she realizes,   449
the ones scattered about,
the ones with their arms inside like that,

like before, are unable to attend to their weapons!
They had quickly placed their arms inside their parkas.*
They had quickly placed their arms inside their parkas!

Then after they had gone some distance,   455
they placed their arms through their sleeves
when she asked them to place their arms through their sleeves.

They are fearsome,   458
it is told, thus it was, the ones they dealt with, but still . . .
They encountered them and once again continued onward.*
They encountered them and once again continued onward, like that.

RESOLUTIONS

ACT II: REACHING HOME

Then,   462
losing their lethargy, those two, like that,
they would remain awake.
Probably because they now have a mother.*
Indeed! It is because they now have a mother.

It is likely that they went to sleep . . .   467
that she fell asleep with her young brother like before
after doing the usual things in the middle of the day.

Sleeping like before,   470
but before they had slept long, it is told,
she, once again, calls to her:
"Time to wake . . . ," she awakens them again, "wake up,
it is time for you two to wake up once again.
Over there is a house, one with no apparent signs of life,
we are about to reach it."

Then,   477
getting up . . . she getting up quickly, sitting up quickly,
also letting her young brother sit up quickly,
she begins to find herself wanting to look at it, it is thus.

When she finally looks at her, it is told,   481
that one, their steerer, their mother now,

her face, it is told, did begin to turn red, thus it was.

"My parents stay in a place like that, I recall," it is told she said.   484
"The house looks like my parent's house," it is told she said.

Then she lands with them quickly, forcefully.   486
They quickly begin to prepare to disembark.
"You two stay here a while.
I will go to see your parents, ME."

Then she is not disobedient,   490
she begins to remain there with her young brother,
when she climbs up.

With no results,   493
she makes her presence known in their immediate outside area;
she does whatever,
she also coughs,
she does this and that, but
they do not make their presence known.

She coughs again and again,   499
she does whatever,
she makes her presence known, but . . .
they do not make their presence known.

Finally then, it is told,   503
through the skylight, after she climbs up,
she proceeds to look in on them,
lifting the corner of their skylight.

Suddenly, she realizes,   507
the two are there inside,
facing each other, it is thus;
she realizes they are lying down!
Probably since that time when they were swept away they had lain.*
Down there, she realizes,
facing each other, like that, they lay.

Then it is told, she called to them down there: 514

"Your children, down there, have arrived, but . . ."

They do not do anything.   516
They do not move.

When they do not move,   518
she once again calls to them:
"Your children are down there.
They have arrived, but . . ."

Her husband, she realizes, it seems, reacted to sound . . .   522
he seemed to react to the sound.
Yes, probably because he hears something.*
Yes, he did hear something.

"Your children are down there;   526
I arrived with them, but . . ."

They begin to expend great effort to get up, but . . .   528
they begin to stumble about.
Then crawling . . . when they come out,
then standing up,
they begin going down there to their children.

Indeed, they fuss over their children down there,   533
that one, his wife, to the boy
and her husband, to the girl.
They pay no attention to this one, their visitor.

Finally then she says to them: 537
"Climb up . . . you two climb up with these two here and carry on.
They probably cannot escape, now it seems, to anywhere.
They probably cannot leave ever again.
You all climb up and carry on."
From up there, she calls to them.

They begin to climb, thus it is.   543
Upon reaching their door,
like before they begin to fuss over them.

Keeping them on their laps,
doing whatever to them,
constantly hugging them.

After they remain like that for a while, she finally tells them: 549
"They probably will not go anywhere now, these two,
they are now safe, thus it is.
I have become hungry, thus it is."

"Yes," it is told they said.   553

Then, they respond quickly.   554

Then, when his wife quickly gets some food from the meat cache,   555
they begin to eat, all of them do.

Then while eating . . . while they are eating,   557
her husband, he says, when they finished eating:
"You should make some clothes for this one.
Her clothes, thus it is, do seem to be in need of replacement."

Sealskins . . . it is told, all her clothes were sealskins,
this one's clothes were.   561
She did not have caribou clothing.

Then,   563
her clothes, these here, precious . . .
she begins to express her wish to keep them,
the clothes she had just taken off.

"You will have plenty of clothes.   566
You do not have to be unwilling to part with these;
you should not do that to your clothes, thus it is."

"I will be insecure without them, thus it is," it is told she said;   569
"I will put them away for safekeeping," it is told she said.
"The clothes I replaced mine with," it is told she said, "these here—
ones that are like our own— *
I find uncomfortable."

CONCLUSION: WOMAN LEAVES

Then, right there, they begin living together.   574
That one was prevented from doing any kind of work:

"You will not do anything, thus it is.   576
It is enough that you eat when you get hungry, thus it is.
You will remain like that right here.
You will have nothing to worry about."

Like that, they begin to live with her.   580
And all winter, it is like that, they live with her.

When summer comes, it is told, she, however, says something.   582
"I want to go home," it is told she said, "thus it is.
However, probably there is no way I can get home."

"You do have a boat down there, it is apparent,"   585
He said to her, the husband of that one did.
"You do have a boat down there, it is apparent;
it is like that, you are able to do thus, thus it is."

"Then I will use it to go home with," they say she said.   589

Then, he begins to load it.   590
Making the inside of the boat level,
he fills it up with fox and caribou skins.

"How do you expect me to pay for these, thus it is,   593
these that you are loading on, how?"

"Do not worry about them;   595
these things here are yours to keep."
Yours to keep.*

"Yes, that is so."   598

Then,   599
after some time, with her drum, after she gets onboard,
after she shoves the boat destined to be hers into the water,
she slowly once again raises her arms up.

And it becomes windy for her, thus it is,
and carries her way over there,
following the same path when they were swept away.

Far out to sea, thus it was.   606
She once again begins traveling.*

Then,   608
like before, they begin living.

She begins to cross to some unknown destination far out to sea.*   610
She begins to cross to some unknown destination far out to sea.

Just before the beginning of autumn,   612
suddenly, they realize, here she is coming again!
Yes, with her boat again.*

She did bring, thus it was, many, many beads with her.   615
She did bring, thus it was, a large bag of beads with her, thus it was.
Beads.*

"These are what others from over there filled
the boat with," it is told she said,   618
"as they took from the load that the boat carried.
Payment for the load that the boat carried," it is told she said.
There they are all around.

Their money.*

Then they begin to spend the winter once again.   623
She continually made clothing trimmed with beads for her,
that woman did.

Then she would react with deference to the clothes, but . . .
they would tell her not to treat them like that:
"Clothes, these are.
They need not be treated with deference, these are clothes."

This time especially, the clothes trimmed with beads are probably very
beautiful.*

They were probably very beautiful.

Then when she said she wanted to go home,   632
they tell her to go home:
"There it is, you have the means of leaving."

Then,   635
after some time, it is told, it became apparent
that she became of the past.
When she went home once again.*
Although they gave her a load just like before, thus it was.

                                                            FINIS

Then that is the end,   640
as my father stopped telling it.
As my father stopped telling it.

                                                            CODA

It is now clear that these beads were the
currency of those of long ago.*   644
It is now clear that these were the currency of those of long ago.
From a place located across over there not visible, from somewhere.*
From somewhere, then, probably from a place located across there not visible.
It is probably the case that they obtained
beads from that place there in the past.   648

2. West

Kwakwa̱ka̱'wakw

Giver

Introduction by Judith Berman

While myth and poetry have received the lion's share of the attention granted to Native American oral literature, on the north Pacific coast at least, nonmythic narratives are also an important part of indigenous literary traditions.[1] Among the Kwakwa̱ka̱'wakw of coastal British Columbia (also known as the Kwakiutl), true narratives were traditionally divided into a sequence of four categories that together span the history of the world. Two of these categories belong to the era of myth, two to the human, "secular" era that followed. The secular-age categories are ḵ'ayuɫ, which one source translates as 'tale[s] about the forefathers', and ḵ'ayoɫa, the personal experiences of living people.

Myths tell of world creation and transformation; many of the secular-era stories focus on human morality, on appropriate behavior, and even, it might be said, on human psychology. These narratives not infrequently contain material that would seem fantastic or magical to a Western audience, but they were all nevertheless considered to have factual accuracy, to be "historical."

The story translated here, "Giver," is a ḵ'ayuɫ, a traditional narrative set in the human era but before the memories of living people. We do not know a great deal about finer-grained divisions of the ḵ'ayuɫ category, although some definitely existed. Ḵ'ayuɫ includes what could be called folktales, recitations listing the generations of chiefly succession, the mourning "cry songs," and more. There is some evidence that "Giver," along with a few other published texts, belongs to a sub-genre of sagalike tales. "Giver" has several unusual characteristics that distinguish it from many other ḵ'ayuɫ. The individual temperaments of the main characters are treated as more important than their social affiliations and specific ancestry. The plot is formed not from connected, linear action but from a number of episodes that skip from character to character, place to place. There is a relatively large dramatis personae, and supporting characters have considerable stage time.

The text of "Giver" was narrated by a Kwakwa̱ka̱'wakw man named Umx'id to anthropologist Franz Boas, probably late in the year 1930. The event most likely took place in the community of Fort Rupert near the northern tip of Vancouver Island. As more than one family in Fort Rupert used the name Umx'id, the narrator's identity is not certain. Perhaps the best candidate is the brother of the first wife of Boas's long-time coworker George Hunt. Boas ultimately published eight stories that he collected from Umx'id, all with only rough, hasty, and sometimes inaccurate translation.[2] Most of the recorded Kwakw<u>aka</u>'wakw narratives in existence were composed in written form by Hunt, so Umx'id's texts are of interest on a number of fronts.

Umx'id's "Giver" is the tale of a nervous and vacillating hero named First in Everything who slowly works his way toward avenging a murder. Both the murdered man and his killer married sisters of the hero, so "Giver" is in a way a family drama. Because Giver, the villain, and First in Everything, the hero, are each the head of a kin group, the events of the story also have enormous impact on their community, at first fragmenting it and then, when revenge is complete, reuniting it. That the threatened dissolution of the community was perhaps the most important theme is suggested by the first line. The narrator tells us that the eponymous villain of "Giver" was the reason why houses were built at a certain site (called Having Cockles), even though that location and those houses do not come into the story in any way.

Some historical, cultural, and geographical information is helpful for reading "Giver." The technology used in the story—for example, Giver's stone battle-ax and his whalebone knife—tells us that it is set in the days prior to European contact, that is, in the first part of the nineteenth century or before. The social practices, too, are those of the nineteenth century and perhaps earlier. For a man of George Hunt's generation like Umx'id, born in the middle of the nineteenth century, the technology would have been archaic but the social life largely that experienced through most of his adult years.

Like their neighbors along the coast, the Kwakw<u>aka</u>'wakw were traditionally fishers and gatherers who lived in permanent shorefront villages long before the advent of Europeans. Until the early twentieth century, they dwelt in large, wooden multifamily houses that were partitioned into bed- and storerooms fronting on a central, shared interior space. The central space contained one or more open hearths. Residence in a house was determined by membership in a *'na̲'mimut,* a kin or descent group, and the house was said to belong to the hereditary chief of that group.

The descent group, in English sometimes called a clan, was in these earlier times the most important social unit. It was internally ranked; each descent group had its own hereditary chief, nobles, and commoners. Ethnohistorical documents tell us that a descent group might number over ninety men, women, and children and fill two or three houses. Members of the descent group usually traveled together, too, with the "men of the house" (the commoners) paddling the chief's large canoe.

The two descent groups headed by Giver and First in Everything are not named in the text—another sharp contrast with most other *k'ayuł*—but the two men were evidently historical or semihistorical figures, and a partial identification of them is possible. To begin with, nearly all of the places named in the story are located in Hope Island and adjacent Vancouver Island and are traditional village and resource sites of the T'łat'łasi̱kwala division of the Kwakwa̱ka'wakw. This division consisted of just three descent groups.

We do not know which of the three First in Everything is supposed to have headed, although many chiefs' names were hereditary, and this information was probably available to the indigenous audience. We can, however, name Giver's clan. When Franz Boas encountered the T'łat'łasikwala at the end of the nineteenth century, one of the three descent groups, called Lala'wiḻala 'Those Going Back and Forth across the Strait', was split into two parts. One part was called "The Givers"—meaning, according to Kwakwa̱ka'wakw descent-group naming practices, the descendants and adherents of a man named Giver. This man is presumably the Giver of Umx'id's narrative, and Umx'id's narrative is in turn presumably a retelling of the events that tore apart the clan—and the larger T'łat'łasi̱kwala community—some time before Umx'id's birth. Despite the ending of Umx'id's story, the continued existence of a rift in the Lala'wiḻala clan several generations later suggests that restoration of social harmony was not complete.

In the story one of the hero's grievances against his brother-in-law Giver is that Giver has taken a second wife. Polygyny was an acceptable practice for chiefs, so the fact that First in Everything feels "sick at heart" probably has more to do with the lack of respect and affection his sister now receives than the fact of the second marriage.

Three other important cultural institutions come into the story, one of a secular nature and the other two belonging to ceremonial and spiritual realms. The secular institution is the seal feast, an event that both First in Everything and Giver attempt to stage. A clan chief's status depended in part on his ability to host other descent groups at bountiful feasts of various kinds, and a feast of harbor-seal meat was among the most prestigious of all. The distribution of meat at seal feasts was determined by hereditary rank: "[T]he chiefs receive the chest, and the chiefs next in rank receive the limbs. They give only pieces of the seal's body to commoners . . . and they give the tail of the seal to the lowest people."[3] Only slaves were lower than commoners, so when Giver hurls the hind flippers at the sons of the man he has murdered, the children of a chief's sister, he has offered a profound insult.

The two institutions belonging to the spiritual realm are the winter-dance complex and shamanism. While entirely distinct in organization, both of these have initiatory narratives of death and resurrection, and in the story they are presented as both reflecting and standing in opposition to each other.

During the course of the narrative, Giver gains the right to be initiated into an Oowekeeno ceremonial through his marriage to the Oowekeeno chief's daughter. During the nineteenth century and perhaps before, a number of real-life marriages like Giver's took place as Kwakw<u>a</u>ka'wakw chiefs sought the prestigious winter dances of the Oowekeeno and the Heiltsuk, their northern neighbors. The highest-ranking and most sought-after northern dance was the Hamat'sa, often glossed in English as 'Cannibal'. According to the initiation myths, the original Hamat'sa initiates, male clan ancestors, were abducted by a predatory spirit with a taste for human flesh. In the spirit's house the novices were killed, eaten, and brought back to life, and they returned home in a wild and dangerous state.

The native winter ceremonial of the Kwakw<u>a</u>ka'wakw has a rather different origin myth, however, in which the ceremonial was acquired in the myth age from the wolves. The wolves are also said to be the source of the *nun<u>l</u>am*, a distinct ceremonial performed by the T'<u>l</u>at'<u>l</u>asi<u>kwa</u>la and only a handful of other Kwakw<u>a</u>ka'wakw groups. Finally, wolves are central to a great many Kwakw<u>a</u>ka'wakw narratives of shamanic initiation, where they take pity on a sick or dead person of any social condition, restore him or her to life, and grant shamanic powers. Thus, in the story, when the Hamat'sa's victim is brought back to life by wolves, it is not only a victory of the native and local over the foreign and distant; it is also a triumph of egalitarian shamanic power over spirit power accessible only through gender, inherited rank, and political alliance.

Several stages of Giver's winter-dance initiation have consequences for the unfolding of the plot:

1. Seclusion. The nineteenth-century Hamat'sa novice lived in seclusion in a hut in the woods for four months. He was said to be in the spirit's house during this time. There were apparently no special restrictions on his activities, and a novice could pass the time hunting, as Giver does in the story.

2. "Surrounding" the novice. The novice came out of the woods in a dangerous state and had to be surrounded, captured, and "tamed." He then wore a black-bear-skin robe, as does Giver in the story, along with head and neck rings of red-dyed cedar bark, and he was called *dzi<u>l</u>ala* 'freshly caught (i.e., not dried) fish'. (The imagery of the initiation invokes the life cycle of salmon, which were thought to return to life after humans ate them.)[4] Red cedar bark is the prime symbol of the power of the winter ceremonial, and the secular noninitiate was in some contexts represented as fearing it. The Hamat'sa in this stage was said to return easily to his wild ways and to be feared for this reason as well.

3. Purification of the Fresh Fish. The new Hamat'sa purified himself regularly for four months by washing with urine, a spiritually potent liquid. In the story Giver keeps his wooden box of urine on the shore opposite his tiny

island fort. His enemy apparently knows the rigorous schedule that the Fresh Fish must follow—washing at four-day intervals, then at six-day intervals, then at eight-day intervals, and so on—because First in Everything knows when to find his brother-in-law at his ablutions.

The form of the story as presented here needs some explanation. As Dell Hymes and others have shown, much traditional oral narrative is a form of poetry in which the poetic units—lines, verses, stanzas, and so on—are "rhetorical" structures defined not through features like meter or rhyme, but rather through particles or patterns of narrative action.[5] In traditional Kwakwaka'wakw narrative, the basic rhetorical unit, which I call a stich, is marked in somewhat different ways according to genre, formality of the occasion, and the narrator's personal style. In "Giver" Umx'id marks each stich solely with the Kwak'wala discourse suffix -*la*. This suffix is attached to the initial auxiliary or verb of the first clause of the stich, or, in the case of quoted speech, to the "he/she said" tag that usually follows. I have not translated -*la*, which occurs in nearly every sentence, but I indicate its presence by beginning each stich at the left margin.

Most stichs are made of a single sentence, but some are more elaborate. Groups of stichs form larger rhetorical units that are demarcated by shifts in setting, character, topic, focus, and by the patterning of action and response; these can be called couplets, verses, stanzas, scenes, and acts. The main pattern-numbers here, as in many Native American traditions, are two and four rather than the European three.

The narrative of "Giver" is divided into four acts. The first, introductory act has two scenes while the rest have four each. Each scene in the story contains four stanzas. Stanzas are generally formed of two or four couplets, although they range in length from a single stich to more complex constructions with as many as nine stichs.

The contrasting parallel is an especially common element of form that appears at many levels. Act II, for example, is framed by paired, opposing sequences involving the orphaned children's growth and future ability to seek revenge. Act III is likewise structured thematically by the already mentioned opposition between winter-ceremonial and shamanic initiations. The story as a whole seems to be framed rather subtly by the image of the two grieving widows. The first and most important widow in the story is, of course, the wife of the murdered Good Maker, the hero's sister. We never see her grieving for her husband; we meet her at the beginning of act II only as the mother of the insulted children, and when she weeps in that scene it is as if her tears are brought on solely by the insult. It's as if the consequences of the original, central crime, the emotional core of the story, were too awful to show—or as if the narrator decided it would be more effective to leave to the imagination the devastation caused by that murder. The second widow, the Ławit'sis woman—a very minor character—is the one whose mourning is shown onstage. Her function is apparently to provide indirect reflection of the grief of the first widow—both for the audience and for First in Everything, whose long-delayed assault on Giver is given a boost by this further evidence of his brother-in-law's villainy.

In the translation stanzas are marked by two line spaces, and their constituent parts (verses, couplets) by one line space.

A NOTE ON ORTHOGRAPHY AND PRONUNCIATION

Kwak'wala words are transcribed here according to the orthography used by the U'mista Cultural Centre of Alert Bay, British Columbia. The underlined <u>k</u> is made further back in the throat than a regular k. The apostrophe (') indicates glottalization, a sound similar to the catch heard at the beginnings of words in the phrase "I ate eight eggs." The underlined <u>a</u> sounds like the initial vowel in English *about;* without an underline, a is pronounced as in *father.* The character *x* is similar to the *ch* in Scottish *loch* and the barred *ł* character is pronounced like a Welsh *ll,* often sounding to an English speaker like the combination *lth.*

Under the onslaught of colonization, missionization, English-only residential schools, and the increasing pressure of the dominant culture, Kwakw<u>a</u>k<u>a</u>'wakw oral tradition has diminished in vitality over the last hundred years. It has not, however, disappeared. Moreover, the Kwak'wala language is taught in schools today, and Kwakw<u>a</u>k<u>a</u>'wakw communities are making a number of efforts to preserve and revitalize both language and culture.

NOTES

1. Judith Berman, "'Some Mysterious Means of Fortune': A Look at Northwest Coast Oral History," in *Coming to Shore: Northwest Coast Ethnology, Traditions, and Visions,* ed. Marie Mauzé, Michael Harkin, and Sergei Kan (Lincoln: University of Nebraska Press, forthcoming).

2. Franz Boas, *Kwakiutl Tales, New Series,* vol. 1, *Translations,* Columbia University Contributions to Anthropology, vol. 26, part 1 (New York: Columbia University Press, 1935); and Franz Boas, *Kwakiutl Tales, New Series,* vol. 2, *Texts,* Columbia University Contributions to Anthropology, vol. 26, part 2 (New York: Columbia University Press, 1943). "Giver" is in Boas, *Kwakiutl Tales,* vol. 2, 134–40.

3. Franz Boas, *Ethnology of the Kwakiutl,* Bureau of American Ethnology Annual Report 35, parts 1 and 2 (Washington DC: Government Printing Office, 1921), 750–51.

4. Judith Berman, "Red Salmon and Red Cedar Bark: Another Look at the Nineteenth-Century Kwakw<u>a</u>k<u>a</u>'wakw Winter Ceremonial," BC *Studies* 125/126 (2000): 53–98.

5. Dell Hymes, *"In Vain I Tried to Tell You": Essays in Native American Ethnopoetics* (Philadelphia: University of Pennsylvania Press, 1981).

SUGGESTED READING

Berman, Judith. "The Seals' Sleeping Cave: The Interpretation of Boas' Kwak'wala Texts." Ph.D. diss., University of Pennsylvania Department of Anthropology, 1991.

Boas, Franz. *Kwakiutl Tales.* Columbia University Contributions to Anthropology, vol. 2. New York: Columbia University Press, 1910.

———. *Kwakiutl Ethnography.* Edited by Helene Codere. Chicago: University of Chicago Press, 1966.

Boas, Franz, and George Hunt. *Kwakiutl Texts.* Memoir of the American Museum of Natural History, Jesup North Pacific Expedition, no. 3. New York: G. E. Stechert, 1905.

———. *Kwakiutl Texts, Second Series.* Memoir of the American Museum of Natural History, Jesup North Pacific Expedition, no. 10. New York: G. E. Stechert, 1906.

Jonaitis, Aldona, ed. *Chiefly Feasts: The Enduring Kwakiutl Potlatch.* Seattle: University of Washington Press, 1991.

Giver

Told by Umx'id
Translated by Judith Berman

ACT I

SCENE 1

Giver was the reason they built houses at Having Cockles.[1]
When it began they were living at Land-Otter Point.[2]

He was sitting in his house.
His uncle Pushed Through came in.[3]

Pushed Through whispered to Giver.
Said he,
   "Kill this man who came to warm himself at your hearth.
     He was sent to spy on you.
   You will be killed, Giver, by First in Everything."

But the man had only come to dry his hair.
He had only been bathing, that Good Maker.

"You are evil, Pushed Through,"
   said Giver.
     "When will I finish my feasts if I kill this man?
     All right, I'll kill him."

1. Having Cockles is a site in Shushartie Bay on Vancouver Island, off the southeast corner of Hope Island. For the identification of place names, I have relied on Franz Boas, *Geographical Names of the Kwakiutl Indians,* Columbia University Contributions to Anthropology, vol. 20 (New York: Columbia University Press, 1934).
2. Land-Otter Point is a site on the southeast corner of Hope Island.
3. Father's or mother's brother; most likely the former as Pushed Through belongs to Giver's descent group and membership was most often acquired through the paternal line.

Up rose Giver, and he grabbed his stone battle-ax and threw it at Good Maker.
Good Maker was dead.

He just pushed him onto his hearth fire and barred his door.
Good Maker's friends tried to enter when they learned that Good Maker was
dead, but they could not.

SCENE 2

Giver moved away from Land-Otter Point and went to Deer Place,[4] going across
with all his people, the single clan that was Giver's people.
First in Everything and his clan stayed at Land-Otter Point.

First in Everything said,
"Let's invite Giver here so we can avenge Good Maker's death.
    Go hunt seals so we can feed them to Giver."

The seals arrived.
    He invited Giver.
Giver entered the house with all his clan.

First in Everything shot an arrow at Giver.
It missed.

It hit a slave instead.
The arrow struck the slave right in the belly.

Giver became enraged.
    He took his knife and swung it among the guests.
His knife was of whalebone.

Giver just returned to Deer Place.
He ate nothing of what they had served him once he realized First in
Everything had plotted to kill his own brother-in-law.

---

4. Deer Place is present-day Cape James, the northeast point of Hope Island. It is about three miles
along the beach from Land-Otter Point.

Good Maker's children said to their mother,
   "We're going to see Across the Top at Deer Place."
"Go ahead,"
   said the children's mother.
      These were the late Good Maker's children, the ones going to see Across
      the Top.

The children walked along the shore toward Deer Place.
They reached their aunt Across the Top.[5]

At the invitation of Giver, men were feasting.
They had steamed the seals with red-hot stones.

The seals were cooked.
They removed the pieces from the liquid with tongs.

Giver grabbed a set of hind flippers and took one bite.
He threw them across the house at the children.

"Take these,"
   said Giver.
"Eat these, little babies,"[6]
   said Giver,
"so you'll grow up quickly — if you plan to take revenge against me,"
   said Giver.

The children just left the house and returned to Land-Otter Point.
They told their mother.

"Do you know what Giver said to us?"
   said the children.
"What did he say?"

5. Their mother's sister, who is Giver's wife.
6. K̲'as- 'to bite on or eat meat or fish' was also used metaphorically in the sense of 'to take revenge on enemy'.

said their mother.
"He bit the hind flippers and he threw the hhind flippers at us.
'Eat these, little babies, so you can grow up quickly—if you plan to take revenge
against me,' Giver said to us,"
    the children told their mother.
The mother began to cry inconsolably when she heard her children's story.

First in Everything came in and asked his sister,
    "Why are you crying?"
The woman told her brother what Giver had said when he bit the hind flippers
and threw them at the children.

"We will move across to Na̱'widi,"[7]
    said First in Everything,
        "and leave this evil man."
He and all his clan moved their goods.
    They built houses at Na̱'widi.
Giver moved too and went to Island in Back with all his clan, and they built
houses at Island in Back as well.[8]

                                                                          SCENE 2

Giver went to the Oowekeeno to try to get a wife from Born to Dance.
He returned with a wife, one in addition to Across the Top.

He went to Ma̱'lubax to fish for sockeye.[9]
He roasted them.

His brother-in-law, First in Everything, walked along the shore to see Giver.
Across the Top fed her brother.

First in Everything was truly sick at heart when he saw Giver's second wife.

7. Na̱'widi is a site near Cape Sutil on Vancouver Island, southwest of Hope Island and about nine
miles by water from Land-Otter Point.
8. Island in Back is apparently tiny Rason Island on the north side of Hope Island.
9. Ma̱'lubax is located on the Nahwitti River on Vancouver Island, about two miles upriver from the
ocean. The mouth of the Nahwitti River is itself about three miles along the beach from the village site
of Na̱'widi.

Giver did not love his sister at all.
  The one Giver loved was the Oowekeeno woman.

"Let's go hunting,"
  said Giver to First in Everything.
"Let's go,"
  said First in Everything.

They walked along the beach.
They saw a seal.

First in Everything shot an arrow.
It hit the seal dead on.

The seal floated along on the water.
"Go ahead, swim,"
  said Giver to First in Everything.

First in Everything swam toward the seal.
  But Giver had tricked him into swimming.
Giver threw a stone.

First in Everything just kept diving.
First in Everything arrived on the rocky shore.

They grappled with each other.
"You set a trap for me,"
  said First in Everything.
    "We are going to war."

First in Everything returned home to Na̲'widi.
Giver also returned home, to Island in Back.

First in Everything summoned his clan for an announcement.

He was going to pole up to Ma̱'lubax with the children, the late Good Maker's offspring, so he could try to make them grow at the lake above the river at Ma̱'lubax.[10]

    The children were going to bathe in it all the time.

    This is what he announced to his clan.

"Go ahead,"

      First in Everything's clan told him.

He poled up the river.

In the canoe there were three of them, First in Everything and the two children.

They arrived at the lake.

In the lake sits an island.

There they built a shelter to be their house.

The children went into the water from the flat rocks.

They bathed four times a day.[11]

A season passed.

He measured the children's height on the flat rocks.

He would lay the children on their backs and take a stone to mark the distance between head and feet.

He constantly measured them during that season.

The children grew up quickly.

He made the children wrestle whenever they played.

    For this reason the children became very strong.

ACT III

SCENE 1

Giver went to the Oowekeeno to begin a Hamat'sa initiation.[12]

---

10. Literally "the lake of the river/creek at Ma̱'lubax." At Ma̱'lubax the Nahwitti River is joined by the outlet of a small lake. This outlet is only a half-mile long but plunges three hundred feet from the lake to the Nahwitti.

11. Bathing children in cold water was thought to cause them to become strong and grow quickly. In myth, as it is suggested here, the growth takes place with magical swiftness.

12. As Giver's seclusion should last four months, the narrator has probably gone back to a time soon after the seal-hunting incident, which takes place around midsummer (the end of sockeye season).

Giver entered seclusion among the Oowekeeno.

Giver paddled secretly to where the children were, to Ma̱'lubax, where the
outlet of the lake joins the river.
  Giver was searching for something to kill.

"Let's go hunt loons by firelight,"
    said First in Everything to the children.
They canoed down the river at night.[13]

They lit a fire in the canoe.
They shot at loons.

A loon cried out.[14]
"Go on, put out our fire,"
  said First in Everything to the children who were with him.

And here all at once came Giver, nearly grabbing the stern of First in
Everything's canoe.
  He intended to kill them.
First in Everything slipped away and headed swiftly up the river.
  Giver could not track him because the night was dark.
  First in Everything escaped, his course unknown.

First in Everything went straight to his house on the lake.
Giver returned to the Oowekeeno to be surrounded in his aspect as Hamat'sa.

SCENE 2

Giver finished dancing.
He returned to his house at Island in Back.

He was a Fresh Fish.

When Giver arrives at Ma̱'lubax it is near the end of his seclusion, probably November. He will emerge
to dance in late November or December.
13. Likely the Nahwitti River is meant, rather than the outlet of the lake.
14. The common loon is "usually silent in winter." Roger Tory Peterson, *A Field Guide to Western Birds*
(Boston: Houghton Mifflin, 1961), 3.

He covered himself with a robe.

His robe was of black-bear skin.
On the back of his robe was a man made of red-dyed cedar bark, and imitation
bones were on the back of his robe.

The reason he was so feared, that Giver, was because of his red cedar bark.
In his aspect as Hamat'sa his name was The Hidden One.

SCENE 3

He was always sitting on the roof of his house.

"I will visit The Hidden One,"
   said Causing Potlatches.
"You don't dare!"
   Causing Potlatches was told.
      "He's an evil man."

   "You will see me.
      I will come light a fire on the beach at Perch Place if I am killed by that
      evil man." [15]

First in Everything canoed down the river with the children.
The children had become extraordinarily strong.

Causing Potlatches arrived on the beach at Giver's place.
He was greeted and asked for news.
Causing Potlatches spoke:
      "The news is that the attempt to make them grow was successful, and First
      in Everything has canoed down the river.
   The children are very strong."

"What is he saying?"

15. Perch Place is a beach at the western tip of Hope Island, about three miles across the water from
Na̲'widi.

said Giver.
    He was sitting on the roof of his house.
"This is his news:
He says they have grown up and have canoed down the river.
   He says they are very strong,"
      Giver was told.

Giver became enraged.
"Why is that news so exciting?"
   said he.

Up rose Giver on the roof and he took his stone ax and went to kill Causing
Potlatches, and he cut him open and threw him into the ocean.
He went back and sat down on the roof of his house.

                                         SCENE 4

The children said,
"Let's pull our dead friend out of the water on the far side of the channel,"
   so said the children.[16]

They tied a rope around his neck and towed him to the far side, and pulled him
up the beach to the high-tide line.
It was almost evening.

A great many wolves approached.
The children said,
   "Let's go watch them eat up our friend Causing Potlatches."

The wolves came to eat him.
But they did not in fact eat him up.
They just licked the wound in his stomach to bring him back to life.
The wolves departed.

Causing Potlatches did indeed come back to life.

16. They have found Causing Potlatches drifting on the water and tow him across the strait to Hope
Island. The currents seem to run from Island in Back to N<u>a</u>'widi; in the next stanza Giver's daughter
apparently drifts along the same route.

When darkness fell, Causing Potlatches rose and went to Perch Place to light a
fire on the beach that night.

Those who lived at Na̱'widi saw the fire on the beach.
"Our friend was indeed killed,"
    said Causing Potlatches's people.

"Let's go get him,"
    they said.
They went to get Causing Potlatches.

He told his people the story of how Giver had tried to kill him.
He had been shown mercy by the wolves.

ACT IV

SCENE 1

Giver's people prepared to go visit [the chief of the Ławit'sis].[17]
All of Giver's people went to the Ławit'sis at Women's Voices.[18]

Across the Top carried her daughter to a canoe and sent her to visit First in
Everything.
She whispered to her child.
"'Come attack my father.
    All his people went to the Ławit'sis.'
        Say that to your uncle,"
            Across the Top said to her child.
Her child went on the ocean in the canoe.[19]

She arrived at First in Everything's place.
They called to First in Everything to come lift his niece out of the canoe.

His niece spoke to him.

17. A neighboring division of the Kwakw̱a̱ka'wakw. The text says "visit First in Everything," an error
by narrator or transcriber. It is the Ławit'sis chief's name that should be given here.
18. Women's Voices is a site on Hardy Bay to the south along the coast of Vancouver Island.
19. The text is not clear as to whether the girl paddles to Na̱'widi or drifts there. The fact that she is
apparently too young to disembark under her own power suggests the latter possibility.

"Go attack my father,"
   said the girl.
"My mother says all his people have gone to the Ławit'sis."

First in Everything and his clan right away prepared to go to the Ławit'sis.
   They wanted to confirm the girl's message.
First in Everything's wife took blood and smeared her face with it.
She accused First in Everything of wanting to die.
   She quickly bought grave wrappings for First in Everything.
But he said he believed the girl's message.
He started believing it when he went out on the water and saw Giver's clan.
   They really were going to the Ławit'sis.

SCENE 2

He quickly turned back to come to Crosswise on Rock.[20]
At Crosswise on Rock there was just one canoe builder, an old man.

First in Everything spoke.
   "I came to hire someone to sharpen my knife — so you could sharpen it, old
   man.
   This is what I'll use to cut open Giver when I kill him."

   "Let your children['s knife] come to me so I can sharpen it."[21]

The old man sharpened it.

"Maybe your knife has a good edge now,"
   said the old man.
He cut his cheek.
   "Your children's knife has a good edge indeed.
   Go kill this evil man.
   As soon as I finish hollowing out a canoe, Giver robs me of it."

20. Crosswise on Rock is a site at the head of Bull Harbor, located on the south shore of the neck
that connects the western and eastern parts of Hope Island. Island in Back, where Giver is now living,
stands just off the north shore of this neck.
21. Apparently a word is missing from the text.

First in Everything crossed the neck to hide on the beach opposite Giver's
house.

    He knew that Giver always came across to bathe.
Now Giver came across with his slaves.

He took off his clothing, a tunic of elk hide.[22]
He began to wash at his box of urine.

First in Everything was afraid that he would not be quick enough to kill him
while he washed at his box of urine.
Giver returned home.

    First in Everything grew afraid.

"We had better kill his people first,"
    said First in Everything,
"so let's go to Deer Place now, to lie in ambush for his people; they will stop at
Deer Place on the way back from the Ławit'sis, because they still have houses
there,"
    said First in Everything.

    He walked back to his canoe and they went to Deer Place.

They concealed themselves behind a reef.
A large canoe approached.

    It came into view around the point.

"These are the ones we are waiting for,"
    said First in Everything.
    "Be ready when they reach us."
Giver's people reached the reef.

First in Everything's people paddled and rammed them.
Giver's people capsized.

22. Clothing of elk hide was most likely armor—that is what elk hide was used for—suggesting that
Giver anticipated attack. Early European visitors to the coast reported that elk-hide armor was proof
even against musket balls, and it would likely repel a whalebone knife. First in Everything has chosen
the time and place for his attack well, even if he does not follow up on it.

They were killed by the children.

"Try to save that Pushed Through,"[23]
 said First in Everything.
Pushed Through's feet were tied to a stone, and they stood him up in the water.
 Now all of Giver's people were dead.

SCENE 4

"Let's go kill Giver now, tonight,"
 said First in Everything to his people.
They arrived at the back of Island in Back.
 It was dark.

They walked along the rocky shore.
They headed for Giver's house.

They heard the sound of someone crying.
They also heard Giver.

"Hai,"
 said Giver.
"They ought to have returned by now,"
 said Giver.
  He was worried about his people.
  They had in fact all been killed.

"Go ask why she's crying,"
 said First in Everything.
One man went secretly to ask the woman,
 "Why are you crying?"
"Giver killed my husband.
 We're Ławit'sis,"
  said the woman.
   "That's why I'm crying."

Giver spoke from inside the house.

23. The uncle of Giver who incited the first murder.

"Why don't you stop that blubbering?"
　　said Giver.
　　　"I am exhausted by all of this weeping."
　　　　Giver seemed to fall asleep.

Said First in Everything,
　　"Let's go into the house."
The strong child on the left side heaved up the door.
It was one-half of a cedar trunk, that door.
The warriors entered.
　　They took hold of Giver.

Giver spoke.
"Don't attack me senselessly.
　　You are going to take your revenge.
　　　But let the wound cross my belly, so my descendants will rightly also be
　　　　marked that way,"[24]
　　　　　said Giver.
"You'll be that way,"
　　said First in Everything.
He cut open Giver.

Giver's younger brother spoke from the next house.
"Have you all finished with your uncle?"[25]
　　said Giver's brother.
First in Everything spoke.
"He is off the fire,"[26]
　　said First in Everything.

24. That is, so his descendants will bear a mark that resembles that wound. The mark may indicate successive reincarnations of Giver.
25. Giver is, of course, First in Everything's brother-in-law, not his ḵ'wali' 'father's or mother's brother' as it says here in the text. Nor would the strong children use this kin term; Giver is their mother's sister's husband. The younger brother's use of the second-person plural here seems to be a reminder to the avenging warriors that the dead man is kin — is the "uncle," in an extended sense, of all of them.
26. First in Everything uses a form here that means both 'he/she/it is divided into two parts in the house' and 'he/she/it has moved off of or away from the hearth fire in the house'. The ambiguity is surely deliberate. Giver pushed the corpse of his first victim, their mutual brother-in-law Good Maker "onto the fire." By cutting Giver "in two," First in Everything has moved Good Maker and the conflict that has torn apart their community "off the fire."

"Well,"

    said Giver's brother,

       "now our weather will grow calm.

Come, load my goods and we will become one tribe again,"

    said Giver's brother.

    This story has reached the end.

Haida

The Sea Lion Hunter

Introduction by Robert Bringhurst

Ghandl of the Qayahl Llaanas was a Haida-speaking mythteller, born about 1851 in the village of Qaysun, on the exposed west coast of the Queen Charlotte Islands, off the coast of British Columbia and Alaska. The Haida people, who have lived in these islands for thousands of years, live in them still, and the archipelago is known locally both as the Charlottes and as Haida Gwaii (or Haida Gwaay; both spellings are now used). The older Haida name for the place is Xhaaydlagha Gwaayaay 'the islands of the exposed surface'.

At the end of the eighteenth century, ten thousand Haida or more were living in Haida Gwaii. By the end of the nineteenth, the Native population was well below a thousand. Smallpox accounts for most of this vast difference. Measles, scarlet fever, and other imported diseases account for the rest. Ghandl survived the epidemics, but a bout of measles or smallpox in early manhood cost him his sight.

The catastrophic drop in population during the later nineteenth century led to the abandonment of many Haida villages. Ghandl and other survivors from Qaysun gave up their village in the early 1880s. After a series of moves, they settled in the 1890s in the mission village of Skidegate — one of two Native towns in Haida Gwaii surviving to this day. Along the way a visiting missionary gave him a new name, Walter McGregor — but Haida, not English or Scots Gaelic, is the language he spoke to the end of his life. In middle age, though he could not fish, hunt, or work in wood like other Haida men, Ghandl was admired for his speech and for his skill in telling stories.

John Reed Swanton, a young linguist who had studied with William James at Harvard and Franz Boas at Columbia, came to Skidegate in September 1900. He stayed in the islands nearly a year, transcribing several thousand pages of Haida narrative poetry, oral history, autobiography, and song. Ghandl and Swanton were introduced in October 1900 and worked together intensely for several weeks.

Ghandl's story of the Sea Lion Hunter is one of twelve narrative poems he dictated to Swanton in October 1900 in the Haida village of Skidegate, on Graham Island, off the British Columbia coast. It is constructed out of three main themes, all well known and often told in that part of the world, yet it remains a distinctive and singular work of art. No other mythteller recorded in any language treats these themes in quite this way or links them in this particular combination.

Sea lions in Haida are called *qaay*. Ghandl belonged to a Haida lineage, or matrilineal family, called Qayahl Llaanas 'the Sea Lion People'. He was born and raised in a village called Qaysun 'Sea Lion Roost' or 'Sea Lion Town'. And in the world of the Northwest Coast, where most of the world's northern sea lions live, the size and power of these beings, their elaborate social order, and their skills in navigation and dealing with rough weather command the greatest admiration and respect.

The five-act story or five-movement poem is as basic to Haida oral literature as the five-act play is to Elizabethan theater. Ghandl is a master of such structures, unfolding his story in tight clusters of clauses and sentences—threes and fives more often than twos or fours—which grow together into little scenes or sections. These grow together in their turn, primarily in threes and fives, to form the acts or movements of the story. These kinds of patterns are widespread and probably universal in Native American oral literature. Though simple to describe in general terms, they can be intricate in practice. Closely studied (as they have been by Dell Hymes), they constitute a set of mental fingerprints or footprints—sufficient, I believe, to identify not just the provenance or culture but the individual speaker of the story.

There are no acoustic recordings of Ghandl's voice; there are only written transcripts. Surface features such as timbre, pause, and intonation, which we usually use to identify a voice, are missing from the record. So, though Ghandl did not write (and no one, so far as I know, has ever *written* a story in Haida), the legacy he leaves is like the legacy of a writer. Like a fossil, it permits us to examine hard structures in great detail, though the warm, soft tissue of the speaking voice has vanished. Yet in the fossil of his language—as in many great pieces of Haida sculpture that survive from the same era—is the signature of a highly accomplished artist.

There is more about Ghandl in my book *A Story as Sharp as a Knife: The Classical Haida Mythtellers and Their World* (Douglas & McIntyre, 1999; University of Nebraska Press, 2000), and more of his work in his own book: Ghandl of the Qayahl Llaanas, *Nine Visits to the Mythworld,* translated by Robert Bringhurst (Douglas & McIntyre / University of Nebraska Press, 2000).

SUGGESTED READING AND REFERENCES

Boas, Franz. *Tsimshian Texts.* Bureau of American Ethnology Bulletin 27. Washington DC: U.S. GPO, 1902.

———. *Tsimshian Texts (New Series).* Publications of the American Ethnological Society 3. Leiden: E. J. Brill, 1912.

Bringhurst, Robert. *A Story as Sharp as a Knife: The Classical Haida Mythtellers and Their World*. Vancouver: Douglas & McIntyre, 1999; Lincoln: University of Nebraska Press, 2000.

Dauenhauer, Nora Marks, and Richard Dauenhauer. *Haa Shuká, Our Ancestors: Tlingit Oral Narratives*. Seattle: University of Washington Press, 1987.

Ghandl of the Qayahl Llaanas. *Nine Visits to the Mythworld*. Translated by Robert Bringhurst. Vancouver: Douglas & McIntyre; Lincoln: University of Nebraska Press, 2000.

MacDonald, George F. *Haida Monumental Art*. Vancouver: University of British Columbia Press, 1983.

Skaay of the Qquuna Qiighawaay. *Being in Being*. Translated by Robert Bringhurst. Vancouver: Douglas & McIntyre; Lincoln: University of Nebraska Press, 2001.

Swanton, John R. *Contributions to the Ethnology of the Haida*. Jesup North Pacific Expedition vol. 5, part 1. New York: American Museum of Natural History, 1905.

———. *Haida Texts and Myths: Skidegate Dialect*. Bureau of American Ethnology Bulletin 29. Washington DC: U.S. GPO, 1905.

———. *Haida Texts: Masset Dialect*. Jesup North Pacific Expedition, vol. 10, part 2. New York: American Museum of Natural History, 1908.

———. *Tlingit Myths and Texts*. Bureau of American Ethnology Bulletin 39. Washington DC: U.S. GPO, 1909.

Walkus, Simon. *Oowekeeno Oral Traditions as Told by the Late Chief Simon Walkus, Sr*. Edited by Susanne Storie and John C. Rath. Mercury Series 84. Ottawa: National Museums of Canada, 1982.

The Sea Lion Hunter

Told by Ghandl
Translated by Robert Bringhurst

A master carver had fathered   [1]
    two children, they say.

They saw game on the reefs,
so he made the harpoon.
He bound it with cord, they tell me.
He used something strong for this purpose, they say.
And he put a detachable barb on the shaft.

They herded the sea lions into a pool on top of a reef,
and he was the one who harpooned them.
One thrust, and he pulled out the shaft
and fastened another barb on the end.   10
This is the way he killed sea lions, they say.

When he had been doing this for a while,
they paddled out early one day
and they put him ashore on the reef.
Then they pushed off
and left him.

His wife's youngest brother turned toward him.

The source manuscript is John Swanton, Skidegate Haida texts, MS, ACLS Coll. N1.5 = Freeman 1543, American Philosophical Society Library, Philadelphia, pp. 397–401, and there is a prose rendering in Swanton, *Haida Texts and Myths*, 282–85. Swanton gives as the title for this story *Qaay kit ttaga nang sta ttl ttsaasdaayagan* 'one they abandoned because he speared sea lions'. The Haida poet Kingagwaaw treated Swanton to another very fine (and very different) meditation on some of the same themes (Swanton, *Haida Texts: Masset Dialect*, 385–92). In 1972 two Tlingit speakers, Kéet Yaanaayí and Tseex-wáa, dictated related stories to Kéet Yaanaayí's daughter, Nora Dauenhauer (Dauenhauer and Dauenhauer, *Haa Shuká, Our Ancestors*, 108–37).

There in the midst of the crew, he tugged at their paddles.
He struggled against them.

The hunter was watching.   20
He called them again and again.
They paid no attention.

They were unable to kill the sea lions.
He was the only one who could do it.
That is the reason they left him, they say.

Alone on the top of the rock, he wept for his children.
He wept for a while,
and then he lay down by the pool.

After he lay there in silence awhile,
something said to him,   30
"A headman asks you in."

He looked around him.
Nothing stood out,
but he noticed that, there in the pool, something went under.

When he had lain there a little while longer,
something said the same thing again.
Then, they say, he peeked through the eye
of the marten-skin cape he was wearing.
Then he saw a pied-billed grebe break the surface of the pool.

After swimming there awhile,   40
it said, "A headman asks you in,"
and then it went under.

He wrapped his fingers round the whetstone   [2]
that he wore around his neck,
and he leaped into the pool, they say.

He found himself in front of a large house,
and they invited him inside.
He went in,

and there they asked him,
"Why is it you are murdering so many of my women?"[1]   50

He answered,
"I have done what I have done
in order to give food to my two children."

In a pool in a corner of the house,
he saw two baby killer whales spouting.
Those, they say, were the headman's children, playing.
In all four corners of the house, he saw the dorsal fins of killer whales
hanging up in bunches.

Then, however, they offered him food.
There was a sea lion sitting near the door.   60
They dragged it to the center.

They lifted the cooking rocks out of the fire
and dropped them down its throat.
They dropped a halibut down the throat of the sea lion too.
When the halibut was cooked, they say,
they set it there before him.

When the meal was over,
they brought one of the fins down from the corner.
They heated the base of the fin.

When they made him bend over,   70

1. In a normal Haida context, *diigi jaatghalang* would mean 'my clanswomen'—i.e., sisters and other women of the speaker's moiety. It could mean the same thing here, if the speakers are brothers and sisters of the slain sea lions. But the social structure of sea lion rookeries is different from that of Haida villages. Sea lion bulls take harems. If only the bulls (the headmen) are speaking—which I think to be the case—the phrase must mean 'my wives' instead. There are good reasons, too, why a sea lion bull should ask about his wives and no one else. The bulls are roughly twice the size of grizzlies and are rarely troubled by hunters. Cows and pups are at greater risk. They surround the bulls on the rookeries, are smaller and less aggressive, and their meat is not so tough. Younger male sea lions are at some risk from hunters too, but not so much as cows and pups. And younger males are not the bulls' concern, because they have no place in the social order except as the bulls' replacements-in-waiting.

There are, however, other complications. The people whom the sea lion hunter meets at the bottom of the pool are plainly killer whales. This does not, of course, prevent them from having sea lion forms as well—but why then do they use a sea lion for a cooking box? Moody and Swanton sidestepped this problem by translating *diigi jaatghalang* as 'my servants' rather than 'my women'. This makes interpretation easy but violates the text.

he slung the whetstone around so it hung down his back.
When they tried to fasten the fin to his spine,
it fell off.
The fin lay on the stone floor planks, quivering.

They went to get another.
They heated that one also, right away,
and they forced him to bend over.

Again he moved the whetstone.
When they tried to fasten the fin to his spine,
it fell off like the other,   80
and it dropped onto the stone floor of the house.

Then they got another.
When the same thing happened yet again,
they went and got a tall one.[2]

After they had warmed it there awhile,
they forced him to bend over once again.
He moved the whetstone round again.
When they tried to fasten that one to his spine,
it too fell shuddering on the stone floor of the house.

After they had tried four times,   90
they gave it up.
"Let him go," the headman said.
"He refuses the fin.
Put him into a sea lion's belly."

Then the headman told him what to do.
"After you have drifted here and there awhile,
and after you have washed ashore four times,
let yourself out.
You will find that you have come to a fine country."

They put him into a sea lion's paunch right away.   100
He sewed it shut from the inside,

2. The dorsal fins of mature bull killer whales tower over those of the cows and younger males.

and they set him adrift.

When he had floated on the ocean for a while   [3]
and washed ashore for the fourth time,
he crawled out.
He had drifted ashore on a sandy beach.

He sewed the paunch up tight from the outside,
and he put it in the water.
It faced upwind
and disappeared to seaward.   110

Then he walked in the direction of the village.
He waited until nightfall on the outskirts of the town.
After dark, he peeked in at his wife.

His wife had singed her hair off.
He saw soot stains on her face.[3]
He saw that both his children sat there too.

He tapped against the wall just opposite his wife.
She came outside.
He said to her, "Bring me my tools."

She brought him what he asked for.   120
"Don't tell anyone I'm here," he said.
"Don't even tell the children."

When he left that place,
he grabbed another of the children who were playing there.
He took the child up the hill.

After walking for a while,   [4.1]
he came to a big lake.
There was a tall redcedar standing on the shore.

He cut the trunk across the front.
When he made another cut across the back,   130

3. In other words she bears the marks of a widow in mourning.

the cedar dropped across the surface of the water.

He split it from the butt end.
After splitting it part way,
he braced it open.

Then he stripped and twisted cedar limbs,
splicing them together to make line.
When the line was long enough,
he tied the child to one end.
Then he lowered it into the lake
between the split halves of the tree.

After letting it touch bottom,   140
he jigged with it awhile.
Then the line began to jerk,
and he began to haul it in.
By then the lake was boiling.

Its forepaws broke the surface first.
When its head broke the surface just behind them,
he sprang the trap by kicking out the brace.

The creature thrashed and struggled.
He clubbed it again and again,
until he had killed it.   150

Then he pulled it from the trap.
He touched his knifepoint to its throat,
but then a lightning bolt exploded,
so he started his cut instead from the base of the tail.

He skinned it.
He liked the way its tail looked especially.
It was curled.

Then he built a fire,
and he dried and tanned the skin.
It was a sea wolf that he caught, they say.   160

After he had tanned it,

he rolled it up
and packed it back to town.

On the outskirts of town stood a hollow redcedar.
He hid it in there.
He put moss over top of it.

Then he walked away from the edge of the village.   [4.2]
He carved redcedar into the forms of killer whales.
He fitted them with dorsal fins
and pushed them under water with his feet and let them go.   170

Just out beyond low tide mark, some bubbles rose.
Then he said, "You're on your own.
Go wherever you can live."

Those are harbor porpoises, they say.[4]

Next he carved some western hemlock
into the forms of killer whales.
When he had ten of them,
he pushed them under water with his feet and let them go.

After they had left,
bubbles rose a little farther seaward.
After that he turned it over in his mind.   180

Then he said, "You're on your own.
Go wherever you can live."
Those are Dall's porpoises, they say.[5]

All this time, the weather was good, they say,
and as long as it lasted, the men were out fishing.

On the following day, after thinking again   [4.3]
about what he would use,

4. Harbor porpoises (*Phocoena phocoena;* Haida *squl*) look a lot like small, misshapen killer whales.
5. There is a pun here. The western hemlock (*Tsuga heterophylla*) and Dall's porpoise (*Phocoenoides dalli*) are both called *qqaang* in Haida. Dall's porpoises look very much like miniature killer whales. On average they are also larger and heavier than harbor porpoises — though still no more than a third the length and perhaps a tenth the weight of full-grown killer whales.

he made ten killer whales out of yew wood.

Their skins were shiny black and splashed with white,
their underbellies white,   190
and they had white patches up behind their mouths.

The dorsal fin of one was nicked along the fore edge.
The dorsal fin of one hooked backward toward the tail.
As he was making them, they moved.

He laid down skids for them to rest on.
Then he launched them,
and he pushed them with his feet to deeper water.
Bubbles rose a long time later, out at sea.

Then he called them in
and hauled them up on shore.   200
They had snapper, salmon, and halibut in their jaws.

Evening came again,   [4.4]
and he went to see his wife.
Once again he peeked inside,
and then he tapped on the wall beside his wife.
She came outside.

He said to her, "Tell your youngest brother
he ought to wear a feather in his hair
when the men go fishing in the morning."

Next day, when they were fishing,   210
he gave the killer whales their instructions.
"Do away with all the humans who are fishing.
Rub your fins on their canoes,
and only save the one who wears a feather in his hair."

Then he nudged them to sea with his feet, they say.
Bubbles rose a while later,
seaward of where the canoes were riding at anchor.

Then the killer whales closed in on the canoes.

Bubbles rose among the boats.
The killer whales rubbed against them with their fins   220
and chewed the canoes and humans to pieces.
Only one, who wore a feather in his hair, continued swimming.

When the whales had destroyed them all,
the one who wore a feather in his hair
climbed aboard a chewed canoe,
and the pod of whales brought him to the shore.
They left him on the beach in front of town.

Then he called the killer whales again.   [4.5]
He told them what to do.

He said to one who had a knothole in his fin,
"Pierced Fin will be your name."   230
To one whose fin was wavy, he said,
"Your name will be Rippled Fin."[6]

Then he told them this:
"Go to House Point.
Make your homes there.
That is a fine country.
People of the Strait will be your name."

Then he went to see his wife
with fish the killer whales had brought him in their mouths.
Both of his children were happy to see him.   240

When he had been in the village awhile,   [5.1]
he went outside
while others were still sleeping.

He dressed in the sea wolf skin.
There at the edge of the village, he reached out
and touched the water with one paw,

6. Ripples along the trailing edge of the dorsal fin are a recognizable sign of age and seniority in bull
killer whales. Nicked or notched fins are also seen from time to time. I know of no confirmed sight-
ings of a killer whale with a punctured dorsal fin, but mutilated fins are not uncommon, and these
sometimes include white scars that look like perforations from a distance. In any case, the pierced fin,
like the doubled fin, is a popular motif in Haida sculpture.

and he had half of a spring salmon.

His mother-in-law, who nagged him all the time,
always got up early in the morning.
He laid the salmon down at the door of her house.

Early in the morning, she came out.   250
She found the chunk of salmon
and was happy.

That night again, he dressed in the sea wolf skin.
He went into the water up to the elbow.
He came back with half a halibut.

He set it down beside his mother-in-law's door.
She found it in the morning.
The people of the village had been hungry up till then, they say.

Again that night, he dressed in the skin of the sea wolf.
He put his foreleg all the way into the water,   260
and he got a whole spring salmon.
He set it at the woman's door as well,
and she found it in the morning.

He dressed again the next night in the sea wolf skin,
and then he let the water come over his back.
He brought in the jaw of a humpback whale
and left it at his mother-in-law's door.
She was very pleased to find it there.

His mother-in-law started to perform as a shaman then, they say.   [5.2]
They fasted side by side with her for four nights.   270
He was with them too, they say.
It was his voice that started speaking through her—
through the mother of his wife.

The next night again, he got inside the sea wolf.
He swam seaward.
He killed a humpback whale.
Fangs stuck out of the nostrils of the sea wolf.

Those are what he killed it with, they say.

He put it up between his ears
and carried it to shore.   280
He put it down in front of the house.
She had predicted
that a whale would appear.

And again, as they were sleeping,
he went out inside the sea wolf.
He got a pair of humpback whales.

He brought them back to shore.
He carried one between his ears
and the other draped across the base of his tail.
He swam ashore with them   290
and set them down again in front of the house.

When night came again,
he swam way out to sea inside the sea wolf.
He got ten humpback whales.

He carried several bundled up between his ears.
He carried others in a bunch at the base of his tail.
He had them piled on his body,
and he put one in his mouth.
He started swimming toward the shore.

He was still out at sea when daylight came, they say,   300
and when he came up on the beach,
the mother of his wife was there to meet him
in the headdress of a shaman.

He stepped outside the sea wolf skin.
"Why," he asked her, "are there spearpoints in your eyes?
Does the spirit being speaking through you
get some help from me?"
She died of shame from what he said, they say.

The sea wolf skin swam out to sea alone.   [5.3]

Then the hunter took the string of whales
and said that no one was to touch them.   310

The sale of those whales made him rich, they say.
And then he held ten feasts in honor, so they say,
of the youngest brother of his wife.
He made a prince of him.

This is where it ends.

TRANSLATOR'S POSTSCRIPT

Like chemical elements, the themes in this story have lives of their own, and they
bond with other elements to form new narrative compounds. The Nishga statesman Sgansm Sm'oogit, for example, telling stories to Boas in 1894, linked the
themes of abandonment among the sea lions, creation of killer whales, and the
taking of revenge much as Ghandl did in 1900, but Sgansm incorporates these
themes into the story of the hero known as Asihwil or Asdiwal. (His work is preserved only in English paraphrase—Boas, *Tsimshian Texts,* 225–29—and Boas calls
him by his English name, Chief Mountain). The Tsimshian writer Henry Tate connects these themes with Asdiwal as well (Boas, *Tsimshian Texts (New Series),* 146–
91), but for Kéet Yaanaayí and Tseexwáa, these are elements of the story of an an-
cestor named Naatsilanéi. At Rivers Inlet in 1969 the Uwikeeno statesman Simon
Walkus also told a story about a sea lion hunter abandoned by his brothers-in-law,
and he too focused on the taking of revenge—but he linked this theme of revenge
against the brother-in-law to another, very widely told, story of a blind hunter's
revenge against his faithless wife (Walkus, *Oowekeeno Oral Traditions as Told by the
Late Chief Simon Walkus, Sr.,* 100–134). The Tlingit mythteller Ḵaadashaan ties the
creation of killer whales to the idea of revenge against a wife's ungrateful brothers
but divorces it from the figure of the hunter abandoned among the sea lions, as
well as from the figure of the hunter who dresses himself in the skin of the sea wolf
(Swanton, *Tlingit Myths and Texts,* 165–69, 230–31). Kingagwaaw, like Ghandl and
Sgansm, links the theme of abandonment among the sea lions to the creation of
killer whales, but he insists that the abandonment was unintentional. Revenge has
no place in his story (Swanton, *Haida Texts: Masset Dialect,* 385–92).

Often, though not always, in such stories it seems clear that killer whales already exist when the carver engenders a new clan of them. So the Tlingit mythteller
Deikinaak'w can combine the figure of the expert carver who creates killer whales
with the figure of the hunter who must rescue his abducted wife from other killer
whales (Swanton, *Tlingit Myths and Texts,* 25–27). And Ghandl's sea lion hunter
can meet killer whales beneath the sea well before he creates them.

Though it dwells on revenge, Ghandl's poem ends on a note of praise for brotherhood and loyalty. It is worth comparing the conclusion of Kingagwaaw's poem (Swanton, *Haida Texts: Masset Dialect,* 392), where the focus is on brotherhood of a somewhat different order. (In Kingagwaaw's poem, the protagonist's name is Guut·tsa.)

> And so, Guut·tsa never went back to his home.
> But because he got inside the sea lion's belly,
> he remains in the sea lion's mind.
> Their minds are human.
> And besides that, he created killer whales.

Kingagwaaw does not, like Ghandl, bring the sea wolf and the hunter who takes its skin into the fabric of this story—but that theme too has a rich existence of its own. It is important to the third and fourth parts of the *Qquuna Cycle,* dictated to Swanton by the Haida poet Skaay of the Qquuna Qiighawaay (Skaay, *Being in Being,* 35–267). It is also central to another classic of Northwest Coast oral literature: Moses Bell's *Maxsmts'iits'kwł* 'Growing Up Like One Who Has a Grandmother'. Bell dictated the latter work in Nishga to Boas at Kincolith in 1894 (Boas, *Tsimshian Texts,* 137–68). Both the master artist Daxhiigang and the northern Haida raconteur Kihltlaayga link the theme of capturing a monster from the water with the theme of revenge against a mother-in-law pretending to be a shaman (Swanton, *Haida Texts: Masset Dialect,* 612–24), but Ghandl is the only classical Haida author who fuses the hunter who traps the sea wolf with the hunter who creates the killer whales.

The Blind Man at Island Point Town and the One Who Went around the Sea as a Halibut

Introduction by John Enrico

Adam Bell was born in 1905, the son of Giid Xiigans (Phillip Bell) of the Ts'àahl 'Laanaas clan and Jad Quyaag (Elizabeth Bell) of the Yahgu Janaas clan. He died in 1987, the last man in Masset to have relatively full knowledge of the old ways. He was a renowned storyteller and boasted about once having told traditional stories for a six-hour stretch in the bar in Masset. That he frequented bars does not mean that he was a drunk, though he liked an occasional binge. He had far too much self-respect to be a drunk. The story presented here was recorded by me in Haida in 1984.

This contribution is an interesting example of story combining, since its two parts were told separately by other storytellers. The first part appears in Swanton's Masset texts as "The Blind Man Who Became a Chief" and relates how an afflicted and neglected person was pitied and helped by animals, a motif that the Haidas understood to have moral significance. The second is the story of Suusduu Gudaal, the Masset version of the Southern Haida story Ruudang Xiiwaad, "He Who Has Quartz for Ribs" (for which see Enrico 1995, 136–58). One clan originating toward the south end of the Queen Charlotte archipelago, the Taaji 'Laanaas, migrated to Langara Island and thence to Alaska. The story of Suusduu Gudaal may have come to Island Point Town from the south that way. The story recounts the cleaning up of marine monsters remaining on earth from the epoch before humans appeared.

While Adam Bell's versions have their typically Haida vivid moments (vide the gulls pulling the blind man into their house, or the herring coming down on his head), they are certainly not as full of detail as the material that Swanton collected, nor is the language as polished. These differences are probably to be expected in the case of a dying language. Otherwise, the telling is masterful, and these and the other stories that Adam Bell recorded are significant as illustrations of Haida narrative. It is already obvious from Swanton's written collections that Haida myths do not have structure that may be captured by a verse format—the "stanzas" in the translation presented here are episodes, not repetitive formal units—and Adam Bell's delivery (as well as that of a traditional Southern Haida storyteller recorded in the 1960s) shows no prosodic evidence of such structure either. There are a couple of interesting prosodic features, however, that Swanton did not notice or ignored. First, quotations are in a slightly higher register than other material. Second, Adam Bell tends to repeat certain quoted lines (and only quoted lines) sotto voce (represented here by a slightly smaller typeface); the significance of these lines is thereby emphasized. Clause-internal pauses are omitted from the translation because the different lexical structure of Haida and English makes it awkward and unrevealing to transfer them to the English version.

The town called Island Point Town lay on the northwest corner of Langara Island, itself at the northwest corner of the Queen Charlotte archipelago and just north of the much larger Graham Island. Cape Knox is the northwest point of the latter. Shaking the Head is a rock just off the site of Island Point Town to the north; it has a small pool and a single tree on it (this is referred to as a "little island" at the beginning of the second part of the translation). It is said to shake when breakers pound it, hence the name. He Who Has Quartz for Ribs is a reef about twenty miles northwest of Langara Island. Cape Saint James is the southernmost point of the archipelago. Skidegate Channel separates Graham Island from the other major island of the group, Moresby. Naden Harbour lies on the northern coast of Graham Island east of Langara, while Rennell Sound, Hippa Island, and Frederick Island are on the west coast of Graham. According to the Haidas, a giant sculpin lived at the mouth of Naden Harbour when humans first appeared on earth, and the many crabs in that harbor are attributed to the giant crab that our protagonist chewed up and spit out there.

Fishing for halibut was done with anchored lines on which wooden hooks were suspended a short distance above the bottom by means of submerged wooden floats. Dried halibut was a staple Haida food. Fishing and hunting in general were undertaken with certain precautions and rites to ensure luck, one of the precautions being that no menstruant woman should walk between a hunter or fisher and the fire or water, or look at his gear. Otherwise her blood would enter his eyes and prevent his finding game or adhere to his weapons and make them useless. So the blind man was probably left behind because he would have been unlucky in any case.

The word *potlatch* (from the Chinook jargon for 'give, giving') refers to any large Northwest Coast ceremonial distribution of property; these had a variety of functions within the various traditional social systems found there. The two major Haida potlatches were ostensibly payments from one moiety to the opposite one for services in house building and erection of mortuary structures, but at a deeper level they validated the entry of children into the society and the departure of deceased persons from it. The cycle of property exchange from one moiety to the other reflected the cycle of human death and rebirth—the Haidas believed in reincarnation. They also believed in the cyclic death and rebirth of other creatures, notably salmon, their other major food source.

The significance of the Haida hat in the first part of the story is unknown. The version that Swanton collected has the blind man wearing a hat when he begins to crawl around but makes no further mention of it. In that version the fact that the man can now see is simply revealed by his opening his eyes, but only after he has made nine potlatches. The Swanton version also has the gulls give the man a magic box that confers luck (or wealth) when one looks into it, something absent from the Adam Bell version. Since the man has his children and wife look into that box, while the Adam Bell version has the man give his hat to his wife, it may be that the hat and box were somehow connected.

The Haida language is moribund, and while there are retention efforts underway in Masset and Skidegate (the latter being perhaps more successful), there is little chance that the spoken language will survive.

The interjection *7aah 7aah* is addressed mostly to children and means 'Don't (you'll make a mistake)!'; the numeral *7* stands for a glottal stop. The interjection *huhu huhu* was one of amazement. The only other Haida appearing in this translation itself is the name Suusduu Gudaal, which does not contain any nonobvious orthographic symbols, and is actually a shortened form of Suusraduu Nang Gudaals 'He Who Goes around the Sea as a Halibut' (the letter *r* in the latter stands for a pharyngealized glottal stop).

SUGGESTED READING AND REFERENCES

Enrico, John. 1995. *Skidegate Haida Myths and Histories.* Skidegate BC: Queen Charlotte Islands Museum Press.

Swanton, John R. 1905. *Haida Texts and Myths: Skidegate Dialect.* Bureau of American Ethnology Bulletin 29. Washington DC: Smithsonian Institution.

———. 1908. *Haida Texts: Masset Dialect.* Memoir of the American Museum of Natural History, vol. 10, part 2. Leiden: E. J. Brill.

The Blind Man at Island Point Town and the One Who Went Around the Sea as a Halibut

Told by Adam Bell
Translated by John Enrico

When Island Point Town was inhabited, people used go out from it to fish.
There are halibut way out from it.
When they would go out fishing from there, they would leave behind a certain blind man.
Although he would make his wife offer him as crew to his many brothers-in-law, they didn't want him because he was blind.

Finally, when his wife returned later than she usually did, he questioned her.
"What's the story?"
"The canoes all left sometime earlier."
Then, since he felt bad, he crawled outside.
He went on his hands and knees along the side of this house toward the trees and crawled around aimlessly.

While he was still crawling, gulls started calling right above his head.
The gulls made a racket.

After he had listened to that for a while, he felt seawater with his hand.
He just sat there.

The gulls were making a racket right above his head.
Someone spoke to him quietly.
"The chief tells you to come in," they said to him.

When he agreed, when they grabbed for him, they caught his hand in the air.
They pulled him in.

The chief greeted him.
"There is news that they left you behind when they went out fishing.
There is news that they left you behind when they went out fishing."

Then they began to work on his eyes first.
When he reached into the corner of his eye to grab something,
"Don't say anything even if your eye hurts.
Try your best.
We're going to help you."
Then he felt him pull something small out of his eye.
When it came off his eye, they did the same to the other eye too.
Again.

Then they asked him,
"Don't you see anything?"
"Yes, I see a little."

Then they reached into his eye for it again and did the same.
When they did one side, then they did the other.
Then they asked him again,
"Don't you see anything?"
"Yes, I see things."
This large landmass forming a point in this direction, he saw clean through
that.

This chief was a very high-class and wise man among the gulls.
When he had heard how the man was, he had watched how things went for
him.

Then he said to him,
"While you're sitting, don't look down.
You might see into the underworld.
Just look at the surface of the ground.
Don't look down,"
He said to him.
He promised not to.

After a while, they gave him a meal, after they fixed his eyes.
They started to feed him.

They put a tray of ooligans before him first.[1]
These ooligans lying there were just bones.
He lo-o-oked at them.
"I wonder if I'll eat them even though they're like that?"
"Yes, eat them.
The Gull People eat them though they're like that.
Eat them."
When he swallowed one, oh, he was eating fresh ooligans!

When he had finished that, they gave another food to him, herring too.
He ate that.

As they gave him different foods, he ate them.

He was able to see even things far away.
They were very happy with him, because he was able to see.

Later,
"As you leave now, wear your hat as you used to, the Haida hat.
And crawl.
When you come to the door, don't mention it even to your wife."

These young girls who were menstruating got up before him and he slept in.
He was awake but he lay in bed.
Because those girls walked around in front of him as he lay there, his eyes went
bad.
That's what they told him.
"After this, as long as you live, get up early.
And walk around outside.
Young women who were menstruating, it's that which went into your eye that
made you lose your sight."

"Later when you get back, make your wife offer you as crew when they go out
fishing again.
Do you own a canoe?"
They asked him.
"Yes, I have a canoe."
"When you have offered yourself four times, then get ready to leave.

1. The ooligan is a small herringlike fish, rich in oil and very important to Native people on the Northwest Coast.

Don't take off your hat.
Behave just like you have always done.
Do you have halibut lines?"
"Yes, I have some."
He answered "yes" to each question.

Then when they paddled away from him, when he crawled in, his wife was
feeling bad.
His wife kept the children alive with seafood that she knocked off the rocks
with her digging stick.

Then, on the fourth day when he offered himself as crew, they went out as usual
to where they got halibut only when it was blowing from the west.
So they wouldn't be unable to get back to land.
So they could sail back in.
When they landed their loads of halibut.

At that time, just when the canoes had all left, when he and his wife had pushed
the canoe into the water, they went out fishing.
"Over there not far from where you live there are some reefs.
Go behind there.
Then when you've stopped, say,
'Hel-l-lp me! Help me!'"

Like when they dump them out of a bucket, these herring came down on him.
He baited his hooks with those and let them down.
They hit the bottom when he first lowered them and he pulled them up floating
a bit close to the bottom.
While the rest were still gone, his canoe was filled and he came back to shore.

"Later, when your halibut becomes sufficient, put your canoe way up from
shore.
Put it way up from shore.
Put it way up at the place where you used to keep it.
As soon as you quit fishing, it is going to start blowing from behind Shaking
the Head.
It is going to start blowing from behind Shaking the Head.
It is going to be impossible to gather things."

Then he gathered these halibut and the back of his house became full of the
dried fish.

His wife dried them in front of the house and his house was very full of them.
He kept packing them up from the beach.
He took them up while the rest were far out fishing.
Much later, when the house was full, when only the place where they slept was
clear, he quit fishing.

Although he could see, he pretended to be blind.

"Let's go, push up the canoe with me."
His wife got herself ready and she was happy.
They shoved the canoe up.
It was up very far from the water.
As they had warned him, it began to blow from behind Shaking the Head.
The sea broke on shore.
There was no way to gather things in that weather.
The waves were so big, they didn't know whether the tide was high or low.
These big waves kept breaking.
There was no way to gather things.

Then he remembered what they had told him.
"When it begins to blow from behind Shaking the Head, it is going to be
impossible to gather things.
People's food will run out.
They are going to buy this halibut from you.
They are going to buy it from you.
Then you will end up with all the townspeople's property."
He didn't tell this to his wife.

He crawled around like when he couldn't see, although he now saw.
His hat too, he put it on as soon as he got up.
Then his wife would cook the food for him and he would eat.
They didn't throw away anything.
They saved all the halibut heads and they ate them.

It blew the who-o-ole winter.
Then, as the food ran out, someone came in his house.
"I want to buy the food from you."
Then he would ask them,
"How many children do you have?"
He gave them a strip of dried halibut and added this fillet to it too.

"When your dried halibut is all gone, the weather is going to become good
again."
So they had advised him.
He continued to sell it, right into spring.
The breakers were still big.
Then, just as they had advised him, when his halibut started to run out, the
weather improved.

And they had advised him,
"Later, when you've got hold of all the townspeople's property, you are going to
potlatch."
They just told him what he was thinking.
"You're going to potlatch.
And when you've potlatched ten times, take off your hat.
Give your hat to your wife.
Give it to her where she sits.
So that she may know that you can see, your wife.
Give it to your wife and then give it to the people on the other side too.
When you have potlatched ten times, when these ten potlatches are done, you
will be a person highly thought of by everyone.
Then you are going to get all the property of these townspeople.
When you get it, you are going to finish everything that you thought you could
do on the same day.
When you take off your hat, go up to where your brother-in-laws are sitting
and go along speaking kindly to them.
Tell them that you can see.
You see them now."

Then when he told them he could see them well, they were happy.
When the weather got better, they went out fishing.

Island Point Town sits here [demonstrates].
Shoreward of the little island here there is deep water.
The rest of it dries up at low tide.
While he was sitting there, he saw an eagle far out flying shoreward.
He saw the tail of the halibut it was carrying waving back and forth.
As he watched it, it dropped it right toward the pond shoreward of the island.

He went to it and it was a little halibut.
He looked at it.

When he tried to cut off its head with a mussel shell he had broken with a rock,
"7aah 7aah 7aah 7aah,"
someone said to him.
He thought about it a while, sitting there.

He was able to see now.
He was destined to do even better still.

When he was about to cut off the tail of this halibut, again "7aah 7aah 7aah
7aah."
"I wonder how I could handle it?"
He tried cutting it at its side.
Again "7aah 7aah 7aah 7aah."

Then when he cut it at the tail end, nothing spoke.
When he had cut it, he pulled off its skin.
Nothing spoke to him.

At the back of Shaking the Head, this rocky bottom is deep.
He came there and sat.
He thought hard.
He sat there.

He picked up the halibut, put his head into it this way, and it slipped down on
him.
He was able to feel what he had become.
He was wearing the halibut skin.
Then when he suddenly moved his feet at the edge of the water where he sat, he
suddenly slipped into the water as a halibut.
It was Suusduu Gudaal that helped him.

When he set off as a halibut around this world, he came upon big supernatural
beings living under water and sucked them into his mouth.
He chewed them up and blew out the remains right there.
Only at Rose Spit did one give him a hard time, he used to say.
These big supernatural beings were big crabs and other things.
He destroyed the one at Rose Spit.
Then after he went around Cape Saint James, he destroyed the supernatural
beings around there.

While he was still going and going, he went back out again to the west coast
from Skidegate Channel.
He went along destroying the big dangerous supernatural beings living out
there.
This Suusduu Gudaal, he was big.
He would chew everything up and spit it out.

While he was still going and going around these islands, the one at Hippa
Island too gave him a very hard time.
I don't know what sort of fish it was.
That too was too much for him.
He used to say that it al-l-lmost killed him.
The supernatural being of Hippa Island was a great supernatural being.
Then he went around these islands.
As he went along after he had killed that one, when he went into Rennell
Sound, a big wolf eel was lying in there too.
Its head stuck out of a hole in this rock.
Then he sized it up and went around it.
After a while, when this big eel came out, he backed away from it.
When he had become as big as it was, he sucked it in.
He chewed it up.
Then when he spit it back out, its head was still alive.
He worked up his courage and he chewed up its head too.
Then he killed it.

He left there too.
He came to Frederick Island too.
He went along destroying the big supernatural beings that were there too.
When he left there, the ones at Cape Knox too.

Something very big was lying in the channel between Langara Island and
Graham Island.
He thrashed that too.
He killed that too.

Then, after he had gone along for a while, he went out to the place far out
where they used to go to fish.
A big supernatural being was lying there.
He was called He Who Has Quartz for Ribs.
When he went around and around him, this He Who Has Quartz for Ribs,
because he was confident, he didn't even glance at him.

He was big too.

Then he sized him up for a long time.

After he had gone around him for a while, he did it some more.

There was no way he could get hold of him.

Finally, when he took him in his mouth headfirst, he thrashed his tail around as he was swallowing him.

When he saw the right moment, he swallowed him.

He gave him a very hard time.

Then behind where this town of Island Point lies, there is a narrow bay.

He swam shoreward with him into there, but this narrow bay was too small for him.

He came ashore far out behind where this town lay when the tide was up.

He spit them out on there, the bones.

As he sat in the house, the sunshine was very bright.

His wife cooked for him and he ate as usual.

His wife didn't question him.

She didn't ask him where he had been.

The Gull People had helped him and the Eagle People had helped him too.

The eagle had brought Suusduu Gudaal for him.

That was how he had gone around destroying the things around this world.

Then he sat there.

After he had eaten, he just sat.

"Huhu, huhu, after He Who Has Quartz for Ribs has acted as he pleased for a while, the sun is beating down on him and spoiling him as he lies there," he said.

His wife didn't know what he was talking about.

His children, who by now were grown up, didn't know what he was talking about.

Then, at dawn, he just sat there.

After he had eaten, he sat.

"Huhu, huhu, after He Who Has Quartz for Ribs has acted as he pleased for a while, the sun is beating down on him and spoiling him as he lies there," he said about him.

Much later, people realized why he kept saying that.

They saw these bones lying there and among them lay the bones of the people the monster had destroyed.

When he had swum away from Island Point Town, when he had come out of
Naden Harbour, he did his last deed.
First, he spit out the sculpin that lived far out of the mouth of Naden.
He spit that one into the harbor.
He did the same to the crab too.

This is where the story ends.

Okanagan

Prophecy at Lytton

Introduction by Wendy Wickwire

The ethnographic archive for south central British Columbia is a valuable source for studying Aboriginal oral narratives. There are hundreds of stories in collections compiled more than a century ago by Franz Boas, Charles Hill-Tout, and James Teit; and there are additional stories in volumes assembled more recently by Randy Bouchard, Dorothy Kennedy, Darwin Hanna, Mamie Henry, Steven Egesdal, and myself. A survey of these sources provides important insights on many issues, in particular, the changing dynamics of the collector-storyteller exchange over time.

Harry Robinson's "Prophecy at Lytton" is a good case in point.[1] After recording this story in 1979, I found six variations of a similar story in sources published between 1895 and 1995. Although all seven stories have core elements in common, they also have major points of difference. In the following discussion I shall track changes that occurred as stories passed from storytellers to collectors and finally to published monographs. My goal is to highlight the importance of historicizing individual stories.

Harry Robinson (1900–1990) was a member of the Lower Similkameen Indian Band, a branch of the larger Salishan-speaking Okanagan Nation of south central British Columbia. I first met him in 1977 while undertaking ethnographic field research on Aboriginal musical traditions in the region. A renowned storyteller, Robinson rented a small bungalow just east of Hedley, having recently sold the large cattle ranch that he had managed with his wife, Matilda, until her death in 1971. During our thirteen-year-long friendship, we spent many hours recording his stories. His capacity for this work seemed to be endless. "I can go for twenty-one hours or more when I get started," he explained to me one day, "because this is my job. I am a storyteller" (Harry Robinson, interview by author, Westbank BC, April 16, 1984).

Robinson was unique among storytellers in British Columbia. Rather than following the usual pattern of telling stories through a translator, he began telling stories in English to accommodate his growing number of monolingual English

listeners. Recognizing the importance of these English tellings, I began recording
and publishing a representative sample (Wickwire 1989; 1992). To retain their special performance qualities, I focused on verbatim transcripts of our audiotaped
recordings. Aided by the first wave of desktop computers, I experimented with
various print formats, opting in the end for the poetic style. Unlike the standard
prose style, the poetic form captures Robinson's distinctive rhythm of speech, his
colloquial English, his emphasis on certain phrases, and his intentional repetitions, dramatic rhythms, and pauses.

"Prophecy at Lytton," one of the first stories that Harry told me, is representative of his general narrative style. Although the main focus is the storyline, em-
bellished with vivid dialogue and character development, he includes a range of
personal detail, for example, a colorful vignette about his quest to learn the fate
of a "spotted rock," a patchwork quilt transformed to stone that forms the core
of the story (Wickwire 1989, 194–97). As with many of his stories, he takes time
to acknowledge his sources — his grandmother, his father-in-law, and an elderly
friend — all Similkameen Okanagan relatives who traveled regularly to the Fraser
River to obtain salmon (1989, 196).

The oldest print version of a story similar to "Prophecy at Lytton" is "Der
Knabe und die Sonne" (The boy and the sun), published in Germany by Franz
Boas in 1895.[2] Boas collected the story at Lytton in July 1888 as part of a large field
project funded by the British Association for the Advancement of Science. It was
one of a number of Nlaka'pamux stories told to him by a small group of people
assembled at the local Anglican church. Concerned that Aboriginal cultures were
being crushed by the onslaught of Europeans, Boas's goal was to recover what
survived of the precontact ways before they disappeared. He had difficulty fulfill-
ing this objective at Lytton. "The people have been Christians for a long time and
that stands very much in my way," he noted in his diary after this session. "I hear
very little about olden times" (Boas Diary, 13 July 1888, in Rohner 1969, 99). As a
missionary center on a major transportation route, Lytton, not surprisingly, did
not yield his desired results.

Despite such problems, however, Boas resumed this work in 1894 through an
ethnographic assistant, James Teit, a young Shetlander based at Spences Bridge,
near Lytton. Married to a local Nlaka'pamux woman and fluent in her language,
Teit was a good choice for such work (Wickwire 1998). Over the course of two decades, he collected hundreds of stories. Three of these have links to "Prophecy at
Lytton." Edited by Boas, the three stories are presented under the following titles:
"The Tale of the Bad Boy; or The Sun and the Lad" (Teit 1898, 51–52); "The Bad
Boy; or The Sun and the Lad" (Teit 1912, 230–31); and "NKE'KAUMSTEM" (Teit
et al. 1917, 34).

Following a long hiatus, Darwin Hanna, a young Nlaka'pamux ethnographer, and Mamie Henry, a Nlaka'pamux elder, initiated a Canada Council project to record oral narratives in the region. One of the stories they published from this work was "The Boy Who Was Abandoned," by Mary Williams of Lytton (Hanna and Henry 1995, 83–85). They also included a fragment of a similar story told by Fred Hanna (1995, 163).

All six of these stories have links with Robinson's "Prophecy at Lytton." The most obvious point of similarity is the main storyline, focused on the fate of a "bad boy" who is abandoned by his community because of his "lazy" and "quarrelsome" ways. With the assistance of an elderly woman (in all but one account, the boy's grandmother), the boy ekes out a living. While he snares birds and rodents, the woman creates blankets from the skins. One day a surprise visitor (in all cases, a male) arrives and offers to purchase the patchwork blankets in exchange for gifts and special knowledge. The boy and the woman agree to the trade and find that it instantly benefits them. Eventually the villagers return to find the boy and the old woman not only alive but thriving.

All but two of the stories present Lytton as the setting for the story, a point established in the opening sentences of four accounts. For example, just as Robinson begins his story with "At one time in Lytton, there was a lot of Indians right at Lytton where the town is now" (Wickwire 1989, 168), so too did the storytellers at Lytton in 1888 open with a reference to Lytton: "Vor langer Zeit lebten veile Menschen in Lytton" (A long time ago many people lived in Lytton) (Boas 1895, 17). Although separated by a century, the opening line of Teit's 1898 account ("There was once a boy who lived with his parents at Lytton" [1898, 51]) has links with Mary Williams's 1995 account: "This story happened right here in Lytton" (Hanna and Henry 1995, 83).

Although clearly related, all seven stories have major points of difference. Unlike the older versions, which present the boy's parents as alive and in full support of the decision to abandon him, Robinson's account portrays the boy as an orphan who was raised by a grandmother who neglected to train him properly. According to Robinson, the woman's neglect led to the boy's rejection: "She [the grandmother] just leave him alone. . . . Never was trained to be a good worker, to be a good boy. He just grow up like wild grass or something. And he don't know nothing" (Wickwire 1989, 170). Fred Hanna makes a similar point: "She never showed her grandchild how to get wood. He just done as he pleased and that annoyed the other people because they were always helping—helping his grandmother—so they all left" (Hanna and Henry 1995, 163). While Boas describes the elderly woman in the story as an "alte Frau" (old woman), the others portray her as the boy's grandmother. But there is inconsistency here as well. According to Teit's 1898 account, the boy is hostile and physically aggressive toward his grandmother. Mary Williams, by way of contrast, presents the grandmother as fond of the boy and therefore opposed to deserting him. Fred Hanna claims that "the grandmother spoiled the little boy" (Hanna and Henry 1995, 163). In Robinson's story, the grandmother is blind.

The identity of the visitor who arrives at the boy's camp varies from story to story. In Robinson's account the visitor is "God" disguised as an old man who introduces new forms of prayer, teaches new fishing and hunting techniques, and foretells of the arrival of strangers who will transform the landscape. This God uses the language of Christianity: "I am the Father. I am God," the visitor tells the boy and his grandmother. "I come from Heaven" (Wickwire 1989, 185).

Boas, on the other hand, presents the visitor as "der Sonnenmann" (Sun Man) who "descended from the sky" and requested a fur coat in exchange for his bow (1895, 17). Teit describes the visitor in all three versions he recorded as "Sun" (1898, 52; 1912, 231; Teit et al. 1917, 35). Mary Williams describes the figure as "Sun [a flashing light] who turned himself into a man and came to earth" (Hanna and Henry 1995, 84).

The visitor's gifts also vary from story to story. In Boas's 1895 recording the Sun exchanges his "Bogen" (bow) for fur blankets (1895, 52); in Teit's 1912 account Sun offers the boy and the woman cooler weather in exchange for four skin blankets (1912, 231); and in Teit's 1917 account "Sun" gives gifts of bows, arrows and a "goat hair robe" in return for bird-skin blankets (Teit et al. 1917, 35). According to Mary Williams "Sun Man" traded his rifle and gunpowder for the woman's fur blankets. In Robinson's story God trades skills and knowledge for the blanket.

Robinson is the only storyteller to shift from the timeless mythical past into the present. Except for the mention of a rifle and gunpowder in Williams's account, the other six stories are firmly fixed in the deep past in which abstract universal teachings prevail, for example, the importance of welcoming strangers and accepting one's youth, however deviant. By way of contrast Robinson's story incorporates "God," who appeared in the deep past to warn the people living there about the arrival of white people a "long time from now" to live among them "till the end of the world." Despite the presence of whites, he warns, Indian land would never transfer hands. "This island supposed to be for the Indians," God explained. "This is *your* place." As such, Robinson's account is an assertion of Aboriginal sovereignty. His search for the "spotted rock" (the fur blanket that turned to stone on God's departure from Lytton) in this context serves as a permanent marker of the important exchange of knowledge between God and the boy and his grandmother. Fred Hanna also made reference to such a "rock" (Hanna and Henry 1995, 163).

The temporal distancing evident in all but Robinson's account may have more to do with the collecting process than with the storytellers. Boas, who assembled and

supervised the recording of the early versions and influenced generations of ethnographers, was driven by the fear that the indigenous cultures of the Northwest
could not survive the onslaught of westernization. He envisaged ethnography as
an urgent rescue mission and the published monograph as key to cultural preservation. Armed with sufficient field data, he was confident that he could produce
textual portraits of traditional cultures that would outlive the cultures themselves.
That his so-called informants were several generations removed from his imagined pristine contact point did not deter him. Over the course of several decades
he produced thousands of pages of written text framed against the backdrop of
his imagined "Golden Age Past."

Stories formed the core of Boas's ethnographic legacy. With his focus on the
deep past, however, these were not everyday stories of the times (about epidemics, missionaries, deaths, floods, etc.), but rather specialized stories—"legends,"
"tales," "myths"—about animals, origins, migrations, and so on set in the deep
past. Theorists Charles Briggs and Richard Bauman have recently analyzed Boas's
preference for "the more canonical genres of putatively authentic folk expression"
as a natural extension of his Germanic education in the "the philological program
of Herder and the Grimms" (1999, 504). "A critical element [in Boas's text-making
project]," they argue, "is that the social opposition between the traditional and
modern worlds that it sought to construct was sustained by texts whose rooted-
ness in modernist discursive practices and interests was suppressed in favor of
producing an aura of authenticity and verisimilitude" (1999, 483).

No analysis of "The Lad and the Sun" stories would be complete without considering the effects of Boas's quest for cultural purity. Boas's objective at Lytton
in 1888, for example, was to collect the oldest and least "contaminated" stories.
Meanwhile, his storytellers were horse packers, construction laborers, and small-
scale farmers who had never known a life without whites. As he noted on the
day he recorded "Der Knabe und die Sonne," it was a struggle to hear anything
about "olden times" at Lytton in 1888. Despite such obstacles, however, Boas proceeded with his recording project, carefully editing out personal detail, such as
individual names and community affiliations, and promoting his narrative collections as valuable living survivals of a distant and wonderful past.

On the surface Boas's efforts to filter out the modern appear to have worked.
Dig a little more deeply, however, and cracks begin to appear. Consider the following questions that arise from the study of "Der Knabe und die Sonne." Could
the "Sonne," "Sun," or "Sun Man" of Boas's account be related to Robinson's
"God"? Could Boas, without realizing it, have mistaken a Christianized story for
a traditional story? Is the forewarning about whites in Robinson's story unique to
contemporary tellings? Or could Boas have eliminated such details to maintain
cultural "purity"?

The following example taken from the 1917 presentation of the story suggests the latter. As noted earlier, there is no mention of anything current in the published accounts that Boas collected or edited. Teit's field notes, however, suggest that this may not have been the case in the original telling. For instance, the Nké-kaumstêm story that Teit sent to Boas listed "a gun" as among the items that Sun traded for the skin blanket (Teit n.d). Yet when Boas edited this story for publication, he omitted the word "gun," noting instead that Sun exchanged "bows and arrows and a goat-hair robe" for the skin robe (Teit et al. 1917, 34). By eliminating the word "gun" from Teit's original, he transported the story out of its early twentieth-century context to a more remote and exotic past.

As stories of whites began to trickle in, one wonders if Boas noted associations that the latter may have had to the "Sonne/Sun" of his earlier collections. Teit, for example, sent Boas a number of stories he collected among the Nlaka'pamux about Simon Fraser, the leader of the first European expedition to reach Lytton in the spring of 1808. These stories claim that when the Nlaka'pamux encountered Fraser, they named him "Sun" (1912, 416).

Contemporary tellings make a clear link between Sun and whites. In the 1980s Annie York, a Nlaka'pamux woman from Spuzzum, explained that the Nlaka'pamux referred to Simon Fraser as the "Son of the Sun" (Hanna and Henry 1995, 124); Louie Phillips, a contemporary of York, claimed that his Nlaka'pamux forebears at Lytton believed Fraser to be "Christ" (interview by author, Lytton BC, March 10, 1991).[3]

These contemporary stories, although a century removed from the earliest recordings, open a range of new interpretive possibilities. Robinson, for example, states that the "spotted rock" was shrouded in secrecy. The lack of mention of such a rock in the early accounts could be attributed to the community's pact to keep it secret.

Robinson's account demonstrates how the listener/collector influences the story. Robinson's "Prophecy at Lytton," for example, was told to me—a young, female, white outsider. One of his objectives in telling this story early in our friendship may have been to convey the extent to which he and I were products of two very different worlds. The storytellers at the Anglican church at Lytton in 1888 may have had similar objectives in telling the story of "Der Knabe und die Sonne" to their white listeners—a young German visitor and a local Anglican missionary.

There is great value in linking stories to their tellers. Like the boy in Robinson's "Prophecy at Lytton," Robinson spent much of his childhood on his own with his blind grandmother while his mother, Arcell, worked to bring home the wages necessary to support her extended family.

Surely what is most important about these stories are the contexts of their tellings. Whereas Boas's motive in recording "The Boy and the Sun" story was to textualize the deep past, the storytellers involved may have had a very different objective. Like Harry Robinson, they may have told "The Sun and the Lad"/"Bad Boy" stories to voice their perspectives on the colonial project rapidly enveloping their world. With limited communication skills and a focus on cultural purity, the visitors may have missed their hosts' messages.

NOTES

1. Because Robinson did not give titles to his stories, I assigned the title "Prophecy at Lytton" at the request of the publisher, who required titles for each of the stories in *Write It on Your Heart.*

2. I am grateful to Ashley Hilliard and Marianne Ignace for providing English translations of this story.

3. For a full comparative analysis of the Simon Fraser stories, see Wickwire 1994.

SUGGESTED READING AND REFERENCES

Boas, Franz. 1895. "Indianische Sagen von der Nord-pacifischen Küste Amerikas." In *Donerabdruck aus den Verhandlungen der Berliner Gesellschaft für Anthropologie, Ethnologie und Urgeschichte, 1891 bis 1895.* Berlin: A. Asher & Co. (English translations by Marianne Boelscher and Ashley Hilliard.)

Briggs, Charles, and Richard Bauman. 1999. "'The Foundation of All Future Researches': Franz Boas, George Hunt, Native American Texts, and the Construction of Modernity." *American Quarterly* 51 (3): 479–527.

Hanna, Darwin, and Mamie Henry, eds. 1995. *Our Tellings: Interior Salish Stories of the Nlha7kapmx People.* Vancouver: UBC Press.

Teit, James A. 1898. *Traditions of the Thompson River Indians.* American Folk-Lore Society Publication. London: Houghton, Mifflin.

———. 1912. *Mythology of the Thompson Indians.* Memoir of the American Museum of Natural History, vol. 12; Publications of the Jesup North Pacific Expedition vol. 8, part 2. New York: G. E. Stechert.

———. n.d. Field notes. Anthropology Archives, American Museum of Natural History, New York City.

James Teit, Marian K. Gould, Livingston Farrand, and Herbert J. Spinden. 1917. *Folk-Tales of Salishan and Sahaptin Tribes.* Publication of the American Folk-Lore Society. New York: Stechert & Co.

Wickwire, Wendy. 1989. *Write It on Your Heart: The Epic World of an Okanagan Storyteller—Harry Robinson.* Vancouver BC: Talonbooks & Theytus Books.

———. 1992. *Nature Power: In the Spirit of an Okanagan Storyteller—Harry Robinson.* Vancouver: Douglas & McIntyre; Seattle: University of Washington Press.

———. 1994. "To See Ourselves as the Other's Other: Nlaka'pamux Contact Narratives." *Canadian Historical Review* 75 (1): 1–20.

———. 1998. "'We Shall Drink from the Stream and So Shall You': James A. Teit and Native Resistance in British Columbia, 1908–22." *Canadian Historical Review* 79 (2): 199–236.

Audiotapes and transcripts of Harry Robinson's storytelling recorded from 1977 to 1991 are in the author's possession.

Prophecy at Lytton

Told by Harry Robinson

At one time at Lytton, there was a lot of Indians
    right at Lytton where the town is now.
Up on the hillside, from there to the east like,
    in the hillside.
That's where the Indians lived at that time.

That's a long time ago.
    I would say now that was before Christ.
That was right after the animal-people,
    shortly after the animal-people,
        when it's become to be real people, Indian.

And those days, there is no Christ yet.

And God came to certain one to talk to 'em.
Not for all of 'em, but certain one.

But, when he going to draw the animal-people from the animal,
    God came at that time,
        and he see all the people at that time.
That was long time before this happens in Lytton.
That's another way.

But this in Lytton,
    God came all right at that time.
There was a lot of people, Indian, live there
    And they got a teepee there and there and there.
A lot of teepees, you know.
Bunch of Indian.

And those days, the Indian,

all they do is hunting and fishing.
And they get the berries, you know, pick the berries,
   and get the digging, you know, the root digging.
That's food too.
And the berries, and the deer, and the fish,
   that's all they do.
They just getting the food.
They busy everyday.
They go out hunting,
   and some people they do something else.
And they were living in one area, like a lot of people there.

And the one old lady, not too old,
   could be around sixty years old, something like that.
And they got a daughter, and they got a son-in-law,
   and these two, they both die,
      not at the same time,
         but I think one of them died first.
And not too long and the other one died.

And these two, they had a son.
And they both died, you know.
But the old lady, they take care of the son of her daughter.
And that was her grandson.
See?
She take care of 'em.

And this little boy,
   he could be around one year old or two when his mother died.
Then his dad died.
But he's living with his grandmother.

And all the people, they hunt, and they getting food.
And whoever is old and they can't hunt,
   and they can't do much work,
      they give 'em from their food what they get to live.
But they can do a little work at the camp, you know.
Might gather in some wood or something else.
Just what they can do.

And at this time this old lady, they raise that boy.

From one or two years old,
   she raise him up to eight or ten years old.
But they don't train him.
They never tell him,
   "Do this work.
   Go with these people to get the meat.
   Pack 'em in."
They just leave 'em alone.

And the boy never was told what to do.
Never was trained to be good worker,
   to be a good boy.

They just grow up like wild grass or something.
And they don't know nothing.
And they were lazy.
But he know enough to eat.
And he can eat like a pig.
He eat lots.

But the other people they know how much work they do
   to get the food.
They got to work.
They all know.

But this boy, he don't know that,
   because was never told about it by his grandmother.
Maybe the other people told 'em, but they wouldn't listen.
Unless his grandmother could tell 'em something,
   he might take her word.
But in another way, they don't care.
And that means he's a bad boy.

Some people, they get a deer.
The next morning, maybe three or four of them,
   they go over there and get the meat.
Those days, no horses, no nothing.
Only pack 'em on their back.

They should go.

His grandmother should tell 'em,
   "You go with these people and help them pack the stuff in."

But he never.

And these people go to get the meat, pack 'em in.
And the boy, he played around.
They don't pay no attention to what his people do.

But he eat as well as these others.

And these other people, they don't like that way.
And they told the old lady,
   "Why don't you make that boy work?
   And why don't you tell him to do something?"

Well, the old lady, they wouldn't tell him for a while.
And they always give him food, you know, to live.

And one day, the bunch of Indians,
   they decided they're going to leave this boy and his grandmother
     because it was his grandmother,
      it was her fault for that boy to be like that.
That's why they're going to leave 'em,
   the both of 'em, and they can go away.

And they can stay there just themselves.
See what they'll do.
They could be starve to death.

So all the people, they decided they'll do that.
And they talk to one another without the old lady know.

And one day, the people, they told the boys,
   like the same age as that bad boy,
     told these boys,
   "You take that boy out, away, way out some place.
   Play and go away.
   And tell him some kind of thing to go out of sight.
   When they go out of sight, you guys come back,

and when you get here, we all go away.
When they come back, there'll be nobody here.
But they wouldn't know which way the people went."

And they tell the ladies the same way for his grandmother.
And they all go out, and they digging some roots or picking berries,
    and they tell this lady,
        "There's a lot of berries over there," or something,
        "You go over there and see 'em."

So, she go over there by herself.
Alone.
And she went out of sight.
And these other ladies come back,
    and they all go to the camp,
        and they gather the stuff, not much, you know.
Just get something and pack and go away.

And they hide their tracks.
They went in the place where the tracks couldn't be seen.

And the boy, they were out there and come back.
And the other boys, they're not there.
They missing the other boys.

The same way the old lady.
They come back and the other ladies, they're not there.
So finally the old lady get back to the camp first.
Nobody.
Everybody go.
They don't know which way it went.

And the boy came back.
Nobody at the camp.
Only his grandmother.

And they ask one another,
    "Why? Where's the other ones?"

They don't know.

And they figure they're going to look around
   and see if they could see the tracks, which way they went.
And they looked around.
They couldn't see no track because these people,
   they hide their tracks.
They pick out hard ground so the tracks wouldn't be show.
They couldn't find the tracks
   and they don't know which way their people went.

They go away.
They know they were left.
They know these people, they left them.
So nothing they could do but stay there.

And when the people were there, before they leave,
   and they eat the meat, the bone of the deer,
      they put 'em away from the camp.
And they're there.
And they go over there and pick them up
   and bring 'em and boil 'em.
And all they can do is to drink the soup of that bone.
But that's not good, you know.
They can't live on that kind of food.

Then, the old lady is kinda old.
They can go out and pick berries and dig—root digging.
But she can't do much because she's old.
And the boy is too young.
And, in another way, he don't know nothing.
He can never bring the food in.

So the way it look like,
   they going to stay there till they die by starving.
No eat nothing.

And these people, the other people, they go away.
Make another camp over there.
And then they hunt and they getting the food.
   "To heck with the boy and his grandmother!
   Let 'em starve to death!"

Because they blame the old lady.
That was the old lady's fault.
That's why the boy was no good.
If she train that boy, when that boy grow up,
   he'll be a good boy like the others.
And that'll be all right.
But they didn't.
That's why they leave 'em.

But, they all mad,
   like they all mad to that lady and that boy, these Indian.

But God did not mad for these two.
Didn't.

So, they were live there for quite a while
   and they try to do what they can.
But still, it was all right in the summer.
But when winter comes, what they going to do?
They going to die by starving.

And the old lady, they make a bow and arrow.
Small.
And they give 'em to the boy.
And they said to the boy,
   "You go out.
     If you see a squirrel or magpie or blue jay or robin,
       whatever it is, the bird and the squirrel, or rabbit,
         if you see them,
           you shoot 'em with a bow and arrow.
     And bring 'em in. We can eat 'em."

All right.
Now they try to train that boy.
But it seems to be kinda late before they try to train 'em.

So anyway, the boy, he go out and he look around.
And he see the magpie.
Shoot 'em with the bow and arrow and he got 'em.
And bring 'em.

When he get them in, and he skinned 'em, you know.
He pull the skin and he skinned 'em.
And stretch out the skin while they're raw.
Just like the skin you throw over there.
And stretch 'em out and leave 'em dry.
He want 'em to be dry.
That would be blue jay skin.

Then next time, they mighta get a magpie.
Yeah, he get a magpie and he do the same.
They bring 'em in and skin 'em.
Then they eat the meat.
They boil 'em and eat 'em.
But they skin 'em and stretch out the skin.
Little pieces.
Magpie skin and blue jay skin.

And they do that till they had a few of that skin.
And they put it in.
They sewed 'em together.
Like, they put the blue jay skin, like, put it in here.
Magpie skin in here.
And blue jay skin, like, from one to another.
They mix 'em, this blue jay, magpie, and blue jay and magpie again.
Just like that all the way.
Then, they had 'em pretty good size.
It's all mixed, but it's all spotted because the magpie,
    it was black and white, and the blue jay, just blue.
But they had the blue jay in one section, and magpie here,
    and magpie here again, and blue jay here again.
It look nice, you know.

They stretch 'em out when they dry and sewed 'em up together,
    and then stretch 'em out.
They no good for nothing,
    because it's easy to tore.

But they laid 'em on the ground.
But only thing is, they just look nice.
That's all.

So, they have that.

And nothing more they can do but getting magpie and blue jay,
    and sometimes they get rabbit.
Or sometimes they mighta get squirrel.
But they never take the skin off that to use for anything.
Just skin 'em and eat 'em.

They live there quite awhile in the summer.
Then, they getting hungry.
They got quite a time to live, you know.
They could hardly eat, because they can't get 'em.
Sometimes the boy, they couldn't get no blue jay
    or magpie or rabbit or squirrel.
They can't get 'em.
But sometimes he get 'em.

And the old lady tried to get the root digging.
But she's old.
She can't do much work.

Then, they couldn't get no fish from the river,
    because they can't do it—and for quite a while.
And they begin to drop, you know.
They going to be weak because no eat.
Nothing to eat.
They eat very little.
That won't do 'em good, you know.
They drop down.
Pretty soon they'll be die by starving.

And this time, the boy went out and got the blue jay and magpie,
    two of them.
And that's a big one, a big food, because they're two,
    one blue jay and one magpie.
They bring 'em in both, and skin 'em and boil the meat.

And they got them cooked.

They were ready to eat.

They got 'em cooked,
   and they make kind of a table
      and put the branches on the ground.
Then they put the meat there.
And then they were sitting down there.

They were just ready to eat and somebody came.
They never see where they come from.
Just like if we could see somebody come,
   we'd say,
      "Here comes somebody."
But this one here, they never see.

The first thing they know,
   somebody stand right here.
Look like it was a man, old man.
And this old man, he says,
   "Looks like I come in time.
   You guys going to have lunch."

Old lady says,
   "Yeah, we're just going to have lunch."

The old lady says,
   "All right, you sit down and we'll all eat
     because you're in time.
   We just going to eat when you came.
   Sit down and we'll all eat."

But that's all the food they got.
Just a blue jay and magpie, that's all.
But still they offer this to their visitor.
They offered something from there.

All right, they all sit down,
   and this man told 'em,
     "I'm going to tell you something before we eat."

All right.
This old man told 'em,

"You close your eyes and you close your eyes.
Two of you, close your eyes.
I'm going to say a prayer."

Well, at that time, they don't say a prayer.
But anyway, they meant that way.
And told 'em,
   "I can do the talking, just a few words.
   Then I stop.
   And then I tell you,
      'All right, you can open up your eyes.'
   And you open up your eyes, and then we eat."

All right.
They close their eyes.
Then listen to him.
And he talk a few words.
And he said,
   "All right, open your eyes."

They opened their eyes.
Instead of magpie and blue jay there to eat,
   but they not there when they open their eyes.
They were different food there were there.
They never see that kind of food before.

And this old man told 'em,
   "We eat this one. There's lots of them there."

They never asked that man,
   "Where is that magpie and blue jay?"
They never said nothing about it.

Anyway, they started to eat this new kind of food to them, you know.
And they eat.
And this man told 'em,
   "Eat all you want."

And the old lady, she think,
   This is not much.

But this man told 'em,
   "Don't have to think that way.
   Eat plenty. You can eat all you want.
   We can eat all we want of this food.
   But still it'll be there.
   We never eat 'em all."

All right.
They eat till they get full.
And they had enough.
But the food is still the same.
There's never any less or any more.
Just about the same amount.

All right.
And this man told 'em,
   "This food that's there,"
   and suppose to be kind of cloth or something
     where the food was,
       and this man told 'em,
   "Put the cloth like that from this side.
   And put it away.
   You eat that again.
   But you got to say your prayer."
And told 'em what word they have to say in their language,
   because he's talking to them in their language.

Then he said,
   "You got to say your prayers.
   You got to say these words first.
   You put this food while it's cold like that.
   Put 'em away and bring 'em like that.
   The food's in there.
   Then you put 'em away.
   When you feel like eating, you hungry,
     bring 'em and put it here.
   Before you open 'em up, say your prayers.
   Say these word.
   And close your eyes and say that word
     just like I say awhile ago.

Say that word.
Close your eyes and say that word.
And after open 'em up and the food is there.
And eat that.
But not for all time.
That's just for so long.
Then there'll be no more.
But they will find there was something else
    when this food was no more, when they're gone.
You're not going to eat 'em all.
They'll be still the same.
But next time you open 'em, they'll be not there.
And then you'll know what to do after that."

All right.
They eat that.
And after they eat this food, and,
    they didn't know that was God yet.
Anyway, they just think he was just another man.
So he told 'em,
    he told the old lady,
        "This boy, did he get the blue jay and the magpie?"
        "Yeah, he get 'em.
        He shoot 'em with a bow and arrow.
        Sometimes he get a squirrel
            and sometimes he get a rabbit.
        That's about all he can get."

And he said,
    "Has he got a bow and arrow?"
    "Yeah."
    "Let me see it," man says.
And he showed it to him.
Only small.

And he told the old lady,
    "You know how to make this bow and arrow?"
    "Yeah, I know how to make 'em."

He says to the old lady,

"You make a bigger one for the boy.
This is only good for the bird, for the magpie, squirrel,
   and things like that.
Too small.
But you can make a bigger one,
   and strong and long arrow, strong,
      so he could shoot the deer with that and kill it.
You make that bow and arrow and finish it
   and the boy could take that and go out."

And he told the boy,
   "When your grandmother finish that bow and arrow for you,
     when she finish 'em,
       then you can take that bow and arrow, big one,
         and you go out this way
           and you go out a little ways, not too
             far, then you can see a deer just standing.
You shoot it with the bow and arrow and you hit it,
   and you kill it.
Then you come back and tell your grandmother.
You both can go over there and cut 'em and skin 'em,
   and cut 'em into pieces and pack 'em.
Pack 'em into the camp and dry 'em.
Next two or three days, then you go out this way,
   and you go a little ways and you see a deer.
And you kill 'em.
Two, three days after that and you go out another direction.
Every time, until you make a round like.
And don't you ever think,
Well, this is lots of 'em. We got enough.
Get all you can get.
Then you can go down.
You can make a net.
You can make a net out of the grass they make a rope out of."

Tell the old lady,
   "You can make a net and you go down to the river.
   And you wait there awhile
     where is good for the salmon to come up.
   And you wait there a little while.

Not too long.
You could see salmon coming and you get 'em with that net.
And you can get five or six, or maybe only two.
And keep them.
And if there's a lot of them,
    cut 'em into pieces.
Dry 'em.
Do that all the time.
And this food will be no more because you're getting some.
Getting some meat and fish, root digging, and berries,
    and things like that.
And then you have a lot of food.
But don't you think this is enough.
Get all you can.
Because these people that were here,
    these people that leave you guys,
        over there where they are, they hungry.
They never get anything.
They couldn't get 'em.
Once in a while maybe they get one deer.
They run out of food and they getting hungry.
And they going to have a heck of a time.
One of these days, they going to come.
Not all of them, but maybe one or two from there.
They're going to come.
And when you have lots of meat already dry,
    and a lot of fish already dry,
        and when you have a lot of them,
            you put them in a place where they keep the food."

And tell 'em in each place where they move,
    their teepee, the place,
        they still there where they put the food, you know.

And tell 'em,
    "Whenever you got lots of this dry meat,
        put them in that place.
    That's for that people.
    And in the other one, that's for that people.
    So many of them.

You can put all the meat you dried,
    and you eat some of that.
But put 'em there.
That's for them when they come back.
And, before they come back,
    maybe only one or two they could come
        to see if you guys were alive yet.
And they don't have to come right here,
    but they might come on the distance
        so you could see them from quite a ways.
Then they go back.
Whenever you see them, the first time just see them,
    pay no attention, just like you didn't see 'em.
But the second time, they could come,
    maybe three or four.
Same way.
They can pick out from the distance.
And you'll be around.
The first time they pick out from the distance,
    just like you didn't see 'em.
Pay no attention.
And they go back.
When they get back to their bunch,
    and they could tell their bunch,
        'These two, they was still there.
        They were alive.'
They were around in that same place.
That's what they'll have to say when they get back
    to the other ones.
But later on in a few days,
    they'll send three or four of them.
And they come the same way, like,
    pick out,
        then you could see there was four of them.
All right.
This time you wave your hand and tell 'em to come.
Tell 'em to come by your hand, you know.
Tell 'em to come.
Wouldn't be long and they'll sneak to you guys,
    and they'll get here.

And as soon as they get here they could look and say,
   'By God, there's a lot of meat over here.'
Then over there, then over there.
Then where you are there's all kinds of meat,
   all kinds of food.
They could look at it.
First they could be wonder how you could get 'em.
And you could tell 'em,
   'All right, you guys, sit down and I'll give you
     something to eat.'
And they'll be glad because they're hungry.
And then you give them some of this meat or fish or berries.
Anything you got, give 'em all they can eat.
And let them eat all they want till they get full.
Then you make a bundle.
Big one.
And tell the other one,
   'You pack this.'
And make another one, and say,
   'You pack this.'
All of 'em.
You make four bundles.
And tell 'em.
   'When you get back to wherever you was,
     and open this and all you people can eat.
   Feed the people over there.'
And this one, they'll take it over there.
Just for that time.
Tell these people, these four, tell 'em,
   'When you get back and eat these,
     in two or three days, come back,
       all of you come back.
   Here's your camp.
   There's a lot of food there.
   And here's your camp.
   A lot of food there.
   And there, and there.
   And the food, it's all ready for you guys.
   Come back and stay here like it was before.'
  You tell 'em that."

All right.
That's what this man told 'em.

And after they told 'em all about this, he says,
    "What's this?"
That was the blue jay and magpie.
It was laid on the ground.
It look nice.

    "And what's this?"

    "That's the blue jay and magpie.
    We sewed 'em together.
    They no good for nothing.
    Only lay on the ground.
    They look nice.
    That's all.
    Just look pretty."

This man says,
    "All right.
    Could you guys give me this?
    I want 'em."
    "Sure, you can take it. We give it to you."
And the man says,
    "All right. I'll take it."
And they reached down and picked 'em up.
And they held 'em in his hand.

And they says to this grandmother and grandson,
    he said to them,
        "You guys give me these. Now it's mine.
        But I'm not going to take it along with me.
        But still it's mine.
        I'm going to set 'em back on the same place.
        Then it's going to be there for all time.
        But it's going to turn in different way."

    "All right.
    You can do as you like.

We give it to you."

"Now this is the time," he told them.
"I am the God.
I'm the Father.
I come from heaven.
And your people left you.
They want you to be starved to death.
But I don't like it that way.
I don't want you people to starve to death,
    and also this bunch.
I want you to live.
But only thing is, these people got to come back and live together
    just like it was before.
But I'm going to leave.
You're going to watch me.
I'm going back to the heaven.
And this place, this country, this world
    not this world, but where you were here,
        all this place, it's yours.
And you going to live there till you die.
But whoever is next is going to be here at all time.
This is yours.
But another thing I'm going to tell you.
There was some people going to come here,
    not right away, it'll be a long time from now.
They going to come.
I want 'em to come.
Different people.
Built just like you, but only taller.
These people they going to get here is white.
More white than you.
You kinda dark.
But the people, they going to come here, is going to be whiter,
    whiter than you.
Long time from now they going to come here.
When they get here, that's going to be your,
    you're going to be amongst with them.
They going to live here.
When they come here, they going to live here for all time.

And you people going to be live together around here.
But these white people, when they come,
   they going to do the work.
They can make the land to be look good,
   just like this blue jay and magpie.
You guys make 'em look nice.
Very nice.
So the white people,
   they going to make this land very nice.
But still, you going to be there.
And whatever they going to make,
   just like I do now,
     give you the food for you to live,
      they can do the same.
When they get here, they can go to work
  and they can change everything,
    what you eating.
And they'll give you from what they do or what they raise,
   because this is your place.
But they going to do the work.
And what they get, they can give you some of that.
And they could use themselves."

That means the white people is going to come.
And that's the way it's going to be.
And that's the way they do now.
The white people came and then they fixed the land,
   make a hayfield, and make a garden.
They do everything nice.
But when the Indian only here, they don't make it that way. Nothing.
All they do, just hunt.

And told 'em,
   "When these people come here,
     they going to be amongst with you people.
   They going to live here with you.
   But this is your place."

And they said,
   "When you go out to get that deer, it's all yours.

It's going to be that way for a long time."

And they don't tell 'em,
    "Later on you going to have a permit to get that deer."
They never say that.
But now, the Indians, they going to hunt.
And they have to go to the government office
    and ask for the permit.
And the government office, they write.
It say, "Here is your permit to hunt."

It should not be that way.
The Indians should be free.
They can go out hunt.
But the white people, that's their way.

They can go to the office and get the permit for what they can shoot,
    buck or doe, or one or three or four, or only one.
That's for the white people, not for the Indians.
Because, at that time, God, they never said for the Indian,
    "Later on you going to have a permit to get the deer."
They never did say that.

As long as they don't say that, well,
    Indians supposed to be free at all times that way.
Not only that way.
For everything.

So they tell 'em all about and they said,
    "These people, when they get here, long time from now," he says,
    "I want 'em to come here.
    But not all.
    The part of it, it's going to be here, but the other part of it
        going to be still over there where they are now."

Well, that means in Europe.
See? The white people came.
But still there's lots more over there.
And now there is a lot of white people over there in England,
    a lot of white people, all over in Europe.

But there's lot of 'em in here.
But that time, when God was there at Lytton,
   there is not a white man in this place.
Only Indian.

And that's the reason why the Indian, they was saying,
   "This is my land."
They don't say,
   "This world is mine."
Because the world,
   it belongs to all person, whoever they were,
      living alive in the world.
You, me, or anybody.
But, in another way, the Indians owns this island.
Not on overseas.
This one, this island, supposed to be for the Indian.
They are living here in the first place.

And that's another stories.
They become to live here in the first place
   long before the white man came.
In the first place was animal-people.
That's when they was "imbellable" stories.[1]
But then, in Lytton, they were already in human people
   when God came and told 'em,
      "Now, tell you all this and you got to remember.
      You will see these people.
      That's going to be your friend.
      When they live here, they going to be your friend.
      Not to fight one another. Not to make trouble.
      Going to be your friend.
      But they going to live here
         from this time till the end of the world."

And who knows when it's going to be the end of the world?
But he told 'em they going to live here till the end of the world.
And you too.

1. This is the English translation Harry was given for *chap*-TEEK-*whl,* stories from "way back" during "time of the animal-people." Once, when seeking an English translation for *chap*-TEEK-*whl* Harry was told these are "unbelievable." Since that time, Harry has called them "imbellable" stories.

But now, nobody here but only you Indian.
He said,
    "Now I leave.
    And you have to see me going up.
    I come from heaven.
    I am the Father. I am God."
He said,
    "This one here, you give me, that's the blue jay skin and magpie.
    They look nice.
    I'm going to put them down, and I'm going to stand."
Because when they sewed 'em, you know,
    then it's a pretty good size.
And they said,
    "I'm going to put them down because it's mine.
    You give it to me.
    And I'm going to put 'em down.
    And I'm going to stand right on 'em.
    And then I'll go."

All right.
He put that down.
Then he walked over there and then stand right on 'em.
Supposed to be a skin, a bird skin, you know.
But they never tore.
He put 'em down and stand there.
It's big, you know.
They sewed 'em together and then they was so big.

Stand there, and then they said,
    "All right.
    Just watch me.
    I'm going back."

Then they was stand on that blue jay skin.
And they stand,
    and they just like,
        jerk!
Down.
Up they goes.

And they don't go fast.

They go kinda slow.
Not too fast.
Not fly up, you know.
You know, they go kinda slow.
And they watch 'em.
Way up.
And they could still see 'em.
Just like a smoke.
Just like a smoke, and they don't see 'em no more.
And they look.
No more.
Went up to the sky.
And then they look at the one they,
    that skin they stand on.
They looked there.
Turn into a rock.
It's a rock.
Turn into a rock, just like this one here.[2]
This is supposed to be wood at one time, but it turn into a rock.

That's how come.
From that time it can happen that way.
Then it was.
And that's supposed to be wood but they turn into a rock.
Because that blue jay skin and magpie,
    it was a skin, but God stand on 'em
        and raise from there.
And instead of watch that, they watch him going up, you know.
It takes awhile.
Watch 'em till he go away.

And then looked there.
As soon as they looked there, it's already rock, just like this.
But still, the spot, it's still there.
Still look nice.
But it turn into a rock.
And it's heavy.
It's thick and big.

2. Harry points to a fossil that he had found and saved for many years.

And that, in Lytton, from town is now,
   up to the hillside, that way,
     that's where that is.
And this rock is there.
For a long, long time, all the Indians, they was seeing 'em,
   they still in the same place.

And he told 'em,
   "This one here, I'm going to stand on.
I'm going to raise from there.
But this one, leave 'em as they are.
Leave 'em there all the time.
Don't take 'em away.
Just leave 'em there."

So, they was there a long time till the white people come.
One at a time, you know, maybe a few this way and a few that way.
Just a very few white people came.

And this one is still there.
But the white people didn't know.
They never seen 'em.

And later on, the white people,
   getting thicker and thicker and thicker.

And finally, the old-timer, like, way back,
   could be around 1850, could be maybe before then,
     maybe 1800, something like that,
       because old John Ashnola, John Shiweelkin
         born in 1820.
And on his time, they already disappeared, that rock,
   when he know.
When this rock disappeared, it might be before 1800,
   something like that.
But the white people, you know, they already came.

And the Indians at that time, they say,
   they decided and they say,
     "We better hide that rock.

We going to sunk 'em in the ground.
Because the white people came, and they might find 'em.
They not very big.
Just so big, and thick.
It's heavy.
But still, the white people,
    they might find 'em and take 'em away.
They'll pack 'em away.
They could steal that from us.
But we could sunk 'em down right there and bury 'em.
So the white people will never see that."

All right.
That's what they figure,
    the Indians at that time.

So, they went over there
    and then they dig just alongside of 'em.
Like, they lay on the hillside.
There is a little dip, like,
    not steep, but it's uphill a little bit.
And they dig on the lower side.
They dig it deep enough
    and just slide 'em and drop 'em in the hole.
And they bury 'em and smooth this.
But they got some kind of mark,
    not there, but a long ways off from there.
But they know how many steps from there to that mark.

Just like they do when surveying.
I work on surveying and we do that.
We put in a stick or nail, the bar, you know, like just about this size,
    and we drive 'em.
Sticking out just a little bit.
And they got to stand on top, you know.
Then they put the line from that to the tree,
    maybe long ways out.
Then they mark that,
    how many feet from that tree to which way,
        which direction, either west or south or north or

    whatever it is,
       or angle, you know,
          how many degrees to the west or to the south, from that mark.
Then the post was there.
And the next surveyor, in seventy, eighty years,
   they could still find that.
Easy to find.

Same thing they do.
They put in the ground
  and they had some kind of mark, way out,
  not one, but maybe two or three.
And they know how far from there to there.
And they know where it's supposed to be,
  in open place, when they bury 'em.

But they never tell the young people, the young Indian.
They tell some.
But later on, they just quit telling 'em.
And they don't tell 'em anymore.

And now today,
  all the young people in Lytton and Spences Bridge and Shulus,
    and Douglas Lake, and everywhere,
      they don't know that.
They never did know they was buried there.
They don't know anything about it today.

That's the way they want,
  the Indian was.
Supposing they figure,
  if they let the young people know,
    and nowadays, that they could tell the white people,
      and they could sell it.
They going to get the money from the white people for that rock.
They might ask five hundred dollars or something like that.
And the white people will give 'em that money.

And whoever they sell that,
  maybe a bunch or something like that,

and then take the money.
Have a lot of money to drink.
It can be that way, they figure.
So they don't let 'em know.

And not yet.
They never did let 'em know.
The way I see, nobody know today about that.

But I know.
And my wife know.
Because I learned that from her father.
And I learn the same stories from my grandmother.
And so she learned that from her father.
And also we learned that from Mary Narcisse.
Mary Narcisse was living until 1944 until the age of 116.
That's how we know that.

But we didn't know if anybody know about that.
We think not, because nobody talked about it.
Not even Slim.
I never tell. I know, but I never tell.
But one time I says to my wife,
"We both know about that spotted rock in Lytton, we know that, you and I."
    "Yeah," they says, "I know."
I said,
    "Next time we go to Josephine George,"
        that's the Indian doctor,
            "next time we go over there," I says to her,
                "because you speak in Thompson,
                    you ask about that, see what she got to say."
She says, "All right, I will."
So next time we get to her,
    we bring some fruit from here and go over there.
We want her to work on us because she's a doctor.
We bring some fruit and some money.
We were there two or three days.
And my wife and Josephine,
    they go to bed together in one bed.
And my wife ask her all about it.

My wife tell her the stories.

Not all.

Just a part of it.

Just a little.

Says,

>"There's supposed to be a spotted rock over in Lytton.
>
>It was there.
>
>What happened with that?"

But we know, but she ask Josephine,

>"What happened?
>
>Did you ever know about it?"

And Josephine, they don't like to say.

They know, but they hide it.

But that's the only one left.

And maybe Antony Joe,

>another old one still alive.

Just a few of them old people know about it

>but they never said a word.

And Josephine, they don't like to say anything.

But my wife explain that she know that we did know,

>just like she does.

So finally she says to my wife,

>"I'm kinda surprised that you two, you and your husband,
>
>>know about this.
>
>We thought nobody know but just a few of us around here.
>
>But how do you know?"

My wife told her,

>"We learned that from my father, and from my husband's grandmother
>
>>and that Mary Narcisse."

They mention all these people.

That's how we learn — from these old people.

Because they go over there to get some salmon

>kinda often in the early days.

From here they go to Spences Bridge, Lytton, Hope, Lillooet,

>on horseback, packhorses those days.

And these old people, when they were over there,

>they learn that, from over there.

Then when they come back, we learn from them.

So my wife told Josephine all about that.

Then she could tell that we did know.

Then she says,
   "They hide that."
I says,
   "We know that already. We know they hide it."
But we just wondering what we got to say.
I could ask 'em myself, but I can't speak in her language.
But my wife can speak in her language.
And she ask her.
And for a while they don't like to say,
   but they can tell that we did know.
So they tell all about it.
They said,
   "We don't want to tell the young people nowadays
      because they're going to sell 'em.
   I never tell nobody since.
   You're the first one because you ask for it.
   And I try to tell some Indians about it.
   I don't tell 'em everything, but I kinda start it.
   They don't care. They don't pay no attention.
   They don't seem to want to know."

So that's about all.

Lushootseed

Coyote and His Son

Introduction by Crisca Bierwert

"Coyote and His Son" was recorded in 1962 by Martha Lamont for Thom Hess, then a graduate student in linguistics at the University of Washington. Hess was documenting and analyzing the Lushootseed language, the language of peoples native to most of the Puget Sound watershed, extending thirty to sixty miles from the present city of Seattle, Washington (see Suttles and Lane 1990, 323). Martha Lamont was in her eighties and a renowned storyteller. She conversed only in Lushootseed, although she understood English and spoke a few words of it.[1] Her husband, Levi Lamont, who helped Hess in transcribing and translating his wife's stories, was bilingual. This couple, along with a half-dozen others residing on and near the Tulalip Reservation, which is about forty miles north of Seattle, provided Hess with a corpus of texts with which to work. His interest at the time was in documenting and defining the grammar. The youngest native speakers were then in their forties, most of them were bilingual, and they rarely used their native language.[2] Hess used these texts as the basis for his first Lushootseed dictionary and for a set of pedagogical texts used to teach Lushootseed at the University of Washington and in reservation communities. His attention to documentation was so great that it was not until later, Hess admits, that he realized the great value of the texts as literature.[3]

Starting in the 1970s, Hess began to work with Vi (taqʷšeblu) Hilbert on transcribing texts from his own collecting efforts and others. Hilbert, a native speaker of the Upper Skagit dialect of Lushootseed, was in her fifties and taught Lushootseed with him at the University of Washington. Their collaborative relationship continues to this day. In addition to working on Hess's recordings, they transcribed recordings made in the 1950s by Leon Metcalf, an amateur anthropologist who collected texts from the distinguished storytellers of that decade. He recorded Hilbert's aunt, Susie Sampson Peter; her in-law Ruth Shelton; and also Martha Lamont, among others, and he deposited the recordings in the Thomas Burke Memorial Washington State Museum at the University of Washington (Seattle). The texts that Hess and Metcalf recorded form the core of Lushootseed literature as we know it today.[4] Since those early years, Vi Hilbert formed a nonprofit organization, called Lushootseed Research, to continue to record and collect Lushootseed texts; her work has augmented, enhanced, and promoted the oral traditions. The work she directs now includes projects as diverse as digital archiving and theatrical production based on archival texts; she is still devoted to bringing her own elders' archived texts to publication and distribution to family members. As native speakers become fewer, the "old" recordings become nearly as precious as the once-living elders who made them.

Lushootseed literature today takes many forms and is expressed in many dimensions: archival documents, publications including scholarly works and children's editions, storytelling to teach language and culture, storytelling on national and international lecture circuits, storytelling at political and environmental gatherings, theater productions, retreats involving performance, interactive storytelling events, multimedia digital organization of texts, televised events, television programs on Puget Sound Native peoples, civic events and ceremony, and private and community ceremonials that are part of religious practice. Most of these uses are in English or use the Native language fleetingly. Exceptions are the locally based cultural preservation programs. Two of the most productive in recent years include the program at Puyallup, where Zalmai Zahir has worked with his elders on language teaching tools and drama. The other is at the Tulalip Reservation, where David Cort has created ways for children learning their ancestral stories to create not only recordings but also digital text and animation for them. Also at Tulalip elder Marya Moses and Toby Langen have worked together on both a cultural education project for "home" and scholarly publications for those both home and "away."

This story, then, comes to us by way of Hess's recording, transcription in collaboration with the Lamonts, retranscription with Vi Hilbert, and my translation. When Hess, Hilbert, and I published *Lushootseed Texts,* we included three of Martha Lamont's stories in Lushootseed transcription and English translation. Hess subsequently published eight other texts in Lushootseed only in two volumes with grammatical information and lessons (Hess 1995 and 1999). Hilbert also included "Coyote and His Son," along with Martha Lamont's other tellings, in *Haboo,* an anthology of Lushootseed literature in English (Hilbert 1986).[5] The translations there are free ones; the one I provide on the following pages is quite literal, with the exceptions noted.

Despite the limited corpus of old texts available, we know enough to identify this story as one of several types of trickster tales in Lushootseed. Mink, Raven, and Coyote are prevalent trickster figures in this area, with Mink and Raven stories overlapping with those from adjacent areas both north and south, and Coyote stories overlapping with those from the Plateau region to the east. Among Lushootseed stories Coyote is the most lascivious character, and it is this naughtiness that is featured in "Coyote and His Son." This Coyote story is one of four in Martha Lamont's recorded repertoire. All four portray Coyote in traditional trickster character. His talents include his being able to tell a convincing story, to cast a spell of conviction, and to render his fictions believable. He is stingy and wily in "Rock and Coyote," greedy and then very clever and charismatic in "Eyes of Coyote," lustful to excess in "Coyote Marries His Own Daughter." In "Coyote and His Son" Coyote transgresses social convention as he plots to satisfy his desire for his own son's wife. His central deceit in this, as in two of the other stories, is that he impersonates someone else. In every case he fools a woman (for varying motives, but always a woman) into thinking he is an intimate relative. In every case he uses trappings of this relative as a disguise; in one story he pretends to be a grandmother, in the other two he feigns to be a lover.

Since Coyote stories expose the constructed nature of social order, when Coyote has family, the stories expose tensions that can or could wreck havoc with kinship relations. The problematic premise of this story is established in its first lines. Coyote and his son live together, and the household is polygynous. Coyote's son has two wives, and he is neglecting one. To think about the story, we should know that, historically, extended family residence was usual, and polygyny was quite acceptable in Lushootseed kinship relations. A man's having more than one wife was not prevalent; rather it was a mark of distinction. Marriages, especially the first marriages, were traditionally arranged by the prospective in-laws. If a second marriage was planned, the first wife and her family would not necessarily take part in discussions directly, but relations between two sets of in-laws were a major strong form of social alliance, and offenses would not be introduced lightly. A second wife was considered to be a help to the first, at least in documented theory. A consequence for both or all spouses was that they were expected to support their kin's alliances by getting along. On the other hand, marriages could be dissolved, and such dissolutions apparently were without violent repercussions. Serial marriage was not discouraged. In short, we can presume that Coyote's son's household was founded agreeably. It is the fact that Coyote's son neglects his first wife that helps set the stage for trouble here. The fact that his father is known for his uncontrollable lust suggests what is coming.

This is the only Lushootseed story in which Coyote *has a son,* and the temptation of his living in a household with his daughters-in-law provides an usual opportunity to see rivalry between men played out in a story about Coyote. More typically, Coyote's flagrant violations are usually his own undoing, and he remains central to his own story. If he runs up against a male authority figure, he is rather quickly seen through and moves on to another episode. In "Coyote and His Son" the narrative dynamics involve a bit of contest between the men, providing a redemptive opportunity for other characters. Coyote's son, the one redeemed,

receives supernatural assistance in this story, suggesting that the Coyote tale—
typically one that upsets the social order—is balanced here by a questing story.
This tension is unusual in Coyote tales, and I must admit to accentuating it here
by closing the translation at the end of this sustained episode rather than following Coyote at the end of the story into another episode where he operates again
alone.

I truncated Martha Lamont's story here primarily to keep it short enough for
this anthology. In the subsequent episode, Coyote transforms himself, first into a
wooden platter (to hold salmon caught by his unwitting hosts) and then into a
whiny baby (again to be fed). Although the longer story tells more about Coyote,
I have rationalized my decision by recalling that Martha Lamont's corpus is not
the whole story of Coyote, after all. It was once and remains a part of a larger
tradition. As others have said, the ability to grasp Coyote is thwarted by his very
elusive nature.

I have also altered the particularity of Martha Lamont's 1962 storytelling by in-
serting into this text two passages from a 1952 version of this same story, a version
that was recorded by Leon Metcalf and transcribed later by Hess and Hilbert. The
first insert is a scene in which Coyote sends sparks to Sawbill's feet, providing an
amusing elaboration on Coyote's longing and detailing a solicitation of sorts that
provides a prelude for his dangerous liaison. The scene also adds another layer
of Coyote's ingenuity and power. The second insert describes how Coyote's son
prepares himself with regalia for the hunt. This passage clarifies later scenes, and
the patterning it adds to the text is characteristic of Lamont's other narratives (see
Bierwert 1995).

I have presented the story in a rather simple format, especially compared to
my representation in *Lushootseed Texts.* There I sought to highlight the repetitions
that provide rhythm and ornamentation to the telling, and in those other stories
these features are more remarkable (see Langen 1995). Here I simply distinguish
between the narrator's voice (lines set flush with the left margin) and the characters' voices (indented lines) except in a couple of instances. First, when Coyote's
son is pursuing Sapsucker, I use indentation with a tilde (~) to show the alterna-
tion of action between the two. Second, I use this same device differently for two
lines near the end of this same section and one slightly later. This use marks the
narrator's explanatory voice where she clarifies that Coyote is acting supernaturally. The two lines state, "he is working" and "he is making something happen,"
meaning that Coyote is acting in the background to make Sapsucker lure the son
on. The later single line states, "Coyote took that, his thing, and then he waved
it," meaning that Coyote took his penis and waved it to make the world foggy—
one of the extraordinary talents he is known for in this literature.

The reader who is new to Northwest Coast literature in contemporary translation will no doubt be struck by a certain awkwardness in my use of "And," "And then," and "Then" at the beginning of sentences. These words translate the Lushootseed *gwel, gwel huy,* and *huy,* which Dell Hymes has clearly demonstrated are marking devices in storytellings. These markers do not divide this story, or most of Lamont's narratives, into segments as neatly as they do stories that Hymes and others have studied (see, for example, Hymes 1981, Kinkade 1987). Nonetheless, they do provide a structure to the telling that would be lost without them. My translation is quite literal, working to preserve the structures and rhythms of the original telling, not so much as those in *Lushootseed Texts,* but nearly so (cf. Langer and Moses 1998 for a different strategy with Lamont's narrative).

Two particular glosses interrupt what is otherwise a fairly smooth tone of translation. I use the word *heaven* to translate a phrase more literally meaning 'world above' when Coyote's Son travels there. I also use the phrases "place high up," "the first world," and "other world." Each of these glosses marks a slightly different usage in Martha Lamont's telling. The word *heaven* may be jarring in this old — and logically pre-Christian — story; it is also clear that this is not a Christian heaven. There are no angels, for example, but merely a rather dirty character. I use the term to disrupt the idea that this spiritual place was untouched by the influence of Christianity. Martha Lamont was a member of the Indian Shaker Church, a syncretic religion that incorporates Christian concepts and such Christian signifiers as altar cloths, candles, and bells. The "world above" idiom is, in practice, the Lushootseed expression for heaven in the Indian Shaker understanding and also means heaven to Lushootseed-speaking Christians. I use the term *heaven* in this polyvalent sense, then, to resonate perhaps like a Shaker bell. My second breach of tone is rowdy. I used "Heya!" in a section where Coyote tells his son to take off his clothing to climb a tree. In the Lushootseed, the Coyote includes "you" a bit emphatically, four times in close succession. "Heya!" was thus my attempt to convey "Hey you, get on with it!" without the same degree of insubordination that the English would express. The added exuberance definitely exceeds that in the recorded version, but it seeks to express the flair of Coyote's persuasion. Please see the footnotes for a few other remarks about particulars of the translation.

To open the story, Martha Lamont identifies all the characters — Coyote, his son, and the son's two wives, who all live together. To make matters complicated (as if Coyote's presence were not enough), the son favors one wife, Pigeon, and is neglecting the other, prettier one, Sawbill. Coyote, perhaps attentive to opportunity, sets his sights on Sawbill, and the story is set in motion.

As the narrative develops, Coyote demonstrates several kinds of special abilities. First, we see his ability to create magical effect from ordinary things when he arranges a cedar fire to send sparks out at Sawbill, the wife his son is neglecting. Second, Coyote appeals to his special advisors for a method to secure the favors of this wife. These advisors he calls his "little brothers," and their identity would be well known to the story's traditional listeners. They are his feces, truly a source of inspiration as naughty as Coyote himself. Another, more ordinary cunning that can be surmised from this telling is that Coyote steals the supply of feathers his son uses to prepare arrows for hunting. This draws his son into Coyote's next manipulation, as Coyote "directs" little Sapsucker to lure his son up a very tall cedar tree, with the son in pursuit of her for the needed arrow feathers. Coyote sets still another dimension of his plot in motion when he tells his son to take off his clothing in order to pursue this prey, thus making this hunter's signature garments available to Coyote as a disguise. That Coyote is exerting some magical powers is evident from the narrator's telling us that he is "working" as his son pursues Sapsucker up the tree, and then by his son's suspicions and finally his son's declaration that he has become lost up in another world because of the connivance of his father. The grand deception is Coyote's pretending to be his own son. Decked in his son's clothing, he mourns that his *father* is lost, and he makes off with both wives. Since he completely fools Sawbill, something more than ordinary charm may be working here as well.

Coyote's son is not an ordinary man either. First, he is a hunter of land animals, with particular ornaments he wears for the hunt. This hunting ability is what we can also assume allows him to track down his wives when he eventually returns to this world from the one he was lured into. Up above, in a place that remains ambiguous but which I have called "heaven" (see my earlier comments on the translation), Coyote's son has some unusual guidance. First, he is "moved" by "somebody." Second, he gains direction from an unnamed old woman. Third, he is lowered by Spider back into this world. This extraworldly assistance marks him as a worthy man. His persistence in going after his wives and his father shows strong character. He reveals some Coyote-like coyness after he has tracked them down, moreover, as he toys with them in a curious way, as if playing at being invisible since they all think he is somewhere else. Finally, his blunt dismissal of his father when he confronts him tells us that he has learned something through the narrative. The point is not only that he is fed up with his father's exploits, but also that he is no longer willing to do this other's bidding. He has taken charge of himself, and of his favored wife.

What of the women in this story, and what do we make of their different fates? Multiple readings are possible. Clearly Pigeon is the more discerning of the two wives. Coyote's preference for the more attractive Sawbill is probably an indication not only of his superficial motives but also of Sawbill's shallow character. Similarly, as Coyote's son turns out to be more honorable on the whole, we might see his neglect of Sawbill as a judgment of her character. On the other hand, Sawbill is in a marriage without much reward, it seems. Coyote may be a vehicle through which she is discarded; he may also be the vehicle of her freedom. That she is hoodwinked tells us she is not very smart, and that she goes, in the end, "wherever she went" tell us again that she is not important. Perhaps she gets away to her own, separate story. We cannot interpret these characters against the social context of the story's origins; we do not know enough about Lushootseed life in earlier times to know what impact they might have had in the past. What Martha Lamont gave us came from the mid-twentieth century, however, which is not so remote. And from her, we can see that how well these wives know their husbands certainly affects their outcomes. This little bit of spousal agency does not contest the construction of gender nor the fact that Coyote and his son dominate the story. This is a woman's tale about men and about wives, not about women.

The nature of the world in this story, as is evident from the commentary I have made so far, is one in which invisible forces operate. The tree that Coyote's son climbs seems to be an ordinary one, though an especially large one, yet it brings him into another world. That world has characters both strange and knowing. The more important of these is Spider, who bridges the two worlds and yet is not a creature viewed as particularly marvelous. Indeed, he is called "pitiable Spider" at one point, and then we learn why. What he produces sticks all over the place in an ungainly way, it seems, and it is "ugly." Moreover, the reason for Spider's putting his "rope" down into our world below is that his food is comprised of little creatures — mosquitoes and flies and "things" — that are presented as a rather dirty collection. Spider is kind, however, and expresses a humorous demurral when Coyote's son offers to pay him for returning him to his world. A bit decrepit, without apparent glamour, Spider resembles a European folk hero's ally more than the Spider of other First Nations literatures or other Lushootseed tales for that matter. Perhaps Lamont has turned this character into something a bit different from what he may have been; perhaps he has changed crossing cultural borders; perhaps this was always a face of Spider. Whatever the image, however, his ability to connect the worlds is invaluable to the lost young man.

The other mystery in the landscape here are three rivers that Coyote's son, Pigeon, Coyote, and Sawbill must cross to reach the end of the episode. These have been "made for them," and each one is larger than the last. Again we see a bit of storytelling that resembles a magical tale. Yet the sorting out of peoples by rivers is, of course, a locally appropriate motif. Historically, each river descending to Puget Sound was a regional dialect area, so the "sorting out" of people by rivers may be an allusion to such differences. That the final river's current pulls the characters in different directions allows us to think that an appropriate destiny has been played out by the end of the episode. We are left to interpret what the characters and their motives have contributed to this ending.

The style of this storytelling is very typical of Martha Lamont's repertoire and in fact for the recorded Lushootseed literature. The story shifts scenes frequently; sometimes actions in subsequent scenes overlap what has come before, and sometimes the narrative backtracks in time. There are disjunctive moments, but shifting is characteristic of a Puget Sound episodic narrative style. I included the synopses from Coyote's and the son's perspectives in my discussion in part to make the story easier to understand on first reading. The story is best read (or listened to) more than once, so its development can be appreciated. The narrator *intends* the experience of the listener to be jolted, I believe, to be surprised, and to be caught somewhat in the disjunctions experienced by the characters. In a Coyote story where deception and partial knowledge are integral to the plots and to the genre, it seems appropriate that the storyteller keep the audience a bit off balance.

NOTES

1. Lamont spoke a Snohomish dialect of the language, originally from the Snohomish River watershed area, which rises in the Cascade mountains just east of the Tulalip Reservation. She and her husband sometimes commented on dialect differences in pronunciation and vocabulary when they helped Hess parse the texts he had transcribed from their recording sessions.

2. The residential schooling, involving year-long and years-long separation of children from their families, was compulsory. An explicit and sometimes brutally enforced policy was that the children not speak their native languages. Thus, even elders who knew their languages then (and know them now) often associated the language use with punishment.

3. See Bierwert 1995 for a detailing of Hess's work.

4. Earlier publications documented the oral traditions. Transcriptions were rough and translations were not refined, however, and it is not possible to discover the aesthetic forms within the texts. The emphasis then was on obtaining storylines or narrative rudiments more than narrative arts. In addition to Hess's and Metcalf's work, Warren Snyder published some excellent transcriptions of Southern Lushootseed texts (Snyder 1968); like recordings, these sources document the art of Lushootseed narrative that the earlier narratives did not. There are no extant recordings of Snyder's sessions, however.

5. *Haboo* is an utterance, rather than a word, spoken during a storytelling to signify that a person is listening and is unobtrusively urging the teller to continue. The title *Haboo* reflects Vi Hilbert's relationship to the storytellers whose work she included; she was both listener and the one carrying the stories on. Thus, the title effectively dedicates the volume to them. The title also suggests that her readers listen attentively — and that they become aware of their ability to play a part in encouraging the telling of the stories. In *Haboo* (Hilbert 1985) this story is titled "Coyote's Son Had Two Wives."

SUGGESTED READING AND REFERENCES

Bierwert, Crisca, ed. 1995. *Lushootseed Texts: An Introduction to Puget Salish Narrative Aesthetics.* Lincoln: University of Nebraska Press.

————. 1999. *Brushed by Cedar: Coast Salish Figures of Power.* Tucson: University of Arizona Press.

Harmon, Alexandra. 1999. *Indians in the Making: Ethnic Relations and Indian Identities around Puget Sound.* Berkeley: University of California Press.

Hess, Thom. 1995. *Lushootseed Reader with Introductory Grammar.* Vol. 1, *Four Stories from Edward Sam.* University of Montana Occasional Papers in Linguistics no. 11. Dallas: Summer Institute in Linguistics and the University of Montana and the Tulalip Tribes.

————. 1999. *Lushootseed Reader with Intermediate Grammar.* Vol. 2. University of Montana Occasional Papers in Linguistics no. 11. Dallas: Summer Institute in Linguistics and the University of Montana and the Tulalip Tribes.

Hilbert, Vi. 1985. *Haboo: Native American Stories from Puget Sound.* Seattle: University of Washington Press.

Hilbert, Vi, and Jay Miller, trans. 1995a. *Aunt Susie Sampson Peter: The Wisdom of a Skagit Elder.* Seattle: Lushootseed Press.

————. 1995b. *Gram Ruth Sehome Shelton: The Wisdom of a Tulalip Elder.* Seattle: Lushootseed Press.

Hymes, Dell. 1981. *"In Vain I Tried to Tell You": Essays in Native American Ethnopoetics.* Philadelphia: University of Pennsylvania Press.

Kinkade, M. Dale. 1987. "Bluejay and His Sister." In *Recovering the Word: Essays on Native American Literature,* edited by Brian Swann and Arnold Krupat. Berkeley: University of California Press.

Langen, Toby C. S. "Nostalgia and Ambiguity in Martha Lamont's 'Crow and Her Seagull Slaves.'" In *Memory and Cultural Politics: New Approaches to American Ethnic Literatures,* edited by Amritjit Singh, Joseph T. Skerrett Jr., and Robert E. Hogan. Boston: Northeastern University Press.

Langen, T. C. S. 1995. "Annotator's Introduction." In *Lushootseed Texts: An Introduction to Puget Salish Narrative Aesthetics,* edited by Crisca Bierwert. Lincoln: University of Nebraska Press.

Langen, Toby C. S., and Marya Moses. 1998. "Reading Martha Lamont's Crow Story Today." *Native American Oral Tradition: Collaboration and Interpretation,* edited by Larry Evers and Barre Toelken, special Native American issue of *Oral Tradition* 13, no. 1: 92–129.

Snyder, Warren Arthur. 1968. *Southern Puget Sound Salish: Texts, Place Names, and Dictionary.* Sacramento CA: Sacramento Anthropological Society, Sacramento State College. 1968.

Suttles, Wayne, and Barbara Lane. 1990. "Southern Coast Salish." In *Handbook of North American Indians,* vol. 7, *Northwest Coast,* edited by Wayne Suttles, 485–502. Washington DC: Smithsonian Institution.

Coyote and His Son

Told by Martha Lamont
Translated by Crisca Bierwert

This is the way it was.[1]

And Coyote and his son lived together.
Coyote's son had two wives.
   Pigeon was the wife of Coyote's son
   and the other was Sawbill.
      Sawbill was the first wife.
      She was beautiful.
      She was white.
      She was a beautiful woman.
And then
      There was Pigeon.
      She was sort of ordinary,
      just an ordinary woman.
      Pigeon was not a good-looking woman.
      And yet this one was a wife of his son.
      She was Coyote's daughter-in-law.
They lived all together with his son.

§

Coyote was lusting for this wife, Sawbill.
   Coyote's son ignored this one, Sawbill.
   She was the one Coyote's son ignored, this Sawbill.
   Pigeon was the one who was his wife.

1. This story is set in a time when all the animals were people. Lamont would have heard and told the story with Coyote, his son, and the son's wives being imagined as human people, not as animal figures behaving like people.

   This opening is characteristic of some of Lamont's stories. The second line, identifying that people are "living there" or "dwelling there," is also a conventional opening. It is possible that the first line here, like others of her recorded stories, is a frame added for outsiders.

She was the wife he desired.
And that Coyote, Old Coyote, was lusting for his daughter-in-law, Sawbill.

And yet, how could he get her from his son?

§

Coyote gathered the firewood there where his son was.
He gathered cedar.
It was cedar he gathered for fire.
It was cedar lying about.

Then he burned it.
He just wanted a fire to see his daughter-in-law.
He was lusting for Sawbill.
   Why is his son ignoring Sawbill?
   Sawbill is so beautiful,
     so white.
The fire crackled toward this woman's feet, of course.
It sparked right at those feet.

And she said,
   "What is happening with this fire?
   It seems to spark right at my feet."

He saw the feet of his daughter-in-law.
   She is so white,
   so beautiful.
He was lusting for her.
He wanted her.

§

Suddenly, he went for a walk.
He prepared to get his daughter-in-law, who was being ignored.

Then he thought about the ones over there,
who *always* advised him when he would go.
And he would squat where he was.
And then he would finish.
And he would ask, where he squatted,
   "Oh, my little brothers, what can I do about this?"

"You say, as always, that you alone are so clever!
You just go and you—
You just make him confused.
He gets lost.
Then your son will die somewhere.
If he is lost,
Then you can have his wives."

"Oh, hold it down you, little brothers.
I'll do it that way."

Coyote went home.
And then, then, he prepared himself to do it that way.

It was not long
And he went and walked,
and he returned again.
And he spoke to his son.

                                                                              §

His son was at home.
He was a kind of hunter.
He was one who hunted game on the land.[2]
He was a tracker.

There is something he does when he hunts.
He outfits himself to do it.
He wraps his legs.
He wraps his arms with his array.
He wears a kind of ornamental waistband.
He has fine moccasins and leggings.
Then he hunts for whatever he is after.

Now he went to prepare.
Then he ran out of what he uses for the arrows he shoots.

---

2. The term for hunting game animals is distinguished from that for hunting sea mammals on and along the water.

Why did he run out?

§

Then Coyote walked.
Soon Old Coyote arrived.

Then he spoke to his son,
    "There is your prey, my son.
    It is climbing over there.
    That's where it is, on a very old tree, a cedar tree.
    It is climbing over there.

    That sapsucker is climbing over there
    That is a beautiful sapsucker.
    That has the stuff you need for your arrows."

    "Oh, I will go after it."
He went.
    "I have none of that."
So his son went.

    "There, there it is, my son.
    That is it."

She was climbing on that, that little—
What is it called? Sapsucker? What is it?
It circles the tree trunk.
There it goes, the little creature.
There is something sort of red on that bird's wing.
And that resembles what he uses with his own bow,
    the shooting gear,
    his son's hunting gear.
He went.

§

So it was a set up for him.
He [Coyote] had just arranged it to be that way.
It was a set up now.

Old Coyote managed to direct Sapsucker:

"If that one, my son, climbs,
    you just be going, be climbing.
    Now you are near him, and he cannot get you,
    and you go again
    and you make him go
    and you make him go
    and he will come to be a way up.

    And then, now it will become foggy.
    And that one, my son, will be lost.
    This is my intention."
So, the little creature acted that way.

                                                                    §

He said now,
    "There it is.
    Your prey is climbing there, my son.
    There it is.
    Spot it. Heya!
    There it is.

    Take off your leggings,
    what you wrap on your legs,
    what you tie on your arms,
    those things of yours,
        Heya!
    Take them off over there.
        Heya!
    And pile up your clothing.
    Just go without clothing,
        Heya!
    that regalia,
    what you tie on your legs for regalia."

Then his son prepared himself that way.
And he climbed.
        Yes.
He was very high up there.

He [Coyote] was there.

He was standing.
He was looking.
   "Over there now.
   It's going again.
   Over there again, my son."

He went.
   ~And it circles the trunk.
The he nears it again.
   ~And just then it goes.
He almost catches up.
   ~And it will go again.
And he went.
   ~And it took his son over there a way.
   ~It went over there again.

Then his son looks around.
   "Oh, something so strange is happening.
   When you wink your eye at my prey, at that!
   There is something so strange that you are doing.
     Suddenly again, it is up high again."

   "No.
   I am just fixing my eye, my son.
   I am just fixing it, this eye of mine."

Then he goes again.
He climbs again.
   ~But he is working.
   ~But he is making something.
He goes.
   ~And it goes.

And he was lured, made to climb,
away up on this very old cedar tree.
And then he came to be away up.

                                    §

Then eventually it became foggy.
   ~Coyote took that, his thing, and then he waved it.

And then it became foggy.
And nothing could be seen anywhere.
That son was lost in that place high up.

Then it might be this way . . .
And he was made to go somewhere by someone.

Instead of being here, he was on the other side now.
Instead of being here, he was in heaven.
Suddenly now, he was going along above, in the first world,
in that place, in heaven.
Then he saw now it was different.

He was walking.
  "Oh, no.
  It is different now where I am traveling."
Then he traveled now.
He was dazed now.
He was traveling now in this other world.
He traveled now, yes.

§

And he found an old woman.
And she spoke to him.
The old woman said to him,
  "Oh, my grandson, oh!
  Where have you traveled from, my grandson?"

  "Oh, grandmother,
  I became lost.
  My father, Coyote, made me travel.
  And he made me lost.
  He is the one who arranged this.
  That is why I am traveling.
And I am just asking if I can get down to the place I came from."

  "Oh, grandson, there is that one . . .
      (What is that called?
      That one that stretches something out?

⟨That's Spider.⟩[3]
Yes, Spider.)
. . . Old Spider.
He is an old person.
Spider is your grandfather.
And you will reach there, not far off.
And you say,
'Can you return me down below?'"

That is the one who stretches something down below.
And Spider will bring him down.

Then he went now.
"Oh, grandmother, I will go."

§

He reached this old one.
And he said,
"I reached you, grandfather.
Oh, my grandfather,
I was confused by my father, Coyote.
And I became lost up above instead of being in my place down below.
How can I get down there?
That is why I have reached my grandfather.
Can you lower me downward?"

Then the old one said to him,
"Oh, my grandson,
Why are you saying I should do this for you,
why are you that way?"

"I would pay you."

"Don't pay me, grandson.
Go on! You pay me?
What has your father done to you, poor thing!
It is a good thing for me to return you.

3. "That's Spider" is added by Lamont's husband, Levi Lamont, in Lushootseed, as she gropes for the
name of the character.

There is a hole over there where I go.
I open it, not for long, because suddenly wind comes through the hole.
People would find out.
And so we will go fast.
There is my rope to get you down."

It was a rope; the thing might be his rope.
That was from himself, just something at his sacrum.

And then he would take his body.
And he would stretch that, having tied him on to be lowered.

"You will drop
and as soon as you land down below, pull gently three times.
As soon as you land, you are there.
As soon as you untie yourself,
that rope of mine will come back
because I take it into my body."

"Then that will be what I do, grandfather.
Then,
what am I paying you?"

"You are not paying me anything.
Only—what do we call it?—tallow, or something,
Just that alone.
And just how can you do this?
You just figure this out.
Then, that's good."

And that pitiable Spider went.
And he opened his climbing place.
And he proceeded through.
And he proceeded to stretch his rope.

Then, there it was.
The rope was there inside him.
He would stretch it out;
Spider is the one who stretches and stretches that.
So he stretched and stretched it as he made it.

He stretched and stretched it on things,
   on the world, on the *trees*,[4]
   at the base of the trees, and that.
It was very ugly.
What he would stretch is where everything got caught:
   the mosquitoes,
   these things,
   the flies,
   all the little creatures that are made.
That is what he gathered now.
That is what he ate.

Then, that one, the son of Coyote, traveled now.
He traveled now again.
Yes, he traveled now.

§

That guy Coyote had gone now.
He took his wives now.
Then they were married now, of course.

Coyote was going around mourning,
   when his son was completely gone now.
   He was completely lost.

   "Umm, my father may be there.
   Umm, my father may be there.
   He is getting really old, my father, my father.
   Umm, my father may be there,
   Umm, my father may be there.
   He was getting really old, my father."
He pretended now he was fatherless.
He pretended now it was his father, Coyote, who had died.
But it was Coyote who was saying that over and over.

He went home now to the women, the wives of his son.
He was lusting.

4. Lamont says "trees" in English here, and she uses a Lushootseed term for the base of the tree in the next line without using the generic word for tree there.

Then Pigeon knew.

   "Oh, this is that one, that nasty old man,

   that one who killed my husband.

   This is that nasty old man.

   He is the one who is saying that over and over."

But she did not express this.

She was just angry inside.[5]

Then he came to the one who is his daughter-in-law.

And he said,

   "For now, I will let you be.

   For now, I will go to Sawbill.

   She is the one I will go around with.

   And for now, I will set you aside,

   because you are the one your own father-in-law wanted."

He is talking to Pigeon.

But she was angry.

She knew it was Coyote who was talking to her,

This was her father-in-law.

And it was a bad situation with Sawbill being fooled.[6]

She did not know.

Then, she married her father-in-law.

§

They went.

They walked now.

They walked now.

Pigeon was behind, last.

Was crying.

She was a little behind them.

They were walking.

---

5. The site of Pigeon's anger "inside," as I have put it here, is different from either "heart" or "mind." The Lushootseed term, *xech* (using a typographical transcription), is located in the chest; encompasses the senses of both English terms; and includes capabilities of thought, reckoning, and sentiment. Pigeon's capacity to carry anger knowingly here may be as much a sign that she has a "long" (capacious) *xech,* as it is a sign of her being stuck for the moment in a bad situation.

6. Vi Hilbert sees Sawbill's being fooled as a sign that the woman lacks some basic awareness in this situation, no matter how strong Coyote's powers of deception may be. Hilbert interprets this line, loosely, as "Leave it to someone as lame-brained as Sawbill."

They walked to the place where they had made camp.
And that Pigeon was sent off at a distance.
　　"Don't come.
　　Stay away.
　　Stay where you are over there.
　　Don't come to us."
They send her off over there.
She was just broken-hearted.
There she was.

They walked again until that one—
There was something as they were walking,
　　from that other one.
And her tumpline was stepped on as it trailed.
It was her belt.
And something stepped on it.
And she said,
　　"Whatever is happening?
　　Whatever is it that is happening to my belt?
　　What's happening?"
And again, later,
and again it was taut,
again it was pulled.
Then she turned around.
But somehow it was her late husband who was truly there.

Then, he would look for them.
He followed where they walked as his father walked his women.

Then she saw the one who was her late husband.
　　"Oh, it's you somehow."
Pigeon had been crying, since she wanted her late husband.

Sawbill and her father-in-law were over there.
They were married now.

Pigeon realized this one was her husband.
And then she said,
　　"I have been sent off by that couple.
　　I went at a distance,

and I was sent off.
I just stayed where I was there, making camp a way off.
And what's the matter with that?
It's better that way, because they are married.
Also, he is wearing your things,
    your arm wraps,
    your leg ties,
    the ceremonial gear.
Coyote remade himself to be appealing."

And then, he said to her where they made camp,
    "Go ahead.
    Go, even though they will send you off.
    You just go up close.
    No, even though they send you off,
    you just go up close."

                                                          §

That Pigeon went, and the other stayed hidden.
Then Pigeon went now.

And Coyote said,
    "S-s-s-s-s.
    Don't come, Pigeon.
    No.
    Stay where you are over there.
    Go off, Pigeon."

No, Pigeon simply went up close.
And she got there.
And she stood there.
These two were standing there.
His son was standing.

He ran to his son right away.
And,
    "For my son,
    your arm wraps,
    your leg wraps,
    your things,

your leggings."

"Why are you taking off your clothing?
It's better for you to wear them,
since the clothing is your own."
His son spoke to him.
"You had better keep them,
since they are your clothing.
What is the matter with you now?"

Then, then they traveled now.
They traveled now.
They went now.

"Go ahead.
Go with Sawbill.
I don't want you to come and give her back.
It's better for you to have Sawbill now."

Then Coyote went on.
They went now, of course.
Those two, Pigeon and her husband, went walking.
They walked on now, where they were walking.
Yes, that Coyote came a little behind now.
They were last, he with his wife Sawbill.
Sawbill was left.

§

Then someone made a river for them.
So they crossed.
That Coyote crossed.
He swam, because he always swam.
So they came ashore.
And they walked on again.

Yes, a river was made for them again,
    a still bigger one, if a river it was.
They crossed again.
They got themselves ashore again.
Then there was a last one now.

A very big river was made for them,
   where they were pulled along.
Then these two crossed.
And they came ashore.
And they walked on.

Then Coyote crossed.
He just got pulled far away, carried downstream somewhere.

Then Sawbill went now.
So Sawbill was good at swimming, of course.
And then she too was just pulled along.

They just came ashore, then, on the other side.

Then he went now, that pitiful Coyote.

She got pulled now.
She went now, wherever she went.

So, those two walked on, of course.

And he [Coyote] stuck into the shore
where Snipe and Magpie made something for hunting,
the trap they tied to their poles.

[and here begins another episode. . . .]

Sahaptin

Celilo

Introduction by Virginia Hymes

In the mid-1980s, Larry George, a Sahaptin artist and storyteller from Toppenish, Washington, sent a cassette titled "Celilo" to my husband and me. The note that accompanied it said simply, "Do what you do with this." For this paper I have done "what we do," that is, verse analysis; I have "translated" an oral text into a written one in a way that shows the poetic artistry of the original.

We had come to know Larry in the 1970s, and in the fall of 1974, when the American Folklore Society held its annual meeting in Portland, Oregon, he and a Warm Springs Sahaptin, Nathan Jim, a mutual friend, spent part of one night in our room. In the course of that evening Larry proclaimed the famous speech attributed to Chief Seattle. What he proclaimed was of course an English translation. Chief Seattle spoke a Salish language, and his speech reached English by way of being noted down at the time in Chinook Jargon. A few years ago Vi Hilbert, a speaker of that Salish language, Lushootseed, worked with several of her elders to reconstruct the original.

Transmission through several languages was hardly new in the large coastal and plateau areas of Washington and Oregon. Long before French or English speakers appeared, speakers of three quite different language families, Chinookan, Salishan, and Sahaptian, had traded, intermarried, and in many cases learned one another's languages and customs. Bilingual and even multilingual individuals were not rare. Charles Cultee dictated myths and historical narratives to Franz Boas in both Kathlamet Chinook (a language he learned when he lived with his mother's people on the Oregon side of the Columbia River) and Shoalwater Chinook (presumably learned among his father's people). He knew Chehalis Salish, which he used with his wife and children, and Chinook Jargon, which he used with Boas.

This was certainly the case with the Columbia River Sahaptins who were the ancestors of Larry George and other residents of Yakima Reservation in Washington, and it was the case for the Sahaptins and Wasco Chinookans of the Warm Springs Reservation, where Dell and I have worked. At Warm Springs a small number of Paiutes added to the mix. By 1955, a hundred years after the treaty that triggered the removal of those living along or near the Columbia to reservations roughly one hundred miles north (Yakima) and south (Warm Springs) of the river, a switch to English as first language had accelerated. English had been the only language of the reservation schools, the Christian churches (which many attended), and the government offices for well over fifty years. After the Second World War English became the language in most homes. When I interviewed a teacher at the Warm Springs school in 1956, she said that only some of the children from one small district, Simnasho, were coming to first grade knowing no English. By the time I began to study Sahaptin there in 1972, there were just two very old sisters in Simnasho who were monolingual, and people who had been raised with it as their first language were scarce and into their thirties and forties.

Fear of the death of the languages prompted a project (for which I was the linguist) to prepare teaching materials for language classes in Sahaptin, classes that had that year been introduced at the school — for half an hour each day. The teachers were three women, eighty, seventy, and forty years old. Their supervisor was a sixty-year-old man. Larry George, whom we met at around that time, was about the age of the youngest. As an artist, trained elsewhere in his youth, he had begun to illustrate some of the traditional narratives, presenting them in English with slides of his paintings. (We were present at one of these events, arranged by Nathan Jim when he was cultural heritage director at Warm Springs.)

In such a context it is not surprising that the words of Larry's "Celilo" are English words. Evidently he wanted to reach as many people as possible, both Indian and non-Indian. And although the words are English, the patterns that organize them are not. The patterns are those of Sahaptin oral narrative, just as the concerns are those of someone devoted to Sahaptin ways of life.

There is originality as well. The narrative on the cassette Larry sent us is unlike any I had heard before in several years of work with speakers of Sahaptin and with personal experience narratives told in Sahaptin. Its characters, if it could be said to have characters, are the ocean, the earth, the river, the salmon, the people, the other people who built town and cities and dams, and at the end an "I" who has been the teller of the tale and whose voice will be heard no more.

I had, by the time I listened to the Celilo tape, transcribed, translated, and verse-analyzed a dozen or so hours of narrative from six Sahaptin speakers. I had come to know well the patterning of these narratives in groups of lines, predominantly in groups of three and five, and the linguistic devices that achieve them. One hearing of the tape convinced me that it cried out to be shown on the page, so as to bring out this organization. Doing so, I hope, makes it easier for a reader to "hear" the beauty of Larry George's creation.

But why "Celilo"? Celilo was the name of a community and a great falls on the southern side of the Columbia River, a few miles east of the Oregon city called The Dalles. Because of channels on the Celilo side of the river, it was a very favorable site for dip-netting for salmon during the spring and fall runs from platforms built out from the rocky shores. Chinookan and Sahaptin Indians gathered there, and other Indians came from considerable distances, especially in the fall, to fish, trade, gamble, socialize. The Celilo site was known far and wide, and the salmon caught during those runs provided a significant part of the diet of the Chinook and Sahaptin people of that stretch of the Columbia. With the building of The Dalles dam above the falls in the mid-1950s, the channels disappeared, as did the fishing and the gathering of people. Larry George's narrative traces the story of the place from beginning to end.

A few words might be said here on the concept of "the Great Spirit," which is mentioned by Larry George. The concepts expressed by this term and by "the Almighty" were not part of the precontact Sahaptin universe. That universe was one in which everything in it had a spirit, not just each human being but all animals, trees, fish, and so on. The elements of the Sahaptin world were believed to be mutually responsible for one another as are members of the family. No one was above all others. The sun was termed "father" and the earth "mother." Thus it was that when the missionaries came to the Middle Columbia in 1834 and began to teach the Sahaptins about their God, trying to explain this concept (through interpreters) with terms like *Great Spirit* and *the Almighty* and *Our Father,* the Sahaptins used their words *nami piap* meaning 'elder brother' for the last of these terms. An elder brother has more authority than a younger but is not great or all-powerful. Those who actually became Christians or were taught Christianity in mission schools became familiar with the terms *Great Spirit* and the *Almighty* and the *Creator.* Under the influence of the Prophet Movement begun by the Sahaptin man Shmuxala (more familiarly known to English speakers as Smohalla), the Waashat or Seven Drum or Longhouse religion incorporated these elements of Christianity into the precontact religion, and these terms thus came into usage outside of Christian churches and schools. The religion that Smohalla (1820–95) brought to the Middle Columbia Sahaptin world survives and even thrives. It has become the main symbol of continuing Sahaptin identity at Warm Springs and Yakima, the two reservations to which the river Sahaptins as well as the neighboring Wascos and Wishram Chinooks were removed a number of years after the treaty.

Finally, a note on the phrase "the earth is my mother," which Larry George uses in the section I have called "The Other Men." This stanza echoes a speech by Smohalla as his movement became increasingly a resistance means of subsistence! The speech, given in Eugene Hunn's chapter on language (1990, 83), which Hunn offers as an example of the excellence of Sahaptin oratory, is as follows:

You ask me to plow the ground!

Shall I take a knife and tear my mother's bosom?

You ask me to dig for stone.

Shall I dig under her skin for her bones?

Then when I die I cannot enter her body to be born again.

You ask me to cut grass,

and make hay

and sell it

and be rich like white men.

But how dare I cut off my mother's hair?

On reflection it occurs to me that Larry George's "Celilo" is in fact a superb example of modern Sahaptin oratory, sent on tape to an audience of two and now available to a wider audience on the printed page.

SUGGESTED READING AND REFERENCES

Frey, Rodney, and Dell Hymes. 1998. "Mythology." In *Handbook of North American Indians,* vol. 12, *Plateau,* edited by Deward E. Walker et al., 584–99. Washington DC: Smithsonian Institution.

Hunn, Eugene S. 1990. *Nch'i-Wana "The Big River": Mid-Columbia Indians and Their Land.* Seattle, University of Washington Press.

Hunn, Eugene S., and David H. French. 1998. "Western Columbia River Sahaptins." In *Handbook of North American Indians,* vol. 12, *Plateau,* edited by Deward E. Walker et al., 378–94. Washington DC: Smithsonian Institution.

Hymes, Virginia. 1987. "Warm Springs Sahaptin Verse Analysis." In *Native American Discourse,* edited by Joel Sherzer and Anthony Woodbury, 62–102. Cambridge: Cambridge University Press.

———. 1992. "How Long Ago We Got Lost": A Warm Springs Sahaptin Narrative." *Florence M. Voegelin Memorial Volume,* special issue of *Anthropological Linguistics* 34, Nos. 1–4: 73–83.

Walker, Deward E., and Helen H. Schuster. 1998. "Religious Movements." In *Handbook of North American Indians,* vol. 12, *Plateau,* edited by Deward E. Walker et al., 499–514. Washington DC: Smithsonian Institution.

Celilo

Told by Larry George

A co . . . ld, icy wind
   blows across the mountains.[1]
The mountains
   of an unnamed land.
It comes from the northwest.
It comes from the direction
   of the big salt waters.

The sun rises.
It casts its golden rays of light upon the land.
And
   upon an ocean.
A new day
   at the beginning of time.

Fa . . . r beneath this ocean,
   there is movement,
   there is life.
Salmon,
   great schoo . . . ls of salmon,
   thousands upon thousands of them.
They are going
   to a place
     of sweet water,
       driven by an unknown force
         within them.

1. The first word of each stanza is set in boldface type.

By early spring,
   these salmon
      enter the mouth of a mighty river,
        a river of
          clear, sweet water.
From this point on
   they will swim to the upper reaches of this great river.
They will swim
   until they finally reach
      quiet streams
        and clear lakes.

They go there
   to spawn.
They go there,
   there
      a place of their birth.
They go there
   to die.

This u . . . rge within them
   drives them
      pushing them.
Nothing will stop them.
Nothing
   must stop them.
For it is
   through these very salmon
      that others of their kind
        will live on.
Only the strongest
   shall survive.

Many
   will die.
Long miles of water.
Long,
   long miles
      of sweet water.

MAN, THE PEOPLE

Then
    there is man.
Man,
    a member of the people.
Man,
    the enemy;
        on stone cliffs he leaves his mark.

He tells of the Great Spirit.
He thanks the Great Spirit
    for life,
        his village,
    for the days
        and for the nights.
He writes
    of man,
        his hunger,
           and of death.

Again he thanks the Great Spirit,
    the Almighty.
For the sun,
    duck,
    bear,
        deer.
Even the turtle!
He thanks him for the river.
For the swallow,
    the swallow which will tell him
        of the arrival
        of the first great salmon.

For hundreds and thousands of years
    these salmon have come back from the depths of the ocean.
And for hundreds and thousands of years
    the Indian
        has fished these very same, pure waters.
Every year
    year after year

the people have waited
for the first salmon to appear.

But before the spring salmon run
only a few
will be permitted to fish.
These chosen few
would fish for
the coming feast.

No one
would be permitted to fish
until after the feast.
No person
could fish for his own
until the Almighty had been thanked.

For this reason
the feast.
And *this*
the people must do together.

They came
from near and far.
They came
from *both* sides of the river.
They came to this place called Celilo,
a place of
great white water,
a place
of the great falls.

After the songs of prayer,
the thanks for all food,
the people
would now fish
for their own winter's food.
The winter,
which was like night,
cold

and hostile.
Salmon was dried.

Some of the salmon
   was pounded into *ch'lai,*
     pímisan.
The *ch'lai*
   would be like powdered gold
    and just as useful.
For in the late summer months
   and early fall
    this *ch'lai*
     and other dried fish
      would be traded with tribes
       far to the north,
        east,
         and south,
      traded for
       other needed things.

The salmon fight their way through the swift white water.
Some
   only to be washed back
    by the strong current.
Do . . . wn,
  do . . . wn,
   down into the falls.

Others
   would find a channel *skirting* the falls
    only to find
     another dead end.
Others would be scooped from the waters by man,
   man and his nets.
The Indian
   must live too.

THE OTHER MEN

The . . . n,
   then *they* came,

        the other men,
            men of different ways.
These men,
    they built things.
Bridges,
    roads,
        towns,
            factories,
                cities,
                    giant highways,
                        and dams.

Dams that *slow* the mighty waters.
Bonneville.
Grand Coulee.
Rocky Reach.
Rock Island.

Still
    the people came.
Now
    they came with modern nets.
No . . . w
    they crossed over to these basalt islands
        by small cable cars,
            not by the canoe.

The world had changed.
Yet these people,
    they still thanked the Almighty.

They still prayed.
They still feasted,
            laughed,
            and sang.
Wanapam.
Priest Rapids.

The earth,
    the earth is my mother.

The Almighty has made her so.
How could I trade my mother?
How could I sell my mother?

Fish there,
    people.
Fish there
    for all time.
Fish for
    as long as the mountains stand.
Fish
    for as long as the river flows.
For as long
    as the sun shall shine.

More towns.
Cities.
Cities.
People.
Highways.
Roads.
Lights.[2]
McNary.
Chief Joseph.
The Dalles.

Still
    every spring
        the *núsux,*
            which the young salmon are called by the people,
                the *núsux* came.
The Indian came
    just as he had for generations.

Generation after generation,
    father to son,
        father to son.
Now he built scaffolds of lumber,

2. The three italicized words were spoken in a loud voice.

lumber cut from the mother earth
   and milled
      by the other men.

The river,
   the river *still* makes its way to the ocean.
The salmon,
   they still
      make their way up the many tributaries still open.

But time,
   time moves too fast for men.
It moves so fast
   that things
      and places
         soon have no meaning.
Words become words
   blowing in the wind
      lo . . . st.

THE ENDING

And now the sun
   sets for the last time
      on a place called Celilo.
No more will the people meet here.
No more will they sing,
   pray,
      and thank the Almighty from *these* rocks.

The *mountains* still stand.
The sun,
   it still shines.
The grass
   grows.

So . . .
   if you should see the swallow,
      the swallow
         which tells the people
            of the salmon's arrival,

> you will know
>   that the *núsux will* soon pass this way.
They will come.
Not as many,
>   *not thou . . . sands upon thou . . . sands*
>   but they *will* come.

They will pass a place
>   once called by man
>   Celilo.
Most of the people are gone now.
They have moved away.

They have
>   taken with them
>   their laughter.
They have taken
>   their singing.
They have
>   taken their prayers
>   to *another* place.

So when you
>   pass this way
>   don't look for me.
I am gone.
I live only
>   in the memory of a few.
To you . . .
>   I am dead

>   *and* gone.

One might think that dams began with whites, but one of the myths about the
world being set right for the Indian people has a dam as well. There were sisters
who had a dam that kept salmon from the river and from the people who were
to come, but Coyote broke it. This story was in fact the first myth I was told by
the late Susan Moses, then, at age eighty, the oldest of three women I worked
with in the spring of 1973 on developing an orthography and teaching materials
for the language program at the Warm Springs school. During my brief visit to

Warm Springs during the winter of 1974, she performed for the group and my
tape recorder the story of the Swallow Sisters and Coyote in which Coyote disguised himself as a baby floating down river on a raft, was rescued and adopted
by the sisters, and left propped up on a cradleboard when they went off to work
for the day. While they were gone each day, he began breaking through the dam
until finally he succeeded, freeing the salmon and predicting (or laying down the
rule) that no one in future was to dam up the salmon for his or her own use.

After she had finished the story, for which her friend Ellen Squiemphen provided the requisite responses to a performed narrative of *ii* 'yes', there was laughter
and some general discussion. Then suddenly Susan added the coda that follows
in English translation.

Since then it is,
   in regard to Coyote,
     that he decides e . . . everything.
On the one hand, it was
   that he would do right,
   on the other, that he would sometimes do wrong.
That's how he was,
   Coyote.

And there was that dam,
   the Swallow sisters had it
     right where today the whites are following
       and damming up the salmon.
There,
   right there
     Coyote broke down the dam,
       and the salmon went out
         along the river.
It will go on being Coyote's decision:
   "Here salmon travel along the river."
Thus did Coyote have it predicted,
   everything here in this land.

That's all now.

Upper Coquille Athabaskan

Two Tales of Power

Introduction by William R. Seaburg

The following two texts, "Gambler and Snake" and "Wind Woman," were recorded by Elizabeth D. Jacobs (1903–83) from her Upper Coquille Athabaskan consultant, Coquelle Thompson Sr. (ca. 1849–1946) in the late fall of 1935 at the Siletz Reservation in western Oregon. Jacobs worked with Thompson for about two months, recording by longhand myths, tales, personal experience narratives, and historical narratives, as well as ethnographic notes. She and her anthropologist husband, Melville Jacobs (1902–71), also recorded on phonograph records a variety of song types that Thompson sang for them.[1] Most of this rich collection of oral and musical tradition remains unpublished.

Jacobs was not formally trained as an anthropologist, but she was a very bright and capable person and quickly learned phonetic transcription and field methods from her husband. Although the Jacobses worked at separate field sites during the day, in the evening hours they would rehash the day's findings, and Melville would assist Elizabeth in compiling the next day's queries. Her work with Coquelle Thompson was not her first fieldwork; for several months in 1933 and again briefly in 1934 she recorded ethnographic notes and stories from her Nehalem Tillamook consultant, Clara Pearson.[2]

Jacobs's ethnographic field questioning was rather unstructured, especially at the beginning of her work with Thompson. She would suggest a topic and let Thompson lead the way. Most of the narratives Jacobs recorded from Thompson seem to have emerged quite naturally from the discussion of a particular ethnographic or historical topic. Whenever Thompson volunteered a story, Jacobs wrote it down.[3] She explained in later years that a nondirective approach "was our way of letting the informant run the show and showing our respect. It was their culture, not something we were supposed to dig out. They were telling us how they lived and how they felt."[4]

Jacobs's goal was to transcribe faithfully Thompson's words verbatim, especially in the narratives. Evidence for this can be seen in her preservation of Thompson's nonstandard grammatical forms, pronunciations, rural English colloquialisms, certain lexical choices, and phonetic transcriptions of Indian words.

Occasionally Jacobs's voice intrudes in the text, usually in the form of lexical choice or brief paraphrase. There is no evidence of bowdlerization. In editing her texts, perhaps the biggest frustration is not always knowing when an explanatory aside, enclosed within parentheses in the notebook, represents Jacobs's or Thompson's voice.

Coquelle Thompson Sr. was born around 1849 in an Upper Coquille Athabaskan village in the Coquille River valley, southwest Oregon. After the disastrous Rogue River Wars of 1855–56 he and his people, as well as many other coastal southwest Oregon Indian groups, were removed from their aboriginal homelands and resettled some one hundred miles north on land that eventually become the Siletz Reservation. Many did not survive the emotional and physical deprivations of the early days on the reservation, but Coquelle was a survivor and he lived there the rest of his long life.

Thompson was either a participant in, a witness to, or an oral recorder of all the major events at Siletz from 1855 to 1946, including an offshoot of the 1870 Ghost Dance, known at Siletz as the Warm House Dance. He was a noted singer and dancer of both Native and nativistic songs and dances. He knew virtually everyone on the reservation—and their kinship ties—as official heirship testimonies amply demonstrate. He spoke Indian English as well as the local lingua franca, Chinook Jargon, and his native Upper Coquille Athabaskan, a language that only a few still spoke at the time of his passing in 1946.

Thompson worked at various times as a farmer, hunting and fishing guide, teamster, tribal policeman, and expert witness for six different anthropologists over a period of nearly sixty years, from 1884 to 1942. Most of what we know about the Upper Coquille Athabaskan language and culture comes from the memory of this incredibly able and willing consultant. Thompson was a perceptive, intelligent observer, and he had a phenomenal memory. He was also a master storyteller, and both Elizabeth Jacobs and Bureau of American Ethnology ethnologist and linguist John P. Harrington recorded hundreds of notebook pages of myths, tales, and historical-event narratives from him. The two texts presented here represent only a very brief sampling of his rich heritage.[5]

Aspects of Thompson's features of expressive style have been described in some detail elsewhere.[6] Style elements exhibited in these two texts that are generally characteristic of Thompson's narrative repertoire include extensive use of dialogue; descriptive specificity with regard to time, numbers, and measurements; frequent expressions of moods and sentiments both by and for the characters; explicit mention of characters' motives and thoughts; and explanatory or evaluative comments, sometimes attributed to a character, more often to the narrator himself, thus providing valuable cultural-insider exegesis.

The dominant cultural theme in "Gambler and Snake" is one man's encounter with a spirit power that provides the means for extraordinary success in gambling at the stick game. An Upper Coquille audience would have strongly identified with such an individual: his appropriate ritual preparation, his resourcefulness in dodging the snake shamans' medicines, his success in cutting the snake's insides, and his catching hold of the snake's dentalia as he is thrown to safety. The gambler also understands that such dentalia will magically multiply when kept hidden in a hollow log or tree, and he acts accordingly.

Not only is the gambler successful in his encounter power experience, but he fulfills proper social responsibilities following his good fortune as well: his invitation of the chief and other high-class folks to a meal so generous they are unable to finish it in one sitting, his distribution of his new-found wealth among these worthies, and his deference to the chief's decision-making authority.

Perhaps most of all the audience would have thoroughly enjoyed the resounding defeat of all those who had previously gambled against them and had won everything. Indeed, because of his encounter power experience the gambler and his cohorts are now so successful that no one can play against them and win.

Several cultural themes are apparent in Thompson's "Wind Woman" narrative; the two dominant ones involve sibling and in-law relations. Kinship was vitally important everywhere on the Northwest Coast. A man or woman who lived alone, who had "no folks at all," would have been pitiable; even someone as powerful as Wind Woman desired kin. In the first half of the text, a baby magically emerges from behind the bark of a tree she is cutting. In response to their mutual needs, this unnamed child and the older woman form a close, mutually beneficial sibling relationship, perhaps suggesting the importance of the brother-sister bond in the culture. Wind Woman raises her adopted brother, teaches and encourages him in adult-male skills, and ultimately helps him acquire a wife and in-laws. In turn, Wind Woman's brother provides her with abundant food and with companionship.

In the second half of the narrative, the young man leaves home to find a wife—indeed, he finds two wives, sisters—but his marriage is repeatedly challenged by his new neighbor, the powerful and dangerous Thunder, who forces the man to stay with him and *his* two daughters. The man is presented with a series of son-in-law tests, similar to tests found in oral traditions throughout the Northwest, but with an interesting twist: the already married young man is not being tested by his actual father-in-law; he is only courting Thunder's daughters under duress. Because of his spirit power, which he kept "in his hand all the time, but no one could see it," the resourceful man handily passes the first seven tests that Thunder imposes. He barely survives the eighth test, though, and Wind Woman comes to his rescue in the form of a tremendous storm that smashes Thunder's house, breaks him into pieces, and scatters his remains. She assures her brother that he is safe now and welcomes him to return home whenever he wishes.

The young man in this story represents a kind of culturally romantic ideal: a wholly masculine and admirable man. His masculinity is highlighted by the fact that he only needs one arrow to hunt—he never misses his mark—and that he fearlessly faces and outwits Thunder. He is admirable because he provides quantities of food and hides for his sister, and he has successfully acquired a strong spirit power, one that allows him to survive the tests of the supernaturally potent Thunder.

In preparing these texts for publications I have consulted the original notebook version as well as an unpublished edited version prepared by Jacobs.[7] Words and phrases enclosed within brackets in the texts presented here indicate (1) where Native words have been translated into English and the original phonetic transcription moved to a footnote, (2) where words have been added to turn a sentence fragment into a complete sentence (although to avoid a distracting proliferation of brackets, not every *a* or *the* is so indicated), and (3) where assumed cultural knowledge or explanations of potentially confusing or ambiguous phrasing have been added. Verb tenses have been made consistent. None of Thompson's words has been deleted from the texts.

A NOTE ON ORTHOGRAPHY AND PRONUNCIATION

The following special symbols occur in Upper Coquille Athabaskan words that appear in the notes to the texts:

d	no equivalent in English; similar to the *t* in English *stop.*
ɛ	the *e* of English *met.*
ə	the *u* in English *but;* the *a* in English *sofa.*
g	no equivalent in English; similar to the *k* in English *skull.*
γ	no equivalent in English; similar to the x̣ but with voiced pronunciation.
ł	no equivalent in English; similar to the Welsh pronunciation of *ll* in *Lloyd.*
t'ł	no equivalent in English; a combination of the *t* and the ł but with an explosive release, indicated by the apostrophe.
t'	no equivalent in English; similar to the *t* of English *team* but with an explosive release, indicated by the apostrophe.
tc	the *ch* in English *church.*
t'c	no equivalent in English; similar to the *ch* of English *church* but with an explosive release.
t's	no equivalent in English; similar to the *ts* in English *cats* but with an explosive release, indicated by the apostrophe.
q'	no equivalent in English; similar to the *k* sound of English *cod* but

further back in the throat and with an explosive release, indicated by
the apostrophe.

x̣   no equivalent in English; similar to the *ch* in German *Ach.*

ˀ   a brief glottal stop or pause, represented by - in English *uh-oh.*

NOTES

1. William R. Seaburg, *Guide to Pacific Northwest Native American Materials in the Melville Jacobs Collection and in Other Archival Collections in the University of Washington Libraries* (Seattle: University of Washington Libraries, University of Washington, 1982).

2. Elizabeth D. Jacobs, *Nehalem Tillamook Tales* (1959; Corvallis: Oregon State University Press, 1990).

3. William R. Seaburg, "Collecting Culture: The Practice and Ideology of Salvage Ethnography in Western Oregon, 1877–1942" (Ph.D. diss., Department of Anthropology, University of Washington, Seattle), 153–54.

4. Elizabeth D. Jacobs, interview by author, tape recording, Seattle, summer 1975.

5. For a detailed biography of Coquelle Thompson, see Lionel Youst and William R. Seaburg, *Coquelle Thompson, Athabaskan Witness: A Cultural Biography* (Norman: University of Oklahoma Press, 2002).

Coquelle Thompson's first name has been spelled several different ways. The spelling *Coquelle* best reflects the way he pronounced it: kokwél. The name of the tribal group, Upper Coquille, is sometimes pronounced kokwél and sometimes kokíl, where the second syllable rhymes with English *keel.*

Jacobs's original Upper Coquille Athabaskan notebooks and field notes are part of the Melville Jacobs Collection, Manuscripts and University Archives, University of Washington Libraries, Seattle, Washington. Harrington's original field notes from western Oregon are in the National Anthropological Archives, Smithsonian Institution, Washington DC.

6. William R. Seaburg, "Expressive Style in an Upper Coquille Athabaskan Folktale Collection Recorded in English," *Northwest Folklore* 12, no. 1 (1997): 23–34.

7. Several unpublished edited versions of the texts prepared by Jacobs are in my possession.

SUGGESTED READING

Beckham, Stephen D. *The Indians of Western Oregon: This Land Was Theirs.* Coos Bay OR: Arago Books, 1977.

Jacobs, Melville. *The Content and Style of an Oral Literature: Clackamas Chinook Myths and Tales.* Chicago: University of Chicago Press, 1959.

Miller, Jay, and William R. Seaburg. "Athapaskans of Southwestern Oregon." In *Handbook of North American Indians,* vol. 7, *Northwest Coast,* edited by Wayne Suttles, 580–88. Washington DC: Smithsonian Institution, 1990.

Seaburg, William R., and Pamela Amoss. *Badger and Coyote Were Neighbors: Melville Jacobs on Northwest Indian Myths and Tales.* Corvallis: Oregon State University Press, 2000.

Gambler and Snake

Told by Coquelle Thompson Sr.

One man had a card's bed.[1] He [was] the last to go swim, swam right down the middle of the river, got down to the riffles, went down—a big flat-headed snake swallowed him.[2] He felt just like he was coming in a house. [There was] no water [inside]. He sat down there. He had a little knife [of flint][3] and that [gambling bed] with him. Now he kind of realized he's in a snake's belly. He tried to cut its heart. He wanted to get out. Oh, that snake hollered, went [thrashed] all around. Finally the snake gave up. He came back in his house.

Big, deep water—that's snake's house. That fellow kept cutting.

The snake people talked. "What's the matter with you? You're always hungry, have to eat everything?[4] Now you've swallowed poison! Where did you swallow that man?"

"Oh, I don't know, except one place up river I felt something go in my throat."

"Yes, you have to eat anything. You eat timber."

They abused him because he just ate and drank anything and never had enough. In every river he'd watch, open his mouth, a stick [would] come in, he'd swallow.

The snake chief said, "You go get that doctor Big-Deep-Water Chief. He might know that [swallowing-everything] medicine."[5]

All right, one fellow went. This man had beat that snake. He knew everything the snake was doing. The snake [was] making noise; he was a pretty good sick man. Every so often the man inside would cut a little.

"Now they're coming, make more room."

That doctor didn't come in the door. He came down the smoke hole. The man inside had cut till he could see through. He saw everyone sitting around—that doctor standing up there.

"What's the matter with this fellow?" the doctor said.

1. The "card's bed" or "gambling bed," *ntɛɬ*, was a buckskin blanket on which the stick or hand game was played.
2. *sɛq'ɛ hu·li* was the name for the big flat-headed snake.
3. *t'cənt'i* 'flint knife'.
4. *ngətɛlsa ɣilxətla* 'you have to eat everything'.
5. The notebook reads: "ngətɛlsa medicine."

They told him, "Well, he's a pretty sick fellow. He ate a person at that place, up the river."

"Uh-huh, all right, I've got medicine," the doctor said. He reached in his pocket, took out medicine, put it in a cup—a shell cup. He came, he said, "Hold his head up."

The man went under the snake's heart so he could dodge the medicine. Presently something dropped, dropped. It was the medicine. He kept out of the way. It didn't affect him in any way.

The doctor said, "Well, that's all I know, just that medicine."

The man inside cut more. It hurt more. In [that] big belly, wide as this house, he could dodge anywhere. Now he cut more.

"U·····h," the snake groaned.

Now they talked it over, talked it over. "Who knows that kind of medicine?"

The chief said, "Maybe that Along-the-River Chief knows that kind."

The doctor chief said, "Go get him. I'll go back now. I've done the best I can. I can't do any more. He ate a person all right. That person's in his belly now. It takes strong medicine to kill a person."

That [doctor] fellow left. A man had already started out to get the Along-the-River Chief.

Pretty soon that mail carrier [messenger] returned. "He's coming, make ready! Make more room, that fellow takes lots of room," he told them.

It took a long time for that doctor fellow to come down. Now the man went to one side of his [the snake's] heart. He figured the medicine [would] come down the other way. He cut, made [the snake] sick. Now that doctor was opening that medicine. The fellow inside was getting sick. "Must be strong medicine. I guess I'll get killed." He heard the medicine drop to one side. He had shut his mouth and nose. As long as the medicine didn't touch him, he's all right, but kind of paralyzed. [If] one drop touched him, he would have died.

Now that sick snake was having a little rest. They decided this new doctor had helped. He said, "That's all I do. If he doesn't get better today, he never will get better." Then that doctor left.

[As] soon as the doctor went out, that man cut a little more. Oh, that snake fellow cried.

Well, they talked. "What are we going to do?"

"Around-Gravel Chief, he knows something about it," one said.

"All right, go get him."

They went. Now the man inside got ready. They might kill him this time. [It] didn't take long, the mail carrier [messenger was] back.

"He's coming, make big room."

He came, came down tail first, winding around and around [until] the room [was] half full. "How's the sick man?"

"No better at all," the people answered.

"Did he get medicine?"

"Yes."

"Well, I've got some medicine. Maybe it'll help him." He took his medicine out.

The fellow saw it; it just paralyzed him there in the snake's belly. "I'll have to cut the whole thing," he thought. "That medicine will sure kill me." He took his knife and just cut right down. Everything spilled out. He got two or three handfuls of money. The water boiled around him; that ocean was mad. It just spilled him right up on the side hill. Now he was safe. Now he looked at his money: he [had] two, three, four, five long ones.[6] He put it away.

Down home they missed him. He had been gone a day and a half. They thought sure he drowned. Now he fixed his money: put one on the [gambling bed],[7] put the others together. Now he thought he'd go home.

They saw him. "Oh, he's come back, he's coming."

He got in the house. He went to the sweathouse, he sweat, he swam, he came back in the house. Then he ate.

Someone asked, "Where have you been?"

"Oh, I've been around all over. I've been camping somewhere." He didn't say he had been that way; he wouldn't tell.

The next day he went away again to see his money in that hollow log. Oh, he saw lots. He got, oh, maybe a basketful. In four, five days he told his wife to clean up the house. "I'm going to bring money in," he said. "We'll have to work." He fixed [a mat][8] in that room. He brought that basketful of money, poured it right down on that [mat] so he can pick up the big ones. She helped too. They picked up the big ones, put them together in one place, in one little basket. They were busy all day, he and his wife. He told his wife that evening, "Make lots of acorns. I want to call the chief tomorrow morning."

She [was] busy that night. She mashed acorns until ten that night, with one woman helping her. By sweating time in the morning she had everything nearly all cooked, nice. They put [a mat] down [and] he went after the chief.

The chief said, "You are giving us a meal?"

"Yes, I made you breakfast."

"Well, how about this fellow, that fellow, that fellow, and that fellow?"

"Bring them all," the man said. "That's for you to say. I just called you; you have to say about the rest."

"All right," the chief said, "that's good."

6. Long dentalium shells, a form of currency.

7. tɛɫ.

8. mətci 'mats woven from grass'.

People [were] coming in, coming in; pretty soon [there was a] full house of leaders, high [class] people. Everybody got a little bucket of acorn soup, put his spoon in. They started in eating. They ate all morning and in the afternoon they [were] all done eating—they had to take grub away [with them].

And they had fixed already how much money they would give away. The man said, "Sit down now before you go home, I have something to tell you folks. Now I leave it to the chief, whatever he says. I got [a gambling bed] and swam with it. I think it is all right. Now, I got a little money. You folks have to go ahead and gamble with it. So the chief has to decide when to get ready."

Everybody talked. One said, "Well, we have to do the best we can with whatever money we have. I don't know how I myself can bet. I got no money."

His wife held a basket pan.[9] He took that little pan and dipped. Each man got a panful. He issued, issued, issued money. What was left in the bottom, that [was] for the chief. That's his chief's money. Now he put the basket before the chief. "This is yours. You're my chief. I'll help you that much, help my people."

Well, they all got money. No one opened his mouth. Only the chief talked. "You people get ready. We'll go the day after tomorrow morning. I'll go with you, soon as you get ready, get your cards [gambling pieces] ready and make your money ready."

They decided it was fine. "All right, I'll be ready," everyone said.

Where people had [previously] won everything from them, that's where they were going to gamble. Come time, everyone ready, they went. This fellow [Gambler] went too. He had that [gambling bed] with him. They got there. Soon as they got in the house, "Which side shall we put our bets on?"

"Oh, over there, where you put them before."

"All right."

They got ready. The other side [was] all ready quick. They wanted to have a good time.

They started to bet, bet—bet big money. Everybody bet. They had to make one bunch [pile of bets]. Now they started to gamble. The first game, they won it. It took a long time to place bets again. Soon as [the bets were] ready, they started the game. Before twelve o'clock at night they just had one game, a pretty tight game. The sticks went back and forth. It took all twelve sticks to make a game. Maybe [by] two o'clock they got [won] another game. They played all [through the early] morning until about six-thirty, then they got another game. They had won lots of money in three games. They played all forenoon and got another game.

Now those people [the hosts] talked it over. "We have to give up. We haven't got enough money to match what we have lost. You take it, we give up," the man said.

9. *gása* 'basket pan'.

They took their money, went home, had supper at home. They didn't go any-where to gamble then. That was the end of that. He sent word to two places, but they didn't go because those other people didn't have enough money to match bets.

Now when everybody [was] back in the sweathouse that man told where he had been.

One old man said, "I just thought that's where you'd been. That [big flat-headed snake] swallows anything that swims across."

So no one could win from him. They were always lucky. No one [other group] could play against them [successfully].

Wind Woman

Told by Coquelle Thompson Sr.

Wind Woman stayed alone. [She had] nobody, no folks at all, just she alone. Once in a while she got wood in a basket, got lots of wood, kept it on hand all the time. One morning she went [to get wood]. There was a big tree. She ran around it. It was hard to get that [tree] bark. She had a long pole. She sawed the bark open in that one place. She pulled there, then she twisted, then the whole bark came down and one baby dropped out. She threw the pole away; she picked the baby up. That baby just cried, cried, and cried—never quit crying. She held that baby; she told it, "You are my baby." Everything [different kinship terms] she called it. At last she told it, "You're my brother." Then that baby quit crying.

She had all kinds of things in the house: beaver skin, coon, rabbit skins. All [were] nice, everything. She made them for [the baby].[1] Now the baby's all right. [She made a cradleboard][2] for packing the baby. He slept there at night. Then [she] cleaned it, took it [the baby] out again. Finally that boy got to be two, three years old, can walk around, play. He was good company to her. She thought about a little bow for him. She made him a tiny bow and arrows. She had everything. She gave it to him [and] that little boy would play [at] shooting, outdoors. Oh, that woman was glad.

Now when he was ten, twelve years old, she made a bigger bow, bigger arrows. She told him, "Now you go around over to that open place, you look around. [When] you see a rabbit sit up on his hind legs that way, you shoot him."

He went. He saw a rabbit but he missed [and] he lost his arrow. He came back. "Sister, I lost my arrow. I want another arrow."

"Oh, all right, I'll make you another one." She made one, gave it to him.

He went around again, every day. Finally he killed one rabbit. Oh, it tickled him. He hollered. He put a string on it; he packed it on his back like deer are packed. He took it to his sister.

Oh, she hollered. She said, "All right, now, you're old enough now to kill deer. You have to hunt. You are old enough now."

1. The notebook version says: "She make them for ga·yu." *ga·yu* is the Upper Coquille word for 'baby'.
2. The notebook version reads: "ga·yu thing for packing baby," apparently referring to a cradleboard.

He went to hunt now. "Give me only one arrow, not two." [He said.] She dug up the best arrow she had. He never missed anything. [It was a] big bow he carried. He hunted. He fixed his own sweathouse. He slept there then.

That young man went [hunting]. About ten o'clock he [would] bring a big deer home. Oh, that young woman almost danced, she was so glad. I don't think she had ever been married.

She heard in the evening, someone coming. Her brother had already gone to the sweathouse. She thought, "I wonder what he wants? What's he coming back for?" Then she saw a woman standing outdoors.

The woman asked, "Does Wind's brother stay here?"

"Yes, I am Wind." Wind thought, "Well, she is a pretty woman." She said, "You can come in."

She took that good-looking woman in the house and fed her. It got late. They went to bed. In the morning they arose, cooked; that visiting woman was lively. She wanted to get that boy. She wanted to marry him.

That boy came back about ten o'clock. He saw a woman sitting there with his sister, but he never noticed her. He ate his breakfast, got his bow and arrow, and he went. He never noticed that woman.

His sister told him, "This young woman came to see you."

He never answered his sister. He went to hunt. About eleven o'clock he brought one deer. That Wind Woman was busy. She was a stout[3] woman too. He never noticed that [visiting] woman, just ate, went away again to hunt. [He] just kept on that way for three or four days.

Finally that pretty woman left. She told Wind Woman, "Goodbye. I guess your brother doesn't like me, so I don't have to stay here." She knew that boy didn't care for her.

About two, three, four o'clock two women came in. They had heard his name, [and that] Wind's brother was a good hunter, a good man. They came in the house. That young man didn't stay in the house. He stayed in the sweathouse, but he saw two women coming by. They were good-looking women.

They asked her, "Is this Wind Woman's house?"

"Yes."

"Well, we've come to see your brother."

Wind Woman said, "You folks come in, eat something. My brother never stays in the house; he stays in the sweathouse."

He came to supper, saw two women sitting there, eating. He said nothing, did not greet them or anything.

Well, those two women talked to each other. Each said, "Well, I don't have to

---

3. *Stout* in this and other contexts in this story means 'strong'.

stay here and take care of him if he doesn't like me." Then, "Let's go," they said. Then they returned home.

He packed deer in all the time. Pretty soon there were lots of hides. Wind Woman worked on those hides. She's so stout, she made them soft, just like a blanket. She worked day and night.

As that young man hunted, he studied: "Well, I've got to go away now pretty soon. I have enough food for my sister now." One day he sat down in the house [and] asked his sister, "Can I go away? Can I get a good woman somewhere?"

She laughed. She said, "Why, lots of good women came here to see you. You didn't sit down, talk to them, or anything. Why's that? What kind of woman do you want?"

He didn't answer. He just said, "Oh, I must go away, somewhere."

"Well, when are you thinking of going?"

"Oh, I might go in the morning," he said.

"All right. I've got everything ready for you to wear. You have to go like a man, not like a poor person. You take your arrow and bow."

He went in the morning, but she had told her brother, "Now you watch right across the river. Thunder lives right there. I know where you are going to see a girl. You better watch or he'll pick you up and kill you. Hammering-all-the-time[4]— he's a dangerous man."

He answered his sister, "What do you think I am? I'm not a coward. I'm no coward." By that he meant he had his power. He's got a power to get away from any place. He went. He was traveling all day, all afternoon.

Now she had fixed a stone [pestle]. [She had] tied it up in otter-skin strings and tied it to the front of the house, the line stretched across the house. She told that stone [pestle],[5] "Now, if they abuse my brother over there, or he gets into trouble, you have to fall down, break that string." That fellow was gone, that Wind Woman sat night and day, working.

Finally he arrived. Now he heard *dul, dul,* that hammering. Now he got to that house [in the] late evening. No one was around outdoors. He thought, "That [Thunder] fellow hasn't seen me."

But [Thunder][6] had seen him and said, "I'll fix him all right." So the next morning, not early, around breakfast [time] Thunder opened the door where he [the young man] stayed. "Who is it here?" Thunder [in a harsh voice] said, "I've come to get my son-in-law. You people are no good!" The boy had stopped at the next house [across the river from Thunder]. "I have two *good* daughters. Come on,

4. The notebook version reads: "t'cədətni· (sənsalt'səł hammer all time—you hear long ways)." In Jacobs's editing of the text she renders this as Thunder's name, "Hammering-all-the-time."
5. The notebook reads: "mɛ·lt'si· (to pound meal) She told that stone". *mɛ·lt'si·* is the Upper Coquille word for 'grinding stone' or 'pestle'.
6. Here Thompson renders Thunder's name as "sənsəldyɛł (Thunder)."

son-in-law." Then that boy had to go. That old couple was afraid to answer a word to Thunder.

That boy went with him. Now they went, crossed in a canoe. Thunder took him in the house, where pretty women were. One woman had fingernails *that* long [seven inches]. She was the one who killed people. This young man thought, "I'll have to be ready for her and for old man Thunder." He [the boy] had his power in his hand all the time, but no one could see it.

Now Thunder told the young man, "You go over there a little ways. I've got a [fish] trap over there. You'll get all kinds of eels there and bring them here."

"All right."

He got there. Oh, all kinds of rattlesnakes [were] there. He took his power, he took a stick and strung those snakes on the stick and took them [back].

Old Thunder was sitting by the fire. The young man opened the door and threw them [the snakes] right in the door, said, "Here's your fish." That old man got scared, jumped up. He had expected those rattlesnakes to kill that young man. Now the young man came back in the house. The old man took those snakes and threw them back down to the river. Those two women sat, one on each side of the fire. The one was ugly, but the other one looked pretty good.

Now the young man knew they would try a different way. The old man said, "Let's sweat."

"All right," the young man answered.

So they went to the sweathouse. That sweathouse was awfully hot. Old Thunder kept moving around. He was getting ready to do something. Well, the old man got out, so the young man got out too. Then they went to the river to swim.

"Dive!" the old man said.

Now the young man knew what he [Thunder] was going to do. The young man dived. Thunder caused thick ice to cover the water. The young man tried to come up, but his head hit the ice. He swam up [stream] about fifty yards, put his power up through that ice—he had it in his hand all the time—and got out and sat down.

Down a little ways stood Thunder, laughing. "Ha! ha! You were going to beat me, eh? Now you can't get out."

Back home that [pestle] began to move. Wind Woman thought, "Oh, my poor brother. He's having a hard time now."

The young man went back to that first house where he had been staying across the river. Now those two daughters [in this household] were his wives. They treated him good, fixed him food.

Near sundown Thunder made the ice go. He saw no one dead in the water at all. Now he thought, "Oh, that young man beat me after all."

The next morning about ten o'clock Thunder came after the young man. He growled at those poor old people and scared them. "You have no business to keep my son-in-law here," he said, "You folks [are] no good, [you] got nothing."

The old man never answered. [He was] afraid. He had no boys, just two daughters.

Thunder said, "Come on, son-in-law, let's go back. You need not stay with these dirty people." He took him back across the river.

Thunder studied what to do. But that young man knew what he thought. Thunder said, "We'll have to wrestle now." Thunder wanted to mash his [the boy's] ribs. He was stout.

The boy said, "All right."

Then they stood together, all ready. He [the boy] told his power, "I want big chest muscles, big back, a strong body like a log."

Thunder grabbed him, tried to mash [crush] him, couldn't do it. He tried to throw him down; couldn't throw him down. They wrestled for half an hour. The young man had beat him. He couldn't throw him.

"All right, son-in-law, let's go back in the house."

The young man had to do that. He went back in the house with him. They sat down.

That ugly-looking girl said, "Let me look for lice in your head. Put your head right here in my lap."

He said, "All right."

He already talked to his power, had his head fixed for her. She looked for lice. She was [really] looking for a place to tear his head off. She tried it once.

He said, "What's the matter?"

Her fingernails were all broken. She fell over dead. She [would] pull people apart and sling them down the hill. It was her own fault.

Now they were going to sweat again. They went in the sweathouse. Oh, [it was] hot! Just red, all those stones! Now Thunder jumped out quick. He closed the sweathouse door. It was burning up in there. He thought, "Now that young man will burn up."

Now that young man just took his power, made a passageway under the ground to the river, swam across.

Old Thunder stood in front of the burning sweathouse, laughing. "Oh! Ho! You thought you'd beat me, eh? Now you're burning now," he said.

The fellow [was] already back in the house across the river.

Back home that [pestle] moved. [His] sister thought, "My poor brother, he is having a hard time now."

Now the next morning Thunder came again to abuse those old folks. He found no bones where the sweathouse had burned. He took the boy back across the river again. He took him back in the house and studied what to do. "All right, son-in-law, come on."

The boy acted like he didn't know what was going on. He just did whatever he was told. They went outdoors. Thunder caught hold of a good-sized tree, caught the top, and pulled it down slow. He sat on the top; he told the young man to sit near the base. "You sit here," he said. Now that young man knew Thunder would jump off. Thunder said, "All right, you set on good?"

"Yes."

Thunder jumped. The tree snapped up. That young man had jumped too, but Thunder didn't know it. The young man went back across the river while Thunder stood there laughing. "You thought you were going to beat me, but where are you now?" He thought that young man had gone way off somewhere like an arrow. He went back in the house.

In the morning Thunder came again [to the house where the young man was staying]. "Well, you'll have to come back with me son-in-law."

"All right."

They went back again. Thunder told him, "I have a little bird's nest up in that tree. I want you to get it." That bird was making a noise to fool him.

Now he had to go. He pulled himself up that pole [tree trunk]. He never looked back. Finally he looked down. He was way up to the sky. He could hardly see the ground. "All right. I'll get out [of this situation] some way." He studied. He got a little moss, rubbed himself all over [with it]. He said, "I'll just be that moss, weigh nothing, wind will carry me down."

That devil Thunder was laughing, dancing around at his house.

Now that piece of moss rolled off. He came down, down, [for a] long time. "What's the matter? I haven't hit the ground yet!" He waited a long time. He opened that moss so he could look out. There he was, hanging on a maple tree. He removed that moss and jumped to the ground. It wasn't high. He went home across the river.

His sister watched that thing [pestle] moving. She thought, "Oh, he's having a hard time. He suffers now."

The next morning Thunder came for him again, saying, "Oh, I just came to get you. Let's go across. We'll have to hunt. I'd like [some] meat."

The young man thought, "I know what he'll do now," but he said, "All right."

They went. They went a little ways on the mountain somewhere. It got cloudy, dark. Snow came down. That devil Thunder ran home. The young man came back slow. He couldn't tell where to go. He had to use his power to guide him. Now he came, came, [in the] cold. He got home, half dead. He scratched on the house by his wife [where she slept]. She opened the grass [and] saw his hand. They dragged him in. They built a big fire.

Back where his sister was, that string [holding the pestle] broke. Wind Woman cried. "I'll fix you!" she thought.

Toward daylight he was getting better. They gave him some hot soup.

He told his wife, "My sister will come here, pretty soon."

About ten o'clock they heard something, a big storm coming. It was coming now. Trees [were] just like straws [in that] big wind. The top of the house went [blew] off.

"That's my sister," he said.

Wind Woman took Thunder's house, mashed it. He [Thunder] broke in pieces. Wind Woman threw one part one way, another part, another [way]. She had killed him now. She had let her hair loose on just one side.[7]

Her brother told her, "These old folks don't have any wood."

"I'll go get some," she said. She went, didn't take long. She made lots of noise, brought two sticks, trees, right under her arm. She put them right by the door, took her pole [and] chopped them right up, bark and all. "Now, I'm done," she said. She told her brother, "Now there'll be no more trouble. You need not travel any more. You have two women now. You stay here, come home whenever you're ready."

They gave Wind Woman all kinds of food: Indian oats,[8] dried berries, clams, camas. "I'll have to go back. I have lots of things at home," she said. Now she went back. She was all done there. She got home; everything was all right.

7. In Thompson's version of this narrative recorded by John P. Harrington, Thompson notes: "The wind woman always kept her hair tied on both sides. She never let it loose" (reel 27, frame 0420).
8. Thompson uses the Upper Coquille word *t'ɬu·dɛ'* here, which he translates as 'Indian oats'.

Lake Miwok

How Coyote Remade the World

Introduction by Catherine A. Callaghan

It is an honor to contribute a translation of a Lake Miwok sacred text to this collection, intended to awaken awareness of the literary merit of Native American narratives. There is desperate need for such a volume. As a beginning professor, I remember my dismay when a professor of French asked me why I spent my time on languages "with no literature and only a few speakers." Although I was used to such queries from the general public, it was shocking to hear one from an academic. I now realize they result from ignorance. Few good translations of such texts are readily available. They are not included in comparative literature courses. If Native American literature is studied at all, it is usually for its anthropological or linguistic content. This neglect is interpreted even by the educated public as evidence that no such literature exists or that it has no value.

Lake Miwok is a central California Indian language formerly spoken south of Clear Lake in Long Valley and the surrounding foothills, about one hundred miles north of San Francisco (see Callaghan 1978a for a map of the Lake Miwok area, including former settlements). Much of this territory is now privately owned. The Lake Miwok Indians were part of the Pomo culture area. Bert W. and Ethel G. Aginsky (1971) have presented a highly readable account of daily life in that area just before the time of contact.

The Lake Miwok language is now remembered by fewer than half a dozen people and is rarely used in conversation. It is closely related to Coast Miwok, once the language of the Marin Peninsula across the Golden Gate Bridge from San Francisco. Lake Miwok is more distantly related to the Eastern Miwok languages, formerly spoken on the western slopes of the Sierra Nevada Mountains from the Fresno River north to the Cosumnes River, and across the northern portion of the San Joaquin Valley to a point west of Mount Diablo. The Miwok language family is in turn related to the Costanoan family, those languages once spoken along the coast of California and inland from San Francisco south to Big Sur. Miwok and Costanoan comprise the Utian family of languages, not to be confused with Ute, which is unrelated.

"How Coyote Remade the World" describes the end of the prehuman cycle, populated by animal personages with human attributes, and the beginning of the current cycle. It reinforces and sustains the Lake Miwok world-view by explaining the origin of landmarks and other natural phenomena as well as the bow and arrow and the art of fire making. The personality of Old Man Coyote, a being with great power who combines animal cunning with human nature in all its sublime and ridiculous aspects, pervades throughout.

Coyote is a scavenger who eats dead meat, a cunning survivor, a powerful beast who thunders when he runs. He is an old man who dribbles acorn mush when he eats. He is a loving grandfather who takes his grandson, Bullet Hawk, around Old Place to show him Pointed Hill, Rocky Mountain, and a powerful tree with hardly any limbs.

Coyote is a trickster who teases Bullet Hawk unmercifully. In one story he disguises himself as his grandson and tries to seduce Bullet Hawk's wife. That episode ends badly, since he cannot hide all his coyote hair. Coyote is sometimes a fool, such as when he tries to climb a pine tree to get nuts for two pretty girls. He falls, leaving the imprint of his knee on a rock below.

In his sublime aspect Coyote brings on the great flood that puts out Weasel's world fire as well as all other fires. He stands on the newly barren earth and calls forth birds, trees, animals, and finally people of the present cycle of existence. "Old Man Coyote, the one that made us, the one that was before us and knew everything, he also made a mistake in everything. That's why we, too, can make mistakes," James Knight once said. I know of no Western figure comparable to Old Man Coyote.

Tules, local marsh grasses, parts of which are edible, play an important role. When Bullet Hawk steals Weasel's beads, Weasel sets the world on fire with his fire spear, which, according to Merriam (1910, 143), was the stick he used to hold his hair in place. Because beads served as money, such a theft could disrupt the Lake Miwok community. When Bullet Hawk flies off, his wings go *wekwek wekwek wekwek,* sounding out his name (Wekwek). A pair of helldivers (grebes, a type of duck) save his life when he grows tired, allowing him to rest on their backs, asking only that he be careful not to disturb their heat sores, which old people get from sitting too close to the fire. James Knight was a hunter, and he reported that a bullet hawk would not eat a helldiver, because helldivers had once saved Bullet Hawk's life. Crane, the Sentinel, also sounds out his name (Waak) when he cries in the night. It is obvious that these narratives are central to the preservation of the Lake Miwok world-view and culture and that we are all poorer if they are lost. They constitute a powerful argument for language revival and revitalization.

This account was one of the narratives transmitted in the homes by skilled storytellers on rainy winter days. The audience was mostly children, who would be inside when it was raining, but there was no fixed format, and the storytellers were free to adapt their rendition to those present. They spoke in high narrative style, which James Knight had mastered. What follows is a synthesis of two of his renditions of the account, told twenty-two years apart. The first has been published previously (Callaghan 1978b). An earlier version of the creation account appears in the Merriam collection (1910). James Knight owned a copy of this book and was probably influenced by it, although he learned the account primarily from one of his uncles. Because there was no tradition of word-for-word transmission, any two renditions would differ, even if they were by the same person.

Incorporation of postcontact elements is more common in later versions. According to Merriam (1910, 145), it rained for ten days and ten nights to produce the world flood. In his 1958 version James Knight claimed it rained forty days and forty nights, obvious syncretism from the biblical account. In Merriam (1910, 149–51), two shrew-mice steal fire from Crow, with the help of a fire bug, and Coyote stores it in the buckeye tree, telling people how to rub the buckeye stick to make the fire come out. In James Knight's first version two shrew-mice steal fire with the help of Crane alone. The black cat and the lamp of James Knight's 1980 version are recent additions, since both are postcontact introductions.

Certain elements in the story are hard to explain. Bullet Hawk's age (twenty years) when he sets out to explore Lake Miwok territory is mentioned only in the 1980 version. I know of no special significance for that number, so it is probably an arbitrary figure designed to let the listener know that Bullet Hawk has come of age. Also, I do not know why Coyote cooked the mud hens carelessly and ate them while they were still bloody unless James Knight wanted to emphasize the unrefined tastes of Coyote the Scavenger, in contrast with Bullet Hawk, who ate only the breasts, presumably the best part.

My elicitation strategy for both versions was to allow James Knight to record the entire account at a single sitting. In the case of the 1958 rendition, I relied on his older brother, John Knight, for a sentence-by-sentence translation. Although John Knight knew the traditional stories well and had a better command of Lake Miwok, he lacked his brother's dramatic flair and refused to relate them. He did make corrections where James Knight had used slang, an inappropriate word, or a substandard grammatical construction.

Lake Miwok narratives are marked by declamatory style, high words, and certain particles. The hearsay particle *weno* 'it is said' indicates that the narrator is relating something he or she has heard. Another particle, *kasha* 'said', marks direct quotations.[1] Words such as *kelats* 'used to' and *kelatskelats* 'long ago' occur frequently. Repetition and backtracking furnish continuity between episodes.

The problem of how to translate this account into English is not an easy one to solve, especially since it is a performance piece that cannot be adequately reduced to the printed page, and we are considering it as a work of literature rather than a source of purely linguistic or ethnographic information. Under such circumstances the principal goal of a translator is to render the text into a style in the target language that reflects as closely as possible the spirit of the original, in the mind of the reader as well as that of the translator. Since the creation account is in Standard Lake Miwok, I have translated it into Standard English, rather than some other type of English such as Red English, roughly analogous to Black English. Anthony Mattina (1987, 129, 137, 139) prefers to translate his narratives into this style. Although Red English might better reflect how an American Indian would retell the account in English, it would be less faithful to the literary style of the original, especially from the standpoint of the reader, who has no means of judging its speech level and quality other than through the translation.

I believe that high narrative style should be recognized as a legitimate genre in and of itself, as it certainly would if major oral traditions had survived into our literate culture. This style should be distinguished from poetry, which better applies to chants within such narratives and to traditional songs. Of course, even in English there is a continuum between metered verse, free verse, a prose poem, and rhythmic prose, the latter two being written in prose form. I would classify Lake Miwok narratives as rhythmic prose.

Several scholars have opted to capture the internal rhythmic patterns of Native American oral texts by treating them as poetry and writing them out in lines (Swann 1994). While this may be a valid heuristic device, I believe it serves little purpose to cast the English translations into corresponding lines, especially in cases where they read more like prose than poetry and the original is not included. The compactness of prose style also heightens suspense and interest for the average reader.

In a volume such as this one, translators have an obligation to readers who are neither linguists nor anthropologists. If the translation is not in Standard English, we risk the assumption that the native language lacks such an elegant style, however wrongheaded this assumption may be. The appearance on the page is also important. If the translation is too literal, including every occurrence of hearsay particles, for instance, we risk reducing rather than enhancing the overall dramatic effect.

I emphasize reader response for a reason. Native American languages and traditions are undergoing a period of renewal and revitalization, both of which cost money (see Hinton 1994). We must convince the educated public of the wealth that lies in these traditions, not only for Native Americans but for everyone. Examples of their literature should be included in anthologies, and the scholars who choose the subject matter for anthologies are neither linguists nor anthropologists. When Native American literature is studied in the classroom, we will hear fewer questions like the ones I discussed earlier.

NOTES

1. I use *sh* for an *s* with the tongue curled back. This sound is usually represented by an *s* with a dot under it.

SUGGESTED READING AND REFERENCES

Aginsky, Bert W., and Ethel G. 1971. *Deep Valley: The Pomo Indians of California.* New York: Stein & Day.

Bright, William. 1993. *A Coyote Reader.* Berkeley: University of California Press.

Callaghan, Catherine A. 1978a. "Lake Miwok." In *Handbook of North American Indians,* vol. 8, *California,* edited by Robert F. Heizer, 264–73. Washington DC: Smithsonian Institution.

———. 1978b. "Fire, Flood, and Creation." In *Coyote Stories,* edited by William Bright, 62–68. International Journal of American Linguistics: Native American Text Series, Monograph 1. Chicago: University of Chicago Press.

Hinton, Leanne. 1994. *Flutes of Fire: Essays on California Indian Languages.* San Bernardino CA: Borgo Press.

Mattina, Anthony. 1987. "North American Indian Mythography: Editing Texts for the Printed Page." In *Recovering the Word: Essays on Native American Literature,* edited by Brian Swann and Arnold Krupat. Berkeley: University of California Press.

Merriam, C. Hart. 1910. *The Dawn of the World: Myths and Weird Tales Told by the Mewan Indians of California.* Cleveland: Arthur H. Clark.

Swann, Brian. 1994. Introduction to *Coming to Light: Contemporary Translations of the Native Literatures of North America.* New York: Random House.

How Coyote Remade the World

Told by James Knight
Translated by Catherine A. Callaghan

Long ago, before the world was destroyed, Old Man Coyote was the most power-ful of all beings. Bullet Hawk was also great. Weasel was great, too. Everything was filled with wonder.

My father and mother told me this story the way the old-timers used to tell it. The story was here before my brothers and sisters, before all my relatives. It began in Old Place, where Old Man Coyote lived with his grandson, Bullet Hawk. They had a home there. Right there is where Bullet Hawk grew up with his grandfather.

All the Lake Miwok Indians originally came from Deep Place. After they filled it up, they spread out from there, and some of them ended up in Old Place, which they also called Lake Miwok Indian Place. Guenoc Lake was nearby. There was a tree standing next to that lake, and it was powerful, just as I've been saying.

Bullet Hawk was a great bird, and Old Man Coyote was also powerful. He had four legs like a dog, but he made the whole world. When he said, "I wish," then everything came out the way he wanted. He was just like the Great Man Above; whatever he commanded came to pass.

One day, Bullet Hawk wanted to explore. His grandfather told him he could travel to the end of the valley, so he went over that way. He went farther up and climbed into the mountains. He looked over the valley. He saw the creek. He saw the lake, Rocky Mountain, and Pointed Hill. Bullet Hawk wondered about every-thing, how the valley was filled with all kinds of birds. He saw the meadowlark and the quail and examined them all. He kept going further, far enough to see Guenoc Lake. Then he said, "Grandpa, there must be a lake there."

"Yes," said Coyote. "There's a lake there. They call that lake Guenoc; that's the lake you saw. Did you see the two mountains on the other side of it? Those are great mountains, too. One is Pointed Hill and the other is Rocky Mountain." Old Man Coyote knew everything in olden times; he was the greatest of all.

Weasel was around there, too, and he was also powerful, but not as great as Old Man Coyote. And there was a big tree standing next to Guenoc Lake. It didn't have any limbs. It was like a resting place where a pretty bird could perch in the morning. There was a type of small green fish in the lake, which the Indians used to eat. Suckers, salmon, trout, and little chubs were in that lake, too. Later, people planted catfish and a lot of the fish we have there now.

One day Bullet Hawk was getting big, you know; growing up. "Grandpa," he said.

"What?" said Coyote.

"What can I use to kill these with, these birds and geese?" Mud hens and meadowlarks—Guenoc Lake was full of them, you know.

"Well, I'm going to get a bow," Coyote said. "A bow and arrow, that is." Before getting it, he went into the sweathouse. He smeared his eyes with spit and pretended to cry.

"What are you crying for, Grandpa?"

"This bow and arrow I'm giving you belonged to my father and my father's father. I feel sad, so I'm crying," Coyote said.

"What's that green stuff growing around Guenoc Lake?" Bullet Hawk asked.

"Well, that's tule. We eat that, too, the tender young sprouts." He wanted to eat some but couldn't get into the water.

When you look at this lake from down below, it's pretty. There are two mountains standing just like a sweathouse. The name of the lower one is Shalshal. That's Weasel's home. There's a sweathouse somewhere around there, Weasel's sweathouse. Bullet Hawk perched in the tree and kept watching it for three or four days.

He got up early in the morning and went around to get food for himself. Then one day, after his grandfather had given him the bow and arrow, he caught all kinds of mud hens. He caught them, but he didn't eat them all—just the breasts. And his grandfather ate everything bloody—he just threw the birds into the fire a little while and ate them with the blood dripping. That went on for a long time.

Then Bullet Hawk spotted Weasel from across the lake, going in and out of his sweathouse. He went out in the morning, going after his bow and food. After he left, Bullet Hawk told his grandfather, "I'm going to visit that man." He was planning to go inside Weasel's sweathouse, so he left early and went to Weasel's home. Bullet Hawk found lots of things there. He was twenty years old when he went in there, inside that sweathouse. Every kind of food was in there—pinole, acorn bread, rabbit meat, deer meat, little fish—every kind of good food was there. The meat was in a sack, they say. They used to make deerskin sacks, then stored all kinds of acorns inside.

There were beads in one of those sacks. Weasel's sweathouse was full of all kinds of food. Bullet Hawk didn't know if he was going to try it, so he stuck his hand into the acorn mush and tasted it. There was even sugar there. After he finished

eating part of it, he stuffed straw in the sack, filled it with water, and tied it up
again.

Weasel had buckeye in his sweathouse, too—clover and all kinds of old-time
food—he had it all right there. Then Bullet Hawk saw a sack of beads and considered stealing it, but he was afraid of getting caught. So he packed half of the
beads and hid them in a ditch above Guenoc Lake, pretty close to his grandfather's
home. He replaced the beads with tules, grass, and all kinds of leaves. This went
on for three or four days.

After Weasel came back, he felt something was wrong. "What's the matter with
me?" he said. "Something must be wrong around here. I'm going to stay home
today." So he stayed home and swept his house. Then he searched all around, but
his beads were gone. His acorn mush was gone. His meat was gone. Bullet Hawk
had stolen all his good things. They say Weasel only missed his beads—his sack
was half full of grass.

"I don't know what's going on," Old Man Weasel said. "It's not right if someone's living high off this. It isn't right if someone's doing fine."

He got mad. "Oh, yeah, I know you. I know who you are, and now, I'm going
to look for you," he said. Then he went to the back of his sweathouse and got his
spear, his fire spear. He pointed it toward the Lower World. He pointed it toward
the Upper World. He pointed it west. He pointed it east but didn't see anybody.
He pointed it north—he pointed it that way, but still didn't see anybody.

Finally, he pointed it south and saw him. "Well, now, you think I don't know
you?" said Weasel. "Did you really think I wouldn't find you out?" People were
dying wherever he pointed his spear—burnt up. The fire was spreading all over.

Meanwhile, Bullet Hawk had returned to his grandfather, Old Man Coyote.
He was glancing toward Clear Lake when the fire broke out. "Grandpa, there's
smoke." he said.

"Yes."

"Why is it smoking over there? Are they burning something?"

"Oh, yes; that's what they're doing. This time of year, they burn tules so that
new shoots will come up later for us to eat, so don't be scared. They always do
that." That's what Coyote told his grandson as the fire was approaching his house.

"Grandpa, this fire is getting closer and closer."

"Yeah, it seems like that when the tule's thick. Then the smoke goes higher and
higher," said Coyote. He was teasing his grandson, because he knew everything.
No one can fool Old Man Coyote.

Bullet Hawk went on that way three or four times. Old Man Coyote already
knew that his grandson had stolen the beads, but he didn't say anything.

Finally, Bullet Hawk said "Grandpa!"

"What?" Coyote said.

"Somebody must be living below Guenoc Lake that you didn't tell me about. Whoever it was, I took his beads. I took some food, too. I got his bow, and I took some clothes," Bullet Hawk told his grandfather. He had stolen it all, you see.

Coyote said, "Oh." He knew that already.

Weasel destroyed the earth, then Old Man Coyote flooded it; that's how the old people told it to me. I heard it, so that's how I know. When I was little, they would tell this story as I was about to go to sleep in the evening, when it was raining outside. They recited it while it was raining so the little ones would learn it. If the old people had told it on a good day, the children would be thinking about eating, swimming, and playing, and they wouldn't learn very much. When it was raining, they listened carefully inside the house and learned things properly.

If they said something once or twice, the little ones would pick it up fast. I believed that, and I liked it that way, too, when the old people were teaching what happened and teaching it right. That's how they transmitted things up to now. Look, I'm putting it all into the tape recorder. At some point the little ones will read it in a book and learn it. Yes, what my uncle underneath the tree once said will be written down, and they'll note the time and place. It's already being recorded the way the Indians used to tell it. It won't die out. This story will continue on and on. Look at the little ones now; they learn what they read in a book. What comes out will be published from the tape, so they'll read it and learn.

This is the Lake Miwok story that the old people used to tell, and this is how they would tell it long ago. They knew it and recited it. Some people know it now but can't recite it the way they should. That's what I did just now. They know it, too. That's why we're putting it on this tape. The machine will make it talk. That's how one can learn it, and it's good to translate it, but only if you translate it correctly. If you make even a small mistake, it will turn out bad.

I'm happy today to be telling as much as I know in proper style, the way the old people taught me. They left me with these beautiful stories. I know them from what they shared long ago, what the young ones used to know, and that's what I'm sharing now. If the children learn it, perhaps they'll transmit it a bit further. For this reason, I'm grateful for the story I'm telling.

Bullet Hawk lit right at Guenoc Lake. He returned from there to his grandfather's sweathouse.

"Please, Grandpa, stop this fire! I'm going to burn up. The fire's getting hot, and I don't like it," he told his grandfather.

Then his grandfather said, "All right, I'll stop the fire." He took a big horn, an elk horn, and tied it securely to the center pole.

He went to the back of the sweathouse behind the drum, picked up a sack, and hit the center pole. It started to drizzle, but that wasn't enough. He got another sack, which produced a foggy rain. Then he hit the pole with a rain sack, and it rained hard. That still wasn't enough; he needed something more. He got another sack and slammed it against the center pole, making it snow. Each time he used a different sack, he got more. Then he crawled inside the horn and stayed there. He didn't leave; he just stayed there.

It rained a long time, and the world was all full of water. Then Bullet Hawk flew up above his grandfather. Old Man Coyote started teasing his grandson. "Mama," said Coyote—he was inside the elk horn teasing his grandson, who had lit right on the point of the sweathouse, right there. "Give me meat! Give me fish! I want that dry fish, Mama," said Coyote. He named every kind of food to tease his tired, hungry grandson—Coyote didn't have a mother and he wasn't eating anything. Bullet Hawk must have heard all that through the top. The drum makes the echo carry up through the center pole and all around the sweathouse.

Just as Bullet Hawk was about to fly away, the water came up to the top of the sweathouse. Then he flew off, going *wekwek wekwek wekwek wekwek wekwek wekwek wekwek wekwek* as he went.

Water was everywhere, and he didn't know which way to fly. Mount Kanaktai was the only mountain he could see, and its peak seemed to be going in and out. The water covered everything as he watched. I don't know how many days he flew before he saw two helldivers, one male and the other female. He was tired, and his wings were drooping just above the water. After flying around like that, he came up to the two divers.

"Friends," he said, "help me. I'm tired, and I'm getting sick." Bullet Hawk had been flying around for a long time, you know.

"All right, Grandson," one of them said, "but light on my back gently. You might knock off the scabs there." They're called heat sores. "You might break my sores."

First one diver carried him, then the other, and he slept there. When that one got tired, the other one would dive under the water and hold Bullet Hawk up. This went on until it had rained forty nights. After it rained forty days, the whole earth was flooded. By that time only four people were left; the two helldivers, Bullet Hawk, and Old Man Coyote, who had done it all for his grandson. Whatever his grandson wanted, Coyote made for him.

The two divers gathered up driftwood, made a nest for Bullet Hawk on top of the water, and laid him inside. By now the water was going down. They kept feeding him fish. Whatever they saw, they would feed him. After a long while everything dried up and he slept. He kept on resting for three or four days while the divers watched over him.

After the water went way down, Bullet Hawk told the two helldivers he was going for a walk down the river. "I'm going to look for my home, where I used to live." He went down the edge of the creek and saw an old man on the other side.

"Old man!" he said.

"What? What's your name?"

"How about you? What's your name?"

"I want to know your name, too, so you'd better tell me."

"Oh, yeah? It's me, Bullet Hawk. I just came from the lake up there, Clear Lake."

Then the old man was glad. He jumped up and said, "Grandson, Grandson! I'm your grandfather. Stay there awhile, and I'll come over." He backed up and came down running, going *kool kol kol kol*, jumped across the creek, landed on the other side, and fell down.

"Grandson, Grandson, Grandson!" he said, and then he cried. He cried when he hugged Bullet Hawk.

"Don't cry, Grandpa," he said.

"I haven't seen you for a long time. That's why I'm crying," said Coyote. "I've been looking for you and couldn't find you. Come with me and let's go home."

"All right, but I can't go there right now, Grandpa. There's an old lady and an old man waiting for me. I've been staying with them, so I have to go over there and tell them what happened. Tomorrow, I'll come back here," Bullet Hawk said to Old Man Coyote.

"Fine, I expect to see you again this time tomorrow," Coyote said.

Then Bullet Hawk returned to Old Man Diver and Old Lady Diver. "I saw an old man over there who said he was my grandfather. He told me to come back tomorrow, so I'm going to go with him."

"Oh, yeah, we know him. Go with him then, and let him take care of you. He's a great old man, that one," the divers said.

Bullet Hawk left the next morning. He went to the creek and saw his grandfather. He flew to the other side and came up to him. "Now, I'll go with you," Bullet Hawk told his grandfather. So they turned around and went back to the sweathouse in Old Place, where they're still living together now.

But the earth was empty and barren. "Grandpa!" said Bullet Hawk. He had been there several days, and he was sad. "Is there nobody around here? Aren't there any birds or things like that?" he asked.

"Yeah, lots of them. All kinds of birds, and they'll be coming tomorrow morning," said Coyote. He then named some of the birds. He named the geese. He named the ducks, mud hens, woodpeckers, doves, quail, yellowhammers, crows, sapsuckers, robins, chicken hawks, all the birds the Indians used to have around here. They all have a name: valley birds, tufted tits, mockingbirds, cranes, killdeer, brown birds, towhees, eagles, hummingbirds. All the birds on this earth that the Indians named—billy owls, spotted owls, bats, hoot owls, Oregon woodpeckers— all the birds that were around here long ago.

After naming them, he said, "They're going to come." And the next morning all these birds were talking. The wild mud hens and the geese were singing pretty songs.

"That's good, Grandpa. That's what I like to hear. I just didn't want to keep living here with everything quiet," said Bullet Hawk.

Sometime later Bullet Hawk noticed that there was no sun. He said, "Grandpa, is it always going to be dark like this? Can you make it light here?"

"Yes, I could make it shine. Let me call my helpers," he said. He then summoned two doves, an older brother and a younger brother. "Those two will bring out the sun."

The doves had a sling. "Little Brother, you hurl first," said the older one.

"Big Brother, you're stronger. You ought to go first."

The younger one hurled first, but he only grazed the sun, yet it made Old Man Coyote blink. "Ep, ep, ep, ep," he said, blinking because his eyes hurt.

"You see, Big Brother? If you'd gone first, we could have hit it. The sun would have come out, now. Why don't you try?"

"All right," he said, "I'll do it."

The little one got a big, beautiful rock, and his brother hurled it. He hit the sun right square in the middle, and from then on till today, we've had a sun sitting up in the sky, a beautiful sun. The two doves brought it out.

They went on like that, but early in the morning and in the evening, it kept getting cold. Then Bullet Hawk again said, "Grandpa!"

"What?" he said.

"Can't you get fire anywhere? It gets cold. We could cook with it and eat, too."

"Yes. You and I could get it. I'll fetch my helpers now," he said. "We'll go after that fire by night."

They were going to steal the fire, now. There was a shrew somewhere up in the mountains among the rocks. He was somewhere around there, and his name was Fire Thief, that little shrew. Coyote went for him. "All right, Fire Thief. My grandson wants fire, so get it for me," he said to the shrew.

"I can't do that all by myself. I need Crane and a black cat, too. Weasel and his helpers are guarding that fire. I might get it if those two help me," said Fire Thief.

"All right, we'll get them." They enlisted a black cat and Crane, too. Crane was a sentinel. He watched everything and noticed where everyone was going, since he can see in the dark. When Crane yelled, "Ready!" the cat kicked over the lamp inside Weasel's sweathouse. That's what the crane does; he cries at night. When he sees something, he goes *waak,* the crane at nighttime. That's how they got fire; Fire Thief took it.

After he stole it, Weasel and his helpers came looking for him. "Right here, right here's where he went," they said. Then Fire Thief crawled under the leaves, and they couldn't find him. They looked all over, but he'd hidden the fire inside dead wood, and it looked like white cotton. That's where he stored the coals when he stole fire. That's why we have fire today and build it like that. Bullet Hawk wanted it.

"All right, Grandpa. I want the trees to be green and pretty, too," Bullet Hawk said.

"Fine. That's what we'll get," said Old Man Coyote. "Let me try."

There was nothing on earth a long time ago. Everything was bare—no trees or green grass, no hills either. Old Man Coyote is just like a god—that's how they tell this story. He makes everything, he destroys everything. That's how he runs the earth. The Lake Miwok Indians think of him as a powerful god from above. That's the way the story is told around here. I think all the Indians believe that some of these old stories are true. Wonderful birds, great snakes, wonderful freak birds—the earth was full of wonder a long time ago. But now everything is being improved. The white people have tamed the earth.

I know some plants, too—mush oak, flat tule, young oak, elderberry, gray willow and willow, tan oak, yellow pine—all the trees here have a name, but I forget some of them. I will dictate whatever I know into the tape recorder; smoke brush, pine, elderberry trees, yellow pine—I have named all the trees I know.

When Coyote made all those trees, Bullet Hawk was happy. Coyote named them. Then he put people on the earth last of all. He made them out of sticks— all kinds of sticks, which is why people are here now. White people, there are a lot of white people on the other side of the lake, too. That's how Coyote made us and why we're here now.

This is how they told the story long ago. This is what I heard. I know it because they told me. I'm telling it now, at this time, on this fine day. They used to recite it when it was raining, but I'm repeating it now on a beautiful day. I'm glad that I have this much to say when it's not raining, what I'm telling on a nice day. This is how I'm going to talk, traveling around from one place to another. I'll teach the little ones, so they'll learn, so they'll see, so they'll hear. Then they'll have to tell it, too, someday when the time comes. If someone asks them, they'll say, "Yes, I heard it. My uncle told this. My grandfather told this." That's what they'll say, just as I'm going around now, repeating what my relatives taught me, what I heard. I tell as much as I know. That's all I can do.

That's why everything we have on earth is like what they had long ago. They made lovely things and left fine descriptions. They behaved properly when they made everything and left what we have right here. At that time there was the rule of kindness. That's the way we lived. I'm glad that I'm talking like this today, about how the world was destroyed once. That's what I'm describing, what they wanted and what kind of rules they lived by. They lived by great rules, splendid rules long ago, as the older people have told me.

Everything was filled with wonder long ago: the water, the birds, the trees, the rocks, the mountains, the sun, the fields. They used to sing for these things long ago, the old Indians. That's why they were great. And they knew who was great—they didn't just make it up. Something different made them. People knew deep inside that the Man Above had made them. They knew that's the way it was.

I'm glad I know as much as I do. Take care of my children, take proper care of my grandchildren. Take good care of my friends from now on, so they'll become aware and learn all the rituals, all the songs, the beautiful language.

All right, that's all.

Miguelino Salinan

Snake

Introduction by Katherine Turner

The Miguelino Salinan story that follows is one of the eleven written down by J. Alden Mason on his second trip to the Salinan Indians in 1916. In 1910 J. Alden Mason had transferred from the University of Pennsylvania to the University of California to complete his graduate work in anthropology. He had no experience with linguistic fieldwork and only a sketchy acquaintance with Spanish, but he was soon doing fieldwork with Salinan-Spanish speakers. The next year, 1911, Mason received his doctorate with a dissertation on "The Ethnology of the Salinan Indians." In 1916 Mason had a fellowship at the University of California and returned to his linguistic fieldwork with Salinan. Mason had a speech impediment (stutter) and had no language in common with the Salinan speakers he interviewed, so he hired Spanish interpreters, primarily J. Alonzo Forbes, a justice of the peace. Perhaps this helps explain why he often mixed the two Salinan dialects.

The Salinan language, a member of the Hokan stock, is comprised of two mutually intelligible dialects. The language was spoken in an area of central coastal California. Spanish intrusion came swiftly at the end of the eighteenth century. Two Franciscan missions were established in the area, the first less than two years after the first recorded Spanish expedition in 1769. By 1810 most of the Salinas River Valley groups and peoples from the Inner Coast Ranges were missionized. The death rate was extraordinary in the missions, and the Indians who survived were expected to speak Spanish. By the twentieth century only a handful of fluent speakers remained.

Maria Ocarpia gave this mythological tale of the origin of rattlesnakes to J. Alden Mason in 1916. Ocarpia was also known to other linguists as Maria de Los Angeles. The daughter of Anesmo Bailon, she was first married to Fernando Ocarpio and then to Tito Encinales. She served as a teacher of Miguelino Salinan from 1901, when she worked with A. L. Kroeber, until 1932, when she last worked with J. P. Harrington. Mason describes her as an elderly woman in 1916.

"Snake" shows the Christian influences of the Franciscan missionaries. The story takes place in mythological time and features the personifications of animals and natural phenomena, such as Hawk, Raven, Snake, and Whirlwind. This power-of-place story appears to be part of a larger tale because it is comparatively short. Still, it is a self-contained whole by itself. The "dream-helper" is a West Coast specialization of the "guardian spirit" found throughout almost all of North America. In Salinan the dream-helper was a song *and* a physical object, often a flute. The object was held in the hand to invoke its power. When it was not in use, it was usually hidden in a distant rocky crevice. The dream-helper is found in south central California among the Tulare Yokuts and the Western Mono Indians. There are also a few scanty references to a dream-helper among the Southern Yokuts, the Chumash, and the Kitanemuks.

Based on my experience with other records of the Salinan language, I have retranslated Mason's text after phonemicizing and grammatically analyzing the story and working out a literal translation. With this translation we have a clearer reflection of the beauty of Maria Ocarpia's retelling of this dramatic episode. Of the places mentioned in the story—Me:neka (Maynekah), Lo:yam (Loiyum), and Lesa:m (Laysahm)—only Lesa:m can be identified as the historical Moro Rock.

SUGGESTED READING

Mason, J. Alden. 1912. *The Ethnology of the Salinan Indians.* University of California Publications in Archaeology and Anthropology, vol. 10, no. 4. Berkeley: University of California Press.

———. 1918. *The Language of the Salinan Indians.* University of California Publications in Archaeology and Anthropology, vol. 14, no. 1. Berkeley: University of California Press.

Turner, Katherine. 1988. Salinan Linguistic Materials. *Journal of California and Great Basin Anthropology* 10 (2): 266–70.

Snake

Told by Maria Ocarpia
Translated by Katherine Turner

Snake that ate Indians was born from Whirlwind, which fed it.
Hawk heard it, and Raven said, "What shall we do?
How great are your dream powers?"
Hawk answered, "I have the power to catch Snake. I am ready."
"Good, mine is two or three mountains from here," Raven said.

"Where is that?" asked Hawk.
Raven told him, "At Me:neka."
"Where is that place again?" asked Hawk.
"At Lo:yam. Where's yours?"
"It's around my neck," Hawk answered.
"Good."

Hawk asked again, "Where is that place?"
Raven answered again, "My most potent dream-helper is hidden at Lesa:m."
"Good. I've been there," Hawk said.
"We will target that Snake."

While they were on their way, Snake opened its eyes,
screaming as it woke.
Whirlwind was broken; it snapped.
Whirlwind smashed and broke.

"Good! Run! Let's go now!" they cried.
Snake was coming after them.
"Up!" "No, down!"
"Be strong, use your dream-helper. You can overcome the Snake."

Snake was upon them shouting, "You better remember how to pray!"

Snake was getting nearer.

(Raven) "I am going to cry."
(Hawk) "Don't cry. Use your dream-helper."
(Raven) "O.K. My dream-helper is at Lo:yam."
(Hawk) "Fly up. I remember it at Lesa:m; get it quickly!"
(Raven) "But I am already tired."
(Hawk) "Call upon your power or the Snake will get it. Up! Go!"

Hawk hurtled upward ahead of Snake.
Snake was already winding itself around Lesa:m from below
when Raven and Hawk got there and landed at the top.

Snake coiled itself around and around Lesa:m.
Hawk jumped and grabbed his dream-helper.
He killed Snake, cutting it into four pieces.

That is why there are rattlesnakes.
Coyote also has poison.
There are little rattlesnakes at the coast.

Snake said, "Live forever."
"I am dead but they live."

Yana

Young Blue Jay's Journey to the Land of the New Moon

Introduction by Herbert W. Luthin

Little is known of Sam Batwi, the narrator of this tale, and that little is quickly told. He was one of the Yanas, the "People," and spoke the Gataa'i dialect of his language, which makes him what we today would call a Central Yana. (Apparently he spoke a more southern dialect as a child, though by the time he dictated this story of Young Blue Jay's adventures to the linguist Edward Sapir in 1907, there were so few Southern Yana speakers left that he remembered but little of his childhood dialect.) His father was a Central Yana, his mother Southern Yana and Maidu. He married a Central Yana woman, though, which probably explains his ultimate shift to the Central dialect. Indeed, having lived for so long with only his wife to talk Yana with, he found himself a bit rusty in the use of the special "male" patterns of speech that Yana men used among themselves and frequently slipped into "female" speech during his sessions with Sapir—a tendency that seems to have amused them both.

Sam Batwi was no stranger to the role of linguistic consultant. Over the course of his life, he worked as an interpreter for Jeremiah Curtin on Curtin's 1895 tour through Yana territory and subsequently served both Roland Dixon and Sapir as a consultant for Central Yana, providing them with narratives and grammatical information. (The nine narratives he gave Sapir are published in Sapir's *Yana Texts*, the present story being the fourth in that sequence.) Later, following the discovery of Ishi, the last Yahi Indian, in 1911, Sam was brought down to Berkeley to help interpret Ishi's closely related dialect.[1]

THE YANAS

The Yanas were a mountain people, living on the long, rugged western slopes and plateaus of Wahganup'a, or Mount Lassen, as it is now called. They hunted deer and waterfowl, trapped small game, fished for salmon in the tributaries of the upper Sacramento, and gathered the seasonal bounty of acorns, pine nuts, roots, seeds, and berries. Their language, spoken in four close dialects, forms one of the dozen or so branches of the ancient Hokan language phylum, which means that they and their ancestors had been "Californians" for as many as ten thousand years—until they were rubbed out as a people by American soldiers and settlers during the holocaust years of the gold rush. (Sam Batwi, an old man at the time of his work with Sapir and Ishi, must have been one of the last few Yanas to speak their language fluently, or even to think of themselves primarily as Yanas.)

From what we know of California prehistory, it is likely that the Yanas were not always mountain dwellers, at least not exclusively. But with the expansion of the Penutian-speaking ancestral Wintus into and down the Sacramento Valley about two thousand years ago (Whistler 1977), the ancestral Yanas must have been forced off the richer, more luxurious bottom lands of the Big Valley and pressed up into the rough high country, where they learned to live small and hardy and acquired a reputation for being scrappy, tough survivors (Kroeber 1925, 336).

THE STORY

I mention this migration scenario not just for its own intrinsic interest but because key aspects of the story presented here, recounting Young Blue Jay's journey to the land of the New Moon people, may actually manifest tensions that derive—ultimately—from this age-old shift in status quo. Oral history done in the early decades of the twentieth century suggests that the Yanas traditionally held at least some stretches of the east bank of the Sacramento River, though perhaps only seasonally, and tenuously at that (Sapir and Spier 1943, 241–42). Against their more powerful and numerous Wintu neighbors, the Yanas necessarily refrained from full-scale conflict.[2] Skirmishes, such as the ones described in Ishi's "A Story of Lizard" (Hinton and Luthin 2002), must long have been the Yanan response strategy—but skirmishing, as a rule, doesn't secure large tracts of contested land for long, especially against a populous rival.[3]

In the story New Moon is the chief of a fair-sized Yana village on the Sacramento shore—the extreme western edge of the Yana homeland—directly across the wide river from an extensive Wintu settlement, described in the story as being large enough to boast six chiefs.[4] New Moon has gotten a bad reputation throughout the region for magically poisoning any young man who comes to seek his daughter's hand in marriage.[5] Despite the danger (or because of it; a hero needs glory, after all), Young Blue Jay, who has his own reasons for seeking his manhood early, arrives to challenge New Moon for his daughter's hand. With the help of his Uncle Silkworm, he succeeds.

The story of Young Blue Jay's journey is divided into three main parts. Part I outlines the unwell state-of-affairs back home that drives Young Blue Jay to his quest, and part II details his triumph over New Moon. Part III, in resolving both spheres of conflict, ultimately concerns nothing less than the preservation of the

Yana homeland itself. If the Yanas could not risk all-out conflict with the Wintus, at the same time no Yana group could afford to show weakness against such powerful neighbors. So when the Yaa'wis of the story, inexplicably enraged by Young Blue Jay's presence across the river, challenge the New Moon villagers to a salmon competition and begin besting them in a humiliating manner, Young Blue Jay, as the newly resident hero, has no choice but to step in to salvage the village's reputation. (New Moon himself seems to lose both nerve and authority once his tobacco magic is rendered ineffectual.) This he does, in a series of three increasingly nasty encounters with the Yaa'wis and their animal assassins. Finally, though, having renewed Yanan sovereignty over this stretch of the Sacramento, restored health and balance to New Moon Village, and won high-ranking brides for himself and his brother, Young Blue Jay packs up and heads back to the land of his birth. His *own* reputation—and by extension, of Blue Jays everywhere, who have been generically "tarred" by the behavior of his father—has been reclaimed in the process.

Sapir categorizes this story as "one of the suitor tales characteristic of Northern California" (1910, 66). Yet, despite the centrality of courtship to the story as a whole—part I sets up the conditions that necessitate Young Blue Jay's exogamy, part II accomplishes it, and part III explores the consequences in terms of the expanded political responsibilities it entails—Sam Batwi's story of Young Blue Jay is a far cry from a love story. Winning the chief's daughter seems to be little more than a by-product of foiling her father at his deadly game; indeed, it is presented as little more than an afterthought. Once he has told it, Batwi pays this element of his plot no further attention at all. Instead, "Young Blue Jay's Journey" is much more a hero tale than a romance, failing at the latter genre in much the same way that the early Middle English protoromance *King Horn* does. And that makes the extraordinary portrait of domestic life and marital strife in part I all the more striking.

Mic'aahba ay K'ec'iwaala, Batwi notes in the opening passage of the story: "Blue Jay always had good luck."[6] In a sense the story that follows is an account of how he *lost* his luck—a fall from grace that sets the stage for the still more glorious restoration of the Blue Jay lineage and its hereditary luck by his firstborn son. As the story unfolds, it is clear that the father's downfall is entirely self-inflicted. Unable to tear himself away from the hunt, he becomes increasingly careless of the taboos associated with pregnancy and childbirth. He even fails to come home for either of his wife's two births. Wildcat Woman is forced to care for her newborns by herself, bathing each one alone in the night after her labor. Indeed, the story may be implying that Blue Jay's excessive absences from home have opened the door for his cuckold's paranoia over the parentage of his second son, who apparently takes after Wildcat Woman rather than Blue Jay himself. His suspicion, once entertained, becomes an obsession, and he begins behaving abominably, throwing the infant out the smoke hole of their house and eventually banishing mother and child from the home altogether. Young Blue Jay, growing up with a magical rapidity that betokens his destiny as a hero, resolves to right his father's wrong, and as part I closes, the two boys run away from home.

From this point on, Blue Jay *per*, having squandered his luck, spoiled his reputation, and destroyed his family in a fit of jealous rage, ceases to be a significant figure in the story, and the torch is passed to Blue Jay *fils*. Once the latter's adventures begin in earnest, we never again return to the lingering, intimate domesticity that Batwi portrays in part I, with its dandling scenes and midnight bathings, its children's games, its tears and fights, and its bitter, irremediable remorse.

In a sense, then, the audience gets to have it all: Sam Batwi's story runs the stylistic gamut from domestic melodrama to supernatural horror story to action-adventure tale. It's a rich narration whose multiple depths I've only been able to suggest in this introduction.

THE TRANSLATION

My efforts to bring Sam Batwi's stories into latter-day English would be impossible without Sapir's antecedent. Because the language is extinct, there are no living speakers we can turn to now for clarification of a line or passage. Virtually everything we know of Central Yana comes from Sam Batwi's lips via the stories glossed and translated by Sapir in *Yana Texts*. Thus when Sapir says that *Wawulpawsik'uwa'a, na gasi'wanaa'i* means 'He must have been come to for wooing, therefore they are making merry', we have little choice today but to take him at his word. My debt to Sapir's earlier analysis and translation is therefore profound and one I'd like to acknowledge properly here, with gratitude for his keen ear and clarity of expression — much of which has, of necessity, persevered into the present translation. That said, I have tried nonetheless to do more than merely modernize Sapir's now somewhat formal-sounding translational style. For instance, a micro-analysis of the quoted line reveals that the words parse this way:[7]

> wa-wul-paw-si-k'u-waʔa,
> woo-entering-to him-PRES-DUB-PASS

> na   gasi-ʔwanaa-ʔi
> therefore   celebrate-son·in·law-INF

From these nuts and bolts I can make a new go of it: "Someone must have come in courting to him, / so they are celebrating the son-in-law." Thus the present translation is at once more literal than that of Sapir, who had a tendency to fold contextual information into his glosses, and less formal.[8]

Sam Batwi was a fine traditional storyteller and must have been in great demand around the campfire and the kitchen table. If he had children, which he most likely did, they must always have been clamoring for "just one more." At any rate, from examining his performances in Sapir's *Yana Texts,* there is little evidence that his talent had grown rusty from disuse, as can sometimes happen when elders are dragged out of "retirement" by inquiring linguists or heritage-minded in-laws with tape-recorders, though exactly who his audience was at this late stage in the Yana demise is not clear—his wife, perhaps. Regardless, his stories are not mere bare-bones treatments but fully developed and well-imagined performances. Ribald and stately, comic and serious, fantastical and matter-of-fact by turns, his narratives possess a surprising, essential liveliness. Somehow, in delivering these stories to Sapir, Sam Batwi managed to transcend the deadening effects of the dictation process, which is how Sapir took his words down more than ninety years ago: phrase by phrase, by hand, in detailed phonetic transcription. I have worked with the Sapir/Batwi texts off and on now for more than a decade and have always found great pleasure in translating the fruits of their work together. This story was no exception.

NOTES

1. Theodora Kroeber's biography of Ishi, *Ishi in Two Worlds,* includes some photos of Sam Batwi with Ishi and A. L. Kroeber. The book's cultural background on the Yahi people transfers well to the Central Yanas, too.

2. The Yanas called their Wintu neighbors the Yaa'wi, with whom they were—at least in recent times, if not in myth-time—on terms of "chronic friendliness" (Kroeber 1925, 340).

3. Kroeber, after noting the Yanan reputation for superior "military prowess and cunning," observes: "The hill dweller has less to lose by fighting than the wealthy lowlander. He is also less exposed, and in time of need, has better and more numerous refuges available. All through California, the plains peoples were the more peaceably inclined, although the stronger in numbers" (Kroeber 1925, 336).

4. This unusual number of chiefs is possibly the temporary result of some special or seasonal ceremonial gathering, rather than a full-time complement. In any case, the number implies that the Yaa'wi settlement is *much* larger than New Moon Village during the time frame of the story.

5. This proclivity seems to alternately delight and appall the neighboring Yaa'wis, who keep a keen gossip's eye on the goings-on at New Moon Village. (New Moon's scary, homicidal sorcery may indirectly protect his village by making the Yaa'wis leery of getting mixed up with his people.)

6. From this statement we can see how intimately the concepts of *luck* and *observance* are intertwined in Yanan philosophy.

7. Abbreviations: DUB = dubitative mode; INF = infinitive; PASS = passive voice; PRES = present tense. The verb takes passive form because the true subject (the "agent") is unspecified and of less importance to the story than the dative object (i.e., New Moon).

8. Out of a preference for ethnopoetic presentation, I have also broken the text into

lines, each of which, for the most part, represents a syntactic sentence—that is, one independent clause, together with any appositives or subordinates attendant upon it. Each such sentence begins flush left; successively indented lines indicate extensions of the main clause that exhibit linguistic evidence for separate prosodic phrasing. The division into numbered sections is based largely on the occurrence of the discourse suffix -'anti 'now' and various scene-shifting temporal phrases, such as "In the morning" and the like. The divisions into scenes and parts are not manifest in the original; I've added them as guideposts for the reader.

SUGGESTED READING AND REFERENCES

The complete Native-language text of this story may be found in Sapir's *Yana Texts* (1910), where it is accompanied by word-by-word interlinear glosses and a free translation. Eight other Batwi stories are included in this collection, along with a comparable sampling of Northern Yana narratives. Curtin's *Creation Myths of Primitive America* ([1898] 1967) presents English versions of nine more Yana myths. For ethnography, see Sapir and Spier's *Notes on the Culture of the Yana* (1943) and Kroeber's entry on the Yanas in his *Handbook of the Indians of California* (1925). There is no real grammar of the Yanan languages, though Sapir and Swadesh's *Yana Dictionary* (1960) contains a brief grammatical sketch. An overview of California linguistic prehistory may be found in Foster's "Language and the Culture History of North America" (1996). For more on ethnopoetic presentation, see Luthin 1991, Hymes 1981, and Tedlock 1983.

Curtin, Jeremiah. [1898] 1967. *Creation Myths of Primitive America, in Relation to the Religious History and Development of Mankind.* Reprint, New York: Benjamin Blom.

Foster, Michael K. 1996. "Language and the Culture History of North America." In *Handbook of North American Indians,* vol. 17, *Languages,* edited by Ives Goddard. Washington: Smithsonian Institution.

Hinton, Leanne, and Herbert W. Luthin. 2002. "A Story of Lizard." In *Surviving through the Days: Translations of Native California Stories and Songs,* edited by Herbert W. Luthin. Berkeley: University of California Press.

Hymes, Dell. 1981. *"In Vain I Tried to Tell You": Essays on Native American Ethnopoetics.* Philadelphia: University of Pennsylvania Press.

Kroeber, Alfred L. 1925. *Handbook of the Indians of California.* Berkeley: California Book Company.

Kroeber, Theodora. 1963. *Ishi in Two Worlds: A Biography of the Last Wild Indian in North America.* Berkeley: University of California Press.

Luthin, Herbert W. 1991. "Restoring the Voice in Yanan Traditional Narrative: Prosody, Performance, and Presentational Form." Ph.D. diss., University of California at Berkeley.

Sapir, Edward. 1910. *Yana Texts (together with Yana Myths, collected by Roland B. Dixon).* University of California Publications in Archaeology and Ethnology, vol. 9, no. 1. Berkeley: University of California Press.

Sapir, Edward, and Leslie Spier. 1943. *Notes on the Culture of the Yana.* University of California Anthropological Records, vol. 3, no. 3. Berkeley: University of California Press.

Sapir, Edward, and Morris Swadesh. 1960. *Yana Dictionary.* Edited by Mary Haas. University of California Publications in Linguistics, no. 22. Berkeley: University of California Press.

Tedlock, Dennis. 1983. *The Spoken Word and the Work of Interpretation.* Philadelphia: University of Pennsylvania Press.

Whistler, Kenneth W. 1977. "Wintun Prehistory: An Interpretation Based on Linguistic Reconstruction of Plant and Animal Nomenclature." *Proceedings of the Annual Meeting of the Berkeley Linguistics Society* 3:157–74.

Young Blue Jay's Journey to the Land of the New Moon

Told by Sam Batwi
Translated by Herbert W. Luthin

I. THE STORY BEGINS

1   There were lots of people there, they say,
       dwelling there with Blue Jay.
    He had a sweat house, they say—
       for killing deer.
    Blue Jay had Wildcat Woman as a wife.
    Wildcat Woman was pregnant,
       while Blue Jay was off killing deer.
    Blue Jay always had good luck.
    He had deer meat hanging all over the place to dry.

II. WILDCAT WOMAN GIVES BLUE JAY A SON

2   It rained, it snowed.

3   Now the woman gave birth to a child, they say,
    gave birth in the house-place, inside;
    Blue Jay's not there watching while she gives birth to her child.
    Wildcat Woman bathed him,
       her child.
    Blue Jay arrived back home.
    "I have a baby," said Wildcat Woman,
       speaking to Blue Jay.
    "Ah!"
    He spoke in a small voice, they say;
    he spoke just drawling it out slowly, they say,
       answering her.

4   Now, in the night, now she's bathing her child.

5   In the morning, Blue Jay stood outside the house.[1]
           He shouted around to them,
               waking up the people:
           "Get up, everybody!"
           He was heard shouting east;
           he was heard shouting west.
           "Flake your flints!
           Warm up your bows at the fire!
           Let's find some deer!"

                                III. BLUE JAY DELIGHTS IN HIS CHILD

6   So the people did,
           they got up before it was day.

7   Now the people went off deer hunting.
           "I'll just go along beside them," said Blue Jay.
           "I've had a child born to me."

8   Now these people go off,
               these other people,
                   deer hunting now.
           Blue Jay did not hunt deer;
           he merely went along.

9   Blue Jay arrived back home after dark,
           sat down at his seat.
           Blue Jay had a child, they say, just one.
           It's only two days that he's been growing.
           "Give me the child!"
           Wildcat Woman,
               she placed it in his arms.
           Blue Jay fondled him in his arms.
           "He is very good, very good, our child!"
           He played with his child.

1. The generic Yana word for "house" translates literally as 'sweat house', though it's the regular permanent dwelling place that's meant, not an actual sweat house. I have translated simply 'house', to avoid any confusion.

10   Now he grew older, they say,
           the already-a-toddler Little Blue Jay.
      The youngster looked just like the elder, they say.

                    IV. WILDCAT WOMAN BEARS ANOTHER SON

11   Young Blue Jay played outside.
      He played at rolling a ball uphill, Young Blue Jay,
           on a hillside a little ways off to the south.
      It was smooth downhill to the south.

12   It was morning again.
      Blue Jay went outside,
      shouted around to them:
      "Wake up, everybody!
      Hunt the deer!"
      Rising up, the people did so.

13   Now they went off deer hunting.
      Blue Jay,
           he arrived back home after dark.
      "I am pregnant for you again now," said Wildcat Woman—
           she spoke to Blue Jay.
      Blue Jay laughed,
           as the woman was telling him.

14   It was morning again.
      Blue Jay went off,
      went east, they say,
           not really deer hunting,
                merely going about.
      She gave birth to a child again,
      gave birth to a child over on the north side.
      (Blue Jay always lay over there on the south side.)
      Blue Jay arrived back home.

15   Now she had another baby.
      "I have given birth to a child," she's telling Blue Jay.
      "Aah! That's good!"   *said Blue Jay*

16   Now the woman's bathing it in the night.

17   In the morning, Blue Jay didn't go away.
       "Give him to me!" they say he said.
       The Young Blue Jay was playing outside,
           playing at rolling a ball uphill.
       He made a hill-rolling ball out of a buckeye, they say.

18   Every morning, she gave her child to Blue Jay in his arms.
       He held his child in his arms,
       looked at his baby's eyes, they say.

V. BLUE JAY BELIEVES HIMSELF A CUCKOLD

19   It snowed down snow outside.
       Blue Jay was angry:
       "I don't like your child," he told his wife.
       He gave it back to her;
       she took her child back into her arms.
       "This one here is not my child —
       another man has given the child to you."
       The woman cried,
           the way Blue Jay had spoken to her.
       "Go outside!" Blue Jay said to the woman,
       "Stay outside!
       I don't like you staying in the house.
       Keep your baby outside!"
       But the woman's not going outside.

20   Now Blue Jay rose up:
       "Hand over your child!"
       Blue Jay,
           now he snatched her child away from her,
       threw the child out the smoke hole to the north.
       The woman's crying,
           weeping for her child.
       "I am not the one whose child that is!
       His eyes are big;
       he is big-eyed.
       Look at his hands!
       Those don't look like my hands," said Blue Jay,
           speaking to the woman.
       "Your child doesn't even have a crest on his head —

YOUNG BLUE JAY'S JOURNEY

he doesn't!"

So Blue Jay rejected him as his child.

"*My* child is the one outside;

he *does* have a crest on his head."

The woman went outside after it,

came back into the house with her child in her arms.

Blue Jay snatched it away from her again.

Again he threw it back north through the smoke hole.

"Get out! Get out! Get out!"

The woman,

   she gathered her child back up into her arms.

Weeping, the woman did not go back into the house.

21   Now she stayed outside,

          building a house out there with dead bark,

              the woman.

VI. THE CHILDREN RUN AWAY FROM HOME

22   By and by the Young Wildcat ran around.

      "Why is it that you stay outside, Mother?"   *Young Blue Jay asked*

      "He has driven me out of the house."

      "Mother!

      I'm going to play right there a little south on the side of that hill,

      I'm taking him along there."   *said Young Blue Jay*

      "Take him along! Take him along!

      Play with him! Play with him!"

23   Now they went off, going out to play;

      now they played all day, a little to the south on the side of the hill.

24   Now they went west, in play.

      Young Wildcat had grown older.

      Young Blue Jay sat down on a rock.

      Young Blue Jay looked around, thinking.

      "Hmm, hmm," Young Blue Jay said in his heart:

      "The way you've thrown my brother out of doors, Father . . ."

      He stood up.

25   Now they went west all day.

      They went as far as Wiicuma'na.

They played at bathing.
"You will not see *me* again, Father!"
Wildcat Woman shouted for them,
   her children;
they were gone.

26   Now the woman ran around,
      looking for them now,
        not finding her children.
    Blue Jay did the same,
      looking for them.

27   Now Blue Jay wept.
    He put dirt on his face.
    "Waaiii!" Blue Jay said.
    "Come back, Son!
    How could you have done this?"

28   Now Young Blue Jay and Young Wildcat   *i.e., "Meanwhile . . ."*
        went west.
    They went as far as Jicintpaamawna.
    Young Blue Jay sat down.

29   Now they're weeping in the east.
    Young Blue Jay stood up,
    went as far as C'iiyu,
    remained there.

PART II

VII. YOUNG BLUE JAY VISITS UNCLE SILKWORM

30   Silkworm dwelled at C'iiyu, they say, alone.
    "Let's go that far and rest overnight with our uncle,"
      he told Young Wildcat.   *Young Blue Jay did*
    "May there suddenly be:
      bows, two of them,
        and many arrows!
    May there suddenly be:
     otter-skin quivers,
       filled with arrows!"

It happened like that:
    arrows and bows appeared to them.

31   Now they shot,
      shooting arrows against each other.   *in sport*
    Both kept shooting with all their might, they say.
    Young Blue Jay shot,
    shot it up there, way far off to the south.
    "Ready, shoot!" Young Blue Jay said.

32   Now Young Wildcat shot,
    shot his arrow up there, way far off.
    "That's pretty good now," Young Blue Jay said.
    Young Blue Jay slung the otter-skin quiver over his shoulder;
    Young Wildcat did the same.

33   Now they went west when it got dark.
    They looked into the house;
    Young Blue Jay went inside Silkworm's house.
    He had his javelin sticking in the ground beside his sitting-place, they
        say.
    Silkworm looked outside.
    "Hey!" said Silkworm, they say.
    He reached back for his javelin.
    "Who are you two?"
    "It's me, Uncle!"
    "'It's me,' do you say!
    Aha!" Silkworm said.
    "Sit yourselves down!"

The two sat down, they say.

    "Why have you run away from there?"
    "We're the ones who started out from Ba'nxa."
    "Aha!"
    "My father has thrown my brother here out the house,
      rejecting him as his child."
    "Aha!" the old man said.
    "Where is it you are going?"
    "Me, I'm about to go out after New Moon Chief."

(New Moon Chief lived to the west on this side of the river, they say.)

"I'm going to court his daughter,
I want his daughter."
"Aha!" said Silkworm.
"Hey-hey! That one's being bad.
Many people has he killed so far,
    for coming to woo his child.
And he has killed all those people."

(His children, his own people, were numerous,   *New Moon's*
        they say.)

"How do they say they are being killed?"   *asked Young Blue Jay*
"He fills his pipe with dead people's bones.
He makes tobacco from dead people's bones.
He fills his pipe with dead people's brains," Silkworm said.
"He smokes first,
then offers the people his pipe.
The people smoke who have come to woo —
they smoke,
and then they drop down dead.
New Moon Chief,
    he throws them north through the smoke hole,
        once they've died.
So there are a lot of them there,
    these dead people."

VIII. YOUNG BLUE JAY CHALLENGES NEW MOON

34   Young Blue Jay's been listening to him:
      "Well then! Let's go after him!"
      "I'm going with you," Silkworm said.
      "O nephews!"

35   Now they went west,
      now they went downhill to the west.
      There were two women,
          they were sitting over on the east side of the house, they say.
      Blue Jay tied his hair up into a topknot, they say,
      put a wrap around his hair, they say.

"Set me down in your hair," said Silkworm.

He sat down in there, they say.

"I shall look down from your south side, like this," Silkworm said.

"If you go into the house,
   pray do like this:

pray sit with your back to the west,   *so as not to be seen*
   if you sit."

Silkworm spoke,
   as if talking to himself.   *whispering?*

36   Now they entered the house during the night;
      now they sat down with the women.
      New Moon Chief turned to look;
      he looked across east.
      "What sort of person is that one over there?"
      "I don't know, he is a stranger."
      "Get the pipe!
      I'm going to fill it with tobacco."

37   Now he rolled his tobacco around between his hands,
      now he filled it up,
      now New Moon Chief smoked.
      "Well now!
      Offer it to my 'son-in-law'!
      My son-in-law will be smoking."
      The woman herself carried the pipe.
      "Take it," the woman told Young Blue Jay.

38   Now Young Blue Jay smoked.
      (But Young Blue Jay's not really smoking;
      Silkworm, *he* smoked the dead people's bones.)
      He knocked out the ashes,   *Blue Jay*
      handed him back the pipe.
      He filled up his pipe again.   *New Moon*
      "Why is it, then, that he doesn't just perish?"
         New Moon said in his heart.
      New Moon filled up his pipe yet again.
      "Well now!
      Give it to my 'son-in-law,'
      he will smoke."

Young Blue Jay, he smoked.
New Moon, he looked across east.
"Why is it, then, that he won't perish?"
(But truly, they say, it was *him* there, Silkworm, who smoked—
Young Blue Jay just *acted* like he was the one who smoked, they say.
Young Wildcat was another one who didn't smoke, they say.)

39   Now New Moon was afraid:
Young Blue Jay did not perish.
He stopped filling up his pipe with tobacco.

40   In the middle of the night,
     Young Blue Jay unwrapped his hair.
He took him out of there,
     Silkworm, from his hair hiding place!
He put him over to the north by the ladder near the fireplace.
Silkworm went to sleep.
Silkworm wrapped his blanket about himself,
     sleeping by the ladder near the fireplace.[2]
New Moon's not seeing Silkworm.

IX. YOUNG BLUE JAY WORKS A MIRACLE WITH DEER FAT

41   "We are meatless people,
our deer meat just isn't there to be eaten," she said, so they say!

In the morning that's what the woman was saying to him.
Said Young Blue Jay,
     "Ah! Give me a basket pan!"
He had put a big, round lump of deer fat in his quiver, they say.

42   Now Young Blue Jay cut the deer fat down in slices into the basket pan,
          they say.
He gave it to New Moon.
"Give me another basket pan!"
One was given to him.
He cut the deer fat down in slices,
     gave it to him again,

2. The foot of the smoke-hole ladder was traditionally the spot where persons of low social station were relegated. Silkworm's positioning himself here may have been a way of disguising his presence: no one would pay him any attention there.

placed it over on the west side.

"Give me another basket pan!" said Young Blue Jay.

Talking to the deer fat:

    "Don't disappear completely!

      Keep on being big!"

At last the deer fat was gone.

PART III

X. THE YAA'WIS CHALLENGE THE NEW MOONS

43   "Do go ahead east across the river!" said the Yaa'wis.

"They are celebrating a suitor across the river to the east.

They don't usually sound like that."

That's what they were saying.

"Someone must have come in courting to him,

    so they are celebrating the son-in-law."

One person went east across the river.

44   Now one did so east across the river.

That one person saw Young Blue Jay and Young Wildcat.

"Hey!"   *said New Moon*

He chucked rocks at him.   *New Moon did*

"What is it *you're* looking at?

Do you think *I'm* the one who's dead?" New Moon said.

The Yaa'wi ran off back home,

hurried back cross river to the west.

"Someone has come courting to him,"

    the Yaa'wi is telling them.

(Many are the Yaa'wis on the west side of the river.)

"Have you seen him?" said the Yaa'wis.

"Oh, yes!"

"Who do they say he is?"

"An Easterner."[3]

"Aha!"

All the Yaa'wis were angry:

    Fish Hawk Chief,

    Crane Chief,

    the chief of the Yaa'wis,

---

3. The Yana word translated here as 'Easterner' is Chunooyaa, the Yana designation for Hat Creek Indian—in short, an Atsugewi. It's possible that the Yaa'wis are under the impression that Young Blue Jay and Young Wildcat are Atsugewis, not Yanas.

the Heron Chief,
the Yaa'wi Salmon Trout Chief,
the Big Acorn Pestle—
    that many were chiefs, they say.
"What are we going to do?" said the Yaa'wis.
"Let us go salmon fishing!"

45   So now they did salmon fishing,
    shooting for salmon in the water at the river place.
"Hurry east across the river!
Go and get the New Moon people!"   *said Fish Hawk*
One went to get them:
"Fish Hawk is salmon fishing!
You all have been sent for!"
"Aha!" said the New Moon people.

XI. THE YAA'WIS CALL FOR A SALMON-SPEARING CONTEST

46   They shot for salmon.
New Moon's people speared salmon,
but they pulled the salmon across to the   *Fish Hawk's people*
        west side—
Fish Hawk's people pulled them across to the west side,
    not letting them have any salmon.
"Where is he?" said the Yaa'wis.
"Where is this friend come from the east?"

"Don't you two go away!" the woman said to Young Blue Jay.
"Stay right here at home!"
"We are tired," said Young Blue Jay.
"We're going to watch the people shooting for salmon;
we're going off after them."

47   So they did;
    they went off after them,
        he and Young Wildcat.
They stood around at the river place, they say.
"Hey-hey! It's the two friends from the east!"   *said the Yaa'wis*
They looked east across the river.
They hadn't taken any salmon out of the water;   *the New Moon people*
only the Yaa'wis had a lot of salmon.

"Give it to me!" said Young Blue Jay to his wife's brothers.[4]

"Give me that salmon-spear shaft;

I'm going to shoot for salmon."

He was given the salmon-spear shaft.

Fish Hawk, he did his salmon shooting like this,   *gesturing*

       they say.

There was one big salmon in the middle of the river, they say.

48   Now Young Blue Jay shot at the salmon.

Young Blue Jay speared the salmon,

and Fish Hawk speared the salmon, too—

    the same salmon.

Fish Hawk,

    he pulled the salmon across to the west side,

      hard.

Young Blue Jay did likewise,

    hard,

      so hard he pulled the salmon across to the east side.

Young Blue Jay jerked it across to the east side,

    the salmon together with his spear-shaft.   *Fish Hawk's*

He pulled it right out of his hand!

Blue Jay and the New Moon people went off back home.

Young Blue Jay packed the salmon back home on his back.

Said the Yaa'wis:

    "Hey! He has beaten us out,

      this Easterner."

XII. THE YAA'WIS SEEK REVENGE WITH A WATER GRIZZLY

49   "What are we going to do?" said Fish Hawk.

"Let us fish with the seine net;

let us go seine-net fishing!

Go get New Moon!

Let us go seine-net fishing tomorrow."

One hastened east across the river.

"You all have been sent for!"

---

4. From this oblique reference we learn that Young Blue Jay's marriage to the chief's daughter has taken place off-scene. (It is also just possible that Young Blue Jay's odd remark, "We are tired," ten lines earlier is an equally oblique reference to a surfeit of lovemaking in the aftermath of their double wedding ceremony. Batwi's narrative priorities seem to lie elsewhere here, but such ribald humor is by no means beyond him.)

"Aha!" said New Moon.

50   Now many of the New Moons went off.
        "Go!" Fish Hawk said.
        They swam into the water,
            seine-net fishing.
        They put in a water grizzly, they say.[5]
        "Pray catch Young Blue Jay!"
            the Yaa'wis told that water grizzly there, they say.

51   Now the water grizzly stayed in the water,
            deep down.

52   Well!
        He swam in the water —
            now Young Blue Jay swam south in the water with a seine net.
        The salmon did not swim into the net,
            having already done otherwise themselves,
                swum south already to the river place.
        There were ten people,
            five Yaa'wis,
                five New Moon people.

53   Suddenly he was pulled down at the river place!
        The water grizzly,
            now he caught Young Blue Jay.
        Young Blue Jay did not come up again from the river place.
        The commoners all started out of the water;
        no longer did they fish with seine nets, then.

54   Now the Yaa'wis shouted.
        He got dragged back down into the river place by the water grizzly.

55   Now all the New Moon people are weeping for him;
        now they're going back home to cry!
        "He is dead, my sister's husband;
        he has been pulled under by the water grizzly."

5. A mythological creature common to several Northern California cultures.

56   Now the Yaa'wis are shouting,
            clapping their hands.

XIII. YOUNG BLUE JAY IN THE WATER GRIZZLY'S DEN

57   Young Blue Jay, he spoke to the water grizzly:
        "It's me, Uncle!"
        "Aah!" said the water grizzly,
        "It *could* be you . . .
        Take off my skin!"

58   Now he did so,
            now he skinned the water grizzly.
        The water grizzly had not killed Young Blue Jay, after all!
        "Take my hide home with you,
            go on back home!"
                said the water grizzly to Young Blue Jay.
        "This here hide of mine,
            pray hang it up outside the house!"

59   Now Young Blue Jay went back home from the river place.
        Now he hung up the water grizzly hide,
            having now arrived back home.

        Said Young Wildcat:[6]
            "Hold in your weeping, all of you!"
                — speaking to the New Moon people.
        "Maybe he's not dead, Young Blue Jay;
            soon he may come back home."
        They wept no more;
        they put down their weeping.

XIV. THE YAA'WIS SEEK REVENGE WITH A RATTLESNAKE

60   "Listen!" the Yaa'wis said.
        "They have put down their weeping.
        One of you ought to go on east across the river!
        Go to see!" said the Yaa'wis.

---

6. The remaining lines of this scene have a kind of "meanwhile back at the ranch" function, backtracking in time in order to dwell further on the grieving rites mentioned earlier.

One Yaa'wi hurried east across the river,
   going to see.
The water grizzly hide was hanging up outside!
The Yaa'wi hurried on back,
   having seen the water grizzly hide.

61   Now he reported to the Yaa'wis:
"The water grizzly has been killed;
Young Blue Jay has made it back home."

62   Now those Yaa'wis wept,
   weeping for their water grizzly.
"What are we going to do?" the Yaa'wis said.
"Let's go deer hunting!
Let us make a rattlesnake!
Someone go get the New Moon people!"

63   Now they did so,
   going west across the river,
      deer hunting.
The rattlesnake was put down along the trail place.
The Yaa'wis went north,
   deer hunting.
"Where are the Easterners?"   *said the Yaa'wis*
"That's probably them there,
   coming from the south,"
     the New Moon people told the Yaa'wis.
Just then those two came up from the south along the trail.
They had let the rattlesnake down on the ground   *the Yaa'wis*
     at the trail place—
   it was coiled up around some brush.
Young Blue Jay stepped on the rattlesnake.
The rattlesnake darted up!
The rattlesnake wound around his legs,
   coiling itself all around him now.
He trampled it down with his feet,
pounded the rattlesnake all up with his feet,
cut it into pieces with his feet, Young Blue Jay did.
He killed that rattlesnake.

64   Now the Yaa'wis wept for themselves once more,

their rattlesnake having been killed.

65   Now Young Blue Jay went on back home.

XV. YOUNG BLUE JAY RETURNS HOME

66   "Come morning, I'm going to go back home,"
        Young Blue Jay said to his wife.
    "Tell the New Moon people for me:
    I'm going on back home.
    I am now tired of this place here.
    You two could come home with us,   *their new wives*
        if you wanted to,"
            he said to his wife, they say.

    "He's going to be going back home,"
        she told New Moon, her father.
    Said the old man:
        "Aah! His is right; his way is right."

67   Now he's going on back home when morning comes,
        together with his wife.

68   Now he went back east,
        back as far as Jiicintpaamawna,
            back as far as Wiicuma'na.
    "Get closer, Place!
    Don't be so far away!"
    He went back as far as Xawp'uk'ayna.

69   Now he arrived back home to the old place of his father,
        the old place of his mother.

Quechan

Old Lady San^yu·xáv

Introduction by Amy Miller

The Quechan (also known as Kwtsaan or Yuma) people once lived along the flood-plain of the lower Colorado River, between Blythe, California, and the Colorado Delta. Their population is estimated to have numbered between four and five thousand at the time of first contact with whites. Today the Quechan Indian Nation occupies the Fort Yuma Indian Reservation, located on a portion of their original territory on the west side of the Colorado near its confluence with the Gila River.

The Quechan language, often referred to as Yuma, belongs to the Yuman family (which extends from western Arizona through much of San Diego County, California, and into Baja California). It is now spoken fluently by fewer than 150 people. Abraham M. Halpern began work on this language in the 1930s, and his grammar later appeared as a series of articles in the *International Journal of American Linguistics*. In the 1970s, after retiring from a career in international relations, he returned to the study of Quechan language, literature, and culture. He published bilingual versions of numerous stories, songs, and personal reminiscences, as well as detailed descriptions by Quechan elders of the mourning ceremony known as the Kar²úk. Halpern's legacy also includes a large collection of oral literature, ethnographic information, and local history, recorded on cassette tape in the Quechan language.

The story of Old Lady San^yu·xáv that appears here was recorded by Halpern in 1979.[1] The storyteller, born in 1923, is now an elder in the Quechan community. She asked that her name not be revealed.[2] The story was translated by Millie Romero and Amy Miller in 1998. Millie Romero explained that stories like this are important in teaching young people about social and personal relationships and about the dangers of a world in which some people have more power than others.

Supernatural power, manifested in curing, magic, and witchcraft, played a prominent part in traditional Quechan life.[3] The story of Old Lady San^yu·xáv, like many Quechan stories, is concerned with supernatural power and its consequences for the people touched by it. The version presented here tells of twin

young men, born in magical circumstances, who decide to marry against the
wishes of their mother. Being twins, the sons of Old Lady Sanᵞu·xáv are particularly powerful; they change shape at will and do as they please. The old lady's
powers are no match for theirs, and she tries with little success to persuade them to
do her bidding. The twin young women who marry the sons are powerful enough
to overcome the old lady on one occasion but cannot escape her wrath in the end.

Three different versions of the story of Old Lady Sanᵞu·xáv are found in the
Halpern collection, each told by a different storyteller. While the present version
focuses on the old lady and her relationship with her sons and their wives, another is concerned with the family of the twin young women, and the third focuses
on the great power of the younger twin and its effect on his relationship with his
brother. Details differ across the three versions of the story, and their plots develop
in different directions, but two versions end with the disappearance of the old lady
into the ocean in the west. The name Sanᵞu·xáv is based on the verb *axáv* 'to enter;
to set (in the west, said of the sun)' and is said to refer to her disappearance.

The story is presented here in a broken-line format intended to capture aspects
of the Quechan oral delivery in the physical layout of the text. Each line provides
a coherent translation of a prosodically motivated unit of Quechan speech.[4] Blank
lines separate prosodic "paragraphs", or units of speech bounded by a long pause
and often falling to a low pitch. This broken-line format forces the flow of information in the English translation to follow that of the Quechan original. It also
highlights stylistic devices such as repetition and parallelism.

NOTES

This material is based on work supported by the Abraham Halpern Memorial Fund and by
National Science Foundation Grants no. SBR-9728976 and no. BCS-9910654. Any opinions,
findings, and conclusions or recommendations expressed in this material are those of the
authors and do not necessarily reflect the views of the National Science Foundation.

1. Quechan words are given in the orthography of Halpern (1946–47, 1997). *X* has a
sound similar to that of *x* in the Spanish pronunciation of *Mexico,* and ʔ is glottal stop, the
sound that separates the vowels of the English negative *uh-uh.* Before voiced consonants
such as *v,* the stressed vowel *á* has the sound of *a* in English *father;* at the end of a word
it is shorter and may be followed by aspiration. The stressed vowel *ú,* when it appears before a voiceless consonant such as *k,* has a short sound closer to that of *oo* in English *look*
than to that of *u* in English *Luke,* while the unstressed long vowel *u·* is closer to the latter
than to the former. For a full discussion of the sound system of the Quechan language, see
Halpern's "Yuma I" in the *International Journal of American Linguistics.*

2. See Forde 1931, 149–50, for some discussion of traditional views on personal names.

3. Further information on these topics may be found in Forde 1931, 181–207.

4. Prosodic criteria used to determine line breaks include the presence of a pause; a
lengthened final segment; a coherent intonation contour; unit-final intonational characteristics (usually a conspicuous fall in pitch over the last stressed syllable and any subsequent

unstressed syllables, but sometimes a level or slightly rising pitch spanning the last stressed syllable and any subsequent unstressed syllables); and an increase in the rhythm of stressed syllables at the end of the line (this most often occurs when the line ends in an auxiliary construction). Typical prosodic lines meet several of these criteria. For further discussion, see the introduction to Halpern 1997.

SUGGESTED READING AND REFERENCES

Bee, Robert L. 1983. "Quechan." In *Handbook of North American Indians,* vol. 10, *Southwest,* edited by Alfonso Ortiz, 86–98. Washington DC: Smithsonian Institution.

Forbes, Jack D. 1965. *Warriors of the Colorado: The Yumas of the Quechan Nation and Their Neighbors.* Norman: University of Oklahoma Press.

Forde, C. Daryll. 1931. *Ethnography of the Yuma Indians.* University of California Publications in American Archaeology and Ethnology, vol. 28, no. 4. Berkeley: University of California Press.

Halpern, A. M. 1946–47. "Yuma I, II, III, IV, V, VI." *International Journal of American Linguistics* 12:25–33, 147–51, 204–12; 13: 18–30, 92–107, 147–66.

———. 1976. "Kukumat Became Sick: A Yuma Text." In *Yuman Texts,* edited by Margaret Langdon, 5–25. International Journal of American Linguistics Native Texts Series, vol. 1, no. 3. Chicago: University of Chicago Press.

———, ed. 1984. "Quechan Literature." In *Spirit Mountain: An Anthology of Yuman Story and Song,* edited by Leanne Hinton and Lucille Watahomigie, 291–344. Tucson: University of Arizona Press.

———. 1997. *Karʔúk: Native Accounts of the Quechan Mourning Ceremony.* Edited by Amy Miller and Margaret Langdon. University of California Publications in Linguistics, no. 128. Berkeley: University of California Press.

Harrington, J. P. 1906. "A Yuma Account of Origins." *Journal of American Folk-Lore* 21: 324–48.

Old Lady Sanɣu·xáv

Told by an elder of the Quechan Tribe
Translated by Amy Miller and Millie Romero

This old lady was living over there,
and something told her
to go swimming.
"I'll go swimming," she said.

And so,
"Duck down under the water,
do it four times,
and come back up.
You'll gather willow roots."

Something told her this, they say.

When she went —
the old lady went swimming —
she went along and ducked down under the water,
and she went along,
and halfway there she came back up.

Then she ducked down under the water again,
and she went along,
a little way,
and in a little while
she came back up again.

She went along, until
the third time,
she went along and ducked under the water again,
and as she went along,

all of a sudden,
"Oh!" she said,
and she came back out.

She came back out,
and there she was—
there had been something there under the water!

So,
something was there,
but she ignored it
and went farther,
and as soon as she went down again,
she cut the willow roots.
She cut them,
two of them,
and she picked them up,
and came out,
and came back;
she went home and there she was.

She went home,
and she set about making flutes,
she made two of them and put them away.
There she was,
she was a really old lady, and yet
she gave birth to twins.

She gave birth and there she was,
the old lady.
She went out and went along,
and as soon as she went out and went along,
they came from the house—
the doves,
they came flying out,
they headed off toward the rising sun,
and she stood there watching them.
"Somehow they seem to be my children,"
she said,
and she stood over there watching them.

All of a sudden,
they came back,
and as soon as they went back into the house,
"It's them," she said,
and she watched them.
"Oh,
this is very bad."

They were there,
and they went off.

When they came back out again,
she was still standing there,
and they went back inside.

They were crying.

She saw them,
and she went back inside,
and she gave them things,
and they were about to eat.

There they were,
they stood up again, and suddenly,
they turned themselves into lizards and away they went!
"Why is it
that they are making such trouble?" she said.
The old lady was watching them.

There she was,
and finally they were growing up,
there they were,
and she said to them,
"The things you do,
you go too far with them.
Be careful when you do things.
One of you will have a bad time."

She said this,
but they didn't pay attention.

They didn't pay attention,
well,
they were in their lizard shapes,
and off they went,
and there they were, underneath something.

Suddenly,
some kind of thing—
it was a snake or something,
and it was going to swallow them—
they saw it and ran home,
they went into the house, and so,
they were people again.

They stayed that way, until
finally they grew up,
and the old lady kept after them,
and they paid attention to her and settled down.

They settled down.
They picked up the flutes,
they were grown up now, and so,
they picked them up.
The west,
they went into the west,
and they sat on the top of a mountain over there,
and they played their flutes.

She heard them,
the old lady heard them, standing here.

"They've picked up the flutes I made,
and they are making music,
and it's very pretty,"
and she stood there in the distance.

Suddenly,
in the east,
someone else was there in the east.
It was young women—

and they were twins.
They were twins too,
they were over there,
and they were listening.

"Listen!
It's twin young men!
There are twin young men playing flutes,
and it's very pretty!
Do you hear it?"
one of them said to her sister.
"Yes,
I hear it."

They heard that tremendous sound;
the young men were doing something on the top of the mountain,
and it made a tremendous sound, they say.

"Shall we go see?"
she said,
and they went after the other set of twins.

They didn't get anywhere near the house—
the old lady,
her powers were tremendous,
and all of a sudden,
she took control of their actions,
and they got just so far and then went back!

They went back,
and the young men watched them,
they were watching—
and the old lady's anger was tremendous.

The young women were back at home.
There they were;
"We might take a walk,"
they said,
the young men,
and off they went.

They went off into the east, and all of a sudden
something over there stopped them and forced them back!
The people over there didn't want them!
They came back and here they were.

The old lady was angry, but
there she was,
and she pretended to be happy.

So,
they played their flutes again,
there they were, when all of a sudden
the young women,
the young women did it,
they went after them,
and somehow they went through and got there!

They got there,
and the young men,
they were playing their flutes,
when they got there.

They were laughing flirtatiously,
and she heard them,
the old lady heard them,
and she stood up;
"They're on top of the mountain," she said.

"They got here!
This was bound to happen!
I kept saying so!
I forbade them to do it!
And in spite of my power they got through, didn't they?"
she said.

And so,
she stood there thinking.

She stood there thinking;
"They have gone there to get married,"
she said.

"So,
all right,
they'll get married, no matter what I say.
They'll get married, but
it won't turn out well,"
she said,
the old lady said it.

And when they could hear her,
the old lady,
she said "You are going to get married,
aren't you?"
she asked the young men;
"Yes," they said.
"All right.
We'll have a gathering."

They had a gathering,
they went on and on inviting people,
and so,
"We're going to have a dance,
you'll have a good time there,
you'll have a good time,
you'll enjoy it,
and then go on with your lives,"
she said.

She said it,
and when they heard her,
one person
went from house to house telling about it
and inviting the people.
"They're having a feast!
They're going to have a feast!"

They had a feast,
and the people were singing,
and they were dancing.
One of the young women was laughing flirtatiously,
and the other was laughing flirtatiously,

there they were,
and the old lady's hatred was extraordinary.

There she was,
and one of them was standing there laughing about something,
and all of a sudden,
the old lady put a curse on the young woman—

She put a curse on her—

And in a little while she fell face down!
The young woman died
in the middle of the dancing!

When she died,
when she died,
they all sat here,
and finally,
they were going to prepare her body for cremation.
The next morning they were going to prepare her body for cremation.

All of a sudden,
the young man's heart was about to break,
there he was.

The next morning,
they finished preparing the young woman's body for cremation.

And when they finished preparing her body for cremation,
the young man,
he was there too.
He was there too,
and he did just what she had done.
In a little while he died too,
the boy twin.

Now there was one twin from each pair,
one of each was left,
and they were together,
with the old lady.
There they were.

The old lady was going to go back home.
"I'll get that young woman taken care of," she thought.
Well,
it's called a parching tray,
that thing.
She took that tray, and so,
she used it to gather up the ashes, and suddenly
it was full of maggots!

It was full of maggots,
and when she saw this,
right then,
when she saw that it was full of maggots,
she said to the young woman,
the one young woman who was left,
"You,
right now,
right here,
you'll pop these in your mouth like grapes,
that's what you'll do from now on!

"So,
I name you Buzzard,
and that's what you will be,
and this is what you will eat for the rest of your life!"

And so,
she gave the young woman a shove,
she turned her into a buzzard,
and there she is up in the sky,
there she is, they say.

The old lady did it,
Old Lady San^yu·xáv.

And so,
there they were,
there they were, and so,
out of everything,
finally,

nothing was left,
and so they sat there.
They were around here and there, and—
"How can we put up with this!

"What did you think you were doing
when you went about killing them off?
Now that you are finished,
just go,
go away to a place you don't know,
and come to your end there!

"Don't ever come here again!"
they said,
and off they went,
they went off heading west.

They went off,
and in the middle of the ocean
there was an island,
and they abandoned her there,
and there she stayed and stayed,
so they say.

So,
you can see it,
they say.
And that's it,
she is still there.

3. South

Western Apache

He Became an Eagle

Introduction by M. Eleanor Nevins and Thomas J. Nevins

"He Became an Eagle" is a story about desire, transformation, journeys between worlds, marriage, separation, and loss. It is set among the Western Apache people "in the old days," when people lived in mobile village encampments across the mountains of Arizona and New Mexico. Apache marriage conventions required that husband and wife come from distantly related clans, each associated conceptually and sometimes physically with different places on the landscape. In this context marriage often involved spanning geographic as well as conceptual distance between the families of husband and wife. No doubt this story speaks to some aspects of that experience. Paul Ethelbah, who lives on the White Mountain Apache Reservation in eastern Arizona with his wife, Genevieve Ethelbah, and family, performed the story in 1998.

An elder now, Paul Ethelbah spent a good deal of his young life on horseback, first as a cowboy and then working for the tribe's forestry department managing cattle herds and forest resources. But at the center of his life is his role as a *dighíń* (dee-yin), or 'holy man', performing Apache healing ceremonies for those who ask it of him. Paul Ethelbah began his long training in Apache verbal traditions at a young age when his verbal and intellectual gifts were recognized and encouraged by his father and by elders in his community. Learning Apache ceremonies requires that the initiate retain very long sets of stories, songs, and choreographed ritual actions and be able to perform these flawlessly. Paul Ethelbah describes what was for him a supportive educational environment around his family home and community:

> I learned a lot of things in my young days, you know, because there's a bunch of elders sitting around, you know. Sometimes they'd teach me. I was sitting right by my dad. I was little, about eight years old. And they talk and they sing, and then they want me to repeat. So I come out and make a speech like they say, and I sing, the way they do, you know. And they look up: "Hey, that guy is good!" you know. All the way around, you know, nine of them sitting there, elders, talking to me. I never got nervous, you know. I know what to do, I feel it, you know. I did that.

Recognizing his son's ability, his father, also a *dighín,* taught Paul Ethelbah many stories and songs, trained him in the ceremonies that he knew, and sponsored his training by *dighín* in several other White Mountain and Cibecue communities. Today Paul Ethelbah is one of the most important practicing Western Apache *dighín,* a status that frequently takes him to other Apache reservations in Arizona to perform ceremonies. While he knows many stories and songs in conjunction with his work as a *dighín,* none of these is likely to appear in print because their use is restricted to very particular, ceremonially defined contexts. The story presented here, "He Became an Eagle," is one that would be told in a more relaxed home environment, though still proceeding according to certain formalities. Paul Ethelbah describes the protocol followed when he was a young adult: "If we wanted a story from my dad or my mom, we usually get together and make arrangements for what day we should get together and let my dad or mom tell us a story. It would be a legend. And we have to pay them to do that too [i.e., bring groceries, something for them], so that way they are willing to do it. So, that's how we used to do it." This is the environment in which "He Became an Eagle" and other similar stories would be told. Today, however, the conditions of storytelling and prevalence of this kind of storytelling performance within Western Apache homes have changed.

Genevieve Ethelbah is roughly ten years younger than Paul and describes herself as typical of many people her age in being familiar with these kinds of stories but not enough to perform them confidently: "And beginning with me, my age group, I don't think we know how to tell stories like this anymore. I don't know a story of my own. These are all Paul's stories. I don't have any. I just remember bits of it here and there but not a complete story." There also appears to be less demand for these kinds of stories from the younger generations. Paul Ethelbah said he hadn't been asked to tell this story for about fifteen years.

Many Apache people link the scarcity of stories like this and the requisite knowledge to tell and understand them to a profound difference in Apache language fluency between older and younger generations and to changes accompanying this difference in the language used in everyday life. While most adults over the age of twenty-five speak Apache fluently, many perceive a precipitous drop in fluency among young school-age kids. For example, as we were working on the translation together, Genevieve Ethelbah commented:

> *A lot of these words I guess were just everyday words at one time, but now we don't talk like that too. That's why it's hard to translate it. We throw in a lot of English words to make it easy for us to talk. Then, now we try to talk with our kids and we have to talk English with them and that's hard. And we can't tell stories like this to them because it loses the*

meaning, or the fun part in it, the joke in it, you know. It loses that as
you try to speak it in English because it's meant to be told in Apache, I
guess. It has more meaning in Apache. We can't even tell our grandkids
stories like that anymore. They don't understand. They don't speak the
Apache language. It's just sad.

She notes that this drop in fluency is not across the board. Families are different, and there are differences in perceived fluency among different communities: "I think, and good for them, more people in Cibecue speak Apache. Here, I don't know what our problem is. My grandkids spoke Apache but later on picked up English on their own, and now they don't speak Apache anymore. My niece is married out there, and all her kids speak real good Apache."

Many people were involved in the preparation of this manuscript. The central contributor is, of course, Paul Ethelbah, who knows the story and has license to perform it. He performed "He Became an Eagle" in the Apache language at his kitchen table to an immediate audience comprised of his wife, Genevieve Ethelbah, and two graduate students from the University of Virginia, Tom Nevins and Eleanor Nevins. Also present was a potentially wider audience, anticipated by earlier discussions among the four of us about the desirability of publishing bilingual editions of some of the stories that Paul Ethelbah knows. In the days after the performance, we prepared a rough transcript and took this, along with the tape-recording, back to the Ethelbahs' kitchen table. There the four of us worked together on the English translation. A year or so later, we worked with the materials generated from these kitchen-table sessions to prepare the presentation of the story for this volume.

Acknowledging that translation involves an inevitable loss of meaning and, as Genevieve Ethelbah put it, some of the "fun part" of the story, we nonetheless endeavor to convey something of the beauty and meaning of the spoken Apache in this written presentation. Following Dell Hymes (1980, 1981), we have presented the story in print in a way that mirrors the rhetorical features of the spoken Apache. And like Keith Basso in his treatment of another Western Apache oral narrative (Basso with Tessay 1994), we identify the smallest rhetorical elements of the story as narrative passages, which are comprised of one or more sentences or lines. In the Apache version passages are defined by pauses and intonational contours, and they are bounded by initial particles, final particles, or both (discussed later). To reflect these features in the English print version, passages are separated from each other by an extra line space, and we make an effort, when possible, to include a rough English equivalent of particles as they occur. A doubling up of several particles marks the boundaries between larger divisions or episodes within the narrative, and these are marked by section symbols (§).

Paul Ethelbah makes regular use of particles, which act as a kind of punctuation. Many have meanings very similar to 'and then', 'and so', or 'from there'. But some particles are notoriously difficult to translate inside the text without disrupting its narrative flow because they convey understandings that have no comparable shorthand equivalent in English (see, for example, Young and Morgan 1948; Pepper 1993). For example, *léni* (lenny) 'it's said to have happened', conveys the sense that this is something people know, not from seeing it around them today, but from stories about a time and place removed from the present here and now that people know about only through generations of storytellers. A related particle, *shq'* (pronounced "sha," with the *a* pronounced quickly through the nose and ending abruptly with a sharp closure of the glottis) is peppered throughout the narrative, often employed just before the speaker introduces a new point of focus. Outside of storytelling contexts this particle conveys the sense that the speaker is not speaking from personal experience or basing what he says on the surety of patterns of everyday life but is describing something that has potential or hypothetical reality. As it is used here, the particle indexes the relation of the story as a whole to the everyday life of its listeners as well as the relation between the two realities described in the story between the life of people on this earth and that of the Eagle People in the sky. The repeated movement from one of these narrative scenes to the next, and between the story and the everyday life of its listeners, implies a relationship of similarity between what are different places constituted in very different ways.

These relationships are crucial to the motivations of the characters described by the narrative. More than a simple story, the tale is an intellectual exercise, replete with cosmological and philosophical meanings. It is addressed to the fascination of the unknown and the desire to transgress the boundaries encountered in the course of ordinary experience. What motivates the tale's protagonist is curiosity, aroused by stories he has heard, which has the ability to elevate him from his usual universe of experience to another very different one.

The story starts off by drawing a contrast between the world of a man and his people, who live on the surface of the earth, and the Eagle People, who live, it is said, on the surface of the sky. The man is curious about this sky-world of the eagles and inquires of all around him how he might find his way to this place. He finally approaches one of his people's elders. After hearing his questions, the elder instructs him to lie down at a spot were the river flows over a sandy bank and at this place between water and earth to pray to be transformed into an eagle. This he does, and after repeating his prayer four times he effects his transformation and begins to soar upward. He flies, as the story is careful to point out, in the manner of the eagle, wheeling through the sky in four circuits. After the last circuit, he comes to a door made of black obsidian, the passageway to the east. The people who live there open the door for him, and he passes through, completing the first leg of his journey. There he spends the night. The next morning he resumes his journey, making his way to the turquoise doorway to the south. Once there, he passes through and once again spends the night. In a similar fashion he continues through the remainder of his journey, coming next to the red shell doorway of the west and finally to the white shell doorway to the north.

After passing through the last doorway, he finds himself among beings he recognizes as people. These, he concludes, must be the Eagle People and the place he has found himself is the land of the Eagle clan. After spending some time with the Eagle People, he finds that they are at the mercy of what to him are fairly innocuous hazards—tumbleweeds and wasps. He confronts these threatening presences and quickly routs them. The Eagle People marvel at his display of unnatural strength and masculine virtue. No doubt as a result of his good deeds, the Eagle People welcome him among them and soon have him married to one of their own daughters. The man and his new wife have a child together and in time decide to return to visit the man's family below the sky-world of the Eagle People, in the human world.

Just as the man had done several years earlier, they lie down at a place where water flows against a riverbank. They pray, are transformed, and fly through a hole in the ground into what the people below think of as the sky. Downward they fly, traveling in reverse the path the man had previously followed. Over the next four days they pass from north to west and south and finally to the eastern doorway and then find themselves at last on the surface of the human world. Transformed into human form, the couple and their child are greeted by the man's family, who ask him where he has been these past years. The couple lives with the man's family until such time as the wife decides she must return to her people. The man states that he must stay with his people, and they part.

The woman returns to her home, where she tells her people of her time among the people below. After some time, however, she decides to return to the human world to see her husband. She and her child transform themselves and once again descend to the earth. The woman inquires after her husband, only to learn that he has died. Deeply saddened, she spends four days with her former affines, a period of time that marks the ending of their relationship to one another. She and her child return sadly to her family in the sky. While consoling her, her family observes that her time on earth has brought her much sadness.

Along with its air of contemplative melancholy, part of the attraction of the story is the attention it pays to the processes by which, first, the man and later his wife and child travel back and forth between the human and the eagle world. Anthropologists have often noted that in many Native American cultures animals are considered to be, at least in some sense, kinds of people (Brightman 1993;

Fienup-Riordan 1990, 167–91). A given species of animals, such as the eagles of the story, by virtue of their "eagleness," perceive a world unique to themselves, and it is in this world that they seem to one another to be persons, much in the manner humans do. In this story we discover that some individuals are capable of moving between the different worlds that humans and eagles respectively occupy. This wonderful ability allows the unnamed human protagonist to discover for himself what kind of place it is where the eagles fly.

Another striking feature of the story is the importance of four—in the form of the four directions, the four prayers uttered by the man, and the four circuits of the sky the man flies through to pass from one gateway to another on his way to the eagle world. Each of the four directions is always associated with a quality that is both color and substance: black obsidian in the east, blue turquoise in the south, red shell in the west, and white shell in the north. The symbolic power of four and the associated power of repeated sunwise, circular movement, obtains from the way in which these images evoke ideas concerning the place of human life in the larger cosmos. The place of the individual person is always situated at the crossroads of two movements: the sun's passage from east to west and the shifting preeminence of north and south signaled by the change of seasons. In Apache religious thought, this holy tetrad of paired cardinal points is understood to map not just the place of the person on the landscape but also the place of life in a larger encompassing reality. The cyclicity described by the passage of days into seasons is a metaphor for both the finitude of individual lives as they progress from birth to youth, maturity, and old age and the importance of this progression to the infinitely regenerative power of life itself. Considering this, it is not surprising that the characters in the story must move through the domains of each of the four directions in order to effect the transformations necessary to their journeys between worlds.

But the story Paul Ethelbah has related is not an adventure tale, and it concludes with an obliquely cautionary message. The ability to literally move between worlds leads to a relationship that ultimately ends in sadness. Curiosity drives the characters of the story to break through the barrier separating earth and sky, but the joining that is the result of this cannot overcome the need of the human man for the world he was born to and of the Eagle woman for hers. The relationship of the two was possible and even desirable to them and their families, but it was not in the long run sustainable. The story does not pass judgment on the efforts of the man and his wife; it only lays bare the consequences of them. What curiosity leads to may seem at first to be remarkable, but in the end humans and eagles cannot easily inhabit each other's worlds. The passage from one world to the other can be a lonely journey, as the characters of the story discover, that separates as it illuminates.

SUGGESTED READING AND REFERENCES

Basso, Keith. 1970. *Cibecue Apache.* New York: Holt, Rinehart & Winston.

———. 1996. *Wisdom Sits in Places: Landscape and Landscape among the Western Apache.* University of New Mexico Press.

Basso, Keith, with Nashley Tessay Sr. 1994. "Joseph Hoffman's 'The Birth of He Triumphs over Evils': A Western Apache Origin Story." In *Coming to Light: Contemporary Translations of the Native Literatures of North America, edited by Brian Swann, 636–56.* New York: Random House.

Brightman, Robert. 1993. *Grateful Prey: Cree Human-Animal Relationships.* Berkeley: University of California Press.

Farrer, Claire R. 1991. *Living Life's Circle: Mescalero Apache Cosmovision.* Albuquerque: University of New Mexico Press.

———. 1996. *Thunder Rides a Black Horse: Mescalero Apaches and the Mythic Present.* Prospect Heights IL: Waveland Press.

Fienup-Riordan, Ann. 1990. *Eskimo Essays: Yup'ik Lives and How We See Them.* New Brunswick: Rutgers University Press.

Goddard, Pliny E. 1920. *While Mountain Apache Texts.* American Museum of Natural History Anthropological Paper, vol. 24, pt. 4. New York.

Goodwin, Grenville. 1942. *The Social Organization of the Western Apache.* Chicago: University of Chicago Press.

———. [1939] 1994. *Myths and Tales of the While Mountain Apache.* Reprint, with introductions by Elizabeth Brandt and Boni Lavender Lewis, Tucson: University of Arizona Press.

Hymes, Dell. 1980. "Particle, Pause, and Pattern in American Indian Narrative Verse." *American Indian Culture and Research Journal* 4 (4): 7–51.

———. 1981. *"In Vain I Tried to Tell You": Essays in Native American Ethnopoetics.* Philadelphia: University of Pennsylvania Press.

Opler, Morris. [1969] 2002. *Apache Odyssey: A Journey between Worlds.* Reprint, Lincoln: University of Nebraska Press.

———. [1941] 1996. *An Apache Lifeway.* Reprint, with a new introduction by Charles R. Kaut, Lincoln: University of Nebraska Press.

Pepper, Mary. 1993. "Particles in Northern Athapaskan Languages." *Meta* 38 (1): 8–100.

Young, Robert, and William Morgan. 1948. *The Function and Signification of Certain Navajo Particles.* Phoenix: Phoenix Indian School, Educational Division, United States Indian Service.

He Became an Eagle

Performed by Paul Ethelbah
Translated by M. Eleanor Nevins, Thomas J. Nevins, Paul Ethelbah,
and Genevieve Ethelbah

A man was living with a village of people here on the earth's surface.

From here he heard people say that eagles live in a similar way up in the sky.

   "Where the eagle circles through the four directions,
   that is the home of the Eagle People."

That's what people said; they would tell stories about it.

§

And so then, the man started talking like this:
   "How is it possible for me to go over to where the eagle lives?"
He started asking many questions like that.

The elders, there,
   he was continually asking them questions about it.

"I want to go where the Eagle People live. People say that they live in the sky; so
   how is it possible for me to go over there?"

he would talk to them like that.

Well, he goes to this elder and talks to him about it.
This elder says:
   "Well, if you really want to go there, there is a way,"

and he tells him how to do it.

§

Following these instructions, the man goes to the river's edge,

to where the current has left its path in the soft sandy soil.
He rolls around in this sand praying:
  "Let me become an eagle."
He prays like this four times while rolling in the sand.

And then, following this, as he was told, he becomes an eagle.
He becomes a golden eagle.

At this point, transformed, he gets up in the manner of an eagle.
And flies from there as an eagle flies.

Upward from that place,
                            circling,
                    circling,
              circling,
        circling.

                                                                    §

From there, farther on, to a place with an obsidian passageway, just as he was
told,
a doorway was there, as he was told,
an opening in the blackness,
a passageway to that world was there.

And then, as he was told to do, he asks the people who are there:
  "Is this the way to where the Eagle People live?"
                                                        this man says.

  "Yes, go on through here, the path goes through this door,"
                                            those people tell him.

And from there they open the way for him,
he passes through this doorway.

And once through, he spends the first night of his journey there.
After that first night, the next morning, he flies as an eagle flies once again.
He flies, circling along the path of the sun:
                            upward,
                    upward,
              upward,
        and upward.

He is flying as the sun moves along its arc across the sky.
Flying down,
    down,
        down,
           following the sun as it goes down.

And from there he comes to a turquoise passageway.

And again, the people let him through.

And he again spends the night.

From there, the next day he starts flying again as the eagle flies,
            circling,
          circling,
        circling,
      circling.
He comes to a place where there is a passageway made of red shell,
where again a doorway is opened for him, and again he passes through.

From there, he spends the night in the same way, for the third time during his journey.
The next day he again starts flying as the eagle flies,
            circling,
          circling,
        circling,
      circling.

From there he comes to a place where there is passageway made of white shell.
The people there open the way for him, and he passes through.

And then, he spends his fourth night over there, having passed through the white place.

And in the morning, here he sees people living all around there, they say.
These people living there, they are Eagle People, the Eagle clan.
They are living just everywhere around there.
He had finally made it to them.

§

And then, he starts to make his living among them, according to their ways.

And so, time passes.
He's been living with them there for two years, it's said.

And it happened to be that there were things called "tumbleweeds" that were
    being blown around all over the place.
It happened to be that if Eagle People are hit by one of these, they are killed,
    they say.
If the tumbleweeds hit them, they are killed, they say.
This is how it was there, and then he arrived.

And so, this man, he goes to them and jumps up and down on these
    tumbleweeds that were rolling around, flattening them out.

He completely flattens them out.
And in doing so he makes it much easier for the Eagle People to live.

After what happened there, people had seen what he did, and so:
    "Truly, this is a strong man!"
    "Truly this is a powerful man!"
        they said to one another about him.

    "We are proud of him."
        they said, it's said.

                                                                        §

From there, as more time passes,
It turns out to be the same with wasps,
    when Eagle People are stung by them, they are killed.

So he pulled out a bunch of grass, and as a great many of them flew at him,
    he used it to knock them out of the air, it's said to have happened.
He knocks down great numbers of them, killing them, it's said, with grass.

Now, when an Eagle person is stung by a wasp it kills him;
    but not for this man, if he is stung, it's no problem.
So he really killed them all, it's said.

                                                                        §

And so from there, after more time has passed,
A man who lives there announces that he wants to give his daughter to this man
   in marriage:
   "You and my daughter should become married to one another.
   You are truly a man of great strength.
   You are a man who inspires good will.
   You have shown yourself to be a man of truly great strength.
   You can bring happiness to this place.
   Marry my daughter,"
     he says to him, talking about what he hopes for them.

After this, they got married, it's said.

§

From there, after they were married, one year passes.
A child is born and lives with them there.

   "Let me take you back with me to the earth's surface,"
                  he says, hoping to persuade her.
   "I want to go back there."

His wife:
   "I also want to know how it is over there."
           this is what she says to him.
   "So, let's go then,"
     she says in agreement.

§

From there, the three of them go to the river,
   to the sandy riverbed along its edge,
   praying in just the same way as he did before.
Here they roll around and around in the sand.

And they become eagles; his wife turns into an eagle, and their little one too.

§

And, from this, they fly in the manner of eagles,
   circling down through an opening in that earth,
   flying down through it.
Flying down, they come to the white shell passageway.

It is opened for them, and they pass down through.
Down from there, they spend the night.

The next morning they fly down through white shell earth,
flying in the manner of eagles,
        circling down,
           circling down,
               circling down,
                  circling down,
                     falling,
                       falling.

Then they come back to what must be this same red shell passageway.

From there, just down from this, they once again spend the night.
The next day they take off flying, through the red shell earth,
  flying in the manner of eagles, following the arc of the sun,
           circling,
              circling,
                circling
                  circling,
                    following it down, all day.
There they fly through an opening to a passageway made of turquoise.

From there they again spend the night in the same manner as before.
The next day they take off flying again, through the turquoise earth,
       flying,
          flying,
             circling,
                circling,
                  falling downward for the rest of the day.

And then an obsidian passageway is opened for them, and they pass through.
From there they again spend the night.
The next day they fly again in the manner of eagles, through the obsidian earth,
        circling down,
           circling down,
  in this manner circling down to that very cave into which the sun sets here
    on the earth's surface.

Ands so, after the fourth day of their journey they make it to the earth here, it's
said.

From there they roll around in the sand made soft by the currents at the river's
edge, and they turn back into people.

And as people, the three of them start off from there,
to find where his family is living,
to visit his father where he lives.

§

At a certain point they come to where his father has been living.

"Hey, a long time ago you went away from me, my son. Why did you go like
that?"
His father wants to hear him talk about how he has been living.

"I left so that I could go to where the Eagle People live.
This earth is one of many.
I have lived over there,"
he said, wanting to tell him all about it.

And then, his father:
"We cried over you because we didn't know what had become of you, and
now the three of you have come to us."

§

And so, from there, time goes by.
His wife was living with his family on his earth according to their manner.

"I would like to go back with my child, to where my Eagle People live,
I would like to go live with them again,"
she said to him.

"Even though you are both dear to me, as for me, I will stay here.
Will you two really go away from us?"
he had said.

§

From there he went with them to the sandy riverbank
where his wife and child rolled around in the sand,
and becoming eagles, in that manner, flew off.
Sadly, they circled down into the sunset.

They fly through a passageway made of obsidian.
There they spend the night.
The next day, going up, they fly once again in the manner of the eagle.

And flying even so, until coming to a stop at the passageway made of turquoise,
   and the two of them just go through it, at the opening.
And so, there, again, they spend the night.
From there, upward, the next day,
   using their transformation to eagles to go upward,
     using their eagle's bodies to fly in that way.

There that red shell passageway,
   where he alone went through the first time,
     where the three of them had gone through together,
       here the two of them went back through it again.
There they again spend the night.
From here, through this land, they again fly in the manner of eagles,
                 flying back up,
              flying back up.
They go through the opening in a passageway made of white shell.

And so from there, again they spend the night.
The next day, through white shell earth, they again fly in the manner of eagles,
              flying back in this way,
           flying back in this way.

Up just right at the place where the sun goes down,
   flying through that opening
     they go through the cave there to arrive at the place where they live.

                                      §

And so, they roll around in the sandy riverbank.

From there, they become Eagle People again
   so that they can go live with her father and mother there, it's said.

And so, her father questions her about it:
　"A person should stay home. Why did you three leave?"
　　　　　　　　　　　　　　　　her father said to her.

　"Truly, I'm staying here at home. We two have returned to you. And when
　we go indoors, I'll tell you all about those with whom we have been living.
　We'll speak about it many times."

　"You speak truly,"
　　　　　　her father said; they were speaking like this with one another.

And so, time passes,
　many years go by.

And then:
　"The man who is married to me, I really want to go back to him.
　And so, my child and I are going to the earth's surface.
　In the past you have said of me that I am given in marriage.
　You have said that I am not doing anything here."

And so, the two of them start off and prepare themselves to fly back over there.

　　　　　　　　　　　　　　　　　　　　　　　　　　　　§

There: "We two are going back again."

From that place in the sandy soil,
from rolling around in the sand,
from becoming eagles again,
they are able to fly back again in the manner of eagles.

There they get up as eagles, and they fly as eagles through an opening in the
earth.

They go back down through the passageway made of white shell.
And there they again spend the night.

That next day they fly in the manner of eagles down through the white shell
　earth,
　　　　　flying back toward us,
　　　　　　　flying back,

continuing
flying back toward us,
still.
They go back down through this red shell passageway.

From there they again spend the night.
The next day they fly back again in the manner of eagles through the red shell
   earth,
         down from there,
               downward,
                     down,
                           flying down to that person.

They go through an opening, a passageway made of turquoise.

And from there again they spend the night.

And from there the next day they fly down through the turquoise earth,
                 flying back for him, through the passage there.
They go through a door made of obsidian.

And so, from there they spend the night again.

And from there, again, using the next day to fly back through the obsidian
   earth.
Going downward again for a reason,
   they follow the way downward
      until they fly again through an opening onto this earth, it's said.

§

And so, from there, they roll around again
   in the sand where river currents have left a path,
And from that, they turn back into people.
Thus, it came to be that they were once again people on this earth.
In this way the child also became a person again too.

To find out about her husband,
   just for this purpose,
      they went back looking for where his father's village had moved,
         to talk to people about it.

§

And so, from there, despite going back to the very place where they had lived,
   they have to travel all around before they come to some people who were
   living there.

When they come to them,
She starts asking them questions about her husband's whereabouts:
   "Where is my husband, the one I am searching after?
   Where is this person, the one who is married to me?
   They used to live here, they used to stay here.
   This is where we found them when we stayed with them before."
                        The woman was talking to people like this:
   "We have just come for this person, to see how he is doing."

And so, at last, they come to the man's father, and he was the one who tells
   them about him:
   "He has been dead."

And because of that they only stayed there for several days.
They spent four nights with them.

They had come there because they had loved him.
The boy also spent four nights, and his sufferings there were truly great.

   "My son, this one has gone from us, he has gone from you.
   What can we do here? Nothing,"
               she says to him.

Their sufferings were great.

And so, from here they stayed over through four days and nights,
   going through a hard time, feeling down, before going back.

Then,
   "We are not happy here, I am not happy, it is of no use for you two to stay
   here. You have lived as one of us here, but now go back. You want to do it.
   Go back because there is nothing you can do for him."

From there:
   "These two should leave this place where they used to live with him.

There is nothing to do, there is nothing but to let the customary time pass."

And so, it was decided that they would stay over for the expected amount of
    time, and then they would start back.
There was nothing else to do but spend four days with them; it would be four.

From here, they stayed over four days and nights at that place on his behalf.

§

And then, there, they started back.
They went back to the sandy bank of the river.
There they would again become eagles.
Upward, flying in the manner of eagles again, up, they just go back.

They fly through an opening in the passageway made of obsidian.
Right here they spend the night.

The next day, they fly upward again through the obsidian sky,
    still flying around, still in this way.

They fly through a passageway there made of turquoise.
They fly across it, they go through it once again.

From there they again spend the night.

From here, they fly back up again in the manner of eagles,
    the next day, flying through this turquoise sky, going on still.
They pass through this passageway made of red shell.

Again they spend the night there.
The next day, they fly back upward again in the manner of eagles,
    through the red shell earth, and they keep flying.

From there, a white passageway, they just fly across here.

And so, they go through it, and they spend once again spend the night there.
The next day they fly back upward, in the manner of eagles,
    through the red shell earth,
                                flying up,
                            aaaahhhh . . .

to the passageway where the sun sets on their earth.
Thus they return on the fourth day to the village where the Eagle People live.

§

They roll around in the sand at the river's edge,
   and turning back into Eagle People,
      they just go back home.
They go back to where her father and her mother are living.

   "How is it there is no man with you, why is this so?"
                              people say.
   "Where is your husband?"

   "There is no longer such a person."

   "How long has it been?"
   "When did it happen?"
                  they talk to her in this way.

   "There was nothing for us on the earth, so we two came back here,"
                                          she says.

They were very unhappy about what happened to the man on earth, it's said.
They stood there grief-stricken.

   "Hey, that's terrible! What has happened is no good!"

They were very sad about it.

   "For what reason did you stay with them for a while over there?"
                           they ask her.

   "We stayed with them a while to mourn for this one before coming back."
               She told her father's village about it there.

From there,
   here my yucca fruit lie piled up.

Navajo

The Flight of Dzilyi neeyáni

Introduction by Paul G. Zolbrod

The accompanying passage comes from a project now underway — an attempt on my part to recast in a viable literary form Washington Matthews's English rendering of the Navajo Mountain Chant narrative, originally published in 1887 in the Fifth Annual Report of the Bureau of American Ethnology. At first glance the effort would seem futile, for on one level it is impossible to extract an essentially immutable printed text from a dynamic oral tradition with any real fidelity to how the narrative once functioned.

An ongoing celebration of a story that frames it, the ceremony is part of a complex religious system that remains a mainstay of Navajo life, even as the dominant culture continues to encroach. Like some three-dozen known cognate ceremonies held to prevent or bring about the recovery from the effects of illness or misfortune, it occasions a gathering that is at once secular and religious, entailing song, dance, intricate paraphernalia, and detailed social interaction. This is among the best known ceremonies because when held in the late fall it provides the occasion for a spectacular fire dance that attracts local non-Navajo onlookers and tourists from distant places. Yet the underlying narrative that endows the ceremony with much of its meaningful power can stand on its own as literature. It tells of a youth's escape from Ute captors with ample help from the various Yeis, or Holy People — led by the all-powerful Haashch'éélti (anglicized as Yeibichai), or 'Grandfather-of-the-Gods' — and of the fugitive's struggle to reintegrate into his community following that harrowing ordeal.

The hero must determine when to act on his own, when to seek help, and how to accept it. As he makes his way, he must learn what offerings the Holy People expect and what arouses their disfavor. The entire community eventually becomes involved, because he must transmit what he learns to others, who will then use that awareness to heal kinsmen who themselves may suffer the consequences of crucial inaction. In short, he acquires ritual knowledge, but along with that, he gains powerful self-awareness and a growing confidence that makes him virtually godlike.

Nothing I have seen in print can duplicate hearing a Navajo storyteller recite such a tale; seeing a sand painting materialize on a hogan floor in preparation for the ensuing cycle of chants and prayers; watching the dancers appear in the roaring firelight; singing the story's progress through the night; or feasting come dawn on fry bread, coffee, eggs, and green chilies as participants take turns offering closing remarks.

Even so, a deep awareness of what the ceremony celebrates can be recovered from the event and the long tradition it represents. Matthews's ground-breaking publication, with its accompanying description of the ceremony replete with sketches and full-color reproductions of the sand paintings, along with his verse translations of the ceremonial songs, is adequate in many ways. How he acquired the story remains unknown, although I surmise that he listened to various recitations over a period of time, quite likely in Navajo, and then reconstructed the narrative from memory in English. But he wrote it out more as ethnographic data than as poetic narrative. As a result his abbreviated and rather literal translation sidesteps the narrative's essential verbal richness.[1] At the very least it warrants added sensitivity to the leap from orality to print, even if the fixed silence of written prose may displace the dynamic elasticity of telling and retelling. My aim, then, is to adjust the English prose idiom Matthews employed so that the story might survive in a published version whose verbal texture reflects the essential poetry residing within it and honors its outward social function.

I could not listen to what was recited to Matthews, of course, but in reviewing his correspondence and field notes, I developed enough confidence in what he achieved to base my revised version on his text, further influenced by fragments I heard both in Navajo and in English and by my participation in ceremonies. As I grew more familiar with this story in particular, with its songs and procedures, and more generally with Navajo culture and its essentially poetic traditions, I became increasingly aware that as much as delineating the action, the story of Dzilyi neeyáni projects a gradually shifting frame of mind. In a sequence of events whose thematic rhythm registers that subtle change, he moves from a state of inner paralysis to one of growing resolve — a theme common to a number of Navajo ceremonial stories — set fully in motion when he acquires the name that links him with the ceremony for all posterity.[2]

Embedded in that story of transformation and the gathering it frames is no less than a systemic world-view that fuses space and time in seasonal quadrants, aligns the Navajo landscape with the four cardinal directions, and fixes the hero's learning cycle within that framework. Also subsumed in its telling are patterns of repetition in speech as well as in song still evident in many facets of everyday Navajo life; a style of delivery with visible counterparts in such other arts as weaving, sand painting, ceramics, and silverwork; an approach to learning that relies on direct, trial-and-error experience rather than discursive instruction; and a perception of how humans should relate to one another, to animals, and to members of the spirit world.

Wary of sounding trite and fawningly simplistic, I find it difficult to summarize such things, which I have learned only gradually from years of contact that include field research in Navajo communities; social interaction, especially with elders; participation in ceremonial activity; and classroom teaching on the reservation, which requires as much listening and learning as lecturing. In telling about the story and its full cultural setting, I simply cannot repeat all that I have come to know about Navajo life, any more than I can account in such limited space for the cumulative experience of getting to know the narrative more intimately through years of association with those among whom it endures. I can only try to combine some essence of that lived experience with my broad literary experience to forge a text that approximates the abiding beauty of the story when people gather to celebrate it. I hope it thus becomes one modest example of the potential for North America's indigenous tribes to alter the way we define our literary past.

A precautionary word to readers of a transcribed Navajo text such as this one: the narrative should be read on its own terms, so that standards common to mainstream works do not obtrude, because Navajo storytelling has its own distinct conventions. Incidents occur in series of fours, for example, and movement within a section of space, whether small or large, goes clockwise; variations from such patterns can suggest reversal and disorder. Comic traces can sometimes tincture the most dire circumstances, inasmuch as those involved in rescuing the hero might mock him as he learns. Thus, the Yeibechai occasionally laughs at Dzilyi neeyáni, for example, and the owl-masked figure repeats an interjectory expression commonly used in scolding children, "Shúúh, shúúh!" to get the youth's attention. Familiar associations in Western literature do not apply: an owl stands as a figure not of wisdom but of admonishment; the whippoorwill resonates differently here than in an English romantic poem; youth is associated almost exclusively with inexperience rather than with physical strength, at least until some kind of initiation occurs, whereas power resides with age.

Symbolism functions on an entirely different level in stories like this one. I was once asked if the hole the hero struggles to enter for safety from his pursuers might represent a rebirth of sorts. But rebirth as it might be expressed symbolically in a mainstream literary work is not an issue. The issue is spiritual transformation. In other words Dzilyi neeyáni is enlightened more than he is reborn. Following the subtleties of the Navajo language, the second part of the name given him suggests that his mind is lifted upward as he learns to initiate events, so that he can literally take flight to escape while at the same time learning how to propitiate the spirits and deified animals who assist him.

Readers new to works broadly drawn from the oral traditions of the Native

Americans should be advised that they are in another realm wherein *literature* is not only interpreted in new ways but should be defined differently. As I speak of literature when converting a Navajo story to print, I mean to specify only what exists in that medium. On the other hand, I expand the term *poetry* to include both what is written and what is recited, and I define it more broadly to include that art whose primary medium is language whether written, spoken, or sung. For my purposes, then, I do not apply *poetry* just to *verse* as that word is conventionally understood, or to language deliberately spaced line by line on a page. Loosely speaking, what is seen on the page as *verse* represents what I call *lyric poetry,* whose language takes on properties of song, such as rhyme, fixed measures of rhythm, or other such carefully assembled patterns of sound. What appears as *prose,* on the other hand, I take as a term associated with the way print appears on a line from margin to margin. It designates properties of the conversational voice, which I call *colloquial poetry,* in contrast with *lyric poetry,* which is sung or chanted.

While transmuted to *prose* on these pages, a narrative like this one is nonetheless poetic, albeit *colloquial.* What makes it poetic, whether performed orally or placed on the page, is a set of features drawn from a vast repertoire of verbal techniques that assure its survival. Those techniques ensure that those who listen to it will want to hear the narrative again and again, in the way oral tradition promotes variation over time and across the expanse of space, and those who read it will want to do so over and over. Such a refined vocabulary is needed if the conversion of Native orality to print is to reflect distinctions more peculiar to performance in the donor language and its cultural setting than they would otherwise appear in the recipient language.

The numbers at the head of each section in my revision are those assigned by Matthews to individual paragraphs, which I have expanded into cantolike units. That, in addition to the way I have altered his prose, reflects the Navajo ceremonial system, the cadences of its language both sung and recited, conventional storytelling style, and the steady thematic rhythm of the hero's progress.

A NOTE ON ORTHOGRAPHY AND PRONUNCIATION

Although Navajo consonants introduce several unfamiliar sounds and form sound combinations difficult for newcomers to the language, they equate roughly with their Indo-European counterparts, except for two that are rare or nonexistent in English—the voiceless *l* (ł), which sounds a little like *sh* as in *push,* or like the double *l* in Welsh place names; and the glottal stop ('), which resembles the medial clicklike sound in the English expression "oh, oh."

There are only four basic vowels—*a* as in *art, e* as in *met, i* as in *sit,* and *o* as in *note.* However, vowels may be short or long, and length is designated by doubling a letter. A given vowel can take on a high tone. Hence, the second part of the proper name Dzilyi neeyáni includes a long vowel and high-toned one. Vowels may also be nasalized, but I have chosen not to designate those in the Navajo terms reproduced here.

NOTES

1. I summarize Matthews's achievement in originally compiling the *Mountain Chant* text and discuss the narrative as literature in Zolbrod 1997. A modified version of that essay appears in Zolbrod 1998. I explore in greater detail the process and its effects of converting Native American orality to written literature in Zolbrod 1984, 1992, 1995. By way of contrast, see Bahr et al. 1997, especially chapter 1 (3–31). See also Tedlock 1983, Hymes 1981, and the various essays in Swann 1992. For a detailed inquiry into the history of committing Native American oral traditions to printed English, see Clements 1996.

2. Spencer 1957 provides an early list of Navajo ceremonial narratives along with synopses. Although published nearly half a century prior to this commentary, hers remains the most comprehensive survey. More recent guides can be found in Wyman 1983 and in Levy 1998.

SUGGESTED READING AND REFERENCES

Bahr, Donald, et al. 1997. *Ants and Orioles: Showing the Art of Pima Poetry.* Salt Lake City: University of Utah Press.

Clements, William. 1996. *Native American Verbal Art: Texts and Contexts.* Tucson: University of Arizona Press.

Hymes, Dell. 1981. *"In Vain I Tried to Tell You": Essays In Native American Ethnopoetics.* Philadelphia: University of Pennsylvania Press.

Levy, Jerrold E. 1998. *In the Beginning: The Navajo Genesis.* Berkeley: University of California Press.

Matthews, Washington. [1883–84] 1997. *The Mountain Chant: A Navajo Ceremony.* Fifth Annual Report of the Bureau of American Ethnology. Reprint, Salt Lake City: University of Utah Press.

Spencer, Katherine. 1957. *Mythology and Values: An Analysis of Navajo Chantway Myths.* Philadelphia: American Folklore Society.

Swann, Brian, ed. 1992. *On the Translation of Native American Literature.* Washington DC: Smithsonian Institution.

Tedlock, Dennis. 1983. *The Spoken Word and the Work of Interpretation.* Philadelphia: University of Pennsylvania Press.

Wyman, Leland. 1983. "Navajo Ceremonial System." In *Handbook of North American Indians,* vol. 10, *Southwest,* edited by Alfonso Ortiz, 537–57. Washington DC: Smithsonian Institution.

Zolbrod, Paul G. 1984. *Diné bahane': The Navajo Creation Story.* Albuquerque: University of New Mexico Press.

———. 1992. "Navajo Poetry in Print and in the Field: An Exercise in Text Retrieval." In *On the Translation of Native American Literature,* edited by Brian Swann, 242–56. Washington DC: Smithsonian Institution.

———. 1995. *Reading the Voice: Native American Oral Poetry on the Written Page.* Salt Lake City: University of Utah Press.

———. 1997. Foreword to *The Mountain Chant,* by Washington Matthews. Salt Lake City: University of Utah Press.

———. 1998. "On the Multicultural Frontier with Washington Matthews." *Journal of the Southwest* 40:68–86.

The Flight of Dzilyi neeyáni

Storyteller unknown

—29—

It is said that on the twelfth day of his captivity, the youth's Ute captors went out to hunt, leaving two deer skins for him to prepare. They sat stretched across two poles in a small brushwood enclosure close to the tent wherein he was being kept prisoner.

He set to work passively, laboring to scrape and rub, rub and scrape, until the sun reached its midday zenith. By then its heat intensified his hunger. So he entered the tent to see if he could find something to eat.

There he spied a bag, opened it, found in it some dried meat, and placed several pieces over the coals. He then sat waiting for them to cook.

As he watched the meat begin to sizzle, he heard a noise at the tent's deerskin entrance. And looking up, he beheld an old woman crawling on her hands and knees. Moving sunwise, she passed once round the fire and headed for the door, saying nothing as she made her way. But as she moved through the entryway to leave, she turned and addressed him thus.

"My grandson, do something for yourself!" she addressed him.

Having heard what she said, he paused in wonder at this strange vision and what it might mean. Baffled, he rushed through the doorway out of the tent, hoping to overtake his strange visitor, to question her, to learn who she might be, and to determine what she intended by the words she spoke.

But he saw no one.

He circled the tent four times, gazing in each direction to no avail. Not eating after that unsettling incident, he could accomplish little thereafter for the rest of the day. Occasionally he picked up a stone and rubbed the hides a few strokes. For the most part, though, he could hardly do more than loiter and pace, busying himself only with his troubled thoughts.

Who was this woman?

Where had she come from? Why did she crawl so? And with her words—"My grandson, do something for yourself!"—what did she mean for him to do?

— 30 —

The sun set that night, and with its return next morning the Ute hunters filed back into camp carrying an abundance of meat.

Approaching the great lodge where the youth's master made his home, they widened it by moving the anchor pegs at the bottom and extending its base outward from the center so that they could clear a large space therein. Many guests had been invited to gather there that evening to celebrate so successful a hunt— or else to determine his fate.

With darkness about to fall, visitors began arriving in great numbers. As they came, the youth's master ordered his captive to fetch some water. Accordingly, he took two large wicker bottles to a nearby spring, filled them, placed them on the ground at the stream's edge, and set about finding something to fasten into the mouths of the jars. He did not want to return with half the water having spilled to the ground and be beaten or rebuked therefore by his master.

As he did so, he heard what at first sounded initially like a hiss. "Shúúh!" it went, scarcely audible at first and so faint that he could not tell where it came from. He looked around for a minute or two. But seeing nothing and hearing nothing more, he resumed looking; however uncertainly now, he once again set about seeking plants suitable to seal the jars, pacing back and forth but unable to concentrate fully on what he was doing.

But the voice interrupted him again. "Shúúh!" it repeated. "Shúúh! Shúúh!" And again he stopped to look, aware now that it came from somewhere in the water. But in the gray light of oncoming night he could see only shadows flickering darkly against its surface. Somewhat tentatively, he again resumed his search for stopples and found several low branches of mountain mahogany supple enough to break off and pry into the top of first one wicker jar, then another.

But as he set about doing so, he again heard that sinister noise, louder this time and sounding more clearly like that of a speaking creature. "Shúúh!" it repeated. "Shúúh! Shúúh! Shúúh!"

Certain this time that he indeed heard something deliberately uttered, he looked again, focusing on a heavily shadowed spot upstream of where the water descended across a bed of pebbles. And instead of resuming his task of sealing the jars, he sat gazing thereat, aware that his heart was pounding in his chest, as just the stream's muted ripple of water followed the sound of that voice.

Until it again broke the silence. "Shúúh!" it cried. "Shúúh! Shúúh! Shúúh! Shúúh!" And now he could make out a humanlike form sitting in the water. While it had the shape of a person, its head bore a mask like that of a great owl, albeit smoking a pipe. And as the youth gazed on it fixed in his tracks with heart beating wildly, it had this to say.

"You walk around like someone without sense," it said. "Someone without knowledge or purpose. Someone willing to let things happen to him as they may. Why don't you take it upon yourself to do something? When you next hear my voice, you would do well to approach it instead of standing dumb in your tracks as you now do, awaiting what is to happen."

— 31 —

The voice ceased and the owl vanished, leaving the youth with nothing to gaze at but shadows flickering on the dark water, and nothing to hear but the sound of its rippling. So he finished sealing the vessels and dutifully carried them back to the encampment, troubled by that strange encounter and the words that issued from whatever vision it was he had see — "Do something for yourself!"

What indeed was he to do?

When he returned, he noticed two large dogs had been posted at the door of the lodge, one tied on each side. He observed, too, that three doors had been added to the dwelling in his absence, so that four doors in all now covered the entryway.

Once in the tent, he found the lodge filled with Utes, all of them staring at him as he made his way through the door. He also saw four bags of tobacco and four pipes lying about the central fire, one to its east, one south of it, one at its western edge, and one on its northern side, all arrayed in ceremonial fashion. He also noticed a very old man and a very old woman seated at the doorway, one on either side of it.

Tied to the old woman, a cord passed west round the edge of the lodge behind the onlookers. Another, fastened to the man, passed similarly round the edge to the east. Both ends came together near the center of the lodge. His master then commanded him to seat himself on the western side, whereupon one of the cords was tied to his wrist and the other to his ankles so that he was now secured to the elderly pair.

— 32 —

Now he feared more than ever for his safety. Surely his captors intended to torture him to his death.

As four elders lit the pipes, council among all present began. Long into the night their talk continued in their alien tongue. Listening to this strange chatter he could not understand, and looking helplessly from one hostile face to another, he grew more and more afraid.

In his deep fear, however, he fancied that he heard a strangely familiar cry floating through the din of the Ute voices. "Wu'hu'hu'hu'," he fancied he heard, the voice reaching from far in the distance, it seemed.

Whose voice could that be?

As he strained to listen and to be sure he indeed heard it, the voice again made its way across the cacophony of Ute chatter, a little louder now and a little bit nearer. "Wu'hu'hu'hu'," it repeated. Could it possibly be the voice of Haashch'éélti, the Talking God, grandfather of all the other holy people?

Not long thereafter, he heard the voice for a third time. "Wu'hu'hu'hu'," it repeated, now more loudly and distinctly, as if coming immediately from the west side of the lodge. And yes! it was the voice of the kindly old Yeibichai, Haashch'éélti, the Talking God.

He recognized that call.

Upon realizing as much, he heard footsteps at the door and saw a streak of white lightning bolt through the smoke hole and circle round the lodge over the heads of those assembled.

They, however, did not hear what the youth had heard. Nor did they see what he beheld. Nor were they aware that Haashch'éélti, the Talking God, had entered the lodge with the arrival of the white lightning, that he now stood astride the lightning bolt, or that he addressed the youth, demanding this:

"What is the matter with you, grandson?" he demanded.

"Do you take no initiative at any point? Or do you merely sit helplessly as your fate is determined by others? Something you must do for yourself, else come morning you will be whipped to death. That is what the council has decided."

Without pausing, the Yeibichai continued. "Quickly," he continued. "Pull out four pegs that anchor the bottom of the tent. Then push it open there. Then you can shove things through."

Hearing these words, the youth hesitated. "How can I do that?" he objected. "See how I am bound to my captors."

But Haashch'éélti merely continued issuing instructions, as if the youth had uttered no excuse. "As you leave," he instructed, "take those bags filled with embroideries with you. And take with you tobacco from the pouches near the fire." And with those words he vanished.

He had scarcely done so before the youth heard another voice overhead, different this time from that of the Yeibichai. It was that of Hooshdódii the Whippoorwill, who flew down through the smoke hole.

"Woo-woo, wheeoh-wu," it cried in its characteristic sedating way.

"Woo-woo, wheeoh-wu; woo-woo, wheeoh-wu; woo-woo, wheeoh-wu," it called as it circled the lodge four times above the heads of the assembled Utes, then soared back out the way it had entered.

No sooner had this happened than a few of the Utes began to nod and close their eyes. Soon others likewise grew drowsy. Overpowered with drowsiness, in fact, they stretched out on the ground and dozed off. Still others stood up, raised their arms wide overhead, arched their backs and yawned, then filed out to sleep in their own dwellings.

The last ones to fall asleep were the old man and the old woman to whom the youth was bound, seated to one side of the door and the other, respectively. At length their chins dropped to their chests, their eyes closed, their mouths fell open, and they too dozed.

Now fearing no watchers, the youth went to work loosening the cords that bound him. And doing as Haashch'éélti had instructed, he removed four of the pegs that anchored the edge of the tent to the ground.

Through the opening made thereby, he shoved the two bags of embroideries that the Yeibichai had bid him take. Then he made his way through the door of the lodge, where he found both dogs sleeping as soundly as the Utes inside now slept.

Taking along the cords that had fettered him, he circled round the lodge to the back, where he had put the bags and the tobacco. These he carefully bound with the cords, so that they would make an easily balanced bundle, which he then shouldered so that he could move with it easily.

— 33 —

Just then he heard the hoot of an owl.

It came from a short distance south of where he stood. Remembering the words of the owl-like form near the spring at nightfall, he set out in that direction.

He did not go far, however, before he found himself atop a steep bluff formed where two branching canyons converged, its walls rising out of sheer darkness below. Thus it seemed impossible for him to venture any farther. Before him lay a dark abyss whose bottom he could not see; behind him were his Ute enemies, who would surely wake soon and fly after him in angry pursuit. So he again feared for his life.

However, he spied the top of a tall spruce tree that grew alongside the precipice where he stood, apparently growing out of the canyon floor. For day was beginning to break and he could see more clearly.

Even so, he stood indecisively in his tracks as if paralyzed.

Until suddenly he beheld Haashch'éélti, the Talking God, who had again appeared and admonished him thus. "How is it, my grandchild, that you stand there motionless?" he admonished. "Are you ever to initiate something on your own? Are you ever to think and act for yourself? Grab the top of that spruce tree and climb down through its branches to the canyon floor!"

Whereupon the hapless youth put out a hand to seize the tree's topmost branch.

But it swayed beyond his grasp.

Again he reached, this time leaning a little bit forward and extending one arm tentatively to grab it. But again the branch swayed out of reach. Securing the bundle on his back so as to move more freely, he lifted his other hand in an effort to guide the branch into the hand of his outstretched arm. To no avail, however, for the tree's topmost bough again bent away.

"See, my grandfather," cried the youth. "It moves away from me. I cannot reach it."

In desperation he stretched both arms as far as his balance would allow and inclined his body forward even more. And with his doing so the kindly Yeibichai flung a bolt of white lightning around the tree's topmost stem, as if it were a lasso ready to fling around the neck of a horse the way Navajo cowboys now do during roundup time, thus drawing its high branches within the youth's grasp.

"Now descend," he instructed the erstwhile prisoner. "And when you reach the bottom of the cliff, take four sprigs from the tree, each from a different lower branch. One branch must extend to the east; one must extend southward; one must reach toward the west; and the remaining one must reach northward. For you may well need them in the future."

Doing what he was told, the youth made his way down the tree to the canyon floor, where he took the four sprigs as he had been instructed, and he placed them under his clothing.

— 34 —

When he reached the foot of the cliff, he found Haashch'éélti waiting for him. But at the same time he heard a noisy clamor. At first it seemed to come from the cliff's ledge overhead whence the youth had made his escape. But it grew louder and louder from moment to moment, and seemingly nearer at hand.

As he listened, the fugitive recognized the angry shouts of human voices. The Utes had apparently awakened to the discovery that their prisoner had escaped. Now they were in spirited pursuit.

"Your enemies are after you," advised the Yeibichai then. "But yonder on the far side of the canyon do you see some small holes? They are the doors of a dwelling of mine down here, and inside you can hide," he advised. "But you will need my help getting there," he added.

"Large rocks and fallen trees have strewn the canyon floor," he advised. "So you would have a hard time trying to make your way over them by foot. But I can make it easy for you to get there. As for you, you must learn to determine when to act on your own and when to expect help from the Holy People."

Whereupon he inhaled deeply and then blew a powerful breath. Instantly a great white rainbow spanned the canyon floor.

Anxious to get across now that he heard the voices of his pursuers, the fugitive tried to step on it. But first his one foot then the other sank shin deep into its luminescent dust, and he found himself going nowhere, all the while hearing the clamoring voices of his pursuers.

Watching him struggle so, Haashch'éélti merely stood alongside him and laughed at his fruitless efforts to mount the rainbow's shimmering nothingness. But after he had made sport enough of the youth's gyrations, he again drew a breath and blew hard. At once the rainbow's powdery glow took on the substance of hard ice, and the two of them crossed easily to the canyon's far wall. Upon reaching it, the Yeibichai pointed to a small hole therein, saying, "This is the door to my lodge." He said, "Go in."

All the while the youth could hear the angry shouts of his pursuers.

Their voices rang in his ears, so near at hand were they. Surely they had descended to the canyon floor, where they had picked up the fugitive's trail, and were now somehow making their way across to this side. It would not be long until they spied him.

Terrified, he tried to wiggle his way into what he considered the largest of those small holes. But indeed he could barely poke his head into it, so narrow was the passage. And as he struggled, Haashch'éélti again began to laugh. The more he struggled, in fact, the harder the laughter became. As he watched the youth thrust his arms into the hole and try to widen it with his shoulders, the Yeibichai slapped his hips with glee.

Meanwhile, the angry clamor of the pursuing Utes grew louder and louder still, so near now that they seemed to be distinctly upon him. Any second, he feared, one of them or another would grab his feet and pull him away from the hole.

Having laughed his fill by then, Haashch'éélti again inhaled deeply and blew hard at the small hole, which instantly enlarged, and through it they both easily passed, making their way along a passage yielding three rooms and stopping in a fourth.

Once there, the Yeibichai took from the youth's back the bundle he had placed there before descending the tree down to the canyon's bottom. The Holy One then opened the bags and withdrew from them an array of beautifully decorated clothing. He withdrew a pair of moccasins; he withdrew a pair of long fringed leggings; he withdrew a finely crafted shirt; he withdrew a pair of eagle feathers.

He arrayed himself in these and went out, leaving the fugitive alone in the cave. No sooner was the Yeibichai gone when the clamoring voices of his pursuers outside resounded through the passageway, their angry shouts lasting for a long, long time, until at last they died away.

Perhaps they had lost the trail of their escaped prisoner; and after searching the vicinity and not finding him, they now looked elsewhere, likely led away by Haashch'éélti, the crafty Talking God.

Once it was silent, the Yeibichai returned, assuring the youth that he could now leave. "Your enemies have gone," he assured him. "You can safely go forth and begin making your way back to your people."

"But before you go, you must accept the name Dzilyi neeyáni, or Enlightened in the Mountains, inasmuch as you will be helped by various other Holy People along the way and that you will learn amply from them.

"They will protect you against further danger; they will instruct you as to what you must do and must not do; they will teach you songs; they will show you what sacrifices you are to make and how you must do so. And all that you learn from them you must take back to your people."

So, taking a tanned elk skin to cover his back and a pair of moccasins to protect his feet, the fugitive set out from the cave, eager to rejoin his family in the aftermath of this ordeal. He was now able to make his way confidently, as ready to act on his own as to obey, it is said.

Coyote Stories

Introduction by Rex Lee Jim

I trotted into Coyote the other day. Really, I did. And following is more or less what Coyote and I chatted about.

"Do you really want to get to know me," he commands. He does not ask; he demands. I don't even want to know him. He just happens to be there, right in front of my path. And he dares to demand that *I* get to know him.

"No," I say.

"Aren't you curious, not even one bit?" he queries.

"No, curiosity killed a cat." I regurgitate his own medicine onto his ugly face. And I commend Bobcat for a job well done!

"Yes, but satisfaction brought it back," he retorts as though I have just insulted his immortality. This deflates my ego, of course. I feel like punching him out.

Then, out of courtesy, I tell him my plans for sharing his ways with younger people, especially the kids in my family, and, out of curiosity, ask him for his informed opinion.

"Kids in your family? You mean your nephews and nieces?" he almost scolds.

"Why do you want them to know something about me?" He tilts his ears.

"I says to them that they might learn something from you," I say.

"Says?" he guffaws.

Then he laughs at my plan, too. He actually laughs at it. He begins by asking, "For a human being, you don't know much about being human, do you?" That intolerant ignoramus! How arrogant.

He demands that I find more ways to involve the children in activities, rather than just tell them his stories. My plan for passing Coyote stories is dissipated by its own aura of dormancy. If only it weren't for that coyote nose; now I must do everything all over.

"Change," he says. "I am all about change," he continues. "Adoption. Adaptation. Improvement. Challenging the status quo. Now we're beginning to talk," he chuckles.

"Think about the kids," Coyote insists.

I think about the kids, look at my plans, and realize that my plan is geared more toward what I would like to see happen. I think some more and decide to change. Instead of just telling those stories, the children will have more fun drawing the stories or coloring what one of my brothers would illustrate. Camping outside at night and listening to coyotes howl in nearby canyons to the east or out on the plains to the west will help the kids begin to place Coyote within the landmarks they see daily.

"I'm not talk," Coyote says. "I'm all about action," he scolds.

So I decide to take the kids to museums and zoos to learn about the ways of animals. We'll start with the coyote, of course. While we're on these trips, my parents will come along and talk with their grandchildren in Navajo. The kids might as well learn Navajo, too.

"Make them feel high, make them feel low, and I'll speak to them," Coyote says, it is said.

I listen some more and decide to teach acting classes for my nephews and nieces. We will play theater games and learn about movement, voice, and storytelling, guided by Coyote's voice. We'll go high and go low. We'll laugh and cry.

"Let them have fun. Encourage their curiosity," he demands. "Curiosity never kills anyone. Hey, I'm still around. How many storytellers have I run out?" he muses.

When we do the plays, we will use materials from the land around us to make props and musical instruments. This will encourage curiosity as well as promote creativity. At the same time the children will learn more about the environment in which they live. My parents can help with the Navajo names of the materials that we will be using. This way the kids will learn about and know more of the land in detailed and intimate ways. For example, if we're going to make materials from sticks or plants, we can do a whole adventure about plant life. To make it more fun, we can create a detective game by finding sticks and see if we can trace them back to the live plants, bushes, shrubs, and trees from which they come. Then from the top of Limestone Mesa, we can point to where these plants live on the land. We even can make maps of where certain plants live. Again my parents can help with the names of plants. In this way we'll be acting on Coyote's advice.

"Action," he says. "And forget about assessment. Let them speak the language and have fun." Coyote laughs.

"And, Rex," he chides. "Don't forget about technology. The times are changing, and you must learn to embrace the changing. Change with the times. Change the way you tell my stories. Take the camcorder, the cameras, the tape recorders, and the digital cameras out of your closet and teach your nephews and nieces how to use them. Use them. Hey, they're just collecting dust now," he teases.

The teasing stings because, of course, as always, he's right.

"The kids can learn so much about photography, videotaping, and tape-recording. They can play interviewing games in the spirit of Oprah Winfrey's or Barbara Walters's talk shows. Better yet, they can interview me!" He delights in his ingenuity and boldness.

I think about how the children can interview their elders and record them on videotapes that they then can show on the television. With tape recorders they can transcribe their interviews, small sections of them, and turn them into little books using the computer and digital cameras. They will learn about desktop publishing. Like Coyote says, all that equipment needs to come out of the closet.

"You're dealing with kids," he says. "Excitement. Risk taking. Action. Fun. Challenge. These must become part of your daily vocabulary," Coyote instructs.

I think about his ideas some more and they really make sense. Then I realize, too, that Coyote can easily connect all the language choices in my home in fun and exciting ways. He insists on baby-talk Navajo not only during baby-talk time but whenever it becomes useful, just like his nasalized talk.

"That's baby talk all the way, baby," he says.

I flinch at Coyote calling me baby. That jerk.

"While you're doing these projects, the Navajo language will allow you to act on your thoughts, to accomplish your goals, to realize ideas in physical forms. Navajo then becomes a language of action, excitement, working together, and accomplishment. How much more utilitarian can you get than that?" he asks. "This is the language of true love," Coyote says. "You teach the children how to fish way out in the sea of sand. They learn to use Navajo as a way of thinking and acting. Let them be actors, not the ones acted upon." Coyote almost raises his voice. "The Navajo language and I have an intimate relationship," he commands.

"Tell my stories in Navajo and you, too, shall endure," he says, it is said.

"I am the way of transformation," he declares. "In the end I always transform and transcend. I am change, and only I endure," he howls.

Then Coyote runs away. "Now get off your lazy . . . ," he says. I don't catch that last word. Then I hear him howling, "Better get to work. Remember, I'm around and I'll be back!"

I look after him and laugh, "Yeah, right. But don't you forget, Mr. Coyote, I'm much more of a bobcat than Bobcat himself!" He hears, I'm sure.

So that's what Coyote said. That was my encounter with Coyote the other day.

SUGGESTED READING

Bingham, Sam, and Janet Bingham. *Between Sacred Mountains: Stories and Lessons from the Land*. Chinle AZ: Rock Point Community School, 1982.

Wilkins, David E. *The Navajo Political Experience*. Tsaile AZ: Dine College Press, 1999.

Zolbrod, Paul G. *Diné bahane': The Navajo Creation Story*. Albuquerque: University Of New Mexico Press, 1984.

Coyote and Skunk

Told by Rex Lee Jim

One day Coyote was trotting, they say. He started trotting from a place called Narrow Water Canyon. He was trotting that day under a blazing sun. Not even a cloud could be seen in the sky. As he trotted, he looked around for something. Finally, he said, "I wish there was a cloud in the sky." Immediately a cloud appeared and he trotted in the shadow of the cloud. "I would like to trot in a drizzle," he said. He trotted in a drizzle. "I wish to trot with water sprinkling from out between my toes," he said. Right away water started sprinkling from out between his toes. He looked around again. "Hmmm, it certainly would be nice to trot in water up to my knees," he said. Water rose up to his knees. "Perhaps it would be nicer if only my backbone showed while trotting," he said. Only his backbone showed as he trotted. "Let me trot with only the tip of my nose sticking out of the water," he said. Only his nose stuck out. "I wish the water to carry me to a place of many prairie dogs," he said. He started floating and was washed ashore in the bend of the river where there were many prairie dogs. He lay there among the debris.

He was coming for water that day, the Skunk was. He was listening, this Coyote. "Shhhh" was heard. Skunk looked around, no one. He kept going. "Shhhh" sounded again. Again he looked around. Again, no one. This happened four times. Finally, Skunk saw Coyote lying there in the bend of the river, among the debris of washed ashores.

"Come here, my cousin, I should like to speak to you," he said.

Skunk went over and asked, somewhat wary, "What is it, my cousin?"

"Come, don't be afraid," he said. "I would like for us to cook some prairie dogs and rabbits in the ground," he said.

"Let me share a plan with you," he continued. "Now you listen carefully," he instructed Skunk. "This is what I want you to do. Go grab some tall, slim grass and bring it back. Place it all over my body. Here under my armpits, between my toes, in my nose, ears and nose. Lift my tail and stick some in my ass too," he said. "Then run over to prairie dog village and let them know that I am dead. Say, 'The Intolerant One is dead.' Then tell them that you want to have a ceremony for him. When you finally bring them over, dance around me singing, 'Iinao'o, Iinao.'

When you're all into it, say, 'Look, look, see that beautiful thing flying in the sky.' When they all look up, piss up in the air. When they are scrawling around with their eyes, we'll club them to death. We're going to have a feast, my cousin," he said triumphantly.

Skunk thought the idea would work and started for the village.

"Wait, wait," Coyote said.

Skunk went back to him.

"Don't forget to bury big, strong clubs underneath me," he said.

Skunk did so. Then he went to prairie dog village.

There Skunk saw many prairie dogs and even rabbits. "Shoh, shoh, I saw the Intolerant One in the bend of the river among the debris. He is dead!" Skunk said.

Of course, no one believed him. "Who would kill him? No one is capable of that!" they all agreed.

"No, no, he is truly dead," Skunk insisted.

Finally, a small prairie dog reluctantly volunteered to go check. "It is true. I even walked around him," he said upon his return.

Then they sent Rabbit. He returned saying similar things; "I walked around him pretty close."

Big Prairie Dog went and came huffing back. "It's very true. I even got on top of him and danced around!"

Finally, the Jack Rabbit went and returned immediately. "He is truly dead. He must have been dead for some time now. He's beginning to decay; grass is beginning to grow all over him," he said.

Then everybody got silent and began to worry. "What must be done? What should we all do?" they asked themselves.

"Let's have a ceremony for him. Let's dance for him," Skunk said.

They all agreed. They went over and started dancing. "Iinaoo'o, iinao," Skunk started singing. Everyone joined in. Just when everyone was beginning to get into it, Skunk said, "Look, look, see that beautiful thing flying in the sky." They all looked up, and Skunk pissed into the sky.

"My eyes, my eyes," they all screamed sprawling about.

Up jumped the dead Coyote. "Don't just stand around. Club them, club them! There goes another one," he yelled at Skunk. No one survived his club that day!

Skunk started picking up sticks. "No, no," Coyote said. "Let's go over there where there are lots of greasewood bushes. There's plenty of wood over there," he said.

So they went over there, and Skunk carried most of the heavy load. Skunk wanted to eat badly, so he started to work right away.

"Oh, I've been lying there for so long. I need to stretch out a little bit. I'll help you when my bones get back into their places," he said as he lay down and stretched himself out beneath the shade of a big greasewood bush.

Skunk ignored him and went about his work.

"Be sure to dig a hole and build a huge fire there. When the fire goes out, put in the prairie dogs and rabbits. Then cover them with a thin layer of dirt, and make sure the fire doesn't get too hot," he said.

Skunk did all that, for he knew what he was doing.

When Skunk finished, Coyote started pacing. Finally he said to Skunk, "I think we should have a race around that rock over there. Whoever wins get to eat first, to make the choices of what to eat first."

"No, no," Skunk said. "You're just trying to trick me. You know I don't run fast," Skunk argued.

"Well, let's race anyway, just to build an appetite," Coyote said. Skunk still refused. Coyote insisted. "I'll give you a head start. When I see you coming around the rock, then I'll start from here," he urged.

Skunk finally agreed, reluctantly. So he started and barely made it over the first hill. As he was wobbling along, he saw a badger hole and went inside to hide. He placed a large ball of plant in front of the hole. No one could see him. Some time later, Coyote zoomed by with huge balls of smoke trailing him. He had made a long string of bark, tied it to his tail, and lighted it. As soon as Coyote went over the next hill, Skunk came back out and went back to where they were cooking in the ground. He took out everything and eventually decided to leave some for Coyote. He put back some very small prairie dogs and rabbits. Then he carried the rest to a nearby cliff and perched himself in a place where Coyote wouldn't get him.

Skunk started eating. Just when he was beginning to enjoy himself, he saw Coyote coming in the distance. He came so fast and was back at the cooking place so suddenly. He fell on his back beneath a greasewood bush, in the shade, chest heaving. He said, "I wonder how my poor cousin is doing, the poor Skunk!" He rubbed wet sand on his chest to cool himself down. Then he got up and looked into the distance and didn't see Skunk coming. "Oh, I'm hungry," he said and started digging up the prairie dogs and rabbits. He threw away the small ones, saying, "This will ruin my appetite for the real juicy ones." He didn't find any. Then he grabbed what he threw away and gobbled them down so quickly that Skunk barely noticed.

"I know it's you, my cousin, Skunk," he said. He started tracking him and ended up at the foot of the cliff. Coyote couldn't figure out which way Skunk went. Skunk suddenly dropped him a bone. Coyote looked around and downed the bone. This happened four times.

"Shhhh," Skunk said.

Coyote looked up and saw Skunk. "My dear cousin, won't you please share with me," Coyote pleaded.

Skunk continued eating and dropped Coyote his leftover bones, which Coyote gobbled right down. Skunk finally said, "Please, don't ask me to share, my cousin. You're so much faster and cleverer than I am. You hunt. You can hunt because you can run. I can hardly walk. Let me have what little is left. You're so much faster!"

Coyote was pleased to hear that. Forgetting his hunger, he responded, "Of course, that I am! In fact, I run over four big logs in one leap!" Then he left and trotted way. He was trotting, they say. Coyote was trotting.

Coyote and Bobcat

Told by Rex Lee Jim

I

One day Coyote was trotting.
He was trotting, trotting.
He found the Bobcat asleep.
Stretched out in the sun on a rock.
Coyote walked around him.
"You sleep in the day," he mused.
"Just can't lie around," he said.
Then he pushed in the ears.
Then he pushed in the nose.
Then he pushed in the arms.
Then he pushed in the legs.
Then he pushed in the tail.
Then he pushed in the whole body.
Coyote howled with laughter.
"My, isn't he more handsome now," he said.
He walked around him one more time.
Bobcat snored even louder.
And Coyote trotted away, giggling.
He was trotting, trotting.
Bobcat woke up and didn't feel like himself.
"Coyote, my cousin, this is your work," he said.
"I will get you yet," he said, somewhat peeved.
Then he shook himself and started walking.
Bobcat was walking, walking.

II

One day Bobcat was walking.
He was walking, walking.

He found the Coyote asleep.

Stretched out in the sun on a rock.

Bobcat walked around him.

"You too sleep in the day," he mused.

"Just can't lie around too," he said.

Then he pulled out the ears.

Then he pulled out the nose.

Then he pulled out the arms.

Then he pulled out the legs.

Then he pulled out the tail.

Then he pulled out the whole body.

Bobcat meowed with laughter.

"My, aren't you more handsome now," he said.

He walked around him one more time.

Coyote snored even louder.

And Bobcat walked away, giggling.

He was walking, walking.

Coyote woke up and didn't feel like himself.

"Bobcat, my cousin, this is your work," he said.

"I will get you again," he said, somewhat pissed.

Then he shook himself and started trotting.

Coyote was trotting, trotting.

III

Sitting, sitting Bobcat.

Bobcat is sitting in the sun on a rock.

Coyote finds him and walks around him.

Sitting, sitting, Bobcat continues to lick himself.

"So," says the Coyote,

"Yes, it is so," says the Bobcat.

"Let's be friends again," says the Coyote.

"Yes, then let it be so," says the Bobcat.

"Well, then, let's play a game," says the Coyote.

"Yes, what should we play," says the Bobcat.

"Let's play scratching," says the Coyote, for

he couldn't see Bobcat's nails.

"How do you play that?" says the Bobcat.

"Simple," says the Coyote.

"I scratch your back, then you scratch my back," says the Coyote.

"No, no," says the Bobcat.

"You got longer nails than I do," says the Bobcat.

Coyote gets all excited and says, "Let's, let's."

"You just want to tear down my back,

I thought you wanted to be friends," says the Bobcat.

"Yes, yes, my cousin, this is a friendly game," the Coyote says.

Starting with Coyote,

they scratch one another's back.

Each time Bobcat feigns crying out in pain,

"Oh, I feel your scratching even more every time."

Coyote giggles with pleasure.

"I can't feel yours. This is your last time, cousin,

go ahead, give me your best scratch!"

Then Bobcat brings out all those nails

And scratches Coyote's back with all his might.

"Wawaaaaaaaaaoooooooooooooo!" Coyote howls with pain,

and with arched back he runs over the hill,

never looking back, not even once.

To this day he still hasn't returned to Bobcat yet.

IV

Aah,

should

we

play

scratching!

San Juan Pueblo–Tewa

The Oekuu Shadeh of Ohkay Owingeh

Introduction by Hao Huang

The Tewa Pueblos of northern New Mexico maintain a vibrant ceremonial tradition that encompasses music, dance, poetry, costumes, and ritual. The gestures and words of Tewa dance ceremonies symbolically order space by referring to the four cardinal directions and to the point at which they intersect, which is the village center. Dance movements, series of movements, even entire dance appearances are often repeated four times or in multiples of four, creating a nexus of motion and directional order.[1] Ritual ceremonies invoke the power of ancestral spirits to provide the most precious element of life in a dry land: rain. Most San Juan Pueblo ceremonial music is performed by a group of men, who sing in a low register, in unison, and with no harmony, often accompanied by squash rattles and drums. Texted passages alternate with formulaic phrases of vocables (syllables that are not words), which often mark the beginnings and endings of sections.

Ohkay Owingeh (San Juan Pueblo) is the largest, most populous, and northernmost of the six Tewa-speaking Pueblos. Approximately one hundred original seven-hundred-year-old adobe homes remain in the pueblo. Ohkay is situated on the east bank of the Rio Grande, north of the confluence of the Rio Grande and Rio Chama, on a rich alluvial floodplain adjacent to the town of Espanola. The pueblo is renowned as the birthplace of Popay, the leader of the successful Pueblo Revolt of 1680, which drove the Spanish conquistadors out of New Mexico for a dozen years. It is respected for maintaining traditional Tewa cultural practices. The Tewas believe that becoming and remaining Tewa is not a simple birthright but rather a long process of socialization and acculturation. This is achieved through participation in a complex annual cycle of communal activities, which include the performance of ceremonial dances, songs, and prayers, embodying and sustaining the physical and spiritual order of the Tewa world.

I have chosen to feature the Oekuu Shadeh (Turtle Dance) in this volume because, as the most sacred public dance ceremony of San Juan Pueblo, it touches on a core of Tewa sacred beliefs. Described by Parsons and Roberts as a "Maskless Kachina" ritual drama, this dance is particularly intriguing because its choreography, music, and texts are practically identical with the extremely secret and sacred masked ritual ceremonies that are restricted to kivas of the Rio Grande Pueblos.[2] The 1992 Oekuu Shadeh of Ohkay Owingeh was composed by Peter Garcia Sr., who taught the song to me over two summers (1995, 1996), during twenty-five hours of individual sessions and five more spent observing performances. My first article on this particular dance was published as the "1992 Turtle Dance of San Juan Pueblo: Lessons with Peter Garcia," which presents an ethnomusicological perspective on the relationships between sacred meanings, musical structure, and performance practice.[3] This revision integrates commentary by Garcia Sr. within the song text presentation and updates contextual information.

THE COMPOSER AND POET

Peter Garcia Sr., Kwa-Phade (Passing Rain), was born in Ohkay Owingeh (San Juan Pueblo), one of twelve sons of the noted Tewa singer Jose Antonio Garcia, Kaa-Tse (White Leaf). From an early age he participated in the ceremonial life of his community. He was a member of the Sawipingeh, the group of singers and religious elders at San Juan Pueblo who supervise traditional Tewa ceremonial dances, and was widely recognized by many Tewas as "the Singer." A member of the Garcia Brothers, leaders in the Pueblo cultural revival since the 1950s, he made many recordings on labels such as Indian House, New World Records, Tribal Music International, and Music of the World. His songs and dances have been performed at many institutions, including the Smithsonian Institution, Washington DC; the Pueblo Indian Cultural Center, Albuquerque; the Museum of Indian Arts and Culture, Santa Fe; Colorado College; the University of California at Los Angeles; and also in Spain and Canada.

As a practitioner of Pueblo sacred rituals, Peter Garcia Sr. followed the path of a Made Person (religious initiate) by praying to the Oekhuwa of the four directions: "Remember that the words and the method of delivery of all prayers and speeches are the same; only the places mentioned are different. If you are a Made person you always pray to and invoke the authority of the mountains, and the 'Dry Food Who Never Did Become' [Oekhuwa]."[4] The Made People "of the Lake" (of Emergence) mediate between spiritual and human realms and become Oekhuwa after death. They maintain the regular progression of the seasons and promote peace and social harmony through creating and performing traditional ceremonial songs, which reestablish the village as a sacred center at the intersection of the four cardinal directions. At our first lesson Garcia began with an introduction to the basic elements of traditional Pueblo music. He invoked each cardinal direction and its associated color, tracing the traditional directional circuit beginning with north.

The music that I compose (is) not in relation to instruments except for the instruments which I use, which are the drums, the rattle, the turtle.

The motions are also included, but the words are also very important be-cause we are relying on the directions which Mother Earth gave us. First of all, in the Tewa world, we are talking about the north, the west, the south, and the east, and to the heaven and Mother Earth. The directions also have colors—to the north we have blue, to the west we have yellow, to the south we have red, to the east we have white. Those are the main colors that the Tewa world uses, and when it comes to crops, the corn, the wheat are mentioned in the songs.

A preliminary step to gaining access to sacred, nonordinary reality is to visual-ize the sacred reference points of the cardinal directions, believed to be "encoun-tered at the periphery of the horizontal plane."[5] This realm is often associated with beings variously described as *shiwana* or *kat'sina,* katcina, and kachina, whose Tewa equivalent is Oekhuwa, 'cloud beings', who comprise the highest order of deities.[6] Sacred mountains identified with the four cardinal directions define the boundaries of the Tewa world. Each mountain is associated with a sacred lake where the Oekhuwa reside; at the top of each mountain a shrine made of stones arranged in a keyhole pattern marks the *na sipu,* 'earth navel', where the To'way, guardians of ritual order, reside. Closer to the village are four mesas with caves and labyrinths, where the Tsaviyo, masked supernatural beings who discipline the community with whips, dwell. The mesa tops serve as observation posts for the To'way when they come from the mountains to look in at the village during a community ceremonial dance. Most Turtle dances refer to this cosmology.

DANCE INFORMATION

The Oekuu Shadeh (Turtle Dance) is held each year on December 26, marking the winter solstice, thereby straddling the end of one year and the beginning of another. Despite written speculations by scholars about whether the ceremony was performed during precolonial times, Tewas believe that the Turtle Dance has always functioned as a winter solstice ceremony—no less so now than in the past. To understand why the dance is held on the twenty-sixth, rather than, say, the twenty-second, one must bear in mind that the dance itself is merely the public portion of a larger ceremony. As with many Tewa dances, formal preparation for public performance takes place over the course of four days. As such, the winter solstice often coincides with the first of four days of preparation, after which the dancers and singers emerge from the kiva to perform in public (on the twenty-sixth)

The public dance is performed to thank the Oekhuwa spirits of the sacred ever-greens (the Douglas spruce, blue spruce, and white fir, which symbolize everlast-ing life) for the continuing life and good health of the people in the San Juan community. Only men participate, bare-chested and daubed with mud, originally gathered from the distant sacred lakes, currently collected from the banks of the Rio Grande where it passes through San Juan. The dancers wear white kilts, colorful headbands, turquoise and shell necklaces, arm bands holding evergreen sprigs, ankle wrappings of skunk fur over ceremonial moccasins, and turtle shell rattles (made with deer or pig's hooves attached by leather thongs to the top of a river turtle shell) tied to their right knees. Gourd rattles, ritually significant for their evocation of the sound of rain, are used by all the dancers; no drum is used. The messages of the songs refer to the core of Tewa religious belief, and viewers from the community are notably reverent and attentive for this public dance.[7]

Garcia remarked that the turtle is almost never mentioned in Turtle Dance song texts and explained the ritual significance of turtles thus:

> They're river turtles. The Rio Grande has never gone dry, and it keeps us with abundance of water. . . . One of the elders said that the river turtle has the longest life of any reptile. It's a long life that the turtle provides for the world, and nobody thanks him for it. It's ending the year, for the whole twelve months it has carried us through. There's a lot of rituals that are involved in it; it has a lot of power giving us that extension of life that we have completed the whole year and now will give us life for the following year.

An alternate explanation told to Tewa field researcher Danny Lichtenfeld is equally compelling:

> This dance, which signals the beginning of a new annual cycle (rebirth, reemergence), is appropriately named for the first creature in the region to reemerge after winter dormancy. After the annual ceremonial cycle ends in September with the Harvest Dance, traditional activities are literally taken underground. In those years when highly sacred "masked kachina" dances are to be held, they occur in the kiva throughout November and early December. Just as the turtle eventually emerges from the mud of the riverbanks, the people literally emerge from the kiva into public view for the aptly named Turtle Dance.[8]

Peter Garcia's performance impressions of the San Juan Pueblo Turtle Dance provide a personal perspective of this dance:

> December being a winter month, it's usually cold after you put on the Earth paint, and you're all naked, all you're wearing is the kilt and you're painted and you have the leg belts with the turtles and you have a headdress; when you start moving the cold doesn't even bother you. . . . Every-

body is standing in line; there are about a hundred and some. This is all nothing but males; they're painted up and lined up in the plaza in front of the kiva. . . . Everybody follows through; they follow the leader. There's a tribal member who leads you; he's wearing a blanket. When we go out from the kiva, the leader as soon as he gets to the back end of the chapel (that's our sanctuary for participating in dancing), as soon as he gets there, he starts shaking the rattle and everybody starts doing that. As soon as he turns (right), they turn sideways, and then the tail end comes, and when it gets to the tail end, the guy on the tail end makes another turn, and when everybody is facing to the north, that's when the center people like us, we start, and then we emphasize more on the beat.

Then we start the "Ha-a-a-a-e-e-e," and everybody joins in with the same pitch. That's why it is important that the song leader carry a start with a note where everybody can sing. And people are out there observing, they're watching you. Like I said, we have two clans, the Winter Clan like us, we are wearing white moccasins with a little red thing on it, and the Summer Clan are wearing the yellow moccasins. The people are watching that costume, not just paying attention to the singing and the footsteps, they are very attentive and they are observing what the people are wearing. There are more in Winter Clan, I'm not bragging for that. There's me, my brother, and another elderly man, there are two from the Summer Clan, and they're standing with us, and we start, we're the elders. But it's a story. The story the composer is saying is this is how it's formed. In those days I couldn't find the words for lightning and thunder. How inspiring it is to identify what these elements mean. Before we get the rain we get lightning, right? And pretty soon, we get the water in abundance. You have to be patient and consider what elements are being used.

As is the case with almost all Tewa rituals, the 1992 Turtle Dance expresses a theme of regeneration and rejuvenation of life. The dance ceremonies exemplify new life because they are communal experiences that revitalize the Tewa community by bringing it together. Traditional Tewa culture is renewed by ritual performances, which reaffirm a deep relationship between the land and the spirits of the venerated ancestors. For Peter Garcia Sr. performing ritual was a way of regaining a meaningful perspective on life. He sang not only for himself but also to maintain the traditional ways of his people.

It becomes clear that the Turtle Dance celebrates a covenant between the ancestral spirits and current human life, linking both to the land in a ceremonial cycle.

In fact, the Turtle Dance ritually orders Tewa dualities: the human with the spiritual (i.e., the human To'way with the supernatural To'way, the Made People to the Oekhuwa deities); male and female Dawn People, followed by male and female Oekhuwa; north with east and south with west; lightning followed by rain, then thunder ushering rain; corn with wheat; crops before human birth and maturation. The following passage in *Musical Repercussions of 1492: Encounters in Text and Performance,* published by the Smithsonian Institution Press, was attributed to Peter Garcia: "It is living history, a pathway to the future, and an incorporation of the Pueblo interpretation of life and the cosmos around us. It is poetry and philosophy in motion, and it involves intricate and detailed planning. . . . If there was no one here in San Juan Pueblo to carry on the songs and traditional dances, our whole society might fall apart. . . . The songs honor renewal, regeneration, and the continuing process of creation."[9] As poetic as these words are, they are not Peter Garcia's but are, in fact, entirely Julio Estrada's! When Garcia was initially informed about that chapter, he had no idea it was in print or that he was cited as a coauthor.

It is best for Peter Garcia Sr. to speak for himself and, in fact, to explain the motivation behind this chapter. He told me, "If you share this, somebody will learn a little bit out of you, and as it goes on down the line, some of these things are going to be related." The composer of the 1992 Turtle Dance chose to share his knowledge by teaching me how to sing the song. He said quite eloquently,

> *If you start a song, you run out of words, you run out of what happened after that, you leave people standing with their mouths open. What happened next? If we don't explain these things, people are lost, and they get turned off. If you know a portion of it, you just stay with it until the end. That's what some of the people do, the local people. There's a lot who come just for that day, usually everybody's on Christmas vacation. So they come on the twenty-sixth to hear this. When people are standing around the audience, and we're dancing, I look around and you could see people with their eyes closed, and they're into the tone of that music because it's so—I think it does something to them, to their bodies and everything else. When that is true, you feel "I've completed something, I gave a message coming from Mother Earth and the whole community of San Juan." And your pueblo is known for the Turtle Dance.*

NOTES

1. Jill D. Sweet, *Dances of the Tewa Pueblo Indians* (Santa Fe NM: School of American Research Press, 1985), 29.

2. Don L. Roberts, "A Calendar of Eastern Pueblo Indian Ritual Dramas," in *Southwest-*

ern Indian Ritual Drama, ed. Charlotte J. Frisbie (Albuquerque: University of New Mexico Press, 1980), 105.

3. Hao Huang, "The 1992 Turtle Dance of San Juan Pueblo: Lessons with the Composer, Peter Garcia," *American Indian Culture and Research Journal* 21, no. 4 (1997): 171–215.

4. Alfonso Ortiz, *The Tewa World* (Chicago: University of Chicago Press, 1969), 22–23.

5. Dennis and Barbara Tedlock, *Teachings of the American Earth* (New York: Liveright, 1975), xiv.

6. Regarding *shiwana* or *kat'sina,* see Paul Humphreys, "Form as Cosmology: An Interpretation of Structure in the Ceremonial Songs of the Pueblo Indians," *Pacific Review of Ethnomusicology* 5 (1989): 66.

7. Alfonso Ortiz, liner notes for *Oku Shareh: Turtle Dance Songs of San Juan Pueblo,* New World Records NW 301 (1979).

8. Danny Lichtenfeld, e-mail to author, Thursday, March 26, 1998.

9. Julio Estrada, "Bridging the Past and Present," in *Musical Repercussions of 1492: Encounters in Text and Performance,* ed. Carol E. Robertson (Washington DC: Smithsonian Institution Press, 1992), 93.

1992 Oekuu Shadeh

Composed by Peter Garcia Sr.

SECTION A

(Puchenu)

HA- A- A- A- EY- EY- EY

HA- A- A- A- EY- EY- EY

(Khapu)

Daybreak is coming from the horizon.

The Dawn Boys are singing together in unison.

The songs they sing sound beautiful.

LEHEY KWA LEHEY

AYHEY LA-YA-YA-YA

Daylight is coming over the horizon.

The Dawn Girls are calling like trumpets.

It rings out and sounds beautiful.

LEHEY KWA LEHEY

AYHEY LA-YA-YA-YA

> *P. G.: The first one, it starts with the directions; it's the Khapu. First, we're talking about daylight coming from the horizon, close to where the sun comes out. You picture the start of the horizon, and there's Dawn People living in that area. What are they doing when it becomes daylight? You picture them. What are the Dawn People, the Horizon People doing? They're singing, and it is coming out beautifully, what we're hearing of their song. The boys are mentioned first and then the girls. The boys are singing, and when it comes to the girls, they're humming—well, I couldn't really find a word for* tentu. *If you say* tem peh, *that's to say like a trumpet, very loud. And the girls are doing that in their own way, and they're sounding beautifully too, in their own way. And then it goes to the chorus, which is called Khake. That really emphasizes the direc-*

tions; it means loud pitch, I guess. Everybody joins in, and that song
carries in the whole plaza.

H. H.: This pair of opening phrases follow the Tewa ritual order of the sexes: the boys come first, then the girls; later the male elders are succeeded by the females. The spirit world parallels the progression of the natural world. The initial dawning of the horizon is accompanied by the song of the Dawn Boys; the next time, when the horizon shows more of the sun, "when it's just about light" (Garcia), the Dawn Girls make their calls.

(Khake)
Way out in the North, the male Oekhuwa [Cloud Beings]
create lightning.
The lightning flashes, followed by rain,
so that the corn can grow.
HAWEY A-A-A-AWEY

Way out in the West, the female Oekhuwa [Cloud Beings]
make thunder.
The thunder roars, followed by mist,
so that the wheat can grow.
HAWEY A-A-A-AWEY

> *P. G.: And then the second one, its just like saying, What did they*
> *bring? through the elements which they created, you know, the kachina*
> *[Oekhuwa]. So first through the creation of the elements, they created*
> *rain and what comes before that, the lightning, through their powers. In*
> *order for the song and the story that you're telling to be complete, you*
> *have to put in the words that make sense to you in here and in here.*
> *. . . You concentrate. What did they bring through the lightning? They*
> *brought the rain. Then on top of that, they brought the corn and then*
> *the wheat, the growth of the wheat.*

H. H.: In the Khake, Garcia outlines certain central aspects of the Tewa worldview. The outermost points of the cosmos are identified with mountains, which are visible in the four cardinal directions. Each peak cradles a lake where the Oekhuwa, the Cloud Beings, dwell. These mountains constitute sacred sources of precious moisture, evidenced by more rainfall at higher elevations, by trees felled by lightning, and by an almost perpetual presence of clouds overhead, which are taken as signs of the presence of ancestral spirits. In bringing lightning and thunder (light precedes sound), which heralds rain, the Oekhuwa deities "are the sources for all of man's needs" (Ortiz, *Tewa World*, 25); their blessing is translatable as 'life breath blow'. By invoking these deities and describing their powers, the Tewas are praying for rain.

(Khakhanu)
Through these creations, we have become happy.
We are thanking them.
EY-EY-EY-HEY-EY-HEY-EY-HEY-EY-EY-EY-HEY
EY-EY-EY-HEY-EY-HEY-EY-HEY-EY-EY-EY-HEY

> *P. G.: And so, how did you feel by receiving those creators bringing this stuff? Naturally you feel happy. What did you do after you felt happy? You gave thanks. Kudaapoe. We thank them for it.*

H. H.: The Khakhanu features the rhythmically buoyant T'aa, where the normal duple pulsations are supplanted by triplet groupings, and it ends in a long, climactic vocable passage. This subsection publicly acknowledges the blessings provided by the spirits and celebrates the partnership between the physical world inhabited by human beings and the spirit world, which provides water, necessary for life-sustaining crops in the arid Southwest.

It is important to understand that for the Tewas repetition does not automatically indicate monotony but rather suggests a heightening of concentration and ritual meaning. There is also a planned symmetry in lyrics, with each pair of phrases in the Puchenu, Khapu, and Khake leading to the climactic Khakhanu, which highlights the T'aa and extended vocable sections.

SECTION B

(Haapenbay)
Haapenbay, Haapenbay, Haapenbay, Haapen(bay).
Two sacred spirits are coming from the east.
The Tsaviyo come jumping into the kiva.
HAWEY A-A-A-A-WEY

The Tsaviyo come out to the center of the main plaza to see us.
They come to bring us blessings.
HAWEY A-A-A-A-WEY

> *P. G.: Haapenbay is altogether a different tune. The beginning of the Haapenbay, that portion is meaning to say the two spirits in relation to the ceremonial dance of the Turtle [Tsaviyo] came from the east, and they came into the kiva and are jumping. They have whips; their role is*

> *to discipline the community. They come once a year, they're included in*
> *there in the song, they come jumping into the kiva. The second portion*
> *is about the middle of the plaza; they bring blessings to the plaza. . . .*
> *The spirits in the Haapenbay, they're in the form of human things.*
>
> *They're bringing us the blessings; it's a yearly thing, in traditional*
> *talks, in the counseling session, the elders talk. They always mention that*
> *you have to respect these two because they come once a year and they*
> *bring us the blessings, the health, the crops. . . . That's how we live.*

H. H.: Significantly, the Tsaviyo are impersonated only once a year, during the
Turtle Dance preparations and ceremonies, and are invoked only in the Haapenbay. They are a pair of spirits, white and black, who wear masks and carry whips.
Two days before the Turtle Dance, both Tsaviyo appear at dusk. Their ritual directions recall the divergent paths of migration: the white (winter) Tsaviyo enters
the village counterclockwise through the north plaza; the black (summer) Tsaviyo
goes clockwise by way of the south plaza. Ortiz writes about an important physical encounter between these two spirits: "At the 'earth mother earth navel middle
place' (nan e hu kwi na sipu pingeh), the sacred center of the village located on
the south plaza, they meet, shake hands. . . . This symbolic act of meeting and
shaking hands, performed while standing atop the sacred shrine at the center of
the village, is interpreted by informants as affirming the unity and partnership of
the Tsave Yoh" (Ortiz, *Tewa World*, 75).

The Tsaviyo maintain order and moral purity in the sacred center of the village
by symbolically joining as partners from the Winter and Summer moieties, as the
old year ends and the new one begins. Spirits with disciplinary authority, possessing therapeutic as well as admonitory powers, the Tsaviyo exercise the right
to flog any social delinquents of San Juan Pueblo and leap down into the kiva to
admonish the Turtle Dance performers gathered there. The sick of each household are brought out into the public plazas after the Turtle Dance ceremony so
that the Tsaviyo may minister to them. Their curing rite or blessing, translated as
'children illness blow away', can offer temporary relief from bodily ailments. This
should be distinguished from the power of the Oekhuwa, who bestow life itself.

(Khakegi)
Way out in the south, the male Oekhuwa create lightning.
The lightning flashes, followed by rain,
so that children can be born.
HAWEY A-A-A-AWEY

Way out in the east, the female Oekhuwa make thunder.
The thunder roars, followed by mist,

so the human beings can mature.
HAWEY A-A-A-AWEY

(Khakhanu)
Through these creations, we have become happy.
We are thanking them.
EY-EY-EY-HEY-EY-HEY-EY-HEY-EY-HEY-EY-HEY
EY-EY-EY-HEY-EY-HEY-EY-HEY-EY-EY-EY-HEY. HEY.

H. H.: Garcia's emphasis on the uniqueness and ritual meaning of the Haapenbay
offers insights into an insider's interpretation of the special qualities of the 1992
Turtle Dance:

> P. G.: *You're telling a whole story, by golly, there's a whole lot of words in
> it. . . . The meaning—the Haapenbay has a different rhythm right from
> the start, you noticed that, right? So in the Haapenbay the south and
> the east are mentioned, but with different productions. You realize that
> first they brought the crops, and to go into the south, instead of saying
> "corn" you say "the child," "the bringing of the children." . . .*
>
> *I think that's what makes our song so unique, because there is a Haa-
> penbay, and that Haapenbay is altogether different from the start of the
> beginning. But when it gets to the chorus, the Khake, it's the same thing.
> See in this one, we are mentioning different elements. . . . So this is the
> childbearing because the life is also included in our songs. Why would
> we sing it, why would we dance it if there's no child, no children, no ac-
> tivities of humans, you know? What I'm saying the spirits put a lot of
> words into your system so you can share it and express your feelings of
> what we're doing.*

REPEAT SECTION A

(Return to Puchenu section)
HA- A- A- A- EY- EY- EY
HA- A- A- A- EY- EY- EY

(Khapu)
Daybreak is coming from the horizon.
The Dawn Boys are singing together in unison.
The songs they sing sound beautiful.
LEHEY KWA LEHEY
AYHEY LA-YA-YA-YA

Daylight is coming over the horizon.
The Dawn Girls are calling like trumpets.
It rings out and sounds beautiful.
LEHEY KWA LEHEY
AYHEY LA-YA-YA-YA

(Khakegi)
Way out in the north, the male Oekhuwa create lightning.
The lightning flashes, followed by rain,
so that the corn can grow.
HAWEY A-A-A-A-WEY

Way out in the west, the female Oekhuwa make thunder.
The thunder roars, followed by mist,
so that the wheat can grow.
HAWEY A-A-A-A-WEY

(Khakhanu)
Through these creations, we have become happy.
We are thanking them.
EY-EY-EY-HEY-EY-HEY-EY-HEY-EY-EY-EY-HEY
EY-EY-EY-HEY-EY-HEY-EY-HEY-EY-EY-EY-HEY

O'odham

Whirlwind Songs

Introduction by David Kozak

The traditional song-poetry (*ñe'i*) of the O'odham of southern Arizona is a
dreamt-nature poetry. Lyric content, the defining feature of this people's song-
poetry, revels in the verbal representations of the natural world. It is a nature
poetry because it describes gorgeous landscapes that contain mountains, deserts,
and oceans inhabited by plants, animals, birds, insects, the sun, rain, lightning,
and other natural phenomena. But as Donald Bahr, Lloyd Paul, and Vincent Joseph have pointed out (1997, 100), O'odham song-poetics is a nature poetry that
often privileges social relations. The relations between people and spirits and nature are often conspicuous in this music. Whirlwind songs, the subject of this
chapter, are a genre of healing songs sung by shamans (*ma:kai*) and ritual curers
(*s-wusos o'odham*) in the treatment of whirlwind sickness (*siwulogi mumkidag*).
As a sickness-causing entity, whirlwind (*siwulogi*) is one of approximately fifty
etiological agents in the O'odham medical theory. One usually contracts whirlwind sickness as a carefree, disobedient child who plays in the dust devils that are
characteristic of the O'odham desert region.

The symptoms of whirlwind sickness include arthritis-like leg and back pain
and dizziness that emerge in adulthood. To my knowledge whirlwinds are not a
commonly diagnosed cause of sickness today, and so the singing of whirlwind
songs may now be a rare occurrence (although I'm sure that playing in dust devils
is still popular with children). This chapter presents two whirlwind song sets, the
only published examples of this song genre. Despite being recorded over seventy-
five years apart, their poetic kinship is obvious. The first set was recorded, translated, and published by Frank Russell in 1908. The six whirlwind songs were sung
by Ha-ata (Finished Olla). David Lopez and I retranslated this set because Russell's
version contained some flaws. The second song set we present was sung by Vicente
Jose and recorded by Lopez during a cure for one of Lopez's sons. Lopez and I
translated and discussed the set in 1994. At the time we did not pursue their publication, and we left them for a later time. Sadly, David Lopez died in 1998 due to
diabetic complications.

For much of his life David Lopez worked as a cowboy, farmer, school custodian, and occasional ritual curer. He lived in the villages of Santa Rosa and Covered Wells. He worked with three generations of anthropologists (Ruth Under-hill, Donald Bahr, and myself) in the furthering of the world's understanding of O'odham language and culture. His contributions are significant as attested by his coauthoring of three books: *Piman Shamanism and Staying Sickness, Rainhouse and Ocean,* and most recently *Devil Sickness and Devil Songs.* His motivation was a desire to help ensure the continued viability of the O'odham language. In his more pessimistic moods David agonized over the younger generations' seeming am-bivalence toward their native language. His linguistic work was an effort to address language loss. There appears to be a generational difference in language facility; younger people are less likely to know and/or use their native tongue, while older people (perhaps fifty years of age and older) speak O'odham more frequently and consistently. While Lopez didn't see this work on whirlwind songs to completion, I trust—hope—that he would be happy with it.

The singer Vicente Jose was from the village of Santa Rosa. I never met him because he had died before my arrival there. According to Donald Bahr, Vicente Jose was a master of many kinds of curing and social dance songs. He was a re-spected singer with a strong voice and was very knowledgeable in the old ways (*o'odham himdag*). Nothing, to my knowledge, is known of the singer Ha-ata (Finished Olla). Frank Russell does not provide biographical information on this man, who most likely resided on the Gila River (Pima) Indian Community. The O'odham (Pima-Papago) live in southern Arizona and northern Sonora, Mexico. They number approximately twenty-five thousand and occupy four separate reser-vations in the United States, including the Gila Bend, the Sells, and the San Xavier Reservation, and the Gila River (Pima) Indian Community. The various O'odham communities share a language and culture, despite their different adaptations to variations in the Sonoran Desert environment.

In the twentieth century the United States' political and economic culture, as well as popular culture, have gone a long way in changing the peoples' lives. Al-though now much of traditional O'odham culture is a series of memories residing in various academic publications, the song-poetic tradition remains a viable and enduring element of O'odham identity and pride, a symbolic touchstone for many. The basis of this music tradition is the dream and epitomizes what George Herzog (1928, 455–58) called the "dreamt mythic song series" found in the western United States and northern Mexico among speakers of the Uto-Aztecan languages. It is not known how many O'odham today dream songs, but it is arguable that the ma-jority of singers now learn them from other O'odham people in both social and ritual contexts.

Characteristic of O'odham song-poetics is the dream spirit author of the text, the arrangement of songs into compilations or sets, and certain genre-specific tex-

tual/behavioral attributes. Songs are not thought to be the product of human creativity. Rather, songs are gifts sung to humans by spirit-persons (e.g., owl-person,
deer-person, butterfly-person, etc.) in the dreams of humans, fully articulated and
ready for humans to memorize and repeat them. Presumably, the eleven whirlwind songs presented here were gifts from a whirlwind-person to both Ha-ata and
Vicente Jose. While they did not compose the whirlwind songs, they did arrange
them into short song sets, one six and the other five songs in length. Song-set arrangement is an aesthetic and practical act as it serves a storytelling and healing
purpose. Finally, the textual/behavioral attributes or characteristics of the songs
are what distinguish them from other spirit-given forms of music.

The eleven whirlwind songs celebrate botany, sound, and movement. First,
plants. There are five plants rooted in these songs. Overall, four plants are mentioned in the lyrics, with two being specifically identified (*to:ta hanam,* white or
jumping cholla [*Opuntia fulgida*], and *wi:pam,* or climbing milkweed vine [*Sarco-
stemma cynanchoides*]). Two other plants are variously referenced and defined
(*u'us* 'tree', and *u'us* 'bush, shrub, general desert plant growth'). The fifth plant
(*gi:dag u'us,* whitethorn [*Acacia constricta*]) is used in the cure of wind sickness
and is not mentioned in any of the songs, but David Lopez explained its relation
and relevance to me. A branch of the *gi:dag* tree about eighteen inches in length
is selected, cut from the tree, and stripped of leaves so that the small thorns are
exposed, and it is then used to whip the legs of the patient who suffers whirlwind
sickness. The whipping brings small dots of blood to the skin's surface where the
thorns penetrated, thereby releasing some of the sickness-causing substance.[1]

Wind houses are mentioned in each of the whirlwind song sets, and they are
plant based. One may rightly ask, What is a wind house? and Where can it be
found? The answer offered here is tentative. First, a wind house does not refer to a
built structure. Second, "wind house" is referenced in both Mockingbird speeches
and in this people's mythology. Third, in an attempt to answer this question, after
David Lopez and I had translated the Vicente Jose songs we drove to a remote
desert location on the Sells Reservation to visit a wind house. What he showed
me was a paloverde tree (*kek cehedagi* [*Cercidium microphyllum*]) on the bank of
a wash that was covered, tangled and twisted, with the milkweed vine. "Look,"
Lopez said, "this is where the whirlwinds come from."

Now sound and movement. Space limitations do not permit me to discuss each
song individually. Whirlwind songs are striking in that they do not dwell on either
the beautiful desert landscapes so common in other song genres (e.g., *duajida,*
or diagnosis songs) or the interactions between humans and spirits (e.g., *cu:kud,*
or owl songs). Insofar as the following eleven whirlwind songs are representative
of the genre, this poetry emphasizes the auditory aspect of forceful wind and its
movements, thus sound and motion. And while one does not see wind directly,

one may observe its actions. Thus, the wind unexpectedly "thunders"; it wraps around, it runs ceaselessly, incessantly, it twists and swirls. The songs' verbs reveal this genre's behavioral attributes: whirlwinds and therefore the songs are about frenetic and ceaseless movement and deafening sound.

Translation of Native literatures into English, in our way of thinking, demands that the original words and meanings be maintained as much as is possible. For us fidelity to the originating language is essential. Thus, the eleven whirlwind songs are the product of discussions and debates between Lopez and me over the significances of individual words, usually the verbs. Together we tried to produce and believe we achieved "literal" translations. After David's death, I decided not to stray from the versions we agreed on and thus not to present them in a more "free" (although perhaps a more readable and less quirky English) mode, largely because I do not want to say more than the translations that David Lopez and I agreed on. Yet one is tempted to present versions that may help the non-O'odham reader more readily grasp the original meanings and aesthetics of the songs, that is, to make them as compelling in English as they are in O'odham. For example, one might use a kinetic, "concrete" approach to suggest something of the original imagery and energy, to lift the songs off the page. Compare this version with the "literal" version of song 1.

> Wind sing
>   begin
> here
>   the land   stretches   in front of me

Experimenting with word choice and arrangement on the page may assist in cross-cultural understanding. And while this approach does not solve the problem of translation and presentation in Native literatures, it does indicate some of the difficulties inherent in trying to render such literatures in writing.

Now, what do the song sets say? I find the sets to be modest compilations of medicine songs that churn with excitement and power. Modest because they are not "complete" sets of healing songs in terms of O'odham musical theory, according to which a full song set should commence with an easily identifiable series of starting references, possess a "turning" song, and conclude with a series of equally identifiable "ending" or sunrise songs. Only song 1 of the first set is a starting song. Songs 7 through 11 of the second set may all be starting songs. Neither set possesses a turning song or ending songs. This is not to say that the absence is improper or unheard of. Rather, the absence is probably more common than not, although the ideal would be for the sets to possess them. They are also modest in that in translation, as in the original language, the churning excitement, the songs' kinetic energy, is often muffled and resides just beneath the surface. This tendency toward understatement and modesty in O'odham song is common in this people's healing song-poetry.[2]

They are exciting because they engage the hearer/reader in the glories of the turmoil found in nature. Everything is shaking, blowing, churning, and swirling. The songs speak of this turmoil, thereby glorying in the nature or personality of the whirlwind-person. It is, therefore, a whirlwind's nature to spin, swirl, twist, and thunder. That's to be expected, and songs 4, 5, 6, 8, and 11 clearly state this. But what is not expected is how humans can be paired to this behavioral characteristic of nature. Juxtaposing the two song sets reveals a behavioral complementarity. Together, they tell a story that boasts of the frenetic nature of life. In the first song set the whirlwind is dizzy and running pitifully (read, staggering like a drunk human). Songs 5 and 6 tell us of this ecstatic state. In the second set a vine and other desert plants are twisted and swirled by the wind. That is, plants too can be dizzy (song 11 states this most clearly). But this is not to say that any of the plants discussed have intoxicating properties; they do not. Thus, it is a metaphorical rather than an intoxicant-induced dizziness.[3] The complementary relationship is poetically established in song that says that like human beings, plants, whirlwinds, and nature are beautifully dizzy (remember that dizziness is a symptom of this sickness). Hence, yet another complementary association exists with the *gi:dag* branch used as a whip. Just as the *gi:dag* is whipped around by the blowing wind, so too is the *gi:dag* whipped around by a human (ritual curer) against the legs of the patient.

This analysis leads to a final claim and conclusion regarding the healing component. As with many, if not all, O'odham curing song-poetics, healing is at least partly accomplished in a process of abreaction or complementarity that the singer(s) of songs establishes to create a sympathetic link or comparison between patient and the sickness-causing entity. In terms of whirlwind sickness the comparison or abreaction is established between patient and the whirlwind-person via the songs sung by the ritual curer.[4] In this case one is simultaneously sickened by and cured by wind in its frenetic, chaotic, and churning nature. Because health is restored when singers sing songs that "please" the sickness-causing spirit (in this case, whirlwind-spirit), it is technically unimportant for the patient to hear the curing songs. Rather, the spirit who caused the sickness is the intended audience, as it alone has the power to restore a person's health. But patients do, of course, hear and pay attention to the songs. Finally, the practical-aesthetic of song offers the human patient a way to understand his or her illness and therefore to begin the healing process, because to know the cause and hear the cure is to reduce the patient's anxiety over their illness.

A NOTE ON ORTHOGRAPHY AND PRONUNCIATION

The apostrophe in the O'odham language as in the word *ñe'i* is a glottal stop that is pronounced like *oh-oh*. The letter *ñ* in the word *ñe'i* is pronounced like the *ny* in *canyon*. A colon following a vowel, as in the word *ma:kai,* creates a long vowel sound in the O'odham language: *a:, e:, i:, o:,* and *u:* are all long vowels.

NOTES

Thanks go to J. Page Lindsey for her botanical knowledge of the plants discussed herein, and to Donald Bahr, Kris Kozak, and Brian Swann for helping me to think through the songs and my interpretations of them. The Jacobs Research Funds, of the Whatcom Museum, generously funded this research.

1. The shaman Juan Gregorio in Bahr, Gregorio, Lopez, and Alvarez 1974 reported that the whip was also made from greasewood (*kawk u'us* [*Sarcobatus vermiculatus*]). Thus, we have a sixth related plant.

2. A tape recording has been deposited in the Whatcom Museum for those interested in hearing Vicente Jose's whirlwind songs.

3. Refer to Kozak 1991 for a discussion of the dizziness concept that is commonly found in social dance (Swallow-bird) songs.

4. See Kozak and Lopez 1999 for more on the abreaction element of healing.

SUGGESTED READING AND REFERENCES

Bahr, Donald, Juan Gregorio, David Lopez, and Albert Alvarez. 1974. *Piman Shamanism and Staying Sickness.* Tucson: University of Arizona Press.

Bahr, Donald, and Vincent Joseph. 1994. "Pima Oriole Songs." In *Coming to Light: Contemporary Translations of the Native Literatures of North America.* New York: Vintage Books.

Bahr, Donald, Lloyd Paul, and Vincent Joseph. 1997. *Ants and Orioles: Showing the Art of Pima Poetry.* Salt Lake City: University of Utah Press.

Bahr, Donald, Juan Smith, William Allison, and Julian Hayden. 1994. *The Short, Swift Time of Gods on Earth: The Hohokam Chronicles.* Berkeley: University of California Press.

Herzog, George. 1928. "Musical Styles in North America." In *Proceedings of the Twenty-third International Congress of Americanists,* 455–56. New York: n.p.

Kozak, David. 1991. "Swallow Dizziness: The Laughter of Carnival and Kateri." *Wicazo Sa Review* 8 (2): 1–10.

Kozak, David, and David Lopez. 1999. *Devil Sickness and Devil Songs: Tohono O'odham Poetics.* Washington: Smithsonian Institution Press.

Russell, Frank. 1908. *The Pima Indians.* 26th Annual Report of the Bureau of American Ethnology. Washington DC: Bureau of American Ethnology.

Whirlwind Songs 1–6

Performed by Ha-ata
Translated by David Kozak and David I. Lopez

1

Wind sing
here begin[1]
the land extends before me

2

Wind house thunder
wind house thunder
I cover the land with thunder

3

The windy mountains
the windy mountains
the windy mountains
all over the centipedes run

4

Black snake wind
black snake wind
here the song runs
and it wraps around me

5

I am led
I am led

Retranslated from Frank Russell's originals (1908, 324–25, songs 1–6)
1. This song is a conventional beginning song in that it announces its own intention. The "Here begin" is self referential to the purpose of the singing.

quickly I am led to drink
and I drink
dizzily I go
in circles spinning

6

White cholla is budding
white cholla is budding
I come running
pitifully I run[2]

2. "Pitifully" refers to the song's "I," who is in a sorry, in this case, drunken and staggering, state. The "I's" drunkenness is established poetically in the previous song.

Whirlwind Songs 7–11

Performed by Vicente Jose
Translated by David Kozak and David I. Lopez

7

Out of the wind house running
out of the wind house running
over the smooth ground going
off into the far distance it runs

8

I burst out running
I burst out running
distantly over the desert plants running
I will twist the tops of trees

9

I flow over the beautiful earth running
I flow over the beautiful earth running
I thunder four times and run[1]
through the distant trees running
distantly running

10

I emerge and thunder
I emerge and thunder
along the sandy washes
running far away

1. Four is an O'odham sacred number. Songs are sung in multiples of four, with repetition serving as emphasis and as a didactic tool for learning songs.

11

Vine of the milkweed likes me[2]
vine of the milkweed likes me
I grow and grow and come out
and I swirl and twist

2. The word for "likes me" in O'odham is *ñ-hoho'id*. It was unclear to us what this transitive verb means in this song. Asking Vicente Jose the word's meaning would be the only sure way to know.

Kiowa

The Red Wolf Story

Introduction by Luke Eric Lassiter

Among the most important expressions for Kiowa people today is song. As the Kiowa language continues to decline in its everyday use, song is emerging as a dominant symbol for articulating Kiowa heritage and identity. Yet song cannot be stripped of its narrative context; for many Kiowa singers, in particular, story is absolutely critical for translating song. Without story, song is merely sound; with it, however, sound embodies a meaningful memory and history made real through the act of singing.[1]

In the Kiowa community, then, to convey song is also to convey story, and in turn, the process of translating song necessitates the translation of story. The act of narration clarifies and elaborates this sung world of sound that Kiowas have traditionally called *daw-gyah* — literally meaning 'catching power'. The Red Wolf story is one narrative that powerfully engages this process.[2]

The Red Wolf story elaborates the history of a particular Kiowa dance and song tradition today called in English the Gourd Dance. The Gourd Dance was once the Ton-ga gkoon (Rattle Dance) of the Taimpego, one of the Kiowas' warrior sodalities, which began to fade by the end of the nineteenth century. Before and after the First and Second World Wars, however, Kiowas used the dance to recognize Kiowa veterans who had served in the military. But in 1955 at the American Indian Exposition in Anadarko, Oklahoma, a group of Kiowa singers and dancers presented the dance of the Taimpego as a public exhibition. Kiowa people remember that "this presentation brought back memories of our cultural heritage and there were tears and soft crying among the elder spectators."[3]

The impact of this particular presentation created a renewed community-wide interest in the Taimpego, its dance, and its songs. In the two years following this presentation, a few inspired men consulted Kiowa elders, and on January 30, 1957, formed what they decided to call the Kiowa Gourd Clan. No longer a warrior's society, the Gourd Clan focused exclusively on the dance of the Taimpego, which they decided to call the Gourd Dance in English. They defined its new purpose thus: "The purpose and function of this organization was to perpetuate our Indian Heritage and to revive the Kiowa dance as near as possible from the past original ceremonies."[4]

Today the Gourd Dance is a simple dance. Men most often wear jeans or slacks, nice shirts, moccasins or cowboy boots, and silver and bead bandoliers. In their hands they carry feather fans and rattles made of tin. Most women simply wear shawls over their regular clothing. The movement of the dance is restrained and understated: dancers bob up and down in accord with the cadence of the songs.[5]

Many Kiowa people consider the dance itself extremely important; yet most Gourd Dance participants ultimately center the dance's importance—and indeed its very revival—on song. As Taimpego encampments became less and less common in the early twentieth century, its songs lived on with singers who had remembered the songs long after the dance had ceased. Indeed, the dance's revival after WWII would draw its lifeblood from singers. Without these singers and their songs, many Kiowas say, the revival would not have been possible. More than this, however, the continuance of the songs through adverse changes represents the continuance of a collective memory far greater than the songs' obvious use for dancing.[6] Today Kiowa people often tell the Red Wolf story to talk about the origins of the Gourd Dance itself and to communicate the importance of Gourd Dance songs to the Kiowas' past and present lives.

The following Red Wolf story was related in English on April 23, 1994, by Kiowa elder Ralph Kotay. In his mid-seventies, Ralph Kotay is well known in and outside the Kiowa community for his mastery of Kiowa song—especially Kiowa church hymns and powwow songs (which include Gourd Dance songs).

I recorded this story when I accompanied Ralph Kotay and a group of other Kiowa singers on a trip to Lubbock, Texas, where we performed the Gourd Dance. Our hosts asked Ralph to talk about the history of the dance, and he responded accordingly by telling the Red Wolf story. In collaboration with Ralph, I transcribed his public telling for use in *The Power of Kiowa Song,* as reproduced in this volume. Because Ralph's rendition of the Red Wolf story fell within certain types of speech that are not readily rendered on the written page, I chose to employ a kind of transcription that more closely approaches the clear patterns of speech that emerge in public presentations, storytelling, or lengthy narration.[7] Often called ethnopoetics by sociolinguists, this style of transcription helps to translate these patterns together with content, which in turn helps to illustrate the communicated intent that standard styles of writing gloss. For the poetic translation of Ralph's following narration, then, a few general rules applied: breaks in lines represent breathing pauses, breaks between stanzas represent a change in topics, and italics denote a greater emphasis in Ralph's tone.

A particular song is often associated with this story, but I do not transcribe it here.[8] Yet this story is not so much about a particular song as it is about the much larger continuity story that originates from the Kiowas' ongoing commitment to the power of song, its past, and its future promise.[9] While the Red Wolf story is at first glance about the origin of the Gourd Dance as founded primarily on song, in the end Ralph's narrative is ultimately about *belief* and its *confirmation:* Red Wolf tells the Kiowa warrior that as long as the Kiowas take care of the dance and songs, they will continue to receive new songs. And indeed, today Kiowas like Ralph continue to receive new songs as they chart their current lives through the framework of collective memory, history, and identity.[10]

NOTES

Much of this chapter is excerpted from parts of Lassiter, *Power of Kiowa Song,* and reproduced here by permission.

1. See Lassiter, *Power of Kiowa Song,* esp. 139–52.

2. Lassiter, *Power of Kiowa Song,* 157–86.

3. Kiowa Gourd Clan ceremonials program, 1976. Photocopy in the author's possession. See also Lassiter, *Power of Kiowa Song,* 116–28.

4. Kiowa Gourd Clan ceremonials program, 22. See also Lassiter, *Power of Kiowa Song,* 116–28.

5. For a more extensive description of the Gourd Dance, see Lassiter, *Power of Kiowa Song,* 99–115.

6. For a fuller discussion of the Taimpego Rattle Dance and its revival as the Gourd Dance, see Lassiter, *Power of Kiowa Song,* 116–38.

7. Cf. Hymes, *"In Vain I Tried to Tell You,"* and Tedlock, *Spoken Word and the Work of Interpretation.*

8. See Lassiter, *Power of Kiowa Song,* 153–64. The song often associated with the Red Wolf story can be heard on the Web page that accompanies *The Power of Kiowa Song: http://www.uapress.arizona.edu/extras/kiowa/kiowasng.htm.* I do not transcribe the song here because its form resists any clear translation on the written page. The song is like most Gourd Dance songs: it is a "song without words." Even if it did have words, however, representing lyrics on the written page can be very misleading in conveying intent and community meaning, especially with Gourd Dance songs. Gourd Dance "songs with words," for example, may only have a very few lyrics, which do not carry their fullest meaning in and of themselves; they reference much larger narratives. Kiowa singers contend, then, that understanding a song like Red Wolf's rests with knowing the song's larger story, which, in the end—whether it is a "song with words" or a "song without words"—elaborates the song's fullest meaning, not the presence or absence of lyrics.

With this in mind, it might be tempting to use Western notation to represent this song's "vocable" content. I have contended elsewhere, however, that Western notation also does little to communicate the song's intent and community meaning. While it may do much to illustrate the abilities of the author to transcribe music, Western notation strips the song of its performative context, and in the end its use on the written page does more to obscure a song's sound and community meaning than to elaborate it (for a fuller discussion, see Lassiter, "Southwestern Oklahoma, the Gourd Dance, and Charlie Brown."

9. See Lassiter, *Power of Kiowa Song,* 187–216.

10. Lassiter, *Power of Kiowa Song,* 157–64.

SUGGESTED READING AND REFERENCES

Boyd, Maurice. *Kiowa Voices*. 2 vols. Fort Worth: Texas Christian University Press, 1981, 1983.

Ellis, Clyde. *A Dancing People: Powwow Culture on the Southern Plains*. Lawrence: University Press of Kansas, 2003.

————. *To Change Them Forever: Indian Education at the Rainy Mountain Boarding School, 1893–1920*. Norman: University of Oklahoma Press, 1996.

Hymes, Dell. *"In Vain I Tried to Tell You": Essays in Native American Indian Narrative*. Philadelphia: University of Pennsylvania Press, 1981.

Kracht, Benjamin. "Kiowa Religion: An Ethnohistorical Analysis of Ritual Symbolism, 1832–1897." PhD diss., Southern Methodist University, 1989.

Lassiter, Luke Eric. *The Power of Kiowa Song: A Collaborative Ethnography*. Tucson: University of Arizona Press, 1998.

————. "Southwestern Oklahoma, the Gourd Dance, and Charlie Brown." In *Contemporary Native American Cultural Issues,* edited by Duane Champagne, 145–66. Walnut Creek CA: AltaMira Press, 1999.

Lassiter, Luke Eric, Clyde Ellis, and Ralph Kotay. *The Jesus Road: Kiowas, Christianity, and Indian Hymns*. Lincoln: University of Nebraska Press, 2002.

Marriott, Alice. *Kiowa Years: A Study in Culture Impact*. New York: Macmillan, 1968.

————. *Saynday's People*. Lincoln: University of Nebraska Press, 1963.

————. *The Ten Grandmothers*. Norman: University of Oklahoma Press, 1945.

Meadows, William C. *Kiowa, Apache, and Comanche Military Societies*. Austin: University of Texas Press, 1999.

Mishkin, Bernard. *Rank and Warfare among the Plains Indians*. Monographs of the American Ethnological Society, no. 3. New York: J. J. Augustin, 1940.

Momaday, N. Scott. *The Names: A Memoir*. Tucson: University of Arizona Press, 1976.

————. *The Way to Rainy Mountain*. New York: Ballantine Books, 1969.

Mooney, James. *Calendar History of the Kiowa Indians*. Seventeenth Annual Report of the Bureau of American Ethnology, pt. 1. Washington DC: Government Printing Office, 1898.

Nye, Colonel W. S. *Bad Medicine and Good: Tales of the Kiowas*. Norman: University of Oklahoma Press, 1962.

————. *Carbine and Lance: The Story of Old Fort Sill*. 1937. Reprint, Norman: University of Oklahoma Press, 1969.

Palmer, Gus, Jr. *Telling Stories the Kiowa Way*. Tucson: University of Arizona Press, 2003.

Parsons, Elsie Clews. *Kiowa Tales*. New York: American Folk-Lore Society, 1929.

Tedlock, Dennis. *The Spoken Word and the Work of Interpretation*. Philadelphia: University of Pennsylvania Press, 1983.

The Red Wolf Story

Told by Ralph Kotay

In the 1800s,
   I think the *first* time that it had been
     written in history,
   that they could trace it back,
     back to 1838.
That is a long time ago.
That's over,
   over a hundred and fifty years ago.
   About a hundred and fifty years ago.
That's how far back they had traced this dance.

And the legend was this—
There was a warrior,
   lost.
He was by himself.
He was with these—
There was a group,
   of warriors.
For some reason,
   he got lost.
And then from that time,
   he was looking for his people—
     the Kiowa tribe.
   Looking for his people.
And he walked for days,
   nights.
And he was looking for the Kiowa encampment—
   where they camp,
   you know.
You've *seen* pictures

movies of these,
   where they are camping out.
Well, that's where they *used* to *be,*
   a long time ago.
And this young warrior,
and he had come up to a small hill,
   knowing that his tribe was
      encamped over the hill,
         somewhere.

And as he was going up there,
   that mountain,
      he heard some *singing.*
         Some song he had never heard before.
And so,
   as he come up to the hill to look over,
      he saw that *ravine.*
There was a
   a red *wolf*
      there in that ravine.
He had this in his paw.
   A gourd [Ralph shakes his rattle].
And he was keeping time with the music.
So, he was just *amazed* to see something *like* that.

This seems like it's a *fairy* tale . . .
   But people long ago,
      they *all* dressed up—
         like an animal,
         or a *bird.*
And that's the reason why—
   we *really* think a lot of what we
      have here . . .

To this day,
   this modern *time,*
   we're still
   at this drum,
      singing the songs to all the people that wants
      to hear these songs.

But getting back to *this*—
The next day,
   the next day this red wolf,
   he come up and said,
   "I'm giving you this.
   I'm giving you this dance to your people.
   These songs that you've been hearing."
He heard *songs*,
   song after song all night long.
And he remembered these songs.
And the wolf told him that,
   "You take these back to your people.
   Be *proud* of this dance.
   These songs that you have,
   that's what I give you."

And that was way back in,
   like I said,
   around 1838 when this happened.
And this has been passed down through the history.
Our elders always tell us stories about these things.
And of course we know that they are telling us the right things,
   the right way,
   how it's supposed to be and all that.
Today, we respect *all* these things.

Well, after he found his encampment.
That's when he told his people about,
   about what he had experienced.
What he had experienced,
   what he had *seen*,
   and these songs that had been given to him.

Well, they went ahead and accepted it.
They accepted it.
And to this day we are still dancing this particular dance . . .

These *songs* that have been passed down from generation to generation,
   today we have
     many of these songs.

Cherokee

Thunder and the Ukten

Introduction by Willard Walker

I returned to Oklahoma in 1979, after a long absence, to work with Wesley Proctor, an old friend who was fluent and literate in both English and Cherokee. He showed me some issues of *The Cherokee Nation News* in which "Thunder and the Ukten" was printed serially in Cherokee syllabics. I had known its author, Willie Jumper, or Sigwanida Dihltadegi, another bilingual Cherokee who died in 1977.

The cast of characters in this story features the Thunderer, which I transcribed as Ahyvdagwalosgi and which Proctor translated as Thunder in deference perhaps to the expectations of English speakers, who code natural processes as nouns. The Cherokee word has two suffixes, one of which indicates durative or habitual action; the other functions like English *-er* in *farmer, carpenter, swimmer,* and so on.

The notion of Thunderers is widespread in North American Indian mythology. According to Fogelson, the Thunderers are known to Cherokees as

> the sons of Selu, the Corn Mother, and Kanati, the Lucky Hunter, or
> the principal Thunderer. . . . They never really grew up or became old,
> but remained in a state of perpetual youth or suspended adolescence.
> . . . Mankind enjoys an abiding friendship with the Thunderers, for, ac-
> cording to several myth fragments, humans once rendered support and
> assistance in a battle for cosmic supremacy when the Thunderers de-
> feated their arch-enemy, the evil, dragon-like Uktena. Ever since, Chero-
> kees have petitioned the Thunderers for a wide variety of boons, includ-
> ing victory in war or the ballgame, success in love, gambling luck, and
> prevention of and relief from illness.[1]

Willie Jumper's myth has much in common with "The Red Man and the Uk-tena," a nineteenth-century myth.[2] In Jumper's tale two boys shoot the Ukteni to free the Thunderer from its coils. In Mooney's, two brothers shoot it to free "Asga'ya Gi'gagei, the Red Man of the Lightning." According to Mooney, the Red Man is equated with thunder: "The priests pray to the Thunder and call him the

Red Man, because that is the brightest color of his dress."[3] Jack and Anna Kil-patrick wrote that "the present-day Cherokees do not equate 'Ancient Red One' and 'Ancient White One' with either the sun or the fire . . . but with Thunder-Lightning."[4] At any rate, the Thunderer, or Red Man, escapes death in the coils of the Ukteni in both Mooney's and Jumper's version of the tale through the inter-vention of two boys.

The Ukteni, or Uktena, is a prominent figure in the classic Cherokee tales told by Swimmer and others in the nineteenth century and recorded by James Mooney in "Myths of the Cherokee." Mooney described the Uktena as follows:

> Those who know say that the Uktena is a great snake, as large around as a tree trunk, with horns on its head, and a bright blazing crest like a diamond upon its forehead, and scales glittering like sparks of fire. It has rings or spots of color along its whole length, and cannot be wounded except by shooting in the seventh spot from the head, because under this spot are its heart and its life. The blazing diamond is called Ulunsu'ti, "Transparent," and he who can win it may become the greatest wonder worker of the tribe, but it is worth a man's life to attempt it, for whoever is seen by the Uktena is so dazed by the bright light that he runs toward the snake instead of trying to escape. Even to see the Uktena asleep is death, not to the hunter himself, but to his family.[5]

James Adair, a reliable eighteenth-century source on the Cherokees, wrote that

> [b]etween two high mountains, nearly covered with old mossy rocks, lofty cedars, and pines, in the valleys of which the beams of the sun reflect a powerful heat, there are, as the natives affirm, some bright old inhabi-tants, or rattle snakes, of a more enormous size than is mentioned in history. They are so large and unwieldy, that they take a circle, almost as wide as their length, to crawl round in their shortest orbit; but boun-tiful nature compensates the heavy motion of their bodies, for as they say, no living creature moves within the reach of their sight, but they can draw it to them. . . . As they cannot support themselves, by their speed, or cunning to spring from an ambuscade, it is needful they should have the bewitching craft of their eyes and forked tongues.
>
> The description the Indians give us of their colour, is as various as what we are told of the camelion, that seems to the spectator to change its colour, by every different position he may view it in; which proceeds from the piercing rays of light that blaze from their foreheads, so as to dazzle the eyes, from whatever quarter they post themselves—for in each of their heads, there is a large carbuncle, which not only repels, but they

*affirm, sullies the meridian beams of the sun. They reckon it so danger-
ous to disturb those creatures, that no temptation can induce them to
betray their secret recess to the prophane.*[6]

John R. Swanton published a Natchez Uktena myth in English translation, told
to him by Sam Watt, who spoke Creek, Natchez, Cherokee, and English.[7] He mentions that what the Cherokees call Uktena is the Olo'bit in Natchez and "the sharp-
breasted snake" in Creek.

Jack and Anna Kilpatrick's *Eastern Cherokee Folktales* has the following story,
called "Thunder Kills AN UGH(A)DHE:N(A)." The Kilpatricks reconstructed this
story from notes taken by Frans Olbrechts in North Carolina in 1927. A footnote
identifies the UGH(A)DHE:N(A) as "the Cherokee mythical sea dragon."[8]

*Once Thunder was fighting an Ugh(a)dhe:n(a). A man saw the fight.
The Ugh(a)dhe:n(a) asked the man for help. Thunder asked the man
to help him. At first the man wondered whom to help; then he decided
to help Thunder. When the man arrived upon the scene, the fight was
over; Thunder had killed the Ugh(a)dhe:n(a). Thunder said, "You will
be my vghiwi:na [sister's son, clansman of a younger generation]; you
call me edu:tsi [mother's brother, clansman of an older generation]."
Thunder commanded his two sisters to bring "horses," which were two
huge snakes. "Get on!" Thunder said. All got on. They whooped, and at
every whoop, lightning flashed and thunder sounded. When we think it
thunders, it is but the Thunder People whooping in the air.*[9]

In another version of this tale, told to Janet Jordan in Oklahoma in the 1970s,
the Thunderer killed a horned snake with the assistance of Cherokees using "Indian medicine," after which "they made an agreement with tornadoes, thunder
and lightning never to bother [them] any more."[10]

Fogelson has described the Uktena as "a monstrous, dragon-like, anthropopha-
gous, aquatic serpent" that "represents a primeval being, a survivor from the prehuman era of world creation."[11]

Charles Hudson's "Uktena: A Cherokee Anomalous Monster" is a fourteen-
page essay on the Uktena. Elsewhere he wrote that creatures like the Cherokee
Uktena "existed in the beliefs of most southeastern Indians."[12] But such creatures
were also known far north of the Mason-Dixon Line, far west of the Mississippi,
in the Valley of Mexico, and far beyond. Five versions of a late nineteenth-century
myth featuring a horned, sea-going serpent with supernatural powers were recorded from Maliseet-Passamaquoddy speakers in Maine and New Brunswick.[13]
At Zuni Pueblo, in western New Mexico, where all boys between the ages of eight
and twelve are initiated into one or another of six kiva societies, a prominent

feature of these initiations is *koloowisi,* a giant, plumed, sea-going serpent represented by a fetish "constructed of deerskin, . . . about 5 feet long and 8 inches
through the thickest part of the body. . . . The back is black, covered with duplicate
curves in yellow and blue-green to designate the scales of the serpent. . . . A deerskin tongue, colored red, hangs from the mouth, which is provided with teeth."[14]
A picture of a horned serpent in a body of water during a thunder and lightning storm appears as figure 8 in M. Dale Kinkade and Anthony Mattina's "Discourse."[15] The caption reads: "Horned serpent depicted in a struggle with its traditional enemies the Thunder-beings, who are often described as hurling lightning
bolts. Variants of this motif were found over a wide area of North America, and
the horned or plumed serpent was found as far south as Chile (Wissler 1922:212;
Michelson 1930:54–550.) Pen and ink drawing by the Cattaraugus Seneca artist
Jesse J. Cornplanter, 1908."

The Uktena is well known to Oklahoma Cherokees as well. The Wahnenauhi
Manuscript of 1889 refers to a "legend of a large serpent, called the 'Ground Snake,'
being the color of the ground [which] was said to betoken death to the one who
saw it; if it appeared to several persons a National Calamity was apprehended."[16]
In a footnote Jack Kilpatrick wrote that "this 'Ground snake' is undoubtedly the
mythical sea-Dragon, the Ugh(a)dhe:n(i) (the spelling of this word in manuscripts
is variable)."[17]

The Uktena appears also in *A Cherokee Vision of Eloh',* which tells how, long
ago, a Cherokee Seven-Clan Council prophesied an invasion by thousands of
enemy soldiers coming "across the great waters." The Cherokees mobilized for
war and sent some men to kill the "*oocatene*" and get its poison. When the enemy
landed, the Cherokees spilled the Uktena's poison out of gourd containers near
the enemy forces and then decoyed them into the poison, which made them "faint
and fall down." After that, they were easily "slaughtered."[18]

A NOTE ON ORTHOGRAPHY AND PRONUNCIATION

The letters *a, e, i, o,* and *u* are pronounced much as they are in Spanish or Italian,
except that word-final vowels and vowels preceded or followed by *n* are nasalized.
A sixth vowel, written as *v,* is pronounced like the French word *un* and is always
nasalized. Stressed vowels are marked with an apostrophe. The consonants *n, l,*
w, and *y* may be preceded by *h.* The glottal stop, as in English *uh-oh,* is represented by a question mark without a dot (ʔ). The letter *s* is pronounced as in English by Western Cherokees, as English *sh* by most Eastern Cherokees. Cherokee
has a complex sound system in which semantic distinctions are often governed
by vowel length (duration) or pitch, crucial features that are not marked in the
transcription used here.

THE TRANSLATION

Willie Jumper died two years before Wesley Proctor showed his syllabic text to me in 1979, but I had no difficulty in persuading Proctor to translate it. It is his translation that is given here.

Cherokee often requires specificity where English does not. The past tense of Cherokee verbs, for example, is marked by one or the other of two contrasting suffixes: -v(ʔi) and -e(ʔi). The first indicates that whatever happened was witnessed by the speaker or narrator. This suffix appears in the fourth sentence of the first paragraph of the syllabic text in a word that I transcribed as *unihnohehlv'ʔi* and that Proctor translated as "[others] have told it." In so doing he omitted the information that the narrator claimed to have direct, personal knowledge that they told it. The same suffix appears also in the first sentence of the second paragraph in a phrase that I transcribed as *Gohi'gihno jigesv'* and that Proctor translated as "[it was] long ago." As in any narrative about events in the mythical past, however, the past-tense verbs in the story itself are all marked with -e(ʔi), indicating that things happened evidently, reportedly, allegedly, or seemingly. But to make his English translation clean and smooth, Proctor discarded this information. Thus "there were [two people]," "they used to hunt," and so forth are presented as known facts without qualification.

The Cherokee text routinely conveys other types of information that do not appear in the translation. Every Cherokee verb has a prefix providing information about its subject. First- and second-person subjects are obligatorily marked as singular, dual, or plural, and some prefixes mark verbs for person and number of both subject and object. I transcribed a verb in the second sentence of the fourth paragraph as *yisginiyo's;* Proctor translated the whole sentence as "Will you look for something for me to eat?" preserving the information that a single person is making the request, but omitting the fact that "you" refers to two people.

Some transitive Cherokee verbs require an affix indicating that their objects are either liquid, living, flexible, long and rigid, or none of these. The fifth paragraph of Proctor's translation includes the phrase "they brought him some birds and squirrels." The verb he translated as "they brought [them to him]" is in my transcription *dunihnohe'le',* which is used only with flexible objects. It indicates, therefore, that the birds and squirrels are not living but flexible, that is, dead. This information is omitted in the translation but implied by the context.

A verb in the sixth paragraph of the syllabic text that I transcribed as *unvkewse'* must be glossed as 'they forgot it', as opposed to *anvkewse'* 'they forgot him/her'. I transcribed the verb in the very next clause as *wi'unandadeʔi,* which Proctor translated as "they remembered it." This verb is ambiguous as to whether its object is animate or not, but, having used "it" with the preceding verb, Proctor used "it" again here.

A word near the end of the story is worthy of note. I transcribed it as *dagilvwis-danehesti,* and Proctor translated it as "I will be working." The Thunderer is promising the boys that he will "work" to help them escape. Any traditional Cherokee would know instantly that the "work" would consist entirely of conjuring, and this was surely in the mind of Willie Jumper when he wrote this word and in that of Wesley Proctor when he read it. But this information is not explicit in Proctor's translation, which is as euphemistic and oblique as the syllabic text itself.

A verb in the thirteenth paragraph that I transcribed as *yigalihwogi* was translated by Proctor as "he will die." There are two contrasting verbs for dying in Cherokee: one if the subject is human and another, this one, if it is a plant or animal. Proctor's translation, "he [the snake] will die" specifies a human subject. Stretching the grammar here to anthropomorphize the snake seems appropriate, given the way Jumper's text deals with speech acts, which figure prominently in this story. Everyone talks, not only the boys, but the snake, the Ukten, and the Thunderer.

THE TEXT

The way speech acts are coded in Jumper's text reflects his traditional understanding of the nature of the universe and of human beings' place in it, all of which is obscured by the English translation. The boys *unosele'* 'said' (something) in the eighth paragraph. This same verb, inflected for singular subject and nonsingular object, is *duwosele',* which appears in the thirteenth paragraph, when the Thunderer *duwosele'* 'said' (something to the boys), and again in the eighteenth paragraph, when the Thunderer "said" (something to them). Clearly the Thunderer is being presented as a being that can talk to people, like any well socialized and enculturated Cherokee.

The snake's speech acts are coded in the same way. In the third paragraph he *duwosele'* 'asked' (the boys to stop); in the fourth paragraph he *duwosele?i'* 'told them' (he was hungry); and in the ninth paragraph he *duwosele'* 'said' (something to the boys).

Another verb that translates as 'do' or 'say' (something) is used to describe speech acts of the boys and also those of the Thunderer and the Ukten: the boys *unadvhne(?i)* 'said' (something to the snake) in the sixth paragraph and *unadvhne* 'said' (something) again in the eleventh. The Thunderer *udvhne'* 'said' (something) in the sixteenth paragraph and again in the nineteenth. The Ukten *udvhne'* 'said' (something) in the fourteenth paragraph. Thus the speech acts of the boys, the snake, the Ukten, and the Thunderer are all coded with the same terminology in this story.

Jumper's story, then, equates the speech acts of reptiles, which are associated with subterranean aquifers and Mother Earth, with those of the Thunderer, associated with supraterrestrial forces and Father Sky, and with those of the two boys, who represent terrestrial humans, forever situated between Father Sky and Mother Earth.

There is, however, a verb in Cherokee that is commonly used to designate the vocalizations of birds and animals, for example, the barking of dogs, the howling of coyotes, the cawing of crows, the crowing of roosters. This verb is never used in the story to describe the speech acts of the snake, the Thunderer, or the Ukten, but it does appear in the final paragraph when we are told that the story is what *gohigi janehv'ʔi* 'people who lived long ago' *nuniwesv'* 'said'. Just as the snake and the Thunderer could talk like people, the people who lived long ago could talk like animals and natural forces, which qualified them to mediate, not just between man and animals, but between all the contending natural and supernatural forces of an awesome universe.

NOTES

1. Fogelson, "Cherokee Little People Reconsidered," 94.
2. Mooney, "Myths of the Cherokees," 300–304.
3. Mooney, "Myths of the Cherokees," 257.
4. Kilpatrick and Kilpatrick, "Foundation of Life," 1390–91.
5. Mooney, "Myths of the Cherokees," 297–98.
6. Adair, *Adair's History of the American Indians,* 514.
7. Swanton, *Myths and Tales of the Southeastern Indians,* 245–46.
8. Kilpatrick and Kilpatrick, *Eastern Cherokee Folktales,* 391 n. 15.
9. Kilpatrick and Kilpatrick, *Eastern Cherokee Folktales,* 391–92.
10. Jordan, "Politics and Religion in a Western Cherokee Community," 122.
11. Fogelson, "Windigo Goes South," 139.
12. Hudson, *Southeastern Indians,* 132.
13. Fewkes, "Contribution to Passamaquoddy Folk-Lore"; Leland, *Algonquin Legends of New England or Myths and Folk Lore of the Micmac, Passamaquoddy and Penobscot Tribes,* 324–27, 327–30, 330–33; Gatschet, "Water Monsters of the American Aborigines."
14. Regarding Zuni initiation practices, see Ladd, "Zuni Social and Political Organization," 482–91. Regarding the appearance of the *koloowisi,* see Stevenson, "Zuni Indians: Their Mythology, Esoteric Fraternities, and Ceremonies," 506.
15. Kinkade and Mattina, "Discourse," 254.
16. Kilpatrick, *Wahnenauhi Manuscript,* 186–87.
17. Kilpatrick, *Wahnenauhi Manuscript,* 187.
18. Meredith and Milan, *Cherokee Vision of Eloh',* 21–23.

SUGGESTED READING AND REFERENCES

Adair, James. *Adair's History of the American Indians.* 1775. Edited by Samuel Cole Williams. Reprint, New York: Johnson Reprint, 1969.

Fewkes, Jesse W. "A Contribution to Passamaquoddy Folk-Lore." *Journal of American Folk-Lore* 3 (11) (1890): 257–80.

Fogelson, Raymond D. "Cherokee Little People Reconsidered." *Journal of Cherokee Studies* 7 (1982): 92–98.

———. *The Cherokees: A Critical Bibliography.* The Newberry Library Center for the History of the American Indian Bibliographical Series, ed. Francis Jennings. Bloomington: Indiana University Press, 1978.

———. "Windigo Goes South: Stoneclad among the Cherokees." In *Manlike Monsters on Trial: Early Records and Modern Evidence.* Edited by Marjorie M. Halpin and Michael M. Ames. Vancouver: University of British Columbia Press, 1980.

Gatschet, Albert S. "Water Monsters of the American Aborigines." *Journal of American Folk-Lore* 12 (1899): 256.

Hudson, Charles. *The Southeastern Indians.* Knoxville: University of Tennessee Press, 1976.

———. "Uktena: A Cherokee Anomalous Monster." *Journal of Cherokee Studies* 3 (2): 62–75 (1978).

Jordan, Janet. "Politics and Religion in a Western Cherokee Community: A Corporate Struggle for Survival in a White Man's World." Ph.D. diss., University of Connecticut, 1975.

Kilpatrick, Jack F. *The Siquanid Dil'tidegi Collection: Sacred Formulas of the Western Cherokees.* Series 1, no. 1. Dallas: Southern Methodist University, Bridwell Library, 1962.

———. *The Wahnenauhi Manuscript: Historical Sketches of the Cherokees.* Smithsonian Institution, Bureau of American Ethnology, Bulletin 196, Anthropological Paper no. 77. Washington DC: Government Printing Office, 1966.

Kilpatrick, Jack F., and Anna G. Kilpatrick. *Eastern Cherokee Folktales: Reconstructed from the Field Notes of Frans M. Olbrechts.* Smithsonian Institution, Bureau of American Ethnology, Bulletin 196, Anthropological Paper no. 80. Washington DC: Government Printing Office, 1966.

———."The Foundation of Life: The Cherokee National Ritual." *American Anthropologist* 66 (6), Pt. 1 (1964): 1390–91.

———. *Friends of Thunder: Folktales of the Oklahoma Cherokees.* Norman: University of Oklahoma Press, 1964.

Kinkade, M. Dale, and Anthony Mattina. "Discourse." In *Handbook of North American Indians,* edited by William C. Sturtevant, vol. 17, *Languages,* edited by Ives Goddard, 244–74. Washington DC: Smithsonian Institution, 1996.

Ladd, Edmund J. "Zuni Social and Political Organization." In *The Handbook of North American Indians,* edited by William C. Sturtevant, vol. 9, *Southwest,* edited by Alfonso Ortiz, 482–91. Washington DC: Government Printing Office.

Leland, Charles. *The Algonquin Legends of New England or Myths and Folk Lore of the Micmac, Passamaquoddy and Penobscot Tribes.* Boston: Houghton Mifflin, 1898.

Meredith, Howard L., and Virginia E. Milan, eds. *A Cherokee Vision of Eloh'.* Muskogee OK: Indian University Press, 1981.

Michelson, Truman. *Contributions to Fox Ethnology.* Vol. 2. Smithsonian Institution, Bureau of American Ethnology, Bulletin 95. Washington DC: Government Printing Office, 1930.

Mooney, James. "Myths of the Cherokees." Part 2. In *The Nineteenth Annual Report of the Bureau of American Ethnology for the Years 1897–98,* 3–576. Washington DC: Smithsonian Institution, 1900.

Stevenson, Matilda Coxe. "The Zuni Indians: Their Mythology, Esoteric Fraternities, and

Ceremonies." In *The Twenty-third Annual Report of the Bureau of American Ethnology for the Years 1889–90.* Washington DC: Government Printing Office, 1904.

Swanton, John R. *Myths and Tales of the Southeastern Indians.* Norman: University of Oklahoma Press, 1929.

Walker, Willard. "Cherokee Curing and Conjuring, Identity, and the Southeastern Co-Tradition." In *Persistent Peoples: Cultural Enclaves in Perspective,* edited by George P. Castile and Gilbert Kushner. Tucson: University of Arizona Press, 1981.

Wissler, Clark. *The American Indian: An Introduction to the Anthropology of the New World.* 2nd. ed. New York: Oxford University Press, 1922.

Thunder and the Ukten

Told by Willie Jumper
Translated by Wesley Proctor

This is the story of an Ukten and Thunder having a fight. Sometimes, when others tell the story, it is a little different. When I hear others tell the story, their version of the story sometimes seems better. This story is similar to the way others have told it. Old-timers have told this story that I know. This is a story of Ukten and Thunder, of their first meeting.

Long ago there were two people who always hunted with bows. Sometimes they shot rabbits and other wild things.

One time these boys were walking in a deep valley and in rough and rocky terrain. They found a big snake lying on top of a rock as they walked among the big, sharp rocks. He was big enough to eat squirrels. The snake was lean and hungry and asked the boys to stop. He wanted to ask the boys something.

He said, "I am very hungry. Will you look for something for me to eat? I will eat birds or squirrels. When I become strong, I'll become your helper. Whatever you do, I will help you as much as I can as long as we live."

The boys decided to help the snake. When morning came, they brought him some birds and squirrels. Many times they brought him something to eat, and he grew bigger and stronger.

Some days later, again, they brought him squirrels. And now the snake was very big. About this time, for a little while, the boys forgot about the snake. Later they remembered. They said, "Let's go see the snake and take him some more birds and squirrels."

When they got to the place where the snake lived, they called for him. He came out of the rocks. He was much bigger now, and he had horns. As he was coming out, they saw something like lightning before they saw his horns. They gave him the squirrels and birds that they had brought him.

They said to him, "You have really grown and gotten big."

"Yes, but don't forget, forever we will be friends," the snake said to the boys. Really the snake just wanted to kill the boys soon, and that's why he was just saying this.

When morning came, the boys went near the snake. When the boys went into the valley, they heard something popping. It popped many times, but then it seemed to just get quiet.

The boys said, "Something is happening to somebody. Let's hurry and go near where the snake is." The boys hurried and went in that direction.

Soon they saw the snake they were feeding. They saw the snake wrapped around something. Thunder and the snake were fighting. The snake was coiled around the Thunder. The Thunder could not get away, because the snake was tightly coiled around him, and he could not move.

And the Thunder said, "Boys, my nephews, this snake that is wrapped around me is fierce and kills people. If you can, do something to kill him! Shoot him on the seventh spot. He will soon die."

Ukten hollered, "No, don't! Kill the Thunder instead. Thunder is meaner than I am. The popping will kill you," said Ukten. (The snake that the boys were feeding later became Ukten.)

The boys didn't know what to do.

Thunder said, "Do not do this. You boys are my grandsons, and I'm your helper, your helper forever. This snake that tells you he's your helper is just deceiving you. He just wants to kill you. That's why you better shoot him in the seventh spot."

The boys believed what the Thunder said to them and did what he told them to do. The Ukten fell to the ground, and the Thunder got away.

When the Thunder got away, he told the boys, "Go back to where you came from. As you go back, build seven fires. As you walk along, keep building those fires. These fires will do away with the smell of the Ukten. The first fire will give you enough time to build the second fire, and the second fire will give you enough time to build the third fire. By the time you build the seventh fire, you will have saved yourselves from the smell, and I, too, will be working to help you as you go along." That is what the Thunder said.

"You can depend on me forever. As long as we live on earth and until the end of the world, we must watch out for one another and keep one another safe. I am the master of all things that are fierce here on earth," said the Thunder.

The boys believed what the Thunder said to them and did what he told them to do. They ran through the valley and escaped. People that lived long ago, this is what they said.

Yuchi

Trickster Tales

Introduction by Mary S. Linn and Jason Baird Jackson

For a host of reasons, the Yuchis (alternatively Euchees) occupy a unique place among the Native societies of eastern North America. Yuchi is one of only a small number of language isolates, a term used for a language that is not demonstrably related to any known language, still spoken in the Americas and the only one still surviving in the eastern part of the continent. This singular achievement, signaling an ancient history as a people and a power of cultural resilience into the present, has meant that the Yuchis have long captured the interest of scholars. Despite this attention the Yuchis do not have a very high profile in the public imagination or even in Indian Country. The Yuchis are probably the least well known indigenous people in the east. They are little noticed even in the Oklahoma communities where they reside today. The reasons for this status are political and historical.

Like most of the world's minority and indigenous populations, the Yuchis are a distinct people who have been denied sovereignty, even of the limited type accorded to other Native North American nations. Forced from their southeastern homeland by the U.S. government in the 1830s, the Yuchis were pressured into political amalgamation with their more numerous Muscogee (Creek) neighbors. Despite being misrecognized as Muscogees by government officials and misdescribed as culturally extinct by countless encyclopedists, the Yuchis today have a strong identity, a rich cultural life, and a remarkable sense of social solidarity. Their community life focuses on a seasonal round of ancient calendrical ceremonies as well as secular social gatherings that bring active ceremonialists together with those Yuchis who have made the United Methodist Church an additional focus of community life.

While some Yuchi people have settled throughout the country, Yuchi territory is today found straddling Route 66, America's most famous highway, as it runs through the region just west of Tulsa, Oklahoma. The Yuchis live in three distinct settlements, known in English as Duck Creek (near the town of Bixby), Polecat (in and around the cities of Sapulpa and Kellyville), and Sand Creek (south of Bristow). Each community has its own social and religious life, but Yuchis also participate in an array of broader activities. One such community-wide endeavor is language classes and camps. These gatherings are a positive response to the threat of language loss that is facing Yuchi. Such a gathering provided the setting for one of the texts we present here.[1]

Yuchi language, rituals, beliefs, and social order are unique, but they do share commonalties of culture and history with the other Native American people of the eastern, particularly southeastern, United States. One of these (partially) shared traditions is a series of animal stories in which Rabbit most often assumes the role of trickster. Like his unpredictable peers elsewhere in Native America, Rabbit, or Sachwane, sometimes victimizes his neighbors while at other times he gets his due when his outraged compatriots endeavor to tame his greed, self-indulgence, and trickery. Linking the tradition of Rabbit stories to the more serious domain of sacred narrative, Rabbit is sometimes credited with causing the world to take its current shape through his mischief. Occasionally Rabbit plays the role of hero and achieves some good for ancient humanity, as when he steals fire from distant peoples and brings it back to his own community of animal and human companions.

Among the Yuchis, Rabbit understands both nature and culture but regularly seeks to subvert either or both. He is a great singer and dancer, but he is also a ne'er-do-well who seeks to obtain wives, meals, and social prestige via clever schemes that sometimes achieve their ends but also further Rabbit's poor reputation. Rabbit sometimes shares the mischievous spotlight with other animals. This is the case with the story of Wolf and Fawn, presented here. Speaking English, Yuchi people refer to this genre of stories alternatively as Rabbit stories or, more broadly, as animal stories. The Yuchi term *de'ile* refers specifically to this genre. Its etymology is obscure, and only a few speakers use or recognize the term today. Another term, *k'ala 'a'yagwa*, which means 'something that is told', is more common today and refers to animal stories as well as all other genres of storytelling.

In the world of Yuchi storytelling, animal stories were traditionally told only in winter, but this prohibition had fallen away among the Yuchis by the early twentieth century.[2] As experienced by older Yuchis, such stories were once told at night around family fireplaces in winter and on porches in summer. Tellers would take turns telling such stories and, having completed their turn, end (during winter) with a customary gesture—spitting into the fire. In such sessions Rabbit stories shared the stage with other popular genres, particularly ghost stories (*gothlēne*) and humorous anecdotes. A story-telling session was most likely when visitors called. In the late nineteenth and the early twentieth century, Yuchis devoted considerable time to both visiting and hosting friends. While this pattern continues in certain respects today, old-time visits in the days before Yuchis entered the wage economy would often last several days, and one visitor would follow quickly on the heals of another. In this way political opinion and cultural knowledge flowed regularly around the Yuchi community during the fall and winter seasons when larger communal gatherings were not being held.

Those older Yuchis we have known have uniformly commented that traditional Yuchi animal stories are always much more funny when told in Yuchi. This has presented a paradox for current efforts by the Yuchis to preserve this repertoire, as elders feel the stories lack expressive power in English, but language shift means that most people today can only appreciate them in English. The stories also seem to native speakers to make less sense in English, as if some intangible cultural context is also lost in the move to English. One result of this process is that these stories are most often told today in the context of language camps and classes in which younger Yuchis, both children and adults, seek to learn Yuchi as a second language while gaining knowledge of other aspects of traditional culture. In such settings speakers often try to (re)contextualize stories by attributing to them morals or purposes that either were absent in earlier tellings or were self-evident to older audiences. This pattern occurs in the brief tale of Wolf and Fawn that serves as our focus.

The two contexts of animal storytelling in Yuchi are represented in the two stories we present here. The first is a widely known Southeastern Indian tale in which Rabbit plays a disfiguring joke on his neighbor the Alligator. This tale, recorded by Waxin Tiger in the course of linguistic research with William L. Ballard in 1970, can stand as an example of the compressed, self-evident style of tale telling that was probably typical of situations in which listeners and tellers shared full fluency in Yuchi. His telling contains both the formulaic beginning and ending. He begins with *kæshtale* 'long time ago', which puts the hearer back into ancestral time. He ends with *'ahõgwajē* 'that's what they said', which attributes the storyteller's knowledge to those who came before.

The more complicated nature of Yuchi storytelling today is represented by another classic southeastern tale, here told by William Cahwee. In this story Fawn behaves as the trickster, and Wolf is the victim of a particularly macabre joke, perhaps in retaliation for his own usual predatory conduct. Cahwee told this tale at a Yuchi language camp held at the Pickett Indian United Methodist Church, Sapulpa, Oklahoma, on March 25, 1996. On that occasion he first told the story in Yuchi and then presented it again in an English telling. In essence, he provided for his audience a free translation of his own narrative. We present this story in two forms. First, we provide Cahwee's Yuchi telling in translation. This translation was prepared with the assistance of Josephine Keith and Josephine Bigler. These women are knowledgeable Yuchi speakers who have been actively involved in Yuchi language revival efforts. While we regret not presenting the Yuchi text here, the English translation struggles to be literally faithful to the Yuchi of Cahwee's original telling. This is followed by Cahwee's own English translation.

For thinking about the nature of translating American Indian oral literature, the translation of Wolf and Fawn is a particularly instructive case, as comparison of the two texts reveals the possibilities and the limitations posed by any translation effort. Cahwee was faced with constraints — grammatical, social, cultural, and artistic — that are typical of translation situations. Most crucial is the elaborate pronoun system central to Yuchi grammar. Throughout the story Cahwee uses three different pronouns to refer to Wolf and Fawn talking, but all are translated as 'he said' in his English telling (and by the women, who felt that it was just easier). The Yuchi pronouns with their more accurate English translations are given here.

> hõgwa
> *hõ-gwa*
> *he [Yuchi male actor; spoken by a male]-speaks*

> 'ogwa
> *'o-gwa*
> *he [older Yuchi male actor; spoken by a female, showing respect]-speaks*

> wegwa
> *we-gwa*
> *he [any non-Yuchi living being, including all animals]-speaks*

Shifts in these pronouns reveal issues of responsibility and authorship. These can be seen clearly in the women's close English translation. For instance in line 19 and at the end in lines 54 and 55, Cahwee shifts away from taking full responsibility for the story and briefly moves into the stance of reporting the story as it was told to him by an (unknown) female narrator. This shift is signaled by the grammatical forms available to male and female speakers of Yuchi, as Cahwee moves from *hõgwa* 'he said' in men's speech to the women's speech *'ogwa* 'he said'. This movement away from full performance and into the role of reporting on older, more authoritative performances is a common feature of traditional storytelling in contexts of American Indian culture change.

Also taxing to translation is the epistemological status of the animal personages in Cahwee's tale. As noted, Yuchi has clear grammatical markings that differentiate animate beings into two categories, Yuchi and non-Yuchi. The non-Yuchi class contains various kinds of non-Yuchi humans, together with animals and other animate entities. Animal stories such as these present a limiting case. The stories are not only told in Yuchi, but, via reported speech, the characters are also represented as speaking Yuchi. While multilingualism was common in the Southeast before English became the region's lingua franca, the use of Yuchi by non-Yuchis was almost unknown. For this reason *speaking* Yuchi is synonymous with *being* Yuchi. The animals present a problem, as they cannot be both animals and Yuchis, despite their fluency in Yuchi and their participation in ancient Yuchi society. As a general pattern, Cahwee resolved this dilemma in his Yuchi text by using the non-Yuchi forms when describing the actions of the animals and by using Yuchi forms when characterizing their actions as speakers in framing narrative for their reported speech. These can be seen throughout the close English translation, but a particularly instructive case is found in lines 22–23.

Our point in calling these patterns to our reader's attention is to suggest the limitations of translation, whether by a talented and fully bilingual speaker such as Cahwee or by a scholarly editor grappling with unfamiliar grammatical, folk-loric, cultural, and social detail. Such limitations seem to be at the heart of the critique made by Yuchi speakers confronting familiar stories glossed in English, a language lacking both the complex grammatical machinery of Yuchi and a rich association with the culture and way of life of earlier generations of Yuchi people.

TRANSCRIPTION CONVENTIONS

Lines are broken whenever there is a pause in speech or a discourse marker that indicates a shift in narrative sequence. Longer pauses are indicated by additional space between lines.

Italics	raised amplitude or pitch
S p a c e d	slower speech
SMALL CAPS	quiet, creaky voice
( )	unclear speech
[ ]	additional grammatical or lexical information not in translation

NOTES

We would like to thank Mose Cahwee and William Cahwee for information on storytell-ing. In addition Mary Linn and Jason Jackson would like to thank Josephine Keith and Josephine Bigler for their contribution to this work and to the study of Yuchi storytelling in general. We are grateful to W. L. Ballard for the assistance he provided to this project. Ap-preciation is extended to the Wenner-Gren Foundation for Anthropological Research for its support of Jason Jackson's ethnographic work among the Yuchis. Mary Linn's studies of Yuchi linguistics were conducted with funds provided by the National Science Foundation.

1. Basic sources for Yuchi linguistics are Linn, "Grammar of Euchee (Yuchi)," and Wag-ner, *Yuchi Tales.* For Yuchi ethnography, see Speck, *Ethnology of the Yuchi Indians,* and Jackson, *Yuchi Ceremonial Life.*

2. Mary Haas reports that, among the other southeastern peoples such as the Creeks, the Seminoles, and the Natchez in Oklahoma, telling stories about Rabbit during the spring

and summer would result in Rabbit coming and damaging the crops, then leaving (letter with attached notes from Mary R. Haas to Raymond D. Fogelson, September 23,1974).

SUGGESTED READING AND REFERENCES

Jackson, Jason Baird. "Of Bears and Rabbits: Animals in Traditional Native American Art and Literature." *Gilcrease Journal* 6:2(1999): 16–29. Another version of Rabbit and Alligator recorded among the Yuchis.

———. *Yuchi Ceremonial Life.* Lincoln: University of Nebraska Press, 2003.

Kimball, Geoffrey. "Two Koasati Narratives." In *Coming to Light,* edited by Brian Swann. New York: Vintage, 1994. Provides a comparable account of a southeastern storytelling, including a discussion of Koasati Rabbit stories.

Linn, Mary S. "A Grammar of Euchee (Yuchi)." Ph.D. diss., Department of Linguistics, University of Kansas, Lawrence, 2001.

Speck, Frank G. *Ethnology of the Yuchi Indians.* 1909. Reprint, Lincoln: University of Nebraska Press, 2004.

Swanton, John R. *Myths and Tales of the Southeastern Indians.* Bulletin of the Bureau of American Ethnology 88. Washington DC: Bureau of American Ethnology, 1929. Both Yuchi tales presented here have Muskogean analogues, available in Swanton's collection. For Rabbit and Alligator, see Creek texts 54 and 55. For Fawn and Wolf, see Creek text number 34 and Natchez text 23.

Wagner, Günter. *Yuchi Tales.* Publication of the American Ethnological Society 13. New York: G. E. Stechert, 1931. Wagner's collection provides the largest number of available Yuchi texts.

Rabbit and Alligator

Told by Waxin Tiger
Translated by Josephine Barnett Keith, Josephine Wildcat Bigler,
and Mary S. Linn

Long time ago,
Rabbit and Alligator were friends.

The Rabbit, he was going around.
He was always going around the creek, like that.

The Alligator was there,
lying right by the edge of the water.

He looked up.
It was hot.
It was really hot.

He was lying there when Rabbit came up.

  "My friend,
  what are you doing lying there?" he said.

  "I'm lying here, looking up.
  And while I was lying here, you come along," he said.
  "Do you see anything up there?" he said.
  "Aren't you able to see God?" he said to him.

The Alligator said to him,
  "No."

  "Do you want to see God?"

  "Yes."

"Well, if you want to see him,
then get up on the bank, in the grass.
Go into the middle of those tall weeds over there.
Lie on your back under there
and look up.
I will go off for a while,
but you lie there and look up."

Alligator went under the tall weeds,
and those weeds were really tall.

The Rabbit went around there,
he went all around.
He set the grass on fire
all the way around.

The Alligator was still lying there.
He saw nothing.
He was looking up,
but still he saw nothing.
He was still lying there.

Suddenly, something must have burned him.
Smoke was going upwards.
But he was looking up,
and still he saw nothing.

And then the fire was coming closer,
but the Alligator saw nothing.

And then he had to move from under there.
He went back into the creek, under the water.
Still, when he got there,
that fire had got him.
His legs were all burnt up.

And when we was back to the creek,
he was lying there under the water.

While he was lying there,
the Rabbit came around again.

"Did you see God?"

"No. I didn't see him at all.
That Rabbit that was around here,
he lied.
He sent me under the grass
and then lit a fire.
It went on me,
and now my feet are all burned.
Now you came back," he said to him.

"Rabbit, he lies," he said.
"He was around here.
Yes, he was probably around here."

Rabbit fooled Alligator.
He didn't see God at all,
but he got all his feet
all burnt up.

That's what they said.

Wolf and Fawn

Told by William Cahwee
Translated by Josephine Barnett Keith, Josephine Wildcat Bigler,
and Mary S. Linn

Long time ago,   1
the old people [now deceased] would get together.
They would talk about bad things [referring to ghosts and evil].
And sometimes one would get scared
when they got together [for the purpose of telling stories].   5

They talked together, sitting there.
They were there talking together.

Someone said that Wolf was there [emphatic, true].
And he [an animal] was going there,
Through the brush, he was going.   10
Wolf,
and Fawn, he was there.

He [animal] said to him,
    "How did you get spotted like that?" [expectation]

    "Like this,   15
    The old people [Yuchis, ancestors] made me like this,"
    he [Yuchi] told him.

    "I want to be spotted like that," he [Yuchi] said.
    The Wolf said [Yuchi, spoken by a woman],

    "I'll be back sometime.   20
    I'll return so that you can be spotted," he [Yuchi] said.

And they [animals] got back together again.

The Wolf [he, Yuchi] says to him,
    "Deer, I told you."

And he [animal] lighted the fire.   25

    "Do you want to get spotted like this now?"

    "Yes! I want to get spotted," he [Yuchi] said.

    "I'm building up the fire now."

And he [animal] put a large cast-iron kettle with legs on the fire.

It was very hot.   30

And the Wolf said to him,
    "Are you ready now?
    Now that it is hot."

He [animal] was sitting in there.

(unintelligible line)   35

    "I'm *hot!*" he [Yuchi] said.
    "I'm *veeery* hot!" he [Yuchi] said.

    "You're almost spotted."

That's the way it was, he [Yuchi] told him.

    "You're just a little spotted,   40
    you're almost there."

He [animal] put more wood on the fire.

And the Wolf now,
    "No more!
    I can't stand it anymore!   45
    I can't take it anymore!"

And he [animal] was still sitting in there.

"I'M VERY HOT!
I'M ALMOST DEAD NOW."

"You're almost ready now."   50

Still he [animal] was sitting there.

And then the Wolf was naked and dead that way.

The Wolf [Yuchi, spoken by a woman] didn't say anything.

He [Yuchi, spoken by a woman] said nothing.   55

Wolf and Fawn

Told and translated by William Cahwee

The story I told was about this Wolf and the Deer.
And this Deer run up to this Wolf,
I mean, this Wolf come up to this Deer and ask him,
he said,
   "You know, I'd like to be spotted like you are," he said.
He said,
   "Can you tell me," he said, "how you got spotted like that?"

He said,
   "Well my, uh, my uh,
   people are the one that spotted me like that," he says.

He said, "Well, I'd like to be spotted like that," he said.

So he said,
   "Okay, if you want to, well," he said.
   "You come back one day," he said,
   "and we'll spot you."

So they waited a few days, and they got back together.

Here come this Wolf up to this Deer,
he said,
or this Deer asked this Wolf, he said,
   "Are you ready to be spotted?"

The Wolf said,
   "Yeah."

So he got this bunch of fire going,
this great big fire going.

So when he got this fire going real good,
he had a big old kettle there.

So he got this kettle on this fire
and got this kettle *real* hot.
So, he turned around and asked this Wolf,
he said,
   "Are you ready to get spotted?"

And Wolf said,
   "Y e a h."

He said,
   "Okay," he said,
   "you gotta get in here," he told him.
   "You gotta get in this kettle."

So the old Wolf
he got into that kettle
and he's sitting there.

Pretty soon he said,
   "Boy," he says,
   "it's getting *hot* in here!
   I'm *really* getting hot!"

So this old Deer told him, he said,
   "Well that's what it takes," he said.
   "You got to stay in there.
   You stay right in there."

So then awhile put some more wood in there
and got the fire going a little bit bigger,
he said, uh,
   "How're you feeling now?"

   "I'm *hot!*
   I'm *really* hot!"

   "Well," he said,
   "you're just about, about ready to be spotted," he told him.

And so he just kept on and kept on,
and just kept on wandering around
and kept on complaining how he was getting hot.

So pretty soon when he asked this Wolf how he was doing,
he said,
   "How are you feeling?" he said,

And Wolf didn't answer him.

And he said,
   "I think," he said,
   "you're just about spotted," he told him.

So he told him, he said,
   "Are you getting hot?" he told him.

Wolf didn't answer him.

It was real quiet.
This Wolf didn't answer him.

The moral of this story was that he didn't want to be spotted,
he just wanted to become a (fool).

Catawba

Four Fables

Introduction by Blair A. Rudes

The Catawbas are one of the few indigenous groups of the southeastern United States that continue to live on ancestral territory. Their current reservation along the Catawba River in Rock Hill, South Carolina, is only a few hours walk from where the tribe was located in the 1520s when Spanish galleys captured Indians from the Carolina coast and sold them into slavery in the West Indies.[1] A short time later, expeditions of Spanish conquistadors under the leadership of Hernando de Soto and Juan Pardo traversed Catawba territory in search of treasure and took captives along their route. The loss of tribal members to slave traders and conquistadors, coupled with deaths from the new diseases that the Spanish introduced, severely weakened the Catawbas.

When the English arrived in the seventeenth century to colonize the Carolinas, they brought with them other new diseases as well as alcohol, which further reduced the Catawbas' numbers. By the early eighteenth century, tensions between the English colonists and neighboring tribes in the Carolinas resulted in the Tuscarora Wars of 1711–13 and the Yamassee War of 1715, which together decimated the Indian communities of the region and turned Catawba territory into a giant refugee camp for the survivors.[2]

Although the Catawbas as a people survived the traumas of the first three centuries of European contact, their culture and language suffered greatly. Unquestionably, the greatest damage was caused by the conversion of the Catawba people to Christianity.

A people's oral literature, in particular its epic legends, are closely linked to its real-world knowledge, values, and beliefs. When the members of a culture adopt en masse a new belief system such as Christianity, they often look back on their traditional oral literature as a holdover of pagan beliefs, and unless recorded in writing prior to the conversion, the great legends of the past are abandoned. For example, the Germanic forefathers of the English—the Angles, the Saxons, and the Jutes—brought with them to England their epic tales of Valhalla. However, their subsequent conversion to Christianity by missionaries from Ireland led to the abandonment of these legends. Furthermore, since these pre-Christian Germanic settlers were illiterate until the Irish missionaries taught them to write, they did not record their legends before adopting the Christian faith. In fact, our knowledge of their legends comes to us secondhand from other Germanic peoples, in particular the Norse, who recorded the legends in written form before they too were Christianized.

The Catawbas first encountered Christian thought early in their contact with Europeans, when the Spanish Father Sabastian Montero, chaplain to Juan Pardo, established a mission in 1567 among the Wateree Indians, neighbors of the Catawbas.[3] Spanish efforts to convert the Catawbas continued intermittently into the 1600s.

Around 1700, German-speaking Protestants began moving into the Carolinas. The first to arrive was a contingent of poor Swiss and persecuted Palatines who settled to the east of the Catawbas in 1710. The Swiss and Palantine settlement in New Bern, North Carolina, was originally separated from the Catawbas by Tuscarora territory. However, in 1711 the Tuscarora wars broke out, and by 1713 the defeated Tuscaroras had fled the area.[4]

The Palatines were soon followed by the Society of Friends (Quakers) and the United Brethren (the Moravians), who settled to the north of the Catawbas in Greensboro and Winston-Salem, respectively. That these German-speaking communities undertook missionary activities in Catawba country is reflected in the presence of at least one German loan word within the Christian vocabulary of the Catawba language, specifically, *hímbare·* 'heaven' from German *Himmel* 'heaven'.[5]

However, neither the Spanish nor the German missionary activities had any lasting effects on the Catawba culture. It was only with the arrival in the early 1800s of Robert Marsh, a Pumunkey Indian who married into the Catawba Nation and became a Baptist minister, that serious conversion of Catawbas to Christianity began.[6] Later in the century, Presbyterian missionaries arrived. Finally, in 1882 the Church of the Latter Day Saints (the Mormons) established a foothold in the surrounding non-Indian community and sought to bring Indians into the church. The first baptism of a Catawba into the Mormon faith occurred in 1884, and today the majority of Catawbas adhere to Mormon beliefs.[7]

Distantly related to Siouan languages of the Great Plains such as Crow, Lakota, and Omaha, the Catawba language was but one of several Catawban languages spoken in the Carolinas since time immemorial. Prior to the conversion of the Catawbas to Christianity, their language was unwritten. All of the efforts by anthropologists, linguists, and the Catawbas themselves to record Catawba oral literature occurred well after their conversion. Thus, we must assume that much of their traditional knowledge had by this time been replaced by Euro-Christian knowledge and forever lost. The oral literature that has survived consists principally of short fables, medicinal and culinary recipes, songs, and historical fragments. We have no way of knowing how representative this material is of the pre-Christian oral literature of the nation.

The Catawbas today are painfully aware that they have lost much of their traditional knowledge, and many in the tribe are working diligently to retrieve what has been lost. For example, the Catawbas, like the Pueblo tribes of the Southwest, were once revered for their pottery. Although the pottery tradition had fallen largely into disuse by the mid-twentieth century, the Catawbas have managed over the past few decades to revive the practice, in part because three elders remembered the art and because numerous examples of finished works were available to serve as models.[8]

However, language is not like pottery; oral traditions are "words on the wind." Unless captured by the ears of the listener and retold to another generation or recorded in writing, the stories are lost forever.

At the opening of the twentieth century, only a handful of fluent speakers of the Catawba language remained. The anthropologist Frank G. Speck gathered texts from four of these speakers: Sally Brown Gordon; her brother, Chief Sam Blue; their mother, Margaret Wiley Brown; and another elder, Susan Harris Owl. Speck's research resulted in the publication of one extensive collection of texts as well as a few isolated texts in various journals.[9] All of the texts that Speck published were presented in Catawba, with free English translations. Unfortunately, Speck was a notoriously poor translator, and many of his English translations are wrong.

Several other anthropologists and linguists collected texts from Sally Gordon and from Chief Sam Blue, including Raven I. McDavid, Frank T. Siebert Jr., and William C. Sturtevant. However, none of the texts they collected were ever published. Like Speck, these other researchers were more interested in the linguistic and anthropological value of the information contained in the texts, and their English translations suffered as a result.

Chief Sam Blue, the last native speaker of the Catawba language, died in 1959. Toward the end of his life he worked for some time with an individual who, although not a Catawba Indian, had acquired a speaking ability of the language by studying Frank Speck's field notes and talking with speakers on the reservation. After Chief Blue's death, this individual—Red Thunder Cloud, né Cromwell Ashbie Hawkins West—worked with G. Hubert Matthews, a linguist, to produce the only other Catawba texts to appear in print. The last non-native speaker of the language, Red Thunder Cloud, died in 1996.[10]

Over the past few years I have analyzed the unpublished texts contained in McDavid's, Siebert's, and Sturtevant's field notes and have reanalyzed Speck's published texts. One focus of this research has been to produce more accurate translations that better reflect the aesthetic qualities of the original Catawba texts.

Fables, which were used to teach moral lessons and calm the fears of the young, were the principal genre of the Catawba literary tradition that survived the tribe's conversion to Christianity. These fables tended to be short, ranging from just a couple of sentences to a few paragraphs, a characteristic that is apparent in the texts collected by all the researchers. I present here new translations of four fairly representative Catawba fables.

Several versions of all four texts were collected by different scholars. The "Comet" story first appears as text 1a in Speck's published collection of texts. It also appears in McDavid's field notes and on a tape recording made by Siebert. It has a classic plot about good versus evil and provides an explanation for how comets come into existence.

A version of "Barred Owl" also occurs in Speck's collection, as text 30, as well as in McDavid's notes. The story provides an explanation for how owls manage to get into the rafters of a house and helps allay the fears of children when they see the owl's eyes looking down at them. I have combined elements from the various versions to give a more comprehensive rendition of the story.

Two versions of the third text, "A Dog's Tale", were recorded. The first version, under the title "A Dog Tells the People How the Tuscarora Killed His People," was taken down by Speck from Margaret Wiley Brown and appears as text 34 in Speck's published collection. The second version was recorded by McDavid from Brown's daughter, Sally Gordon. The two versions differ in important details. First, Brown identifies the murderers in the story as being members of the Tuscarora Nation, with whom the Catawbas had long-standing enmity, whereas Gordon simply states that they were from some other tribe. Furthermore, Brown's version contains a discussion of how the dog raised a child, presumably the child of the people who were murdered, and how the dog's howling attracted the attention of other people, who took the child home. Gordon's version, on the other hand, omits discussion of a child and instead concludes with a moral lesson on what happens to people who make fun of others. The text presented here combines the elements contained in both of the recorded versions.

The last text presented here, "Rabbit Steals the Fire from the Buzzards," appears twice in Speck's published collection, as texts 9a and 9b, and once in Sturtevant's field notes. The first version (Speck's text 9a) was taken down from Brown. It is by far the most detailed version and is the one that I have edited to present here. The other version in Speck's collection (text 9b) was recorded from Brown's daughter, Sally Gordon. It leaves out many of the details of Brown's version, including the rabbit's praise for his own ingenuity. The third known version of the text was recorded by Sturtevant from Brown's son, Chief Blue, and is even more abridged that the version taken from Gordon. The story is above all an explanation of how people came to possess fire. Secondarily, it provides an explanation for why rabbits hop, a characteristic that gives the rabbit its Catawba name, *dapahwą́ʔ* 'thing that jumps'.

A NOTE ON ORTHOGRAPHY AND PRONUNCIATION

In the word *hímbare·* 'heaven' the consonants are pronounced as in English except that *r* is trilled as in Italian or Spanish. The first vowel (*i*) is pronounced like the *i* in *pizza*. The second vowel (*a*) is pronounced like the *a* in *sofa*. The third vowel (*e·*) is pronounced like the *é* in *café*. In the word *dapahwą́ʔ* 'rabbit' the consonants *d* and *p* are pronounced as in English; *hw* is pronounced like the *wh* in words such as *which* and *whale* in British English and some parts of New England, that is, as an *h* immediately followed by a *w*; and ʔ (glottal stop) is pronounced as a brief catch in the throat such as occurs in the English interjection *unh-unh* 'no'. The first two vowels (*a* and *a*) of the word are pronounced like the *a* in *sofa*. The last vowel (*ą́*) is a nasalized vowel, pronounced like the *an* in *élan* or the *on* in *Vermont*.

NOTES

1. Caruso, *Southern Frontier,* 20.
2. Adair, *History of the American Indian,* 224–25; and Rudes, Blumer, and May, "Catawbas."
3. Gannon, *Cross in the Sand,* 31; and Hudson, *Juan Pardo Expeditions,* 154.
4. Johnson, *Tuscaroras,* 55, 161–85.
5. Since the Catawba language lacks the consonant *l,* the word *Himmel* was nativized into the Catawba language as *hímar.* However, since words in the Catawba language cannot end in *r,* the final *r* was reinterpreted as the very frequent suffix *-re·* 'it is'. Finally, beginning in the mid-1800s the Catawba language underwent a regular sound change whereby *m* before an oral vowel became *mb* (and later just *b*), which resulted in modern Catawba *hímbare·* 'heaven'.
6. Brown, *Catawba Indians,* 271.
7. "Mormon Propogandist," *Yorkville (South Carolina) Enquirer,* February 16, 1882, p. 2; and "Missionary Experience: A Cool Reception," *Deseret (South Carolina) Evening News,* May 20, 1884.
8. Blumer, *Catawba Clay.*
9. Speck, *Catawba Texts;* Speck, "Some Catawba Texts and Folklore"; Speck, "Catawba Text"; and Speck with Carr, "Catawba Folk Tales from Chief Sam Blue."
10. Matthews and Red Thunder Cloud, "Catawba Texts"; and Goddard, "Identity of Red Thunder Cloud."

SUGGESTED READING AND REFERENCES

For more Catawba fables and other pieces of Catawba literature, the reader may consult Matthews and Red Thunder Cloud, "Catawba Texts"; Speck, "Some Catawba Texts and Folklore"; Speck, *Catawba Texts;* and Speck with Carr, "Catawba Folk Tales from Chief

Sam Blue." Additional information on the history of the Catawba people may be found in Brown, *Catawba Indians,* and Rudes, Blumer, and May, "Catawbas."

Adair, James. *The History of the American Indian.* London: E. & C. Dilly, 1775.

Blumer, Thomas J. *Catawba Clay: Pottery from the Catawba Nation.* Seagrove NC: North Carolina Pottery Center, 2000.

Brown, Douglas S. *The Catawba Indians: People of the River.* Columbia: University of South Carolina Press, 1966.

Caruso, John Anthony. *The Southern Frontier.* New York: Bobbs-Merrill, 1963.

Gannon, Michael V. *The Cross in the Sand.* Tallahassee: University of Florida Press, 1965.

Goddard, Ives. "The Identity of Red Thunder Cloud." *Society for the Study of the Indigenous Languages of the Americas Newsletter* 13, no. 1 (2000): 7–10.

Hudson, Charles M. *The Juan Pardo Expeditions: Explorations of the Carolinas and Tennessee, 1566–1568.* Washington DC: Smithsonian Institution Press, 1990.

Johnson, F. Roy. *The Tuscaroras.* Vol. 2. Murfreesboro NC: Johnson Publishing, 1967.

Matthews, G. Hubert, and Red Thunder Cloud. "Catawba Texts." *International Journal of American Linguistics* 33, no. 1 (1969): 7–24.

Rudes, Blair A., Thomas J. Blumer, and Alan May. "Catawbas." In *Handbook of North American Indians,* vol. 14, *Southeast,* edited by Raymond Fogelson. Washington DC: Smithsonian Institution Press, forthcoming.

Speck, Frank G. "Some Catawba Texts and Folklore." *Journal of American Folk-lore* 26, no. 102 (1913): 319–30.

———. *Catawba Texts.* 1934. Reprint, New York: AMS Press, 1969.

———. "Catawba Text." *International Journal of American Linguistics* 12, no. 2 (1946): 64–65.

Speck, Frank G., with L. G. Carr. "Catawba Folk Tales from Chief Sam Blue." *Journal of American Folk-lore* 60, no. 235 (1947): 78–84.

Comet

Told by Sally Brown Gordon

Everyone wants to go to heaven. Well, here is a story about how one woman and her son got there.

One day a woman went out to dig up some roots for supper. She took her baby with her, and when she got to the field, she laid him in a ditch where he would be safe while she worked. As the woman gathered roots, she wandered further and further into the field until she was out of sight of her baby. Just then another woman came into the field and stole the baby.

A while later, when she had dug all the roots she needed, the mother returned to where she had laid her baby down and saw that he was missing. Thinking he might have crawled away, she looked everywhere for him. She searched and searched but could not find the boy. Desperate, she went to the nearby village and pleaded for others to help her look. The whole village came out to help, but they could not find the baby either. The woman's grief at the loss of her baby was so great that all she could do was sit in one spot and cry. She refused to eat, and soon there was nothing left of her but skin and bones.

At long last Woodpecker happened by and, seeing her sad state, asked her why she was crying? "I have lost my baby," she replied. Woodpecker took pity on her and said, "If you give me the pair of red earrings you are wearing, I will tell you where your baby is." Of course, she gave him the earrings, and Woodpecker, good to his word, told her she would find her boy down by the river. "You must go there and hide in the bushes. Three boys will come to bathe in the river, the first two finishing before the third arrives. The third one will be your son."

The old woman did what she was told and soon she saw two boys come, bathe, and leave. Then a third boy arrived. Waiting until he had finished bathing and was starting to leave, the old woman reached out to him saying, "I am your mother."

The boy had long felt that the woman who was raising him did not treat him as well as she did the two other boys and thus was not surprised by what the old woman said. "Come with me," he told her. "We will go to the house where I live." She went with her son and, when they got close to the house, he showed her a hollow log in which she could hide.

The boy then went into the house and said to the woman who had raised him, "I'm starved. Cook me a ton of food." The boy ate his fill and took the rest of the food out to his mother. He kept this up day after day until his mother had put some meat on her bones and regained her strength. Then he said to the woman in the house, "We need more food. I'll go up the mountain and shoot us some deer."

After he shot his first deer, he tied a rawhide strap around it and slashed the strap repeatedly so it would split apart when someone pulled on it. Then he went back to the house and told the woman, "I've killed a deer. You go drag it back down the mountain."

Up the mountain she went and found the deer with the strap around it. She began dragging the deer, but when she pulled the strap it broke. She tied the strap back together and pulled again, but again the strap broke. She tied the strap again, and it broke again. This happened over and over again, and each time she cried in despair, "Oh, no! Not again! The load has fallen to the ground."

While the woman struggled with the deer, the boy went and got his mother out of the log where she was hidden. Then he went into the house, packed his clothes, and set the house on fire.

Up on the mountain top the woman saw ashes raining down from the sky. She guessed immediately that it was her house that was on fire. "I should've thought something was strange," she swore to herself, "what with this strap breaking the way it's been doing" and raced back down the mountain.

Meanwhile, the boy had taken his mother by the hand and fled the burning house. The angels on high had seen all that had happened and were moved by all the pair had gone through to be reunited. They determined that the mother and son should be together forever, so they dropped a line out of the sky to carry the two to heaven.

Just as the pair neared the top the wicked woman arrived and saw the angels pulling the rope back up. "Please let the line back down," she begged. "I want to go up to heaven too." The angels let the line back down and she started to climb up, but when she got near the top they cut it. As the woman plummeted back toward the earth, she was transformed into a comet, while the boy and his mother joined the angels in heaven.

Barred Owl

Told by Sally Brown Gordon

There was once an old woman who lived with her family in a house in the woods. One day she fell deathly ill, and no one in the house knew what to do.

A short time later Snail came by and saw the woman's condition. When he was told that no one in the house knew how to cure her, he volunteered to fetch a doctor.

Over two days later, when Snail had not yet returned, the others in the house were sure the old woman was going to die and said to one another that Snail had probably not even gone for the doctor. However, by this time Snail had only gotten as far as the stoop. Hearing what had been said, he spoke up and said, "If you're going to talk about me that way, I won't even go."

He then got down off the stoop and continued on his way. After a while he met up with Turtle, who was heading toward the old woman's house. "Why don't you go for the doctor," Snail said to Turtle, "for you are much faster than I." So Turtle took up the journey and was gone about a year.

Around this time Owl flew by and saw Turtle hurrying along as best he could. Owl asked him where he was heading. "To get a doctor," replied Turtle. "Slow down," Owl said. "I'll get the doctor. I can get to him faster than you," and flew off. Within no time Owl appeared at the home of the old woman with Fish Hawk, the doctor that Snail had originally set off to find.

After examining the old woman, Fish Hawk took out a beetle, broke it in two, and rubbed the bug juice all over the old woman. When she had been completely covered with the juice, he helped her rise and took her over to the fireplace. There he rubbed her with the bug juice again. The old woman was instantly cured and vanished in a flash up the fireplace chimney.

When the people in the house looked outside they saw an owl alighting on the lawn and knew that it was the old woman transformed. She had the appearance of the kind of owl that flies over rivers to warn people of floods, and so Fish Hawk named her Barred Owl.

Every once in a while the old woman flies back across the river at night to the house she once lived in and alights up in the rafters. From her perch she looks down on the children sleeping below. When the children wake and see her eyes shining in the darkness far up in the rafters they get scared, but their parents comfort them by saying, "Don't be afraid, it is just the old woman who had once lived here coming back to see us. Come dawn she will leave again." "But how does she get in the house?" asked the children. "Through the fireplace chimney" is the reply.

A Dog's Tale

Told by Margaret Wiley Brown
and Sally Brown Gordon

Long ago two old Catawba women, who were living out in the woods by them-selves, were killed by warriors from the Tuscarora tribe. A dog that was standing outside the two women's house saw the whole horrible event and was so scared he would be next that he ran away.

The dog kept on running for a day and a half until he collapsed across an old stump. There he just lay, whimpering and howling out of fear and grief.

Not far from the stump were three tents in which lived Catawbas. When they heard the pathetic sounds the dog made, they came out and asked him, "Why are you howling so?" The dog replied, "Tuscarora warriors killed all of my people and ate their bodies. I got so scared they might come after me that I just ran and ran until I got here."

Hearing the dog's story, the people started worrying about their own safety, so they quickly packed up their tents and fled to the nearest large village. There they set up their tents.

A short time later, while the newcomers were still nerve-wracked from the story the dog had told them, some boys came by whistling on bones. The sound startled the newcomers, and they jumped up in surprise.

The boys thought their reaction was hysterical, and they began to laugh up-roariously. They laughed so hard that they swallowed the bone whistles they were playing and choked to death

Rabbit Steals Fire from the Buzzards

Told by Margaret Wiley Brown

In ancient times buzzards jealously guarded fire from all others. They would sit around the fire with their wings outspread, thereby keeping it all to themselves. As a result the rest of the earth was freezing cold.

One rabbit in particular was very cold, and he dared to approach the buzzards, saying, "My foot is very cold. May I please put my foot near the fire?" The buzzards replied, "No, you cannot!"

So the rabbit went away for a while, and then came back again and pleaded, "Please help me, for I am nearly frozen." And so he was.

One buzzard took pity on the rabbit and raised up his wing for the rabbit to approach the fire. Rabbit was overjoyed. Singing all the while, he stuck splinters of pitch pine between his toes to catch fire. He then extended his foot under the buzzard's wing and lit the splinters. When he pulled his foot back the splinters were blazing mightily, and the surrounding woods caught fire.

The fire that resulted was intense, and the rabbit ran to distance himself from it. Because his toes got burnt, the rabbit could not run very well. Rather, he hopped up and down as he coursed through the woods, all the while singing words of self-adulation, "Rabbit is good! The fire is big and hot now, and everyone can come sit around it and get warm."

4. East

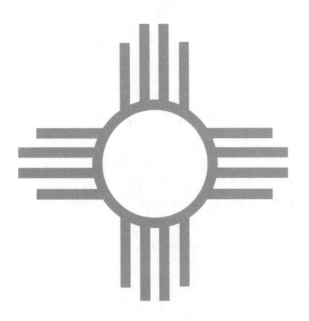

Lakota

Double-Face Tricks a Girl

Introduction by Julian Rice

Until the 1988 publication of her posthumous novel *Waterlily*, Ella Deloria's reputation rested on her achievements in linguistics and ethnology. Few readers realized the literary talents that had produced the little-known collection of sixty-four traditional stories titled *Dakota Texts* (1932), because most assumed that Deloria simply transcribed and translated tales that elderly Sioux people agreed to tell her. These narrators, distrustful of non-Indian anthropologists, spoke freely to Deloria because she needed no interpreter and listened respectfully as a relative, without such inhibiting paraphernalia as a recorder or a notepad. Like generations of Indian storytellers before her, Deloria absorbed the spirit and feeling of the stories; but unlike those earlier storytellers, she retold them in writing—first in Lakota, then in English. Essentially, however, she transmitted the stories as they had always been passed down, renewing them in her own words rather than duplicating a prior performance: "I have honestly tried to recapture these tales as they sing themselves to me, from my memory of the way they sounded as various storytellers told them" (1937, 5: 59).

Since she did not record the stories verbatim, Deloria chose to translate them in two ways: word-by-word translations to assist those with a reading knowledge of Lakota, and free translations, primarily for those unable to read the Lakota versions. The word-by-word translations (given only for the first sixteen stories) make little sense if read for themselves alone, and the free translations are meant to convey the story's meanings rather than to evoke the tone or quality of the original telling. For the story retranslated here I have tried to strike a balance between Deloria's literal and free translations by incorporating some of the narrative conventions that her free translations omit. I have used the quotatives *śke* and *keyapi* 'they say' for emphasis, as I believe the original narrators used them (see Rice 1992a, 52–54), and I have maintained the Lakota style of direct quotation where the narrator names the character and then orally changes to that character's voice without preceding the quote with "he said." Instead, "he said" immediately follows the quote (see Rice 1992a, 57): "Then immediately the man was very angry— 'Sit there, I tell you! If you don't do it, I will throw you in the water,' he said."

My translation also draws from Deloria's notes. For example, just before the woman in "Double-Face Tricks a Girl" elopes with her seducer, Deloria's free translation reads: "She took her pet beaver and went outside and there stood the young man behind the tipi, his blanket pulled up over his head: so she went off with him" (Deloria [1932] 1974, 49). The word-by-word translation reads "So / beaver-little / a / pet / she had / therefore / that one / she took up her own / and / immediately / she came out / and / young man / the / behind the house / head-inside / wearing his blanket / he stood / so / with him / she went" (47).

Neither the free translation nor the word-by-word translation offers a literal rendering of "pet." I felt that a literal translation of the word for "pet" effectively retained the metaphorical connotation of the word: *waniyanpi yuha* 'kept alive one', so I included it in my translation. As I suggest later, *waniyanpi yuha* also enhances the story's theme. For another modification I noted that Deloria's Lakota version describes the Double-Face's head as *pamahel icoma,* which Deloria translates as "his blanket pulled up over his head" ([1932] 1974, 49) and "head-inside / wearing his blanket" ([1932] 1974, 47). Deloria, however, glosses *icoma* as "to wear a blanket held tightly around the body, the arms holding the edges in front of the body" ([1932] 1974, 47 n); my translation inserts the detail "held tightly":

> And so with a little beaver "kept-alive" [a pet],
>   she took that,
>   and right away she came out,
>   while the young man stood outside the tipi
>   with his head tucked in his tightly wrapped blanket,
>   and so together they started out.

My decision to present the story in poetic lines rather than the prose of Deloria's free translation reflects an attempt to convey its tempo. Longer lines express rapid, uninterrupted action, while shorter lines serve to divide speeches by different speakers, to emphasize dramatic acts, and to demarcate particular events.

The quotatives *ške* and *keyapi* 'it is said' or 'they say', phrases which validate any present narration by referring to the storytelling tradition as a whole (rather than to characters in the story), conclude almost every sentence in Deloria's Lakota version, and her decision to use one or the other appears to be a matter of emphasis: *ške* is used less frequently than *keyapi*, because it follows especially significant or dramatic actions, or because it finalizes a section of narrative (see Rice 1992a, 54–56). Deloria does not employ quotatives at all in either her free or word-by-word translations, but I have used the quotative to conclude major events: the girl's consent to marry; her discovery that her "husband" is a monster; the narrator's revelation that the monster's "lice" are actually small toads; the girl's despair, when in her flight from the monster she arrives at the shore of a lake too deep to cross; her safe arrival at her own camp; and the honoring of the girl's pet beaver to the point that "they say he felt like / the best person in that whole camp."

I selected this particular story, because it typifies one of Deloria's favorite themes in both narrative and ethnography. It was imperative for nineteenth-century Lakota women (in "camp circle" communities) to be chaste before marriage. Although formal courting rituals protected them from impulsive elopements, occasionally a young woman could be swept off her feet by an unscrupulous suitor. "Double-Face Tricks a Girl" should be read in light of the strong social pressures women had to bear (see Deloria 1954, 139–52). The story forgives its heroine for being naive, but Lakota society did not tolerate repeated promiscuity before and after marriage, because the incitement of jealousy was a divisive threat. Mistakes might be allowed when a girl followed her heart or her hormones and might even serve to make the woman more protectively alert when advising her children.

Although the circumstance is not stated at the beginning of the story, courting often took place at the summer Sun Dance, where a large gathering of different bands brought eligible men and women together. Since the men of her own *tiyošpaye* 'community' would be too closely related to her, a girl could expect to be courted by many men she had never seen. In such conditions she might well decide on the basis of physical attraction, since she would have no information about the man to mitigate that appeal. The story presents the girl as a person unlikely to be impulsive in her choice. She is a good woman, well liked, even *ksapa* 'prudent', and these qualities make her especially attractive as a wife and relative to a prospective husband's family. Though they all want her, she will consent to none of them.

But suddenly her prudence and goodness are blown aside by a stranger who inexplicably convinces her to run away with him. The lack of narrative preparation for her unaccustomed impulsiveness implies its potential emergence in any girl of that age. That it doesn't follow from anything she has ever said or done is just the point. The girl who has obviously done everything right all her life does not speak to her parents about her choice of a husband, thus ignoring the idea of marriage as a family alliance. With ironic foresight she prepares dried meat and moccasins and mentally rehearses her secret departure. The narrator's attention to detail accentuates the part of the journey she is not prepared for—the reality of a man turned into a monster when his courting blanket is dropped. In the shadows of her ignorance the imminence of unlooked for hardship is suggested by the man's throat clearing. As a preparation for speech, it holds the potentiality of a story she could not imagine.

Since every young person encounters unexpected trials of some sort, the narrator shows how the girl is psychologically equipped for survival. Before starting the journey she takes her pet beaver with her: "The spirit of the beaver was the patron of work, provision, and domestic faithfulness" (Thomas Tyon in Walker 1980, 121). A pet is *waniyanpi yuha,* as mentioned, 'one kept alive', and the qualities represented by the beaver — the disciplined habits of work, endurance, and loyalty — live in the girl. Carrying these qualities in herself, she goes out to meet her enemy, still hidden by his blanket.

The speed with which they travel corresponds to the impulsiveness of her act, the beating of her heart, the excitement of danger and sexuality. The deep lake that he forces her to cross, though she cannot swim, represents the depths of betrayal she has not been prepared to face. Probably the girl has never been forced to do anything against her will; Lakota children were not bullied or intimidated by anyone. The man provokes a fear unfamiliar to a girl surrounded by many brothers, brothers-in-law, and cousins. The entry into the lake while riding the man may also be a sexual euphemism.

In the midst of the crossing the horrified girl sees her husband's second face in the back of his head. The discovery is not a simple reversal of expectation, as the narrator presents it, but a comment on the psychological value of the courting process. The monster is not the man with whom she agreed to elope. That man too might have become a monster if they had not married in the proper way. Breaking the rules can cause even a sincere husband to mistreat a woman whom he feels he can no longer trust.

And as a man transformed by the loss of discipline that creates Lakota identity, the Double-Face immediately evokes repulsion. Once inside his tipi he asks her to pick the lice out of his hair, probably a sexual metaphor. As she puts him to sleep, she herself becomes alert. The lice as toads magnify her recognition and lighten the tone, foreshadowing escape. They also present a workable task for her feminine skills. While men are at their strongest in swift motion outside the camp circle, women are trained to be calm, intent, and dexterous in the tipi.

The girl systematically ties the monster's hair in a spider web pattern to the tipi poles, symbolizing the woman's virtue of industry, traditionally associated with the spider (Powers 1986, 68), a psychological habit that allows her to concentrate confidently in all circumstances. In addition the spider is associated with deception (the name for the Lakota trickster, Iktomi, means 'spider'), and here with poetic justice she has temporarily tricked a trickster.

Her Lakota upbringing also helps her to accomplish her tasks resourcefully and quietly; she does not bang the stones together to kill the toads but carefully puts one down and crushes the toads with the other one:

> Therefore, with two flat stones that were lying there,
>   whenever she caught one,
>   she crushed it to death

by placing one stone in a hole,
while using the other stone
to strike it. (my translation)

When she sets out for home, she again carries the pet beaver, as she has carried the resources for survival throughout, from the meat and moccasins to the quietness and manual skill imparted to her by others. Now she heads back to the people to make their survival the consistent goal of her life.

But first she must learn that any one person's resourcefulness has its limits. Every person must remember that being at home in existence requires the protection of relatives. The beaver, *waniyanpi yuha,* the 'kept alive one', is also the consciousness of interdependence that returns to the girl. A girl should not forsake the protection of her brothers to gamble on the promises of a strange man. Only the beaver, as a representation of her protectors, can bring her back from the deep lake of unfamiliar emotions to the solid kinship relations that define Lakota life. The beaver, like the bridge he builds, is an extension of the male power the girl must remember to respect. His loyalty and industry are also her own female virtues; *she* is the one that weaves the monster's hair into the spider pattern. But the ability to think on the run, in a state of rushing turmoil, is typically a male power, and in the end the beaver represents a separate male being rather than a "side" of the girl.

The Double-Face falls from the bridge because it is so narrow he is unable to cross it before the beaver destroys it from the other side. Calm, deliberate action is not the Double-Face's strength, and he is overcome in the midst of trying to effect it. The narrow passage from immature egotism to the community is impossible for him to negotiate. Although he swims across the lake on the way out, he drowns in its depths at the end because the girl's attraction to danger has now dissolved. Double-Face sinks in the recognition of the woman who is glad to return to those she can rely on. Her parents arrange her marriage to the young man with whom she had originally wished to elope, and they are formally united with honoring of all concerned.

The people's praise of the beaver has the narrator's final attention, since he is an alter ego for the male children listening. He is rewarded for loyalty by being made to feel like the best person in the camp. Of course, all children are supported by adults, *waniyanpi* 'kept alive' like pets, but they are also raised to keep others alive. When they have proved their ability to do so, they will grow from being helpless children to honored heroes. On her homeward flight the girl carries the beaver in her arms until she stops in despair beside the lake. A "boy" then completes the journey by building a bridge to the future. In another manifestation of real life the bridge might be made of food, horses, or coups to keep starvation or an enemy at bay. In the end home is cooperatively established by the defensive alertness of both men and women. Having learned the hard way, the girl acquires the strength to help children surmount their own captivities.

SUGGESTED READING AND REFERENCES

Deloria, Ella. 1937. "Dakota Tales in Colloquial Style." Part 5, page 59, MS 30, x8a.16. Boas Collection. American Philosophical Society, Philadelphia.

———. 1954. Camp Circle Society. Unpublished MS. South Dakota State Archives, Pierre.

———. [1932] 1974. *Dakota Texts*. Reprint, New York: AMS Press.

———. 1988. *Waterlily*. Lincoln: University of Nebraska Press.

Hassrick, Royal B. 1964. *The Sioux: Life and Customs of a Warrior Society*. Norman: University of Oklahoma Press.

Jahner, Elaine. 1983. "Stone Boy: Persistent Hero." In *Smoothing the Ground: Essays on Native American Oral History*, edited by Brian Swann, 171–86. Berkeley: University of California Press.

Powers, Marla N. 1986. *Oglala Women: Myth, Ritual, and Reality*. Chicago: University of Chicago Press.

Rice, Julian. 1991. *Black Elk's Story*. Albuquerque: University of New Mexico Press.

———. 1992a. *Deer Women and Elk Men: The Lakota Narratives of Ella Deloria*. Albuquerque: University of New Mexico Press.

———. 1992b. "Narrative Styles in *Dakota Texts*." In *On the Translation of Native American Oral Literatures*, edited by Brian Swann, 276–92. Washington DC: Smithsonian Institution Press.

———. 1994. "Two Roads to Leadership: Grandmother's Boy and Last-Born Brother." In *Coming to Light: Contemporary Translations of Native American Literature*, edited by Brian Swann, 403–22. New York: Random House.

———. 1997. "Ella C. Deloria." In *Dictionary of Literary Biography (DLB)*, vol. 175, edited by Kenneth Roemer, 47–56. Columbia SC: Bruccoli Clark Layman.

Walker, James R. 1980. *Lakota Belief and Ritual*. Edited by Raymond J. DeMallie and Elaine A. Jahner. Lincoln: University of Nebraska Press.

———. 1992. *Lakota Society*. Edited by Raymond J. DeMallie. Lincoln: University of Nebraska Press.

Double-Face Tricks a Girl

Storyteller unknown
Translated by Julian Rice

A Lakota band was encamped.

At the time, within the camp, a woman was so virtuous
    that they greatly loved her.

She was kind and also prudent,
    and so all of the men desired her
    and wished to marry her,
    but she would not consent.

Then, suddenly, a young man,
    very handsome, came from somewhere
    to court her.

From then on, that woman who had always lacked desire
    was finally well pleased,
    and said that she would marry him,
    they say.

But she did not consult her parents
    and made plans to leave
    and secretly made ready
    and, with dried meat and moccasins hanging from her belt,
    she sat waiting.

Now it was twilight, and then
    according to their plan,
    someone outside the tipi cleared his throat;
    "When I clear my throat outside the tipi, then come out,
    and we will leave," he had said.

And so with a little beaver "kept-alive" [a pet],
   she took that,
   and right away she came out,
   while the young man stood outside the tipi
   with his head tucked in his tightly wrapped blanket,
   and so together they started out.

They moved rapidly,
   until they arrived on the shore of a deep lake.
   Then the man—
   "Ho, I will swim across;
   sit on my back,"
   he said.

But the woman did not want to do it.
   Then immediately the man was very angry—
   "Sit there, I tell you!
   If you don't do it,
   I will throw you in the water,"
   he said.

She was very much afraid,
   so she obeyed him,
   though she had never learned to swim.

Now he swam,
   and as she sat on his back
   looking at the nape of his neck,
   just above it appeared a second face,
   they say.

This was what they call a "Double-Face."
   The young man she had loved before,
   this was not,
   and from then on she realized,
   and she deeply hated him
   and feared his strangeness.

Once across they stopped,
   and in the trees was a large, round, skin tent,

and from it smoke rose,
and into that they entered.

Then right away, the man —
    "I am tired.
    So pick out my lice; I will sleep,"
    he said.

Although she did not want to,
    and felt as if she had been scorched with fear,
    while he lay with his head toward the center,
    she proceeded to remove his lice,
    causing him to go to sleep.

But toads
    of a certain type, very small,
    were what he had for lice,
    so those were jumping
    in his hair,
    they say.

Therefore, with two flat stones that were lying there,
    whenever she caught one,
    she crushed it to death
    by placing one stone in a hole,
    while using the other stone
    to strike it.

Soon he fell into a deep sleep,
    and when he was lying unconscious, as she wished,
    she noticed how long his hair was;
    so she took sections of it
    and tied them around the tent poles
    one by one,
    until they formed a spider web,
    with the man lying in the center.

Instantly, with that same little beaver,
    she set out for home.
    They ran without stopping,

and as they were coming close to home,
   they came to the shore of a deep lake
   that she had no way to cross,
   so she sat down and cried, they say.

But while she wept,
   the little beaver ran to cut down trees,
   and quickly made a solid bridge,
   and so, hurriedly,
   they set out again for home.

Once on the other side
   she stepped on land,
   when someone from behind came shouting;
   she looked back,
   and it was the Double-Face
   waving his hand, as he ran toward her.

He had reached the far shore and paused,
   and now on that same bridge
   he wished to climb,
   but he could come only a short way,
   because its narrowness slowed him,
   and, therefore, the little beaver had time
   to dismantle it.

Starting from the other side,
   he gnawed away to the center
   where he caused it to suddenly break in two —
   the Double-Face fell,
   banged his head on a rock,
   and drowned.

Then the woman, carrying the beaver in her arms
   and running all the way,
   traveled and arrived home,
   and so it happened,
   they say.

Her parents were overjoyed,

and right away they gave her to that same young man
that the Double-Face had impersonated,
honoring them both, ceremonially;
"at last, that woman takes a husband,"
the people said.

The "kept-alive" beaver was so greatly loved,
highly praised,
and even spoiled,
that they say he felt like
the best person in that whole camp.

At that point the story ends.

Ioway-Otoe-Missouria

Rabbit Frees the People from Muskrat

Introduction by Jimm G. GoodTracks

The Ioway-Otoe-Missouria tribes were at one time a single nation with the Winnebago (Hochank) in the area of the Great Lakes; they separated as a single group in the area of Green Bay, Wisconsin. They migrated southward through the area of Wisconsin and Minnesota to the Mississippi River. Those who became known as the Ioway people remained at the junction of the Iowa River, while the rest of the band traveled on, further west and south to the Missouri River. At the fork of the Grand River, a quarrel ensued between the families of two chiefs, and the band of people divided into the Otoe and Missouria tribes. The two communities remained autonomous until the Missourias suffered near annihilation from sickness and intertribal warfare over hunting boundaries aggravated by the fur trade. The remnant group merged with the Otoes in 1798 under their chiefs. However, by the 1830s they had been absorbed by the larger community. In the 1880s the leaders went south and selected lands between the Poncas and the Pawnees in Oklahoma Territory. Their numbers had been reduced to 334 members. The oral tradition of the several communities had ceased, on the whole, by the early 1940s, although several contemporary versions of stories and accompanying songs were recorded by this writer from the last fluent speakers in 1970–87. The final two fluent speakers of the Ioway-Otoe-Missouria language died at Red Rock, Oklahoma, in the winter of 1996. Today the Otoe-Missouria tribe has about 1,700 members. Their tribal offices are located east of Red Rock, Oklahoma.

The Ioways had ceded their lands by 1836 and withdrawn to the Great Nemaha Reservation on the Kansas-Nebraska border. In the 1880s some ninety of the traditional Ioways left the area of White Cloud, Kansas, to establish a village near Fallis, Oklahoma. Later they were relocated on individual allotments along the Cimarron River. They retain tribal offices south of Perkins, Oklahoma, while the northern division have their tribal complex west of White Cloud, Kansas. The Oklahoma Ioways number about 450, while the Kansas-Nebraska descendants are more than 2,000. The tribal members of all three communities are dispersed throughout the United States. There have been no sustained or official tribal efforts made among the three communities to revive, maintain, or preserve the Báxoje (Ioway)-Jiwére-Ñút'achi (Otoe-Missouria) language and oral literature.

The Ioway-Otoe-Missouria people and their close kinsmen, the Winnebagos, divided their prose narratives into two basic types: *wórage* (that which is narrated) and the *wéka^n* (that which is sacred). *Wórage* are stories of the people that have occurred in a known time period and are based on historical facts. On occasion a spiritual intercession and/or aid is rendered by the spirit world. Such stories have a novelistic style. They record local accounts of tribal or personal events and re-call the immediate past way of life. They are meant to inform and entertain one who has previously not heard the story. These *wórage* may be told at anytime, not being restricted to the autumn and winter seasons, as is the case with *wéka^n*.

Wéka^n concern the distant past. The characters and heroes are holy immortal beings, although they may be killed temporarily. Some of these beings take on the appearance of human beings who are also holy, as seen by their ability to communicate with animals. Some of these *Wéka^n* are sad, tragic, even brutal, but the majority are quite comical and all are entertaining with universal appeal to listeners of all ages. All *wéka^n* end with the phrase: "Aré gahéda hagú ke" (That's when I started back). This traditional phrase signals to the listeners that the story is now ended. These stories may be told only during autumn and winter.

The prose narratives grouped the adventures of their heroes into large units. The most important of these for the *wéka^n* are the stories connected with the Rabbit, the trickster Old Man Ishjinki, and the Twin Holy Boys.

The story presented here features the Rabbit, a holy culture hero, a renowned benefactor of mankind. He is born of a human mother in a holy conception with a sacred being. He lives with his grandmother, Hí^{n}na/Hi^{n}kúñi Máya^n (My Mother/Grandmother Earth Spirit). She is differentiated from *máya^n* 'the ground, land' by the use of kinship terms. She calls men her sons and women her daughters. As such, she tells her grandson, the Rabbit: "The women are *rihú^n* ['your mothers' or 'mother's sisters'], and the men are *rijéga* ['your uncles' or 'mother's brothers']." The Rabbit serves as a role model of daring and strength. This insignificant, humble animal is frequently scorned in many of the *wéka^n* and often presumed a coward. But from his humbleness arises an undaunted champion of the common people, as in this story, where he challenges the dauntless, precocious Muskrat, who has forsaken his sacred trust to protect the Native people in favor of sub-jugating them and the animals on earth. Rabbit first prepares himself by making a sacred bundle of rabbit skin, containing various material manifestations of his spiritual power. Then he sets out to find Muskrat, while enlisting his allies. Upon locating Muskrat, he challenges him to a series of contests. He first bets his life and companions against the Muskrat's captive human beings. Then he bets for the animals and plant resources. They play the Stick Game by throwing a bunch of foot-long sticks to the ground and then trying to grab as many as possible with their hands. The one who grasps an even number wins the game. Ultimately Rabbit realizes the Muskrat has carefully hidden away his heart, and he must locate it and destroy the wicked heart before he truly can defeat the Muskrat. His success is assisted by the antics of the Turtle, who consistently arouses the fury of Muskrat. Finally, Rabbit emerges victor and chastises Muskrat for having forsaken the creator Wakánda's trust and world order.

His adventures are a literary satire on humankind, its society, and its institutions. He is a culture hero who saves and secures the welfare and well-being of human beings. Rabbit models the spirit of the warrior as well as that of the common man. His example was surely noticed by the small Ioway-Otoe-Missouria children who regularly heard these stories and adventures of the Rabbit one hundred years ago and even earlier. By the late nineteenth century the three tribal communities had been reduced to a small remnant of people with memories of a former glorious past. Their lives were a flurry of contrasted teachings from their traditional elders and that of the mission and government schools that blatantly sought to strip them of everything considered Indian. Rabbit showed them how to stand up for what is true and right, even against formidable causes and people.

The durability and timeless application of this story and the _wéka^n_ in general is evident today, for the Rabbit, like the Coyote trickster, still thrives. He is found everywhere, even in our city backyards. His small presence stands in quiet testimony to his ability to endure and adjust in a changing world. He is an excellent example of the traditional Native American culture hero.

This story is one of ten Ioway-Otoe-Missouria stories told by Mary Gale La-Flesche (HinágeSta^n, Only Woman; 1826–1909), an Ioway-Otoe married to an Omaha, Joseph LaFlesche Jr. (Í^{n}shtaMa^{n}zé, Iron Eyes).[1] She was the daughter of ÑíGùnaMi (She Starts Back to the Waters) and a U.S. Army doctor, John Marion Gale. While yet a small child, her father died, and her mother married a local French fur trader near Bellevue, Nebraska.

Mary, like her husband, Joseph, was multilingual. Her first language was Ioway-Otoe, then Omaha and French. Her marriage brought her into the Omaha traditional community, and as such, Omaha became her primary language in her latter years and the first language learned by her children. Neither she nor her husband spoke English. She narrated these Ioway-Otoe-Missouria traditional stories to James Owen Dorsey, who collected much ethnographic and linguistic information and traditional stories from the Omaha, Ponca, Quapaw, and Kansa tribes during the 1870s and 1880s. These Ioway-Otoe-Missouria stories remain unpublished, stored on microfilm deposited with the Smithsonian in Washington DC. Inasmuch as Mary was married into the Omaha tribe, Dorsey was able to have her relate the Ioway-Otoe-Missouria stories during this period of his study and collection of oral literature.

The author of the initial English translation is unknown. An English translation of the same story, as told in Omaha by her husband, was published in 1898.[2] The translation did not accurately reflect the Ioway-Otoe-Missouria text and was composed in a manner acceptable to the English (European) audience. As such, I rewrote the Native texts, using contemporary orthography, then composed a literal translation into English. I retained the Native narration style by including in a free English translation the traditional use of frequent introductory terms ("And then," "Again," "Then," "So then"), sentence repetitions, and formula evidential statements at the end of a unit episode ("it seems," "they say"). Thus, I followed the original rhythm and idiom in retranslating into the current English text and only edited and modified to facilitate comprehension for the English reader. The story is formatted as prose with indented lines setting off interactive dialogue of direct quotation. In the Ioway-Otoe-Missouria narration the individual speaking is identified, then the statement, which the narrator may have recounted in a mimicked voice. The completion of the statement is indicated by "he said, it seems" or "he said, they say." The events have been organized into paragraphs describing individual episodes of related events. I chose a title summarizing the theme of the story instead of the original title, which was simply "Rabbit and Muskrat."

A NOTE ON ORTHOGRAPHY AND PRONUNCIATION

Ioway-Otoe-Missouria [AYE oh way-OH toe Mis-sou-ree-ah] vowels and nasal vowels are as follows: *a* as in *father, e* as in *hey, i* as in *ski, o* as in *hope, u* as in *Sue; a^n* as in *ribbon, i^n* as in *drink, u^n* as in *tune.*

Consonants are similar to English, with the following exceptions: *ch* as in *church; j* as in *Jessie; ñ* as in *canyon; r* as in Spanish *rojo, rapido; th* as in *thorn; x* as in German *ch* in *Bach* (a guttural sound, with friction in the back of the throat).

An apostrophe (') indicates a glottal stop, as occurs in *uh-oh!* Accent marks are placed on the appropriate vowel.

NOTES

1. Biographical information was garnered primarily from Norma Kidd Green, *Iron Eyes Family: The Children of Joseph LaFlesche,* sponsored by the Nebraska State Historical Society Foundation (Lincoln NE: Johnsen Publishing, 1969).

2. Giffen, Fannie Reed, and Susette La Flesche Tibbles, *Oo-Mah-Ha Ta-Wa-Tha (Omaha City)* (Omaha: F. B. Festner, 1898).

SUGGESTED READING

Daily, Truman W., and Jill D. Hopkins. "Prayer Songs to Our Elder Brother." Ph.D. diss., University of Missouri, Columbia MO, 1997.

Dorsey, James O. "The Rabbit and the Grasshopper: An Oto Myth." *American Antiquarian and Oriental Journal* 3 (1880): 24–27. (Bilingual text with notes.)

———. "The Sister and Brother: An Iowa Tradition." *American Antiquarian and Oriental Journal* 4 (1882): 286–88. (English text only.)

Skinner, Alanson. "Traditions of the Iowa Indians." *Journal of American Folklore* 38 (1925): 425–507.

Walters, Anna Lee, and Carol Bowles. *The Two-Legged Creature: An Otoe Story.* Flagstaff AZ: Northland Publishers, 1993.

Waters, William T. "Otoe-Missouria Oral Narratives." Master's thesis, Department of Anthropology, University of Nebraska, Lincoln, 1984.

Whitman, William. "Origin Legends of the Otoe." *Journal of American Folklore* 51 (1938): 173–205.

Rabbit Frees the People from Muskrat

Told by Mary Gale LaFlesche
Translated by Jimm G. GoodTracks

At the actual beginning, Waká^{n}da, the Creator, made the earth, it seems.
And again, when he finished making the earth, he made human beings.
Again, indeed he made all the animals for humankind.
Again, plants of whatever kind that they eat, everything he made for them, it seems.

And again, men were not wise, they say.
And when men were not wise, they were not just.
Again, when Waká^{n}da thought on it, a Wise One he would make for them, he decided.
Again, he made Udwá^{n}ge, Muskrat.
And then he made Udwá^{n}ge for humankind, they say.

And Waká^{n}da said:
   "As human beings do not know any thing, you shall teach them.
   You shall govern all the earth," he said to Udwá^{n}ge.
And then Udwá^{n}ge governed the whole world, they say.

Then indeed, he, Udwá^{n}ge, collected all the animals
   and caused them to be guarded;
      the large animals and the small ones too, all of them, it seems.
Again so, indeed, all the plants that grow down in the ground,
   above the ground,
      the fruits that grow on trees and bushes,
All indeed, Udwá^{n}ge said that they were his.
      He possessed them, so he caused them to be hoarded, they say.
      "Everything there on the earth is mine," said Udwá^{n}ge.

And so again, truly, all men were without food,
   so a great many died from hunger, they say.

Then Mother Earth was sorrowful because people were dying, it seems.

And then again, Mother Earth spoke to Míshjiñe, Rabbit.
   "My grandson, you are my grandson.
     The Native women, they are the ones who gave you birth," she said.
And again, she said:
   "All men are mine. I am the one who gave them birth.
     Well now! The women are your mothers," she said.
       "The men are your uncles. They are dying of hunger, and I am
       sorrowful," said she.

And so now, she did not say to him:
   "Go!"
Míshjiñe in his heart knew intuitively her intent.
And so Míshjiñe made a Sacred Bundle.
He made a Sacred Bundle of rabbit skin, it seems.
And then he went. Indeed, he didn't say:
   "I'm going to go."
Instead, he simply went on his way.

Then he met a man, it seems; the man was Hánwe, Day Light.
He acted as a human being, they say.
   "My friend, a long time ago now, they had been saying, you are coming.
     So, I waited for you, but it has been a long time that you did not arrive,"
     he said.
   "Yes! my friend, I have come, but it is just as you say," said he.
From there the two went on, it seems.

And again Kétan, Turtle, he was going along before them in the distance.
When they had overtaken him, indeed, it was Turtle.
And Turtle appeared as a man.
   "My friends, a long time ago they were saying that you were coming. So, I
   have waited for you.
   But for a long time you did not come," he said.
And then they all went on, it seems.

As they went on, Old Man Ishjínke, the Trickster, in the distance
   was going along in front of them.
They went to him. And then Ishjínke said:
   "Wah! My friends, when it was said a long time ago that you were coming,

I waited for you.

But, for a long time, you did not come," he said.

"Yes! my friend," said Míshjiñe.

"We have just come, but indeed it is just as you say," said he.

Day spoke with them:

"Listen now! Even though Udwáⁿge reprimands you, do not argue with him.

Whatever way we decide to do something then, let us do it.

Be quite honest.

Do not be deceived.

Do not lie," he said, it seems.

"Yes!" said they.

They went on to where the animals were guarded, and they reached that country.

When they arrived there, Míshjiñe seized a young spotted fawn that was there.

And then they arrived at the house of Udwáⁿge.

And when they arrived there, Udwáⁿge spoke to them saying:

"Have you come?" he said.

Said he:

"It has been said a long time ago that you were coming.

So, I have waited for you, but you were a long time in coming."

Udwáⁿge:

"Well, what shall we do?" said he.

But Míshjiñe said to Udwáⁿge:

"Do what you decide."

"Well, let us play the Stick Game." he said.

"Whoever wins, the human beings will be his.

Everything is mine. Everything that is on earth is mine.

Therefore, what will you try?"

And Míshjiñe said to him as follows:

"We have nothing, but we will bet for humankind." Because the human beings were theirs.

Now then, it was for the men alone; the women would not be joined with them.

Therefore, Udwáⁿge pretended to be willing.

And Udwáⁿge:

"Yes, all right."

And so he bet all the men of the human race.

And, in like manner he bet all the buffalo.

And so they contested against each other in playing Sticks.
And Míshjiñe won, they say.

"The buffalo are his. What will you bet?" someone said.

"I will bet the elk," Udwáⁿge said.

And when they contested each other,
  it was really not a long time, and Míshjiñe won.
The men were very hungry.
And Míshjiñe called all the buffalo and said as follows to them:

"Well, you will go over the whole earth.

My mothers and my uncles will eat you at last," he said.
And the buffalo scattered and went over the whole earth.
And all the men were very joyful.
And again they contested against each other, and Míshjiñe bet the elk.
He bet with Udwáⁿge.

And so again he bet the deer and the elk because they were large.
Then he bet the small animals — black bear, raccoon, panther.
Then Míshjiñe won, it seems.

"Let us two contest by playing Sticks," Udwáⁿge said, it seems.
Turtle sat in a great hurry, it is said, as he wished to win out soon.
But Day was unwilling. He continued to say:

"Do what is honest."
And Míshjiñe, he won everything.
And when he won:

"All scatter and go on," he said.

"All you animals, go into the world," he said, it seems.

And Udwáⁿge had not yet bet the grizzly bear.

"Let us play another game," Udwáⁿge was the one saying it.
Said Míshjiñe:

"What will we do?"

"Let us play Walking in the Same Tracks," he said.

"Well," said Míshjiñe, "what shall we be?"

"I will be the fawn," said Míshjiñe.
Udwáⁿge said:

"I will be a wild cat," said Udwáⁿge.
They played where there were a great many gooseberry bushes, they say.

And Míshjiñe said as he was speaking to Day:

"Make it snow!"
And just then the snow was falling, they say.
And, it snowed, in the woods too, just so deep.
The fawn made tracks in the middle of the gooseberry bushes.
And the wild cat also made tracks.
And for a long time, they walked in their own tracks.

Again Turtle said:
"Well! What a long time!"
Day standing there said:
"Sit still!" He meant the Turtle.

And again Turtle said:
"My friend," meaning Day,
"They are at it a very long time. Give me some wind."
Into the side of his cheek, as he said it,
Day gave him wind. He blew it into his cheek.
And when Udwá^{n}ge was looking to one side,
"Udwá^{n}ge does not see me," Turtle thought.
And he blew out the wind.

Just then a very strong wind developed.
And then Udwá^{n}ge's tracks blew away.
And then:
"Very big bad Turtle. You are to blame. I will kill you," he said, it seems.
And striking Turtle on the head, he broke in his skull, and the brains spilled out.
Therefore, the turtle has no brains, they say.

Míshjiñe wished to kill Udwá^{n}ge, but Day was unwilling.
He said:
"Do not challenge him. Turtle will live," he said.
And then again, Míshjiñe won everything.
"All you animals, go into all the world," he said.
So then:
"Again, let us play," he said, Udwá^{n}ge.
And Míshjiñe took up his Sacred Bundle.
"Let us play the Stick Game," he said.
And again:
"I bet all the plants and fruits," Udwá^{n}ge said, they say.

Míshjiñe said to his Sacred Bundle:

"Sit and watch them; I'm going to go somewhere."

When Míshjiñe saw Udwá^{n}ge, his heart was not there.

Therefore he was unable to kill him, it seems.

"He does not have his heart, therefore I won't kill him," thought he.

Therefore, he said:

"Sit and watch them."

Again, for a long time, they contested.

And again, Udwá^{n}ge again lost the game.

Udwá^{n}ge said as follows:

"Let us do something different."

Day sat watching, that there should be no wrong.

And Míshjiñe came back and took his Sacred Bundle, and he sat there again in his own body, they say.

"What shall we do?" said Míshjiñe.

Udwá^{n}ge said:

"Let us try keeping our eyes open without blinking."

Míshjiñe sat thinking:

"What shall I do?" he thought.

And Míshjiñe says this as follows:

"Udwá^{n}ge, what will you be?" he said.

"I will be an eagle," said he.

And Udwá^{n}ge said:

"Míshjiñe, what will you be?"

Míshjiñe speaking to him:

"I will be myself," he said.

"If anyone winks his eyes, we shall win," he said.

And Míshjiñe took two acorns and put them on for eyes.

They were not his eyes; they were acorns.

And the Eagle was standing up, and Míshjiñe sat below, it seems.

And Míshjiñe sat looking, and the Eagle sat looking.

And when it was a long while, Turtle was in a very great hurry.

"Leader for our chief, give me some water," he said, they say.

Day said:

"Wait! We shall win in spite of delay," he said.

And Turtle said:

"Leader, give me some water," he said, they say.

And Day gave him some water.

And then, when the Udwáⁿge was not looking, Turtle blew out the water,
and there was a great rain, it seems.

And so, the water got into the Eagle's eyes, for certain.

And then, as he did that, the Eagle blinked his eyes.

Turtle said:

"Well! We have won."

Udwáⁿge said:

"You bad turtle. You are the cause," he said.

So then he struck him extremely hard on the head, fracturing it.

And then all the brains flowed out; there were none left.

Only the actual bone was left of Turtle.

Míshjiñe was angry.

He wanted to kill Udwáⁿge, but Day was not willing.

"Turtle will not die," Day was saying to him, they say, it seems.

Again they tried a different thing.

Again, they gambled with the sticks.

They had thrown the sticks behind them, and they took them back again, is
what is meant.

Míshjiñe took his Sacred Bundle, saying:

"Rabbit, now just as I have been doing, so you do the same," he said, they
say.

And then Míshjiñe went away.

And then the Sacred Rabbit Bundle continued to play exactly as Míshjiñe had
done, it seems.

Míshjiñe arrived there at Udwáⁿge's wife, they say.

Míshjiñe arrived there at Udwáⁿge's wife, saying as follows:

"When I have finished eating, I want to sleep. I've come home."

When he said it:

"You are Míshjiñe," said the wife.

Míshjiñe said, it seems:

"No, I am Udwáⁿge."

"No, you are Míshjiñe," the female muskrat said.

"No, I am Udwáⁿge," said Míshjiñe, it seems.

"No, you are Míshjiñe," she said, it seems.

"No, I am Udwáⁿge," said he, Míshjiñe.

"Cook something!

When you have finished cooking, I want to sleep," he said, they say.

"No, you are Míshjiñe," she continued to say.

"No, I am Udwáⁿge," said he.

And the woman seemed to believe him.

So, the woman cooked something, it seems.

Míshjiñe ate something with the woman.

When they finished eating, Míshjiñe slept with her.

When he had finished sleeping with her, he said:

"I am Míshjiñe," because he too pretended to be a person, they say.

The woman said:

"My husband is very blessed. When he finds out, he will kill you."

"How might you think he could kill me?

How might you think of him being blessed?" he said, they say.

"Tell me straight," Míshjiñe was saying.

"Where is Udwáⁿge's heart sitting?" said he.

"When you tell me truthfully, you will live," he said, it seems.

"Tell me where his heart is!"

And she said, they say, the woman:

"It is sitting there in a really large lake," said she.

"A Tothí, Loon, travels there in the middle of the water.

It is difficult to get," she said, it seems.

"How may you think that you will get it? It is very sacred," she said.

Again he said:

"How might you possibly think that I will not get it? I will get it anyhow," he
said.

"No, it is difficult. It is very difficult," she said.

And the Míshjiñe went on to the lake.

The woman was sorrowful.

When Míshjiñe reached the lake, a Ráwe, Beaver, was there.

And Míshjiñe said:

"My friend, I want to borrow something from you." Beaver is the one who
was meant.

Beaver said:

"What do you borrow from me?"

"I want to borrow your heart," he said.

And again:

"I wish to borrow it from you, but I do not wish to borrow it from you for nothing."

"What will you give me?" Beaver said, they say.

"I will give you a sharp ax," said he.

He meant sharp teeth.

And said Míshjiñe:

"Whatever you wish to do, you shall continue doing it."

And Beaver said:

"Yes, all right."

And taking his heart, he gave it to him, it seems.

And he, Míshjiñe, went on.

He gave him the ax, meaning the teeth.

And then Míshjiñe went on, it seems.

And then he came to a big lake.

And the Loon was sitting there, they say.

Míshjiñe called to the Loon.

And the Loon said:

"Míshjiñe, why have you called me?"

"Yes, I am not Míshjiñe," he said.

And the Loon said:

"You are Míshjiñe."

"I am not Míshjiñe," said he.

"Do not say it again!"

And he believed him, it seems.

And Míshjiñe said:

"My heart is displeased, therefore I want to see my heart.

Something that is bad is touching my heart, it seems,

therefore, my heart feels bad," he said.

And he gave him the heart, it seems.

And taking the heart, he put the Beaver's heart in its place.

And then Míshjiñe took Udwá^{n}ge's heart.

When the Loon saw the heart, he said,

"It is not the heart."

"No, I have made the heart well," said he, Míshjiñe.

And the Loon went on. And Míshjiñe went on back, they say.

He took it back to the house of the woman, it seems.

Míshjiñe said:

"Yes, this is it. I have come back with it."

And she said:

"Yes."

When he had come back with it, he cut the heart into strips and burned it, it seems.

And afterward he went back, they say.

Míshjiñe went back to the place of the contests.

And when he returned, he finished destroying all that belonged to Udwáⁿge.

And when he returned, Míshjiñe spoke to Udwáⁿge.

Udwáⁿge was very angry, because he knew now, at last, that he had slept with his wife.

Míshjiñe said:

"Do not be angry!"

And so, Míshjiñe, talking to Udwáⁿge, said:

"You are very bad. Whatever belonged to men, you wanted to take it all from them.

Therefore, I wish to kill you, but I will not kill you.

Yet, you shall have no soul," he said, it seems.

"Therefore, you will go about poor under the lake.

What grass and roots and things that are under the water, only them will you always eat.

Whenever people see you, they shall do nothing but kill you;

"And thus, shall it always be," he said.

And when he had spoken, Udwáⁿge went away, nothing but a muskrat, not a person, it seems.

He then left his wife, they say.

What things were in his house, he abandoned, they say.

All the muskrats went off on the hunt for food.

And Míshjiñe went back to his house.

"Well, my grandmother, I have finished it all," he said.

"Well, my grandson, you are good," said she.

Aré gahéda hagú ke.

Meskwaki

Two Winter Stories

Introduction by Ives Goddard

Presented here are translations of two winter stories written in the Meskwaki language by Alfred Kiyana in the second decade of the last century.

Alfred Kiyana was born in 1877.[1] His surname is from his Meskwaki name *kya·na·wa,* which belongs to the War Chief lineage of the Fox Clan.[2] Kiyana's father died when he was still a child, and he then lived at different times with his father's two brothers. He learned traditional stories largely from one of these uncles, James Onawat (*a·nawowa·ta,* 1837–1915), and he described in autobiographical reminiscences how he would practice telling them out loud when he was off by himself fishing. He was a superb storyteller, whose skill in employing the Meskwaki language can only be fully appreciated by repeated study of his texts. He attended school for only three months, and that was by running away to Kansas, and his English was rudimentary. He was related in some way to William Jones (1871–1909), a one-quarter Meskwaki who wrote his doctoral dissertation on Meskwaki grammar and published a volume of stories that he had taken down from dictation in the summers of 1901 and 1902 and later edited.[3] Jones's father's mother (*keti·hkwe·wa*) was called "grandmother" by Kiyana, but as she was not the mother of either of Kiyana's parents, she was most likely a sister or parallel cousin of one of his grandparents. Kiyana died in the Spanish influenza pandemic in November 1918.

The Meskwakis (*meškwahki·haki*) are known in history and in the scholarly literature as the Fox and are officially called the Sac and Fox Tribe of the Mississippi in Iowa. They have lived since the middle of the nineteenth century on their own land in Tama County in that state. They speak an Algonquian language nearly identical to Sauk and very similar to Kickapoo; these are generally regarded as the most archaic members of the Algonquian family. In 1906, there were 342 people enrolled as tribal members, though a few of these were ethnically Winnebagos, Potawatomis, and Sauks. By the end of the century tribal membership exceeded 1,200 but included very few speakers of the language under forty years of age.

Writing was introduced to the Meskwakis, probably from the Potawatomis, some time before 1880, by which time the tribe was largely literate in their own language, though very few knew English. The writing system is an alphabet-based syllabary that has evolved from French spelling conventions.[4] It writes all the distinctions of the language except vowel length and *h,* but both of these features distinguish many words and inflectional elements from each other. This means that a single spelling in the syllabary often corresponds to two or more words with different meanings in the spoken language. No punctuation or paragraphing is used except a word divider, and that is often omitted. Consequently, Meskwaki is easy to write fluently but can be difficult to read. When Truman Michelson began fieldwork among the Meskwakis in 1911 for the Bureau of American Ethnology of the Smithsonian Institution, he enlisted many members of the community to write materials for him in Meskwaki, paying them by the page. In this way he obtained, mostly in the first few years, nearly twenty-seven thousand pages of manuscript texts that are now in the National Anthropological Archives, largely traditional folklore but also some ethnographic accounts, personal recollections, and essays on various topics. Of these pages, thirteen thousand were written by Kiyana. This collection of texts, written by a large portion of the adult Meskwaki population and unmediated by any scholastic tradition beyond family instruction in what letters spell what sounds, is an oral literature on paper.

Winter stories (*a·teso·hka·kanaki*), formerly told in endless cycles winter night after winter night, deal with the world in the ancient times before things were as they are today, a world ruled by the manitous (*maneto·wa* 'one with spiritual power, spirit, god, snake'). Human beings were then a tiny band, deep in the forest primeval, beset by monsters, shape-shifters, and cannibal giants, their culture and their spiritual powers not yet fully developed. Fortunately, they were often aided by the culture hero Wisahkeha (*wi·sahke·ha*), the subject of the main cycle of cosmological myths, in which he also appears as transformer and trickster. Wisahkeha, half-human on his mother's side, waged an unrelenting campaign of extermination against the manitous of the earth after they, with the complicity of his grandmother, slew his younger brother Ayapahteha (*a·ya·pa·hte·ha*). He was aided in this by the Apayashi brothers (*apaya·ši·haki*), who are the Meskwaki Lodge-Boy and Thrown-Away, and other heroes. To make the world safe for human beings, Wisahkeha and the other monster slayers removed not only the dangers but also the ambiguities of a world in which firm lines between human and nonhuman and between animal species did not exist, where, for example (as in the stories told here), women might be wittingly or unwittingly impregnated by animals or tree spirits, and to be killed was not necessarily to be permanently dead. In addition to dispatching monsters by killing them, Wisahkeha and others transformed many miscreants and transgressors of the ancient times into life forms found today. And they also instructed people in the cultural practices that enabled them to live their lives as human beings. Since people, or at least Meskwakis, are in the patriline of Wisahkeha's mother, he calls them his aunts and uncles. Accordingly, his dealings with people are always correct, though occasionally buffoonish.

These translations render the Meskwaki originals closely. For example, the enclitic hearsay marker *ipi* 'they say', often used by Kiyana as a highlighter, is always translated. Some liberties are, however, taken in the translation of the quotative verbs ("say," "say to") that follow every direct quotation, which has occasionally been varied for a smoother read. Also inflections of the Meskwaki animate gender have necessarily been translated 'he', 'she', or 'it' even in cases where ambiguity might be desirable, as in referring to creatures that are anthropomorphized or that actually shift between animal and human form. In such cases the English pronoun chosen reflects in part the point of view taken in the narrative.

The presentation on the page employs a phrase-line format in order to follow the phrasing of the original and to reflect the slower pace of oral delivery, but there should be no inference drawn that the texts are somehow poetry rather than prose. A new paragraph is typically indicated where the Meskwaki text has certain delimiting words, expressions, or grammatical devices, generally at the start of each direct quotation, and wherever the narrator employs a proximate shift, a device used in Meskwaki and other Algonquian languages to structure discourse.[5] If there are two animate third persons in a given stretch, only one can ordinarily show inflection and agreement as the primary third person, called the proximate; at least one must instead be treated as a secondary third person, or obviative. Proximate shifts occur when a new proximate displaces the previous one. The new proximate may be a new or reintroduced character, or the narrator may shift the status of a current character, either from obviative to proximate, to show a change of focus or narrative interest or a temporary highlight, or from proximate to obviative, to show backgrounding or a change in point of view. Even an inanimate may be shifted to the proximate to give an effect like that of a cinematic close-up. Also the primary character may be reintroduced into the narrative with a proximate shift and no identification by a noun. Although supplying these nouns in the English version would be justifiable, these translations do not do so, and the reader should be alert to the occasional use of this device. The section divider (§) indicates a larger break, typically corresponding to the passage of time or a change of location. These larger breaks are often marked in Meskwaki by words and expressions like *o·ni* 'and then', *nekotenwi* 'once', and *kapo·twe* 'at some point', though these may also demarcate smaller units of the narrative. Also Kiyana sometimes employs jump shifts at both larger and smaller breaks, with spare or no overt linguistic marking.

The translations were prepared as part of a long-term effort to edit and analyze the texts in the Michelson collection. For the story of the married couple, Michelson obtained a rough translation from an unnamed speaker, which he mostly wrote from dictation; it has gaps and misunderstandings, but I have borrowed its wording in some places. The collection contains no translation for the story of the cannibal giant. I reviewed some individual words and lines from these texts with the late Adeline Wanatee of Tama in 1990 and 1991 and with an anonymous elder in 2001; I am grateful for their assistance. I have also relied on earlier work on Meskwaki by Michelson, James A. Geary, and Leonard Bloomfield.[6]

WHEN THE CANNIBAL GIANT WAS KILLED BY WISAHKEHA

The title is Kiyana's (*"ki·yamowe·wa e·hnesekoči wi·sahke·hani"*), apparently added after he had finished writing. It echoes a line in the text of the story: *ki·yamowe·wani e·hnesa·či wi·sahke·ha* 'And Wisahkeha killed the giant'. The only difference between the two Meskwaki sentences is that in the title the giant is the proximate (with ending *-a*) and Wisahkeha is the obviative (with ending *-ani*), while in the text the giant is the obviative and Wisahkeha the proximate. The verb in each case shows agreement, indicating in the title that obviative is acting on proximate (a construction translated here by the English passive) and in the text the reverse. The reason for the difference in obviative marking must be considered together with the reason for why this is the title in the first place. After all, most of this story (which covers fifty-one pages in the manuscript) is about the giant, who lives with human beings and protects them from monstrous creatures, while Wisahkeha does not show up until page 47 and does not kill the giant until page 50. The choice of the title and the way it is phrased both reflect, I think, the fact that this story is a sliver of a vast oral literature and concerns events that are minor, if characteristic, components of the immense cosmological history that is reported in that tradition. Within the story the giant is the central character, and hence he is the proximate in the title. But within the mythology as a whole, to which the story is linked by the appearance of Wisahkeha at the end, it is Wisahkeha who is the main character, and hence it is Wisahkeha who is the proximate throughout the recounting of his defeat and transformation of the giant.

In Kiyana's 1,110-page manuscript on the life and adventures of Wisahkeha, one of many unwelcome creatures he eliminates is a cannibal giant who wields a large elm tree to keep people off his prairie. In an incident described in a page and a half Wisahkeha battles and defeats the giant, hurls him up in the air, and transforms him into a long-billed curlew (*Numenius americanus*). The present story gives the background and context for this incident, describing the origin and life of the giant amidst other beings emblematic of the broader themes of the cosmology, malign and ambiguous creatures that transgress the boundaries between human beings and nonhumans and between animal species and must be eliminated to make the world livable. And it is within the larger context of the whole

Wisahkeha cycle that the seemingly disparate events of this story can be seen to cohere around these common themes.

Most of the transgressive creatures in the story are eliminated by transformations, typically as part of just-so-story episodes. The giant transforms the were-grizzlies into grizzly bears,[7] and the story accounts for why grizzlies live alone, carry their heads low, smell bad, and have males that are larger than females. Wisahkeha's father, Maminatenoha (*mami·nateno·ha*), transforms wolves with white and green feathers into unnamed species, a slender "young man" and his wife into great blue herons, and a short "man" and his wife into mallard ducks. And Wisahkeha transforms others into puff adders and rattlesnakes.

When Wisahkeha "kills" the giant, that is, defeats and transforms him, the details of the encounter and even the name of the species thus created are omitted in this telling, as if they were common knowledge. The fact that the giant used an elm tree as a weapon is, of course, critical to understanding why he became a long-billed curlew, since it is the bird's elm-wielding in its former existence that accounts for its extremely long, thin bill. In the present version the curlew's bill is prefigured only by the small staff he carries into his first contest. The longer text names the bird as *me·škote·wa·towa·ta* (Geary), which has a variant form (*maškote·we·towe·ha*) that Skinner translates as 'curlew' in the Sauk dialect.[8]

Wisahkeha's elimination of the giant may seem rather abrupt, since this giant never consumes the customary giant fare of people soup and has, in fact, been benevolently protecting the human villagers from harm. The lesson is a hard one: even good giants must disappear as part of Wisahkeha's campaign to rid the world of monsters for the benefit of mankind. It is in this connection that we should probably understand why Kiyana inserts into the story, just before the giant killing, the episode in which Wisahkeha visits his vaguely evil father in the form of a little boy and kills him, permanently, with a giant boulder: to make the world safe for us Wisahkeha even had to kill his own earth-manitou father. The juxtaposition is deliberate, since in Kiyana's longer text the patricide episode occurs hundreds of pages earlier, when Wisahkeha's brother is still alive and they are boys in reality.

THE MARRIED COUPLE: THE MAN WHOSE WIFE WAS WOOED BY A BEAR

For the title of this story Kiyana wrote *owi·weti·haki* 'the married couple' at the top of the page, and some distance below this *mahkwani mi·hketama·kota neniwa*, literally 'the man (*neniwa*, proximate) whose one (unspecified) the bear (*mahkwani*, obviative) courted'. This winter story is an example of the widespread Bear Paramour tale type, but once again the wording of the title points to a significant twist. Jones collected a short version, which he called "*we·na·pe·mita e·ha·manohkata-koči mahkwani*" 'the married woman (proximate) that a bear (obviative) had sex with".[9] He reported that "the same incident [also] appears . . . with a much longer narrative," which is presumably what we have in the version written for Michelson by Sakihtanohkweha as the first part of a story she called "Rolling-Skull Woman" (*we·wi·še·hihkwe·wa*). In these other tellings, the cuckolded husband kills the bear, forces his wife to eat it, and then kills his wife, and in the longer version the slain woman comes back for revenge as a Rolling-Skull ogress.

Why did Kiyana alter the story to have a happy ending, in which the husband and wife are reconciled, and why does he give it a title that presents it as about the husband rather than about the wife, whose activities fill most of the narrative? That Kiyana did, indeed, refashion the story is shown by the traces his telling still contains of the general type reflected in the other two versions. The bear's thoughts at one point foreshadow his being eaten by the woman, but the bear is consumed offstage in Kiyana's telling, and the force-feeding scene has been deleted. Also it is explicit in Sakihtanohkweha's tale and stressed by Jones that the wife's most serious offense is the desecration of her husband's sacred bundle by the use of items from it in her assignations, but in Kiyana's telling this desecration is played down, making it more reasonable for it to be left unatoned for. All three versions mention a red broadcloth blanket, but only in the other two does the woman take this explicitly from the wrapping of her husband's sacred bundle and wear it as a skirt. In Kiyana's version the bear smokes the catlinite pipe from the bundle, but the text seems purposely vague about the provenance of the red broadcloth, which she and the bear use as a robe and a blanket, and of a second broadcloth that the woman does wear as a skirt.

In the story of the giant, Kiyana fashions an ending by bringing in major characters from the larger myth cycle; he makes the story coherent by tying it to the general themes of the whole cosmology. In the story of the married couple, in contrast, he makes an ending that severs the story from its continuation, and he is thus able to distill from the larger tradition a story focused on a particular theme. The theme that interests Kiyana is not the desecration of the bundle or the adultery per se; it is the bear's violation of the cosmically ordained boundary between people and animals, and the story is cast as an example of the consequences of such a transgression. The listener realizes, as soon as the man's luck at hunting suddenly and completely fails, that this cannot be merely a matter of happenstance or narrative convenience. The bear's detailed knowledge of the human family shows that he has planned the events described, and the logic of such tales requires the inference that he has brought these events about by the exercise of his magical powers. The enchantment of the man is eventually broken at the exact moment when the bear has slept with the woman in her own house and has started to think of himself no longer as a bear but as a person. Here the listener readily infers that the heretofore forbearing higher powers have decided that the bear's delusion of actually being human is a transgression that is now seriously disruptive of the order of things and that they must therefore bring to an end.

In taking the husband as emblematic of wronged humanity and thus as the one the story is really about, Kiyana does not recast the story explicitly from his point of view. He lets the clues appear serially without describing the husband as comprehending them, or for the most part even noticing them. In fact, in the entire story no thoughts that the man may have about his wife are reported, only his thoughts about his sons. After the bear accidentally tears the red broadcloth with his claw, Kiyana simply finesses the follow-up scene of discovery, thus both heightening narrative tension and forcing the listener to take the point of view of the husband.

Although Kiyana's stories are still oral literature written down, it seems an intriguing possibility that the changes he has wrought on the tradition reflect a response to literacy and to the possibilities and limitations of the new medium, one that encourages the rearrangement of traditional modular components into discrete stories with more concentrated thematic focus.[10]

NOTES

1. Kiyana was his own spelling when he signed his name in English script, but his descendants spell the family name Keahna. This name was earlier borne, in an older form, by the Meskwaki war chief Kiala, who was captured by the French and shipped to Martinique to be sold as a slave in 1734 (Edmunds and Peyser, *Fox Wars*, 159–80).

2. All Meskwaki words in italics are in a technical phonemic orthography in which long vowels (pronounced roughly as in German) are marked with a raised dot, *š* is English *sh*, and *č* is English *ch*. Capitalization is not used.

3. Jones, "Some Principles of Algonquian Word-Formation," 369–411; Jones, "Algonquian (Fox)," *Handbook of American Indian Languages;* Jones, *Fox Texts.*

4. Walker, "Native Writing Systems," esp. 168–71; Kinkade and Mattina, "Discourse," esp. 274, fig. 13; Goddard, "Writing and Reading Mesquakie (Fox)."

5. Goddard, "Aspects of the Topic Structure of Fox Narratives."

6. Bloomfield, "Notes on the Fox Language," pts. 1 and 2; Goddard, *Leonard Bloomfield's Fox Lexicon;* James A. Geary papers. For Michelson's numerous publications, see Pentland and Wolfart, *Bibliography of Algonquian Linguistics.*

I am indebted to Lucy Thomason for her careful reading of the translations against the Meskwaki texts and for suggesting several improvements.

7. These were-bears are ancient creatures that could adopt human form. They are not to be confused with the bear-witches or bear-shamans of the present age, also sometimes called were-bears, who are human beings that can transform themselves into bears (e.g., Jones, *Fox Texts,* 157).

8. Skinner, *Observations on the Ethnology of the Sauk Indians,* esp. 146. Analysis of these words presents difficulties, but perhaps Kiyana's form was *me·ško·te·wa·towa·ta,* literally 'Peoria speaker', reshaped by folk-etymology from the other variant, which is found in two Meskwaki sources as well as in Sauk (allowing for Skinner's execrable phonetics).

9. Jones, *Fox Texts*, 160–65. The Meskwaki title (here normalized and emended) was probably supplied by Jones, based on a phrase in the text.

10. For further reading on the culture and oral literature of the Meskwakis, see Callender, "Fox"; Goddard, "Some Literary Devices"; Jones, "Episodes in the Culture Hero Myth"; Jones, "Notes on the Fox Indians"; Jones, *Ethnography of the Fox Indians;* and Purcell, "Mesquakie Indian Settlement."

SUGGESTED READING AND REFERENCES

Bloomfield, Leonard. "Notes on the Fox Language." Pts. 1 and 2. *International Journal of American Linguistics* 3:219–32 (1925); 4:181–219 (1927).

Callender, Charles. "Fox." In *Northeast,* edited by Bruce G. Trigger, vol. 15 of *Handbook of North American Indians,* edited by William C. Sturtevant, 636–47. Washington DC: Smithsonian Institution, 1978.

Edmunds, R. David, and Joseph L. Peyser. *The Fox Wars: The Mesquakie Challenge to New France.* Norman: University of Oklahoma Press, 1993.

Geary, James A. Papers. National Anthropological Archives. Department of Anthropology. Smithsonian Institution.

Goddard, Ives. "Aspects of the Topic Structure of Fox Narratives: Proximate Shifts and the Use of Overt and Inflectional NPs." *International Journal of American Linguistics* 56 (1990): 317–40.

———. "Some Literary Devices in the Writings of Alfred Kiyana." In *Papers of the Twenty-first Algonquian Conference,* edited by William Cowan, 159–71. Ottawa: Carleton University, 1990.

———. *Leonard Bloomfield's Fox Lexicon: Critical Edition.* Algonquian and Iroquoian Linguistics Memoir 12. Winnipeg: University of Manitoba, 1994.

———. "Writing and Reading Mesquakie (Fox)." In *Papers of the Twenty-seventh Algonquian Conference,* edited by David H. Pentland, 117–34. Winnipeg: University of Manitoba, 1996.

Jones, William. "Episodes in the Culture Hero Myth of the Sauks and Foxes." *Journal of American Folklore* 14 (1901): 225–39.

———. "Some Principles of Algonquian Word-Formation." *American Anthropologist* 6 (1904): 369–411.

———. *Fox Texts.* American Ethnological Society Publications, no. 1. Leiden: E. J. Brill for the American Ethnological Society, 1907.

———. "Algonquian (Fox)." In *Handbook of American Indian Languages,* pt. 1, edited by Franz Boas, 735–873. Bureau of American Ethnology Bulletin no. 40. Washington: GPO, 1911.

———. "Notes on the Fox Indians." *Journal of American Folklore* 24 (1911): 209–37.

———. *Ethnography of the Fox Indians.* Edited by Margaret Welpley Fisher. Bureau of American Ethnology Bulletin no. 125. Washington DC: Smithsonian Institution, 1939.

Kinkade, M. Dale, and Anthony Mattina. "Discourse." In *Languages,* edited by Ives Goddard, vol. 17 of *Handbook of North American Indians,* edited by William C. Sturtevant, 244–74. Washington: Smithsonian Institution, 1996.

Pentland, David H., and H. Christoph Wolfart. *Bibliography of Algonquian Linguistics.* Winnipeg: University of Manitoba Press, 1982.

Purcell, Edward. "The Mesquakie Indian Settlement in 1905." *The Palimpsest* 55 (1974): 34–
    55.

Skinner, Alanson. *Observations on the Ethnology of the Sauk Indians,* part 3, *Notes on Ma-
    terial Culture.* Bulletin of the Public Museum of the City of Milwaukee vol. 5, no. 3.
    Milwaukee: Public Museum of the City of Milwaukee, 1925.

Walker, Willard B. "Native Writing Systems." In *Languages,* edited by Ives Goddard, vol. 17
    of *Handbook of North American Indians,* edited by William C. Sturtevant, 290–323.
    Washington: Smithsonian Institution, 1996.

When the Cannibal Giant Was Killed by Wisahkeha

Written by Alfred Kiyana
Translated by Ives Goddard

They say a certain woman lived on an island in the sea.
Now, the island was a small island, they say,
one of fairly good size.
And they say there was a lot of little wild plant food there, and there were
Indian potatoes.
All the time she would gather Indian potatoes.
She would always get tremendous amounts of them, they say.
   What's more, it was impossible for her to go anywhere else.
She went on staying right there, with no other person.
At the same time, she was not lonely,
and she knew of nothing to miss.
She just kept on contentedly staying there.
   Then one time as she slept she dreamt that she had a husband.
She had the same dream every time,
and at first she enjoyed it.
Eventually, though, she got tired of it.
   "There's no chance that someone I might marry will come from someplace,"
   she thought.
   For about a year she kept dreaming about married life.
And at some point she began to weep each time,
as she did not want to keep dreaming that.

§

   Then once when she went to get a back-load of firewood,[1]

1. A woman tied the ends of her tumpline around the opposite ends of a pile of sticks she had arranged and then sat on the ground with her back to the wood and her flexed legs to one side. Placing the center of the tumpline on her forehead, she leaned forward on her hands, raising the load onto her back, and then straightened her legs under her before standing up.

just when she raised up her hind end with it (so she thought),

right then she at first thought that that man was in fact right there.

But he was absolutely not there at all.

She was alone by herself on that little island.

And then what kept happening in her dream kept happening outright in fact.

She went one time to get a back-load of firewood,

and just as she loaded it on her back she felt a rush in her womanly parts,[2]

and she could not keep from exclaiming, "Mercy!"

In a strange way it felt very good to her,

and she carried that load of firewood home.

And she went to get another load

and stuck her hind end up further.

Sure enough she found that she felt it even a bit more,

and she brought the load back home to her little house.

And eventually she enjoyed that.

She realized that it felt good to her right in her womanly thing.

"Why don't I really try, after a bit," she thought.

Presently she tried standing with her hind end up for quite a long time,

after loading the firewood on her back.

And sure enough it happened, they say.

And even after she got back home

she was extremely weak.

It was as if she was barely able to get around and do her cooking.

§

In time she realized she was pregnant.

"What's the matter with me?" she thought.

Some time later she gave birth.

And she was only able to give birth with some effort,

giving birth to a boy.

And he was a big boy

and did not look like a child.

He looked quite like a grownup, to tell the truth.

And it seemed as if he grew fast.

In a short time he was able to sit up,

and what's more he was eating like a grownup.

She concentrated her inner thoughts and tried and tried to think,

2. 'Her womanly parts' and later 'in her womanly thing' translate (ota·hwi·hemeki) we·či·ihkwe·wiči, literally '(in her thing) by which she is a woman', the common polite expression.

but she just could not figure out who could have made him in her.

"Who the dickens could it possibly be that made him in me?" she thought.

§

One time as she was getting wood,

while she was chopping to bits a lucky old-lady stick,[3]

a little woodpecker flew up and alighted.[4]

"Don't you know who made your child in you?" it asked her.

"No, so help me, I don't," she said to it.

"Whenever you loaded firewood on your back, didn't it always feel good to
you in a sexual way then?" she was asked.

Only then did she remember.

"So, is that what was happening to me?" she said.

"Well, at those times there was a man having his way with you," she was told.

"Mercy! So, who?" the woman inquired.

"Do you truly not know?" she was asked.

"No, so help me," she declared.

"Wasn't it whenever you loaded firewood on your back that you had that
good feeling?" she was asked.

"So, that's what was happening to me?" she said.

"But I thought there was no particular reason I was having a nice feeling."

"No, don't you see, each time a man was having his way with you," she was
told.

"It wasn't happening to you for no particular reason," she was told.

"Tell me," the woman asked.

"Oh, why not, I'll tell you," she was answered.

"Well, it was a tree spirit," she was told.

"What's more, he's standing right here on this little island now," she was told.

"And to be precise, that's the reason for what happened to you whenever you
loaded firewood on your back,

the reason why it really felt good to you," she was told.

"So then, here's what you should do if that starts happening to you again.

Here's what you should say to him:

3. 'Lucky old-lady stick' translates *metemo·kesakwi,* literally 'old-woman wood'. The term was not
known in the 1990s, but from references in texts it can be inferred that when a woman gathering firewood found a piece that was full of worms, she would split it up and leave it for birds to feast on, thus
gaining long life for herself.

4. 'Little woodpecker' translates *masahkwe·hani,* a hairy or downy woodpecker. When the diminutive
is used later, it is translated 'downy'.

'All right, for goodness' sake, now, take me to where there are people,' you
should say to him, addressing your words at random,
if you start to have that nice feeling," the downy told her.

§

   Then one time when she again went to get a load of wood,
the same thing happened to her.
And it felt good to her.
She could not even speak.
Much later, after she got back home to her little house,
she remembered what the woodpecker had told her,
and she went back.
She loaded a lot of firewood on her back,
but she did not have any sort of marvelous experience,
and she went back.

§

   And then after some time that happened to her again,
and she spoke, addressing her words at random,
and said, "All right, for goodness' sake, now, take me to wherever there are
people."
   Four days after saying that, she saw a large canoe,
and she began to load in what she had.
After some time she finished loading her things.
And right after she got in,
she lost consciousness.

§

   When she came to, it was tied up to the shore.
The place looked different.
And she began to carry her things ashore.
After she had carried her things ashore, she no longer saw that canoe that had
brought her.
   (Now, that son of hers was really big,
and he had a big look to him.)

§

   At some point some other people camped in with her.
Others were quite afraid of her child, they say.
But *she* loved him a great deal.

"He should have been clubbed to death," she would be told, they say.

Eventually, she said to the ones who kept telling her that,
"I'll bet you wouldn't accept it at all
if you'd been told by someone that they were going to club your children to
death."

Some pretty nearly fought back against her.

"Don't you see, he could well be a cannibal giant," she was told.

§

Finally, the men of accomplished deeds held council over him.

And he knew full well that people were talking about killing him.

"All right, at such and such a time is when we'll press ahead and kill him,"
   said the men,
that is, the warriors.

Full well did that child know.

And then, deciding there was nothing else for it, he quickly became big,
and he got terribly big.

(Now, he and his mother were the only two living in their house,
while the others had their houses together in a village.)

§

The villagers could see someone sitting at the edge of the woods,
facing east,
naked.

He was of prodigious size,
sitting there at the edge of the little clearing.

Even his mother did not know who he was,
with his long hair.

The people were beside themselves.

They were extremely frightened.

Some, for instance, ran away without taking anything with them,
abandoning their homes in their flight.

The only people remaining in that village were babies.

The ones that had wanted to club him to death cast away even their children.

§

At some point he thought, "Say, but I might have frightened my mother,
   too,"
and he went back.

He discovered that his mother really *was* gone.

"Oh no, I've frightened my mother along with the rest!" he exclaimed.

He took pity on the babies

and started doing the cooking for them.

He stayed with them on his own for just about a month.

§

And then at some point some men went there,

going to take a look at the place and to see that oversized person.

As they came to the place where the woman had lived on her own, there was smoke coming out.

They could see nothing but children,

and they went there.

They discovered that there really *were* only children.

They came in just as they were eating

and frightened them.

They say it seemed as if they really *were* frightened.

And they asked them what had happened to that giant person.

"Well, we don't know who that is," said the children.

Two of the men were asked to take the news back,

and they set off.

Exactly at midnight they arrived on the run back where they had come from.

And they reported that they had come upon nothing but children.

It is said that they were even able to take good care of the little babies on cradleboards.

§

With their attitude completely changed, they say, it seemed to the children's parents as if dawn barely managed to come.

Arriving over there,

they found that it was true.

They saw every one of their children in good shape.

With a complete change of attitude, they say, they fawned over them.

They say some of them, when they saw their children, even wept.

And with their attitude changed completely, they were grateful to that one of large demeanor.

And his own mother also came,

and he was glad.

And that boy began to have things given to him

and was treated well.

He was treated well by all the people.

(And, incidentally, they say he liked bear meat.)

And then at some point it became known that he liked bear meat.

And whenever men killed bears, they went and left their load of game over there.

§

A certain woman, they say, at some point challenged that oversized boy to a fight.

For they say he was almost grown.

He was big, and he was fat.

Actually, that woman hated that boy.

One time she saw him a little away from everyone

and gave him a whipping.

And he reported it, telling his mother the sorry tale.

And then she admonished him.

"It is out of the question for you to fight with women," he was told.

"Mind you, you'll be shamed by what people will say if you fight her," he was told.

Sometime a bit later she saw him again,

and she gave him even more of a beating.

"I am indeed more powerful than he is," she thought.

"I guess he must not have manitou powers, after all," the woman thought.

(Now, that woman, they say, did herself have manitou powers.)

§

At some point that boy again informed his mother.

"Now she's beaten me up twice," her son said.

And she went to where that woman lived.

When she got there she said to that woman,

"Whatever are you doing,

that every time you see my poor son, you beat him up?"

"So, you don't like it, then?" the boy's mother was asked.

"Just the same as you obviously wouldn't like it

if that were done to your children," she told her.

"Do you challenge these?" replied the other to her.

Her hands were grizzly-bear claws.

"Tell your son," she was told.

"All right, so how come, before, you didn't attack that one who made us all run away helter-skelter?" the other woman was asked.

"We all even cast away our little children," she was reminded.

"I mean, doesn't it seem that you should have scratched up the face of that oversized person who was sitting on the edge of the clearing here?" she said to that other woman.

§

And then that boy became aware that his mother was in an argument.
And he came to the place where his mother was having the big dispute.
Presently, the boy spoke to that woman.
"I see, so your idea is for you and me to fight, is it?" the woman was asked.
"Yes," said the woman.
The woman's hands were already grizzly claws.
"Ah, so then, in four days you shall tear me to pieces," she was told.

§

Four days later the people who wanted to watch the ones that would be fighting streamed out to the clearing.
The woman launched into a speech,
proclaiming that she would kill him.
"And after I've killed him, I have to then have say over you," she said to the people.
"In other words, you have to have me as your chief, in fact," she said to the people.
A roar of assent went up from the people after she finished speaking.
And she said to the boy, "All right, my challenger, now come here."
The boy went to her,
carrying a small staff in his hand.[5]
"You may first make a speech, if you're making a speech," the boy was told.
"Well, obviously no claim I make will be believed," he said to her.
"I might tell a shameful lie if I say anything," he said to her.
The woman had her grizzly-bear hands now.
"So then, how many times shall each of us conjure our power?" she asked him.
"Oh, however many times you want to conjure," he answered the woman.
"Oh, let's say four times each," said the woman.

---

5. 'Small staff' translates *ahtawa·ne·hi,* diminutive of *ahtawa·ni.* This word was no longer recognized in the 1990s, but it was recorded as meaning 'lance' by Prince Maximilian (*Reise in das innere Nord-America in den Jahren 1832 bis 1834,* vol. 2 [Coblenz: J. Hoelscher, 1839–41], 592) and is found in texts as the word for a long, unbladed staff used as a chief's insignia of office, presumably like the one depicted by George Catlin in his portrait of the Sauk chief Keokuk (*North American Indians,* vol. 2 [Edinburgh: John Grant, 1926], 238, no. 280). Later in the story, when Wisahkeha remarks on the staffs that prefigure the fangs of the snake chief, this is the word used.

"All right," she was answered.

"You go first," she declared.

"No, I should say *you* first" was the firm response.

§

And she began to conjure.

She became somewhat larger

and turned into a grizzly bear.

And then that boy became even bigger

and turned into a cannibal giant.

The third time they conjured, the grizzly was unable to make herself bigger

and remained just the same size.

And then that cannibal giant became just frightfully large.

And they went at each other.

As soon as the grizzly attacked,

her head was smashed all to pieces.

But every time, she came to life.[6]

The fourth time the grizzly was killed for good.

§

After she was killed, the grizzly was grabbed by the tail and thrown.

She whizzed off through the air with tremendous noise.

And the whizzing she produced went on until ultimately fading in the distance.

There were shouts of joy when the woman was killed.

Some of the people were pleased,

and some grieved for that woman, some of them.

And they were addressed by him after he had returned to the size he had been before.

§

"If she had killed *me,* she would have killed you *all,*" he said to them.

"In her declarations to you she lied to you.

And here's the reason for what she said:

She was convinced that after she had conjured you were going to run away.

So that's why she said that.

And what's more, she wouldn't have been able to turn back into a person," he told them.

---

6. 'She came to life' translates *e·hmehtose·neniwiči.* The more usual meaning would be 'she became human', but if this was happening every time we would expect more explicit textual support for the repeated transformations.

"At the very moment she began to change her appearance,
right then she became a grizzly bear for good," he said to them.

"Since quite a while ago she had wanted you.
She saw you as tempting morsels to eat, to be precise.
And she didn't realize that you had raised her.
Now, you raised her, all right,
which is actually the reason why she assumed the form of a human being.
And the reason she fled here to where you live was because her husband used to
beat her," he told them.

"So then, when she decided to leave,
well, she decided she would first kill all of you.
She had intended to do that as if to bring food home to her husband," he told
them.

§

"Well then, the ones who grieve for her should go over yonder to Wolf Hill,"
he told them.
"Bear in mind, those grizzly bears are the pets of Maminatenoha," he told
them.[7]
"So then, when you go to Wolf Hill,
you'll see her right over there," he told them.
"But she'll kill all of you that may go.
Actually, she'll assume the form of a person.
And after she has talked with you,
when you get a little ways off at the time you leave,
then she'll shout to you," he told them.

"Those who grieve for her should go there, if they don't believe me," he said,
"those who scoff at the idea that she would kill people."

§

And then her parents said, "Well, she would hardly kill *us*."
And they went to Wolf Hill.
And there was a boy, as well.
When they arrived over at Wolf Hill,
they did indeed see their daughter sitting right on top of the hill,
and a baby, as well.
She was sitting holding a baby.
And they went right to her.

7. Maminatenoha is Wisahkeha's father.

When they got to their daughter,
she said to them, "Gosh, you've come."

And she asked them, "So then, what was that cannibal giant telling you?"

The old man went and told everything.

"Father," his daughter told him, "don't say any more about it.

Don't you see, he has killed me," he was told.

"I was killed, don't you see.

I won't be able to say anything out of line to people again.

I've become something different.

Before, while I was living with you, I loved you.

Now I've changed again," she said.

"Now, daughter," he said to her.

"Well, you'd hardly want to do anything to us," the old man declared.

"Who knows?

Certainly I wouldn't do anything to you if I'm in control of myself," she said to
him.

"All I can say is, whatever I may be told is exactly what I'll do," she said.

Another thing, they say when they held the woman's baby,
it kept trying, without being able to get a good hold on them, to strangle them.
Why, they say the baby pretty nearly overpowered the old woman,
and hurriedly she handed it away.

§

Later on, they say, they left,
telling her, "We should go."

"Well, for goodness' sake, at least take it easy and step softly as you leave,"
they were told.

And they went stepping softly.

When they had almost gotten away, he stumbled.

"Run!

Or at least you should climb a *tree* to escape," they were told.[8]

And they started running.

§

That woman, though, went inside at an easy pace.

And when she got inside, her shape became transformed into that of a grizzly
bear.

And she went rushing out and shouted.

---

8. Climbing a tree is the usual way to escape grizzly bears, as their claws are not adapted to climbing.

"Waho! Waho! Waho! Waho!" came her cry,
as she shouted four times from the east side of the hill.

A second time her shouts came from the west side of the hill,
with the fourfold cry, "Waho! Waho! Waho! Waho!"

§

Meanwhile, the old man's wife had already run a considerable distance away.

Some time later they again heard the shouts, from the north side of the hill,
again, unmistakably, four times, "Waho! Waho! Waho! Waho!"

"Uh-oh!" thought the old man.

Now, he was a fast runner,
and his wife was even faster.

The old man recited his vision,
a vision in which he had received power from a bat.

And he lost his eyesight and flew off.

He truly did have the body of a bat.

And before anything could happen, he arrived on the wing at a grove of trees.

And he hung upside down somewhere, just anyplace.

§

Presently he came to.
Just then she was again starting to shout,
and he heard her calling from the south side of the hill.

Four times she shouted, "Waho! Waho! Waho! Waho!"

And *when* he came to, he found himself hanging from the branch of a
Kentucky coffee tree.[9]

Only then did he regain his eyesight,
and only then did he fly off.

When he got pretty high in the air, he started flying along.

And he watched those creatures as they ran off.

Well, that boy was their grandchild, they say.

And he just let those grizzly bears run,
with the cub running behind, the grizzly bear cub.

§

And then the old woman's daughter managed to get to her and kill her.

9. 'A Kentucky coffee tree' translates *pekimiša·hkoki* (locative form), which is phonemicized and translated on the basis of an uncertain identification of a specimen labeled "pegimīca'kwa" by Jones (Huron H. Smith, *Ethnobotany of the Meskwaki Indians,* Bulletin of the Public Museum of the City of Milwaukee 4[2] [1928], 306). This episode is presumably to be taken as a just-so story accounting for the origin of the long, purplish-brown seed pods that hang from the branches of this tree.

And then the old man beat that grizzly bear cub to death.
And with tired arms he carried it away.[10]

And then she, for her part, carried away in her mouth the one who had been
her mother.

He met up with their daughter,
and he shouted at her,
holding the grizzly cub aloft by the tail as he went.

The grizzly bear let out a loud scream.
And eventually she turned into a person and wept.
She even cast aside the one she had killed
and ran off empty-handed.

§

When the grizzly got back over there, she told her husband.
And the man cried out.
And they ran there.
They came running to where the others had been killed.

And then that old woman was lying there dead.
And they thought they had better bring the old woman back to life.

"All right, you had better go," they told her.

"And when you get back there, here's what they must say to our child:
'All right, go.
Go to where your parents are,' they are to say to him.
And if they don't say that to him,
you must tell him that yourself," the old woman was told.

"You may take your time as you go.
Don't be afraid of us in any way," they told her.
They were both people.
And she left.

§

Some time later she arrived at a walk over where her husband was,
and she found that the poor man had already assumed a widower's mourning
attire.
Also, their belongings had all been divided up and distributed.

---

10. Corresponding to 'with tired arms' the text has the syllabic equivalent of "easkyekwinewiči," which
I take as a miswriting of *e·hayi·hkwinekwe·či* 'he had tired arms or wings', that arose from a hesitation
between *ašk-* (spelled "ask") and *ayi·hkw-* (spelled "ayekw"), the two common roots meaning 'tired'.
The old man has now returned to human shape with tired arms from flying as a bat, but English cannot
reproduce the appropriate ambiguity of the Meskwaki.

What's more, her husband was fasting.[11]

The old man thought he was definitely asleep.

The poor old man spoke to his wife,

saying to her, "All right, woman, for goodness' sake, just take pity on me."

"Don't be making fun of me," he said to her.

"Well, what's this fellow talking about?" said his wife in reply.

After quite some time the old man became aware that he was not asleep.

And his relatives began to arrive.

And the old man provoked shouts of merriment over his being in widower's garb.

Those who had served as the property dividers kept bringing back what they had distributed.

She gave her account of things.

"All right now, it appears this old man killed the cub of some grizzly bears.

So now we must say to it, 'Go,'

must tell it, 'Go to where your parents are.'

And that's the reason why I was revived again," said the old woman.

"Ah, so you really *were* well treated, woman," said the old man.

"Ah, tomorrow at noon we'll send him home," the old guy said.

The entire group of the people was informed.

§

The next day at noon they gathered together.

And after they had gathered, they began to offer Indian tobacco to it,

putting some around its neck and also tying some to its feet.

And then the cannibal giant said to his mother, "Don't *you* do it."

She did not take tobacco to it.

Right away some of them changed their minds, many of them.

(Now, it was in the clearing.

A huge mob went there to offer tobacco to the little grizzly bear cub.)

And the old man was speaking.

He entreated it prayerfully,

the old man did, asking it to have pity on them.

Sure enough, after he had finished speaking to it, it rose to its feet and was stretching.

"Speak to it! Speak to it!" he told the people.

"Don't be afraid of it.

It's a manitou, remember," he said to the people.

---

11. Wearing mourning attire, distributing belongings, and fasting are all components of a bereft spouse's mourning.

And it was sitting there in the middle of where they were seated bunched together.

Actually, that little grizzly cub was thinking, "I'm boxed in."

They spoke to it, revering it greatly.

And at some point it began shouting over and over,

giving four shouts each time, "Waho! Waho! Waho! Waho!"

They, on the other hand, continued addressing their words as if nothing was amiss.

Then at some point, they say, it started running.

Several were injured by it,

but two children were snapped up in one bite together and carried off.

And a noise presently arose among the people,

because some of their children had been carried off.

§

And they, on the other hand, received the news with equanimity.

"It's said that some were killed by it.

It's said that that grizzly bear ran off taking two of the children," was the report they got.

"So that's what happened! It seems that with all that he didn't take pity on them,

when they all gave him tobacco,

when they offered tobacco to him with their children in tow," he said offhandedly.

§

When he got to where his parents were,

they were glad.

"You didn't try to kill them all?" he was asked.

"No, I didn't.

Well, I was really kind of afraid, in a way," he said.

§

And then that one whose father's identity was not known was entreated for help.

"Oh, you folks, now, always believe anyone and then the next one" was the reply the people got.

"Remember, I said what would happen to the ones who didn't believe me," said the boy.

"What's more, if those creatures weren't afraid of me,

you must know that they would come and kill you all.

Not even one of you would manage to be spared by them, either," they were
told.

"So, it wasn't anything *I* did that got you in trouble.
The ones who went there are the ones who, as it were, killed your people.
Those are the ones who brought you grief," he told the people.

The old man dropped his head.

And he continued, "I'll try to go there to them.

"Here's when I'll leave," he said,

"in two days at noon."

§

Two days later at noon he left.

"Anyone who wants to come with me may come with me," he said.

And then there were many men who went with him.
And they went to Wolf Hill,
going to the very top of it.
And they held a dance,
a great war dance.
And after quite a long time they left.

The husband was kind of afraid.

"All right, woman, *you* go and crack some heads," he said to his wife.

And at that the wife at once rushed out
and shouted, "Waho! Waho!"[12]
And as soon as she looked, she saw that that other one was standing right there.
And she was seized.

Then in turn the male also went rushing out.

And just as soon as he rushed out, he was seized.
They were grabbed by their necks and shoved together.

They say the couple immediately became fused together.

He went in, and their offspring was led back out.

"Well?" they were queried.

"Would you not be able to bring back to life the kids this child of yours killed?"
they were asked.

"Oh, I believe we'd be able to revive them," they said.

And the bones were retrieved for them.

Those children looked just the way they had looked before.

12. The text has "child-(proximate) rushed out woman-(proximate) shouted," but in what follows it
is clear that the female is outside and the young grizzly is still inside. I therefore take *child* here as a
narrator's lapse that has been corrected to *woman* on the fly, as if in speech. Subjects may precede or
follow verbs, so the word order presents no problems.

And the poor things were taken back.

§

And those grizzly bears were taken back as well.
They were brought back over to the village
and made to stand some distance away.
And the three of them were stuck together, having been fused into one.
They were fused together quite inseparably.
  And then the people were called to assemble.
  "All right, these are those creatures you were beseeching for life," the people
  were told.
  "So surely this time every one of you must believe me," he said to the people.
  "And here they didn't take pity on anything," the people were told.
  "Well, after this you'll never get me to do your bidding again if these
  creatures do bad things to you," they were told.
  And then he bent their necks down.
  And a young girl who was having her period was sent for.
And she was told, "Pee on them."
  "So *that's* it!" she exclaimed.
  And then her brother said to her, "Come on, do what you're told."
  "I have to tell you, I will cause you shame if you do as you are bidden," the
  female told her.
  "Come on, now," the one with manitou power insisted to her.
And she urinated on them.[13]
And at the very moment when her urine came streaming out, she farted.
And for as long as she kept urinating she kept farting.
  On all sides boys of her age smiled secretly.
  Now she gave forth a terrifically massive fart.
And what's more she was simply unable to stop urinating.
When she did stop urinating, it came pouring out again,
and she farted as well.
  So at that, they say, some of the boys let their laughter get away from them
and were admonished.
  She had utterly befouled those grizzly bears with her urine.
  "I won't kill you," he said to them.
  "And so now, you will not retain your manitou powers," they were told.
  "And *you* won't be able to make yourself look like a person again," she was
  told.

13. We are probably to understand that the female's admonition has spared her from the full flow of
urine, accounting for why female grizzlies do not smell as bad as males.

"And another thing, you'll each live alone, even," they were told.

"You won't live together as a married couple anywhere again," they were told.

They were caused great grief by the actions of their offspring.

§

For just about ten years the male did not stir from where he lay.

After ten years he got up.

And he was not at all the size that he had been.

And the woman was smaller, even more so.

They did not have the manitou powers they had had before.

Later on the woman remembered her husband,

and she went to him.

She found her miserable former husband looking absolutely horrid.

But he for his part just did not know who the woman who came was.

After a long while he recognized his wife.

"So it's you," he said to her.

"Certainly it's me," she said to him.

And now he realized it really was his wife.

§

And then some time after that their master, Maminatenoha, went to see them.

He went right straight to the place.

And when he got near there, he began to sneeze and sneeze,

as he caught their smell.

The odor of his pets was strange, and then some.

And actually, he was unable to enter the place where they were.

Eventually, they say, he spoke to his pets from outside,

saying to them, "Come out."

As soon as they came out, Maminatenoha started throwing up.

He vomited up a huge amount,

because of the awful smell he caught of his pets.

He lectured them.

"All right, I'm not going to come to visit you again," he said to them.

"I imagine you've gotten yourselves into some sort of a mess, for Pete's sake," he said to them.

"Well, after this, never again," he said to them.

"In fact, you shall not even stay here at Wolf Hill," the grizzly bears were told,

and they were driven away.

The husband went off weeping a bit.

§

And then the place was swept out, after a hundred years had passed.
So then, they say, he had wolves as pets, wolf chiefs,
one being white,
and the other having feathers that were green,
together with their wives.
That lodge was nice inside,
and there were always many wolves in it.
(Now, that earth had soils of every kind, they say.
And its soil could change.)
The ones who lived in the cave had their choice of what the soil would be.
And they only went out on good days,
not all the time, they say.
And whenever they were there, they were treated by all the manitous as chiefs.
One time a man went hunting.
And as he went along hunting near there, he was attacked by some of the
wolves,
and they killed him.
The ones standing guard just killed anything at all.
And they even kept continually killing each *other,* they say.

§

And then a long time later Maminatenoha went to see them,
and they nearly killed him.
That is, the very ones he had installed as leaders instigated a plan to kill him.
Presently he began to fight the wolves,
and he lowered the sun.
It was made as unbearably hot for the wolves as could be.
And then the caves were blocked up on the ones that were inside.
Eventually, their hair was singed off down there under the ground.
To that point was the earth heated.
After a long time they were driven out by Maminatenoha.
"Go away," they were told.
Their bodies just reeked and reeked with an overpowering dirty-dog smell.
After they came out they begged to be the same as they were before.
And they looked even a bit more horrid.

§

And so then someone who would stay there was called for, they say.

And a young man was found who was slender,
and a certain woman that he courted.
And there was as well one man who was short,
and his wife.
And they were taken as pets, and both of those fellows were made chiefs.
Then there were many men of the same kind there.
And they were not fastidious.

§

Much later when Maminatenoha went there himself,
his hill looked horribly filthy,
being covered with dung.
It smelled of dung from quite far away.
"Criminy!" he said to them.
"All right, clean this place right up," he said to them.
He went inside and found it covered with dung there as well.
The chiefs were driven out.
And just as the slender one came out, he shoved off with his feet
and defecated hugely.
"There he goes" was the comment he drew,
and he became a great blue heron.
Herons flew off in different directions.
And then the short one likewise, just as he came out, flew up,
together with his wife.
And he became a mallard duck.
Ducks flew off in different directions,
flying in V-formations.

§

And then the place was fixed again.
And after Maminatenoha had made it attractive, he called for ones who would
be the chiefs,
intending, however, to have them as his pets.
It was two men, together with their wives.
And every day they painted up their faces with red ocher.
And then Wisahkeha went there.
Sure enough, they were working out well.
And, sure enough, they were chiefs, wearing buckskin coats.
"Golly, these must be chiefs" was his comment about them.
He sat down where one of them was lying, near his head.
And his head became flat.

"Oh, this one is sure enough a chief," he said.

"Oh, and these things must be his staffs," he said.

Sure enough, they became angry.

And he grabbed them under their arms and threw them out.

They say it turned out that they were snakes,

one puff adder and one rattlesnake.[14]

And he destroyed the hill of chiefs.

§

And then he went to Maminatenoha's house.

And he came as a little boy.

Now, that father of his knew that he would be coming to visit him.

When he arrived over there,

one of the womenfolk reached out and took him in her arms

and said, "It's my younger brother."

Resting in the middle he saw a rock of enormous height, in the middle of the lodge.

Maminatenoha slept with him each night,

as he tried for a while to think of how he would deal with him.

And at some point it dawned on him what his father intended to do to him.

The next morning Maminatenoha smoked a redstone pipe.

And after he had smoked, he slept,

sleeping in a sitting position.

The women, meanwhile, picked wild cherries.

And then Wisahkeha, when he knew that his father was sound asleep,

threw that great boulder up in the air,

and crushed his father with it,

completely flattening him with its weight.

And Wisahkeha had killed his father.

And as for those women, first he grabbed one by the arm

and threw her to the east.

And then he threw one to the south,

and one to the west,

and one to the north.

And after he had thrown one in each direction, he left for home.

§

When he got back there, he then stayed for a little while over at his

14. 'Puff adder' translates *ne·wa*, on the assumption that this is the equivalent of Ojibwa *ne·we·*, the harmless hog-nosed snake, locally called the puff adder, whose breath is widely believed to be deadly.

grandmother's.

And after some time, he said to her, "Well, Grandma, it's time I went to visit my uncles."

"Why, gosh, sure enough, grandson.

That's certainly what your uncles do," said the old woman to her grandchild.

He went to the place where people lived.

And he discovered that there was a cannibal giant there.

He offered a challenge

and attacked on the spot.

And Wisahkeha brought the sky closer[15]

and made it unbearably hot for him.

And Wisahkeha killed the cannibal giant.

After he killed him, he hurled him up in the air.

The cannibal giant hurtled aloft

and revived.

And as he flew right near the sky,

the cannibal giant exclaimed, "Gol-LEE!"[16]

"So you will say," he was told.

§

"That's that," Wisahkeha told the people.

"Now you're free to move to any places you want to move to."

And he returned to his grandmother's.

§

"Grandma, what happened was, I killed a cannibal giant for my uncles," he told his grandmother.

"Woe is me! This one has killed my brother," cried the old woman.

"Say there, Grandma, don't complain.

Since, after all, I didn't think anything of it when you joined in against my younger brother," he said.

"Now, I just gave a gladsome little cry at your return," said the old woman.[17]

§

That is the end.

---

15. The sky is a tier above the earth with portals in it through which the realm above is entered.

16. 'Gol-LEE!' translates *wihihwi·!*, an exclamation of surprise that is taken to resemble the alarm cry of the long-billed curlew, written *cur-lee!* by birders.

17. 'I . . . gave a gladsome little cry at your return' translates *netašinawe·mo·hi,* an archaic word. This whole exchange between Wisahkeha and his grandmother is conventional at the end of episodes in which he kills monsters.

The Married Couple: The Man Whose Wife Was Wooed by a Bear

Written by Alfred Kiyana
Translated by Ives Goddard

This particular married couple was just living somewhere, they say.
The man was constantly hunting,
and he was an exceptionally good hunter.
   And there came a day when he could not kill any deer.
It seemed as if he was unable to kill any temporarily.
Well, to his surprise, he found that he could not kill any from that very point on.
He hunted all day long day after day,
but he did not kill even one.
   They had two children, little boys.
And these lost more and more weight
and were getting quite thin.
In his heart he pitied his sons.
"Golly, my poor sons!" he would always think, they say.

§

   Eventually, they say, the man began fasting,[1]
as he pitied his children for not having meat to eat,
and as, from not having meat to eat, they were quite thin.
They were getting nothing but dried corn to eat,
and there was not anything that was cooked with it.
It was nothing but dried corn.
For about two years, they say, the family went on eating dried corn exclusively.
And they continued to live right there in the same spot.

1. People fasted to elicit the sympathy and blessing of the manitous, in this case by not eating until evening each day.

One time the woman was getting wood,
at a place where stood a great elm of large girth.
And she tapped several times on it with a stick
and said, "Come out, Bear."
(Now, she said it just for fun.)
And the big elm swayed back and forth.
And, to her surprise, a bear actually did come out,
a big bear.
    "Oh my, a bear!" she said to it.
    The bear stood there.
    Every once in a while she said to it, "Oh my, oh my, a bear!"
    The woman was asked, "Woman, what if we get married, would you be
    agreeable?"
    "Oh my, the bear is trying to speak!
Oh my, a bear!" said the woman.
She was very much smitten.
    "You should cut a piece off my belly.
You could take back a little piece of fat.
Then you could cook it for your poor children," the woman was told.
And she cut a piece off the bear at his belly.
    "But don't tell your husband," she was told.
    "Oh, good idea" was the reply to the bear.

§

And then, it seems, when she got back there,
she cooked it for her children.
    The children ate heartily of the bear fat
and their stomachs were filled.
    That night, quite late, their father came back.
What would he be bringing?
He came back empty-handed.
And the woman gave him dried corn.
    He could plainly detect the smell of something,
but he could not tell what it was that he smelt.
And when morning came he left right away.

§

For her part, the woman also did the same.
She left early.

And then, it seems, she really fooled around with the bear seriously.[2]

§

And for their part, the boys stayed home by themselves all day long.
And in the early evening their mother returned home.
And then, it seems, she cooked for them hurriedly.
And hurriedly they ate.
(By the way, the man who was fasting always slept by himself.)
They were very nearly caught at what they were doing when he came.
They only barely finished putting away the dishes in time.
The woman made confused remarks.
And then the next morning the huntsman left.

§

And then the woman left a little later.
They went along watching where their mother went,
keeping out of sight behind her.
At some point over yonder she pounded a stick several times on a great elm.
It was a large bear, of prodigious size,
and their mother ran and grabbed him.
"Jeepers! Look at our mother," said one of the boys to the other.
She had her arms around the bear's neck, hugging him.
The bear was sitting there with his legs straight out.
Their mother was sleeping with him at intervals, showing no concern.
A little bit of her arms could be seen in places as she lay embracing him.
"Jeepers! Darn if she isn't fearless of it," they said.
After a while, their mother pinched up a handful of its belly
and cut off a piece of fat.
"Jeepers!" they said.
When she started walking back, they took off,
running home.

§

They came running back to their house, first one then the other,
looking from the expressions on their faces as if nothing had happened.
And the expression their mother had on her face was as if nothing had
happened,

2. 'Fool around' translates *ana·so-* 'wrestle, roughhouse, tussle amorously, make out'. This can be a euphemism for 'have sex', but it is often unclear how far things went.

and, as if nothing whatever had happened, she was cutting bear fat into small
strips.

After it was cooked, they ate it.

"Our father's rival!" the little boys said to each other on the sly,
and they laughed.

"What the dickens is the matter with these two,
with their rapscallion snickering," said their mother.

The woman had a gnawing suspicion, though,
thinking to herself, "I wonder if I might have been seen by them unawares."
And she scolded her sons sharply.
After a while they finished eating.

And then one boy spoke to his mother.
"Mother," he said to her, "so, shall I save some for my father?"

"Don't, my son.
You might do your father harm," she said to her son.

"So, how come?" he asked her.

"Why, gosh, you see, he can't eat it," she said to him.

"Oh, so that's it," said the boy.

"But don't tell your father, either of you," the woman said.
"He might scold us.
I mean, at least you've been having some meat to eat," she said to her little
sons.

"All right," said the boys.

"And another thing, don't spit in the fire," she told their sons.

§

That night the younger one said, "Older brother,"
he said, "let's play riddles."

"All right," said the older one.
They were saying all sorts of different things.
And after a while their mother stopped scolding them.

But at first she kept telling them, "Go to sleep."

She would say to them, "You should consider your father.
Don't you see, if he should happen to dream of something, we'll be having meat
to eat,
if he has a vision of any game animals."

At some point after one of them had a big mouthful of spit,
he spat in the fire,
and the fire blazed up.
And they kept spitting in the fire.

And after some time they went to sleep.

§

    Very early in the morning their father was trying to start the fire with no
    success,
and they woke up.
    "Here, see, this is how it ought to be done," one said to their father.
And he spat on the fire.
    The fire blazed up.
    When he spat on it twice, it burned with an extremely strong flame.
    "Well look at that!" thought the man.
He was convinced that his son had manitou power.
He thought it meant that he had been blessed with the power to do some thing.
"Or else," he thought, "he probably is indeed a bit of a manitou."
    But the wife, in her heart, was scared.
    Only when nothing was said to them
did the woman say to her husband, as if nothing had happened, "These boys
don't ever help you when you hunt."
    "That's certainly true," said the man.
    After her husband had departed,
she said to her sons, "I'm off now to strip some basswood bark."[3]
    "All right," they replied to her,
and the woman left.

§

    Actually, they once again watched their mother from behind as they went.
    When their mother got over there,
all she did was go straight to the big elm.
And she tapped on it.
Their mother looked like she was ready to catch the bear on the fly.
    "Look at your mother," said one of the boys to the other.
    After fooling around for a while, the ones they were watching sat there
    quietly.
And they began to speak together.[4]
    "All right, woman," the woman was told,

3. The outer bark was stripped off the inner bark, which was used for cordage, after the whole bark
was removed from the tree.
4. 'Speak together' translates *kakano·neti·-*, literally 'converse', the word commonly used for the con-
versations held as part of courtship.

"go and untie your husband's sacred bundle.
And then in it, woman, and the redstone pipe that is in it, you must bring
back," the woman was told.

"And also you must dress up," the woman was told.

"You must wear the red woolen broadcloth as a blanket,[5]
and you must come back with the fine broadcloth on as a skirt," the woman was
told.[6]

"Oh, good idea," she replied,
and she went home.

§

Finding her children gone,
she whistled for them.

After some time one of the boys answered, "What?"

The bear was frightened by the cry.
And in no time the bear was hanging on to the tree halfway up.

And then they went to her, running in from different directions.

"Well, where have you been?" she asked them.

"We've been hunting birds," they told their mother.

She pointed out a different direction for them to go.
"Don't go that way," she told them.
"You must go up the river in this direction,
not down the river," she told them.

"All right," they said to her.

§

And then, it seems, she hurried them off.
But they just pretended and, taking their time, turned back.

Finally the woman scolded them sharply.
And then they left, slowly.
And in time she could no longer hear them.

But by then, they say, they had already arrived back on the run near their
  lodge.
And there they saw their mother combing her hair.
They lay there not far away.
And after some time she went in.

5. 'Red woolen broadcloth' translates *meškwe·kenwi*, a red stroud blanket with an undyed strip of white
along the selvage, referred to as "white-listed" or "white list"; a highly desirable trade item.
6. 'Fine broadcloth' translates *maneto·we·kenwi*, an expensive, deep-indigo broadcloth blanket, also a
highly prized trade item.

When she went in, they ran right up close.

  After quite some time their mother came out,
and she was dressed in her finest clothes.
She was painted on the whole of her cheeks with red ocher,
and she was dressed in her finest clothes.

§

  And then they went along behind, hiding from her,
running along behind.
  Over there, they found the bear up the tree.
It kept peering out up in the tree.
And when the bear saw their mother, it jumped down from right where it was.
  Then their mother said, "Oh my, bear.
You might have hurt yourself, bear.
Oh my, bear."
  The bear smoked profusely,
using the redstone pipe.
After he had smoked, he began fooling around with the woman.
They used the red woolen broadcloth as a blanket,
and they slept with each other.
  The bear's feet were sticking out as he lay.
And as he fixed his covers, he accidentally tore the red broadcloth with his claw.
  The woman did not think it was anything to worry about at all.

§

  The boys, meanwhile, crept over close to where their feet were,
as fast as they could haul themselves.
And they pinched the bear's heel, they say.
And he did not react at all, as if nothing at all was wrong.
And then next they tickled him on the foot.
But, as if nothing at all was wrong, all he did was shift his foot restlessly.
Finally, they say, they stuck a sharp wooden arrow into his heel.
And only then did he jump.
In fact, he even leapt right to his feet,
and their mother had the blanket yanked off of her.
  (Now, remember, the bear had already had part of his belly sliced off.)
  "What the hell took a great whacking bite out of me?" said the bear.
  "You mean something *bit* you?" the woman said.

§

Pretty soon the bear lay down again.

And after the bear was settled comfortably, he began to be tickled on his foot again.

He paid no attention at all to it.

And then at some point he was slashed across the heel.

And he threw his sleeping partner aside.

    The woman was absolutely terrified.

She had been tossed like a small object.

And she lay weeping.

    The bear was scared.

§

And then the bear tried to comfort the woman.

Here, the bear was feeling pain as well, in his heel.

After quite some time, they say, the woman was agreeable.

    The bear kissed and kissed.

    "So help me, it was just because it hurt me right to the quick that I almost smashed you up, girl," declared the bear.

    "Besides, if you're agreeable, we could get married," the bear continued.

    "Well, you have to agree that it's as if we're married as it is," replied the woman.

    "So then, for as long as we may live, we'll speak together," the woman declared.

    "Oh, absolutely.

And your words sound nice when you say that to me," the woman was told.

    "Oh my, you didn't expect me to say anything bad about you, did you, bear?" was the friendly reply the bear got.

    And after that, "Oh my, so help me, what a bear."

    He was delighted.

    "And she would eat me, if her husband kills me," he thought.

    "But for now I'm secretly married to her," thought the bear.

§

That evening he presented some of the fat of his belly.

"After you're alone tomorrow, you must cook it for our children," the woman was told.[7]

"All right," said the woman.

§

7. "Our children" is how a step-parent would refer to a spouse's children.

Their sons came back late,
and her husband came back even later.

Early in the morning the woman finished her cooking.

And, after daubing his face, the man left,[8]
going off to hunt.

But those boys, it is said, got bored with them
and did not follow her over there any more.

§

Some time later, the woman realized that she was pregnant.
"Oh dear," she thought.

After she had been pregnant a little while,
one of the boys told their father everything.

"Father, I can tell you this, our mother's been sleeping with a bear," he said
to their father.

"What's more, she's been doing that for quite a long time," he said to his
father.

"So that's it" was the reply received from him.

He told him all the particulars.
"Also, she takes out the redstone pipe that's in our sacred bundle,
and the bear smokes with it.
And for her part, she dresses up in her finest clothes.
And after she dresses up, she goes to him.
At first they always fool around,
and after they fool around, they begin sleeping with each other," the boy told
their father.

§

And then the next day he went out to hunt.
Some time later he came back.

And then he said to his wife, "Well, wife, I guess I might as well go spend the
night over yonder."[9]

"All right," the woman replied.
She rejoiced in her heart.
"Now we'll really have a time," the woman thought.
And he left.

8. He put charcoal on his face as a sign that he was fasting.
9. It is a stylistic convention to use an expression like "over yonder" in a direct quotation as a substitute
for the name or description of the place that the speaker would actually have used; English, preferring
indirect discourse, would say: "He told his wife he was going to spend the night at such-and-such a
place."

The man really did go a long ways off.
And he really did sleep over there.

§

    And then the bear was taken near there.
And the bear made the children sleep by burning something in the fire.
And sleeping with a woman for real,
the bear thought of himself as very much a person.
    After midnight the man set out.
And he killed a deer, one deer.
And when it was nearly dawn, he arrived where their house was.
    The bear was sound asleep,
sleeping with a woman.
And they had their arms around each other's necks.

§

    The man went in,
and there before his eyes his wife had a sleeping partner.
She was sleeping with a bear.
He saw them without them knowing.
And he put the fire out again
and went a little ways off.
    When dawn came, the bear came out.
And when it had gone a little ways off,
he went and killed it.
    The bear was killed.
    He carried it a long ways off on his back
and arrived with it where the deer was.

§

    At noon he came home with the deer on his back.
The children rejoiced at his return.
"Seems you've killed game," she said to her husband.
"Oh gee, I've really killed game on a large scale," said the man.
"So I believe I'll start to kill game now.
But I know this much, I killed a bear, too," he told her.
"Seems you're making unusual kills," she said to him.
"So then, I'm going to go after it," he said to her.
"All right," said the woman.
He left.

And as soon as the man left,
the woman left.

Expectantly but to no avail she pounded several times with a stick,
expecting to no avail that he would come out.

"Oh, he must be fast asleep," she thought.

§

Meanwhile, when the man arrived back at their house,
only his sons were there, roasting a bit of something for themselves on a spit.
At the same time, no attention had been paid to the deer.
It lay there exactly as he had left it.

Just when the fat had all been cut in strips,
the woman arrived back.

"Seems you're back already," she said to her husband.

"Yes," said he.

And he asked her, "Well, where have you been?"

"My bowels were really loose.
I've been staying over yonder where I go to the bathroom," she said to him.

"So that's it," said the man.

"I thought rather that you might be looking for bears,
when you were doing your pounding on the tree," he said to her.

"So help me, I was just trying the sound of it for fun," said she to her
husband.

"So that's it," he said to her.

§

And then they always ate well.
And whenever he went anywhere, she would instantly run over to that place.

On one such occasion he said to his wife, "This time I'm going far away to
hunt,"
adding, "I'm off."

"All right," said the woman.
She had a pleasant demeanor as her husband left.

"I'm going to make a quick trip for a load of dry sticks," she said to their
young sons,
and she left.

§

"Bear! Come out, bear," she said.
She hit the tree, making it go, "Tonk, tonk, tonk!"

After some time she saw her husband running by.

(He did that to her just for fun.)

Hurriedly she collected dead wood

and took home a back-load of it.

And she ran into him coming the other way.

"So help me, I forgot my stone-headed arrows," he said to her.

§

And then, it is said, the man went and climbed the tree.

And he jumped into the bear hole.

He was naked.

And the woman was back over there in a flash.

"Bear, come out.

Here I am, I've brought myself to you again," said the woman to the bear.

"Please come," she said to him.

"It'll be just as if you're seeing your husband, when you see me," he told her.

"Come here, please," the woman told him.

"You'll no longer see me the way you saw me.

Rather, I will look only like your husband," the woman was told.

"Come on now, come here," the bear was told.

"Okay," the man as bear replied.

When he came out,

it seemed to her that he looked just exactly like her husband.

"Oh my, what a bear!" she said to him.

(But, of course, it was her husband.)

"So, what do you think of your husband?" he asked her.

"Oh my, what a bear!" she said to him,

and put her arms around his neck.

"Well, I hate him.

You're the one I'm always thinking about," she said to him.

"But him I hate,

as well as his children," the man was told.

"As for you, though, I wish I could live with you."

"Well, what if you stay here where I live?" the woman was asked.

"Oh, good idea," replied the woman.

"Now tell me, you're not married?" the woman asked.

"No, so help me.

I'm a bachelor," the woman was told.

(But he was her husband, of course.)

To tell the truth, in his heart the man was very angry.

"All right then, come on, climb up," the woman was told.

And she climbed up and jumped in.

After she jumped in, she was told, "I'll go get some grass for our bedding."

She was thinking, "Oh my, I'm going to live in a tree."

After a while she heard him come back.

And grass began dropping inside,

mixed in with pieces of bark.

She was arranging it with care, as if it was all completely normal.

A bit later there was another huge amount.

"These are for our covers.

I'll bring two more loads, and that's it," she was told.

Sure enough, after some time she heard the sound of the stuff as it was dumped in.

"It's what we do when we're newly married," she was told.

His words were being directed up above.

"Oh my, what a bear!" she thought.

"All right, come here, bear," she said to him.

"Wait a bit."

"Well, where would you expect me to go?"

"I'm coming up there," he told her.

(Now, she was having more and more trouble breathing.)

"When I get up there, I'll tend to you.

I guess it's because you're smothering that you're calling to me to hurry," the woman was told.

"Yes," she said.

"Ah, that's about as much as I would put in there, if that's okay.

And now we'll be toasty," the woman was told.[10]

"Tell me now, what's involved in being toasty, bear," she said.

"One is made toasty.

'You'll be made toasty,' I should say," she was told.

At that very moment the grass was set on fire.

The man departed.

Presently, however, the woman realized that it was burning.

§

Not too far away there was another bear, they say.

And he ran over there

10. 'Be toasty' translates *wa·koso-*, a verb stem containing an element *-eso* 'be acted on by heat or fire' and an unidentified root of uncertain shape, which is unique to this story and intended to be obscure. The translation 'toasty' has been selected to convey the desired ambiguity.

and pulled that woman out.

When the woman came to, she found another bear tending to her.

And she recovered.

"It was your husband that set your place on fire.

The reason he did that to you is that you behaved badly," the woman was told.

"So then, from now on don't do that," the woman was told.

The baby that she was pregnant with was taken out of her.

"And this baby of yours I shall accordingly take care of here," she was told.

"The bears will have that baby for their chief."

§

And that man, when his wife came into the house, said to her, "Hello," as if nothing had happened.

The woman cried.

"Never again as long as I live will I speak together with anyone else," the woman said.

And she put her arms around her husband.

"'Toasty' will be your name," she said to her husband.

"All right," said the man.

"You certainly did a bad thing,

getting involved, as it seems, in being wooed by a game animal," he said to her.

"That's certainly true," said the woman.

"Well, never again," she declared.

§

That's the end of it.

Menominee

Red Swan

Introduction by Monica Macaulay and Marianne Milligan

Menominee is an Algonquian language still spoken by a small number of elders on the Menominee Reservation in Wisconsin. This story was told to Leonard Bloomfield in the early 1920s by Nyahto Kichewano (Nayaēhtow in Menominee) and published in Bloomfield's *Menomini Texts*.[1] Unfortunately, Bloomfield does not tell us anything about the narrator, beyond making the point that none of the speakers with whom he worked spoke English well.

Bierhorst describes Red Swan as "one of the most characteristic of Midwest myths, told by Algonkians and Siouans alike," although the published versions that we have been able to find differ in significant respects from the one presented here.[2] Much of what transpires in the Menominee version is found in the Ojibwe and Fox versions with which we are familiar, but this version ends where the others begin a new episode.

The part that all the versions share (and which is the entirety of the Menominee version) proceeds as follows: There is a set of brothers (eleven, in the Menominee tale). The youngest spots a red swan in a lake and tries to shoot it. After failing to hit it with normal arrows, he takes arrows from someone's sacred bundle (his oldest brother's here) and with those is successful. The wounded swan flies off, and he pursues it. On his journey he stops at a number of villages and marries a woman at each one. Eventually the swan leads him to the house of an old man, who feeds him with food that magically replenishes itself as soon as it is eaten. The old man asks him to retrieve something variously described as his head (in the Menominee version), his scalp, and his hat, which has been stolen. The hero transforms himself into a variety of things (first into plant down and then into a small dog in the Menominee version), so that he can sneak into the enemy's territory and recapture the head/scalp/hat. He brings it back to the old man, who rewards him (with eleven red feathers or with the red swan itself in some versions). On the way back he collects the women that he married and brings them back as wives for his brothers. The brothers are grateful, but eventually the oldest brother decides that he wants the youngest's wife. He hatches a plot to kill his youngest brother (and gets the other brothers in on it), which in the present version involves making a swing, getting the youngest into it, and then cutting the rope. The youngest knows what the others are up to and sends all the women away before it happens. In the Menominee version the hero dies, the brothers go back to their home, find the women gone, and then apparently regret having killed their youngest brother.

In the Ojibwe version, after the hero has returned from the adventure with the scalp, the brothers send him off on a hunt so that they can take his wife.[3] He goes to the land of the dead, and the spirits give him arrows to replace the ones he shot the red swan with. He then goes back and kills his brothers with those arrows.

Thomason describes six Meskwaki (Fox) versions of this story.[4] In one the story turns into the tale of Rolling Skull (with the hero becoming Rolling Skull after the brothers kill him). This is another traditional narrative that Thomason says is "almost certainly grafted onto a tale with which it has no very close traditional association."[5] In all the other Fox versions described by Thomason, however, the youngest brother goes to the underworld and has various adventures there.

Bierhorst says that Red Swan is part of the Hare cycle among the Ho-Chunk (Winnebagos), but that the other tribes who tell it treat it as a stand-alone story.[6] It appears, then, that although the basic story line is shared among a number of Midwestern tribes, there is great variation in how and where different groups (or even different storytellers among a single group) end the story.

As we mentioned, this text was published in both Menominee and English in 1928. We have retranslated it using ethnopoetic methods, following Hymes and others.[7] Such work has established that there is a "rhetorical architecture" to oral narrative signaled by a variety of devices in the text.[8] These devices allow us to treat the text as verse rather than prose (as was done earlier in this century by scholars such as Bloomfield) and indicate major and minor divisions in the structure.

As in so many other Native American languages, a great deal of this narrative structure is communicated through the use of initial particles.[9] Menominee, like some other Algonquian languages, has both predicative and nonpredicative particles. In the former case the particle functions like a verb and in Menominee can even carry certain verbal suffixes. In our translation we reflect the choices the speaker made between predicative and nonpredicative particles by using predicative and nonpredicative English expressions. So, for example, the predicative particle *enewen* is translated as 'it was then', while the nonpredicative *ehpeh* is translated simply as 'at that point'.

No matter how careful one is to replicate—to whatever extent possible—the forms and style of the original, a translation necessarily loses something critical by virtue of its alien audience. In a traditional narrative such as "Red Swan," the intended audience has a wealth of background knowledge that it brings to the story, while the audience for a translation is missing that cultural context which supplies crucial detail. This problem became especially clear to us as we began to realize the amount of foreshadowing present in "Red Swan"—foreshadowing that is entirely lost in the English version.

Two particular instances were entirely due to connotations of the words used in the Menominee version and the lack of similar connotations of the words that were used to translate them into English. The first involves the bundle from which the hero of our story takes the arrows with which he shoots the swan. Bloomfield uses the term *medicine bundle* in his translation of the story and *sacred bundle* in the *Lexicon*.[10] We wondered which term would strike the elders as more appropriate and asked them to translate the Menominee word. They were shocked and told us never to say this word out loud; it was a very dangerous word for a kind of evil spirit, and just talking about it could cause harm or even death. Because there is no corresponding cultural item in the English-speaking world, no term can be used in translation without obscuring an unambiguous signal in Menominee that the use of these arrows will bring death to the hero. We have chosen to use *sacred bundle* to translate the Menominee term, but the reader should keep in mind that this is an imperfect equivalence.

The second such case is the name of the oldest brother, Macehkewes. Bloomfield's *Lexicon* provides this entry for Macehkewes: "man's name in mythology, the eldest of the ten brother Thunderers; eldest of a set of brothers, as common noun and nickname."[11] This, however, omits the connotation of bad behavior that is considered characteristic of eldest siblings.[12] It is significant that the term first appears precisely at the point that the oldest brother comes home and sees that the youngest brother has returned, bringing women with him, leading to the jealousy that will ultimately cause the death of the youngest.

One of our primary goals in doing this translation has been to put the story into a more colloquial English style. Bloomfield, following the fashion of his day, translated the story into very archaic-sounding English (using terms such as *fie* and *hither*, for example); we hope that by using more modern forms we have made it more accessible to today's readers (both Menominee and non-Menominee).

NOTES

We would like to thank Menominee elders Marie Floring, Sarah Skubitz, and Tillie Zhuckkahosee for helping us with some of the more difficult lines, and Rand Valentine and Ives Goddard for their comments. In addition Lev Blumenfeld, Anna Griffith, April Winecke, and especially Rebecca Kavanagh contributed to the analysis of the Menominee as well as with data entry. Of course, all errors in translation are ours alone.

1. Note that the tribe now uses the spelling "Menominee," so that is what is used here.

2. Bierhorst, *Mythology of North America*, 218.

3. For the Ojibwe version, see Bierhorst, *Red Swan: Myths and Tales of the American Indians*.

4. Thomason, "Two Types of Mesquakie Stories: A Comparison of 'The Ten That Were Brothers Together' with Five Variants of 'Feather.'"

5. Thomason, "Two Types of Mesquakie Stories," 6.

6. Bierhorst, *Mythology of North America*, 1985.

7. Hymes, "Discovering Oral Performance and Measured Verse in American Indian Narrative"; Hymes, "Particle, Pause and Pattern in American Indian Narrative Verse"; Hymes, "Some Subtleties of Measured Verse."

8. Hymes, "Some Subtleties of Measured Verse," 18.

9. Cf. Hymes, "Discovering Oral Performance"; and Bright, "A Karok Myth in 'Measured Verse.'"

10. Bloomfield, *Menominee Lexicon,* 212.

11. Bloomfield, *Menominee Lexicon,* 106.

12. Ives Goddard, e-mail to authors, May 17, 2001.

SUGGESTED READING AND REFERENCES

Bierhorst, John. *The Red Swan: Myths and Tales of the American Indians.* New York: Farrar, Straus, & Giroux, 1976. The "Red Swan" story is reprinted and retranslated from Henry Rowe Schoolcraft, *Algic Researches* (New York: Harper & Brothers, 1839).

————.*The Mythology of North America.* New York: William Morrow, 1985.

Bloomfield, Leonard. *Menomini Texts.* Publications of the American Ethnological Society, vol. 12. New York: G. E. Stechert, 1928.

————. *Menominee Lexicon.* Milwaukee Public Museum Publications in Anthropology and History, no. 3. Milwaukee: Milwaukee Public Museum Press, 1975.

Bright, William. "A Karok Myth in 'Measured Verse': The Translation of a Performance." In *American Indian Linguistics and Literature,* by William Bright, 91–100. New York: Mouton, 1984.

Hoffman, Walter J. *The Menomini Indians.* Bureau of American Ethnology Annual Report 14 (1896): 1–328. Washington DC.

Hymes, Dell. "Discovering Oral Performance and Measured Verse in American Indian Narrative." *New Literary History* 8 (1977): 431–57.

————. "Particle, Pause and Pattern in American Indian Narrative Verse." *American Indian Culture and Research Journal* 4 (4) (1980): 7–51.

————. "Some Subtleties of Measured Verse." In *Proceedings of the Fifteenth Spring Conference of the Niagara Linguistics Society,* 13–57. Buffalo NY: Niagara Linguistics Society, 1985.

Keesing, Felix Maxwell. *The Menomini Indians of Wisconsin: A Study of Three Centuries of Cultural Contact and Change.* Philadelphia: American Philosophical Society, 1939.

Thomason, Lucy. "Two Types of Mesquakie Stories: A Comparison of 'The Ten That Were Brothers Together' with Five Variants of 'Feather.'" Unpublished manuscript, 1998.

Red Swan

Told by Nyahto Kichewano
Translated by Monica Macaulay and Marianne Milligan

Their house was a long lodge;
   there were ten men.
But there were really eleven of them;
   they had a younger brother,
     a boy.

And he was the one who took care of the house,
   while the others hunted.

The oldest of all the brothers,
   he was the one who always came back first;
he was the one,
   as they returned,
     coming one by one.

They didn't have wives;
   they were still bachelors.

One time when they were out hunting,
   that boy—
there was a lake
   where they always got their water—
that boy was fetching water;
the water out in the lake was red.

When he got to the water's edge,
   when he looked out on the water,
      a swan floated on it;
         it was entirely red.
And that was why it looked like that,
   that lake.

He ran home for it,
   his bow,
he ran back to the water's edge,
   he shot at it over and over,
      but it kept floating around undisturbed.

Now, his older brothers had left some of their arrows.
At that point he fetched them
   and kept shooting at it.
Finally, he used up all his older brothers' arrows.

It was then that he must have remembered
   that there were probably two more in their oldest brother's sacred bundle.

He pulled down that sacred bundle,
   ran back,
      untied the sacred bundle,
         and spread it open.
There were two arrows.

It was then that he must have used them too.
When he shot at it with the last one,
   it was that one that must have hit it.

The swan flew up.
   After a while it hung at about half the height of the trees;
      it was then that it flew along,
         it was then that the trees looked like that.
It was there that he must have set off;
   he pursued it.

When the sun had set,
   it was then when he reached a village.
He just stood there;
   he looked strange to them.
From somewhere,
   it was then that someone called him.

When he entered,
   after he had been fed,
      it was then that he married.

When they were about to sleep,
   at that point he asked her,
"When was it
   that a swan flew by?"

"When the sun hung very low."

"That's the one that I'm pursuing."

Scene 2

Now, I have to go back to the other place.

The oldest brother,
   when he got home,
      his younger brother wasn't there.
When he called and called him,
   no one was there.

It was then that he must have gone to the lake;
when he got to the water's edge,
   his sacred bundle,
      it was open in plain view.
When he looked out on the water,
   their arrows were floating there.

He went back home,
   it was there that he sat.
      As they came back,
         he told them of his youngest brother.

"Hey, something has happened to our youngest brother;
as for my sacred bundle,
   at the water's edge,
     it's there that he must have untied it;
our arrows are floating there."

Scene 3

Now, as for that boy,
   it was then, the next day, he must have started off,
     again pursuing it.

When the sun had nearly set,
   it was then that he arrived at another village;
     it was then that he was about to sleep again;
       it was then that he married again.
At that point he asked her,
   "When was it
     that it flew by?"

"When the sun was at half a tree's height."

The next day,
   it was then that he must have started off again.
Ten times he had slept on the way;
   and it was there, where each time he got married.

Scene 4

Now, it was there, when for the eleventh time
   he had taken a wife on the way.
Now, having started off again in the morning,
   when it was almost noon,
it was then that there was a small wigwam.

As he stood for a while by the entry,
   it was then that the door flap must have opened:
     "Oh, Grandson, come in!"
When he had entered:
   "Sit down over there across the wigwam, Grandson!"

When he gave it to him in a tiny cup,
  sweet corn,
    and a spoon,
      he could not possibly be satisfied.
It was then, when he would scrape once at that corn,
  when he would scoop it up,
    that was all of it.

After he had taken that mouthful,
  it was then [that there was] as much as before.
That was what he was busy with,
  he was full;
it was then, just a moment before, when he scraped at it.

After he had finished eating:
  "Well, then, Grandson, I want you to do something for me.

Over here, over here nearby,
  this is what they're busying themselves with,
    it is this, my head;
this thing isn't really *my* head;
  they outwitted me;
    they cut my throat.

And that's what I wanted to ask you to do;
as for everyone else,
  that's what they have failed at.
Well, then, and it was you who I thought of;
  this is why I sent out my pet."

A box was there;
  that was what he opened.
The swan lay in plain view.

"Well, then, he is an evil being;[1]
  his house is a long lodge.
And it's there in the middle,
  it's there that he lies on his back.
And he's the one who watches for anything

1. In this line, *he* refers to one of the group who stole the Grandfather's head.

that might fly by.

Well, then, but be on your guard!

If you want to start off right away,
　　it's over here; it's nearby."

"All right!"
　　he said.

"Farther on, on the other side of the hill,
　　it's there,
　　　　it's there that they are busying themselves with my head;
　　　　　　they're swinging it around on a string there.

The strands of my hair are beaded.
　　From here where they dangle down,
　　　　the beads make a clattering sound."

It was then that the boy started off.
　　When he arrived,
　　　　what was it?
　　　　　　A long lodge, of course.

Scene 5

Now, it was then, at that time what he said was,
　　"If it were a bundle twice the size of plant down!"
And that was the body he had.

Now, it was then that he must have risen up.
　　"Well, then, you won't see me!"

It was then that, silently, he must have begun to move.
Just when he was being blown past there,
　　it was then that [the other person] must have seen him.

"Wait! What is it,
　　this thing flying by?"

"Hey, so he does see me!"

It was then that he did it all over again;
   and it was a bundle not even once the size of plant down,
      and it was there that he must have used it.

Now, it was then that he must have been blown into the air again.
When he got to the middle [of the long lodge],
   [the other person] didn't see him.

Farther on, after he had descended,
   on the other side of the hill there was lots of whooping.
He must have walked over,
   now, it was then, really, that they were dangling down;
      the beads made a clattering sound.

"And now, what is it that I should do?
   Well, then, I'll be a little dog;
      I'll be good-looking."

He started to run then,
   running along the side;
      one of them must have seen him.

"Oh, brothers, the one who catches him,
   he will have him as a pet!"

"All right!"
   they said;
      he was pursued,
         and he really took off.

He must have run all around,
   he ran back up towards the woods.
      When he got to the head,
         he cut it free.

After tucking it into his shirt,
   he was blown up into the air again;
      they didn't see him.

After he had descended over there,
   he started off towards his grandfather;
      when he entered the wigwam:
"Now, that's it, Grandson,
   did you bring it?"

"Yes!"

After he took it out,
   he handed it to him.

"Oh, thank you!
But really, they've made a mess of it.
But it didn't look like this!
But it was all made of beads!

Well, then, Grandson, tomorrow you will go home."

The next day, after he had eaten,
   he went and opened that box;
      he took out his pet.
It was actually bright red.

"Well, then, Grandson, these are what I'll pay you with.
   You will take eleven [feathers].
      Your older brothers,
         they will put them in their sacred bundles."

After he had given him eleven,
   it was then that he started off home.
The last house where he had slept on the way,
   it was there that he slept on the way back.

The next day,
   it was then that he took along the woman.

In every place that he had slept,
   it was there, every place that he slept on the way back;
      and it was then, that he picked up the woman each time.
         It was then, every time, that he gave them one of the feathers.

"Your father,
  he'll have some use for it."

And it was then, that he took all those women away with him,
  he remembered his older brothers.

When he reached their long lodge,
  well, no one was there.

"They're hunting, of course!"

The oldest of all the brothers,
   it was then that he pointed it out to her:
     "Now, this is your bed!"

All of them,
   it was then that he placed them,
     where each man had his bed;
the last one whose house he had slept at,
   and this one,
     her too.

ACT 3: BETRAYAL
Scene 1

And now, that Macehkewes,
  it was he who always came first
    when they were hunting.

Well, he had ordered them beforehand
  to cook.

Now, well, when this Macehkewes came in sight of the long lodge—
  Oh! There was smoke.

"Oh! Can it be?
  Could our younger brother be alive?"

When he had laid down his game outside,
  he entered the house,
    now, here sat his younger brother.
What? He was fasting!

"Hey, younger brother, so you are alive!
   Well, I wonder how long you'll live."

As the men came on in,
   it was then, each time he would call out,
"Hey, our younger brother,
   he has come!"
     as he was grasped by the hand.

The women;
   it was over here, when they looked up,
     he had brought women to his older brothers.

"Oh! And that's that!"

Scene 2

Now, it was suddenly,
   it was then, [the oldest brother] must have begun to admire the younger
   brother's wife.

Now, suddenly, aha!
He must have thought something up,
   he spoke to his brothers,
     when they had started hunting,
       now, somewhere over there:

"Well, then, younger brothers, this is what, as for me,
   I'm thinking about.
As for me, at any rate,
   I really admire our younger brother's wife.

Well, then, and it's over here that we'll do this;
you will order your wives
   to gather basswood bark,
when it's a thick rope,
   they should hang it in place.

When they've finished making it,
   well, then, and then we'll tell them
     to make a basket as well.

When they've finished making it,
   now, and then we'll tell our younger brother,
     as for him,
       he'll be the first to go look at the people.[2]

We'll go make it.
   When we've finished making it,
    that's what we'll go tie up.
Well, then, and he'll be the first one,
   our younger brother,
    who will go look at them.

When he has ridden in the basket,
   just when we've pushed it many times,
    and he's started to speed towards us,
     it's then that we'll cut it off.

Well, then, and the one who outruns the others,
   he's the one who'll marry our younger brother's wife."

"Wait, now! Is *that* it, Macehkewes?
Even though he brought them to us,
   even after that, you intend to do away with him that way!"

"Now, younger brothers, whatever an older brother says,
   that's what always happens!"

"Oh, all right!"
   they said.

It was there, later, that they went on hunting.

Now, well, in the evening after they had all come—
   Aha! He must have spoken:

---

2. Bloomfield translates this as 'the first to look at the world from up aloft'. We chose to follow the original more closely, but the sense of it is precisely what Bloomfield's translation gets at: the boy will be the first to view the people (i.e., all of humankind) from the vantage point allowed by the swing they have constructed.

"Well, then, my younger brothers, as for our wives,
   let them gather basswood bark;
     they'll make a long rope for a swing.
Now, it is then, also a basket.

And now, then, as for our younger brother,
   well, and, as for him,
     he'll be the first to go look at the people.
And later, when he's come gliding back,
   it's then, in turn, each one will go look at the people."

"All right!"
   he was told.

Scene 3

Well, now, the women gathered basswood bark.
The next day, well, soon they had made it.

"Now, tomorrow it will be ready,
   our younger brother will start to swing with speed from there."

In the evening, when they were about to sleep,
   it was then that he told his wife,

"Well, then, tomorrow, I'm the one who they intend to swing from there first.
But when I've started to swing with speed,
   it's then that they plan to cut it off.
     And it's there that, as for me,
       I die.

And you are the reason that they plan to do this.

When they've cut me off over there,
   it's there, our older brother will say,

"'Well, then,'
   he'll say,
'the one who outruns the others,
   he's the one who will marry our younger brother's wife.'

Well, then, as soon as we've started off from here,
   at that point, hurry
     and start off.
Where I had taken you from,
   you're going back there."

It was then that he so urged her.

The next day, after they had eaten:
"Well, then!"
   they said,
     setting out in single file,
       they started off.
He started off with his bow.

When they arrived:
   "Now, younger brother, you look at the people first!"

After the men had started off in single file,
   the women began the work
     of getting ready,
       they ran home
         where he had taken them from.

"Now, younger brother, come on, get in the basket!"
   he said to him.

With his bow, he got in the basket,
   he must have been swung by hand from there;
it was pushed hard by hand,
   that basket that he was in.

After a while, when he was swinging with speed,
   it was then that it must have been cut.
That was the last he knew of it.

"Well, then, younger brothers, the one who outruns the others,
   he's the one who will marry our younger brother's wife!"

They started off;
    Macehkewes must have outrun them;
        he ran inside.
            There wasn't even one in there.

At the far end,
    it was there that he ran out;
        he ran in a circle around that long lodge.

Oh, who was the one he would see?
    No one.

"Oh! Younger brothers, we have destroyed our youngest brother!"

That is all.

Ojibwe

The Birth of Nenabozho

Introduction by Rand Valentine

The four stories in this section were told a century ago by Waasaagoneshkang, an Ojibwe man whose name, according to William Jones, the original transcriber and translator of the stories, means "He Who Leaves the Imprint of His Foot Shining in the Snow."[1] As with many authors of oral traditional literature, we know almost nothing about him. He is described very briefly in introductory notes to the original texts as "an old man, bent with age, living at Pelican Lake, near the Bois Fort Reservation, in Minnesota. He grew up on Rainy River, Rainy Lake, and the Lake of the Woods" (Jones 1974, xvii). The narratives were recorded under dictation, with Waasaagoneshkang pausing at the end of each sentence to allow Jones sufficient time to write down forms. Given such an unnatural method of delivery, the general organization, stylistic quality, and accuracy of transcription of the stories are truly remarkable.

Waasaagoneshkang provided many narratives in this fashion, including an extended account of the birth and many exploits of Nenabozho, a central figure in Ojibwe oral tradition.[2] He is sometimes described by scholars unaccustomed to ambiguity as *paradoxically* both a trickster and a culture hero, in that he is very racy, and many of his actions involve imaginative deception while at the same time establishing the basic institutions and practices of Ojibwe life and landscape. The stories associated with him form a loosely defined suite, which different Ojibwe storytellers arrange and elaborate in different ways according to their artistic sensibilities, their audiences, and their purposes for a given telling. There are recognizable Nenabozho stories of particular subtypes, based on organizational structure and thematic content. For example, Christopher Vecsey (1983) has suggested that there is a core set of cosmologic narratives, which basically establishes the order of the world and many Ojibwe cultural institutions. The stories in the cosmologic "cycle" typically include Nenabozho's birth, his theft of fire, battles with one or more of his manitou brothers, his travels with a pack of wolves who eventually part ways with him after providing a talented young wolf to be his helper and provider, the subsequent murder of his wolf companion by the underwater manitous, his killing of the chief underwater manitou in revenge, a retaliatory flood, and Nenabozho's subsequent recreation of the earth. Alongside this particular sequence, there is also another ancient and widespread group of stories that deals with Nenabozho in the form of a giant who battles giant mythic creatures such as a family of beavers and a skunk. There are also stories involving comic and cunning hunting methods, such as capturing ducks or geese by hosting a "shuteye" dance or swimming underwater to tie their feet together. There are many stories of misidentification, such as when Nenabozho mistakes a distant bed of bulrushes blowing in the wind for a group of dancers and can't resist trying to outlast them in their dance. There are many stories in which Nenabozho fills the role of what folklorists call a bungling host, in which he goes visiting and his host produces food for him by some extraordinary method, which Nenabozho then tries to copy, only to make a fool of himself. There are stories in which Nenabozho attempts various sexual escapades, rarely succeeding in his schemes. In many stories clever schemes backfire, though they can sometimes have beneficial results for humanity.

Given Nenabozho's prominence in Ojibwe oral tradition, it is no surprise that of the two volumes comprising William Jones's fieldwork in Ojibwe country a century ago, one entire volume is devoted to Nenabozho stories. Waasaagoneshkang recorded a large number of such stories with Jones, including the cosmological sequence as outlined by Vecsey (1983), interspersed with several other familiar stories, in such a way that it is difficult to know if the storyteller intended them as a logical sequence and a coherent whole. Translations of three of his narrations were published in *Coming to Light,* in a piece introduced by Ridie Wilson Ghezzi. Here I include the first three in the originally published sequence, along with the seventh, and Ghezzi's work provides two others in this sequence, the twelfth and the fourteenth.[3] Obviously, real justice to Waasaagoneshkang's artistry will only be served with the publication of the full sequence, along with the Ojibwe, which would easily fill a volume in itself. The stories I present in fresh translation, though with considerable debt to Jones's sensitive and nuanced work, include Nenabozho's birth, his theft of fire, a battle with a brother that institutes death, and his travels with the wolves.

Appreciating the verbal artistry of a particular individual such as Waasaagoneshkang speaking from a culture and artistic tradition utterly different from one's own requires a lot of background in particulars, to provide some grounding in the relationship between the linguistic and cultural resources available to the storyteller and the ways that these resources are deployed in specific narrations. Information of this sort typically comes under the rubric of style in discussions of European literature. Style has been very little studied in Ojibwe, though what information exists is relevant to appreciating Waasaagoneshkang's narratives.

At the broadest level Ojibwe people traditionally made a distinction between everyday stories and so-called sacred stories. The term for sacred story, *aadi-*

zookaan, varies in its grammatical gender across different dialects of Ojibwe. In some dialects, such as Waasaagoneshkang's, the term is of animate gender, index-ing an important property of *aadizookaanag* (NB, the plural form), namely, that to tell them is to invoke the beings that inhabit them or at the very least to in-vite their audience. For this reason certain *aadizookaanag* were only recounted in winter, when a host of creatures and their associated manitous (Ojibwe *mani-doo,* plural *manidoog*) were hibernating, such as amphibians and reptiles, or had migrated south, such as the thunderbirds.

The concept of manitou is difficult to translate precisely but is typically glossed in English as 'spirit', a potentially misleading term. In traditional Ojibwe society seemingly anything could have a manitou associated with it, and most, though not all, had considerable power, which they would usually share with particu-lar humans according to their level of engagement with the spirit world. Parents blackened the faces of their sons, and often their daughters, and left them to fast and dream in an isolated spot away from human habitation, with the goal that the child humble himself or herself before the cosmos, and by virtue of humility and poverty of spirit, invite the dream visitation of a sympathetic, tutelary manitou, whose help could then be judiciously invoked in situations of crisis, such as in the failure to procure game to the point of starvation or the illness or injury of a loved one.

The relative power and desirability of particular manitous as tutelaries varies somewhat among different groups of Ojibwe people, but a generalization or two can be cautiously put forward. For one, the physical properties of a manitou's biological correspondent often have a bearing on the nature of the assistance a manitou can provide, in essence helping to define the manitou's "specialty." For example, the manitous of birds are often associated with battle, because birds have the ability to fly and with this special powers of movement and reconnaissance, and they are usually small, which confers on their beneficiaries the advantage of being a more difficult target in battle. Small creatures share the property of in-conspicuousness, which makes for good eavesdropping, and their manitous often provide those they bless with critical information about the secret weaknesses of an adversary. In traditional stories of Nenabozho animals are often indeterminate as to whether they represent particular individuals or the manitou of the given species, and typically, events that alter their form or behavior have consequences for the entire species.

Another important property of manitous generally is their capacity to change shape, a power that they can confer on those they bless, allowing them to strategi-cally take on the form of the tutelary in times of need. A basic axiom of traditional Ojibwe life is that things are often not what they appear to be. As a consequence, everything should be treated with respect, or at the very least, never prematurely dismissed in contempt, because the grandest appearing thing can ultimately represent very little, and the humblest thing can be a repository of great power and means. Furthermore, each species is endowed with attributes and abilities that define its uniqueness and provide it with the particular talents needed to carry out its way of living. These skills often exceed the equivalent abilities of humans and thus too provide a basis for respect and admiration.

There are many details of Waasaagoneshkang's narratives that can only be appreciated with an understanding of traditional Ojibwe culture. For example, a child is typically given a name by means of an elder who receives it in a dream. Children do not generally announce their names to their elders, as Nenabozho does! Furthermore, wrapping a body in birch bark was traditionally, at least among some Ojibwe people, a standard burial preparation. Now, in the case of Nenabozho's incubation, it's possible that his grandmother had wrapped up the blood as a part of her daughter's burial; nonetheless, it is consistent with the "upside-down" nature of Nenabozho that he be born by means of a burial. He's a very tricky guy. Notice how he gets fire, by using ice. Note too that he does not use force but rather makes himself among the most harmless of creatures, a bunny rabbit, and wills not that he overpower his adversaries but that they find him adorable. There is also a vast amount of ambivalence with regard to Nenabozho's character—for example, Waasaagoneshkang never reveals his role in his mother's death. And when Nenabozho desires to find his brother, his grandmother objects, and we are left to wonder whether the institution of death is a good or a bad thing. Waasaagoneshkang is consistently and artfully ambivalent in his treatment of Nenabozho and his deeds.

Throughout these stories we find a common motif in Ojibwe traditional stories, the gendered dyad, in which a male and a female live together, according to the traditional household economy, in which men hunted and women took care of most domestic tasks. The two daughters of the fire-hoarder are immediately recognizable to students of Ojibwe oral tradition as well-known sisters who wander the earth in search of ribald adventure, often behaving in a fashion not unlike Nenabozho himself, and are sometimes even said to be his daughters, based in part on resemblances of impulse, appetite, and character. Another prominent dynamic in these stories is the wisdom and discernment of elders as opposed to the impulse and indiscretion of the young. Details and connections of this sort are extremely common in Ojibwe traditional narratives, but are lost on readers unfamiliar with the tradition and contribute to a devalued appreciation of the artfulness of such traditional stories.

With regard to linguistic resources, Ojibwe is vastly different from English in its basic grammatical patterns. To begin, the previously mentioned distinction between animate and inanimate pervades all aspects of grammar, and every noun is classified as to its animacy. Living things such as creatures and most plants are all animate. Objects of manufacture and other inert things that don't operate under their own power are usually inanimate, though anything can become animate if an animating force behind it, such as a manitou, becomes active, which frequently happens in myths and dreams. In addition, many things that are believed to be inherently powerful are animate or conceived in terms of their animating manitou, such as the sun and the moon, the stars, snow, ice, and objects of traditional religious significance, including pipes, tobacco, and in most dialects, drums, and myths themselves. The world is imbued with power, and this is reflected in language in part in the grammatical category of animacy. At the same time sexual gender is not grammaticalized as in English, nor is there any straightforward grammatical distinction between humans and any other animate thing. In part as a result of this, many aboriginal writers claim that the trickster's gender is far more ambiguous than English translations might suggest.[4]

Kinship terms in Ojibwe are grammatically required to have inflections indicating who the relation is being expressed in terms of, so to speak in general terms of, say, "a grandmother" is decidedly marked and not common. This fact is relevant to these stories because Nenabozho's grandmother has come into English literature through Longfellow's poem *The Song of Hiawatha* as Nokomis, which literally means 'my grandmother'.[5] This is indeed the principal way that Nenabozho identifies her, because she is, after all, *his* grandmother. Issues immediately arise as to whether this designation constitutes a specific name or is simply a term of reference particular to Nenabozho. Myth complicates things, because this woman is, as Jones observes in a footnote, mother nature, and so it is arguably appropriate for any of us to refer to her as *nookomis,* particularly in Ojibwe, where ancestors and spirit antecedents are customarily referred to with terms designating grandparents. But I have elected to refer to her with the designation Ookomisan, which literally means 'animate singular's grandmother', that is, 'his or her grandmother', since in these stories it is her relation to Nenabozho that is always at issue.

Among animates an important grammatical distinction often used skillfully by storytellers is that of obviation. Basically, in any given span of narration, one particular animate is chosen to be primary, called *proximate* in Algonquian grammar, and all others are grammatically marked as *obviative.* This in essence provides a kind of narrative perspective roughly corresponding to distinctions of voice in English, and obviation is often translated by means of active and passive voice, something perhaps initiated and very consistently carried out by William Jones in his translations. To this end, for example, when Nenabozho is born and speaks to his grandmother, I have put all of Nenabozho's utterances in the passive, because Waasaagoneshkang has elected here to tell the story from the perspective of Ookomisan, even though the dynamic of the story draws attention to Nenabozho.

By making Ookomisan proximate and Nenabozho obviative, Waasaagoneshkang essentially subverts the climactic development of the narrative, adding further ambiguity to the status of Nenabozho vis-à-vis his grandmother. Subtleties of this sort are, of course, crucial to understanding and appreciating the text, but they are almost impossible to translate with any elegance.

Oral narratives share a set of features across languages that present challenges of many sorts in transfer to the page. Languages typically have conjunctive expressions equivalent to English forms such as "and then," "so then," and so on, which are liberally used to pace, sequence, and orient oral narrative development. Those used to the written standard of English, whether fiction or nonfiction, often react to such devices as constituting unnecessary and artless repetition. But to do so is to fail to appreciate the nature of oral storytelling. Waasaagoneshkang's narrations are essentially organized by means of such devices, most importantly the "discourse" particles *mii* and *dash,* as well as many others. Many such elements are predicative in Ojibwe, which if translated literally, would have the effect of giving a majority of translated sentences the form "it was then that . . . ," which quickly becomes monotonous if applied too rigidly in translation. I have sought to capture the flavor of the original without imposing a formal straitjacket, though in more general terms it must be recognized that rendering an oral performance on the page is to invite injustice by suggesting a kind of fixity and finality that has little place in the original.

Another distinctive feature of formal Ojibwe oral narrative is the use of quotation frames. This device brackets direct expressions of quotation or thought with explicit verbs of speaking or thinking. An example occurs in Nenabozho's discussion with Ookomisan in part II with the following form:

And this he said to his grandmother:
"Well guess what, I'm going to go get that fire!"
he said to his grandmother.

This example illustrates another striking feature of Waasaagoneshkang's style that I have not found as prominently in the narratives of other Ojibwe storytellers, namely, his frequent framing of direct quotations with a formula using a demonstrative pronoun, "And *this* X said (to Y)." It is possible that this is an artifact of the fragmented nature of his delivery under the conditions of dictation, but that seems unlikely to me, simply because Waasaagoneshkang is such a talented storyteller. Rather, it is probably representative of an extremely formal style.

It has become customary in recent years to cast oral narrative on the page in lines, suggesting that it is more akin to European poetry than prose. Depending on what is given prominence in the poetic analysis, lines are determined on the basis of either prosodic or grammatical criteria. Where there is no auditory record, such as with the stories presented here, one steers a safer course with the latter, though it might be possible to reconstruct the prosodics of stories recorded long ago on the basis of contemporary storytellers. I have organized Waasaagoneshkang's narrations according to impressionistic, syntactically based criteria, typically treating each clause as a separate line and using indents to indicate the conjunction and subordination of clauses. This procedure produces a manuscript that allows one to more readily scan the text for parallelisms and other formal features, though at the price of disturbing the overall flow of thematic development. Line-based formats tend to sacrifice appreciation of the whole for attention to the parts.

NOTES

1. As with all cited Ojibwe words, I have converted Jones's spelling to the modern orthography, as exemplified in Nichols and Nyholm 1995, which distinguishes three short vowels — *a, i, o* — and four long vowels — *aa, ii, oo, e.* Consonant symbols are *b, p, d, t, g, k, j, ch, z, s, zh, sh, m, n, w, y,* and ' (apostrophe), this last representing a glottal stop.

2. Nenabozho is also variously referred to as Wenabozho, Menabozho, and Wiizakejaak in different locales.

3. Ghezzi 1994. The twelfth narration is "Nenabozho Eats the Artichokes," and the fourteenth is "Nenabozho and the Caribou." Ghezzi also includes another part of the story that is not part of this sequence.

4. See, for example, Wilson 1998 and Highway 1988, 1989.

5. Spelled *nookomis* in the standard orthography and pronounced NOKE-uh-miss or NUKE-uh-miss.

SUGGESTED READING AND REFERENCES

Excellent overviews of the trickster from an Ojibwe point of view can be found in Lindquist and Zanger 1994, especially separate articles by Gerald Vizenor and Kim Blaeser. For translations of traditional stories, the original Jones collection has been reprinted by the AMS Press (1974). A selection of Jones's English translations, with an essay on Ojibwe worldview, was prepared by Overholt and Callicott 1982. Another accessible collection of Ojibwe traditional narratives is that of Charles and Charlotte Kawbawgam, recorded and translated at the end of the nineteenth century by Homer Kidder (*Ojibwa Narratives of Charles and Charlotte Kawbawgam and Jacques LePique, 1893–1895*).

Ghezzi, Ridie Wilson. 1994. "Nanabush Stories from the Ojibwe." In *Coming to Light: Contemporary Translations of the Native Literatures of North America,* edited by Brian Swann. New York: Random House.

Highway, Tomson. 1988. *The Rez Sister: A Play in Two Acts.* Saskatoon SK: Fifth House.

———. 1989. *Dry Lips Oughta Move to Kapuskasing.* Saskatoon SK: Fifth House.

Jones, William, comp. [1917, 1919] 1974. *Ojibwa Texts.* Edited by Truman Michelson. Reprint, New York: AMS Press.

Lindquist, Mark A., and Martin Zanger, eds. 1994. *Buried Roots and Indestructible Seeds: The Survival of American Indian Life in Story, History, and Spirit.* Madison: University of Wisconsin Press.

Nichols, John D., and Earl Nyholm. 1995. *A Concise Dictionary of Minnesota Ojibwe*. Minneapolis: University of Minnesota Press.

Ojibwa Narratives of Charles and Charlotte Kawbawgam and Jacques LePique, 1893–1895). Recorded with notes by Homer H. Kidder. Edited by Arthur P. Bourgeois. Detroit: Wayne State University Press, 1994.

Overholt, Thomas, and J. Baird Callicott. 1982. *Clothed-in-Fur, and Other Tales: An Introduction to an Ojibwa World View*. With Ojibwa texts by William Jones and foreword by Mary B. Black-Rogers. Washington DC: University Press of America.

Vecsey, Christopher T. 1983. *Traditional Ojibwa Religion and Its Historical Changes*. Memoirs of the American Philosophical Society, vol. 152. Philadelphia: American Philosophical Society.

Wilson, Alexandria. 1998. "How Our Stories Are Told." *Canadian Journal of Native Education* 22, no. 2:274–78.

The Birth of Nenabozho

Told by Waasaagoneshkang
Translated by Rand Valentine

Once some people were living in a wigwam,
  an old woman and her daughter.
And at some point she said to her daughter,
  "Listen, my daughter, be on your guard.
  Take careful heed of what I'm about to tell you.
  I'm terribly afraid, I fear for your well-being.
  Never ever sit facing the west when you go outside to relieve yourself.[1]
  Something bad will happen to you if you sit facing in that direction.
  That's the basis of my fear for you.
  Take heed of what I'm telling you,
    because you could bring great harm on yourself.
  That's what I want to tell you now."

Well, it seems that that young woman was exceedingly careful.
No man ever came within sight of her.

But then once she forgot,
  and at that instant she heard the wind rushing toward her.
And she felt the rush of a cool breeze there at her going out.
And she leapt to her feet.
  "Mother, look at me, this state I'm in.
  Perhaps it's happened to me as you said it might."

Well, the old woman said to her daughter:
  "Oh, most assuredly you've brought great harm on yourself!"

1. Nenabozho's brothers and father were traditionally associated with the cardinal points of the compass.

And the old woman began to weep.
   "That's how it is, you've brought harm on your body.
   Listen to what's going to happen to you.
   Beings have entered your body, and that's what has left you so pitiable.
   They're not humans, those who entered your body.
   And it won't be long until they're born.
   Alas, it's the very ones I feared."

Well, after a while the old woman heard the sound of them arguing with each
other.
And then she knew for sure that her daughter wouldn't survive.
She heard them arguing;
   there within her daughter's belly they rumbled.
And this they were heard to say:
   "It's I who shall be firstborn!"
"No" was heard another,
   "You will not be firstborn — *I* shall be!"

And always the old woman wept when she heard them contending in this way.
She knew what a large number they were.

Well, as they spoke they pushed each other back, seeking in vain to exit.
Some of them said: "Don't! We're going to harm our mother.
   Let us exit in an orderly fashion," some said, in vain.

But those who wanted to be firstborn weren't happy with this.
And so they declared that they would exit through various routes.
One of them saw a light.
   "Well, as for me, I'm going straight in that direction."
And so as they contended as to who would be firstborn,
   they tore their mother apart.

And some time later as the old woman was looking about,
   she found a bit of blood.
And so she peeled some birch bark.
And into the birch bark she placed the blood, repeatedly folding the bark,
   and then she laid it away.

Well, from time to time she took a look at it.
And once, when she unwrapped it,

she beheld a child.
And she was spoken to by the child,
   this is what she was told:
      "Grandmother!"
   she was told when she was spoken to.

And then it spoke to her again:
   "Do you know who I am?
   Why, I am Nenabozho."

II

So the old woman began to raise him.
And at some point he said to his grandmother:
   "Might you not know of people living anywhere here on the earth?"

"Yes," he was told by his grandmother,
   "across Gichigami there are people."[2]

"And by any chance might they not be in possession of fire?"

"Yes," he was told by his grandmother,
   "most certainly they possess fire."

And this he said to his grandmother:
   "Well, guess what, I'm going to go get that fire!"
   he said to his grandmother.

And this his grandmother said to him:
   "You won't be able to do it.
   They keep very close guard over their home.
   There's an old man living there.
   Every day he works at making a net.
   He never goes out but always remains inside.
   But he has two daughters; they're the only ones who ever venture out."

And this he said to his grandmother:
   "Nevertheless, I'm going,"

2. I use the Ojibwe designation for Lake Superior, Gichigami, throughout, assuming that it is known from Longfellow's *Hiawatha,* though the correct pronunciation is GITCH—ih—guh—mih or gih—CHI—guh—mih, with all the *i*s short as in English *pin.*

he said to his grandmother.

"Very well," he was told by his grandmother.

Well, at some point then he said:
    "Let Gichigami freeze over,
    let Gichigami freeze as thick as a sheet of birch bark covering the lodge."

And truly, it happened just as he said.

"And this is what I'll look like," he said.
    "I'll look like a bunny."

And then truly, that's how he looked.

And so he set off across the ice,
    and most assuredly he didn't break through.

And eventually he came in sight of where the people were living.
And when he arrived at the place from which they drew their water,
    he arranged this at the place where they would come to draw their water:
    he was thrown up on the shore by Gichigami;
    he was rolled up there, precisely where the woman drew her water.

And this he said: "Let her find me irresistibly cute."

And so he lay in wait for her to come to fetch water.

And what do you know, but indeed he saw her walking toward him.
And when she arrived where he was,
    she drew up some water.
And he was noticed by her,
    and he was picked up by her,
And so, he was wrung out by her,
    and he was carried away home,
    tucked inside the bosom of her dress, he was.

And when he had been taken inside the lodge,
    indeed he beheld an old man sitting there.
And, truly, the old man was making a net.

And the woman said this to her elder sister:
  "Look at this!"
  She said secretly to her elder sister.

  "Look at what I found, a little bunny rabbit!"

And this she was told by her elder sister:
  "Our father's going to take us to task,"
  she was told by her elder sister;
  that is, secretly she was told this by her elder sister.

And then she searched inside the bosom of her dress,
  and she extracted him and set him down beside the fire to dry off his fur.

And the women were laughing it up,
  they found the bunny so irresistibly cute.
And as a result, they were discovered by their father.
  "Pipe down!" he told them.

"Take a look at this bunny!"

"What!" they were told by their father.
  "Haven't you heard that manitous were recently born?
  And might not this indeed be one of them?
  Go and put it outside,"
  they were told by their father.

But this the woman said:
  "How could it be that a bunny rabbit be a manitou?"
  she said to her father.

And this he said:
  "Truly you're not in the habit of listening.
  Have you never noticed how advanced in years I am?"

But this is what the woman did:
  she exposed the bunny to the heat of the fire,
  and to make its fur dry,
  she kept turning it over and over by the fire.

And this then thought Nenabozho:

"I must be dry by now."

Well, the women kept amusing themselves with him.

And this he thought: "Let a spark fall on me!"

And truly a spark alit on him.
And after he was on fire,
  he leaped out of the lodge.

And the women said this:
  "Look, it's racing out with the fire!"
  they said to their father.

"Oh, no!" said the old man.
  "Truly you don't know how to listen,
    even though people try to tell you.
  Undoubtedly it's a manitou,
  come to rob us of our fire!"

And the old man leaped up
  and ran to his canoe,
  intending to toss it into the water.
But it was of no use,
  because the water had been frozen into ice.

And so they were left to watch helplessly
  as far out in the midst of the great expanse of Gichigami,
  it began to flicker with a blue flame,
  until it faded from their sight.
They were utterly helpless to do anything.

And he came in sight of where they were staying.
And this he had said to his grandmother before setting off:
  "Be prepared because I may indeed return with fire,"
  he had said to his grandmother.

And so he spoke to her as he came in sight of their home;
  this he said to his grandmother upon entering:
  "Extinguish me, grandma, I'm on fire!"

And that is how they came to have fire.

And this said Nenabozho:
  "And thus shall the rabbit appear mottled in the summer."

III

And thus they came to be in possession of fire.

And Nenabozho remained there with his grandmother,
  and all this time the waters of Gichigami were heaving.
Seated-Rabbit is the name of that portion of Gichigami.
And always he went there to sit.

And this he said to his grandmother:
  "So be it, Grandma, that this be the duration of my being a rabbit."

And at that place there was evidently a promontory,
  and there on the height of the rock he would sit.
Indeed, that is the appearance that the rock has there.
And then he said,
  "Seated-Rabbit is what the people shall call it."

And afterward he took on human form.
But no longer did he have the appearance of a child.
And this he said to his grandmother:
  "Do you know who I am?"

"No," he was told.

"I am Nenabozho."

And this he said to his grandmother:
  "Can it really be that I am an only child?"
  he said to his grandmother.

"Yes," he was told.
  "Truly you're an only child," he was told.

And this he answered:
  "Can you tell me this, then?"

he said to his grandmother,
 "Might not I have had a father?"

"Yes," he was told,
 "but whoever it might have been was not visible,"
 he was told.

And this too he was told,
 "She who was your mother is dead.
 That's all I can tell you.
 I would not hide anything from you."

And this Nenabozho said to her:
 "How could it be that I be an only child?
 You must be hiding something from me,"
 he said to his grandmother.

And then he said:
 "Why do you do this,
 hiding from me what transpired with us?
 But be that as it may, I haven't forgotten what happened.
 I know that I have brothers.
 So tell me the truth of what happened to us."

Well, these words frightened the old woman.
And this she said to her grandchild:
 "Very well, I will tell you,
 it's true that you weren't alone when you were born.
 As truly as I speak,
  this is what happened to you:
 You and your brothers killed your mother when you were born.
 But steadfastly I held to what I had purposed,
 and that is why I have raised you."

And this he said to his grandmother:
 "Oh, so that's what happened to me at my birth!
 It was not I who killed my mother."

And then he thought:
 "I'm going to go looking for those brothers of mine,"
 he thought.

Well, then he said to his grandmother,
   "I'm going to go look for the one who made me an orphan."

"Don't!" his grandmother said in vain to him.
   "What is to be gained in your doing this,
    going into battle against your brother?"

"Nevertheless," he said, "I'm going to do it."

And then he set to work making his arrows.
And when he had prepared,
   he set off;
   directly to the south he went,
   because he knew that that was where his brother was.

And when he was near the home of his brother,
   he made four caches of arrows.

And then he came to the place where his brother was.

And Nenabozho said, "So, are you ready to do battle with me?"

"Indeed," his brother said to him.

"Well, then, let the battle begin."

And so they began fighting,
   and they were firing at each other.
And as he was being forced back,
   Nenabozho came to the place where his arrows were,
   where he had cached them.

And from there in turn he drove the other back,
   almost to the place where he lived,
   Nenabozho drove him back.

And from there once more Nenabozho was driven back,
   once again he was driven back to a place where
   he had cached his arrows.
And once more, futilely, he drove the other back,
   near to where he lived.

And then once more Nenabozho was driven back,
  until yet again he reached a cache of arrows.

And at that point he thought:
  "It seems likely now that I'll be vanquished."
He had only a very few arrows left,
  and they were very small.

And so he began to weep.

And this he thought:
  "It's likely now that I'll be killed,"
  he thought.

And then he was addressed by the weasel.
  "What's the matter with you,
    you look as if you've been weeping, Nenabozho,"
  he was told by the weasel.
  "Nothing's going to happen to you.
  Listen, I'll tell you what you must do,"
    said the weasel to him.
  "Listen, shoot him there . . ."
  "Shoot him at the base of his hair knot."

So then Nenabozho gave a war cry.
And no sooner had he begun driving his brother back,
  than he shot him at the base of the hair knot.
And his brother fell forward.
Nenabozho raced up to him,
  and this he said: "Die!"

And this he was told by his brother:
  "You're doing vast harm to those who are yet to live."
And his brother wept;
  he wept for the people.
In vain he sought to avoid being killed.

But Nenabozho was thoroughly determined to kill him.

And at last he succeeded in killing his younger sibling.
And for a short time his brother was out of his wits.

And Nenabozho said,
 "In return, you will be leader over there
 where those who cease to live will come.
 It's there you shall be,
 and there you shall be leader."

And then after his brother had consented,
 he said to him,
 "You've done vast harm to the people who are soon to live."

"Well, the earth would fill up with people.
 And where might those people live who are soon to be born?
 That is why it shall come to pass that people die,
  because otherwise the earth would soon be filled,
  and although we could arrange it such that
  only the aged might die among those who are to come,
  nowhere would they have room were this to come to pass.

 You see, that's why they will also die while yet children.
 Yes, that is what I foresee,
 that it will happen thus to those who are soon to die,
 that it will happen as it now does with you.
 Because it is only a change of place from one earth to another.
 Where you are those who have ceased to live shall meet you."

IV

And once as he was wandering about,
 he saw someone—
 well! they were wolves.

And so he shouted out to them
 to come over to where he was.

And this said the wolves:
 "Don't go anywhere near him,
 he wants to engage you in conversation,"
 the lead wolf said to them.

And so indeed they stood at a great distance from him
 when they spoke to him.

And this he said to them:
 "Why do you always act like this whenever I see you?
  'We are no kin to him.'—
 Is this what you're always thinking?
 But in point of fact I'm quite closely related to you;
  your father is in fact my brother."

And this he said to the old wolf there:
 "My fellow eldest,"
 he said to him.

And this he said to the sons of the old wolf:
 "Why, you are all my nephews,"
 he said to those wolves.

And this he said:
 "Where are you headed?"
 he said to them.

"Well, over here off a ways,
 where last summer your nephews did some killing;
  it's over there that we're headed.
 For it's over there that we always cache
  whatever they've found.
 And it's over to that place where we've made a cache
  that we were planning on going now.

And this Nenabozho said:
 "Well, I'm headed in that direction too,
 so I'll just go along with you,"
 he said to him.

And so indeed he set out with them on their journey.

But he was barely able to keep up with them.
And a cold wind was blowing as they went along.
And now evening was coming on.

"Well, it's time that we look for a place to camp,"
 they said.

And indeed they looked for where they might camp.
And soon they found a place.
But the wind raced through the site they prepared.
"Here is a place," they said.
And at once they lay down.
And after each had circled a spot where he was to lie down,
    then Nenabozho did the same thing.

And this he was told by the old wolf:
    "There in the midst of where your nephews lie,
    you lie too, because it seems you're cold."

"Yes, I'm quite cold."

And his teeth were chattering,
    he was so cold.
And so indeed he lay down in the middle of the pack.
And this said the old wolf:
    "Please, provide your uncle with a top covering."
And so truly one of them tossed his tail over Nenabozho,
    and then another did so,
        until he was able to fall asleep.

And truly he was warm as he slept.
And once when he awoke,
    he was actually sweating.

And so this he said:
    "Damn, these worthless old dog tails have really got me in a sweat!"[3]
And after he had flung them aside,
    he heard this from the old man wolf:
    "Most certainly you wound your nephews with your words,"
    he was told by the old man wolf.

And then after awhile he began to get cold again.
And once again his teeth began to chatter.

"Without a doubt your uncle is freezing to death.
    Why don't you once again offer your uncle a top covering?"

3. Traditionally no insult was more grievous than to call someone a dog.

And so once more one of them offered his tail,
   and then another.
And so once again he began to get warm.

Then when dawn came,
   once again they were eager to set off.
And this he was told by the old wolf:
     "Well, we'll arrive at our destination this evening,
     if only we hurry."

And so truly they set off,
   and Nenabozho tried his best to keep up.
And at one point as they were going along,
     "Well, by now we should have eaten,"
   he was told by the old wolf.
And Nenabozho was told:
     "Please go on ahead and have a fire built up for our arrival."

And so after he piled up some wood,
   he began to look in vain for his flint.
"What on earth are you doing?"
   he was asked by the old wolf.
And one of the young wolves standing there was told,
     "Please, you, start the fire!"

So the young wolf went over to where Nenabozho had heaped up the firewood,
   and the instant he leaped over the pile,
     it burst into bright red flame.

"There, that's what you do when you intend to make a fire."

And so they ate there,
and then they set off again,
   because they were eager to make their destination.
And they did not stop even when the sun set,
   but continued on their way.
"Well, it's near now," he was told.

And so at twilight they arrived.
And after they had established a camp, they built a shelter.

And then they went after the contents of their cache.
And Nenabozho was given some choice firewood.
And he was given some fungus.

"Don't look at it all through the night,
    but later, when it's morning, then you can look at it,"
        he was told.
He was told,
    "Later, when it's morning."

But he grew extremely restless waiting for morning to make its appearance.
    "Now, truly, I'd really love to have a look at it," he thought.
And so in secret he looked at it,
    and what should he see but an enormously large moose gut!

And then after he had bitten a piece off,
    dawn appeared.
And the wolves turned,
    and what should they see but an enormously large moose gut!
And when Nenabozho turned to them,
    he was told,
        "It seemed that in the night you were making the sounds of someone
eating."

And now he too was trying to take out the things
    that he had been given.
And, lo, the marks of his teeth were on the choice firewood,
and the marks of his teeth were on the fungus too.

So they started laughing at him.
    "Why did you do what you did?
    You shouldn't have disturbed it in the night,
        for look at the hardship you've brought on yourself now.
    Truly you're not in the habit of listening,
    and as a result you've brought this hardship on your belly.
    Now what is he going to eat?"

And so at once he needed to be fed.
And he longed for what they had.
And after he had been given food,

then he too ate.
And this he was told by the old wolf:

"Now then, we'll travel about,"
   he was told.
   "With this nephew of yours in particular shall you go about hunting,
   for all time I make you this gift.
   Truly he is good at getting animals."

And so when they broke camp,
   already their companions had left.
Not until a while afterward did they leave.
And ever as their companions set down tracks,
   they followed along after them.
And from time to time as they followed along,
   looking about,
   they beheld the fresh droppings from where their companions had started
   running.

And this he was told by the old wolf:
   "As you go along, take up the top covering of your nephew."

"How disgusting! What would I ever do with an old turd
   that I should want to take it along with me?" said Nenabozho.

And this he was told by the old wolf:
   "Most certainly you wound your nephew with your words."

And the wolf went along finding the turds,
   and when he took them up,
   he shook them,
   and what should he be holding but a blanket!

"Oh my gosh! Bring it here, my fellow eldest,
   I'll carry it on my back,"
   Nenabozho said to him.

And when he brought it to him,
   he carried it on his back.

Well, then, once more they set off.

And once while they were walking along,
   he was addressed by the old wolf, who said to him,
     "Well, it's a big cow moose that your nephews are after.
     And your nephews are at this moment pressing hard on it."

And shortly thereafter he saw a tooth of one his nephews stuck in a tree trunk.

"Look, Nenabozho, maybe it's here that they shot at the moose but missed.
Nenabozho, take up the arrows of your nephews as you come upon them."

"How disgusting!
   What would I ever do with an old dog's tooth
     that I should want to take it up?"

"Truly you wound your nephews with your words."

By giving it a twist, the old wolf pulled it out.
And when he shook it, what should he be holding but an arrow!

"Bring it here, please," Nenabozho said to the old wolf.
And indeed it was brought to him, and he carried it along.

And at some point he saw his nephews lying down.
Nowhere at all in their vicinity
   was the snow at all bloody.

"Behold, Nenabozho," he was told,
   "your nephews must have killed something,
because that's just the way they behave when they've found a moose."

And the old wolf was happy.
"Come on, come on, Nenabozho,
   let's make a place where we can prepare the meat."

"Where in the world is the meat for us to prepare?"

Whereupon he was told by the old wolf:
   "Truly you wound your nephews with your words."

And so against his will Nenabozho agreed to help them make a shelter.

But not at all did he move
   until they had finished and were entering one by one.

What was he now to see?
He too had already been allotted a share.
Half the fat had been given to him.
So he was very pleased.
"It's certain that I too will eat," he thought.
   "Truly we're living well now."

And once when preparing moose meat there,
   "Please, our father is going to boil the broken bones down for marrow.
   So let him be the only one to do the cooking,"
   the young wolves said of their father.

And then truly their father set to work.
And this they were told by him:
   "I beg of you, don't look at me
   when I do this boiling down of the bones for marrow.
   Be careful about this, Nenabozho,"
   he was told by that old wolf.

And indeed.
Well, Nenabozho was wrapped in his old, soiled blanket,
   and as they listened to their father,
   it sounded as if he were gnawing on a bone.

"Oh my, I've just got to take a look,"
   thought Nenabozho.
And so he quietly lifted his old, soiled blanket,
   and indeed he saw the wolf at the exact moment
   that it was biting on an ulna,
   but at just the moment that it slipped from its mouth.
   And its saliva was stringing from its mouth,
   nearly to the ground.

And as Nenabozho watched him,
   at some point the old wolf lost his hold on the bone in his mouth,
   and straightaway it flew into Nenabozho's eye.
   Then there was the constant sound, "Choe, choe."

"Oh, I must have caught Nenabozho in the eye with the bone!"
And then the old one said:
    "Attend to your uncle;
    cool him with water!"

And so indeed they cooled him with water,
    and he was revived.
And the old one said to him:
    "Nenabozho, you were looking at me!"

"No! No!"

"Nenabozho, most certainly you were looking at me!"

Well, then, in the morning,
    how thick was the grease frozen!
So they were fed in the morning with grease made from the boiled bones.

And he says to them:
    "Well, now it's my turn to make the grease from bones broken and boiled!"

And then indeed he started in to making grease.

"Well, it's the same with me,
    I must never be observed
    when I'm making grease from bones broken and boiled!
    So cover yourselves up!"

And then he set to work on cracking the bones.
And the bones were extremely greasy.
And he sucked grease from as many bones
    as had grease in them.

At some distance away,
    rolled up in his blanket and with his head toward the center,
    lay the old wolf.

And with care, Nenabozho selected a very large bone,
    which he had split crosswise,

and with it he struck the old wolf.
And by so doing knocked him unconscious.
And this he said to his nephews:
    "Look! Cool him off with some water!"
    he said to them.

And then he said:
    "My fellow-eldest was most certainly watching me.
    This is the way I behave whenever anyone watches me!"

Well, presently the old wolf revived.
And he said this:
    "Nenabozho hit me,"
        he said.
    "He hit me on purpose,"
        said the old wolf.
    "I was not in the least watching him,"
        the old wolf said.
    "So, not till later will I feed you."

And so morning broke.
And the grease in his kettle was frozen
    as thick as a sheet of birch-bark covering on a lodge.
And once more he fed his nephews with it.

And now they had consumed their moose,
    "It's time now to move camp,"
    Nenabozho was told by the old one.

And the old said to him,
    "I'm giving you one of my sons,"
    he said to him.

And Nenabozho agreed.
    "And by him shall I be well supplied!
    So let him go forth from here to hunt!"
    he said to the old one.

"Well, tomorrow we'll break camp,"
    he was told by the old one.

And indeed they did break camp.

"I'm leaving you one who will keep you supplied with food throughout winter,"

he was told by the old one.

And it was true.

Seneca

Creation Story

Introduction by Wallace Chafe

One of the great classics of Iroquois oral literature is an account of how the world came to be as it is—the origin of the most salient components of traditional Iroquois life, analogous in some ways to the Genesis story in the Judeo-Christian tradition. As with many other oral traditions, transmission of this creation story from one generation to the next declined during the twentieth century, but at the end of the nineteenth century the story was still known and recited by a number of people in the various Iroquois nations and languages. Fortunately, in the latter part of the nineteenth century several versions were recorded by J. N. B. Hewitt, an ethnologist and linguist (we might now call him a linguistic anthropologist), who was employed by the Bureau of American Ethnology (the BAE) of the Smithsonian Institution.

John Napoleon Brinton Hewitt was born in 1859 near the Tuscarora Reservation in western New York. His father was of European ancestry, but his mother was part Tuscarora. Although Hewitt's native language was English, he is said to have learned something of the Tuscarora language from friends at school. He planned at first to become a physician like his father, but his future was completely changed in 1880 when he met Erminnie Smith, a many-talented woman from Jersey City who was then collecting materials on the Iroquois languages for the BAE. Smith invited Hewitt to be her assistant, and after her death in 1886 he was hired by the BAE to continue her work. He remained an employee of that agency for fifty-one years, until his death in 1937.

Hewitt recorded an impressive amount of material on Iroquois customs and languages. An obituary mentions about four thousand manuscript pages of notes on Onondaga, eight hundred pages each on Tuscarora and Seneca, and two hundred pages on Cayuga, plus about six thousand pages on miscellaneous related topics.[1] He also left behind thousands of file slips that he had prepared for a Tuscarora dictionary. They were recently edited, expanded, and published by Blair Rudes.[2]

Hewitt is said to have been a perfectionist, a trait that may have kept him from publishing more of his materials than he did. Early in his career he ventured into linguistic theory with an article on Indian language morphology in which he criticized the views of Daniel Brinton on the nature of polysynthesis.[3] For this presumption he was scathingly attacked by Brinton, a leading figure in the anthropology of the time.[4] This unpleasant exchange may have discouraged Hewitt from ever again expressing in print his ideas concerning the general nature of the languages of which he had such a deep firsthand knowledge.

He recorded five versions of the Iroquois creation story between 1889 and 1900. Three of them—one in Onondaga, one in Seneca, and one in Mohawk—were published in 1903.[5] Another, longer Onondaga version appeared in 1928.[6] The translation here is of the Seneca version, which was dictated to Hewitt in 1896 by John Armstrong, "an intelligent and conscientious annalist" who lived on the Cattaraugus Reservation in western New York. It was subsequently revised for publication with the help of Andrew John, a Seneca who visited Hewitt in Washington.

This Seneca version is very different from the Onondaga and Mohawk versions that were included with it in the 1903 volume. For one thing, it is less than half as long. The others begin with a complex series of events in the world above the sky, events that precede and lead up to the expulsion from that world of the woman who goes on to establish life on earth. The Seneca version omits almost all of that, beginning directly with the jealousy of the chief who then causes the woman's fall from the sky. The Onondaga and Mohawk versions also include various subsequent episodes that are lacking in the Seneca, for example, the animals' repeated diving for mud to place on the turtle's back (the widespread earth-diver motif), the origin of the primal False Face, and the freeing of the sun from a snare. It gives almost no attention to the activities of the second twin, such as his creation of ill-formed beings that contrast with the well-formed creations of the first twin. The formation of hills and rivers is only briefly alluded to at the very end, seemingly as an afterthought.

On the other hand, the Seneca version includes certain elements not present in the others, for example, the acquisition of fat by the animals, the first twin's collection of food for his grandmother, and the origin of menstruation. It treats some episodes quite differently, as when it describes the stipulation by the wind that his son (the first twin) take part in a race (in which he is aided by the False Face) before the animals are made available. It gives special attention to the naming of constellations and the animals.

In general, whereas the Onondaga and Mohawk versions share much of their content and exhibit similar amounts of detail, the Seneca version follows a different path and is relatively abbreviated. Perhaps some of this difference can be attributed simply to Armstrong's own personal background and knowledge, but it may also be evidence for significant differences between traditions on the Cattaraugus Reservation and those on the Grand River (or Six Nations) Reserve in Ontario, where both the Onondaga and the Mohawk version were recorded and where there was intimate contact between the Onondaga and Mohawk communities. In any case, this Seneca version has its own values and exhibits its own internal coherence.

The reader is invited to imagine what it might have been like to listen to this story in a Seneca longhouse centuries ago, perhaps before the advent of Europeans. That experience and the experience of reading this translation are unavoidably different in many ways, some obvious, some not so obvious. The story was originally told to an audience that was, of course, familiar with the Seneca language, but also with a complex web of shared concepts and expectations. Hewitt's own introduction pointed out that the texts he recorded "represent largely the spoken language of today [that is, the late nineteenth century], conveying the modern thought of the people, although there are many survivals in both word and concept from older generations and past planes of thought. These archaisms when encountered appear enigmatic and quaint, and are not understood by the uninformed. The relators themselves often do not know the signification of the terms they employ."[7]

There are other barriers that separate the older experience from that offered here, preventing the latter from being more than a distorted reflection of the former. One can imagine a scene in which Hewitt sat with John Armstrong, trying to record the Seneca sounds and their meanings. Nowadays there are sound-recording machines that let us capture the sounds themselves, so that we can replay them at our leisure. No machines of that sort were available in the 1890s, and the only way to preserve sounds for later perusal was to convert them immediately into visual form: to transcribe them on the run with some kind of writing. Hewitt was quite good at that; he had, as we say, a "good ear."

But telling a story can be done properly only if the teller can follow a natural pace, not stopping after every phrase to give the transcriber time to record relatively unfamiliar sounds. Hewitt must often have asked for repetitions of individual words; he could not have transcribed them as accurately as he did after a single hearing. Armstrong, in short, could not speak in the flowing manner typical of more natural circumstances. There were various effects of this unnatural process. In Seneca there are numerous small words, or "particles," whose meanings are not essential to the ideas being communicated but which add to the overall effect in subtle ways, including linkages between ideas. We can only congratulate Armstrong for the use he did make of these particles, but more natural circumstances might have fostered an even richer deployment of them. Beyond that, the language Hewitt recorded shows a certain choppiness. Armstrong would state an idea, sometimes repeat it, and then move on to the next, not always with the smooth transitions characteristic of a more natural environment.

But of course the most obvious difference between the original and the translation is that they are in different languages. Seneca and English differ in many ways: not just in their sounds, but in the meanings associated with those sounds and in the ways those meanings are combined. Hewitt published his texts in a format that provided a word-by-word translation following each line of the Seneca. An example can be taken from the very beginning of the narrative. I have retranscribed the Seneca sounds in accordance with more modern practices, although I have not shown the transitions between words that are characteristic of fluent speech.

Ne:'	*gwa:h,*	*gyǫ'ǫh,*	*hadinǫge'*	*neh*
that	it seems	it is said	they dwell	the

sgę́ǫ́yadih		*neh*	*hęnǫ:gweh.*
on other side of the sky		the	they (m.) man-beings

Like the words of most languages, Seneca words convey two basically different kinds of meanings. Some express ideas of events or states (such as locations), or the participants in them:

hadinǫge'	they live, dwell
sgę́ǫ́yadih	on the other side of the sky
hęnǫ:gweh	people

In these three examples the English translations are relatively straightforward, although for the third word I have changed Hewitt's 'they (m.) man-beings' to simply 'people'. Hewitt was trying to capture the Seneca meaning accurately, and Seneca *hęnǫ:gweh* does indeed begin with the masculine plural prefix *hęn-*. Hewitt recorded that fact with the notation "they (m.)." Seneca practice, however, is to insert a masculine prefix whenever a group includes at least some men, even if there are women too. In other words *hęnǫ:gweh* does not limit the people concerned to males. Hewitt also believed that these people "belonged to a rather vague class, of which man was the characteristic type." He used the phrase "man-beings" to distinguish members of that vague class from ordinary people. The fact is, however, that the meaning of *hęnǫ:gweh* corresponds closely to the meaning of English *people,* and that is how I have translated it.

The translation of other words can be more problematic. As one of many examples, when the woman falls from the sky she encounters a rather mysterious celestial creature called Gá:šǫje:tha', who gives her food and the implements for preparing it. This word means literally 'it makes the fire fly', and Hewitt translated it 'Fire Dragon'. In the nineteenth century the same word was extended to lions in circuses who jumped through flaming hoops, but of course 'lion' would be inappropriate here. I retained Hewitt's Fire Dragon, although the connotations of 'dragon' are hardly more appropriate than those of 'lion'. There is no English equivalent.

Aside from numerous difficulties that arise in translating content words, the situation is no easier with the particles that serve to orient ideas in various subtle ways. They occur with great frequency, and it is not surprising that they make up five of the eight words in the sentence just quoted. In the following list I substitute my own translations for Hewitt's, but full equivalence in English is impossible to achieve:

ne:'	it is the case that
gwa:h	it seems
gyǫ'ǫh	it is said
neh	the (occurring twice)

Ne:' functions ubiquitously in Seneca to introduce an assertion. English offers no word at all like it, and any attempt to render it in a translation is bound to sound awkward. *Gwa:h* can be translated 'it seems', but it belongs to a range of expressions that show a speaker's attitude toward the validity of what he is saying, in this case a rather high likelihood that what he is saying is true. 'It really seems' might capture this meaning, but it would be jarring here. *Gyǫ'ǫh* is used when people convey information that was acquired, not from their own experience, but from something they were told by someone else. In a folktale it may be used in nearly every sentence, but its one occurrence here simply sets the story on the right course as something that was acquired through oral tradition. *Neh* occurs twice in this sentence, introducing both *sgéǫyadih* 'on the other side of the sky' and *hęnǫ:gweh* 'people'. In other contexts it can sometimes be translated with the English definite article 'the', but elsewhere it means something more like 'the following', a meaning that might be suggested in English with a colon. In this case it introduced the two ideas that amplified the verb *hadinǫge'* 'they dwell' by saying, first, that the dwelling was on the other side of the sky, and then that those who were dwelling there were people. As with *ne:'*, any attempt to capture it in English would be awkward.

Besides transcribing the sounds of Seneca words and adding word-by-word translations, Hewitt composed a running free translation, probably the only part that is read by most who consult his publication. Hewitt's free translations constitute a genre in themselves, uniquely interesting but far from natural English and not always easy to follow. In the present translation I have gone back to the original Seneca, consulting Hewitt where meanings were obscure. I aimed for greater readability and in some cases greater faithfulness to what I understand to have been the intent of the original speaker. Hewitt translated the first sentence of the story as follows: "There were, it seems, so it is said, man-beings dwelling on the other side of the sky." In trying thus to be faithful to the Seneca, he may have impeded to some extent the smooth flow of ideas. My own version is: "It seems there were people living on the other side of the sky." I believe this wording captures what was in John Armstrong's mind, to the extent that English can.

At times Hewitt amplified his free translation in order to clarify certain culturally obscure events. After a paragraph that described how the chief who was living above the sky felt depressed and jealous, Hewitt wrote: "So now this condition of things continued until the time that he, the Ancient, indicated that they, the people, should seek to divine his Word; that is, that they should have a dream feast for the purpose of ascertaining the secret yearning of his soul [produced by its own motion]." What was being said here is indeed difficult for an English-speaking reader to understand, but Hewitt's additions may not have made it much easier. At the heart of the problem is the Seneca word *aǫwǫwęníhsa:k,* which means literally 'they should look for his word', an idiomatic way of referring to the practice of dream-guessing, or interpreting a dream. Important to the Iroquois was the belief that a person's unconscious desires are manifested in dreams.[8] In the passage at hand the chief was inviting members of his community to use that method of determining what was bothering him. Hewitt used 'the Ancient' to translate the Seneca word *hagéhjih,* which is more or less equivalent to 'old man', although in Seneca more emphasis may be placed on maturity than on years. A chief, for example, would naturally belong to the class of people referred to in that way, as opposed to the younger and less mature class of warriors. With these considerations in mind, I replaced Hewitt's lengthy phrasing with the following: "It continued that way until the old man indicated that they should try to interpret his dream."

The reader unfamiliar with Native American oral literature should be prepared for what may seem to be inconsistencies or omissions in the narrative itself. The Western notion of consistency owes much to a literate tradition in which writing calls attention to things that are unnoticed when stories are transmitted orally. For example, there are several references here to "where there were people," but the creation of people was never described. When the woman from the sky world establishes the sun and the stars, it is said that she "stood outside," although we were not told that she lived in a house, and the establishment of dwellings on the earth was never mentioned.

But there are other devices that make this narrative effectively coherent. It may be noticed, for example, that the gifts of the Fire Dragon—the corn, the mortar and pestle, the pot, and the bone—are introduced at the beginning and then reappear twice at the end, when first the grandmother and then her grandson, following the same steps, establish the traditional Iroquois method of preparing food. The beginning and the end of the story are thus neatly tied together. I have added section headings that may aid the reader in following the progress of the whole. I hope that the overall effectiveness of this story will be evident, even if its language and context are those of another time, place, and culture.

A NOTE ON ORTHOGRAPHY AND PRONUNCIATION

In the spelling of Seneca words, vowels have the pronunciation typically given them in European languages such as Spanish, French, or German, except that ę and ǫ are nasalized vowels, like those in English *men* and *on* but pronounced through the nose. Accented vowels are pronounced with a higher pitch. The colon indicates a lengthened vowel. The apostrophe is used for a glottal stop, as in the middle of English *uh-oh.*

NOTES

1. Swanton, "John Napoleon Brinton Hewitt."
2. Rudes, *Tuscarora-English / English-Tuscarora Dictionary.*
3. Hewitt, "Polysynthesis in the Languages of the American Indians."
4. Brinton, "Characteristics of American Languages," 33–37.
5. Hewitt, *Iroquoian Cosmology,* first part.
6. Hewitt, *Iroquoian Cosmology,* second part.
7. Hewitt, *Iroquoian Cosmology,* first part, 133–34.
8. Anthony F. C. Wallace, "Dreams and the Wishes of the Soul."

SUGGESTED READING AND REFERENCES

Brinton, Daniel G. "Characteristics of American Languages." *The American Antiquarian* 16 (1894): 33–37.

Chafe, Wallace. *Seneca Thanksgiving Rituals.* Bureau of American Ethnology Bulletin 183. Washington DC: GPO, 1961.

———. *Seneca Morphology and Dictionary.* Smithsonian Contributions to Anthropology 4. Washington DC: GPO, 1967.

———. "Seneca Texts." In *Northern Iroquoian Texts,* edited by Marianne Mithun and Hanni Woodbury, 45–55, 96–103, 143–48. International Journal of American Linguistics Native American Text Series, no. 4. Chicago: University of Chicago Press, 1980.

———. "Sketch of Seneca, an Iroquoian Language." In *Handbook of North American Indians,* edited by William C. Sturtevant, vol. 17, *Languages,* edited by Ives Goddard, 225–53. Washington DC: Smithsonian Institution, 1996.

Hewitt, J. N. B. *Iroquoian Cosmology.* First part. Bureau of American Ethnology Annual Report 21. Washington DC: GPO, 1903.

———. "Polysynthesis in the Languages of the American Indians." *American Anthropologist* (old series) 6 (1893): 381–407.

———. *Iroquoian Cosmology.* Second part, with introduction and notes. Bureau of American Ethnology Annual Report 43. Washington DC: GPO, 1928.

Morgan, Lewis Henry. *League of the Ho-De'-No-Sau-Nee, Iroquois*. Rochester NY: Sage & Brother, 1851; reprint, under the title *League of the Iroquois*, New York: Corinth Books, 1962.

Rudes, Blair A. *Tuscarora-English / English-Tuscarora Dictionary*. Toronto: University of Toronto Press, 1999.

Swanton, John R. "John Napoleon Brinton Hewitt," *American Anthropologist* 40 (1938): 284–90.

Wallace, Anthony F. C. "Dreams and the Wishes of the Soul: A Type of Psychoanalytic Theory among the Seventeenth Century Iroquois." *American Anthropologist* 60 (1958): 234–48.

Seneca Creation Story

Told by John Armstrong
Translated by Wallace Chafe

ON THE OTHER SIDE OF THE SKY

It seems there were people living on the other side of the sky. And there in the middle of the town stood the house of the chief. There he had his family, his wife, and their one child, a girl.

The old man suddenly realized that he was beginning to feel sad. And then he became very thin. The reason for his unhappiness was the fact that they had a child. It seems that the circumstances were such that he may have been jealous. It continued that way until the old man indicated that they should try to interpret his dream. So they all assembled, and they kept trying to discover what it was that he desired. After a while one of them said, "Now I may have interpreted the excrement of our chief. His desire may be for this tree to be uprooted, this tree close to his dwelling."

"Thank you," said the chief.

Then they said, "Let us all help each other as we uproot this tree. Let a few take hold of each root."

So they uprooted it and set it aside. The earth fell through where they had uprooted it, leaving a hole. They all looked, and it was strangely green down below. When they had had their turns at looking, the chief said to his wife, "Come, let us go and look."

So she put her child on her back, and he made his way there with difficulty, walking slowly. They arrived at the hole, and the chief himself looked. When he was tired of it, he said, "You look next."

"Oh dear," she said. "I'm afraid."

"Come and do it," he said. "Look!"

So she took the clothing she wore in her mouth, and she leaned down on her right hand, and she leaned down on her other hand too—she held on with both hands, and she looked down below. As soon as she bent her head, he took hold of her leg and threw her down.

THE FALL

So then she was falling. Floating there was the White Fire Dragon, and it was he of whom the old man was jealous. He took an ear of corn and gave it to her. She took it and placed it in her bosom. Next he took a small mortar and a pestle and gave them both to her. Next he took from his bosom a small pot. Then he gave her a bone. And he said, "This is what you will be eating."

The way it was below, there were beings with magic power—the White Fire Dragon, the Wind, and the Dark Night.

Then the creatures down below held a council. They said, "We may not be able to help the woman who is falling."

Each one spoke, saying, "Perhaps I could help her."

Bass said, "Perhaps I could."

They said, "You certainly can't, because you don't have any sense."

Next Pike said, "Perhaps I could."

And again they said, "You certainly can't, because you're a glutton."

Then next Turtle spoke, saying, "Perhaps I could help the woman."

And they all agreed. So Turtle floated directly to where the woman was falling, and she landed there on Turtle.

THE EARTH

Then the woman wept. After a while she remembered that she was holding some earth. She opened her hands and scattered it on Turtle. As soon as she did that, the earth increased in size. So then she scattered a lot of it, and soon the earth became very large. She noticed that she was the one who was making the earth.

So she kept traveling about. She knew that as she traveled, things were growing. Before long bushes were growing, and all kinds of plants. Before long she saw potato vines.

Then she stood outside and said, "Now there will be a heavenly body called the sun."

Indeed in the morning the sun appeared, moving toward the west. When it set, it became dark.

Then again she stood outside and said, "Now there will be stars in the sky."

That is what happened. Then as she was standing outside she pointed, saying, "The stars will have names. Certain stars in the north will be called They Are Chasing a Bear."

Next she said, "There will be a large star that will rise when it is nearly day; it will be called It Brings the Day."

Then she pointed again and said, "That group of stars will be called the Pleiades. It will show the time of year. It will be called They Are Dancing. Still another one will be She Is Sitting. And it will accompany the Pleiades. It will be called Stretched Out Beaver Skin. When people go forth at night, they will look at it."

Later the old woman said, "Far away there will be people living. And beavers will be living too, where there are rivers."

That is what happened, because the voice of the old woman was good.

THE CONCEPTION AND BIRTH OF THE TWINS

After a while the old woman's daughter had grown. And there were lots of woods. Nearby was a tree where the girl played, swinging on it. When she got tired she came down and knelt in the grass. It gave her great pleasure when the wind entered her; she noticed it when the wind entered her body. It gave her pleasure.

After a while the old woman looked at her and thought, "It looks as if my daughter's body is not alone."

"Aha," she said. "Didn't you see someone?"

"No," said the girl.

Then the old woman said, "It appears that you are going to give birth."

The girl said, "When I knelt down there, I felt the wind enter my body."

The old woman said, "If that is so, it is uncertain what our fortune will be."

Soon there were two children growing in the girl's body, and they were arguing. They said, "You will be the older one."

"No, you," they said.

Now the one who was very ugly, covered with warts, said, "You will be born first."

The other said, "No, you."

The warty one said, "You will be born first."

"All right," said the other. "You will endure your fate."

"All right," said the warty one.

And the older one was born. Soon the old woman noticed that there was another one still to be born. When the first one had been born only a short time, the next was born. The two had been born only a short time when their mother died. The warty one emerged from his mother's navel.

Then the old woman wept. Before long she attended to the twins. When she had finished, she made a hole nearby and placed her dead child in it, with her head toward the west. And she talked to her, saying, "Now you have set out on the path from the earth to the sky. When you arrive in the sky, you will prepare a place to live and a place for us to come also."

Then she covered it. It was left for her to care for the twins, the two children.

THE FIRST TWIN VISITS HIS FATHER

After another period of time the two had grown and were running about. Finally the older one, now a young man, asked a question. He asked his grandmother, "Grandmother, where is my father? And who is my father? Where does he live?"

The old woman said, "Your father is the wind. From whatever direction the wind is blowing, that is the direction of your father's house."

"All right," said the young man.

Then he stood outside and watched the direction from which the wind was blowing. And he said, "I need to see my father, because he could help me." He said, "The house of my father, the wind, lies in that direction. I will help him make all the animals, and he will help me in all other ways."

So he set out. He hadn't gone far when he saw where his father's house was. Then he arrived where the man lived, with four children, two male and two female. He said, "Now I have arrived. Father, I need you to help me. What I need are the game animals and certain other things."

All of them were pleased to see him. The old man, their father, said, "All right. I will do what you want in coming here. But first I want you, my children, to amuse yourselves by running a race. I have a flute that you will enjoy competing for. You will circle the earth, taking this flute with you."

So they stood at the starting line. The young man said, "I want the False Face to stand here in order to help me."

So that is what happened; the False Face stood there. Then the young man said, "You must go fast, and I will follow in your tracks."

So that is what happened. The two were always in the lead as they circled the earth. As they ran, the young man followed in the fast tracks of the False Face. Soon they made the circuit, easily beating the other two.

Then the one who carried the flute gave it to his father. The old man took it and said, "Now indeed you have won everything you wanted me to do for you."

He laid down his bundle, a bag that was heavy and full. And he gave the bundle to his son who had come from elsewhere, and he gave him the flute, and he said, "This will belong to you and your younger brother."

THE ANIMALS

So the young man took up the bundle and put it on his back. As he traveled, he got tired and it weighed him down. So he thought, "Maybe I should rest. And this belongs to me."

So he opened and uncovered it. As soon as he opened it, there was a lot of pushing, and they emerged, all the animals his father had given him. He was surprised to see them all emerging. That is what happened as soon as he opened it all the way. And they trampled on him there.

The last to emerge was the fawn, and he shot it. He hit it on its front leg, a little above its hoof, but it escaped from him. Then he said, "It will always be that way with you. You will never be able to recover. And the fat in it will always be a medicine, a good medicine. When anyone has sore eyes, they will apply a compress with it, and they will recover."

So then he set out again. He arrived back at the place where their house was, and he talked to his younger brother, Flint, saying, "Look what our father has given us."

Then he arrived back at his grandmother's, and he said, "I have returned from my father's. He granted me something important."

He sat down and examined it, thinking, "Let me examine them. Now, you go outside. You will hear what a great sound is made by all the animals."

So they went out, and they heard the loud noise made by all the animals. Then the grandmother, the old woman, stood up and spoke, saying, "Here will stand the one to be called the elk. And here will stand another that is a little smaller; this one will be called the deer. Next another will stand here; it will be called the bear. And next another will stand here; it will be called the buffalo. That is how many large game animals there are. As soon as people live here, those will be their names. When people live here, they will refer to all the animals with names."

Then the young man said, "I want there to be a ditch that will be full of oil." And that is what happened.

Then he said, "Let the buffalo come here." Soon it stood there, and he said, "Dive in there." And that is what happened. It came out fat on the other side.

Then he said, "Let the bear come next." Soon the bear stood there. And he said, "You dive into the oil next." And that is what happened. It came out fat on the other side.

Then he said, "How will you help people?"

"I will run away," it said.

So he put meat in its legs. Now its legs are big.

Then he said, "Next the deer will stand here." As soon as it stood there, he said, "Dive into this oil." It jumped in and came out on the other side, and it was fat.

And he said, "How will you help people?"

"I will not run away," it said.

He said, "What will you do?"

"I will bite them," it said.

So the young man said, "This is how it will be with you." And he removed its upper teeth. Then he said, "The buffalo, and the elk, and those with horns will all share in this change." That is why they don't have upper teeth.

All the small animals—the raccoon, the woodchuck, the porcupine, and the skunk all jumped in there—they all dove in. Those are the ones that were accepted.

Next came those that were not accepted—the fisher, the otter, the mink, and the weasel. They were the ones that were set aside, and they assembled nearby. Then the mink jumped into the oil. As soon as he came out, the young man caught him and held him up and stripped him through his hands, and that is why he became somewhat longer. And that is what happened. The fisher, and the otter, and the mink, and the weasel shared in this change.

Next the wolf, and the wildcat, and the fox were all set aside.

THE FATE OF THE SECOND TWIN

So then the two boys kept going off. Every day they went somewhere, setting traps far away. Every day they went off. And they came to be hated by those who had evil power. They had been going off together, but one day the older one said, "You go alone for now. Look by yourself at the traps we have set." And that is what happened.

When the younger one was far away, those with evil power killed him. Then the older one noticed that they had killed his younger brother, and he wept. When it affected him most, when he was weeping, there was the sound "ęh, ęh, ęh, ęh" in the sky.

Then those with evil power became afraid. They said, "It may be that soon, when he weeps a lot, the sky will fall. It is better that his younger brother come back to life."

Then the young man became ashamed, because many people noticed that he was weeping. So he closed up his house, all the places where there were openings. When he had finished closing them up, his brother Flint spoke outside, saying, "Older brother, I have returned."

The older one said from inside, "You can't come in. Just leave. Set out on the path taken by our mother. That is where your tracks will be. Follow our mother's tracks. Sit down not far from here and watch how people live on the earth. Where you are sitting the path will divide. One way will lead to God, and one way will lead to the devil. And you will have servants who live in caves. Take this flute, and keep blowing it. When people's breath ends, they will hear the flute speaking."

FOOD

After a while the young man wondered, thinking, "Why is it that my grandmother doesn't eat potatoes?"

Then he asked her, saying, "Grandmother, why is it that you don't eat potatoes?"

"I am by myself when I eat," she said. "I do eat them."

Then he decided, "I will watch her as soon as it is night."

So he made a hole in his clothing. Then he lay down, pretending to be asleep. But he was looking out through the hole. As he lay there he was looking through the hole in his blanket, looking at where his grandmother was sitting. Then the old woman went out. She looked toward the east. The morning star had risen. She said, "Now I will take the pot from the fire."

So she took the pot from the fire and put the potatoes in a bowl. There was just one helping. Then she rummaged through a bag she had and took out corn. She parched it, and it popped. There was quite a pile of it. Then she took out a small mortar. She kept striking it, and it grew until it was just the right size. Then she took the pestle from her bag. Again she kept striking it, and it grew also. Then she pounded the parched corn and made meal. She went to her bag again and took out a small pot, and she kept striking it, and it grew also. Then she hung the pot over the fire and made mush. As soon as it was done, she rummaged in her bag again and took out a bone, a beaver bone, and scraped it. She poured the scrapings into the pot, and immediately there was fat floating on the mush. Then she took the pot from the fire and ate. And the young man went to sleep.

When it was morning, the old woman set out again to dig potatoes. As soon as she was out of sight, the young man went to the place where his grandmother stayed and began to rummage through her things. He took out an ear of corn that had only a few kernels on it, maybe three and a half rows. Then he began to shell the corn and finished all of it. Then he parched it and it popped, and there was quite a pile of it, quite a large amount. Then he rummaged again. He took out the small mortar and the pestle. He used the pestle to strike with, and both of them grew. Then he poured the parched corn into the mortar and pounded it, and it became meal. Then he looked in her bag again and took out the small pot. He used something else to strike it with, and it grew also. Then he hung up the pot and put water in it, and he poured all the meal into it. So he made mush. Then he looked in his grandmother's bag again. He took out the bone and put it in the water, and the mush expanded.

"Ah," he said, "it tastes good."

Soon his grandmother returned. She said, "What are you doing?"

"I have made mush," said the young man. "And it's very good. Eat it, Grandmother. There is a lot of mush."

Then she wept. She said, "I think you have killed me. That is all I had."

"Oh dear, that's not good," he said. "It makes you feel bad. I will get more corn and bone."

The next day he made preparations, and when he was ready, he said, "Now I will leave." And so he set out, and he arrived where people lived. When he approached the village, he got ready. From his bow he made a deer, and then from his arrow he made a wolf. Then he said, "When you run through the village, one of you will come close to catching up with the other." Next he made himself into an old man. Then he arrived at the house where people lived. Some time after he arrived they gave him food. While he was eating they heard the wolf coming, barking. It was evidently chasing something. So they all went outside. They saw the wolf chasing the deer, and it nearly caught it. They all ran toward it, and so the old man was eating all alone. As soon as they had gone, he jumped over to where strings of corn were hanging. He took two strings, put them over his shoulder, and left. He was running far away when they noticed it, but they did not chase him at all. He arrived home and threw it down where his grandmother was sitting. "Here," he said. "Do as you like with this. Maybe you will decide to plant some of it."

The next day he said, "All right, I will go and kill a beaver." Then he went to the river where his grandmother had said beavers would be plentiful. When he arrived there, he saw where the beavers' lodge was. Then he saw one standing, and he shot and killed it. He put it on his back and set out. After a while he arrived at their house, and he did the same thing again. He threw it down where his grandmother was sitting. "Here," he said.

"Thank you," said the old woman.

MENSTRUATION

So then they skinned the beaver outside, helping each other with its body. When they were nearly finished there was blood on the hide. So the old woman took a handful of the blood and threw it at her grandson's groin.

"Hah," the old woman said. "Now, my grandson, you will menstruate."

"Nonsense," said the young man. "It won't be happening to us males. But it will be happening to you females every month."

Then he took another handful of clotted blood, and he threw it between his grandmother's legs, and he said, "Now you will menstruate."

Then the old woman wept, saying, "How long will it last?"

The young man said, "As many days as there are spots on the fawn. That is how long it will last."

Then the old woman wept again. And she said, "I can't accept that."

"How many then?" he said.

"I would accept as many as there are stripes on the chipmunk's back," she said.

"All right," said the young man. And he said, "She will stay outside for four days. Then as soon as she has washed all her clothes, she will return to where her family is staying."

HILLS AND RIVERS

After a while the old woman said, "There will be hills on the earth." And that is what happened. "And there will be rivers on the earth," she said also. And that is what happened.

THE RETURN TO THE SKY WORLD

Then the young man said, "Now I think we should return home. We should go to the place my mother has prepared, and there we should stay."

"All right," said the old woman.

So he and his grandmother left, and went on high. And that is the end.

Oneida

The Origins of Man

Introduction by Herbert S. Lewis

Andrew Beechtree was one of approximately fifteen Wisconsin Oneida men and women who participated in a unique WPA project from 1938 through March 1942. These people were hired to collect and record linguistic, folkloric, historical, auto-biographical, and ethnographic material from their own culture and society. Working under the direction of university students who acted as supervisors or foremen, they were given the opportunity to write down their own accounts and to record those given to them by their relatives, friends, and neighbors. Conceived and begun as the Oneida Language and Folklore Project (see Hauptman 1981), by the time Andrew Beechtree wrote down this story in March 1941, it had been converted into the Oneida Ethnological Study. This enterprise included record-ing history, autobiography, and accounts of contemporary Oneida life in all its aspects.

All the participants were bilingual speakers of both Oneida and English, and those taking part in the language study were taught to write down accounts pho-nemically in the Oneida language and to analyze them for translation. (They were trained by Floyd Lounsbury, the project's first supervisor, who at the time was an undergraduate student at the University of Wisconsin in Madison.) For the ethnological study they usually wrote directly in English, as Andrew Beechtree seems to have done with his account of the creation of the world.

Like most of the participants in the project, Andrew Beechtree had received his education at boarding schools for the training of Indians. He attended schools on the Wisconsin Oneida reservation, in Tomah, Wisconsin, and the famous Car-lisle Indian Boarding School in central Pennsylvania. He completed twelve years of study, but as he points out ruefully in an autobiographical account, Carlisle was stronger on training in the "practical arts," work, and extra-curricular ac-tivity than it was on academics. His own special subjects were carpentry and "me-chanical arts," which prepared him to begin work at the Ford Motor Company in Detroit in 1917. Like many of his contemporaries, he worked at various jobs in industry (in Detroit, Milwaukee, Green Bay, and elsewhere) until the start of the Great Depression in 1929, after which he was laid off, could not find work, and depended on WPA projects and relief for most of his living.

Keenly aware of the limitations of his education, Andrew Beechtree evidently did a lot of reading on his own, and he was pleased to be working on the WPA project, which offered him an opportunity to learn, speculate, and write, as well as to earn enough money to scrape by during the Depression. This narrative is the product of his researches and of his appreciation for both the Oneida and the English language.[1]

THE WISCONSIN ONEIDAS

The Oneidas of Wisconsin are members of one branch of the Oneida Nation of the Six Nations of the Iroquois Confederacy. About 1822 their ancestors left New York for the area southwest of Green Bay, Wisconsin, impelled by the disturbed conditions in their New York State homeland and induced by the offer of money with which to buy land from the Menominees. By the time they migrated, most of the Oneidas were Christian, primarily Episcopalian or Methodist. Most could not speak English at that time, but they attended church services and heard the sermons of white missionary preachers translated into their language by skilled Oneida interpreters. By the time this account of the origins of man was written down, the Oneidas had been Christians for more than 150 years and their lives, activities, and thought were deeply influenced by their new faith. It is no surprise that biblical and Christian elements and language readily enter this narrative. On the other hand, much of the story has its genesis in Iroquois tradition that predates the coming of the Europeans to their land.

It appears that by 1941 this tale was not viewed as a source of power, nor did it have deep meaning to the Oneidas of Wisconsin at that time. As Beechtree notes at the start, "There are now not many Oneida interested enough in their race to retain this old legend." By then few young people were interested in the Oneida language or traditions.[2] (This does not mean, however, that they did not regard themselves fully as Indians or Iroquois; they certainly did. But they were more interested in modern ways of being Oneida, doing such things as singing Christian hymns in the Oneida language, engaging in sports, and working responsibly at skilled wage labor, often in groups with other Indians.) But Andrew Beechtree, like many of those working with him on the project, was interested in Oneida tradition, and he seems delighted to be telling good stories and drawing morals and history lessons from them.

ANDREW BEECHTREE'S ACCOUNT

The author says that he has built his account out of "those bits of information which I have been able to gather here and there." This text is his creative retelling of numerous stories with his own imagery and sense of morality and history.

Although it contains some of the episodes and themes detailed in Hewitt's great collection of Onondaga, Mohawk, and Seneca accounts (see Chafe, this volume), and although he was aware of Hewitt's account, there is much that is different in Beechtree's telling of the story. His narrative is different from the others in both outline and detail, and it even diverges considerably from the Oneida version from Ontario, told by Demus Elm and Harvey Antone (2000). (Robert Ritzenthaler, doing fieldwork with the Oneidas in Wisconsin during the same year that Andrew Beechtree was writing this story, recorded a brief and rather different version of the creation story from an elder, Aaron House, who may also have contributed something to Beechtree's stock of information. William A. House apparently contributed other episodes, including how the earth was "rewashed" [Ritzenthaler 1950].)

The Beechtree account contains the following major elements of the "ancient" Iroquois creation story.

1. There is a preexisting sky world from which a woman is expelled because of actual or suspected wicked (sexual) behavior.
2. The woman falls through a hole in the sky into a watery world, where she is saved and aided by aquatic animals that are also responsible for the creation of the land.
3. Twin boys, one good and one evil, are born to the woman, who then dies.
4. The competition of the twins creates the good and the bad things on the earth (Ritzenthaler 1950, 43; Wonderley 2000, 27).

Andrew Beechtree takes his tale well beyond this basic outline, however, with those "bits of information gathered here and there" and with his own love of language and imagination.[3]

The author apparently wrote the narrative in English, but he introduced quite a few Oneida words into the text, including a number of complicated literal translations followed by simpler English equivalents. For example, according to Andrew Beechtree *élhal* or *lolhalé·* is translated 'he is prepared and waiting', and its English meaning is 'dog'. *Ya·dliyós* is glossed as 'they kill each other' and then 'fighters'. In some cases I have edited out the Oneida word or at least cut the literal interpretations, because they complicate more than they inform and they tend to bog down the story. They have been left in when they seem to add something interesting. Otherwise editorial intervention has been limited to changing some punctuation, correcting the inevitable slips of the pencil that crop up in any manuscript, and changing occasional words for clarity or accuracy. On rare occasions I have made minor changes in word order for ease of reading or to eliminate redundancy. With these slight modifications, the words and the voice are those of Andrew Beechtree throughout.

A NOTE ON ORTHOGRAPHY AND PRONUNCIATION

Oneida words tend to be very long compared to those of English; in fact they usually represent phrases rather than distinct single words as in English. While few of the sounds recorded in this text offer problems for English speakers, the clusters and combinations of sounds may be difficult. The vowel sounds are the same as those noted by Chafe for Seneca, sounded more or less as in Italian or Spanish, with the addition of ^, which represents a nasalized vowel, as in English *bun,* but pronounced through the nose. The ? symbol in a word represents a glottal stop, as in English *uh-oh.* In several words there is an *h*—an aspirated sound as in *here* that is found in words where English would never have it. A dot after a vowel indicates a lengthened vowel, and an accent mark indicates a stressed syllable.

NOTES

1. The material from the "Oneida Language and Folklore Project" has been in continuous use by the Oneidas and by linguists and other scholars since it was first spoken and written down. The much larger body of material from the "Oneida Ethnological Study" lay forgotten in a carton in the basement storeroom of the anthropology department at the University of Wisconsin from 1948 until 1998. This amnesia was at least partly due to the sudden death of H. Scudder Mekeel, who was caring for the original notebooks and maps. (The whereabouts of two of the three copies of typed transcriptions of these materials is still unknown.) A series of fortunate coincidences led me to them and to their identification. Thanks are due in particular to James B. Stoltman, Harold C. Conklin, and Clifford Abbott.

2. Sixty years later there are only a few native speakers of the language left, and almost all are elders. Some people study the language at the University of Wisconsin–Green Bay and through a language program offered by the Oneida Nation, but it gets more and more difficult to preserve a self-sustaining Oneida language community.

3. In fact Beechtree's narrative has three parts, and he carries his story through the beginnings of society and on into historical time. Only the first part and the beginning of the second are included here, however, because as he continues, the account becomes less literary and storylike and more an attempt at etymological and historical speculation.

SUGGESTED READING AND REFERENCES

Campisi, Jack, and Laurence M. Hauptman, eds. 1988. *The Oneida Experience.* Syracuse: Syracuse University Press.

Elm, Demus, and Harvey Antone. 2000. *The Oneida Creation Story.* Translated and edited by Floyd G. Lounsbury and Bryan Gick. Lincoln: University of Nebraska Press.

Hauptman, Laurence. 1981. *The Iroquois and the New Deal.* Syracuse: Syracuse University Press.

———. *The Iroquois Struggle for Survival: World War II to Red Power.* Syracuse: Syracuse University Press.

Hauptman, Laurence, and L. Gordon McLester III. 1999. *The Oneida Journey: From New York to Wisconsin, 1784–1860.* Madison: University of Wisconsin Press.

Ritzenthaler, Robert E. 1950. "The Oneida Indians of Wisconsin." *Bulletin of the Public Museum of the City of Milwaukee* 19 (1): 1–52.

Wonderley, Anthony. 2000. "The Elm-Antone Creation Story in Comparative and Historical Context." In *The Oneida Creation Story*, by Demus Elm and Harvey Antone, translated and edited by Floyd G. Lounsbury and Bryan Gick, 7–27. Lincoln: University of Nebraska Press.

The Origins of Man

Told by Andrew Beechtree

There are now not many Oneidas interested enough in their race to retain this old legend, so I shall try to reconstruct it, taking for my material those bits of information that I have been able to gather here and there from the people whom I have contacted in my work as an interviewer and gatherer of information.

THE STORY

It seems that at one time those we now know as people lived only in the blue sky. What we now know as the world was only a vast expanse of water inhabited by such water-loving animals as beaver, turtle, muskrat, mink, and others.

The home in the blue sky was under the rulership of a father and his son. In the course of time the son became envious of the worship paid to the father. Therefore, he sought means whereby he could command the admiration of some of the subjects, who were all women.

He became evil. He did it on the sly at first, but as more of the women gathered about him and laughed and did not disapprove of his actions, he became bolder. Finally he became openly disobedient and defiant of his father's wishes. Several times he was verbally reprimanded. The climax had to come because the son would not reform.

One time the ruler went away to inspect some of his other creations, as he often did. As usual he put his son in charge of his place. While the father was away the son invented a weird musical instrument. This instrument was known as *gaye nigalhzo dalhu* (four thongs spanned over something). It is said that the evil son caught a purring cat, killed it, and cut its intestines into fine strips and used that as sound-producing vibrators fastened over a support. By passing another string across these it produced a long moan or wail.

The sound, or a combination of sounds, or music, which this instrument emitted, seemed to create evil sensations and thoughts in the listeners. He now sought to entertain his subjects by playing on this instrument. The bad part of this instrument was that it was played with the fingers, and words could be added by the player to further stimulate the sensuality of the listeners. With this new invention they were having great revelry. They were singing bawdy songs, and some of the women were doing suggestive dances, forsaking their former teaching and their other duties.

In the midst of this revelry the good king returned and beheld the madhouse. This exhausted his patience, and in just anger he told his son and his adherents that they would have to get out of his kingdom. He caused a hole to appear in the surface of the place where they were, and into this chasm he cast them, to live in the dark space below, outside the home of the good people.

The people now lived in two regions. Their original home became known as Galuhyage (On the Blue Sky). This place was still ruled by the good king Lowni·yÓ (God; His Word Is Good). The other and newer region became known as Onihsuh-lolu·ge (The Place of the Covered Hole). This place became governed by the out-cast son, who was now known as La²niguhláks^ (The Evil Minded).

In the course of time one of the outcast women became pregnant by the wicked ruler. As the time of her confinement approached and she gave consideration to her present circumstances, she began to regret her past actions, mostly on account of her unborn child. At last she appeared humbly before the entrance of her former home and pleaded with Lowni·yÓ to forgive her and take her back into his kingdom for the sake of her child, which was soon to be born.

He kindly listened to her pleading, and when she had finished he told her to come back later when he will have given her request his earnest consideration. When she returned some time later he told her that he would forgive her, but he could not let her reenter his kingdom before she gave birth to her child. Inasmuch as she was conceived by the Evil Minded, her child might be imbued with evil tendencies. If she had such a child in his kingdom, then the seeds of evil would again be planted in his kingdom, his Laowezclagu (His Place of Happiness). He told her if she was in earnest in her repentance she should agree to live on the Ohwajage (Light on the Sea; earth), which he would create upon the waters and where her mother, her children, and herself would be placed for a period of probation. Her mother was included because Lowni·yÓ wanted the penitent to reenter his kingdom, and the only way for her to reenter his kingdom from this earth would be by way of the death of the body, at which time the spirit, the true person, would leave this vale of trials, and at which time those who were good on the earth would reenter the home of their original father.

Lowni·yÓ had foreseen that the Evil Minded might be angry with her, who had renounced him, and he would cause her to die at this, her ordeal. The grandmother would then have the care of the child or children. The pregnant woman gladly accepted any penance as long as she was assured that she would be allowed, at some time, to reenter *uwez^cla·gú*, or heaven.

Now Lowni·yÓ, or God, caused a beam of light to be cast upon the dark waters wherein lived the water animals. As this beam of light shone upon the waters, the animals, shyly at first, came to investigate. They looked, and they saw flying about in this beam of light this woman who had come to redeem her soul and her mother.

One of the animals asked what they wanted. He was told that she was looking for a nestling place on which to bear her young. When they learned of this, they held a council to decide what was to be done to help the unfortunate *yeluhyaʔ·gehlo·lú* (inhabitant of the blue sky; angel). The animals thought she was an angel because the beam of light radiated from heaven and she seemed to have traveled down on this beam of light.

Finally the turtle said, "I will float my body upon the surface of the water, and one of you dive deep down and see if you can get some sediment or mud. Bring it up and put it on me, and it will make a soft place for her to settle on." The muskrat said, "I will volunteer to get that mud," and with these words he dove into the water. After a while he returned and said, "I could not find any mud." The mink looked at him scornfully and then said, "I will resume the attempt." And down he went. He was gone such a long time that the other animals had almost given up hopes of ever seeing him again. At last his body reappeared. He was almost dead, but his mouth was full of the boggy substance, as were also his paws.

The animals quickly took this substance and put it on top of the turtle's back, and with his tail the beaver spread the mud out nicely on the turtle's back. To their surprise, the supply multiplied faster than the beaver was able to spread it, until there was enough to cover the whole of the large turtle's back. (All these animals were very large at that time.)

As the beam of light was shining and heating the sediment, it quickly dried and became earth, or land. And as the light and heat continued, there sprouted from the ground vegetation, marsh grass having long and bladelike leaves. The beaver cut some of these down and placed them in such a manner as to form a mat. The woman landed on her feet on this mat. There they waited for the coming event. Hunger and work were not known to the two women at that time because the animals had acknowledged them as a superior creation, and the privilege to supply them with food was considered a great honor.

It so happened that this young woman was carrying twins. Even before they were born, it was evident that they were opposites. One was fair and good, like his mother, and the other was ugly and evil-minded, like his father. The body of the ugly one was covered with scabs or scales, and on his head was a row of horny sawtooth projections running from the front to the back. The fair one wanted to be born in a natural manner, but the ugly one wanted to cut his mother open in the flank and get out that way. As the fair one would not agree with the ugly one, the ugly one said, "All right, but you must go first and I will come later." So the fair one was properly born, but in spite of his promises the ugly one cut his mother open in her side with his jagged head and came out that way.[1]

Of course the mother died, and dying under these circumstances her spiritual self was readily permitted to reenter the kingdom of Lowni·yÓ. Lowni·yÓ had always felt sorry for those of his children he was forced to cast out. Now he had found a way for them to earn his forgiveness and a chance to reenter the place where there is no sorrow or tomorrow. Thereafter all requests for forgiveness were granted on the same basis as the first. And like the first two mothers and two sons, all other people may choose the good or the bad.

At the death of the mother it became the duty of the grandmother to raise the boys. All through early life the boys differed in action and policy. This opposition continued into the time when they were able to create things and conditions.

The Fair One created food plants; the Evil One created insects to eat up the plants. The good one created food animals such as rabbits and deer; the Evil One created snakes, lizards, and rodents. The Evil One created a dragon to live in the ocean where Lowni·yÓ had created the fishes. The good one created the Thunderer to smite the dragon with his lightning bolt whenever the dragon came out of the water to devour the fishermen. The good one created springs from which to water his plants and his animals; the bad one polluted the waters with the blood of dead animals, poisoning the fishes and many animals. (The time when these things happen is what is known as the dog days of the summer.) The good one had to create rivers to drain off this polluted water.

The good one created day birds with their pretty colors and melodious voices; the bad one created voiceless bats and the eerie sounding owl. The good one created the faithful dog; the bad one created the sly fox. Most of the animals created by the bad one were sneaky and destructive.

One day, as the Fair One returned from the south, where he harvested the seeds during autumn, he could not find the animals, and the people's bodies were strewn around. And all the land about was covered with a white substance. Even the trees seemed dead. Finally he found the swift-running rabbit. The rabbit, all nervous, huddled under a bush. He asked the rabbit where all the animals were. The rabbit (*o'cugalo·lÚ* 'split lip') got his lip split open when he was trying to escape from the Evil One. That is why he is so timid. His and the deer's tail were also lost during several close escapes from the Evil One. The rabbit said the Evil One had caught most of them and had placed them in a cave that he, the bad one, had dug. He asked the rabbit what had happened to the people. The rabbit said that the Big Mosquito, which the Evil One had created, had stung the people and they had become unconscious and helpless. The Fair One placed a number of these people's

1. Henceforth in the account they are referred to as "the Fair One" (or "the good one") and "the Evil One."

bodies together and covered them with his fire and bark, which protected them from this freezing and icy cold.

This made the Fair One exceedingly angry. He now went in search of the Evil One, who was running away and hiding. The white substance stayed on the ground during the time that the Fair One chased the Evil One and until after the fight. He chased him for the length of winter.

When he found the Evil One, he talked harshly to him and told him that he would have to undo this—his last unlawful act. The Evil One spoke right back at every command of the Fair One, so that it now became a quarrel. Like most heated quarrels it developed into a desire for combat, so they agreed to fight. They agreed for each one to chose his own weapons.

The Fair One asked the Evil One what he desired to use as a weapon. The Evil One considered awhile until he noticed that the Fair One was shivering, shaking from violent emotion. He mistook that agitation of emotion as shivering from the effects of the cold white substance around about at their feet. So he thought that by putting a lot of that white substance on the Fair One it would cause him to become frozen and hurt. So he said, "I will take from my creation this white substance, which I desire to use as a weapon. What will you use?" Now the Fair One thought of a tree. So the Fair One said, "From all my creation I desire to choose a branch of a tree." So next they set a time at which they were to begin the fight. In the meantime they stored up a supply of their weapons.

The Evil One made balls of snow. Actually he made light or puffy spheres to hit the Fair One. He made many of these snowballs. The Fair One took branches from a tree and formed them into missiles, which acted like boomerangs. He made a number of these but not many. The prearranged time for the duel arrived, and the fighters arrived on the field of battle. The Evil One hurriedly threw these snowballs at the Fair One. As the snowballs flew in a direct line, the Fair One easily dodged them, and those that did hit him just squashed or broke into pieces. Now the Fair One threw his weapon, but instead of throwing it directly at the Evil One, he threw it way off to one side. The Evil One thought, "He'll never hit me by throwing it way off like that" and continued throwing snowballs, his eyes on the Fair One all the time. The bent club was so made that it made a wide circle and if no object obstructed its path it would return to where it started from, and as it traveled through the air it whistled along. Also, as this club flew through the air, it created a violent motion in the air, the snowflakes twirling about, and caused a blizzard.

The branched sticks that the Fair One had thrown suddenly came around and crashed square into the Evil One. Of course the object broke so that it was useless, and the Evil One could not pick it up and throw it back. However, it produced enough force to cause seams or cracks in his armor of ice, an invisible crystal glaze. The Fair One threw another stick. The Evil One was able to dodge this and also several more. But those he did dodge flew back to the thrower. When he was struck the third time, his covering scattered and fell off. The fourth blow laid him low. When the Fair One came up to him, he saw that the Evil One was dead.

Some of the swiftest animals, like the deer, had been onlookers on this scene of battle, and they, too, had now come up. The Fair One now looked at his weapons and became exceedingly proud of them. Now he fondled them and was about to place them on the ground and then he thought better of it. He looked about and saw the beautiful deer (*osganudú* from *osga·wá yau·dú* 'branches attached') standing there. He went up to him and said, "I would like to preserve these weapons by placing them on your head. I know you will go far displaying this, an article that was useful in preserving the land."

The Evil One, covered with ice, was just left lying there, and the Fair One hurriedly went to awaken the people. Next he went about dispersing the clouds that had covered the land so that the sunlight could make summertime. Next he breathed new life into the animals that were buried. And now he decided to chase and kill the Big Biter, or Big Mosquito, for having bitten and paralyzed his people. For a weapon he took a blade of marsh grass and caused it to become so tough that he could use it as a sword.

He now called the burro and said to him, "Will you help me chase the big monster, the mosquito?" The burro said, "I will. Get on my back and I will carry you wherever you want me to." When he got on the burro's back, the dog was there prepared and waiting. He said, "Master, I would like to help you." The Fair One said, "What can you do?" The dog said, "I can tell you where Big Mosquito went by smelling along its trail on the ground."

When the sun arose from where it reappears, the east, they started out on the hunt. Soon the dog took up the tracks of Big Mosquito, and the Fair One followed on his burro, or donkey. Every so often the dog barked. As the light receded toward the west ("where the wall is"), it was not long before they knew that Big Mosquito was going west to keep in the darkness. They soon caught up to Big Mosquito. Then the fight started. The mosquito would fight back awhile and then run away. The Fair One kept cutting and thrusting with his sword into this monster. As they struggled, the blood of the monster flew in every direction. These blood drops became the little mosquitoes.

The Fair One and Big Mosquito were so supernaturally powerful that wherever they struggled they made large depressions in the earth. The water that filled these huge depressions has formed the Great Lakes. In the vicinity of the Great Lakes, the Fair One killed Big Mosquito. The Fair One knew of the great wall, the Rocky Mountains, so after he succeeded in killing Big Mosquito he sent the faithful dog back to the people to report, and ever since then the dog has been a hunter for man. The Fair One continued on the burro's back to the great wall.

As the marsh grass was first to grow on this land, so it is that grasses are the first to appear in the spring. The turtle, mink, and beaver are also given special consideration. The turtle carries his own house on which is marked the rivers and mountains of the earth. The mink is swift, beautiful, a great diver, and very prolific. And the beaver builds himself a house and mats twigs and bark on the water as if still in anticipation of the coming of the celestial being. Also, every winter the deer produces a new set of antlers as if in readiness to present them to the Fair One for his battle with the Evil One. Likewise every winter many of the animals, especially the slower ones, go underground to hibernate, or die for awhile, in commemoration of the time, long ago, when the Evil One killed and buried them and the Fair One resurrected them.

The people used to cover their homes with the bark of trees to protect themselves from the cold as the Fair One did to them to preserve them from the cold that the Evil One had caused to prevail over the land. Every year between winter and spring the air at times moves very violently, as if large, invisible bodies are moving swiftly through it, as one would suppose to have happened at the great battle between the good and the evil force. Likewise, to this day, people shake from cold and from excitement, and we still find mosquitoes in marshy places and at night. As the water animals held a council regarding the descending being, the people likewise perpetuate the holding of councils. As the turtle, mink, and beaver cooperated in the forming of the earth, so do his people progress by cooperation or working together, each doing a part. Likewise, to the Oneidas the greatest deed that one can do in this life is to assist a woman at childbirth.

Soon thereafter, a blanket seems to be removed from the earth and all nature comes forth again in its most splendid raiments (as people are wont to be, to greet the return of a distinguished, or worshipped, benefactor), to look up again into the clear blue sky from which the Fair One had removed the haze of Indian summer. And there is nothing that a dog likes better than to hunt another animal for his master, the man. The imprints of the feet of the beast of burden are still visible in the rocks just west of the Great Lakes. And the burro itself, after depositing the Fair One near the wall, retired to the south end of that wall, where it humbly transports man and his possessions.

Inasmuch as it was a woman who first arrived here, so woman has ever been the stem of family relations. Yet as Lowni·yÓ and La²niguhláks^ in the other world were masters of women, so man is master of a woman, who abides by his bidding, even unto doing evil things. As the Evil One died only after a violent struggle that disrupted the calm air, so it is now that tempest precedes the death of those that do evil before death.

As the Evil One and the Fair One were antagonistic even in the time before birth, so it is today that it is better to trust a stranger than a brother. But as right and fair triumphed over evil at the great battle, so it has always been that in the final accounting right and fair always triumph. So it is with us; when we have conquered the evils of this world and go west from this earth, we shall enter triumphantly into the light and summer of our home in the blue, where want and suffering there is none.

These people from that time on have preserved memory of events and people by giving them names describing a happening. So the Evil One is called Dawisgala (originally *totihawisgalah*ʸ), which means 'he the ice or frost, left abandoned or just left lying there without paying any further attention to him'. The Fair One is named Dehaluhyawaʿ·gu. This means 'the controller of the skies'.

After the slaughter of Big Mosquito, Dehaluhyawaʿ·gu retired to the great wall from where he watched his people, the Ugwehu'we, the original people, the drummers—the Iroquois. The evil had been conquered and the people lived good and happy lives for many winters.

[END PART I]

After many winters of happiness and security, many generations later, the Ugwehu'we forgot the teachings of the Dehaluhyawaʿ·gu. The Ugwehu'we country became the land of sinners again. The reason evil keeps appearing in this land is because the people who came here originally were sinners. Here is where they are given a chance to redeem themselves.

Now it became necessary to wipe out the evil from this place again. Yet there were a few who were still trying to do the right thing, so Lowni·yÓ had compassion on these people. He sought a way by which he could save these good people and yet destroy the evil people. He finally decided on a plan. He would cause a flood of water to swallow the wicked people, but he would build a number of boats. The good and faithful people would be allowed to board these boats, along with a number of animals and birds. So Lowni·yÓ's representative was instructed to build such boats with the help of the faithful. The people were told of the coming disaster. They would have a chance to get on these boats and be saved but they must be conscientiously good. In due time the boats were finished. The people were pleaded with for some time to enter the boats. At last the big rains came and covered the earth in a large manner, and the doors had to be closed. It was at that time that Lowni·yÓ rewashed the earth (the Great Flood).

At that time the people, birds, and animals used to talk the same language. So after the boats had floated around for a long time, the leader asked for volunteers from the birds to go see if any land had yet appeared above the water. A pair of crows hastily offered their services.

The crows at that time were pure white. When these crows volunteered their services, they were instructed to fly out in search of land, and if they found any land they were to return at once without resting or eating from the earth. They started out after agreeing to carry out the instructions. It was not long before they saw land in the distance. When they came to it, they decided to land. When they landed, they found carcasses of animals and corpses of people. Death by drowning causes the body to become dark. When the crows saw the carcasses, they remembered that they were hungry so they decided to eat the carcasses. As they ate, some of the discolored blood splashed unto their white feathers.

After they had their hunger satisfied and had a little rest, they flew back to the boats. They reported to the leader that they had found land. He asked them if they had rested. They said not. He asked them if they had eaten; they said not. He asked them if they had landed; they said they hadn't. Then he said to them, "You two have lied to me. You have spoiled your fine feathers from the splashing of the decomposed bodies. Your bodies are full and not like that of the hungry ones. For your lying you shall no longer be able to talk; for spoiling your feathers you shall hereafter be black, and for getting your food on a sneak, you shall be a thief and a robber. These shall apply to you and to the future of your kind." Even to this day an albino crow is occasionally seen. However, a black crow will not associate with him. Also, it is said that a crow can be made to talk by an operation. They live in flocks or communities and are ever watchful, even in flight. They are intelligent and work in cooperation with their fellow crows.

All haste was now made to go in the direction where the crows had reported the land to be. On approaching the land the people noted that the land resembled a large rock standing on the water. The man, who proposed to build the boats that would float on the water and thus save the people from drowning, was said to want to be like a turtle, floating on the water. Therefore, in mockery he was called *aˀno·wa'lhe* (turtle), which by the process of contraction is now called *nówa* (Noah). And the people having landed on what resembled a standing rock, they called themselves "The People of the Everlasting Standing Rock," *On^yoteˀa·ká* [Oneida].

Maliseet

The Legendary Tom Laporte

Introduction by Philip S. LeSourd

At the time of the first European incursions into their territory, early in the seventeenth century, the Maliseets occupied most of the region that is drained by the Saint John River and its tributaries in what is today New Brunswick and northern Maine. Early European accounts describe them as living in large villages along the river during the summer months, fishing and tending their gardens, but dispersing during the winter, when hunting in the interior country became the primary focus of their economic activity. During the era of the fur trade, Maliseet hunters and trappers increasingly turned their attention to collecting hides and pelts to exchange for European goods, often ranging as far as Montagnais country along the shores of the Saint Lawrence River. Traditional settlement patterns were disrupted as well, both by Mohawk raids and by steadily increasing competition for land and resources with European settlers. The majority of the Maliseet population became Catholics during the period of French control of the region, although many traditional beliefs persisted alongside the new religion.

Some Maliseet families were able to maintain the old pattern of seasonal migration into the last years of the nineteenth century.[1] By this time, however, the majority of the population had come to be concentrated on five reserves located along the Saint John River in New Brunswick: Oromocto, farthest down the river; Saint Mary's, across the river from Fredericton; and Kingsclear; Woodstock; and then Tobique, upriver from there. Early in the nineteenth century, several families from Tobique relocated to the Saint Lawrence country in Quebec. A reservation was set aside for them at Viger, but this population ultimately dispersed. There is still a significant Maliseet community, however, across the international border in Aroostook County, Maine. There is also a substantial expatriate population in and around Bridgeport, Connecticut, where many Maliseets migrated in search of work in the decades following the Second World War.

The Maliseets are closely affiliated, both culturally and linguistically, with the Passamaquoddy Indians of eastern Maine, who are concentrated today on two reservations in Washington County. The two groups speak mutually intelligible dialects of a single Eastern Algonquian language. English has made inroads into the use of the traditional language in all of the contemporary communities, how-ever, and most of the fluent speakers today are over the age of forty. Current estimates place the total number of speakers of Maliseet and Passamaquoddy at around five hundred, a minority of the population.[2]

The seven stories that follow were told in Maliseet by Charles Laporte at the Tobique Reserve in 1963. They were recorded by the linguist Karl V. Teeter on four occasions in June and July of that year, when he visited Laporte in the company of his principal consultant, Peter Lewis Paul of the Woodstock Reserve.[3] Paul had set out that summer to introduce Teeter to the best storytellers he knew in the generation of Maliseet speakers who were born in the last years of the nineteenth century. One of these was Laporte, who grew up at Saint Mary's but spent most of his adult life at Tobique, where he died in 1964.

Despite his small and atypical audience, Laporte told his stories for Teeter and Paul with great enthusiasm, employing many features of traditional Maliseet style, on which other speakers of the language have commented favorably when I have had occasion to play Teeter's recordings for them. Indeed, the stories I have brought together here were clearly among Laporte's favorites. All of them tell of the adventures of a legendary figure in the Laporte family, whom Charles Laporte calls Túma Láhpult, or Tom Laporte. They are set in a mutable past, which Laporte shifts according to his narrative purposes from the era of Mohawk raids and the fur trade to a relatively recent period in the history of the Tobique Reserve.

In Maliseet, traditional stories are called *atkuhkàkonol* (singular *atkuhkákon*). Laporte explicitly identifies five of the following tales as belonging to this type, using the verb *ktatkuhkewolòniya* 'I'll tell you people an old story' in his opening remarks. The other two are designated only as *akonutomàkonol,* a more general term for stories, through the use of the corresponding verb *ktakonutomuloníya* 'I'll tell you a story'.

Many *atkuhkàkonol* are told as true. Among these are stories of the culture hero Koluskap, who shaped the landscape, reduced the size of various wild animals to manageable proportions, and served as a benefactor to all of the Wabanakis or northeastern Algonquian peoples. Others tell of animals who can transform themselves into people or of people who are capable of equally astonishing feats. Many such stories are told about the distant past, but others make it clear that such events can take place even today.

Not all *atkuhkàkonol* are true stories, however. Indeed, a Maliseet narrator will often note that the story he or she is about to tell is not merely an *atkuhkákon* but reflects events that really happened. Laporte makes no such assertions, however, in the stories I have translated here. In fact, his tales of the exploits of Tom Laporte are clearly fictions. They are tales told in fun, set in the past, but not reports of past events.

While these tales are not to be read as history, they nonetheless draw on authentic Maliseet traditions of winter hunts and Mohawk raiders. Laporte also turns the history of his family to his purposes. In the first tale, he reports that the Laportes once lived at Matane, Quebec, on the south shore of the estuary of the Saint Lawrence River. He confirmed the Quebec connections of his family in a more specifically historical narrative that he recorded for Teeter, in which he described how a party of seal hunters, including several of the Laportes, were swept away by flood waters from the Saguenay River after setting out from Tadoussac, on the north shore of the Saint Lawrence.

Laporte was apparently something of skeptic about at least some Maliseet traditions. After telling a brief version of the tale of Koluskap's battle with a giant beaver, for example, he added the comment, "It probably can't be proved, the way one tells the story. It's just what the old Indians say." His stories of Tom Laporte nonetheless presuppose a traditional Maliseet view of the world, for Tom Laporte is not simply an ordinary man: he is a man who can wield extraordinary personal power and accomplish feats that others find astonishing. He is what anthropologists call a shaman and Maliseet speakers call a *motewolòn*.

The power of a Maliseet *motewolòn,* who is as likely to be a woman as a man, is often exercised through an animal form, called a *puwhíkon.* The *motewolòn* is described sometimes as sending out the *puwhíkon* to do his or her work and sometimes as transforming himself or herself into the *puwhíkon.* Perhaps the most powerful *puwhíkon* that any *motewolòn* can call upon is the fearsome aquatic monster known as a *wiwìlomeq.* This creature is sometimes described as a gigantic lizard, while other accounts liken it to a huge slug, with horns like the eyestalks of a snail. It is this monster that Tom Laporte employs as his *puwhíkon* in the first of the tales. As is typically the case in such stories, the listener is left to wonder just how Tom accomplishes this feat, for he walks off into the brush before he begins to exercise his power.

Tom's power is never explicitly mentioned in the second tale, to which, following Teeter, I have given the title "Tom in the Woods." No Maliseet listener would have failed to notice the implications of the events in the tale, however. Here Tom is pictured as having such bad luck in hunting that he cannot even obtain bait for his traps. In desperation, he cuts some flesh from the body of a dead sailor that he has found washed up on the shore, solely in order to use it for bait. But when two Montagnais visitors come unexpectedly to his camp while he is away baiting his traps, they mistake some of the sailor's flesh for moose meat that has been hung out to freeze. Before Tom even knows that they have arrived, they have cooked the meat and eaten it: his actions have led to cannibalism. This is a horrible offense against the moral order, and he is responsible for it. Dire consequences are sure to follow, and they do. No sooner have the visitors left than a *cipélahq* appears. This is another monstrous creature, capable of flying through the air and known in particular for carrying off children and devouring them. It has no body as such, just arms and legs that emerge from directly beneath its head. Contrary to the listener's expectations, however, Tom is not frightened in the least—but he is, after all, a *motewolòn.*

Tom's power seems to be entirely suspended in the two stories given next. In "Tom and the Mohawks," our hero is taken prisoner by these historical enemies of the Maliseets and barely escapes with his life. "Tom and the Moose" is a frankly Christian tale of a vision that reminds the protagonist that he should not be hunting on Easter Sunday. In the last three stories included here, however, Tom's power is back, but now Laporte puts this element of his material to use, not for dramatic effect, but for humor. In one tale he sets Tom to fighting with a ghost who may or may not be a figment of his imagination. In another Tom uses his power to obtain whiskey by tapping a maple tree, while in the last tale Tom temporarily changes wood chips into paper money to buy supplies for his winter hunt—after he has lost all his money by gambling.

The overall picture of Tom that emerges from these stories is not altogether flattering. He is clearly subject to a number of human failings, despite his power as a *motewolòn.* He has a tendency to drink too much on occasion, and he can be an immoderate gambler. He also has a decided fondness for the ladies, as we learn in "Tom Fights a Ghost." Despite these weaknesses, however, he is basically a decent and honest man. After all he is careful to pay back the storekeeper he has cheated, once he comes back from hunting and sells his furs.

Two sources independent of Teeter's work confirm the popularity of some of the tales that Laporte told, as well as giving an idea of the extent to which these stories were community property. The incident in which Tom changes wood chips into paper money to fool a storekeeper occurs in a tale collected by students of the folklorist Edward D. Ives in 1962.[4] The story was told by Henrietta Black, then thirty-three years old, who reported that she had heard it from her mother, Viola Solomon, when she was growing up at Tobique. Black calls the protagonist in her story Jack LaPorte, rather than Tom, and makes no mention of his having lost his money by gambling, but the story is otherwise essentially the same. Like Charles Laporte's Tom, Jack is quick to go back to the storekeeper he has cheated, once he has sold his furs, in order to repay him. In a study published in 1957, the anthropologists Wilson D. Wallis and Ruth Satwell Wallis report that one of their consultants at Tobique told them a story about her grandfather that centered around an incident of the same kind.[5] Their consultant also informed them that her grandfather had once bored a hole in a tree with an auger and obtained molasses. Here we clearly have another version of the story given here as "Tom and the Whiskey," although the Wallises' consultant evidently provided the visiting anthropologists with an expurgated version of the tale.

Several traditional stylistic features of Laporte's stories are also worthy of note. By convention Maliseet storytellers often speak as if they had themselves been present at the events they describe. This accounts for the fact that Laporte often refers to the setting of a tale as "here" and also makes sense of his abrupt shift into direct quotation when he is describing Tom's predicament in "Tom and the Mohawks." The same convention is reflected in certain stock phrases that Maliseet storytellers use in bringing a tale to a close. Laporte employs such formulas twice in the tales presented here: "I ran away from there, too" and "I set out from there, too."

Another traditional feature of Laporte's tales is his frequent use of two exclamations, *nìta!* and *kí!* The first of these is an emphatic form of the demonstrative pronoun meaning 'that' and is most often used in ordinary conversation to mean 'that one in particular', 'right there', or 'just then'. It is also used as a warning, however, with much the same force as English *uh-oh!* In stories it serves to admonish the listener to pay attention. *Kí!* more specifically advises listeners to listen closely, telling them, "Here comes the good part!" Speakers who have listened to Laporte's stories with me have noted his use of these expressions with approval, commenting that this is the way their elders always spoke when they were telling stories. I have accordingly left them untranslated here.

A NOTE ON ORTHOGRAPHY AND PRONUNCIATION

Maliseet words are given here in their usual spellings in a practical writing system that is now widely used by native speakers. The vowels of the language are *a* (as in *father*), *e* (as in *bed*), *i* (as in *machine*), *o* (as in *apron,* or like the *a* in *about*), and *u* (as in *sue*). The letter *c* is pronounced much like the *ch* in *church,* while *q* has the sound of *qu* in *squeal.* Between vowels, however, *p, t, k,* and *q* are pronounced like *b, d, g,* and *gw.* Maliseet is a pitch-accent language, in which each word must be pronounced with its proper "tune." The acute accent written over a vowel letter indicates that the corresponding syllable is pronounced at a higher pitch than surrounding syllables. The grave accent indicates a relatively low-pitched syllable.

NOTES

1. Much of the historical information summarized here is taken from Erickson, "Maliseet-Passamaquoddy," 123–47.

2. Leavitt, *Passamaquoddy-Maliseet,* 1.

3. My translations of Laporte's tales are based not only on Teeter's recordings but also on his notes from his sessions with the speaker and from his subsequent work on this material with Peter Paul, carried out over a period of several years.

4. Ives, "Malecite and Passamaquoddy Tales," 49.

5. Wallis and Wallis, *Malecite Indians of New Brunswick,* 32.

SUGGESTED READING AND REFERENCES

Alger, Abby Langdon. *In Indian Tents: Stories Told by Penobscot, Passamaquoddy and Micmac Indians*. Boston: Roberts Brothers, 1897.

Erickson, Vincent O. "Maliseet-Passamaquoddy." In *Handbook of North American Indians*, vol. 15, *Northeast*, edited by Bruce G. Trigger, 123–36. Washington: Smithsonian Institution, 1978.

Ives, Edward D., ed. "Maliseet and Passamaquoddy Tales." *Northeast Folklore* 6:1–81 (1964).

Leland, Charles G. *The Algonquin Legends of New England or Myths and Folk Lore of the Micmac, Passamaquoddy, and Penobscot Tribes*. Boston: Houghton, Mifflin, 1884.

LeSourd, Philip S. "The Passamaquoddy 'Witchcraft Tales' of Newell S. Francis." *Anthropological Linguistics* 42 (4) (2000): 441–98.

Leavitt, Robert M. *Passamaquoddy-Maliseet*. Munich: Lincom Europa, 1996.

Wallis, Wilson D., and Ruth Satwell Wallis. *The Malecite Indians of New Brunswick*. Ottawa: National Museum of Canada, 1957.

The Legendary Tom Laporte

Told by Charles Laporte
Translated by Philip S. LeSourd

TOM AND THE *WIWÌLOMEQ*

Níta. So now I'll tell you an old story about Tom Laporte, one time when he had gathered up a supply of furs. He had been trapping somewhere far away, up on the Saint Lawrence. Then he went to trade his furs in Quebec, for a gun.

He had to pile all of the furs up just so. As high as the length of the gun. When he had them all set so that he could buy the gun, he had a good many layers of beaver skin—beaver skins, and moose hides, and hides of every kind. So finally he got the gun and some bullets.

This was when those guns first started to appear around here, when they were brought here from over in France. A gun was really prized. Any Indian who owned a gun was rich. He was a real big shot.

So finally Tom finished trading for everything—clothes and supplies, everything. He was taking a woman along this time, too. Finally he had everything stowed on board. Then the woman got in, with the gun lying crosswise on the canoe so that she could hold onto it as they traveled along. She was feeling very proud.

Níta. Then they started off. They traveled and traveled, over to some place near Matane. Back there somewhere where he was trapping, out toward Montagnais country. To get to that place, he had to paddle some 250 miles.

Kí! Finally, as they were traveling along, they rounded a point and suddenly came upon a ledge of rock that juts out into the river, about where the current runs. Here he had to shoot through the eddy, and all at once he was paddling in the swift current of the open water. As he paddled out into the current, the canoe tilted over this way a little.[1]

And that's when the woman dropped the gun, when she was startled. Down into the water it sank. Boys, did she ever wail![2] She felt terribly discouraged.

1. Said with an accompanying gesture.
2. Laporte uses the English word *boys* here and later in the stories, not as a term of address, but as an exclamation.

So Tom paddled to shore and pulled the canoe up on the ledge. He said to the woman, "Now you sit right here."

So she sat right by the edge of the rock, where the ledge stuck out into the river. He set off, walking up the bank. Finally he went off into the brush, out of sight.

All at once, right where the woman was looking, a spout of water shot up out in the river. What the devil![3] Up came this giant lizard. With horns. There on its horns — where there were little horns on its head — lying across there was the gun, the one that she had been so upset about dropping.

Níta. Then, as this *wiwìlomeq* emerged, it started to swim along in a circle, coming toward her. It seemed to be swimming right to where the woman was sitting, close by the shore. Finally the gun even touched her clothing. But she couldn't move at all. She was scared to death.

Kí! Again it swam out into the river, this *wiwìlomeq*. Again it swam around in a circle. Again it swam up to where the woman was sitting. Where the barrel of the gun stuck out, it touched her clothing. Still the woman didn't take hold of the gun.

Kí! Yet a third time. As it swam around for the third time, the gun was practically knocked off the horns of the *wiwìlomeq*. But still she didn't take hold of it. Then the *wiwìlomeq* headed straight out into the river and sank down into the water.

After just a little while, Tom came walking out of the brush. Oh! He was as pale of face now — just like something made of cotton — as he had been dark before. It must have been pretty serious, whatever he had been doing.

Níta. Then he said to the woman, "You must really have been sorry about that gun. Get into the canoe. It looks like we have lost it for good."

Kí! They set out again. They traveled on for a good many days before they arrived at their town, Matane, where the Laportes used to live long ago. The woman told the people there about the things that Tom had done. Boys, they were amazed at him. Everyone avoided Tom. He seemed to them to be something of a *motewolòn.*

That's all I can tell you for now. Some other time I'll tell you another little story about the many things he is said to have done.

TOM IN THE WOODS

Níta. So now I'll tell you another old story, about one time when Tom was still trapping. He was having awfully bad luck, they say. Finally, he got hungry, here where he was trapping. Oh, he was hard up. He couldn't even kill a squirrel. Not

---

3. The Maliseet expression that Laporte uses here is *kinahantuwínaq,* an exclamation based on the noun *kinahànt* 'great devil'.

a thing. He was at a loss. He couldn't even catch anything to use for bait, so that he could bait his traps.

Finally, at one point, he was worried to death. He was already hungry. Then he took a walk along the shore by the sea.[4] As he was walking along the shore by the sea, here was the body of a sailor of some sort, apparently washed up on shore. He must have been one of the white ones.

So then he decided that he would have to use him for bait. So he cut a piece from the sailor's leg, where the flesh was thick, for bait. It was almost Christmas already, too.

Finally, when he had cut a few slices from him, he took them to his camp. It was already cold enough then for them to freeze. He hung them up at the entrance to his camp, this human flesh.

He went trapping again right away, then again the next morning. There were still two slices hanging there, of this bait of human flesh.

Nita. It just so happened that two Montagnais men came unexpectedly to pay him a Christmas visit. They thought to themselves, "This young moose meat here looks really good. It's really nicely skinned, this young moose meat."

"Let's cook right away," one of the Montagnais told his friend.

So then they fried up the meat. Oh, they had a hell of a meal of this young moose meat or whatever it was—although it was actually human flesh.

Finally, when it was already starting to get dark, Tom came clattering on back. He went in. Here they were, telling him all about how they had eaten, these two Montagnais who had come to visit him.

Kí! Finally they said to him, "Hey, Tom, you have some, too. Go right ahead, go right ahead! We've saved that meat over there for you. You go right ahead and eat, too. You must be really tired."

"Oh, no thanks," he told them. "I had my tea on my way here. I'm not at all hungry now that I'm here, since I ate then."

Oh, he didn't say a thing. He was shocked. "Why did I ever hang up that human flesh here at the entrance? Now I have done wrong."

Nita. They had their spree on Christmas Eve. They all had a good time. Then, after Christmas, the two visitors were once again getting ready to set out.

"My friends," he said, "what would you think if I told you the story of that meat that you ate that you liked so much?"

"Oh, that would be no problem. How could it? It tasted so good! We would think nothing of it."

"As for me," he said, "when I was hunting, I was having awfully bad luck. I wasn't even killing anything to bait my traps with. And then I went walking

---

4. It is presumably the estuary of the Saint Lawrence River, and not the ocean as such, that Laporte has in mind here.

around down by the sea. I found a sailor. I cut a steak off him. A few slices, for some kind of bait. I hung them up there outside so they would freeze. Then when these two friends of mine came along, they cooked up a big meal for themselves. They thought it was young moose meat. And they said it tasted awfully good. It was already too late to think anything about it. They had already eaten it the day before."

Ah, boys, they all had a big laugh, they say. Then the two of them left. But just as his two friends were walking away, he could hear something hollering as it moved along up above, as if it were up by a cloud. But he couldn't see it. It made quite a noise when it hollered, but he couldn't see it.

"If I can just spot that devil of an animal! After a while, it will scare away all of the game around here. I won't be able to kill a thing as long as it's around."

Then, some days later, a thaw set in, and he went out to check his traps. There, wandering around beneath a tree, was some person—or some creature. He couldn't make out what he was. One of his forearms was broken, they say. And this creature that was walking around there, his crotch was way the hell up at his throat, and below that were just his arms and his legs, which spread out like roots from beneath his throat and his head. He had a coat on, too, that was made of fur.

"Hey, my friend! Help me!" the creature said. "I've fallen and broken my arm."

Nita. So then he helped him. He pulled his coat on tight, a sort of pullover coat made of something like sheepskin or the hide of some sort of animal.

Nita. In the end, he took care of him. Right away he started to have good luck. Oh, within about three weeks his arm was healing up, the arm of this devil, or whatever he was.

So then Tom explained to him, this creature that he had been doctoring, "Someone has been hollering around here. He makes so much noise that he scares away all the animals."

"Oh, Tom, that's me," the creature replied. "It's me. It's this coat of mine. Whenever I put it on, the louder I can holler, the farther I go. If I holler about three times, I come to France."

"Oh, so it's you that's been scaring away my animals."

After that, when they went out, he crept up behind him and gave him a good whack on the head, this *cipélahq*.

Nita. Then he finally slipped the coat on himself. It occurred to him to go someplace, so he went to Quebec to get some liquor.

Once he had put the coat on, he hollered really loud, but at first nothing happened. Then, they say, he rose right up into the air. About the second time he hollered, he landed way off in town. And in no more time than it took to get his supplies, he was back again. Hollering twice, he was back here again where he had been before.

Níta. After that, he could always get to town in short order. That was all it took.

Finally, when spring came, he hung up the coat somewhere, and it caught on fire—or rather, it went up in flames when he left it somewhere near his fire. It was no more. That was the end of Tom's travels.

So then he quit trapping and went to sell his furs. I ran away from there, too.

TOM AND THE MOHAWKS

Well, I'll tell you another story about Tom, one time when he had finished trapping in the spring. It was just about summer, June already.

When he had sold his furs, he headed this way across the carry, toward this place on the Saint John River. He always left one canoe here, they say, as far as he usually went by water, where he would cut across to a point on the Saint Lawrence River.[5]

But when he got there, they say, there were five Mohawks waiting for him. They grabbed him right there. They tied him up by the feet. And then Tom was dragged away. He was taken away somewhere, he didn't know where.

For four days, five days he was led along on a rope. Then at last they arrived at the little village of these Mohawks, or whoever they were. Ah, then they tied him up securely. They threw him into this house of some kind. Well, boys, he was sure that he would die in the morning.

Suddenly that evening—when it got dark, he could hear someone slipping in, here at the base of the house. And then he saw the flash of a knife. He thought to himself, "Someone is going to stab me."

"But no," he said. "Instead, someone suddenly cut the leather cords off me that my feet and my hands were tied with, and took hold of my clothes, to signal that we should go out together. So I went outside with this person, and here was a woman, or rather a girl."

She went with him for a little ways. After that he went on just as fast as he could. He thought he would head toward here.

Then, when he had grown tired from traveling, he climbed up a big tree. He went to sleep way up in the tree, where there were a lot of limbs close together.

Before long, they say, he could hear the Mohawks in pursuit. They walked right by the place where he was hiding. They looked all around for him, for a long time. Finally they gave up, and then he set out for here right away. He had to travel for some days, but eventually he got here.

5. Laporte later explained to Teeter that Tom would have had only one canoe, but that he would have taken along a temporary skin boat that he could take apart and stow away. It was this skin boat that he took across the carry on his way to the Saint Lawrence country. The canoe itself, he noted, would have been impractical for use the following spring, when the rivers would still have been choked with ice.

Tom was very nearly done in. It was at that point, I guess, that he stopped trapping up along the Saint Lawrence River. He was scared to death.

TOM AND THE MOOSE

Well, I'll tell you another story about Tom, back when he was hunting, when he and his partner were collecting moose hides for the French in Quebec. Just moose. They killed a lot of moose.

At one point he lost count of how many days he had been in the woods. Then, when he woke up one morning, he thought, "Well, now I'll go and bag a good moose." There were tracks all around the place.

So then he picked up his kettle to make his morning tea. He went to fetch water from a stream nearby. But when he got there, here was one hell of a big moose, standing there facing him. Boys, was he glad. He dropped his kettle right there. He went to get a gun.

When he got back, the moose was still standing there.

Nita. He took careful aim. But as looked along the barrel of his gun, here was a gold cross, standing above the moose, where its antlers forked out.

Nita. He was truly astonished. He didn't shoot it. Instead, he put his gun away and went to fetch water.

As he went into his camp, here was the stick on which he always carved notches to keep track of the number of days that he had been in the woods. Much to his surprise, it was Easter today.

"That's why I had the vision when I was going to shoot that moose, because it's such a great Sunday."

He didn't go out again to shoot it. He was scared to death.

TOM FIGHTS A GHOST

I'll tell you an old story now about Tom, Tom Laporte. One time when he had been trapping out along the Saint Lawrence River, and he had a fight with a ghost.

They grabbed one another. When Tom tried to throw him, he couldn't. He couldn't move him at all. That ghost tried with all his might to throw Tom, but he couldn't do it either. Neither could move the other.

So they wrestled and wrestled, until the first light of day was about to appear.

Then the ghost said to Tom, "Tom, let go of my eggs![6] You will catch lots of game!"

---

6. Here Laporte uses the verb *punawonenìn*, which includes a medial element *-awone-*, meaning 'egg', and thus literally means 'let go of me, as of an egg'. This is a clever euphemism that allows him to avoid making a literal statement of the ghost's meaning: "Let go of my balls!" The joke is effective, since it takes Maliseet speakers a moment to realize the implications of this unusual word.

But Tom didn't let go of him. He held on to him still, and they went on wrestling and wrestling until there was just about enough light to see. Finally there was a little light, but Tom still couldn't make out who he was.

"Hey, Tom, let go of my eggs!" the ghost told him. "You will come by money with no trouble at all! Money will come to you from all directions! You will hardly have to work!"

Tom didn't let go of him. He still kept a good grip on him.

Then, after a while, Tom could just about make out who he was, since there was very nearly enough light to see.

And then the ghost told him, "Tom, let go of my eggs! You'll get lots of women! Just about any woman you want, you will get!"

At that, they say, he let go of the ghost.

Finally, after a little while, full daylight came on. Then, when there was enough light to see, and he had had a good rest, Tom looked at this thing that he had been wrestling with. And here, they say, was an old stump! And it was thickly covered with moss. At times he had almost been able to uproot it. Then it would slip back again. It was too heavy.

So he left it, went and sat by the fire, and had a smoke. That's all.

TOM AND THE WHISKEY

Well, I'll tell you another old story, about one time when he had been hunting out toward Montagnais country, with the Montagnais who live up north, farther north than we do. At that point, boys, he was having good luck. And he had gotten in a little hard liquor, too, to have when Christmas came.

Two Montagnais men were walking their trap lines about twenty-five miles away, with some other hunters. Just before Christmas, they came to visit him.

Kí! Then they had a spree. They had a good time. By the time they had all sobered up again, Christmas had gone by. They were horribly sick. No one had eaten. Not a thing.

Tom was really feeling sick after their spree on Christmas Eve, but all of a sudden he looked over at the others. He went and picked up a little kettle and a small auger. Then he went on out the door. So they watched what he was doing. There he was, boring a hole in a huge sugar maple.

Then, when he had finished boring the hole, he made a spile. He hung up the little kettle, his teakettle. Ah, he stood there and stood there. He didn't seem to have been gone for very long, when he suddenly appeared with the kettle full. He brought it in and set it on the table. Then he said, "Come on, have a drink!"

The two other men were really feeling sick. They looked at each other. They didn't believe him. They didn't want to drink water.

"If you're feeling sick," he told them, "have a drink! This will do you good."

Then one of them picked up the dipper. He ladled out some of the liquid. He took a big drink. Damned if it wasn't the very best whiskey, hard liquor!

What the devil! Right away he handed the cup to the other fellow. And he, too, took a big drink. Boys! They both started to feel good again. So did he. By the time they had all drunk twice, they had drunk it all. They had all started feeling pretty good again.

Well, when they had gotten over feeling good, and when they weren't feeling sick anymore, they said goodbye to one another. In times to come, they would all visit one another every Christmas. They all got together to have a good time, these hunters.

So when they had all finished saying goodbye, the two Montagnais men set out to go hunting again. Then I set out from there, too. But Tom must have gone right on hunting.

TOM AND THE STOREKEEPER

Níta. So now I'll tell you an old story about Tom, when people had finished trapping and were through trading.

At that point they all played cards here at Tobique until they had cleaned each other out. It was almost time to go trapping again in any case. So they went to get their supplies of food, enough to last all winter while they were trapping. Tom, though, had already spent all of his money. He didn't have any money. But he went to ask for credit. By then the Bears and the Moultons, they had all gotten their supplies. They all had money.

Kí! He sidled on up to the counter. And he asked the storekeeper if he could let him have enough food to last him until spring while he was trapping, and then when he got back he would pay him.

"I couldn't do that, Tom," the storekeeper told him. "Already, I've sold almost all of my stock. I have to live, too."

"Ah!" Tom said to the other Indians. "I know how to work this man. Wait just a minute. I'll be right back. Stay right here."

He headed on out. They could see him going around picking up some thin wood chips, the leftover chips lying around with the firewood. He was sticking them into his pocket. After a little while he came back in here where everybody was.

Finally he walked up to the counter. He said to the storekeeper, "How much do you charge for that rifle?"

"Sixty-five dollars, Tom," he told him, "with two boxes of cartridges."

"Ah. I'll buy it then."

"But how can you pay for it? You couldn't pay for your food before."

"Don't worry about a thing. Of course I can pay for it." And he ordered flour, everything he would use over the winter. Then he stowed everything away—tobacco, a trap, everything one would use in trapping.

Then he pulled a sheaf of paper money out of his pocket. His bill came to more than a hundred dollars. He paid him.

Kí! He hauled everything away and loaded up his canoe, so he could hurry out into the woods and set up his traps, out where people were trapping.

Kí! Finally, when spring came, and he had sold his furs in Quebec and come back across the carry, he got back here and went to see the storekeeper.

"How much do I owe you?" he asked him.

"Oh, you don't owe me anything, Tom. You already paid me."

Níta.

"But I do owe you. Didn't you find some wood chips, there in the box where the money is stacked, a little while after I had gotten my supplies?"

"Yes, I did," he told him. "I couldn't figure out where the wood chips could have come from in that pile of money."

"That was me," Tom told him. "You were too stingy back then. When I really needed stuff so that I could trap until spring came without having to worry, I paid you with wood chips.[7] That wasn't money that I gave you. But now I'll pay you."

He paid him then and there. That storekeeper was awfully surprised.

7. Laporte in fact used the English word *stuff* at this point in his story.

Mìgmaq

Three Stories

Introduction by Jennifer Andrews and Robert M. Leavitt

"The Floating Island," "The Mìgmaq Cinderella," and "Bapkubaluet the Gambler" examine the themes of power and society's relationship to the "unseen" world from a distinctly Mìgmaq perspective. In particular the three tales portray the importance of perception and vision from youth to death, a concern that is reflected in the subject matter of the stories.

The versions of the three stories included here are by E. Nàgùgwes Metallic, a Mìgmaq who lives at Listuguj (formerly known as Restigouche), Quebec, just across from Campbellton, New Brunswick. Metallic has been actively researching his Native heritage for over thirty years, and he has become an expert on Mìgmaq language. Through his study of etymology and the development of the language, he has also made substantial contributions to the study of Mìgmaq heritage, culture, and spiritual beliefs. Currently, he is writing a series of conversational texts that use an auditory-cognitive approach rather than the grammatical or syntax-based approach of his previous work. The present tales first appeared in Metallic's weekly columns for the Campbellton *Tribune,* a local newspaper with a mixed Native and non-Native readership. These columns have enabled him to publish his research on Native spirituality and to retell many Mìgmaq stories and legends for a wider audience.

The three stories presented here appear in early forms in previous collections of Mìgmaq oral tradition. "The Floating Island," for example, is thought to be one of the earliest Mìgmaq narratives still in circulation. It appears in Silas T. Rand's *Legends of the Micmacs,* under the title "The Dream of the White Robe and the Floating Island," though notably Rand's version concludes with the coming of Christian missionaries and the successful conversion of the Mìgmaq, a section that he may have added himself.[1] A Baptist missionary, Rand dreamed of converting the Mìgmaq, and though his efforts failed, the outcome of the story reflects his commitment to this task.

"The Mìgmaq Cinderella" is descended from an ancient celestial myth and has appeared previously in various, more extended forms in Rand's *Legends,* Elsie Clews Parsons's "Micmac Folklore," Charles G. Leland's *Algonquin Legends of New*

England, and Marion Robertson's *Red Earth.*[2] Metallic's story concentrates on the challenges that several brides-to-be face in trying to win the hand of the invisible hunter; his narrative concludes when one contender, an ugly young girl covered in scars and sores, sees the hunter and becomes his wife. In Rand and other accounts, however, the narrative emphasizes the relationship between the hunter and his sister prior to his marriage and her eventual betrayal of her brother, which results in his murdering her. Clearly, the story has changed substantially over time from a narrative primarily about a brother-sister bond to one of love and marriage based on the power of vision, as exemplified in Metallic's version. Finally, the story of "The Gambler" first appears in Chrestien LeClercq's seventeenth-century collection of Mìgmaq stories.[3]

These stories address a diverse range of issues, including colonization, marriage, death, the immortality of the soul, and the existence of an afterlife. Yet all three are linked by a central concern with vision and power, namely, the ability to see and to shape experience. "The Floating Island" explores the importance of a young girl's prophecy after the creation of the earth and the seasons. This narrative combines a commentary on the passage of the seasons, by naming the young girl Summer, with an examination of how the ability to perceive becomes a source of conflict within the community: someone who is not seen as possessing power gains it through her dream. The story reveals the need to respect the forces of the universe, as manifested through the girl's vision, and not to dismiss a dream simply because of the status of the dreamer. It also vividly demonstrates the ability of the Mìgmaq to use story to reimagine the world. The dream of a floating island with tall trees and bears is later reread by the community when the explorers arrive, as the dream becomes reality. The conclusion of the story hints at the radical reshaping of traditional Mìgmaq practices and structures. The giving of a prophecy to such a young and insignificant girl anticipates the dramatic changes that are about to take place with European colonization. Seeing and perceiving are especially important survival tools for bridging the vast gulf between those aboard the sailing ship and the Mìgmaq residing on Cape Breton Island.

Metallic's other two stories also stress the power of seeing the world and its complexities in a fundamental rather than superficial way. "The Mìgmaq Cinderella" turns the ability to see into a test that rewards truth and inner beauty. The youngest sister is covered in sores and scars, which makes her the butt of community abuse and ridicule. Unlike the other contenders, she takes the challenge seriously and prepares to visit the Hunter by sewing wampum onto her moccasins and making a birch-bark dress decorated with ancient symbols of the Mìgmaq. Her commitment to her Mìgmaq heritage and her description of the Hunter's tumpline as a rainbow, a natural phenomenon that takes a discriminating eye to perceive, become correctives to the elder sisters' abusive treatment and their own inability to see the Hunter.

"Bapkubaluet the Gambler" traces the afterlife of one man and a couple's attempt to regain their son from the Land of Souls. In this story vision is crucial because the grieving parents, when they try to rescue their child, are able to see Bapkubaluet even though he is in spirit form, and they manage to persuade him to gamble for the life of their son. The successful recovery of the child depends on his immediate return to the Land of the Living, where his soul is to be put back into his body. But when the Gambler gives them the tightly wrapped body of their son, the parents make the mistake of trying to sneak a peek at him; his soul escapes, and he is lost to them forever. Their desperate desire to see their child thwarts the parents' ultimate goal, the recovery of their son and his return to the Land of the Living. Here exercising restraint when using one's sight is crucial. As with the Cinderella story, successful connections with the unseen world depend on effective use of vision and power. Both stories can be read as cautionary narratives that instruct listeners to think carefully about how they interact with the seen and unseen worlds and to reflect on the power and limits of sight.

Metallic originally wrote these stories in Mìgmaq, based on his reading of textual sources and his knowledge of oral tradition. He later prepared the translations found here, which are stylistically influenced by the English sources, especially Rand. Mìgmaq is an Eastern Algonquian language spoken in New Brunswick, Prince Edward Island, and Nova Scotia, as well as in communities in the Gaspé Peninsula, Newfoundland, and Maine. It is closely related to Abenaki, Penobscot, and Passamaquoddy-Maliseet. Mìgmaq remains strong today, though recent years have seen a rapid decline in most communities in the number of fluent and first-language speakers.

Interestingly, Mìgmaq has been written, in various forms, since at least the seventeenth century. According to Schmidt and Marshall, the Recollect missionary Chrestien LeClercq, on a 1677 visit to the Miramichi River, in what is now New Brunswick, devised a set of "definite characters," or hieroglyphs, which he used to teach prayers. "Reading and writing soon became competitive pastimes among the [Mìgmaq] people," and the hieroglyphic system spread throughout Mìgmaq territory, reaching Cape Breton by 1735. The hieroglyphs were used by the general Mìgmaq population for secular as well as religious writing and reading. They sustained Mìgmaq Catholicism during the seventy years following the departure of the French in 1762, a period when there were no priests in Mìgmaq territory, and they were an important factor in keeping the Mìgmaq from converting to Protestantism.[4]

Although a number of the Catholic priests had developed alphabetic writing for their own use in learning Mìgmaq, they did not teach it to their Mìgmaq parishioners for fear of giving them access to secular material, which in turn might lead to unrest. It was not until the tenure of Father Pacifique at Listuguj, at the turn of the twentieth century, that a writing system using roman letters became widespread among the Mìgmaq. Although Pacifique encouraged the use of the hieroglyphs and published a book of sacred texts, he used alphabetic writing in a series of Mìgmaq prayer books and a monthly newsletter.[5] In more recent years, linguists and native speakers have collaborated to develop several improved orthographies. Metallic has developed his own orthography, which is used here. He is one of several Mìgmaq writers who have begun to develop a new literature in the Mìgmaq language.

A NOTE ON ORTHOGRAPHY AND PRONUNCIATION

Metallic's orthography uses *a* (like the *a* in English *father*), *e* (as in *bed*), *i* (as in *ski*), *o* (as in *rose*), and *u* (as in *sue*). These vowels are marked with a grave accent (*à, è, ì, ò, ù*) to indicate a lengthened sound. Consonants are like those in English, with *g* always as in *go* and *q* representing a light guttural sound, similar to that in *loch*. *Wiguom* (WEE-goo-ohm) is the origin of the English word *wigwam*. Wabnàgiewaq (wah-b'-NAAH-gee-eh-wakh) may be more familiar to readers in its anglicized form, Wabanakis. The word *buowin* (boo-OH-ween), a person with extraordinary spiritual powers, does not have a convenient English translation free of stereotypes.

NOTES

1. Rand, *Legends of the Micmacs,* 101–9, 225–27.
2. Parsons, "Micmac Folklore"; Leland, *Algonquin Legends of New England;* Robertson, *Red Earth,* 55–58.
3. LeClercq, *New Relations of Gaspesia.*
4. This account is elaborated in Schmidt and Marshall, *Mi'kmaq Hieroglyphic Prayers,* 5–15. The quoted text appears on page 6.
5. Pacifique, *Manual of Prayers, Instructions, Psalms, and Hymns in Micmac Ideograms.*

SUGGESTED READING AND REFERENCES

DeBlois, Albert D. *Micmac Texts.* Hull, Quebec: Canadian Museum of Civilization, 1990.

Leavitt, Robert M., and David A. Francis, eds. *Wapapi Akonutomakonol—The Wampum Records: Wabanaki Traditional Laws.* Fredericton: Micmac-Maliseet Institute, 1990.

LeClercq, Chrestien. *New Relations of Gaspesia.* 1691. Reprint, edited by W. F. Ganong. New York: Greenwood Press, 1968.

Leland, Charles G. *The Algonquin Legends of New England.* London: S. Low, Marston, Searle, & Rivington, 1884.

Murray, Laura J., and Keren Rice. *Talking on the Page: Editing Aboriginal Oral Texts.* Toronto: University of Toronto Press, 1999.

Pacifique, Father (Henri Buisson de Valigny). *Manual of Prayers, Instructions, Psalms, and Hymns in Micmac Ideograms.* Restigouche, Quebec: Micmac Messenger, 1921.

Parsons, Elsie Clews. "Micmac Folklore." *Journal of American Folklore* 38 (1925): 55–133.

Rand, Silas Tertius. *Legends of the Micmacs.* 1893. Reprint, New York: Johnson Reprint, 1971.

Robertson, Marion. *Red Earth: Tales of the Micmacs with an Introduction to the Customs and Beliefs of the Micmac Indians.* Halifax: Nova Scotia Museum, 1969.

Sark, John Joe. *Micmac Legends of Prince Edward Island.* Charlottetown: Ragweed Press, 1988.

Schmidt, David, and Murdena Marshall, eds. *Mi'kmaq Hieroglyphic Prayers: Readings in North America's First Indigenous Script.* Halifax: Nimbus Publishing, 1995.

Whitehead, Ruth Holmes. *Stories from the Six Worlds: Micmac Legends.* Halifax: Nimbus, 1988.

The Floating Island

Written and translated by E. Nàgùgwes Metallic

This is a story about a dream that was really a prophecy. It happened a long time ago, so far back in fact that no one really remembers those old times. The time is many winters ago. In those days the people counted their passing years by winters. A year is thirteen moons, and a new year starts with the spring equinox.

When in the sky-above-sky it was decided to create life on Mother Earth, it was only a watery domain. The two Creator Twins paddled their large stone canoe down from the galaxies and landed it on the ocean depths and created the Wabnà-giewaq, the People of the Dawn. Eventually the canoe transformed into Unamàgi, the Land of Fog, present-day Cape Breton Island. This then has always been the headland of the Mìgmaq.

On this island veiled by fog and surrounded by the sea the people enjoyed the mystery of creation for thousands of years. Now there lived in one of the settlements a small, young, insignificant girl named Summer. She was no different from any young woman. Eventually she might choose a great, young, handsome hunter and prove herself as a woman of her people to him and their children. So it was way back then.

One night while the little girl slept she had a dream, an amazing dream like none other before. She dreamt of picking blueberries on the low promontories before the coast and sea. She looked from her picking toward the water and saw an unusual sight: an island floating and moving on the sea, an island with tall trees, and bears climbing in the trees. In complete wonder she awoke.

In the morning, after the *wiguom* had been tidied up she described the dream to her mother. Her mother listened attentively but thought little of it. However, that same evening she related all to her husband. He was sympathetic but not greatly moved. However, as things progressed he told his parents, and soon this amazing dream got around the whole place. The whole community was abuzz about it. It seemed pretty amazing to everyone!

Now in those days dreams that seemed to be of some significance were not taken lightly. Some dreams could be important to everyone. Some were prophetic; maybe this was such a dream. In those days when a *buowin* knew the unseen world and a dream-interpreter took the task seriously, this dream inevitably came to everyone's attention. They all tried to ascribe some meaning to it, but in the end all disagreed. The fact that the amazing dream had been given to a small, insignificant person and not to one of them also did not escape their attention. Yet as much as some things seem important for a while, they can soon be forgotten. Such was the case now.

For the passing of one winter all remained the same. Pretty young lady Summer soon returned. Then, much to everyone's great surprise and amazement, all saw the incarnation of the floating island dream. For upon the sea and horizon there appeared in fact the floating, moving island with the tall trees and the bears climbing in the trees.

What it was, of course, was a European sailing ship. It moved as it sailed with the wind. It had masts like trees. The bears were the bearded French sailors manning the rigging. The dream was reality.

When all was said and done, this strange and unusual event foretold great changes. That the prophecy had been given to someone so young and unworthy surely foretold great changes for the people. And so it was.

The Mìgmaq Cinderella

Written by E. Nàgùgwes Metallic

On the shores of Indian Lake, back of Listuguj, a long time ago there lived a great hunter who was also invisible. The people told many strange tales about him, about his prowess as a hunter and how he might look; but as no one ever saw him, no one could prove the truth. Many went to his *wiguom* and sat by his fire and ate the food his grandmother gave them. They saw his moccasins when he removed them from his feet and his coat when he hung it on a peg in the *wiguom,* but they never saw him. So many girls begged for a glimpse of him that he eventually promised that he would marry the first one who could see him.

All the girls in the village flocked to his *wiguom* to try their luck. They were kindly treated by his grandmother and invited to sit by the fire. In the late afternoon she would ask them to stroll with her along the shore of the lake and, as they walked, she would ask, "Do you see my grandson there on the opposite shore?"

Some said that they did; others answered more truthfully.

Those who said they could see him she asked, "Of what is my grandson's tumpline made?"

Some answered, "It is made of the ash tree" or "It is made of beaver skin covered with white wampum beads."

As they answered she invited them back to the *wiguom.* When her grandson entered, the girls saw his moccasins when he dropped them on the floor, but they never saw him.

In the far end of the village lived three sisters who had the care of their father's *wiguom.* The two elder sisters were rough with the youngest, especially the eldest, who made her do all the heavy work and often beat her and pushed her into the fire. When they heard that the Invisible Hunter would marry the first girl who could see him, the two elder sisters hurried across the village to his *wiguom.* In the late afternoon they walked along the shore of the lake, and the grandmother of the Invisible Hunter asked them, "Do you see my grandson?"

The eldest sister answered, "I can see him on the farther shore like a dark shadow among the trees."

The other sister said, "There are only trees on the farther shore."

The grandmother of the Invisible Hunter turned to the eldest sister and asked, "Of what is my grandson's tumpline made?"

She answered lightly with a toss of her head, "It is a strap of rawhide."

They hurried to the *wiguom,* and when the Invisible Hunter entered, the sisters saw his moccasins and his hunting pack when he dropped them on the floor, but they could not see him.

The sisters went home pouting and were angry because they could not see the Invisible Hunter. When the youngest sister asked for some of the shells their father had brought them to make wampum, the eldest sister slapped her and pushed her into the fire and shouted at her, "Why should anyone as ugly and as covered with scars and sores as you want wampum beads?"

But now the other sister gave her a few shells, and she made them into wampum and sewed them on an old pair of moccasins. She then went into the woods and gathered pieces of birch bark and made a dress, and with a charred stick she decorated it with ancient symbols of the Mìgmaq. She made a cap and leggings, and dressed in these and her father's moccasins and the bark dress, she walked across the village. Many people laughed and jeered at her: "Look at Scars-and-Sores going to the *wiguom* of the Invisible Hunter!" But the grandmother of the Invisible Hunter greeted her kindly and invited her into the *wiguom*. In the late afternoon she walked with her along the shores of the lake and asked her, as she had asked all the girls, "Do you see my grandson?"

The girl answered, "Yes, I see him."

The grandmother asked again, as she had asked all the others, "Of what is his tumpline made?"

The girl answered, "His tumpline is a rainbow."

The grandmother of the Invisible Hunter smiled and drew her back to the *wiguom*. She dressed her in soft skins, rubbed her scars and sores with a salve that shone, and with another oil made her hair grow long and straight and very black.

"Go now and sit on my grandson's side of the *wiguom,* nearest the door, where the wife of the *wiguom* sits."

She who was despised and covered with scars and sores sat in the place of the wife of the *wiguom,* and when the Invisible Hunter came home, he sat beside her and made her his bride.

Bapkubaluet the Gambler

Written by E. Nàgùgwes Metallic

Millennia upon millennia ago there lived at Unamàgi a Mìgmaq man who fell dangerously ill. Sometime later he died, and his soul went to the Land of Souls. There he met Bapkubaluet, the ruler of the Land of Souls, who gave him a mission to perform. He had to return to his body and to the Land of the Living in order to tell everyone about the existence of the Land of Souls, the survival of the soul, and about the afterlife and reincarnation. This he promptly did and so was born again.

Now, in the same village there lived an elderly couple who had always been childless. But finally, at an advanced age, they had a son. Years later, when this boy was now a young man, he had a canoeing accident and drowned. His parents could not be consoled in any way, because they had loved him dearly. The father implored all his friends and neighbors to accompany him to the Land of Souls so that he might bring back his son.

Soon the party left. This was a perilous trip. They traveled for seven months. Many were numb with fatigue. The four who remained arrived at length at the Land of Souls, which they had sought so very long.

Coming toward them they saw a man, or rather a giant, carrying a huge club. He was in spirit form, but they could see him.

"Whoever you are, prepare to die!" he thundered. "Men of flesh are not welcome here." But the father, still keenly feeling his grief, implored Bapkubaluet to forgive them. Bapkubaluet, out of consideration for a father who blamed himself because he had too much tenderness and affection for his boy, now softened his anger and invited the father to play a round of the Mìgmaq dice game with him. This is a gambling game. The father staked all the meager belongings he had brought with him. Bapkubaluet, for his part, staked the corn, pumpkins, squashes, peas, and tobacco that were part of the bounty of the Land of Souls.

They played from morning until night. The father eventually won. He won all of the loser's bounty. Also, for being the winner, he received the soul of his son. It was wrapped very tightly in a little leather bag. Bapkubaluet told the father to return at once to the Land of the Living. He instructed him to lay out the mummified body of his son immediately after his return and to replace the soul in the body.

Before all this could be done, however, the parents, out of affection and because of their curiosity to see their beloved son, opened the small leather bag containing his soul to sneak a peek at him, his soul, which Bapkubaluet had reduced to the size of a small hazelnut. It immediately escaped and returned at once to the Land of Souls.

Gespiadoqsi, I have finished telling my story.

Naskapi

Umâyichîs

Introduction by Julie Brittain and Marguerite MacKenzie

"Umâyichîs," which translates loosely into English as 'Little Shit Man', belongs to the *âtiyûhkin* (traditional tales) genre of Algonquian oral literature. This version of "Umâyichîs" was narrated by the late John Peastitute, a Naskapi elder, in the summer of 1968 at the Naskapi community of John Lake, near Scheffer-ville, northern Quebec. This community has since relocated several miles to the north, to Kawawachikamach. "Umâyichîs" is one of a number of oral narratives recorded that summer by students working with the Laboratoire d'anthropologie amérindienne, under the supervision of Rémi Savard. Although the presence of the anthropologists may have been the catalyst for telling these stories, it is evident from the sounds of audience participation that this telling of "Umâyichîs" was an authentic performance and that the audience was comprised mainly of chil-dren; they can be heard laughing, and at one point in the story, presumably out of consideration for the youth of his listeners, John Peastitute takes a moment to describe how people used to dress in the days when this story is set.

The Naskapi Grammar and Lexicon Project at Kawawachikamach has tran-scribed these stories and provided a word-for-word translation into English. The initial transcription and translation of "Umâyichîs" was done by Alma Chema-ganish and Silas Nabinicaboo under the supervision of Bill Jancewicz. The English translation of "Umâyichîs" that we present here goes some way beyond this early word-for-word translation; we have endeavored to reproduce the elegance and style with which John Peastitute told his tale and to do so with minimal sacrifice to its original content. We have also sought to recreate the oral performance by employing formatting conventions introduced by Woodbury and Moses in their translation of "Mary Kokrak: Five Brothers and Their Younger Sister."[1] The dis-tinct typefaces we use correspond to the various tones of voice John Peastitute employs throughout the story, and his pauses are represented in the following manner: a line break signifies a pause of less than one second, and a line space signifies a pause of one second or more. In the following section of "Umâyichîs," for example, John Peastitute made a short pause after "he goes from tent to tent," and the line space between "looks like a person" and "Now then" signifies a longer pause:

This Umâyichîs, he goes from tent to tent
because he already looks like a person.

Now then,

he's looking for something,
he's looking for anything he might be able to use for clothing.

The following is a summary of the formatting conventions employed in our translation of "Umâyichîs."

Line break	A pause averaging slightly less than one second
Line space	A long pause within a sentence or a drop in the pitch of the narrator's voice to mark the end of a sentence or group of sentences.
Large capital	Episode break, marked by vocal features and/or determined by a shift in scene.
Small caps	Harsh or raspy voice quality, low pitch.
Italics	Mild voice quality, higher pitch.
Italic small caps	Mild voice, low pitch.

Our aim has been to create a literary work that mirrors, insofar as is possible, given that typologically Algonquian and English are quite different, John Peastitute's performance of "Umâyichîs."

PLOT SUMMARY

This is the story of a manlike creature created from the human waste left behind after a group of Naskapis breaks camp. This creature is Umâyichîs, the Little Shit Man. The first half of the story sees Umâyichîs, dressed in the fine clothes of a chief, wander from one abandoned campsite to the next looking for signs, literally, of the people from whose excrement he is formed. Referring to himself at this stage of the story in the first-person plural ("That's who must have been living here, our long-lost kin"), he is, in spite of his fine attire, still less than human, still a composite and therefore plural entity. When he finds his kin, he becomes whole and refers to himself in the singular from the moment of his initial interactions with the community: "It should be a leader who comes to fetch me." He demands to be treated with respect, as if he were a chief, and the community—who sees him as nothing but a handsomely dressed stranger—receives him with due graciousness. Only the flies can see through the fine clothes; ridiculing the naivety of humans, the flies say to the children, "You treat your shit as if it were a person." Umâyichîs stays long enough in the village to see an eclipse of the moon and then goes back into the woods, pursued by two sisters, where he dissolves into the river, losing his human form. The story ends with the "death" of Umâyichîs and with the younger of the two sisters, who has been gathering up his discarded clothes as he stumbles toward the river, declaring a romantic attachment to him; she will keep his clothes because, she claims, "I will not have a husband."

It is a characteristic property of the oral tradition that each unique performance of a story omits certain details that the members of the audience are presumed to be able to fill in for themselves. This is evident in this performance of "Umâyichîs"; other community members at Kawawachikamach confirm that they know more complete versions of the Umâyichîs story. There are also references in this story that none of the Naskapis we consulted could explain to us. The section in which the eclipse of the moon occurs, for example, feels disconnected from the rest of the story; one feels that it should be more complete in order to fit smoothly into the narrative. Significantly, it is in this section that the phrase *mâtut pisimw* occurs to describe the eclipse of the moon. (*Pisimw* means 'moon' but, because no one could remember the meaning of *mâtut,* the phrase "mâtut pisimw" has been left in Naskapi.) Clearly, as the story has been passed down through the generations, parts of it have become opaque to the contemporary listener.

WHY WE SELECTED THIS STORY

We chose "Umâyichîs" from all the other stories simply because we liked it. We were drawn to it because it has obvious universal appeal; it was a story that we — who are not Naskapi — felt we could relate to. We empathize as Umâyichîs searches for his "long-lost kin"; he seems to be like the Wizard of Oz's Tin Man, who wanted a heart, or Frankenstein's monster, who wanted to be accepted by the villagers around the castle. Of course, we asked the Naskapis what "Umâyichîs" was about. We asked, "Is it a warning against taking people at face value?" People agreed that on some level it probably was. Certainly, the narrator and the audience side with the flies, laughing at the folly of the community that serves its best food to their own excrement just because it is well dressed and so petulantly demands respect. We asked, "Is it a love story?" People said it could be viewed that way. And we asked, "Does it have an ecological message?" Again people agreed that it could have this interpretation; as one man we spoke to about this observed, "One thing's for sure, Umâyichîs is always there when you break camp."

In fact, we turned out to be wrong on all counts in our determination of what "Umâyichîs" is about. We almost missed the whole point of the story because we had been asking the wrong question of the Naskapis. We were asking, "What is this story about?" when we should have been asking, "What is this story for?" It wasn't until we had done with our own speculations on the meaning of "Umâyichîs" that its real significance casually emerged as we were chatting and packing up our books after an afternoon of work. "Umâyichîs" is told at night, in winter, in order to make the weather of the following day milder. It is one of a series of "weather-changing stories." The person who told us this then narrated another story that is told during slushy weather, to make it colder the next day, to facilitate travel. To the Naskapis gathered around the table, the purpose of telling these stories was so completely obvious that no one had thought to mention it.

WEATHER-CHANGING MAGIC

In his book *Bringing Home Animals,* Adrian Tanner describes a set of "weather control rites" used by the Cree hunters of the Quebec-Labrador peninsula.[2] Tanner identifies two basic types of "weather magic": techniques that make winter weather colder and (less numerous) techniques that make winter weather warmer. Rites that make the weather colder might typically be performed during a period of mild winter weather that has turned the snow to slush, making for poor travel conditions. Rites that make the weather warmer, on the other hand, are typically performed in the spring in order to hasten the end of the dangerous break-up period, when the ice is melting. To the set of rites identified by Tanner, we must now add the telling of "weather-changing stories" such as "Umâyichîs"; the act of telling the story is, in fact, the magical rite. This is consistent with the fact that chunks of story that are no longer understood continue to be included in the narration. It is the act of telling the story that creates the magic, and not the actual content of the story. This is not to say, however, that the function and content of "Umâyichîs" are unrelated. In the light of the new information we had received about the function of this story as a weather-warming rite, we realized that weather amelioration is, in fact, a central theme.

Lisa Philips Valentine, in an analysis of Ojibwe oral narratives, observes that repetition of utterances is a stylistic device used to highlight the theme of the narrative; she refers to these sequences of repetitions as "doublets."[3] Roger Spielmann also makes this observation of Ojibwe discourse.[4] John Peastitute makes use of this technique, not exclusively, but nonetheless significantly, it would seem, in the parts of the story in which he describes the weather becoming warmer. The third paragraph of "Umâyichîs" opens with repetition of the fact that he begins his travels in the winter: "It's winter. / It's winter when he sets off walking." By the time he finds fresh tracks of the people he is searching for, it is already spring. At this point in the narrative repetition is again used, and there is reference to the snow being slushy: "Now, by this time it's spring. / Already it's spring. / Already the days are getting longer. / The snow must have been slushy at that time." There are further references to the snow having melted as Umâyichîs carries on through the forest: "he sees that there's already, already, / no snow at all in some places. / But there are patches of bare bare ground, / bare ground where there must once have been a camp." And slightly further on in the narrative: "Then he reaches a place / where there's no snow at all. Already the snow has gone. / Already it's summer."

In addition to this highlighting of parts of the text having to do with the amelioration of the weather, it is also the case that Umâyichîs, because he is made from a substance that dissolves in water (or any type of liquid), is completely at the mercy of the weather. He eventually "dies" because he stumbles into a stream: "And from that place, he is being washed away, / he's dissolving, / he's being swept away by the current." This is, in fact, the demise that he predicts for himself at an earlier point in the story, another stylistic device, perhaps, for drawing our attention to the important role water—or, to give it its correct prominence in the context of this story, thawed ice—is to play in the narrative. Had the weather been colder, the lakes and rivers would have been frozen and there would have been no story because Umâyichîs would not have been in constant peril of dissolving. He avoids contact with liquids throughout the entire story. When the elder comes to pick him up, he has the man turn the canoe sideways so that he can pole-vault into it without touching the water: "'Bring your canoe sideways,' says Umâyichîs. / The man in the canoe turns it sideways, but he doesn't go ashore. / And then, using his spear, Umâyichîs jumps aboard. / He jumps into the canoe." He disembarks in the same manner. When he is in the camp, the very sight of the blood soup causes him to begin to dissolve: "So the blood soup was prepared. / When Umâyichîs saw it, when he saw that blood soup, / he began to come apart, / aahaa / he began to come apart."

Before we discovered the function of "Umâyichîs," it didn't seem that weather played a significant role in the story. After discovering the unusual function of this story, however, the significance of the state of the weather became clear; the two main characters in this story are, arguably, the weather and Umâyichîs, who is the victim of the weather. While there is more to this story than merely the opposition of its principal character to the weather—there is humor, suspense, and romance, all the ingredients of a good yarn—the content of "Umâyichîs" is clearly related to the function it serves.

In *Bringing Home Animals* Tanner explains that, ideally, a "summer-born person" should perform rites that make the weather warmer and, conversely, rites having to do with making the weather colder should be performed by a "winter-born person." Members of the community at Kawawachikamach whom we consulted on this matter agreed that ideally "Umâyichîs" would be told by a summer-born person but that John Peastitute, irrespective of the season of his birth—and no one was sure what it was—had full authority to tell this story because he was an elder.

THE NASKAPI PEOPLE AND THEIR LANGUAGE

"Umâyichîs" is not a uniquely Naskapi legend. A longer Ojibwe version exists in which the creature is constructed by a group of men who want to punish a girl who is too proud to marry any of them. The girl's brother and his peers create Umâyichîs, breathe life into him, and commission him to go out and make the girl fall in love with him. When she discovers what her lover really is, she is humiliated, her rejected suitors reaping what they view to be an appropriate revenge. A monster with a mission, the Ojibwe Umâyichîs is more like the Jewish golem than his Naskapi counterpart. Presumably there are versions of this story told in other Algonquian-speaking communities. The rendition of "Umâyichîs" presented here, however, is Naskapi.

Originally nomadic caribou hunters, by the mid-1950s the Naskapis had divided into two more or less sedentary groups—the Western Naskapis, now resident at Kawawachikamach, and the Eastern Naskapis of Natuashish, Labrador. While distinct subdialects of Naskapi have emerged within each community (Western Naskapi and Eastern Naskapi), the people of Kawawachikamach and Natuashish retain much in common. Members of both communities have family connections that stretch across the Quebec-Labrador peninsula, attesting to their recent common history, and both groups have adopted English as their second language. A unique subset of linguistic properties common to speakers of Eastern and Western Naskapi reflects the fact that the Naskapis at one time constituted a single linguistic community. Among older Naskapis in particular there exists a common pool of lexical items, and Eastern and Western Naskapi share a number of phonological features.[5] A characteristic difference between Eastern and Western Naskapi is that the latter is a "y dialect" while eastern is an "n dialect"; these terms refer to the surviving reflex of the Proto-Algonquian consonant *l. Although in his later years John Peastitute was a member of the Western Naskapi community, his speech retained many Eastern Naskapi features, including the use of n in some contexts where a Western Naskapi speaker uses y.

In 1978, after several years of negotiations between the Quebec provincial government and the Native peoples of the area (Inuit, Crees, and Naskapis), the Western Naskapis signed the North-eastern Quebec Agreement, under which they surrendered their claims to traditional lands in exchange for exclusive rights to limited territory and the promise of provincial and federal funding for social and economic development. One of the many benefits of self-determination has been the creation of the Naskapi Lexicon and Grammar Project, a community-funded project that operates under the auspices of the Naskapi Development Corporation. Since 1981 they have employed a full-time linguist and a team of Naskapi language consultants. To date, a trilingual dictionary (Naskapi-French-English) has been produced, and work on a descriptive grammar is underway.[6] The Naskapi

Lexicon and Grammar Project is also undertaking the task of transcribing John Peastitute's stories into the Naskapi system of orthography (syllabics) to make them available to the Naskapi-speaking community. While the primary goal of the project is to make the literature available to Naskapi readers, ideally the stories will also appear in French and English translation, thereby reaching as wide an audience as possible. "Umâyichîs" is the first of John Peastitute's stories to appear in English translation.[7] Finally, as far as we know, "Umâyichîs" is also the first published example of a "weather-changing" story, at least in Algonquian literature, if not more generally.

NOTES

1. Anthony C. Wallace and Leo Moses, "Mary Kokrak: Five Brothers and their Younger Sister," in *Coming to Light: Contemporary Translations of the Native Literatures of North America,* ed. Brian Swann (New York: Vintage Books, 1994), 15–36.

2. Adrian Tanner, *Bringing Home Animals: Religious Ideology and Mode of Production of the Mistassini Cree Hunters,* Social and Economic Studies 23 (Saint John's NL: Institute of Social and Economic Research, 1970).

3. Lisa Philips Valentine, *Making It Their Own: Severn Ojibwe Communicative Practices* (Toronto: University of Toronto Press, 1995).

4. Roger Spielmann, *You're So Fat! Exploring Ojibwe Discourse* (Toronto: University of Toronto Press, 1998).

5. Marguerite MacKenzie, "Fort Chimo Cree: A Case of Dialect Syncretism?" in *Papers of the Tenth Algonquian Conference,* ed. W. Cowan (Ottawa: Carleton University, 1979), 227–36; Marguerite MacKenzie, "Toward a Dialectology of Cree-Montagnais-Naskapi" (Ph.D. diss., University of Toronto, 1980).

6. Marguerite MacKenzie and Bill Jancewicz, *Naskapi Lexicon* (Kawawachikamach, Quebec: Naskapi Development Corporation, 1994).

7. Several Eastern Naskapi stories (from the Davis Inlet community) appear in Brian Swann, ed., *Coming to Light: Contemporary Translations of the Native Literatures of North America* (New York: Vintage Books, 1994), 208–21.

SUGGESTED READING

Byrne, Nympha, and Camille Fouillard, eds. *It's Like the Legend: Innu Women's Voices.* Charlottetown PEI: Gynergy Books, 2000.

Clouston, James. *River Runners.* New York: Penguin, 1979.

Einish, Jimmy Peter, and John Pratt, eds. *Nine Lives, Naskapi Survival on Thin Ice.* Kawawachikamach, Quebec: Naskapi Nation of Kawawachikamach, 1992.

Henriksen, Georg. *Hunters in the Barrens: The Naskapi on the Edge of the White Man's World.* Newfoundland Social and Economic Studies 12. Saint John's: Institute of Social and Economic Research, Memorial University of Newfoundland, 1973.

Murray, Laura J., and Keren D. Rice, eds. *Talking on the Page: Editing Aboriginal Oral Texts.* Toronto: University of Toronto Press, 1999.

Nichols, John D., and Arden C. Ogg, eds. *Nikotwâsik Iskwâhtêm, Pâskihtêpayih! Studies in*

Honour of H. C. Wolfart. Algonquian and Iroquoian Linguistics Memoir 13. Manitoba: Algonquian & Iroquoian Linguistics, 1996.

Speck, Frank. *Naskapi.* Norman: University of Oklahoma Press, 1935.

Turner, Lucien. *Ethnology of the Ungava District.* Washington DC: Smithsonian Institution, 1889–90.

Umâyichîs

Told by John Peastitute
Translated by Julie Brittain, Alma Chemaganish, Marguerite
MacKenzie, and Silas Nabinicaboo

Even then, way back then in the past, people told legends. They told stories, in
the fall.
So people say.

Now then, so the story goes, there was this shit that looked like a person.

And so it was called Umâyichîs
because it looked like a person.

Now then, as legend has it,

it was in a camp that people had abandoned, a camp they had left behind one
winter, it was here that Umâyichîs was born.[1]

This Umâyichîs, he goes from tent to tent
because he already looks like a person.

Now then,

he's looking for something,
he's looking for anything he might be able to use for clothing.

And then he finds just the thing,
clothing.

He puts these things on,

1. These are the people for whom he searches and whom he eventually meets.

he clothes himself,
he put these things on, pants and all.

And then he goes to look for

a spear,
a spear,

a spear.
He goes to look for a spear.
He finds a good one.
He uses this spear as a walking stick.

And when he had everything he needed to look like a person, well then, he left.

It's winter.
It's winter when he sets off walking

Now then, while he's walking,
he comes across an abandoned camp.

And it seems to him that his kin have been here,
for he can see that whoever had been living here was human.

The impressions in the snow show him that they must have been here a while
ago.

"That's who must have been living here, our long-lost kin,
it must have been them," he says.

He says this to himself; he's speaking to himself.

And then he sets off walking.

And he again reaches what seems to be yet another camp.

For the whole winter he's been walking.

Again, he leaves this camp behind.

Again, he sets off walking.

Again, he arrives at a camp.
And it's here that the impressions in the snow look different.
He sees fresh tracks.

"This must be our long-lost kin," says he.
For once again, he sees where they have camped.

Again, he sets off walking.
Now, by this time it's spring.
Already it's spring.
Already the days are getting longer.
The snow must have been slushy at that time.

Sometimes he comes across recently abandoned camps.

Again, he sets off walking.
Now then, while he's walking again,
he sees that there's already, already,

no snow at all in some places.

But there are patches of bare bare ground,
bare ground where there must once have been a camp.[2]

"*Now then,*

now then,

here are the traces of our long-lost kin."
Again, he sets off walking.

Then he reaches a place
where there's no snow at all. Already the snow has gone.
Already it's summer.

It must already have been summer when they were setting up this camp.

2. Wherever possible, we have tried to mirror the techniques used in the original Naskapi; for example, we have replicated in English the Naskapi "reduplicated" verbs (e.g., the verb 'it is bare ground'
pânâkutâyuw appears in its reduplicated form *pipânâkutâyuw,* which is translated 'bare bare ground').

He isn't bothered about them not being there anymore, he just wants to go off
and look for them.
HE SETS OFF WALKING.

While he's walking,
he stops to make a fire.

And as it burns, the smoke becomes visible.[3]

"Well, well, look at that.
That has to be a stranger making that smoke," they say.[4]

"It's a stranger all right,"
the elders say.

Then, a little while afterward
and from the same direction,

right from that very same direction, again the smoke goes up.
"Just look at that.
He's coming this way.[5]
There's that smoke again, getting closer and closer," they say.

"So let's go see him then, let's go on over there.
Whoever he is, he's going to come out of the bush at that bit of shore just over
there," [speaker points across the water][6]
the elders say.

They look out across the water toward the place where they think this stranger's
going to emerge from the bush.

THEY GO OFF TO GET HIM.
The smoke looks close now.
He's going to be here today.

3. The "there" referred to in this sentence is the camp of the people for whom he has been searching,
the same people from whose excretion he has been created. The deictic terms the narrator uses from
this point in the story onward locates him in the camp with the people.
4. The "they" who are speaking here are the people in the camp.
5. There is no gender specified in Algonquian pronouns. I have translated the pronoun as 'he' because
the reader already knows the stranger is male.
6. The deictic term *mâniyâyuwa*, which appears in this sentence, is accompanied by a pointing gesture.

Later on, as the day fades into dusk,
UMÂYICHÎS CAN BE SEEN COMING OUT OF THE BUSH RIGHT AT THE PLACE
WHERE THEY GUESSED HE WOULD.

"Go and pick him up in the boat," the elders said to some of the young
unmarried men.[7]

And off they go to fetch him.

THEY'RE COMING TOWARD HIM.[8]

They're almost right at him now.

"What are you up to!" Umâyichîs says.

"We've come to take you back with us," they reply. And Umâyichîs says,

"Are you leaders among your people?"

"No," replies one of the young men.

"It should be a leader who comes to fetch me."

[Audience and narrator laugh]

"But none of us is a leader,"
they say.

One of the young men says,
"But my friend here in the boat with me,
his father usually accompanies us,
and he tells the people what to do.
It's him that people listen to
any time there's a decision to be made."

Says Umâyichîs, *"He's the one, he's the one, the one to come and get me!"*

7. Traditionally men married at a relatively young age. The fact that these men are unmarried indicates both their youth and their lack of social status within the community. They are the ones who are likely to be sent off by the elders to do errands that nobody else wants to do.
8. At this point in the story the point of view changes. The story is now told from the point of view of Umâyichîs rather than that of the people in the camp.

The young men go back home in their canoe,
THEY LEAVE UMÂYICHÎS BEHIND.

They don't have Umâyichîs with them,
when they return to the shores of the camp.

"Why haven't you brought him with you?"
the elders say.
"He said something really strange to us," the young men reply.
"He says to us, '*It should be a leader that comes to fetch me,*'" say the young men.

"Well then," says one of the elders, "what does he look like?"
"He looks like a person, of course," they say.
"His clothes are very beautiful."

"He's dressed like a person.
He's wearing mittens
and he's wearing a hat,
and his coat is beautiful."

Now,
long ago, so legend has it.
people wore leggings, and the ones Umâyichîs wore were beaded right here.
[Narrator gestures to show audience how leggings used to be beaded.]
His clothes are so very fine.

Now then, so the story goes, there's a man over there,
and he's making a canoe.[9]
People think of him as a leader.
He's invited to go and fetch Umâyichîs.

He sets off in his canoe to get him.
He knows
just where the stranger is. "Bring your canoe in sideways," says Umâyichîs.
The man in the canoe turns it sideways, but he doesn't go ashore.
And then, using his spear, Umâyichîs jumps aboard.[10]

9. The narrator reenters the world of the story. His use of the term "over there" relocates him physically in the fictitious camp.
10. Umâyichîs knows he will dissolve if he touches water. He asks the man in the canoe to come in sideways, close to shore, so that he will not have to wade through the water. He uses the spear to pole-vault into the boat, clear of the water.

He jumps into the canoe, breaking one of the seats clean in two.
He lands right on one of the seats,
breaking it clean in half.

He doesn't sit down.

He stands there, just like this.[11]
HE STAYS STANDING UP.
The leader takes Umâyichîs back across the water.

AS THEY'RE PADDLING

Umâyichîs says to the leader, "What's that place over there, that place where it
looks like there's a stand of tamarack trees?"

"It's a creek," replies the chief.
"The children used to play there," the chief says.

"It has a lovely pebble beach."

"The person who broke the seat of this canoe will be washed away from that
place over there. He'll break into pieces and vanish," Umâyichîs says.

"WHAT CAN HE BE TALKING ABOUT?" THE LEADER THINKS TO HIMSELF.
Then he paddles Umâyichîs in to shore.

So, once again the leader turns his boat sideways and Umâyichîs jumps ashore.

Mmm.
Umâyichîs jumps ashore.

He's been invited into one of the tents.
They think he's a man of high status because his clothes are so handsome.
They think he's a leader.

HE IS TAKEN INSIDE,

INSIDE HE GOES.

---

11. Possibly the narrator accompanies this sentence with a gesture, showing his audience how Umâyichîs stands in the canoe.

"What on earth are we going to feed this stranger! There's nothing for us to feed him," the people say.

"At the very least, let's make him some blood soup," they say.
"He'll eat that," they say.

So blood soup was prepared.

When Umâyichîs saw it, when he saw that blood soup,
he began to come apart
aahaa
HE BEGAN TO COME APART.[12]

Now then, already it is truly night,
already the sun has set.

In run the children.

"Those flies,
they were talking,
we heard them!"

"'You treat your shit as if it were a person,' that's what it seems we heard those flies say."

[children laugh]

"It's a well-known fact about flies, that they can talk," says Umâyichîs.

"My, my late father,"

says Umâyichîs.
"My late father once said,
'it's at just this time of the year, that flies can talk.'"

And as we all know, Umâyichîs's father never tells a lie.[13]

---

12. As was the case with the water (and getting out of the boat), Umâyichîs cannot make contact with soup. This too causes him to dissolve. It is not clear whether the very sight (and prospect of ingesting) the soup causes him to begin to fall apart, or whether we are to assume he eats some of it.
13. This is an aside to the audience.

[narrator and children laugh]

Nobody says anything.
You see, those people must have thought that Umâyichîs knew an awful lot.

When everyone's ready to go to sleep,
the children say,
"The moon, the moon, it's hiding!"
Everyone goes out to see, THEY ALL GO RUNNING OUTSIDE TO SEE THE MOON.

"This will be the first eclipse of the moon
I'll ever have seen,"
SAYS UMÂYICHÎS.
He goes outside,
he goes out to look at the moon.
"It looks as if,
the moon has been hidden behind something,"
he says.
"When the moon looked like this," Umâyichîs says, "my father used to call it
'mâtut pisimw.'"[14]

[child laughs]

"He really seems to know everything," the people think.

He goes over there, out of sight behind the trees, and it seems that he's leaving.
That's what he does.
As soon as he's completely out of sight,
as soon as he's a little farther on,
he drops the mitten that is his hand.

When his mitten tears away, there's only shit there, there in the mitten.

And again he sets off walking,
and again he drops his moccasin.

Then he walks on. And again his sock,

14. Although *pisimw* is the standard word for 'moon', the phrase *mâtut pisimw* could not be translated. People we asked said that they felt it was a very old word and that no one now remembered what it meant.

his sock comes off.

And his hat,
his beaded hat comes off too.

And so it was that Umâyichîs was nowhere to be found.

"Go on and look for him; go and look for this stranger who has left us, who is
nowhere to be found,"
the young people were told.[15]

Now, some of the girls say, *"We'll go and look for him ourselves."*

AND OFF THEY GO.

There was his moccasin sitting there.

Now, there's this one young girl who has her older sister along with her.

"Older sister," she says. *"I'm going to keep this moccasin, because I will not have a
husband."*

And she puts the moccasin on.
All over her foot there is shit.

"WHAT CAN THIS UMÂYICHÎS BE DOING?"[16]

And off they go on their way again.

AND THERE IS
HIS MITTEN
SITTING THERE.

"Older sister," says the young girl, *"I'm going to keep this mitten, because I will
not have a husband."*
And she puts the mitten on.

15. The first group of young people seems to have consisted of just two boys. This group of youths is
comprised of at least some girls too.
16. Since this comment isn't attributed to either of the girls, it is assumed to be the narrator asking the
question of the audience.

ALL OVER HER HAND THERE IS SHIT.

[child laughs]

Now, again, Umâyichîs drops his hat.

"Older sister," says the young girl, *"I'm going to keep this hat, because I will not have a husband."*

And she puts the hat on her head.
ALL OVER HER HEAD THERE IS SHIT.

[children laugh]

And off they go on their way again. And there are his leggings sitting there.

"Older sister," says the young girl, *"I'm going to keep these leggings, because I will not have a husband."*

AND SHE TAKES THE LEGGINGS
AND PUTS THEM ON
AND ALL OVER HER LEGS THERE IS SHIT.

[narrator and children laugh]

Now the girls have reached the bank of that creek
where the children used to play.

Right there sits his coat,
and it seems to be completely covered in shit.

And from that place, he is being washed away,
he's dissolving,
he's being swept away by the current.[17]

That is the length of the story.

17. This is the demise he predicts for himself when he is in the chief's canoe traveling toward the camp.

Contributors

Jennifer Andrews is an associate professor in the English department at the University of New Brunswick. She has published several articles on Native North American literatures and coauthored *Border Crossings,* a book on Thomas King.

John Armstrong was a Seneca storyteller who lived on the Cattaraugus Reservation in western New York State. He told a version of the creation myth to J. N. B. Hewitt in 1896.

Sam Batwi was a Yana Indian from the Mount Lassen area of northern California and one of the last fluent speakers of Central Yana. In the course of his long life he served as a consultant for several of the key collectors of California languages and literatures. One of them, Edward Sapir, published a collection of his masterful narratives, *Yana Texts,* in 1910.

Andrew Beechtree (born August 1895) was a Wisconsin Oneida writer and researcher who attended Carlisle Indian School and later participated in a WPA project (1938 through March 1942). As part of the WPA project, Beechtree was hired to interview other Oneidas about themselves and the history and culture of their community.

Adam Bell (1905–87) was a renowned Haida storyteller and the last man in Masset to have relatively full knowledge of the old ways. He is known for having told traditional stories for a six-hour stretch in the bar in Masset.

Judith Berman is a research associate at the University of Pennsylvania Museum of Archaeology and Anthropology. She has worked for twenty years with the Kwakwa̱ka̱'wakw linguistic, ethnographic, historical, and literary materials collected by Franz Boas and George Hunt.

Crisca Bierwert is assistant director of the Center for Research on Learning and Teaching and a research scientist with the Institute for Research on Women and Gender at the University of Michigan. She is the author of *Brushed by Cedar: Coast Salish Figures of Power,* an ethnography, and other articles on cultural history and politics. She is also the editor and cotranslator (with Thom Hess and Vi Hilbert) of *Lushootseed Texts: An Introduction to Puget Salish Narrative Aesthetics*.

Josephine Wildcat Bigler is a full-blood Yuchi. Active in the United Methodist Global Ministries, she worked for seven years in New York City serving Native Americans. Since her return to Sapulpa, Oklahoma, in the mid-1990s, she has taught and documented her language and written poetry in Yuchi.

Robert Bringhurst is a well-known Canadian poet and the author of several books on Native American art and literature. Perhaps the most important of these is *A Story as Sharp as a Knife: The Classical Haida Mythtellers and Their World* (1999). He is also the translator of two volumes of Haida myth texts: Ghandl's *Nine Visits to the Mythworld* (2000) and *Being in Being: The Collected Works of Skaay of the Qquuna Qiighawaay* (2001).

Julie Brittain is an adjunct professor in the Department of Linguistics at Memorial University, Newfoundland. She is the author of *The Morphosyntax of the Algonquian Conjunct Verb: A Minimalist Approach* (2001) and has written numerous articles on the structure of Cree, Montagnais, and Naskapi.

Margaret Wiley Brown was born in 1837 and spent her entire life on the Catawba reservation. She was raised at a time when the Catawba language was still spoken widely in the Catawba community. She died in 1922 at the age of eighty-five.

William Cahwee served in the Pacific during World War II. When he returned to Oklahoma after the war and realized he could not speak easily with his father in Yuchi, he began a lifelong endeavor to improve his ability to speak Yuchi and to understand the intricacies of his language. Known as an eloquent speaker, he taught Yuchi in Glenpool and Sapulpa, Oklahoma, for many years and was instrumental in the current Yuchi language revival.

Catherine A. Callaghan received her Ph.D. at Berkeley for her Lake Miwok grammar, under the direction of Mary R. Haas. After teaching at Ohio State University, she is now semiretired and is revising her dissertation.

Wallace Chafe is professor emeritus in the Department of Linguistics at the University of California, Santa Barbara. He is the author of *Seneca Thanksgiving Rituals* (1961) and *Seneca Morphology and Dictionary* (1967) and is currently preparing an expanded dictionary and a comprehensive grammar of the Seneca language.

Alma Chemaganish is a member of the Naskapi Nation of Kawawachikamach. She has worked for the Naskapi Development Corporation as a Naskapi translator and proofreader. She has contributed to the translation and editing of a collection of Naskapi stories and legends and serves as the main copyeditor for all corporation documents in Naskapi.

Nora Marks Dauenhauer was born in Juneau, Alaska. Her first language is Tlingit, and she has worked extensively with Tlingit oral literature, doing fieldwork, transcription, translation, and explication. Her own poetry, prose, and drama have been widely published. She is a freelance writer and independent scholar.

Richard Dauenhauer has lived in Alaska since 1969. He is a former poet laureate of Alaska, and his poetry, translations, and essays have been widely published. With Nora Dauenhauer he has coauthored and coedited Tlingit grammars and bilingual editions of oral literature. He is a freelance writer and independent scholar.

John Enrico is an independent scholar presently living in British Columbia. He has worked on the Haida language since 1975 and has written books on Haida phonology, syntax, and (with Wendy Bross Stuart) music, as well as a book of translations from the Southern dialect. He is currently finishing a tridialectal dictionary of the language.

Ericklook was born around 1880, according to one of his granddaughters, somewhere on the north slope of Alaska. Ericklook's extended family sailed into Barrow, Alaska, from the Colville River delta in the late 1950s. He began performing his *unipkaat* 'legends' for Suvlu in the early 1960s and continued until his death in the late 1960s.

Genevieve Ethelbah is from North Fork, on the White Mountain Apache Reservation in Arizona. She is of the T'iis Kaadn clan. After completing a program of study at the Haskell Institute (now the Haskell Indian Nations University) in Lawrence, Kansas, she worked first in governmental agency offices in Phoenix and then at the Bureau of Indian Affairs office in Whiteriver, Arizona. Now she is retired and living with her husband, Paul, and family at their home in North Fork.

Paul Ethelbah is a White Mountain Apache, born in the community of Cedar Creek to a long line of *dighíń*, or ceremonial specialists. Paul is of the Nágo-dishgizhn clan. He was trained by religious specialists in both Cedar Creek and Cibecue. In addition to his role as a *dighíń*, Paul worked as a range technician, managing cattle herds grazing on tribal lands. He is now retired from the cattle business but is still a practicing *dighíń*. He lives with his wife, Genevieve, and family in the community of North Fork on the White Mountain Apache Reservation.

Peter Garcia Sr., Kawa-Phade (Passing Rain), was born in Ohkay Owingeh (San Juan Pueblo). From an early age he participated in the ceremonial life of his community. A member of the Garcia Brothers, leaders in the Pueblo cultural revival since the 1950s, he made many recordings on labels such as Indian House, New World Records, Tribal Music International, and Music of the World.

Larry George is a Sahaptin artist and storyteller from Toppenish, Washington.

Ghandl of the Qayahl Llaanas was one of the last of the traditional Haida mythtellers. Born about 1851 in the village of Qaysun, Ghandl lost his eyesight but became an accomplished storyteller. In 1900 he was introduced to the young linguist John Reed Swanton, who transcribed a number of Ghandl's stories.

Ives Goddard is senior linguist in the Department of Anthropology in the National Museum of Natural History, Smithsonian Institution. He has conducted fieldwork on Meskwaki since 1990. He has written extensively on Native North American languages, cultures, and ethnohistory, particularly those of the speakers of Algonquian languages. He edited volume 17, *Languages,* of the *Handbook of North American Indians* (1996).

Jimm G. GoodTracks is the collector, author, and editor of the *Báxoje-Jiwére-Ñút^achi—Ioway-Otoe-Missouria Language Dictionary (1st ed., 1992),* which contains over nine thousand entries, and the *Ioway-Otoe-Missouria Bibliography* (1998) on all known publications on the Ioway-Otoe-Missouria language. He is currently working on an amplification of the dictionary and a collection of bilingual personal narratives and traditional story texts. He is a licensed master social worker employed as a case manager with the Native American Health Coalition, Kansas City, Kansas.

Sally Brown Gordon (1865–1952) was the daughter of Margaret Wiley Brown. Raised without formal schooling in the closed society of the Catawba reservation, Sally Gordon was described by Frank T. Siebert Jr. as having been a true lady of the deprived, rural antebellum South. She and her half-brother, Chief Sam Blue, were the last two native speakers of the Catawba language.

Minnie Gray lives in Ambler, Alaska, and is a retired teacher of the Iñupiaq language. She is a traditional storyteller and has published a number of books of Iñupiaq stories as well as works on traditional subsistence and healing practices. She is also a coauthor of the *Kobuk Iñupiat Junior Dictionary.*

Little is known about the O'odham singer *Ha-ata* (Finished Olla), whose songs were recorded and translated by Frank Russell in the early twentieth century. He likely lived in the Gila River (Pima) Indian Community.

Austin Hammond (1910–93) was a fisherman. He became a clan leader, steward of the Raven House in Haines, Alaska, and an activist for many Tlingit social, political, and cultural issues. He was deeply involved in Indian education and received many honors in the last decade of his life.

Hao Huang is a four-time United States Information Agency Artistic Ambassador who has performed in the Middle East, Asia, Africa, Europe, and North America. An associate professor of music and artist-in-residence at Scripps College, Huang has published articles on Tewa dance songs in the *College Music Society Symposium* and the *American Indian Culture and Research Journal.*

Virginia Hymes has worked with Sahaptin speakers on the Warm Springs Reservation on the Oregon Plateau since 1972. She did graduate work in anthropology and linguistics at Indiana University and UCLA in the 1950s and at the University of Pennsylvania in the early 1970s. She was a lecturer in the Folklore Department at the latter university from 1975–87, and in the Anthropology Department at the University of Virginia from 1988 until her retirement in May 2000.

Jason Baird Jackson is assistant curator of ethnology at the Sam Noble Oklahoma Museum of Natural History and assistant professor of anthropology at the University of Oklahoma. Since 1993 he has been involved in projects in collaboration with the Yuchi community. He is the author of *Yuchi Ceremonial Life: Performance, Meaning, and Tradition in a Contemporary Native American Community,* an ethnography of Yuchi ceremonial life.

Rex Lee Jim was born and raised in Rock Point, Arizona. He is of the Red House People and born for the Red Streak into Water People. He teaches at Diné College in Tsaile, Arizona. He has published two Navajo-language books of poetry, *Áhí Ni' Nikisheegiizh* (1989) and *Saad* (1994), and recently founded the Ohodiiteel Acting Ensemble, a Navajo group performing in the Navajo language. His essay "A Moment in My Life" appears in *Here First: Autobiographical Essays by Native American Writers,* edited by Arnold Krupat and Brian Swann (2000).

Vicente Jose was known to be a capable singer of social dance songs, and he knew many healing songs. He was a ritual curer and also a cowboy who lived in the Santa Rosa area of the Sells Reservation. He died in the mid-1980s.

Willie Jumper (1910–77) was the head medicine man of the Seven Clan Society at the head fire of the Nighthawk Keetoowahs for nine years. Because of his expertise in decoding arcane Cherokee manuscripts and his familiarity with Cherokee medical practices and with curing and conjuring formulas, he played a critical role in the work of Jack and Anna Kilpatrick.

Lawrence Kaplan is professor of linguistics at the Alaska Native Language Center, Fairbanks. He has taught and worked with the Iñupiaq language and is the editor of *King Island Tales,* a collection of stories from the Alaskan Inupiat of Bering Strait.

Josephine Barnett Keith is a Yuchi language teacher in Sapulpa, Oklahoma. After thirty years of service as the school cook, she retired from Lone Star School, the same school she attended as a child with no understanding of English. She is actively involved with the Pickett Indian United Methodist Church and the Yuchi master-apprentice program.

Alexander D. King is lecturer of anthropology at the University of Aberdeen in Scotland. He has cumulatively spent over two years in Kamchatka, Russia, since 1995, conducting linguistic and ethnographic research with Koryaks and other people of northeast Asia.

James Knight was the last Lake Miwok storyteller and a master of the high narrative style.

Ralph Kotay is a well-known Kiowa singer whose singing is featured on numerous recordings, including *Kiowa Hymns Sung by Ralph Kotay, Songs of the O-ho-mah Lodge* (Indian House), and *Songs of Indian Territory* (State Arts Council of Oklahoma).

David Kozak is associate professor of anthropology at Fort Lewis College. He is the author of many publications on Tohono O'odham song, religion, and theory of sickness and is a research associate for the National Institutes of Health Clinical Research Unit, Phoenix Indian Medical Center.

Nyahto Kichewano was a Menominee who worked with the linguist Leonard Bloomfield in the early 1920s.

Alfred Kiyana (1877–1918), Kyanawa, was an outstanding Meskwaki storyteller who learned many traditional stories from his uncle, James Onawat. Beginning in 1911 Kiyana wrote thirteen thousand pages of text in the Meskwaki language for the Smithsonian Institution.

Mary Gale LaFlesche (1826–1909), Only Woman, was raised as a member of the Ioway-Otoe community and was the wife of Joseph LaFlesche Jr. In her adult years she lived with the Omaha community and told Ioway-Otoe stories to the researcher James Owen Dorsey.

Martha Lamont was educated in the Snohomish language and oral traditions of the Lushootseed (Puget Sound Coast Salish) language area. She was born about 1880, and she lived on the Tulalip Reservation, some forty miles north of Seattle. As an elder she was a well-known storyteller. She was also a leader and orator in the Indian Shaker Church, a syncretic religion inspired by Native visionaries around the time of Lamont's birth and continuing to this day.

Charles Laporte was one of the best Maliseet storytellers of the last generation born in the nineteenth century. Born at Saint Mary's Reserve, he spent most of his life at the Tobique Reserve and died in 1964.

Luke Eric Lassiter is associate professor of anthropology at Ball State University. His publications include *The Power of Kiowa Song: A Collaborative Ethnography* (1991), and, with Ralph Kotay and Clyde Ellis, *The Jesus Road: Kiowas, Christianity, and Indian Hymns* (2002).

Robert M. Leavitt is a professor in the Faculty of Education at the University of New Brunswick and director of the Micmac-Maliseet Institute. The author of numerous articles and monographs on Native language and education, he is currently codirecting the Passamaquoddy-Maliseet Dictionary Project.

Philip S. LeSourd is associate professor of anthropology at Indiana University, Bloomington. He is the author of *Accent and Syllable Structure in Passamaquoddy* (1993), a Maliseet-Passamaquoddy and English dictionary, and various articles on Algonquian linguistics. With Karl V. Teeter, he is currently editing a volume of Maliseet tales.

Herbert S. Lewis is professor emeritus of anthropology at the University of Wisconsin-Madison. He has conducted research and published works about peoples of Ethiopia and Israel and on theoretical and historical problems in anthropology. In 1998 he had the good fortune to discover the material from the Oneida Ethnological Study. He is currently preparing some of this material for publication.

Mary S. Linn is assistant curator of Native American languages at the Sam Noble Oklahoma Museum of Natural History and assistant professor of anthropology at the University of Oklahoma. She has worked with the Yuchis since 1994, completing a grammar and now working on a dictionary with them. She is a founding member of the Oklahoma Native Languages Association, which promotes indigenous language maintenance through training in linguistics, language teaching methodology, and literature development.

David I. Lopez (1940–98) was a farmer, cowboy, and ritual curer who worked with three generations of anthropologists translating and interpreting O'odham oral literature. He coauthored three books.

Herbert W. Luthin has studied the Yanan languages for fifteen years. His book on Native California oral literatures, *Surviving through the Days: Translations of Native California Stories and Songs,* was published in 2002. He teaches linguistics at Clarion University in western Pennsylvania, where he lives with his wife and daughter.

Monica Macaulay is professor of linguistics at the University of Wisconsin–Madison. She has worked on various topics in Menominee linguistics and has assisted in the tribe's language revitalization program since 1997.

Marguerite MacKenzie teaches linguistics at Memorial University, Newfoundland, and works with speakers of Cree, Innu (Montagnais), and Naskapi on dictionaries, grammars, and language training materials. She is coeditor of the *East Cree Lexicon: Eastern James Bay Dialects* (1987) and the *Naskapi Lexicon* (1994).

Edna Ahgeak MacLean is Iñupiaq. Currently she is president of Ilisagvik College located in Barrow, Alaska, her hometown. While she taught at the University of Alaska in Fairbanks from 1973 to 1987, she wrote a grammar of Iñupiaq, a dictionary, and other educational books in Iñupiaq.

Willie Marks (1902–81), the father of Nora Marks Dauenhauer, was a fisherman and a well-known carver, the teacher of many of today's leading Tlingit artists. He was commissioned to replicate many traditional art pieces burned in the catastrophic Hoonah, Alaska, fire of 1944.

E. Nàgùgwes Metallic is a Mìgmaq historian and linguist from Listuguj (Restigouche), Quebec, whose principal interest has been the insights language affords into heritage, culture, and spirituality. He is coauthor with Gilles Delisle of the *Mìgmaq Teaching Grammar* (1976) and is presently writing a dictionary of Mìgmaq.

Amy Miller, a linguist, is affiliated with the Santa Barbara Museum of Natural History. She is the author of *A Grammar of Jamul Tiipay* and an editor of

Kar?úk: Native Accounts of the Quechan Mourning Ceremony. She has studied the Quechan language since 1989.

Marianne Milligan is a graduate student in the Department of Linguistics at the University of Wisconsin–Madison. She is writing her dissertation on the metrical structure of Menominee and works with the tribe on issues of language preservation.

Katherine Mills (1915–93) was a gifted stylist and storyteller in English as well as Tlingit. She was deeply involved in the Tlingit language restoration movement, teaching language, singing, dancing, and culture for many years in Hoonah, Alaska. She performed at the Festival of American Folklife on the National Mall in Washington DC and was the author of a Tlingit math book.

Silas Nabinicaboo is a member of the Naskapi Nation of Kawawachikamach. He is trained as a Naskapi translator and works for the Naskapi Development Corporation as a Naskapi language editor and technician. He is the editor of the Naskapi Hymn Book (1999) and has collaborated on a number of Naskapi language projects for the corporation.

Tadataka Nagai is a graduate student in linguistics at the University of Alaska Fairbanks, studying the Iñupiaq language. He has visited Ambler, Alaska, several times since 1996 and done fieldwork with Minnie Gray, collecting texts in Iñupiaq and working with the language.

M. Eleanor Nevins is completing her dissertation in linguistic anthropology at the University of Virginia. Since 1996 she has conducted research on contemporary innovations in White Mountain Apache narrative practices.

Thomas J. Nevins is completing his dissertation in cultural anthropology at the University of Virginia. Since 1996 he has researched representations of social change in contemporary White Mountain Apache culture.

Maria Ocarpia (known to other linguists as Maria de Los Angeles) was a Miguelino Salinan storyteller. She taught the language from 1901, when she worked with A. L. Kroeber, until 1932, the time she collaborated with J. P. Harrington.

Paqa was a young or middle-aged Koryak woman, an exceptional storyteller, who lived in the village of Waikenan on the north shore of Penzhina Bay in the early twentieth century.

John Peastitute, Naskapi elder and storyteller, was born circa 1890 and died circa 1981, in Matemekosh, Quebec. He was a respected community member and a skilled teller of stories, familiar with Naskapi life and traditions. His children and grandchildren still live in Kawawachikamach and fondly remember his stories.

Wesley Proctor lived in Bull Hollow, Oklahoma. The son of traditional Cherokee Keetoowahs, he was fluent in Cherokee and English and fully literate in both languages. He collaborated with Willard Walker on analyzing Cherokee texts and interpreted for his mother, Lucille Bark Proctor, when she testified before the U.S. Senate Special Subcommittee on Indian Education in 1968.

Until his retirement in 1997, *Julian Rice* was professor of English at Florida Atlantic University. He is the author of six books on the Lakota oral tradition: *Lakota Storytelling: Black Elk, Ella Deloria, and Frank Fools Crow* (1989), *Black Elk's Story* (1991), *Deer Women and Elk Men: The Lakota Narratives of Ella Deloria* (1992), *Ella Deloria's Iron Hawk* (1993), *Ella Deloria's The Buffalo People* (1994), and *Before the Great Spirit: The Many Faces of Sioux Spirituality* (1998).

Harry Robinson (1900–1990) was a master storyteller and a member of the Lower Similkameen Indian Band, a branch of the Okanagan Nation of south central British Columbia. Unlike his contemporaries, he adapted his stories himself in English.

Millie Romero, an elder of the Quechan Tribe, was born in 1939 and raised on the Fort Yuma Indian Reservation in Winterhaven, California. She spent much of her married life at Laguna Pueblo, New Mexico. She devoted years of energetic work to the preservation of Quechan language and literature, collaborating with A. M. Halpern in the 1970s and with Amy Miller in the 1990s. Millie Romero died on December 30, 2000.

Blair A. Rudes is assistant professor in the Applied Linguistics Program of the Department of English at the University of North Carolina at Charlotte. He has published numerous works on the indigenous languages of the Carolinas and Virginia. He is currently working with the Catawba Cultural Preservation Project on the Catawba Indian Reservation to develop a grammar of the Catawba language.

William R. Seaburg is associate professor of interdisciplinary arts and sciences, University of Washington, Bothell. He is coeditor, with Pamela Amoss, of *Badger and Coyote Were Neighbors: Melville Jacobs on Northwest Indian Myths and Tales* (2000); coauthor, with Lionel Youst, of *Coquelle Thompson, Athabaskan Witness: A Cultural Biography* (2002); and editor of *The Nehalem Tillamook: An Ethnography,* by Elizabeth Jacobs (2003).

Lee Suvlu was born in 1901 in Barrow, Alaska. He helped to build the first hospital in Barrow before becoming the manager of the Native store in the early 1960s where he and his wife, Mary, recorded *unipkaat* 'legends' and *quliaqtuat* 'life experience stories' from local Iñupiat until his death in 1987.

Brian Swann is the author of many books of poetry, short fiction, and poetry in translation, as well as books for children. He has edited a number of volumes on Native American literatures, including *Smoothing the Ground: Essays on Native American Oral Literature* (1982), *Essays on the Translation of Native American Literatures* (1992), and *Coming to Light: Contemporary Translations of the Native Literatures of North America* (1994). He is a graduate of Queens' College, Cambridge, and Princeton University. He teaches at the Cooper Union for the Advancement of Science and Art in New York City.

Coquelle Thompson Sr. (ca. 1849–1946) was an accomplished Upper Coquille Athabaskan storyteller, singer, and dancer. During his long life, he worked as a farmer, hunting and fishing guide, teamster, tribal policeman, and expert witness for anthropologists.

Waxin Tiger was a founding member of the Pickett Indian United Methodist Church in 1907. He worked throughout his life for the continuation of Yuchi cultural and social traditions. He was an uncle of Josephine Keith and was related to Josephine Bigler through her father's line.

Katherine Turner has spent twenty-five years studying the Salinan language, the last eight years as a linguistic consultant to the tribe. She has written several articles on the language and is currently working with the J. P. Harrington sound recordings of both dialects of Salinan.

Boas published eight stories narrated by *Umx'id* in his last volume of Kwak'wala texts. Because more than one family in Fort Rupert used the name Umix'id, the storyteller's identity is not certain. Perhaps the best candidate is the brother-in-law of Boas'a longtime coworker George Hunt. This man, the younger brother of Hunt's first wife, would have been born circa 1870. Umx'id probably narrated "Giver" in 1930.

Rand Valentine teaches linguistics and Ojibwe language and literature at the University of Wisconsin. He is the author of a grammar of an Ojibwe dialect, Nishnaabemwin, has done extensive work on Ojibwe dialectology, and has authored several essays on Ojibwe oral tradition. He is very active in programs to help preserve and promote the Ojibwe and Cree languages in Wisconsin and Ontario.

Little is known about the Ojibwe storyteller *Waasaagoneshkang,* an elderly man who told many tales to William Jones at the turn of the twentieth century. Waasaagoneshkang apparently grew up on Rainy River, Rainy Lake, and the Lake of the Woods.

Willard Walker is professor emeritus of anthropology at Wesleyan University and has published a number of articles on the linguistic anthropology and ethnohistory of American Indian ethnic groups, including the Oklahoma Cherokees.

Wendy Wickwire is professor of history and environmental studies at the University of Victoria and has written extensively about the oral traditions of the First Nations peoples of south central British Columbia. Her work with the Okanagan storyteller Harry Robinson has been published as *Write It on your Heart: The Epic World of an Okanagan Storyteller* (1989) and *Nature Power: In the Spirit of an Okanagan Storyteller* (1992).

Paul G. Zolbrod is the author of *Diné bahane': The Navajo Creation Story* and *Reading the Voice: Native American Oral Poetry on the Written Page,* among other works. He is also coauthor with Roseann Willink of *Weaving a World: Textiles and the Navajo Way of Seeing.* He is emeritus professor of English, Allegheny College, and has served as senior curator of the Museum of Indian Arts and Culture, in Santa Fe, New Mexico. Currently he teaches English and art history at the Crownpoint, New Mexico, campus of Diné College.

Index

Books by Brian Swann

Selected Poetry of Andrea Zanzotto (with Ruth Feldman)

Shema: Collected Poems of Primo Levi (with Ruth Feldman)

EDITED COLLECTIONS

Coming to Light: Contemporary Translations of the Native Literatures of North America

Here First: Autobiographical Essays by Native American Writers (with Arnold Krupat)

I Tell You Now: Autobiographical Essays by Native American Writers (with Arnold Krupat)

Native American Songs and Poems: An Anthology

On the Translation of Native American Literatures

Poetry Comes Up Where It Can: Poetry from the Amicus Journal, 1990–2000

Poetry from the Amicus Journal

Recovering the Word: Essays on Native American Literature (with Arnold Krupat)

Smoothing the Ground: Essays on Native American Oral Literatures